LIKE GRANDMA
USED TO MAKE

Reader's Digest

LIKE GRANDMA USED TO MAKE

A Treasury of Fondly Remembered Dishes

Reader's
Digest

The Reader's Digest Association, Inc.
Pleasantville, New York/Montreal

Like Grandma Used to Make

Contributors

Editorial Director
Spectrum Communication Services, Inc.

Graphic Designer
Linda Vermie Design

Photographer
Michael Jensen

Illustrators
Susan Fitzpatrick Cornelison, Gary Palmer, Thomas Rosborough

Food Stylist
Lisa Golden Schroeder

Asst. Food Stylist
Pegi Lee

Prop Stylist
Juli Hanssen

Recipe Developers and Testers
Sandra Granseth, Elizabeth Woolever

Text Researcher and Editor
Rosemary Hutchinson

Copy and Production Editor
Sharyl Heiken

Nutrition Analysis
Marge Steenson

Color Separators
Event Graphics, Inc.

Staff

Project Editor
Lee Fowler

Design Director
Henrietta Stern

Prepress Manager
Garry Hansen

Quality Control Manager
Ann Kennedy Harris

Reader's Digest Illustrated Reference Books

Editor-in-Chief
Christopher Cavanaugh

Art Director
Joan Mazzeo

Operations Manager
William J. Cassidy

The acknowledgments that appear on page 360 are hereby made a part of this copyright page.

Library of Congress Cataloging in Publication Data

Like grandma used to make : a treasury of fondly remembered dishes.
p. cm.
At head of title: Reader's digest.
Includes index.
ISBN 0-89577-890-4
1. Cookery, American. I. Reader's Digest Association.
TX715.L696 1996
641.5973—dc20 96-14091

Printed in the United States of America
Fourth Printing, March 2001
Address any comments about Like Grandma Used to Make to
Reader's Digest, Editor-in-Chief, Illustrated Reference Books, Reader's Digest Road, Pleasantville, NY 10570.

To order additional copies of Like Grandma Used to Make, call 1-800-846-2100.

Visit us on our website at: www.readersdigest.com.

COVER PHOTO Pork Pot Roast with Garden Vegetables (page 112), Green Beans with Onion (page 242), Sour Cream Biscuits (page 299), and Iowa Corn Relish (page 287)
PREVIOUS PAGE Best-Ever Shortcake (page 326)

Contents

About this Book

This unique cookbook has been written to preserve the legacy of old-fashioned cooking. Based upon the reminiscences of dozens of grandchildren and the history in stacks of old cookbooks, it is a tribute to the memorable meals of yesteryear and the women who made them.

What's Inside

As you turn the pages, you'll discover more than 500 recipes that will enable you to recreate the best of the old-time cooking. In addition, each chapter features a page of Grandma's Treats, time-honored recipes created especially to delight children. You'll also find family activities that have been enjoyed by generations of Americans. Try gathering everyone around to give a tea party outdoors, color Easter eggs with natural dyes, or make a real gingerbread house.

Updated for Today

Professional recipe developers have updated these old-fashioned recipes to fit today's lighter eating patterns and busy schedules. Each recipe has been written with an easy-to-follow, step-by-step method and streamlined so that it's quicker to prepare. In addition, you'll find preparation and cooking times to help you in meal planning.

Each recipe has been tested time and again to make sure your meals will taste just as good as grandma's. Fat, sodium, cholesterol, and calories have been reduced where possible, but without jeopardizing the rich old-fashioned flavor. You'll find a complete nutritional breakdown for each recipe. Where a recipe lists two alternatives, the first ingredient was used in determining the nutritional values. Optional ingredients were not included in the figuring.

Take a few moments to leaf through this colorful cookbook and rediscover some of our most cherished recipes. Then, head for the kitchen and create mouthwatering meals with the flavor of long ago.

Our Cooking Heritage

Many of us yearn for dishes like our grandmothers used to make—hearty, comforting, and good to the last bite. Why is grandma's cooking so fondly recalled? There's no single answer, but taking a look at how women cooked years ago, where they lived, and the foods they used, will help us understand what made grandma's meals so tasty.

Practice Made Perfect

Unlike many of us today, our grandmothers learned to cook at their mothers' knees. Cookbooks were rare, and if a woman did find a recipe, it often was a list of ingredients with few, if any, directions. So, young girls were taught by their mothers to cook by the feel of the dough, the look of the batter, or the taste of the stew. Forced by necessity to cook day in and day out, they soon became excellent cooks. Today, many a struggling cook would love to know how grandma judged when fried chicken was done just right or how she made such tender pie crust. The answer is practice made perfect. Many of our grandmothers' tips and much of their timeless wisdom have been included in this book, along with their recipes.

Time-Tested Dishes

Many of the dishes grandma made were tried and true, handed down from generation to generation. Of course, what those dishes were depended on grandmother's ethnic heritage. Women of English ancestry prepared roast beef with Yorkshire pudding, meat pies, and hot cross buns. African-American grandmas specialized in hoppin' john, gumbos, and fried catfish. Women of German background served sauerbraten and dark rye bread, while Mexican-Americans made arroz con pollo and enchiladas. Over the years, our grandmothers molded and shaped these recipes, adding a spice here, a bit of cream there, so that the traditional dishes became deliciously their own.

Store-Bought Groceries

Grandma's cooking also was influenced by the fact that store-bought ingredients often were a luxury. In the 1800's, women purchased staples, such as spices, sugar, and coffee from the general store. As villages grew into cities, our grandmothers were more likely to get foods from several stores, such as the butcher shop and bakery. And still later, grocery stores became the norm.

But typically, grandma's trips to the store were infrequent—no more than once a week. So in-between, she turned to her pantry, garden, or root cellar.

Using Fresh, Regional Ingredients

Grandmother's cooking was shaped by the fresh ingredients she had near by. Women along the eastern seaboard took advantage of the lobster and clams that were so plentiful. Southern cooks relied on bountiful supplies of rice, sweet potatoes, collard greens, peaches, and grits. Midwestern farm wives made hearty meals with beef, pork, freshwater fish, and dairy products. In the West, women cooked with crab, salmon, and a lot of fresh fruits and vegetables.

Depending on fresh ingredients meant that women served only what was in season. In the spring, fresh greens, asparagus, and peas appeared on the table. Summer was the time for tomatoes, corn, strawberries, and peaches. Fall meant a new crop of apples, pears, and acorn squash. In winter, grandma served the vegetables that could be stored in her root cellar, such as potatoes, onions, parsnips, and rutabagas.

Putting Foods By

Some of our favorite dishes from long ago came about out of necessity. In the days before refrigeration, women had to preserve fresh ingredients before they spoiled. They salted and smoked meats to keep them for months. They made cheese from milk. They dried berries and canned vegetables so they could serve them all winter long. They turned cucumbers into pickles, cabbage into sauerkraut, and fruits

into jams. These foods gradually became a treasured part of our food heritage.

From Icebox to Refrigerator

With the arrival of the icebox, it was much easier to keep fresh foods longer. Although the earliest iceboxes were simply boxes that held chunks of ice, they soon became more sophisticated— having insulated walls, shelves, and a compartment to hold the water from the melting ice.

In the early 1900's, the proliferation of refrigerators changed the whole world of cooking. Cooks were able to make perishable dishes, such as potato salad and cream pies, any time of year.

Later, with the growth in popularity of home freezers, our grandmas invented many new dishes, including frozen fruit salads and ice cream tortes.

From Wood To Electric

Our grandmas' meals also were affected by their cooking equipment. In the era of fireplace cooking, women could only make one or two foods at once and most of the hot dishes they served were simmered in big pots. If they were lucky enough to have a brick oven, it took hours to heat the oven and bake bread. Even then, the uneven heat made baking tricky, so housewives could only make simple breads, like corn bread. With the coming of cookstoves, women had a lot more choices. Some of the fancier models had as many as six stove-top burners, plus baking and warming ovens. These stoves meant women

could cook several dishes at once and they could bake bread quickly and evenly. The invention of gas, and then electric, ranges revolutionized cooking. With these more accurate ranges, our grandmothers could bake even the most delicate cakes and soufflés.

Waste Not, Want Not

Grandma never let anything go to waste. In fact, many of our best loved meals were actually her innovative ways of using up leftovers. She turned those extra bits of vegetables or meat into a scrumptious soup. The day-old bread became French toast or went into stuffing, and supper's leftover potatoes became the next day's hash.

Company's Coming

Years ago, most socializing revolved around food, and many of grandmother's hallmark dishes were created for special occasions. There were ice cream socials, church suppers, family picnics, holiday meals, and dozens of other gatherings. A Christmas dinner menu from days gone by might have included ten or more dishes, with everything from shrimp cocktail as an appetizer to several types of pie for dessert. These special company dishes, such as veal scaloppine or sour cream raisin pie, often became the ones we remember.

Nourishing Meals

Last but not least, grandma's meals were good because they were so hearty. She usually served numerous courses, with generous portions, and always one or two sweets for dessert.

Her meals also were healthful for their day. As early as the mid-1800's, nutrition experts were urging housewives to serve whole grains, fresh fruits, and green vegetables. Later, the experts contradicted themselves. Some said serving cooked vegetables more than three times a week was unhealthy. Others advised against fish more than once a week. Still later, the four food groups became the standard for good nutrition. In general, women tried to make sure that they served lots of meat, vegetables, milk, eggs, butter, and cheese, so no one ever left the table hungry.

Cooking Like Grandma

The wonderful cooking of yesteryear will always have a special place in our hearts. Now, you can enjoy great meals like grandma's with the vintage recipes in this book. They have been updated to fit today's busy schedules and health concerns, yet they still have the same good taste as those grandma used to make.

APPETIZERS, SNACKS, & SANDWICHES

The elegant teas and receptions of days gone by featured fabulous finger foods, tidbits, and other dainties that grandma showed off on her best china and table linens. Those enchanting recipes have evolved into today's appetizers and snacks. This chapter highlights a company-pleasing array of old-fashioned favorites that are perfect for today's parties. You'll find delicate tea sandwiches and canapés; hearty meatballs and cheese spreads; and a delicious assortment of punches, dips, and nibbles—all made lighter and more healthful.

Blue Cheese Tart (page 22)
Egg-Anchovy Canapés (page 36)
Nutty Cheese Balls (page 14)

Lime and Honey Dip (top), Curried Onion Dip (left), and Shrimp 'n' Dip (right)

Curried Onion Dip

Creamy dips accompanied by potato chips were standard fare at 1950's cocktail parties. This recipe has been updated with lower-fat sour cream and mayonnaise to reduce the calories.

1 cup reduced-fat sour cream
½ cup reduced-fat mayonnaise
2 large green onions with tops, finely chopped
¼ cup finely chopped sweet green, red, or yellow pepper
2 tablespoons low-fat (1% milkfat) milk
½ teaspoon curry powder
⅛ teaspoon garlic powder

1 In small bowl, stir together sour cream, mayonnaise, green onions, green pepper, milk, curry powder, and garlic powder. Cover and refrigerate for at least 1 hour (will keep for 2 days). Serve with an assortment of fresh vegetables and/or reduced-fat chips. Makes 1½ cups.

Prep Time: 10 minutes Chilling Time: 1 hour

1 Tablespoon: Calories 27. Total Fat 2 g. Saturated Fat 1 g. Protein 0 g. Carbohydrate 2 g. Fiber 0 g. Sodium 31 mg. Cholesterol 5 mg.

Shrimp 'n' Dip

If you're short on time, you can substitute 1 can (4½ ounces) canned shrimp for the fresh.

2 cups low-fat (1% milkfat) cottage cheese
2 tablespoons low-fat (1% milkfat) milk
¼ small yellow onion
4 sprigs parsley
1 teaspoon dried dill weed
1 clove garlic, halved
¼ teaspoon black pepper
6 ounces cooked peeled shrimp, finely chopped

1 In a food processor or blender, process the cottage cheese, milk, onion, parsley, dill weed, garlic, and pepper until smooth. Stir in shrimp. Cover and refrigerate for at least 1 hour (will keep for 2 days). Serve with an assortment of fresh vegetables and/or reduced-fat chips. Makes about 2⅓ cups.

Prep Time: 15 minutes Chilling Time: 1 hour

1 Tablespoon: Calories 14. Total Fat 0 g. Saturated Fat 0 g. Protein 3 g. Carbohydrate 0 g. Fiber 0 g. Sodium 60 mg. Cholesterol 9 mg.

Lime and Honey Dip

Southern cooks often use citrus to enhance flavor. This cool, creamy, lime dip is best with fresh fruit, such as strawberries, pineapple, papaya, kiwi, and/or melon.

1 package (8 ounces) Neufchâtel cream cheese, at room temperature
½ cup plain low-fat yogurt
2 tablespoons honey
2 tablespoons low-fat (1% milkfat) milk
1 tablespoon lime juice
1 teaspoon vanilla
⅛ teaspoon ground mace or nutmeg
¼ teaspoon grated lime rind

1 In a small bowl, with an electric mixer on *High*, beat the Neufchâtel cheese, yogurt, honey, milk, lime juice, vanilla, and mace until creamy. Stir in the lime rind. Cover and refrigerate for at least 1 hour (will keep for 2 days). Serve the dip with an assortment of fresh fruits. Makes about 1⅓ cups.

Prep Time: 10 minutes Chilling Time: 1 hour

1 Tablespoon: Calories 38. Total Fat 3 g. Saturated Fat 2 g. Protein 1 g. Carbohydrate 3 g. Fiber 0 g. Sodium 47 mg. Cholesterol 9 mg.

HEALTHFUL DIPPERS

The crackers and potato chips served with dips are usually high in fat and sodium. For more colorful and healthful appetizers, surround your dips with one of the following:

SERVE RAW
♦ jicama or celery sticks
♦ baby carrots
♦ mushrooms
♦ cherry tomatoes
♦ apple wedges
♦ pineapple chunks

TOAST
♦ pita triangles
♦ tortilla wedges
♦ French bread, thinly sliced

LOOK FOR
♦ fat-free crackers or chips
♦ fat-free pretzels
♦ melba toast rounds
♦ rice cakes

STEAM AND CHILL
♦ whole green beans
♦ broccoli flowerets
♦ cauliflower flowerets
♦ asparagus spears

Herbed Cheese Spread

Many grandmothers made their own cream cheese from milk and rennet. Today, you can get that rich old-fashioned taste—with less fat—by making yogurt cheese. Then, just stir in fresh herbs and spread on crackers.

1 **cup plain low-fat yogurt**
1 **tablespoon minced fresh basil or thyme or 1 teaspoon dried basil leaves or thyme leaves**
¼ **teaspoon garlic powder**
¼ **teaspoon grated lemon rind**
¼ **teaspoon black pepper**

1 Line a sieve with 100% cotton cheesecloth, coffee filter, or a white paper towel and place over a bowl. Spoon in the yogurt. Cover and refrigerate for at least 6 hours or until it is cream-cheese consistency. Discard the liquid in bowl.

2 Transfer the yogurt to a small bowl. Stir in the basil, garlic powder, lemon rind, and pepper until well mixed. Serve the spread with an assortment of crackers or party rye or pumpernickel bread. Makes ⅔ cup.

Prep Time: 10 minutes Chilling Time: 6 hours

1 Tablespoon: Calories 11. Total Fat 0 g. Saturated Fat 0 g. Protein 1 g. Carbohydrate 2 g. Fiber 0 g. Sodium 11 mg. Cholesterol 0 mg.

Raspberry Cheese Spread Prepare as for Herbed Cheese Spread, omitting the basil or thyme, garlic powder, lemon rind, and pepper and adding **2 tablespoons seedless raspberry jam.** Using tiny cookie or hors d'oeuvre cutters, cut shapes from home-style sandwich bread. Serve spread on the bread cutouts.

1 Tablespoon: Calories 20. Saturated Fat 0 g. Total Fat 0 g. Protein 1 g. Carbohydrate 4 g. Fiber 0 g. Sodium 12 mg. Cholesterol 0 mg.

Nutty Cheese Balls

In the early 1900's, cheese and crackers were served with coffee after dessert. By the 1950's, cheese had become an appetizer, and nothing was more popular than cheese balls.

1 **container (8 ounces) reduced-fat soft-style cream cheese, at room temperature**
1 **cup shredded smoked Cheddar cheese (4 ounces), at room temperature**
1 **cup shredded Monterey Jack cheese (4 ounces), at room temperature**
½ **cup reduced-fat mayonnaise**
2 **tablespoons dry white wine or low-fat (1% milkfat) milk**
¼ **cup finely chopped sliced almonds, toasted**
¼ **cup finely chopped pecans, toasted**
¼ **cup finely chopped walnuts, toasted**

1 In a small bowl, with an electric mixer on *High*, beat the cream cheese, Cheddar cheese, Monterey Jack cheese, mayonnaise, and wine until well mixed. Wrap in plastic wrap; shape into a ball. Refrigerate for at least 2 hours (will keep for 2 days).

2 Place the almonds, pecans, and walnuts on separate sheets of wax paper. Unwrap the cheese mixture and divide into thirds. Form each third of cheese mixture into a ball. Carefully roll 1 ball in the almonds, 1 ball in the pecans, and 1 ball in the walnuts, coating each completely. Rewrap in plastic wrap and refrigerate until time to serve. Serve the cheese balls with an assortment of crackers. Makes 16 servings.

Prep Time: 15 minutes Chilling Time: 2 hours

1 Serving: Calories 122. Total Fat 10 g. Saturated Fat 4 g. Protein 5 g. Carbohydrate 3 g. Fiber 0 g. Sodium 161 mg. Cholesterol 18 mg.

TOASTING NUTS

For a rich, toasty flavor, bake nuts in a 350°F oven for 5 to 10 minutes or until they are golden, stirring occasionally.

Cream Cheese Log with Dried Beef

Cream Cheese Log with Dried Beef

*Dried beef has been used in American kitchens since pioneer days. Only in the last few decades
was it used for appetizers like this intriguing combination of cream cheese, horseradish, and chives.*

1 **container (8 ounces) reduced-fat soft-style cream cheese, at room temperature**
¼ **cup reduced-fat mayonnaise**
1 **teaspoon drained prepared horseradish**
½ **cup shredded Swiss cheese (2 ounces)**
2 **ounces dried beef, finely chopped**
1 **tablespoon drained canned pimientos, chopped**
½ **cup finely chopped chives or green onion tops**

1 In a small bowl, with an electric mixer on *High*, beat the cream cheese, mayonnaise, and horseradish until creamy. Stir in Swiss cheese, dried beef, and pimientos.

Shape the mixture into an 8-inch-long log. Wrap log in plastic wrap and refrigerate for at least 2 hours (will keep for 2 days).

2 Spread the chives on wax paper. Unwrap the log and carefully roll it in the chives, coating it completely. Rewrap in plastic wrap and refrigerate until time to serve. Serve the cheese log with melba toast slices. Makes 14 servings.

Prep Time: 20 minutes Chilling Time: 2 hours

1 Serving: Calories 72. Total Fat 6 g. Saturated Fat 3 g.
Protein 4 g. Carbohydrate 2 g. Fiber 0 g.
Sodium 239 mg. Cholesterol 18 mg.

Favorite Salmon Mold

Favorite Salmon Mold

*Salmon mousses and pâtés traditionally were served for luncheons
or light summer suppers. This tasty mold, made with chopped olives and
chili sauce, is spicier than most—perfect for an appetizer spread.*

Nonstick cooking spray

¼   cup cold water

1   envelope unflavored gelatin (2 teaspoons)

¼   cup bottled chili sauce

1   cup plain low-fat yogurt

1   package (8 ounces) Neufchâtel cream cheese, at room
temperature

1   teaspoon dried fines herbes or thyme leaves

¼   teaspoon black pepper

8   ounces cooked fresh salmon, flaked, or 1 can
(6½ ounces) skinless, boneless salmon,
drained and flaked

1   hard-cooked large egg, peeled and chopped

¼   cup finely chopped celery

¼   cup finely chopped pimiento-stuffed green olives

1 Coat 3-cup decorative mold with cooking spray; set aside. Put the cold water in small saucepan; sprinkle gelatin on top. Let stand 1 minute to soften. Stir in chili sauce. Cook over moderate heat for 5 minutes or until gelatin is completely dissolved. Transfer to medium-size bowl; let stand at room temperature for 15 minutes.

2 Add yogurt, Neufchâtel cheese, fines herbes, and pepper. With electric mixer on *High*, beat until creamy. Fold in salmon, hard-cooked egg, celery, and olives. Spoon into mold. Cover with plastic wrap and refrigerate for 3 hours or until set. Unmold onto a plate. Serve with melba toast slices. Makes about 24 servings.

Prep Time: 10 minutes Cooking Time: 5 minutes
Standing Time: 15 minutes Chilling Time: 3 hours

1 Serving: Calories 58. Total Fat 4 g. Saturated Fat 2 g.
Protein 5 g. Carbohydrate 2 g. Fiber 0 g.
Sodium 141 mg. Cholesterol 22 mg.

Country Pâté

Elegant hostesses often served French pâté as a first course at formal dinners. Today, this lower-fat version doubles nicely as an appetizer or picnic food.

8 ounces lean ground pork or beef
8 ounces ground veal
1 medium-size yellow onion, chopped
1 clove garlic, minced
½ cup low-fat (1% milkfat) milk
2 large egg whites
½ cup fresh bread crumbs (1 slice)
3 sprigs parsley
½ teaspoon dried oregano leaves
¼ teaspoon salt
¼ teaspoon dried thyme leaves
⅛ teaspoon ground sage
⅛ teaspoon black pepper

1 Preheat the oven to 325°F. Line an 8" x 4" x 2" loaf pan with foil, extending the foil about 1 inch above the pan on all sides. Lightly grease the foil. In a 10-inch nonstick skillet, cook pork, veal, onion, and garlic over moderately high heat for 10 minutes or until browned. If necessary, drain off fat.

2 In a food processor or blender, process the pork mixture and milk until almost smooth. Add egg whites, bread crumbs, parsley, oregano, salt, thyme, sage, and pepper. Process until almost smooth. Spread in foil-lined pan. Cover pan with foil, place it in a larger baking pan, and pour hot water around loaf pan to a depth of 1 inch. Bake for 1 hour or until an instant-read thermometer inserted in the center registers 170°F.

3 Cool on a wire rack for 30 minutes. Refrigerate for at least 6 hours (will keep for 2 days). Grasp the edges of the foil and lift the pâté out of the pan. Carefully remove the foil. Using a thin-bladed sharp knife, thinly slice pâté; halve slices. Arrange pâté slices on a lettuce-lined plate and serve with rye bread or an assortment of crackers. Makes about 24 servings.

Prep Time: 15 minutes Cooking Time: 1 hour 10 minutes
Cooling Time: 30 minutes Chilling Time: 6 hours

1 Serving: Calories 37. Total Fat 2 g. Saturated Fat 1 g.
Protein 4 g. Carbohydrate 1 g. Fiber 0 g.
Sodium 44 mg. Cholesterol 12 mg.

Fiesta Bean Platter

Community cookbooks frequently include recipes for fancy Tex-Mex appetizers. This party-size platter combines layers of black bean spread, cream cheese, Monterey Jack, and tomato.

1 container (8 ounces) reduced-fat soft-style cream cheese, at room temperature
½ cup reduced-fat sour cream
¼ cup reduced-fat mayonnaise
½ teaspoon garlic powder
1 can (15 ounces) black beans or pinto beans, drained
¼ cup salsa
1 small bunch leaf lettuce
½ cup shredded Monterey Jack cheese with jalapeño peppers or Cheddar cheese (2 ounces)
½ cup shredded leaf or iceberg lettuce
¼ cup chopped tomato
Toasted Tortilla Chips (recipe, below)

1 In a medium-size bowl, with an electric mixer on *High,* beat the cream cheese, sour cream, mayonnaise, and garlic powder until creamy.

2 In a food processor or blender, process the beans and salsa until almost smooth. Line a serving plate with the lettuce leaves. Spread the cream cheese mixture over the lettuce. Spread the bean mixture over the cream cheese layer. Top with the Monterey Jack cheese. Cover and refrigerate for at least 1 hour (will keep for 4 hours). Sprinkle the shredded lettuce and the tomato over cheese just before serving. Serve with Toasted Tortilla Chips. Makes about 18 servings.

Prep Time: 25 minutes Baking Time: 5 minutes
Chilling Time: 1 hour

1 Serving: Calories 156. Total Fat 6 g. Saturated Fat 3 g.
Protein 6 g. Carbohydrate 19 g. Fiber 2 g.
Sodium 276 mg. Cholesterol 11 mg.

Toasted Tortilla Chips

Preheat the oven to 350°F. Cut each of **12 flour tortillas** into 8 wedges. Place the wedges on baking sheets. Bake for 5 to 10 minutes or until crisp. To store, place in a plastic bag and seal tightly (will keep for 3 days). Makes 96 chips.

1 Chip: Calories 14. Total Fat 0 g. Saturated Fat 0 g.
Protein 0 g. Carbohydrate 2 g. Fiber 0 g.
Sodium 21 mg. Cholesterol 0 mg.

Surprise Cocktail Meatballs

Surprise Cocktail Meatballs

When this sweet and sour dish first became popular, the surprise inside was a cube of cheese. Today, water chestnuts, green pepper, or pineapple make more healthful fillings.

For the meatballs:
- 12 ounces lean ground beef
- 1/2 cup fresh bread crumbs (1 slice)
- 1/4 cup finely chopped yellow onion
- 1/4 cup shredded carrot
- 2 tablespoons minced parsley
- 2 tablespoons low-fat (1% milkfat) milk
- 1/2 teaspoon dried marjoram leaves
- 1/4 teaspoon salt
- 1/8 teaspoon ground sage

- 1/8 teaspoon black pepper
- 1 large egg white, lightly beaten
- 18 water chestnut halves, pecan halves, pineapple tidbits, and/or small sweet green pepper squares

For the sauce:
- 1/2 cup apple juice
- 1/3 cup firmly packed dark brown sugar
- 1/4 cup red wine vinegar or cider vinegar
- 4 teaspoons cornstarch
- 1 tablespoon lower-sodium soy sauce
- 1/4 teaspoon garlic powder

1 Preheat the oven to 350°F. To prepare the meatballs, in a large bowl, mix the beef, bread crumbs, onion, carrot, parsley, milk, marjoram, salt, sage, pepper, and egg white. Divide into 18 pieces (tip, below). Wrap each piece around a water chestnut half. Place the meatballs in a 13" x 9" x 2" baking pan. Bake for 15 to 20 minutes or until the meatballs are no longer pink. Transfer to paper towels and drain well.

2 Meanwhile, to prepare the sauce, in a medium-size saucepan, whisk together the apple juice, brown sugar, vinegar, cornstarch, soy sauce, and garlic powder. Bring to a boil and cook for 2 minutes or until thickened, stirring often. Stir the meatballs into the apple juice mixture and simmer for 3 minutes or until the meatballs are heated through. Place in a small chafing dish or shallow serving dish. Use cocktail forks or toothpicks to serve. Makes 18 meatballs.

Prep Time: 20 minutes Cooking Time: 23 minutes

1 Meatball: Calories 51. Total Fat 1 g. Saturated Fat 0 g.
Protein 5 g. Carbohydrate 6 g. Fiber 0 g.
Sodium 80 mg. Cholesterol 10 mg.

STUFFING MEATBALLS

1. Pat the meat mixture into a 6x3-inch rectangle. Then, with a knife, cut the meat into eighteen 1-inch squares. Separate the squares and flatten each square slightly.

2. Wrap each square around a water chestnut half or one of the other fillings. Be sure the meat is completely sealed around the filling so it doesn't poke out during baking.

Saucy Chicken Bits

Chicken strips or bits dipped in a zesty sauce were popular long before Buffalo chicken wings. This updated version is made with breast meat to reduce the fat.

- 4 skinned and boned chicken breast halves (about 5 ounces each)
- ½ cup apricot preserves
- 1 tablespoon lower-sodium soy sauce
- 1 clove garlic, minced
- ¼ teaspoon ground ginger
- ⅛ teaspoon hot red pepper sauce

1 Preheat the oven to 350°F. Cut the chicken breast halves into bite-size pieces. Arrange the chicken pieces in a single layer in a lightly greased 13" x 9" x 2" baking pan. Bake for 10 minutes or until chicken is cooked through. Drain juices from cooked chicken.

2 Meanwhile, cut up the large pieces in the apricot preserves. In a small bowl, stir the apricot preserves, soy sauce, garlic, ginger, and red pepper sauce until well mixed. Spoon the apricot mixture over the chicken pieces in the baking pan. Bake for 5 minutes more or until heated through. Place chicken pieces and apricot mixture in a small chafing dish or shallow serving dish and use toothpicks to serve. Makes 10 to 12 servings.

Prep Time: 10 minutes Cooking Time: 15 minutes

1 Serving: Calories 102. Total Fat 1 g. Saturated Fat 0 g.
Protein 12 g. Carbohydrate 11 g. Fiber 0 g.
Sodium 85 mg. Cholesterol 31 mg.

Saucy Orange Turkey Bits Prepare as for Saucy Chicken Bits, substituting 1¼ **pounds turkey tenderloin portions** for the chicken and ½ **cup orange marmalade** for the apricot preserves. Bake for 15 minutes or until turkey is cooked through. Drain juices from cooked turkey. Spoon orange marmalade mixture over turkey. Bake for 5 minutes more or until heated through. Serve as for Saucy Chicken Bits.

1 Serving: Calories 104. Total Fat 1 g. Saturated Fat 0 g.
Protein 14 g. Carbohydrate 11 g. Fiber 0 g.
Sodium 85 mg. Cholesterol 38 mg.

Button Ham Biscuits

This bite-size variation of old-fashioned biscuits makes a perfect party appetizer.

- **1 cup all-purpose flour**
- **1½ teaspoons baking powder**
- **½ teaspoon dry mustard**
- **¼ teaspoon baking soda**
- **¼ teaspoon onion powder**
- **½ cup reduced-fat sour cream**
- **¼ cup ground cooked lower-sodium ham**
- **3 tablespoons low-fat (1% milkfat) milk**

1 Preheat the oven to 450°F. In a medium-size bowl, stir together the flour, baking powder, dry mustard, baking soda, and onion powder until well mixed. Using a wooden spoon, stir in the sour cream, ham, and milk; mix just until a soft dough forms.

2 Knead for 30 seconds on a floured surface, then pat into a 7-inch circle. Using a well-floured 1-inch scalloped or round cutter, cut into biscuits; reroll and cut scraps. Place biscuits 1 inch apart on a lightly greased baking sheet; brush the tops with additional milk if you like. Bake for 10 minutes or until golden. Makes about 30 biscuits.

Prep Time: 15 minutes Cooking Time: 10 minutes

1 Biscuit: Calories 22. Total Fat 1 g. Saturated Fat 0 g.
Protein 1 g. Carbohydrate 4 g. Fiber 0 g.
Sodium 38 mg. Cholesterol 2 mg.

Pirozhkis

The Priekulis family of Des Moines brought its prized recipe for pirozhki from Latvia. You can make this quick adaptation using store-bought bread dough. If you have time, try the superb homemade version.

- **4 ounces lean ground beef**
- **¼ cup finely chopped raw potato**
- **2 tablespoons finely chopped yellow onion**
- **½ teaspoon dried basil leaves**
- **⅛ teaspoon each salt and black pepper**
- **1 loaf (16 ounces) frozen white bread dough, thawed**

1 In medium-size skillet, cook and stir ground beef, potato, and onion over moderately high heat for 5 minutes or until beef is no longer pink. Using slotted spoon, transfer to bowl. Stir in basil, salt, and pepper.

2 Preheat the oven to 375°F. On a lightly floured surface, roll dough into a circle, ³⁄₁₆ inch thick. Cut, fill, and shape pirozhkis (tip, below). Reroll scraps and cut, fill, and shape. Place on a lightly greased large baking sheet. Bake for 15 minutes or until golden. Serve warm with brown mustard. Makes about 30.

Prep Time: 30 minutes Cooking Time: 20 minutes

1 Pirozhki: Calories 47. Total Fat 1 g. Saturated Fat 0 g.
Protein 2 g. Carbohydrate 8 g. Fiber 0 g.
Sodium 82 mg. Cholesterol 2 mg.

Old-Fashioned Pirozhkis Prepare as for Pirozhkis, but omit frozen bread dough and make the traditional dough as follows. Pour ⅔ **cup lukewarm (105° to 115°F) low-fat (1% milkfat) milk** into a large bowl. Stir in **1 package active dry yeast** and **2 teaspoons sugar** and let stand for 10 minutes or until foamy. Stir in **2 egg whites, lightly beaten; 2 tablespoons butter or margarine, melted;** and **¼ teaspoon salt.** Using a wooden spoon, beat in **2¼ cups all-purpose flour,** half at a time, until a soft dough forms. Knead the dough on a lightly floured surface for 4 minutes or until smooth and elastic. Transfer the dough to a large buttered bowl, turning to coat with the butter. Cover loosely and let rise in a warm place for 45 minutes or until doubled. Punch down dough. On lightly floured surface, roll into a circle, ¼ inch thick. Cut, fill, and bake as directed above.

1 Pirozhki: Calories 53. Total Fat 1 g. Saturated Fat 1 g.
Protein 2 g. Carbohydrate 8 g. Fiber 0 g.
Sodium 43 mg. Cholesterol 4 mg.

CUTTING PIROZHKIS

1. Using a 2½-inch round cutter, cut dough into circles. Spoon a rounded teaspoon of the meat mixture onto each circle as shown.

2. Fold half of the dough circle over the mixture to make a semi-circle. With the tines of a floured fork, seal the edges tightly.

Old-Fashioned Pirozhkis and Button Ham Biscuits

Cheddar Sticks

*Flaky cheese pastries, shaped into rounds
or sticks, are an old Southern favorite, especially
when seasoned with ground red pepper. These
are lower in fat because they are made with a
yeast dough rather than a butter pastry.*

1½ **cups all-purpose flour**
1 **package active dry yeast**
1 **teaspoon dried thyme leaves**
¼ **teaspoon baking soda**
¼ **teaspoon salt**
¼ **teaspoon garlic powder**
⅛ **teaspoon ground red pepper (cayenne)**
1 **cup shredded reduced-fat Cheddar cheese (4 ounces)**
⅔ **cup water**
2 **tablespoons butter or margarine**
¾ **cup all-purpose flour**

1 In a medium-size bowl, combine the 1½ cups flour, the yeast, thyme, baking soda, salt, garlic powder, and red pepper. Stir in Cheddar cheese. In a small saucepan, heat the water and butter over moderate heat until very warm (120° to 130°F).

2 Using a wooden spoon, beat the butter mixture into the flour mixture until a soft dough forms. Place dough on a lightly floured surface and sprinkle the ¾ cup flour over it. Knead for 5 minutes or until smooth. Transfer the dough to a medium-size buttered bowl, turning to coat with the butter. Cover and let rise in a warm place for 30 to 40 minutes or until doubled.

3 Preheat the oven to 400°F. Punch down the dough and roll out on a lightly floured surface into a 16x12-inch rectangle. Use a pastry wheel or serrated knife to cut dough into 4x¾-inch sticks. Place dough sticks onto lightly greased baking sheets. Prick the top of each stick several times with tines of a fork.

4 Bake for 10 minutes or until browned and crisp. Serve warm or cooled. Makes 48 sticks.

Prep Time: 25 minutes Rising Time: 30 minutes
Cooking Time: 15 minutes

1 Stick: Calories 30. Total Fat 1 g. Saturated Fat 0 g.
Protein 1 g. Carbohydrate 5 g. Fiber 0 g.
Sodium 23 mg. Cholesterol 2 mg.

Blue Cheese Tart

*A truly American food, blue cheese was
developed in California in 1918 and quickly
made its way into salads and appetizers.
You also can serve this tart for lunch.*

1 **store-bought or homemade pie crust (page 337)**
1 **tablespoon all-purpose flour**
½ **cup shredded Swiss cheese (2 ounces)**
½ **cup crumbled blue cheese (2 ounces)**
2 **large egg whites**
1 **large egg**
1 **cup evaporated skimmed milk**
¼ **cup finely chopped chives or green onion tops**
⅛ **teaspoon each salt and black pepper**

1 Preheat the oven to 400°F. Line a 9-inch tart pan with removable bottom with the pie crust, pressing the crust firmly against the side. Line the crust with foil and fill with dried beans. Bake for 15 minutes or until light brown. Cool pie crust on a rack for 5 minutes; discard the foil. (Save the beans for future pastry baking.)

2 Meanwhile, in a small bowl, toss the flour with Swiss cheese and blue cheese. Spread in pie crust.

3 In a medium-size bowl, whisk the egg whites and egg with evaporated milk, chives, salt, and pepper. Pour over the cheese mixture in pie crust. Bake, uncovered, for 20 minutes or until center is set. To serve, cut warm tart into wedges. Makes 12 servings.

Prep Time: 15 minutes Cooking Time: 35 minutes

1 Serving: Calories 145. Total Fat 8 g. Saturated Fat 7 g.
Protein 6 g. Carbohydrate 11 g. Fiber 0 g.
Sodium 221 mg. Cholesterol 27 mg.

Swiss-Cheddar Tart Prepare as for Blue Cheese Tart, substituting ½ **cup shredded Cheddar cheese** for the blue cheese and ¼ **cup finely chopped yellow onion** for the chives.

1 Serving: Calories 145. Total Fat 8 g. Saturated Fat 7 g.
Protein 6 g. Carbohydrate 12 g. Fiber 0 g.
Sodium 172 mg. Cholesterol 28 mg.

Clam Stuffies

Clam Stuffies

Along the Atlantic shore, stuffed clams often are called stuffies on clam shack menus.
If fresh clams aren't available, substitute ½ cup chopped canned clams and use clam juice in
place of the liquor. Then, bake the clam mixture in large mushroom caps.

12 **large hard-shell clams**
¾ **cup fresh bread crumbs (1½ slices)**
¼ **cup grated Parmesan cheese**
2 **tablespoons finely chopped chives or green onion tops**
1 **teaspoon dried basil leaves**
½ **teaspoon dried oregano leaves**
1 **clove garlic, minced**
1 **strip lean bacon, finely chopped and cooked until crisp**

1 Buy the clams the day you plan to cook them. Ask your fishmonger to shuck them, reserving the liquor and the shells. Cover the clams and liquor and refrigerate until ready to prepare the recipe. Separate shells. Scrub 12 of the shell halves and set aside.

2 Preheat the oven to 375°F. Coarsely chop the clams (you should have about ½ cup). In a medium-size bowl, combine the chopped clams, bread crumbs, Parmesan cheese, chives, basil, oregano, and garlic. Stir in enough of the reserved clam liquor to moisten (about 1 tablespoon). Stir in the crisp-cooked bacon.

3 Spoon a slightly rounded tablespoon of the clam mixture into each clam shell half. Arrange on a large baking sheet. Bake for 10 to 15 minutes or until hot. Makes 12 stuffies.

Prep Time: 25 minutes Cooking Time: 10 minutes

1 Stuffie: Calories 48. Total Fat 1 g. Saturated Fat 1 g.
Protein 6 g. Carbohydrate 3 g. Fiber 0 g.
Sodium 82 mg. Cholesterol 15 mg.

❋

Clam-Stuffed Mushrooms Prepare as for Clam Stuffies, spooning a rounded teaspoon of the clam mixture into each of **18 large mushroom caps** instead of into the clam shell halves. Bake as directed. Makes 18.

1 Mushroom: Calories 37. Total Fat 1 g. Saturated Fat 0 g.
Protein 4 g. Carbohydrate 3 g. Fiber 0 g.
Sodium 56 mg. Cholesterol 10 mg.

Shrimp Cocktail in Tomato Cups

Shrimp Cocktail in Tomato Cups

Appetizers long have been a part of the culinary tradition in Europe, but they're relatively new to America.
One of the first to appear in American cookbooks, at the turn of the century, was shrimp cocktail.

For the tomato cups:
  5 **medium-size tomatoes**

For the cocktail sauce:
  1 **tablespoon tarragon vinegar or vinegar**
  1 **teaspoon drained prepared horseradish**
  1 **teaspoon Worcestershire sauce**
  ¹⁄₂ **teaspoon sugar**
  ¹⁄₂ **teaspoon chili powder**
  ¹⁄₄ **teaspoon onion powder**
  ¹⁄₈ **teaspoon garlic powder**
  ¹⁄₈ **teaspoon hot red pepper sauce**

For the shrimp:
  1 **small yellow onion, quartered**
  2 **bay leaves**
  ¹⁄₄ **teaspoon salt**
 16 **fresh or frozen and thawed large shrimp, peeled and deveined with tails left on**

1 To prepare tomato cups, cut off the top third of 4 of the tomatoes, making a decorative zigzag edge. Reserve tops. Gently scoop out seeds and pulp and discard. Invert tomato cups onto paper-towel-lined baking sheet; cover and refrigerate 1 hour (will keep for 1 day).

2 To prepare the cocktail sauce, seed and chop remaining whole tomato and enough of tomato tops to measure 1 cup chopped tomato. In food processor or blender, process the chopped tomato, tarragon vinegar, horseradish, Worcestershire sauce, sugar, chili powder, onion powder, garlic powder, and red pepper sauce until smooth. Transfer to a small bowl. Cover and refrigerate for at least 1 hour or until cold (will keep for 1 day).

3 To cook the shrimp, half-fill a large saucepan with cold water and add onion, bay leaves, and salt. Bring to a boil over high heat. Stir in shrimp. Lower heat and cook, uncovered, for 3 minutes or just until shrimp turn opaque. Drain in a colander; cool under cold running water. Transfer to shallow dish. Cover with plastic wrap; refrigerate for at least 1 hour (will keep for 8 hours).

4 Line the tomato cups with leaf lettuce. Stir cocktail sauce; spoon some into each cup. Arrange 4 shrimp in each cup. Serve immediately. Makes 4 servings.

Prep Time: 25 minutes Cooking Time: 8 minutes
Chilling Time: 1 hour

1 Serving: Calories 68. Total Fat 1 g. Saturated Fat 0 g.
Protein 7 g. Carbohydrate 10 g. Fiber 2 g.
Sodium 220 mg. Cholesterol 47 mg.

Crab Cocktail in Tomato Cups Prepare as for Shrimp Cocktail in Tomato Cups, substituting **8 small crab claws, cooked, or 1 package (8 ounces) frozen and thawed, crab-flavored, salad-style fish** for the shrimp. Omit the onion, bay leaves, and salt and the cooking shrimp step of method.

1 Serving: Calories 96. Total Fat 2 g. Saturated Fat 0 g.
Protein 13 g. Carbohydrate 8 g. Fiber 2 g.
Sodium 190 mg. Cholesterol 57 mg.

Pretty Crab Puffs

This 1930's appetizer was originally called a "Washington canape" and was made with buttered toast topped with cheese and creamed crab. This more healthful version skips the butter and puts the cheese in the creamed crab mixture.

10 **slices home-style white bread, toasted**
3/4 **cup evaporated skimmed milk**
 2 **tablespoons all-purpose flour**
1/4 **teaspoon black pepper**
 3 **tablespoons grated Parmesan cheese**
 8 **ounces lump crab meat, picked over and flaked, or 1 package (6 ounces) frozen and thawed crab meat**
20 **thin strips canned pimiento**

1 Preheat the oven to 400°F. Using a 2-inch round cutter, cut toasted bread into rounds.

2 In a small saucepan, whisk together the evaporated milk, flour, and pepper. Cook over moderate heat, whisking constantly, until mixture starts to thicken. Cook and whisk for 2 minutes more or until thickened. Remove from heat. Stir in the Parmesan cheese. Stir in the crab meat.

3 Using a tablespoon, mound the crab meat mixture onto the bread rounds and place onto a baking sheet. Bake for 5 to 6 minutes or until lightly browned. Top puffs with pimiento strips. Makes 20 puffs.

Prep Time: 10 minutes Cooking Time: 10 minutes

1 Puff: Calories 91. Total Fat 1 g. Saturated Fat 0 g.
Protein 7 g. Carbohydrate 13 g. Fiber 0 g.
Sodium 173 mg. Cholesterol 9 mg.

Rainbow Fruit Cup

This popular first course from the early 1900's is refreshingly seasoned with mint. If you can't find fresh mint leaves, soak 1/2 teaspoon dried mint in 1 teaspoon water for 5 minutes before mixing it with the fruit.

 1 **cup diced fresh pineapple or 1 can (8 ounces) pineapple chunks packed in juice, drained**
 1 **orange, peeled and sectioned**
 1 **cup sliced fresh strawberries**
 1 **tablespoon minced fresh mint**
1/2 **cup chilled ginger ale**

1 In a medium-size bowl, gently stir together the pineapple, orange sections, strawberries, and mint. Spoon fruit mixture into sherbet dishes. Pour some of the ginger ale over each serving. Serve immediately. Makes 4 servings.

Prep Time: 15 minutes

1 Serving: Calories 56. Total Fat 0 g. Saturated Fat 0 g.
Protein 1 g. Carbohydrate 14 g. Fiber 2 g.
Sodium 3 mg. Cholesterol 0 mg.

Eggplant Caviar (shown in artichoke cup), Farm-Fresh Marinated Vegetables (top),
Sweet Pepper and Olive Antipasto (right), fresh fruits and vegetables, assorted cold cuts, cheese cubes, and tortilla chips

Sweet Pepper and Olive Antipasto

*Italian cooks traditionally started meals with an assortment of tidbits designed
to whet the appetite. In this recipe, the peppers are roasted for extra flavor.*

1 **large sweet red pepper**
1 **large sweet yellow or green pepper**
½ **cup green olives**
½ **cup black olives**
3 **tablespoons red wine vinegar**
1 **tablespoon olive oil**
1 **teaspoon dried oregano leaves**
½ **teaspoon dried basil leaves**
1 **clove garlic, minced**

1 Preheat the broiler. Place the whole sweet peppers on a baking sheet. Broil 6 inches from the heat for 15 minutes or until the pepper skins are black, turning frequently. Using tongs, transfer to a clean paper bag,

close tightly, and let stand for 10 minutes or until cool enough to handle. Pull off the skins with your fingers and discard skins. Cut peppers into bite-size pieces.

2 In a medium-size bowl, stir together the pepper pieces, green olives, black olives, vinegar, olive oil, oregano, basil, and garlic. Cover; refrigerate for at least 6 hours (will keep for 1 week), stirring occasionally. Using a slotted spoon, remove vegetables from marinade. Serve with toothpicks. Makes about 2 cups.

Prep Time: 15 minutes Cooking Time: 15 minutes
Standing Time: 10 minutes Chilling Time: 6 hours

¼ Cup: Calories 43. Total Fat 4 g. Saturated Fat 0 g.
Protein 1 g. Carbohydrate 3 g. Fiber 1 g.
Sodium 248 mg. Cholesterol 0 mg.

Eggplant Caviar

Vegetable relishes made with eggplant, mushrooms, and beets were favored by Russian cooks as a substitute for caviar. But these zesty spreads are so flavorful they have become a delicacy in their own right.

- 1 **small eggplant (about 1 pound)**
- 1/4 **cup finely chopped yellow onion**
- 2 **tablespoons minced parsley**
- 2 **tablespoons lemon juice**
- 1 **tablespoon drained capers**
- 1 **tablespoon olive oil**
- 1 **clove garlic, minced**
- 1/2 **teaspoon salt**
- 1/8 **teaspoon freshly ground black pepper**
- 1 **artichoke (optional)**

1 Preheat the oven to 400°F. Using a sharp fork, pierce the eggplant in 3 or 4 different spots. Place the eggplant on a baking sheet and bake, uncovered, for 35 to 40 minutes or until almost tender. Let the eggplant cool until it is easy to handle.

2 Peel the eggplant and finely chop the pulp. In a medium-size bowl, stir together the eggplant pulp, onion, parsley, lemon juice, capers, olive oil, garlic, salt, and pepper until well mixed. Cover and refrigerate for at least 6 hours (will keep for 2 days).

3 In a large saucepan, cook artichoke (if using) in a large amount of boiling water for 25 minutes or until a leaf pulls out easily. Drain; place artichoke upside-down on paper towels and let cool 30 minutes. Use a large spoon to remove center leaves and choke. Serve eggplant mixture in the hollowed-out artichoke or in a serving bowl with tortilla chips. Makes about 2½ cups.

Prep Time: 15 minutes Cooking Time: 35 minutes
Chilling Time: 6 hours

¼ Cup: Calories 24. Total Fat 1 g. Saturated Fat 0 g.
Protein 0 g. Carbohydrate 3 g. Fiber 1 g.
Sodium 123 mg. Cholesterol 0 mg.

Farm-Fresh Marinated Vegetables

This old-timey marinade adds wonderful flavor, but few calories, to fresh vegetables.

- 2 **medium-size carrots, cut into bite-size pieces**
- 1½ **cups small whole mushrooms**
- 1 **small yellow summer squash and/or zucchini, cut into bite-size pieces**
- 1 **small cucumber, cut into bite-size pieces**
- 1 **medium-size red onion, halved and cut into thin wedges**
- 1/3 **cup white wine vinegar or vinegar**
- 1/4 **cup water**
- 1/4 **cup olive oil**
- 1/2 **teaspoon each dried marjoram leaves and whole black peppercorns**
- 1/4 **teaspoon each coriander seeds and mustard seeds**
- 1/8 **teaspoon salt**

1 Half-fill a large saucepan with water; bring to a boil over high heat. Add the carrots. Lower the heat and simmer, uncovered, for 3 minutes. Add the mushrooms and squash; simmer, uncovered, for 3 minutes more or until almost tender.

2 Drain in a colander, rinse with cold water, and drain again. Transfer to a large bowl. Stir in cucumber and remaining ingredients. Cover and refrigerate at least 6 hours (will keep for 1 day), stirring occasionally. Using a slotted spoon, remove vegetables from marinade. Serve with toothpicks. Makes about 5 cups.

Prep Time: 15 minutes Cooking Time: 11 minutes
Chilling Time: 6 hours

½ Cup: Calories 44. Total Fat 3 g. Saturated Fat 0 g.
Protein 1 g. Carbohydrate 4 g. Fiber 1 g.
Sodium 21 mg. Cholesterol 0 mg.

ANTIPASTO, THE EASY WAY

An antipasto tray makes a great party appetizer. If you're short on time, you can put one together with foods straight off the supermarket shelves. Begin with a few prepared relishes, then add some cold cuts, cheeses, and fresh fruits or vegetables.

PREPARED FOODS	COLD CUTS AND CHEESES	FRUITS AND VEGETABLES
◆ marinated artichokes	◆ salami	◆ melon slices
◆ olives	◆ smoked turkey	◆ fresh figs
◆ roasted red peppers	◆ prosciutto	◆ kiwi slices
◆ marinated mushrooms	◆ ham	◆ cherry tomatoes
◆ canned anchovies or sardines	◆ mozzarella cheese	◆ carrot sticks
	◆ Cheddar cheese	◆ cauliflower flowerets
	◆ Muenster cheese	◆ asparagus spears
		◆ jicama sticks

Shrimp-Stuffed Celery

In the 1930's, celery was stuffed with
cheese and served with French dressing as a salad.
Today, it makes a quick and easy appetizer.

- 4 ounces Neufchâtel cream cheese, at room
  temperature
- 2 tablespoons reduced-fat French dressing
- 1 large green onion with top, finely sliced
  Few dashes hot red pepper sauce
- ½ cup chopped cooked, peeled shrimp
- 8 stalks celery, cut into 3-inch-long pieces

1 In a small bowl, stir together the Neufchâtel cheese, French dressing, green onion, and red pepper sauce until well mixed. Stir in the shrimp.

2 Using a table knife, spread some of the Neufchâtel cheese mixture into the cavity of each celery piece. Makes about 24 pieces.

Prep Time: 15 minutes

1 Piece: Calories 20. Total Fat 1 g. Saturated Fat 1 g.
Protein 1 g. Carbohydrate 1 g. Fiber 0 g.
Sodium 46 mg. Cholesterol 8 mg.

Chutney-Stuffed Celery Prepare as for Shrimp-Stuffed Celery, substituting **2 tablespoons finely chopped chutney** for the French dressing and omitting the shrimp.

1 Piece: Calories 17. Total Fat 1 g. Saturated Fat 1 g.
Protein 1 g. Carbohydrate 1 g. Fiber 0 g.
Sodium 34 mg. Cholesterol 4 mg.

Party Perfect
Oven-Fried Vegetables

An old American favorite, crisp fried vegetables
are even better when they're oven-fried to reduce
fat and calories. You also can make this recipe
with diagonally sliced carrots or zucchini.

- 1 cup fine dry bread crumbs
- 3 tablespoons butter or margarine, melted
- 4 to 5 teaspoons dry Italian salad dressing mix
- ⅛ teaspoon ground red pepper (cayenne)
- 2 large egg whites
- 2 tablespoons water
- 1 large yellow onion, halved and cut into eighths
- 1 large baking potato, cut into ¼-inch-thick slices
- 16 small fresh or frozen and thawed okra pods

1 Preheat the oven to 450°F. In a large plastic bag, combine the bread crumbs, butter, dry salad dressing mix, and red pepper until well mixed. In a medium-size bowl, with a fork, beat the egg whites and water until well mixed.

2 Dip the vegetables into the egg white mixture. Put the dipped vegetables in the bag, half at a time; shake until they are well coated. Transfer the vegetables to 2 lightly greased baking sheets, spreading them in a single layer. Bake for 12 minutes or until the vegetables are tender and golden. Use toothpicks to serve. Makes 16 servings.

Prep Time: 20 minutes Cooking Time: 12 minutes

1 Serving: Calories 67. Total Fat 3 g. Saturated Fat 1 g.
Protein 2 g. Carbohydrate 9 g. Fiber 1 g.
Sodium 90 mg. Cholesterol 6 mg.

Deviled Snack Mix

Snack mixes date back to the 1950's
when a savory mixture of cereals and nuts, often
called scramble, was served at card parties.

- 3 cups bite-size wheat cereal squares
- 3 cups bite-size corn cereal squares
- 3 plain rice cakes, broken into bite-size pieces
- 2 cups unsalted pretzel sticks
- 3 tablespoons vegetable oil
- 1 tablespoon Worcestershire sauce
- 2 teaspoons each chili powder and dry mustard
- ½ teaspoon garlic powder

1 Preheat the oven to 350°F. Place cereal, rice cakes, and pretzel sticks in a 13" x 9" x 2" baking pan and stir to mix. In a small bowl, stir together the vegetable oil, Worcestershire sauce, chili powder, dry mustard, and garlic powder until well mixed.

2 Spoon chili powder mixture over cereal mixture and toss to coat. Bake for 20 minutes or until crisp and golden, stirring several times. Makes 10 cups.

Prep Time: 10 minutes Cooking Time: 20 minutes

½ Cup: Calories 102. Total Fat 3 g. Saturated Fat 0 g.
Protein 2 g. Carbohydrate 17 g. Fiber 1 g.
Sodium 102 mg. Cholesterol 0 mg.

Eat-It-By-the-Handful Popcorn and Nut Mix

Eat-It-By-the-Handful Popcorn and Nut Mix

This honeyed snack tastes a lot like old-fashioned popcorn balls, but is much easier to make.

10 **cups air-popped popcorn**
 1 **cup lightly salted dry-roasted mixed nuts**
¼ **cup honey**
 2 **tablespoons orange juice**
 2 **tablespoons butter or margarine**
 1 **teaspoon grated orange rind**
¼ **teaspoon ground cinnamon or nutmeg**

1 Preheat oven to 350°F. Place popcorn and mixed nuts in a 13" x 9" x 2" baking pan.

2 In a small saucepan, stir together the honey, orange juice, butter, orange rind, and cinnamon until well mixed. Bring to a boil over moderate heat. Drizzle the honey mixture over the popcorn and nuts. Using a wooden spoon, toss until well mixed. Bake for 15 minutes, stirring twice.

3 Spread popcorn mixture onto a large sheet of foil. Cool completely. To store, place in a tightly covered container. Makes 7 cups.

Prep Time: 10 minutes Cooking Time: 18 minutes

1 Cup: Calories 228. Total Fat 14 g. Saturated Fat 4 g.
Protein 5 g. Carbohydrate 24 g. Fiber 4 g.
Sodium 166 mg. Cholesterol 9 mg.

Hot Cinnamon Cider

Every fall the Strait family of Minnesota made cider with apples picked from their own orchard. After the work was done, Granny Mary served big mugs full of her memorable hot cider. Her secret—simmer the cider, never boil it.

4   cups (1 quart) apple cider
1   cup orange juice
2   tablespoons honey
12 whole allspice berries
4   cinnamon sticks, each 3 inches long
1   whole nutmeg
½   teaspoon grated orange rind
1   small red apple, cored and cut into wedges

1 In a medium-size saucepan, bring the cider, orange juice, honey, allspice berries, cinnamon sticks, whole nutmeg, and orange rind to a boil over high heat. Lower the heat and simmer, uncovered, for 10 minutes. Add apple wedges and simmer for 3 minutes more.

2 Remove from heat. Strain into a heat-proof pitcher, reserving apple wedges. To serve, place a few of the apple wedges in each cup and fill cups with cider. Makes four 7-ounce servings.

Prep Time: 5 minutes Cooking Time: 18 minutes

1 Serving: Calories 194. Total Fat 1 g. Saturated Fat 0 g.
Protein 1 g. Carbohydrate 49 g. Fiber 1 g.
Sodium 9 mg. Cholesterol 0 mg.

Hot Cinnamon-Cranberry Cider Prepare as for Hot Cinnamon Cider, substituting **2 cups cranberry juice cocktail** for 2 cups of the apple cider.

1 Serving: Calories 208. Total Fat 1 g. Saturated Fat 0 g.
Protein 1 g. Carbohydrate 52 g. Fiber 1 g.
Sodium 7 mg. Cholesterol 0 mg.

Buttered Rum Toddy

In colonial days, folks made their toddies potent to chase the chills away. This milder version has the same flavor but less alcohol.

1¼ cups water
¼   cup honey
3   tablespoons lemon juice
½   cup dark rum
    Butter or vanilla ice cream
    Ground nutmeg

1 In a medium-size saucepan, heat the water, honey, and lemon juice over moderate heat until heated through. Remove from heat and stir in the rum.

2 Pour the rum mixture into mugs. Float a small pat of butter or a tiny scoop of ice cream on each toddy. Sprinkle nutmeg over the butter or ice cream. Makes two 8-ounce servings.

Prep Time: 5 minutes Cooking Time: 5 minutes

1 Serving: Calories 309. Total Fat 4 g. Saturated Fat 2 g.
Protein 0 g. Carbohydrate 37 g. Fiber 0 g.
Sodium 42 mg. Cholesterol 10 mg.

Hospitality Punch

Punches made with tea and fruit juice were popular in the 1930's and 1940's. Some cookbooks contained detailed recipes, while others just instructed readers to add brewed tea to a fruit punch.

2   cups hot brewed tea
½   cup sugar
2   cups unsweetened pineapple juice
1   cup orange juice
½   cup lemon juice
3   cups chilled ginger ale (24 ounces)

1 In a heat-proof pitcher, pour the tea over the sugar and stir until the sugar dissolves. Add the pineapple juice, orange juice, and lemon juice. Cover and refrigerate at least 4 hours (will keep for 1 day). To serve, pour the tea mixture into a small punch bowl and pour in the ginger ale. Makes twelve 6-ounce servings.

Prep Time: 10 minutes Chilling Time: 4 hours

1 Serving: Calories 89. Total Fat 0 g. Saturated Fat 0 g.
Protein 0 g. Carbohydrate 23 g. Fiber 0 g.
Sodium 6 mg. Cholesterol 0 mg.

Orange Eggnog Punch (top right), Hospitality Punch (bottom right), and Buttered Rum Toddy (left)

Orange Eggnog Punch

*This traditional holiday beverage gets fresh sparkle
and flavor from the addition of ginger ale and orange juice.*

1 **quart reduced-fat dairy eggnog or 1 can (1 quart) eggnog**

1 **can (12 ounces) frozen orange juice concentrate, thawed**

1 **can (12 ounces) ginger ale, chilled**

1 In a pitcher, stir eggnog and orange juice concentrate until well mixed. Pour in ginger ale and stir gently. Makes eight 7-ounce servings.

Prep Time: 5 minutes

1 Serving: Calories 177. Total Fat 4 g. Saturated Fat 2 g.
Protein 7 g. Carbohydrate 28 g. Fiber 0 g.
Sodium 82 mg. Cholesterol 97 mg.

Garden Tea Party

In the 1930's, tea parties were the ultimate in elegance. Women wore frilly dresses and sat at tables elaborately decorated with flowers. Tea was poured from silver teapots into delicate china cups. Between sips, the refined ladies nibbled on dainty sandwiches and small cookies.

In the summer, these parties often were held in the garden. To recreate the gracious pleasures of long-ago tea parties, set a table in your favorite outdoor setting. Then, serve tea accompanied by these tiny pinwheel sandwiches.

Tea Party Pinwheels

- 1 package (8 ounces) Neufchâtel cream cheese, at room temperature
- 2 tablespoons orange marmalade
- ¼ cup finely chopped watercress, chives, or parsley
- 1 tablespoon low-fat (1% milkfat) milk
- 1 teaspoon minced fresh basil or ¼ teaspoon dried basil leaves
- 1 unsliced loaf whole-wheat or white bread or ½ unsliced loaf whole-wheat bread and ½ unsliced loaf white bread

Tiny edible flowers (tip, opposite)

Tiny watercress leaves or chive blossoms

Divide cream cheese in half and place each portion in a small bowl. Stir the orange marmalade into one portion of the cream cheese. Stir the ¼ cup watercress, the milk, and basil into the other portion of the cream cheese.

MAKING THE SANDWICHES

1 Using a long bread knife, slice crusts from all sides of loaf. Trim bread into a rectangular loaf with straight sides. Carefully slice loaf lengthwise into ¼-inch-thick slices, as shown above.

2 Spread half of the bread slices with the orange marmalade mixture and the other half with the watercress mixture.

Carefully grasp the narrow end of a slice and roll it up to form a telescope shape, as shown above right. (If the bread breaks while rolling, place the slice, bread side down, on a damp paper towel until slightly moistened and then roll up.)

Place the roll, seam side down, on a sheet of foil and wrap the foil around roll. Repeat with remaining bread slices, wrapping each roll separately in foil. Refrigerate for at least 1 hour (will keep for 1 day).

3 Unwrap sandwich rolls, one at a time, and, using a sharp knife, slice into ½-inch-thick pinwheels. Place a tiny edible flower on top of each marmalade pinwheel and a tiny watercress leaf on top of each watercress pinwheel, pressing gently into filling to secure. Makes about 42.

GARNISHING WITH EDIBLE FLOWERS

Edible flowers do more than just provide eye-catching color to party sandwiches; they also add intriguing flavor. Like herbs, the more fragrant an edible flower is, the more flavor it has. To find the ones you like best, sample several from the list below.

- ◆ Chive blossom (onionlike)
- ◆ Daylily (slightly sweet, nutty)
- ◆ Dianthus (spicy)
- ◆ Geranium (different flavors depending on variety—apple, lemon, mint, nutmeg, and rose)
- ◆ Lavender (mild, lemon)
- ◆ Nasturtium (radish or pepperlike)
- ◆ Pansy (lettucelike, slightly spicy)
- ◆ Rose (slightly sweet)
- ◆ Squash blossom (sweet)
- ◆ Viola, violet (sweet, sometimes tangy or spicy)

The best way to have a steady supply of edible flowers is to grow them yourself. But if you don't garden, look for chemical- and pesticide-free flowers in supermarket produce departments or buy them from a restaurant supplier. (Flowers from florists are often chemically treated.)

Easy Pâté Sandwiches (top) and Ladies' Luncheon Cream Cheese-Date Sandwiches (bottom)

Easy Pâté Sandwiches

This savory pâté combines liverwurst for old-world flavor and Neufchâtel cream cheese for creamy texture.

- 6 ounces braunschweiger or other liverwurst
- ¼ cup low-fat (1% milkfat) cottage cheese
- 2 teaspoons dried basil leaves
- 2 teaspoons onion powder
- 2 teaspoons lower-sodium Worcestershire sauce
- ½ teaspoon garlic powder
- ¼ teaspoon black pepper
- 4 ounces Neufchâtel cream cheese, at room temperature
- ⅓ cup minced parsley
- 6 thin slices home-style whole-wheat and/or white bread

1 In a small bowl, with an electric mixer on *High,* beat the braunschweiger, cottage cheese, basil, onion powder, Worcestershire sauce, garlic powder, and pepper until almost smooth. Add the Neufchâtel cream cheese. Beat until smooth.

2 Wrap the Neufchâtel cheese mixture in plastic wrap and shape into a ball. Refrigerate for at least 2 hours (will keep for 1 day).

3 Spread the parsley on wax paper. Unwrap the pâté and carefully roll it in the parsley, coating it completely. Rewrap the pâté in plastic wrap and refrigerate until time to serve.

4 Trim the crusts from the bread. Using small cookie cutters (or hors d'oeuvre cutters), cut bread into desired shapes.

5 Spread or pipe the pâté on bread cutouts and decorate with radishes, pickles, tomato, olives, or other toppings as desired. (Or, place the pâté on a serving platter and surround with an assortment of crackers.) Makes 24 sandwiches.

Prep Time: 25 minutes Chilling Time: 2 hours

1 Sandwich: Calories 56. Total Fat 4 g. Saturated Fat 2 g.
Protein 2 g. Carbohydrate 4 g. Fiber 1 g.
Sodium 142 mg. Cholesterol 15 mg.

Ladies' Luncheon Cream Cheese-Date Sandwiches

Old-time cookbooks often did not give specific recipes for sandwich fillings. They just listed ingredients and expected cooks to know how to put them together. One favorite combination was cream cheese mixed with dates or raisins and nuts.

- 4 ounces Neufchâtel cream cheese, at room temperature
- ½ cup chopped pitted dates
- ¼ cup reduced-fat mayonnaise
- ¼ cup chopped pecans, toasted
- 8 thin slices cinnamon-raisin or raisin bread

1 In a small bowl, stir together the Neufchâtel cream cheese, dates, and mayonnaise until well mixed. Stir in the pecans.

2 Trim the crusts from the bread. Using small cookie cutters (or hors d'oeuvre cutters), cut bread into desired shapes.

3 Spread the Neufchâtel cheese mixture on half of the bread shapes. Top with the matching remaining bread shapes and decorate with cream cheese, raspberries, fresh mint, or other toppings as desired. Makes about 16 sandwiches.

Prep Time: 20 minutes

1 Sandwich: Calories 89. Total Fat 4 g. Saturated Fat 1 g.
Protein 2 g. Carbohydrate 12 g. Fiber 1 g.
Sodium 97 mg. Cholesterol 6 mg.

Ladies' Luncheon Peanut Butter Sandwiches
Prepare as for Ladies' Luncheon Cream Cheese-Date Sandwiches, substituting ½ **cup reduced-fat peanut butter** for the Neufchâtel cheese.

1 Sandwich: Calories 119. Total Fat 6 g. Saturated Fat 1 g.
Protein 3 g. Carbohydrate 15 g. Fiber 1 g.
Sodium 103 mg. Cholesterol 1 mg.

Open-Face Chicken Tea Sandwiches

In days gone by, dainty sandwiches, like these, were served with afternoon tea. Today, they are perfect for receptions or cocktail parties.

- 1 **cup finely chopped cooked chicken**
- ⅓ **cup reduced-fat sour cream**
- 2 **tablespoons finely chopped almonds, toasted**
- 1 **tablespoon finely chopped celery**
- ¼ **teaspoon paprika**
- ⅛ **teaspoon each salt and black pepper**
- 4 **thin slices home-style whole-wheat and/or white bread**
- 1 **tablespoon minced canned pimiento and/or minced parsley**

1 In a small bowl, stir together the chicken, sour cream, almonds, celery, paprika, salt, and pepper until well mixed. Trim the crusts from the bread. Using small cookie cutters (or hors d'oeuvre cutters), cut bread into desired shapes.

2 Spread the chicken mixture on the bread shapes. Arrange a little of the pimiento and/or parsley around the edge or in the center of each sandwich. Makes 16 sandwiches.

Prep Time: 20 minutes

1 Sandwich: Calories 49. Total Fat 2 g. Saturated Fat 1 g.
Protein 4 g. Carbohydrate 4 g. Fiber 0 g.
Sodium 61 mg. Cholesterol 10 mg.

Hot Ham Sandwiches

The combination of ham, mayonnaise, and dill pickle comes straight out of the 1940's, but it tastes just right for today.

- 4 **slices white sandwich bread, toasted**
- 1 **tablespoon reduced-fat mayonnaise**
- 8 **thin slices cooked lower-sodium ham**
- ¼ **cup reduced-fat mayonnaise**
- ¼ **cup shredded reduced-fat Cheddar cheese**
- 1 **tablespoon finely chopped dill pickle or dill pickle relish**

1 Preheat the broiler. Spread the bread slices with the 1 tablespoon mayonnaise. Place 2 slices ham onto each bread slice; cut each diagonally in half.

2 In a small bowl, stir together the ¼ cup mayonnaise, Cheddar cheese, and pickle until well mixed. Spread the cheese mixture evenly over the ham. Broil 4 inches from the heat for 2 minutes or until cheese melts and starts to brown. Serve hot. Makes 8 sandwiches.

Prep Time: 10 minutes Cooking Time: 2 minutes

1 Sandwich: Calories 83. Total Fat 4 g. Saturated Fat 1 g.
Protein 4 g. Carbohydrate 9 g. Fiber 0 g.
Sodium 228 mg. Cholesterol 9 mg.

Egg-Anchovy Canapés

A 1904 recipe collection, called Dainties, advised our great grandmothers to serve these tasty tidbits "at dinner or luncheon in the place of shell-fish, immediately before the soup..."

- 2 **hard-cooked large eggs, finely chopped**
- 1 **tablespoon reduced-fat mayonnaise**
- 1 **teaspoon anchovy paste or 1 anchovy fillet, minced**
- ⅛ **teaspoon onion powder**
  Dash black pepper
- 3 **slices home-style white, whole-wheat, and/or rye bread, toasted**

1 In a small bowl, with a fork, stir together the eggs, mayonnaise, anchovy paste, onion powder, and pepper until well mixed.

2 Trim the crusts from the toasted bread; cut each bread slice diagonally into quarters to form a total of 12 bread triangles. Spread the egg mixture on the bread triangles. Makes 12 canapés.

Prep Time: 10 minutes

1 Canapé: Calories 39. Total Fat 1 g. Saturated Fat 0 g.
Protein 2 g. Carbohydrate 4 g. Fiber 0 g.
Sodium 61 mg. Cholesterol 36 mg.

Grandma's Treats

Loony Lips

Kids will eat these up as fast as you can make them.

- ¼ cup chunk-style peanut butter
- 2 tablespoons reduced-fat soft-style cream cheese
- ⅛ teaspoon ground cinnamon
- 1 medium-size red apple, cored and cut into 16 wedges
- Miniature marshmallows

1. In a small bowl, stir peanut butter, cream cheese, and cinnamon until well mixed. Spread 1 side of each apple wedge with a thin layer of the peanut butter mixture.

2. Stick together 2 wedges to make "fat lips." Tuck in a few marshmallow "teeth." Makes 8 servings.

The Best Cocoa

On a cold, blustery day, have the children help you make cocoa the old-fashioned way. There's nothing quite like it.

- 2 tablespoons sugar
- 1 tablespoon unsweetened cocoa
- ¼ cup water
- ¾ cup low-fat (1% milkfat) milk
- Miniature marshmallows (optional)
- 1 cinnamon stick, 4 inches long (optional)

1. In a small saucepan, combine the sugar and cocoa. Stir in the water. Bring to a boil over moderate heat. Lower the heat and simmer for 2 minutes, whisking constantly.

2. Stir in the milk. Increase the heat to moderate; cook until heated through. Do not boil. Pour into a cup. Top with several marshmallows and add the cinnamon stick for a stirrer if you like. Makes 1 cup.

Veggie Kabobs

Here is an enticing, fun, and nourishing snack for kids 10 and older.

- 1 medium-size carrot, cut into 8 pieces
- 4 cherry tomatoes
- 1 stalk celery, cut into bite-size pieces
- ½ small cucumber, peeled and cut into bite-size pieces
- 8 pieces sweet green pepper
- 4 wooden skewers, 10 inches long
- ¼ cup reduced-fat sour cream
- 2 tablespoons Thousand Island dressing

1. Thread some of each vegetable onto each skewer. Use kitchen shears to snip off sharp ends of skewers.

2. In a small bowl, stir sour cream and Thousand Island dressing until mixed.

3. To eat kabobs, slide a vegetable down to the end of the skewer and dunk it in the sour cream mixture. Repeat with remaining vegetables. Makes 4.

NOTE: Instruct children to be careful when eating from skewers. Don't give skewers to young children.

Little People Sandwiches

Use ham and cheese slices that are about the same size as your bread.

- 4 slices whole-wheat or white bread
- 4 slices Swiss cheese
- 2 slices cooked ham
- Reduced-fat mayonnaise or Dijon mustard
- Olive and canned pimiento slices for facial features

1. With a girl or boy cookie cutter, cut a "person" from each slice of bread, cheese, and ham.

2. Spread 1 side of each bread shape with the mayonnaise. Assemble the sandwiches and use dabs of mayonnaise to stick on olive and pimiento slices for "eyes" and "mouths". Makes 2 sandwiches.

NOTE: Use your favorite cheese and luncheon meat instead of the Swiss cheese and ham.

THE SALAD BOWL

Vegetables or fruits fresh from the garden or greengrocer were the foundation of the marvelous salads that grandma made for everyday meals as well as for picnics, potluck suppers, and holiday feasts. Gran used greens for tossed or wilted salads and cabbage for coleslaw. She sliced carrots, snapped beans, and cut corn off the cob for marinated salads. Ordinary "taters" were turned into extraordinary hot or cold potato salad, and fruit cups showed off plump melons and berries. You can make those same exquisite salads today with these easy recipes.

Deviled Potato Salad (page 44)
Farm Country Four-Bean Salad (page 43)
Salmon Olive Starbursts (page 59)

Tomato and Cucumber Aspic

In the old days, cool aspics usually were served in the summer when tomatoes were ripe. Today, you can enjoy this zesty salad any time because it's made with hot-style vegetable juice cocktail.

- 1 envelope unflavored gelatin (2 teaspoons)
- 3 cans (5½ ounces each) hot-style vegetable juice cocktail
- 1 teaspoon lower-sodium Worcestershire sauce
- ⅛ teaspoon hot red pepper sauce (optional)
- 1 teaspoon dried dill weed
- ½ teaspoon grated lemon rind
  Nonstick cooking spray
- ½ cup seeded and finely chopped cucumber
- ¼ cup finely chopped sweet green, red, or yellow pepper
- 2 large green onions with tops, finely sliced

1 In a medium-size bowl, sprinkle the gelatin over 1 can of the vegetable juice; let stand for 1 minute. In a medium-size saucepan, bring the remaining vegetable juice, Worcestershire sauce, and red pepper sauce (if using) to a boil. Add to gelatin; stir until gelatin dissolves completely. Stir in the dill weed and lemon rind. Cover gelatin mixture with plastic wrap; refrigerate for 2½ hours or until thickened but not solid (a spoon will leave an impression when drawn through it).

2 Coat a 3½-cup mold with cooking spray. Fold the cucumber, green pepper, and green onions into juice mixture. Spoon into mold. Cover and refrigerate for 2½ hours more or until firm.

3 To serve, unmold salad onto plate. Tuck leaf lettuce around base of salad. Makes 6 side-dish servings.

Prep Time: 15 minutes Cooking Time: 5 minutes
Chilling Time: 5 hours

1 Serving: Calories 24. Total Fat 0 g. Saturated Fat 0 g. Protein 2 g. Carbohydrate 5 g. Fiber 1 g. Sodium 291 mg. Cholesterol 0 mg.

Cranberry Pecan Mold

Handsome, shimmering gelatin molds were the traditional accompaniment to holiday roasted turkey. This recipe also goes well with roasted chicken or pork.

- 1 can (11 ounces) mandarin orange sections
  Orange juice
- 1 package (3 ounces) cherry-flavored gelatin mix
- ½ cup cranberry-orange or cranberry-raspberry sauce
  Nonstick cooking spray
- ½ cup finely chopped Granny Smith apple
- ¼ cup chopped pecans or walnuts, toasted

1 Drain orange sections, reserving syrup. Add enough orange juice to syrup to measure 1¼ cups liquid. In a medium-size saucepan, bring the orange juice mixture to a boil. Remove from heat. Add gelatin to hot mixture; stir until gelatin dissolves. In a medium-size bowl, combine gelatin mixture and cranberry-orange sauce.

2 Cover gelatin mixture with plastic wrap; refrigerate for 2½ hours or until thickened but not solid (a spoon will leave an impression when drawn through it).

3 Coat a 3½-cup mold with cooking spray. Fold the mandarin oranges, apple, and nuts into gelatin mixture. Spoon into mold. Cover and refrigerate for 2½ hours more or until firm.

4 To serve, unmold the salad onto a plate. Tuck red-tipped leaf lettuce around base of salad. Makes 6 side-dish servings.

Prep Time: 10 minutes Cooking Time: 5 minutes
Chilling Time: 5 hours

1 Serving: Calories 172. Total Fat 4 g. Saturated Fat 0 g. Protein 2 g. Carbohydrate 35 g. Fiber 1 g. Sodium 47 mg. Cholesterol 0 mg.

UNMOLDING SALADS

Coaxing a gelatin salad out of its mold is easy if you know these simple tricks.

1. Dip the mold in warm water for a few seconds.

2. Loosen the salad edges with the tip of a knife.

3. Invert a serving plate over the mold. While grasping the plate tightly against the mold, quickly flip both over. Shake gently until the salad slides out of the mold.

Cranberry Pecan Mold

Aunt Ruth's Marinated Vegetable Salad

Aunt Ruth's Marinated Vegetable Salad

*Plastic self-sealing bags weren't available in the old days, but they're
great for marinating salads. Just place everything in the bag and seal it. Then,
turn the bag a few times to distribute the marinade and refrigerate.*

1 **cup sliced broccoli and/or cauliflower flowerets**

1 **cup cherry tomatoes, halved**

1 **large carrot, cut into $1^1\!/_2$x$^1\!/_2$-inch sticks**

1 **small yellow summer squash and/or zucchini, cut
  into $^1\!/_2$-inch-thick slices**

$^1\!/_4$ **cup sliced celery**

For the marinade:

$^2\!/_3$ **cup vinegar**

$^1\!/_2$ **cup olive or vegetable oil**

$^1\!/_4$ **cup minced parsley or cilantro**

3 **tablespoons sugar**

2 **tablespoons finely chopped fresh dill or 2 teaspoons
  dried dill weed**

$^1\!/_2$ **teaspoon salt**

$^1\!/_4$ **teaspoon black pepper**

1 In a large heavy-duty plastic bag, combine the broccoli, tomatoes, carrot, squash, and celery.

2 To prepare the marinade, in a jar with a tight-fitting lid, combine the vinegar, oil, parsley, sugar, dill, salt, and pepper. Cover and shake well. Pour the marinade over vegetables. Close bag and refrigerate for 8 hours or overnight, turning bag occasionally.

3 To serve, use a slotted spoon to transfer vegetables to a serving bowl. Makes 4 side-dish servings.

Prep Time: 25 minutes Chilling Time: 8 hours

1 Serving: Calories 121. Total Fat 9 g. Saturated Fat 1 g.
Protein 1 g. Carbohydrate 10 g. Fiber 2 g.
Sodium 289 mg. Cholesterol 0 mg.

Farm Country Four-Bean Salad

1   small yellow onion, halved crosswise and
    thinly sliced
½   teaspoon salt
1   package (10 ounces) frozen lima beans
1   cup frozen cut green beans
1   can (15½ ounces) red kidney beans, rinsed and
    drained
1   can (15 ounces) garbanzo beans, rinsed and drained
1   medium-size carrot, shredded
1   small sweet red, green, or yellow pepper, cut into
    bite-size pieces

For the marinade:
⅔   cup white wine vinegar or vinegar
3   tablespoons sugar
3   tablespoons water
3   tablespoons olive or vegetable oil
2   teaspoons dried basil leaves
2   cloves garlic, minced
½   teaspoon black pepper

1 Sprinkle onion with salt. In a medium-size bowl, cover onion with cold water. Soak for 20 minutes. Rinse onion under cold running water. Drain well.

2 Meanwhile, cook lima beans and green beans according to package directions. In a large heavy-duty plastic bag, combine onion, all of the beans, carrot, and green pepper.

3 To prepare the marinade, in a jar with a tight-fitting lid, combine the vinegar, sugar, water, oil, basil, garlic, and black pepper. Cover and shake well. Pour over the vegetables. Close bag and refrigerate for 8 hours or overnight, turning bag occasionally. To serve, use a slotted spoon to transfer the salad to a serving bowl lined with lettuce. Makes 8 side-dish servings.

Prep Time: 25 minutes Chilling Time: 8 hours

1 Serving: Calories 185. Total Fat 4 g. Saturated Fat 0 g.
Protein 9 g. Carbohydrate 31 g. Fiber 9 g.
Sodium 87 mg. Cholesterol 0 mg.

✳

Three-Bean Salad Prepare as for Farm Country Four-Bean Salad, increasing green beans to **2 cups** and omitting garbanzo beans. Makes 6 side-dish servings.

1 Serving: Calories 179. Total Fat 4 g. Saturated Fat 0 g.
Protein 8 g. Carbohydrate 30 g. Fiber 9 g.
Sodium 113 mg. Cholesterol 0 mg.

Granny's Taste-As-You-Make Macaroni Salad

*Sandra Mapes says her grandmother never
made this salad the same way twice. She would
always add a bit more of this or that.*

1   cup medium-size shell, corkscrew, or elbow macaroni
½   cup cubed Cheddar or American cheese (2 ounces)
2   large green onions with tops, finely sliced
¼   cup finely chopped sweet green, red, or yellow pepper
¼   cup chopped sweet pickles
¼   cup sliced pitted black olives

For the dressing:
¼   cup reduced-fat mayonnaise
¼   cup reduced-fat sour cream
2   tablespoons low-fat (1% milkfat) milk
2   tablespoons pickle juice
2   tablespoons minced parsley
1   teaspoon dried dill weed
¼   teaspoon each salt and black pepper

1 Cook the macaroni according to package directions. Drain well. Rinse with cold water; drain again.

2 Meanwhile, in a large bowl, combine cheese, green onions, green pepper, sweet pickles, and olives. To prepare the dressing, in a small bowl, whisk together mayonnaise, sour cream, milk, pickle juice, parsley, dill weed, salt, and black pepper; pour over cheese mixture. Toss lightly to coat. Fold in macaroni. Cover and refrigerate for 4 to 24 hours. Makes 4 side-dish servings.

Prep Time: 15 minutes Cooking Time: 10 minutes
Chilling Time: 4 hours

1 Serving: Calories 220. Total Fat 12 g. Saturated Fat 5 g.
Protein 7 g. Carbohydrate 23 g. Fiber 1 g.
Sodium 546 mg. Cholesterol 27 mg.

✳

Macaroni 'n' Green Pea Salad Prepare as for Granny's Taste-As-You-Make Macaroni Salad, substituting **¾ cup frozen and thawed peas** for the Cheddar cheese and **2 tablespoons low-fat (1% milkfat) milk** for the pickle juice.

1 Serving: Calories 168. Total Fat 6 g. Saturated Fat 2 g.
Protein 5 g. Carbohydrate 24 g. Fiber 3 g.
Sodium 394 mg. Cholesterol 10 mg.

Deviled Potato Salad

If you prefer a milder salad, omit the mustard. Choose long-white or round-red potatoes. They have a firm, waxy texture that is ideal for boiling.

4 medium-size potatoes (about 1⅓ pounds total)
1 stalk celery, thinly sliced
½ cup finely chopped red onion or yellow onion
¼ cup chopped sweet or dill pickles
½ cup reduced-fat mayonnaise
½ cup reduced-fat sour cream
1 tablespoon prepared mustard or Dijon mustard
2 teaspoons sugar
2 teaspoons vinegar
½ teaspoon salt
¼ teaspoon black pepper
2 hard-cooked large eggs, yolks discarded
2 to 3 tablespoons low-fat (1% milkfat) milk

1 In a large saucepan, cover the potatoes with water. Bring to a boil over high heat. Lower the heat and simmer, covered, for 20 to 25 minutes or until almost tender; drain well. Cool slightly. Peel potatoes if you like, then cube potatoes. Set aside.

2 Meanwhile, in a large bowl, combine the celery, onion, and pickles. In a small bowl, whisk together the mayonnaise, sour cream, mustard, sugar, vinegar, salt, and pepper. Pour mayonnaise mixture over celery mixture. Toss to coat. Chop egg whites. Carefully fold potatoes and egg whites into celery mixture. Toss to coat. Cover and refrigerate for 4 to 24 hours.

3 Before serving, if necessary, stir in milk to make the salad the consistency you like. To serve, transfer the potato salad to a serving bowl lined with lettuce. Makes 6 side-dish servings.

Prep Time: 15 minutes Cooking Time: 20 minutes
Chilling Time: 4 hours

1 Serving: Calories 205. Total Fat 8 g. Saturated Fat 3 g.
Protein 5 g. Carbohydrate 28 g. Fiber 2 g.
Sodium 424 mg. Cholesterol 87 mg.

Old-Country Bacon And Potato Salad

This well-loved German recipe should be served warm. To avoid some of the last-minute work, cook, peel, and slice the potatoes ahead and refrigerate them. Then, assemble the salad just before mealtime.

4 medium-size potatoes (about 1⅓ pounds total) or 1¼ pounds tiny new potatoes
2 strips lean bacon, chopped
4 large green onions with tops, finely sliced
1 tablespoon all-purpose flour
1 tablespoon sugar
½ teaspoon celery seeds
¼ teaspoon each salt and black pepper
½ cup water
¼ cup tarragon vinegar or vinegar
2 tablespoons minced parsley

1 In a large saucepan, cover the potatoes with water. Bring to a boil over high heat. Lower the heat and simmer, covered, for 20 to 25 minutes or until almost tender; drain well. Cool slightly. Peel medium potatoes if you like, then slice (leave tiny new potatoes unpeeled and whole). Set aside.

2 Meanwhile, in a 10-inch skillet, cook bacon over moderate heat until crisp. Remove bacon, reserving 1 tablespoon drippings in the skillet. Drain the bacon on paper towels; set aside.

3 Add the green onions to reserved drippings in the skillet. Cook over moderate heat until the onions are tender but not brown. Stir in the flour, sugar, celery seeds, salt, and pepper and cook for 1 minute or until bubbly. Add the water and vinegar. Cook, stirring constantly, until mixture starts to thicken. Cook and stir for 3 minutes or until thickened.

4 Carefully stir in potatoes and bacon pieces. Cook for 2 to 3 minutes more or until heated through, stirring gently. Sprinkle with parsley. Serve immediately. Makes 4 side-dish servings.

Prep Time: 15 minutes Cooking Time: 30 minutes

1 Serving: Calories 195. Total Fat 5 g. Saturated Fat 2 g.
Protein 4 g. Carbohydrate 34 g. Fiber 3 g.
Sodium 212 mg. Cholesterol 6 mg.

Summer Corn and Cabbage Salad

Summer Corn and Cabbage Salad

In late summer, farm women created recipes to use their surplus fresh corn.
This delicious garden salad is just one example. When you're buying corn on the
cob, look for green, healthy-looking husks; they tell you the corn is fresh.

  3 **medium-size fresh ears of corn or 1 package**
     (10 ounces) frozen whole kernel corn
1½ **cups shredded green cabbage**
  1 **medium-size sweet red, yellow, or green pepper, cut**
     into bite-size pieces
  1 **stalk celery, thinly sliced**

For the dressing:
 ¼ **cup olive or vegetable oil**
 ¼ **cup lemon juice**
  1 **to 2 tablespoons honey**
  1 **teaspoon dry mustard**
 ½ **teaspoon salt**
 ¼ **teaspoon black pepper**

1 In a Dutch oven, bring 2 quarts lightly salted water
to a boil over high heat. Carefully add fresh ears of
corn; return to a boil. Lower the heat and simmer, covered, for 6 to 8 minutes or until corn is tender. (Or, cook

the frozen corn according to package directions.) Drain
corn well. When fresh corn is cool enough to handle,
cut off corn kernels. Hold an ear of corn at an angle so
that one end rests on cutting board. Using a sharp knife,
cut down across tips of kernels toward board. Repeat
with remaining ears.

2 In a large bowl, combine the corn, cabbage, red pepper, and celery. To prepare the dressing, in a jar with
a tight-fitting lid, combine oil, lemon juice, honey, mustard, salt, and black pepper. Cover; shake well. Pour
dressing over corn mixture. Toss to coat. Cover and
refrigerate for 2 to 24 hours. To serve, spoon the salad
onto leaf lettuce. Makes 4 side-dish servings.

Prep Time: 20 minutes Cooking Time: 11 minutes
Chilling Time: 2 hours

1 Serving: Calories 226. Total Fat 15 g. Saturated Fat 1 g.
Protein 3 g. Carbohydrate 25 g. Fiber 3 g.
Sodium 298 mg. Cholesterol 0 mg.

Tomato Rose Salad

In the 1930's, a whole tomato was trimmed with soft, white petals of cream cheese to look like a rose. This decorative salad was especially popular fare at fancy ladies' luncheons.

- **2 medium-size tomatoes**
- **2 tablespoons Creamy French Dressing (recipe, below) or reduced-fat French dressing**
- **4 ounces reduced-fat soft-style cream cheese**
- **2 teaspoons reduced-fat mayonnaise**
- **½ teaspoon grated lemon rind**

1 Peel the tomatoes if you like. Cover and refrigerate. Prepare the Creamy French Dressing. Cover and refrigerate while preparing the salad.

2 Arrange leaf or butterhead lettuce on 2 salad plates, overlapping the leaves slightly. Shape tomato roses (tip, right).

3 Place 1 teaspoon of the mayonnaise on the top of each tomato. Add lemon rind (tip, right). Serve the salads with the dressing. Makes 2 side-dish servings.

Prep Time: 25 minutes

1 Serving: Calories 215. Total Fat 16 g. Saturated Fat 7 g.
Protein 7 g. Carbohydrate 16 g. Fiber 1 g.
Sodium 400 mg. Cholesterol 21 mg.

Creamy French Dressing

In a food processor or blender, process ⅓ cup vinegar, ¼ cup sugar, 2 tablespoons minced yellow onion, ½ teaspoon paprika, ½ teaspoon dry mustard, ¼ teaspoon garlic powder, ¼ teaspoon salt, and ⅛ teaspoon ground red pepper (cayenne) until smooth. With food processor running, add ¼ cup olive or vegetable oil in thin, steady stream and process for 2 to 3 minutes or until mixture thickens. Cover and refrigerate (will keep for 1 week). Makes ¾ cup (six 2-tablespoon servings).

2 Tablespoons: Calories 117. Total Fat 9 g. Saturated Fat 1 g.
Protein 0 g. Carbohydrate 10 g. Fiber 0 g.
Sodium 89 mg. Cholesterol 0 mg.

ASSEMBLING THE TOMATO ROSE SALAD

1. Fill a flatware tablespoon completely with some of the cream cheese. Then, level it off with the flat edge of a table knife.

2. Hold the tomato in one hand and position the spoon so the cheese side rests near the top of the tomato. Gently pull the spoon down so the cream cheese forms a petal as shown.

3. Continue around the tomato until petal design is complete. Place the tomato on 1 of the lettuce-lined plates. Repeat with the remaining tomato and the remaining cream cheese.

4. Gently sprinkle the lemon rind over the mayonnaise on top of each tomato.

Shaker Cucumber Salad

Shaker women "watered out" the cucumbers before making this salad, so the fresh dill flavor of the dressing wouldn't be diluted. Select firm, well-shaped cucumbers—the withered ones are usually tough and bitter.

1 medium-size cucumber, halved lengthwise

¼ teaspoon salt

2 large green onions with tops, finely sliced

¼ cup thinly sliced radishes

For the dressing:

½ cup reduced-fat sour cream

2 tablespoons tarragon vinegar or white wine vinegar

1 tablespoon finely chopped fresh dill or 1 teaspoon dried dill weed

1 teaspoon sugar

½ teaspoon prepared mustard or Dijon mustard

¼ teaspoon black pepper

1 Scoop seeds out of cucumber; discard. Thinly slice cucumber. Measure 2 cups. Sprinkle slices with salt; let stand for 30 minutes. Drain well.

2 In a small bowl, combine the cucumber, green onions, and radishes. To prepare the dressing, in a small bowl, whisk together the sour cream, vinegar, dill, sugar, mustard, and pepper. Pour the dressing over cucumber mixture. Toss to coat. Cover and refrigerate for 1 hour. To serve, spoon the salad onto shredded lettuce. Makes 4 side-dish servings.

Prep Time: 10 minutes Standing Time: 30 minutes
Chilling Time: 1 hour

1 Serving: Calories 60. Total Fat 4 g. Saturated Fat 2 g. Protein 2 g. Carbohydrate 6 g. Fiber 1 g. Sodium 158 mg. Cholesterol 12 mg.

Black-Eyed Pea Salad

This Southern favorite is perfect for summer luncheons. If you cook the peas from scratch, be sure to boil them until they are just tender—not mushy.

1 can (15 ounces) black-eyed peas, rinsed and drained, or 2 cups cooked black-eyed peas

2 large tomatoes, seeded and chopped

1 cup frozen whole kernel corn, thawed

½ cup finely chopped sweet green, red, or yellow pepper

2 large green onions with tops, finely sliced

¼ teaspoon hot red pepper sauce

Black-Eyed Pea Salad

For the dressing:

⅓ cup olive or vegetable oil

2 tablespoons vinegar

2 tablespoons lemon juice

1 teaspoon dried basil leaves

1 tablespoon Dijon mustard

¼ teaspoon black pepper

1 In a large bowl, combine black-eyed peas, tomatoes, corn, green pepper, green onions, and red pepper sauce. To prepare dressing, in a jar with tight-fitting lid, combine oil, vinegar, lemon juice, basil, mustard, and black pepper. Cover and shake well. Pour dressing over vegetable mixture. Toss gently to coat. Cover and refrigerate for 2 to 4 hours. To serve, use slotted spoon to transfer salad to serving bowl lined with lettuce. Makes 6 side-dish servings.

Prep Time: 20 minutes Chilling Time: 2 hours

1 Serving: Calories 141. Total Fat 5 g. Saturated Fat 0 g. Protein 6 g. Carbohydrate 21 g. Fiber 5 g. Sodium 102 mg. Cholesterol 0 mg.

Gran's Alligator Pear Salad

*Gran called it an alligator pear because
of its bright green, bumpy skin, but we know it
as the Florida avocado. It's larger than
the dark green California or Haas avocado.*

- ²/₃ cup Sweet 'n' Sassy Dressing (recipe, below)
- 5 cups bite-size mixed salad greens
- 2 medium-size oranges, peeled and sectioned
- 1 large avocado, peeled, pitted, and sliced
- 1 medium-size grapefruit, peeled and sectioned
- ½ cup thinly sliced celery

1 Prepare Sweet 'n' Sassy Dressing. Cover and refrigerate while preparing the salad.

2 In a large salad bowl, place the greens, oranges, avocado, grapefruit, and celery. Shake the dressing well; pour over the salad. Toss lightly to coat. Makes 6 side-dish servings.

Prep Time: 20 minutes

1 Serving: Calories 195. Total Fat 15 g. Saturated Fat 2 g.
Protein 2 g. Carbohydrate 17 g. Fiber 4 g.
Sodium 16 mg. Cholesterol 0 mg.

Citrus and Crab Salad Prepare as for Gran's Alligator Pear Salad, gently folding in **1 pound lump crab meat, picked over and flaked, or 1½ packages (8 ounces each) frozen and thawed crab-flavored, salad-style fish, chopped.** Makes 5 main-dish servings.

1 Serving: Calories 309. Total Fat 18 g. Saturated Fat 2 g.
Protein 18 g. Carbohydrate 22 g. Fiber 4 g.
Sodium 277 mg. Cholesterol 52 mg.

Sweet 'n' Sassy Dressing

In a jar with a tight-fitting lid, combine ½ cup olive or vegetable oil, ½ cup raspberry vinegar or vinegar, 3 tablespoons honey, 1 teaspoon dried mint leaves, 1 teaspoon dry mustard, and ½ teaspoon paprika. Cover and shake well, then refrigerate (will keep for 1 week). Makes 1¼ cups (ten 2-tablespoon servings).

2 Tablespoons: Calories 120. Total Fat 11 g. Saturated Fat 1 g.
Protein 0 g. Carbohydrate 6 g. Fiber 0 g.
Sodium 0 mg. Cholesterol 0 mg.

Garden Seed Salad

*In winter, farm women would order
garden seeds from a catalog and plant them
as soon as the spring sun warmed the
soil enough. At harvest time, they would find
flavorful ways to show off their bounty.*

- Lemon Dressing (recipe, below)
- 4 cups bite-size mixed salad greens
- 1 cup alfalfa sprouts
- 1 medium-size sweet yellow, green, or red pepper, cut into bite-size pieces
- ½ medium-size red onion, thinly sliced and separated into rings
- ½ cup thinly sliced cucumber
- ½ cup sliced radishes
- ½ cup crumbled blue or feta cheese (2 ounces)

1 Prepare Lemon Dressing. Cover and refrigerate while preparing the salad.

2 In a large salad bowl, place the greens, alfalfa sprouts, green pepper, onion, cucumber, radishes, and cheese. Shake the dressing well; pour over salad. Toss lightly. Makes 6 side-dish servings.

Prep Time: 20 minutes

1 Serving: Calories 123. Total Fat 10 g. Saturated Fat 3 g.
Protein 4 g. Carbohydrate 5 g. Fiber 1 g.
Sodium 165 mg. Cholesterol 9 mg.

Lemon Dressing

In a jar with a tight-fitting lid, combine **3 tablespoons olive or vegetable oil; 3 tablespoons lemon or lime juice; 2 tablespoons minced parsley; 1 teaspoon dried oregano leaves; 2 cloves garlic, minced; ½ teaspoon sugar; and ⅛ teaspoon black pepper.** Cover and shake well, then refrigerate (will keep for 1 week). Makes about ½ cup (four 2-tablespoon servings).

2 Tablespoons: Calories 99. Total Fat 10 g. Saturated Fat 1 g.
Protein 0 g. Carbohydrate 2 g. Fiber 0 g.
Sodium 1 mg. Cholesterol 0 mg.

Garden Seed Salad

Hostess Salad Bowl

Hostess Salad Bowl

The old-fashioned way to grate onion for salad dressings was to scrape it with a spoon, but you'll find it easier to use a cheese grater.

Tangy Tomato Dressing (recipe, below)
4 cups bite-size mixed salad greens
1 medium-size yellow summer squash or zucchini, halved lengthwise and sliced ¼ inch thick
2 medium-size carrots or 1 small jicama, cut into 1½x½-inch sticks
1 cup red and/or yellow cherry tomatoes or baby pear tomatoes, halved
1 cup small whole fresh mushrooms
1 cup sliced cauliflower or broccoli flowerets

1 Prepare Tangy Tomato Dressing. Cover and refrigerate while preparing the salad.

2 In a large salad bowl, combine the greens, squash, carrots, tomatoes, mushrooms, and cauliflower. Shake the dressing well; pour over salad. Toss lightly to coat. Makes 6 side-dish servings.

Prep Time: 25 minutes

1 Serving: Calories 85. Total Fat 5 g. Saturated Fat 0 g. Protein 2 g. Carbohydrate 10 g. Fiber 2 g. Sodium 24 mg. Cholesterol 0 mg.

Tangy Tomato Dressing

In a jar with a tight-fitting lid, combine ¼ cup lower-calorie, lower-sodium catsup; 2 tablespoons grated red onion; 2 tablespoons olive or vegetable oil; 2 tablespoons lemon juice or vinegar; 2 tablespoons water; 1 teaspoon drained prepared horseradish; ½ teaspoon sugar; ½ teaspoon lower-sodium Worcestershire sauce; and ⅛ teaspoon black pepper. Cover and shake well, then refrigerate (will keep for 1 week). Makes about ¾ cup (six 2-tablespoon servings).

2 Tablespoons: Calories 55. Total Fat 5 g. Saturated Fat 0 g. Protein 0 g. Carbohydrate 4 g. Fiber 0 g. Sodium 5 mg. Cholesterol 0 mg.

CLEANING SALAD GREENS

This traditional way of washing greens is still the best because it doesn't bruise the leaves.

1. Start by discarding any damaged leaves.

2. Place greens in a large bowl of cold water. Let stand for 5 minutes to remove any dirt or sand. Lift the greens out and discard the water.

3. Refill the bowl with cold water. Dunk the greens repeatedly until no more dirt or sand collects in the bowl.

4. Drain the greens in a colander. Break off and discard any stems.

5. Place greens on a clean kitchen towel or several layers of paper towels. Place a second kitchen towel or more paper towels over the greens. Gently pat the greens dry. Refrigerate.

Church Supper Carrot and Raisin Salad

Social gatherings of yesteryear wouldn't have been complete without this tried-and-true salad.

4 medium-size carrots, shredded
2 stalks celery, finely chopped
½ cup raisins or chopped pitted dates
¼ cup chopped pecans or walnuts, toasted

For the dressing:
½ cup reduced-fat mayonnaise
3 tablespoons low-fat (1% milkfat) milk
¼ teaspoon salt
⅛ teaspoon black pepper

1 In a medium-size bowl, combine the carrots, celery, raisins, and pecans. To prepare dressing, in a small bowl, whisk together the remaining ingredients. Pour dressing over carrot mixture. Toss to coat. Cover; refrigerate for 2 to 24 hours. Makes 4 side-dish servings.

Prep Time: 25 minutes Chilling Time: 2 hours

1 Serving: Calories 220. Total Fat 11 g. Saturated Fat 2 g. Protein 3 g. Carbohydrate 30 g. Fiber 3 g. Sodium 344 mg. Cholesterol 8 mg.

Wilted Dandelion Salad

You can make this salad with spinach or sorrel. But for true old-time taste, use the young, tender wild dandelion leaves you find in early spring (before the yellow flower develops). Make sure the leaves haven't been treated with chemicals.

6 cups bite-size dandelion greens, sorrel, or fresh spinach

1 cup sliced fresh mushrooms

2 strips lean bacon, chopped

¼ cup finely sliced leek or 2 large green onions with tops, finely sliced

1 clove garlic, minced

2 tablespoons vinegar or dry sherry

2 tablespoons honey

¼ teaspoon black pepper

1 In a large salad bowl, combine the greens and mushrooms. In a 10-inch skillet, cook the bacon over moderate heat until crisp. Remove bacon, reserving 1 tablespoon drippings in skillet. Drain bacon on paper towels; set aside.

2 Add leek and garlic to the reserved drippings in the skillet. Cook over moderate heat until the leek is tender. Stir in vinegar, honey, and pepper.

3 Bring to a boil. Add the greens mixture. Toss for 30 to 60 seconds or until greens just start to wilt. Transfer back to the salad bowl. Top with the crisp-cooked bacon. Makes 3 side-dish servings.

Prep Time: 10 minutes Cooking Time: 8 minutes

1 Serving: Calories 173. Total Fat 8 g. Saturated Fat 3 g. Protein 5 g. Carbohydrate 25 g. Fiber 4 g. Sodium 180 mg. Cholesterol 8 mg.

Calico Coleslaw

If you want to serve this salad right away, crisp the shredded cabbage in a bowl of ice water for a few minutes. Then, drain it on paper towels and toss with the dressing.

½ small green cabbage, quartered

1 large carrot, shredded

½ cup finely chopped sweet green, red, or yellow pepper

2 large green onions with tops, finely sliced

For the dressing:

⅔ cup reduced-fat mayonnaise

2 tablespoons vinegar

2 tablespoons low-fat (1% milkfat) milk

1 tablespoon sugar

1 teaspoon caraway seeds or ½ teaspoon celery seeds

¼ teaspoon salt

⅛ teaspoon black pepper

1 Shred the cabbage (tip, below). Measure 2½ cups shredded cabbage. In a large bowl, combine the cabbage, carrot, green pepper, and green onions. To prepare the dressing, in a small bowl, whisk together the mayonnaise, vinegar, milk, sugar, caraway seeds, salt, and black pepper. Pour the dressing over cabbage mixture. Toss to coat well. Cover and refrigerate for 2 to 24 hours. Makes 4 side-dish servings.

Prep Time: 25 minutes Chilling Time: 2 hours

1 Serving: Calories 153. Total Fat 9 g. Saturated Fat 1 g. Protein 2 g. Carbohydrate 19 g. Fiber 3 g. Sodium 370 mg. Cholesterol 10 mg.

Calico Red Coleslaw Prepare as for Calico Coleslaw, substituting **2½ cups shredded red cabbage** for the green cabbage and **1 small Red Delicious apple, chopped,** for the green pepper.

1 Serving: Calories 147. Total Fat 8 g. Saturated Fat 1 g. Protein 1 g. Carbohydrate 18 g. Fiber 3 g. Sodium 358 mg. Cholesterol 10 mg.

SHREDDING CABBAGE

For coarsely shredded cabbage, hold a quarter-head of cabbage firmly against the cutting board. Using a knife, slice the cabbage to make long shreds.

For medium cabbage shreds, push a quarter-head of cabbage across the surface of the coarse blade of a hand shredder.

Summer Melon Mix

Summer Melon Mix

"My grandparents always used melons from their garden in salads,"
remembers Jai Hall. "Grandma told me never to remove the seeds when I
store cut melons in the refrigerator—the seeds help keep the fruit moist."

¾ **cup Berry Honey Dressing (recipe, right)**

½ **small cantaloupe, seeded**

½ **small honeydew melon, seeded**

1 **pint strawberries, halved**

1 Prepare Berry Honey Dressing. Cover and refrigerate while preparing the salad. Peel the cantaloupe and honeydew melon; cut into thin wedges.

2 To serve, place butterhead lettuce on salad plates. Arrange cantaloupe, honeydew, and strawberries on top of the lettuce. Drizzle the dressing over fruit. Makes 6 side-dish servings.

Prep Time: 25 minutes

1 Serving: Calories 85. Total Fat 1 g. Saturated Fat 0 g.
Protein 1 g. Carbohydrate 19 g. Fiber 2 g.
Sodium 13 mg. Cholesterol 0 mg.

Berry Honey Dressing

In a food processor or blender, process 1¾ **cups strawberries, quartered; 3 tablespoons honey; 2 tablespoons lemon juice; 1 tablespoon olive or vegetable oil;** and **1 teaspoon grated lemon rind** until smooth. Cover and refrigerate (will keep for 1 week). Makes about 1¾ cups (fourteen 2-tablespoon servings).

2 Tablespoons: Calories 28. Total Fat 1 g. Saturated Fat 0 g.
Protein 0 g. Carbohydrate 5 g. Fiber 0 g.
Sodium 0 mg. Cholesterol 0 mg.

Frosty Strawberry Salad Circles

Frosty Strawberry Salad Circles

In the 1940's and 1950's, whipped cream salads frozen in baking powder cans were the rage.
To serve, all the hostess had to do was push the salad from the can and slice it into circles.

1 **can (8 ounces) crushed pineapple packed in juice**
1 **container (8 ounces) reduced-fat soft-style cream cheese, at room temperature**
1 **cup reduced-fat sour cream**
1/4 **cup sugar**
1/2 **teaspoon vanilla**
2 **cups chopped strawberries**
1/2 **cup chopped pecans or walnuts, toasted**

1 Drain pineapple, reserving 2 tablespoons of the juice. In a medium-size bowl, with an electric mixer on *High,* beat the reserved juice, cream cheese, sour cream, sugar, and vanilla until smooth and fluffy. Fold in the pineapple, strawberries, and pecans. Spoon the mix-ture into three 12-ounce juice concentrate cans. (Or, spoon the mixture into a 9" x 5" x 3" loaf pan.) Cover and freeze for 6 hours or until firm.

2 Tear off the paper from the juice cans and let the salad stand at room temperature for 35 to 45 min-utes to thaw slightly. (Or, let the salad in loaf pan stand for 15 to 20 minutes.) Cut into 9 round slices. (Or, cut the loaf pan salad lengthwise in half, then crosswise to make 8 equal pieces.)

3 To serve, place on salad plates lined with butterhead lettuce. Makes 8 or 9 side-dish servings.

Prep Time: 20 minutes Freezing Time: 6 hours
Standing Time: 35 minutes

1 Serving: Calories 227. Total Fat 14 g. Saturated Fat 6 g.
Protein 5 g. Carbohydrate 24 g. Fiber 1 g.
Sodium 173 mg. Cholesterol 22 mg.

Harvest Fruit Salad

This creamy fruit salad, a variation on classic Waldorf salad, takes advantage of the harvest season's bountiful produce—crisp apples and juicy pears.

1   medium-size green apple, chopped
1   medium-size red apple, chopped
1   small pear, chopped
1   tablespoon lemon juice
¼   cup seedless green grapes, halved
¼   cup raisins or dried tart red cherries
⅔   cup plain low-fat yogurt
¼   cup reduced-fat mayonnaise
2   tablespoons low-fat (1% milkfat) milk
1   tablespoon sugar
⅛   teaspoon ground nutmeg
2   tablespoons chopped pecans or walnuts, toasted

1 In a medium-size bowl, combine the apples, pear, and lemon juice; toss to coat. Stir in the grapes and raisins. In a small bowl, whisk together the yogurt, mayonnaise, milk, sugar, and nutmeg. Spread the yogurt mixture over the top of apple mixture to help seal out air and keep the fruit fresh longer. Cover and refrigerate for 2 to 24 hours.

2 To serve, fold the yogurt mixture into apple mixture. Spoon the salad onto salad plates lined with lettuce. Sprinkle with pecans. Makes 5 side-dish servings.

Prep Time: 20 minutes   Chilling Time: 2 hours

1 Serving: Calories 153. Total Fat 5 g. Saturated Fat 1 g.
Protein 3 g. Carbohydrate 26 g. Fiber 2 g.
Sodium 92 mg. Cholesterol 5 mg.

THE RIGHT APPLE FOR THE JOB

For eating raw, choose apples that stay crisp. For pies and sauces, you'll want ones that cook up tender. Here are the varieties to look for.

• **Salads and Eating-Out-of-Hand**   Cortland, Empire, Gala, McIntosh, Newtown Pippin, Northern Spy, Red Delicious, and Stayman.

• **Cooking and Baking**   Newtown Pippin, Rome Beauty, Stayman, and York Imperial.

• **All-Purpose**   Crispin, Criterion, Fuji, Golden Delicious, Granny Smith, Jonagold, Jonathan, and Winesap.

Overnight Fruit Salad

In the 1930's and 1940's housewives made fancy fruit salads by folding whipped cream into a cooked homemade dressing. This lighter version uses vanilla yogurt to reduce the fat.

For the dressing:

2   tablespoons sugar
1   tablespoon all-purpose flour
⅓   cup orange juice
1   large egg yolk, lightly beaten
2   tablespoons lemon juice
1   carton (8 ounces) vanilla low-fat yogurt

For the salad:

2   medium-size peaches or nectarines, peeled, pitted, and thinly sliced
2   cups seedless green or red grapes, halved
1   pint strawberries, quartered
½   cup miniature marshmallows

1 To prepare the dressing, in a small saucepan, whisk together the sugar and flour. Whisk in the orange juice and egg yolk. Cook over low heat, whisking constantly, for 2 minutes or until thickened and mixture bubbles at the edge. Stir in the lemon juice until smooth. Remove from heat. Refrigerate for 20 minutes. Fold the yogurt into the cooked mixture.

2 To prepare the salad, in a large bowl, combine the peaches, grapes, strawberries, and marshmallows. Pour the dressing over fruit mixture. Mix gently. Transfer the salad to a serving bowl. Cover and refrigerate for 8 to 24 hours. Makes 8 side-dish servings.

Prep Time: 25 minutes   Cooking Time: 2 minutes
Chilling Time: 8 hours 20 minutes

1 Serving: Calories 111. Total Fat 1 g. Saturated Fat 1 g.
Protein 3 g. Carbohydrate 24 g. Fiber 1 g.
Sodium 22 mg. Cholesterol 28 mg.

Frozen Cherry Reception Salad

When refrigerators with freezers first came on the scene, innovative homemakers concocted rich frozen salads by teaming ice cream with sweetened fruit. Soon these dessert-like salads became popular items on reception menus.

1 quart frozen cherry yogurt, softened
1 can (21 ounces) cherry pie filling
1 teaspoon vanilla
3 medium-size bananas, chopped
1 can (11 ounces) mandarin orange sections, drained
½ cup coarsely chopped almonds, toasted

1 In a large bowl, stir together the yogurt, pie filling, and vanilla. Carefully stir in the bananas, mandarin oranges, and almonds. Pour into a 13" x 9" x 2" baking pan. Cover and freeze 10 hours or until firm. To serve, let salad stand at room temperature 30 minutes to thaw slightly. Cut into squares; arrange on a platter. Makes 15 side-dish servings.

Prep Time: 15 minutes Freezing Time: 10 hours
Standing Time: 30 minutes

1 Serving: Calories 153. Total Fat 3 g. Saturated Fat 1 g.
Protein 4 g. Carbohydrate 29 g. Fiber 1 g.
Sodium 37 mg. Cholesterol 3 mg.

Black-Eyed Susan Salad

This dainty salad was inspired by the gloriously colored flower called the black-eyed susan.

4 cups shredded romaine or iceberg lettuce
3 medium-size oranges, peeled and sectioned
2 medium-size red grapefruit, peeled and sectioned
½ cup vanilla low-fat yogurt
4 teaspoons currants or raisins

1 Line 4 salad plates with cabbage leaves. Place 1 cup of the romaine in center of each plate. On top of romaine, arrange orange and grapefruit sections in petal fashion, alternating fruits. Place 2 tablespoons of yogurt in center of each "flower" and top each with 1 teaspoon of currants. Makes 4 side-dish servings.

Prep Time: 35 minutes

1 Serving: Calories 127. Total Fat 1 g. Saturated Fat 0 g.
Protein 4 g. Carbohydrate 29 g. Fiber 4 g.
Sodium 25 mg. Cholesterol 2 mg.

German Herring Salad With Apple

German and Scandinavian immigrants frequently used pickled herring in salads. Look for it at your local deli or in the refrigerated section of larger supermarkets.

3 medium-size beets or 1 can (16 ounces) diced beets, well drained
2 medium-size potatoes
1½ cups bite-size pieces pickled herring (9 ounces)
1 medium-size tart green apple, chopped
2 large green onions with tops, finely sliced
¼ cup finely chopped sweet green pepper or celery

For the dressing:
½ cup reduced-fat mayonnaise
½ cup reduced-fat sour cream
2 tablespoons vinegar
1 tablespoon sugar
1 tablespoon coarse-grain brown mustard

1 Trim fresh beets ½ inch above the stems. In a large saucepan, cover beets with lightly salted water. Bring to a boil. Lower the heat and simmer, covered, for 40 to 45 minutes or until almost tender; drain well. Cool slightly. Peel by slipping off skins while still warm; cut into ½-inch cubes. (Or, use canned diced beets.)

2 Meanwhile, in a medium-size saucepan, cover potatoes with lightly salted water. Bring to a boil. Lower the heat and simmer, covered, for 20 to 25 minutes or until almost tender; drain well. Cool slightly. Peel and cut into ¾-inch cubes.

3 In a large bowl, combine the herring, apple, green onions, and green pepper. To prepare the dressing, in a small bowl, whisk together mayonnaise, sour cream, vinegar, sugar, and mustard. Pour the dressing over herring mixture. Toss to coat. Carefully fold in beets and potatoes. Toss lightly to coat. Cover and refrigerate for 6 to 24 hours.

4 Before serving, if necessary, stir in a little milk to make salad the consistency you like. To serve, place bite-size pieces of romaine on each plate; top with the salad. Makes 4 main-dish servings.

Prep Time: 15 minutes Cooking Time: 40 minutes
Chilling Time: 6 hours

1 Serving: Calories 371. Total Fat 20 g. Saturated Fat 5 g.
Protein 12 g. Carbohydrate 39 g. Fiber 4 g.
Sodium 710 mg. Cholesterol 26 mg.

Italian Rice and Tuna Salad

Italian Rice and Tuna Salad

Traditionally this salad was made with Italian Arborio rice, which has a slightly softer,
creamier texture that soaks up the dressing. However, you also can use long-grain or basmati rice.

1½ **cups cold water**

½ **teaspoon black pepper**

½ **cup uncooked Arborio rice or long-grain white rice**

1 **large tomato, seeded and chopped**

1 **jar (6½ ounces) marinated artichoke hearts, drained and quartered**

½ **cup chopped sweet green, red, or yellow pepper**

½ **cup chopped red onion**

1 **can (2¼ ounces) sliced pitted black olives, drained**

1 **tablespoon drained capers, rinsed**

⅓ **cup lemon juice**

¼ **cup water**

3 **tablespoons olive or vegetable oil**

1 **can (6 ounces) water-packed, chunk light tuna, rinsed, drained, and flaked**

3 **anchovy fillets, drained, rinsed, and chopped**

1 In a medium-size saucepan, bring the water and black pepper to a boil over high heat. Stir in rice. Lower the heat and simmer, covered, for 20 minutes or until the rice is tender. Drain and cool rice slightly (about 10 minutes). Fluff with a fork.

2 In a large bowl, combine the warm rice, tomato, artichoke hearts, green pepper, onion, olives, and capers. Pour lemon juice, water, and oil over rice mixture. Toss to coat. Carefully fold in tuna and anchovies. Toss lightly to coat. Cover; refrigerate for 4 to 6 hours.

3 To serve, spoon the salad onto plates lined with curly endive. Makes 4 main-dish servings.

Prep Time: 25 minutes Cooking Time: 20 minutes
Chilling Time: 4 hours

1 Serving: Calories 413. Total Fat 21 g. Saturated Fat 4 g.
Protein 22 g. Carbohydrate 38 g. Fiber 5 g.
Sodium 761 mg. Cholesterol 18 mg.

Mandarin Chicken Salad

Mandarin Chicken Salad

*You also can make this ladies' luncheon
favorite with 12 ounces of cooked shrimp
in place of the chicken.*

Lime and Poppy Seed Dressing (recipe, below)

2 **large firm bananas**

1 **tablespoon water**

1 **tablespoon lemon juice**

4 **cups bite-size mixed salad greens**

2 **cups bite-size pieces cooked chicken breast**

1 **can (11 ounces) mandarin orange sections, chilled and drained**

1 **can (8 ounces) pineapple chunks packed in juice, chilled and drained**

1 **cup seedless red grapes or pitted dark sweet cherries**

½ **cup coarsely chopped pecans, toasted**

1 Prepare Lime and Poppy Seed Dressing. Cover and refrigerate while preparing the salad. Slice bananas. In a small bowl, combine the water and lemon juice. Add bananas; toss gently to coat.

2 In a large salad bowl, place the greens, chicken, orange sections, pineapple chunks, and grapes. Add bananas. Shake the dressing well; pour over salad. Toss lightly to coat. Sprinkle salad with pecans. Makes 4 main-dish servings.

Prep Time: 15 minutes

1 Serving: Calories 465. Total Fat 21 g. Saturated Fat 2 g.
Protein 28 g. Carbohydrate 47 g. Fiber 3 g.
Sodium 68 mg. Cholesterol 66 mg.

Lime and Poppy Seed Dressing

In a jar with a tight-fitting lid, combine **3 tablespoons lime or lemon juice, 2 tablespoons walnut or vegetable oil, 2 tablespoons honey, 1 tablespoon finely chopped fresh chives,** and ½ **teaspoon poppy seeds.** Cover and shake well, then refrigerate (will keep for 1 week). Makes about ½ cup (four 2-tablespoon servings).

2 Tablespoons: Calories 98. Total Fat 7 g. Saturated Fat 1 g.
Protein 0 g. Carbohydrate 10 g. Fiber 0 g.
Sodium 0 mg. Cholesterol 0 mg.

Tuna Olive Starbursts

*Fashionable hostesses of years ago often served
tuna or chicken salad in "starbursts"—a tomato cut
in wedges to look like the points of a star.*

1 **cup cubed reduced-fat Cheddar cheese (4 ounces)**

½ **cup chopped sweet green, red, or yellow pepper**

½ **cup thinly sliced celery**

¼ **cup sliced pimiento-stuffed green olives or finely chopped sweet pickle**

¼ **cup minced parsley**

2 **tablespoons chopped red onion**

½ **cup reduced-fat mayonnaise**

1 **teaspoon prepared mustard**

¼ **teaspoon black pepper**

1 **can (6 ounces) water-packed, chunk light tuna, rinsed, drained, and flaked**

3 **large tomatoes**

1 In a large bowl, combine the cheese, green pepper, celery, olives, parsley, and onion. In a small bowl, whisk together mayonnaise, mustard, and black pepper. Pour mayonnaise mixture over cheese mixture. Toss to coat. Carefully fold in tuna. Toss lightly to coat. Cover and refrigerate for 4 to 24 hours.

2 With a sharp knife, remove ½ inch of core from the stem end of each tomato. Invert tomatoes and cut to but not through the stem end to make 6 wedges. To serve, place each tomato on a plate lined with lettuce. Spread wedges slightly apart; fill with the tuna mixture. Makes 3 main-dish servings.

Prep Time: 25 minutes Chilling Time: 4 hours

1 Serving: Calories 343. Total Fat 17 g. Saturated Fat 6 g.
Protein 29 g. Carbohydrate 20 g. Fiber 3 g.
Sodium 742 mg. Cholesterol 55 mg.

Salmon Olive Starbursts Prepare as for Tuna Olive Starbursts, substituting **1 can (7½ ounces) salmon, drained, flaked, and skin and bones removed,** for tuna.

1 Serving: Calories 381. Total Fat 22 g. Saturated Fat 7 g.
Protein 28 g. Carbohydrate 20 g. Fiber 3 g.
Sodium 915 mg. Cholesterol 68 mg.

El Paso Steak Salad

2/3 cup lime or lemon juice

3 cloves garlic, minced

1 tablespoon grated lime or lemon rind

2 teaspoons dried oregano leaves

1/2 teaspoon ground cumin

1/2 teaspoon crushed red pepper

1 pound boneless beef sirloin steak, 1 inch thick

3 tablespoons olive or vegetable oil

1 tablespoon sugar

6 cups bite-size pieces romaine

1 cup small fresh mushrooms, halved

1 cup cherry tomatoes, halved

1/2 medium-size red onion, thinly sliced

1 In a jar with a tight-fitting lid, combine lime juice, garlic, lime rind, oregano, cumin, and red pepper. Cover and shake well. Pour half of lime mixture into large heavy-duty plastic bag. Add steak. Close bag. Refrigerate for 6 hours or overnight, turning bag occasionally. Add oil and sugar to remaining lime mixture. Cover and shake well. Refrigerate until serving time.

2 Preheat broiler. Remove steak; discard mixture in bag. Slash fat edges of steak; place on broiler pan. Broil 4 inches from heat for 5 to 6 minutes on each side for medium-rare. Thinly slice. Toss romaine, mushrooms, tomatoes, and onion; top with steak. Drizzle with lime mixture. Makes 4 main-dish servings.

Prep Time: 20 minutes Chilling Time: 6 hours
Broiling Time: 10 minutes

1 Serving: Calories 323. Total Fat 18 g. Saturated Fat 3 g.
Protein 29 g. Carbohydrate 14 g. Fiber 2 g.
Sodium 69 mg. Cholesterol 77 mg.

Sunday Night Salad Platter

On Sunday nights, Sharon Vogel's grandma, Mabel Wright, would set out a platter of cold meats, cheeses, and fresh vegetables and let everyone make a salad.

Blue Cheese Salad Dressing (recipe, right)
Thousand Island Salad Dressing (recipe, right)

6 cups bite-size mixed salad greens

2 cups fresh vegetables, such as mushrooms, sliced cucumber, broccoli flowerets, and cherry tomatoes

1 cup cubed Colby, Swiss, Cheddar, American, Muenster, and/or Gruyère cheese (4 ounces)

4 ounces cooked chicken, turkey, beef, pork, ham, and/or lamb, cut into thin strips

1 Prepare Blue Cheese Salad Dressing and Thousand Island Salad Dressing. Cover and refrigerate while preparing salad. Place greens in a large salad bowl. Arrange vegetables, cheeses, and meats on a large platter lined with leaf lettuce. Serve with dressings on the side and let each person make an individual salad. Makes 4 main-dish servings.

Prep Time: 40 minutes

1 Serving: Calories 334. Total Fat 22 g. Saturated Fat 10 g.
Protein 21 g. Carbohydrate 16 g. Fiber 3 g.
Sodium 552 mg. Cholesterol 72 mg.

Blue Cheese Salad Dressing

In a food processor or blender, process 1/2 **cup reduced-fat sour cream**; 1/2 **cup reduced-fat mayonnaise**; 1/4 **cup crumbled blue cheese (2 ounces)**; 3 **tablespoons low-fat (1% milkfat) milk**; 1 **large green onion with top, finely sliced**; 2 **tablespoons tarragon vinegar**; and 1/4 **teaspoon black pepper** until smooth. Pour dressing into a small bowl. Stir in 1/4 **cup crumbled blue cheese (2 ounces)**. Cover and refrigerate (will keep for 1 week). Before serving, if necessary, stir in a little milk to make the dressing the consistency you like. Makes 1 cup (eight 2-tablespoon servings).

2 Tablespoons: Calories 90. Total Fat 7 g. Saturated Fat 3 g.
Protein 3 g. Carbohydrate 4 g. Fiber 0 g.
Sodium 205 mg. Cholesterol 16 mg.

Thousand Island Salad Dressing

Finely chop the white of 1 **hard-cooked large egg**; discard the yolk. In a small bowl, stir together the egg white; 1/2 **cup reduced-fat mayonnaise**; 1/3 **cup lower-calorie, lower-sodium catsup**; 1 **tablespoon lemon juice**; 1/2 **teaspoon paprika**; 1/2 **teaspoon lower-sodium Worcestershire sauce**; and 1/8 **teaspoon ground red pepper (cayenne)**. Stir in 2 **tablespoons finely chopped sweet green pepper** and 1 **tablespoon finely chopped dill pickle**. Cover and refrigerate (will keep for 1 week). Makes 1 1/4 cups (ten 2-tablespoon servings).

2 Tablespoons: Calories 40. Total Fat 2 g. Saturated Fat 0 g.
Protein 1 g. Carbohydrate 5 g. Fiber 0 g.
Sodium 88 mg. Cholesterol 3 mg.

Grandma's Treats

Fruit Wobblies

The children will delight in cutting this salad into their favorite shapes.

1½ cups cranberry juice cocktail

3 envelopes unflavored gelatin

   (2 tablespoons total)

1 can (6 ounces) frozen pink or regular lemonade concentrate

1. Pour cranberry juice cocktail into a medium-size saucepan. Sprinkle the gelatin over the cranberry juice cocktail. Let stand for 1 minute.

Bring the mixture to a boil over moderately high heat, stirring constantly until gelatin dissolves. Remove from heat. Stir in the lemonade concentrate.

2. Pour mixture into a foil-lined 8" x 8" x 2" baking pan. Cover and refrigerate until firm. Invert the gelatin mixture onto a cutting board. Remove the foil.

3. Use tiny cookie cutters to cut the gelatin into different shapes or a table knife to cut it into squares. Makes about 25.

Sailboat Salads

The little sailors in your family also can use Swiss or mozzarella cheese slices for the sails on their boats.

2 small cucumbers, zucchini, or yellow summer squash

½ cup frozen peas

¼ cup cubed Cheddar cheese (1 ounce)

2 tablespoons reduced-fat mayonnaise

1 tablespoon drained canned pimientos, chopped

½ teaspoon lemon juice

   Dash black pepper

1 slice American cheese

1. For the boats, cut a thin horizontal slice from tops of cucumbers. Hollow out cucumbers; chop pulp and reserve ¼ cup. For the cargo, in a small bowl, combine the chopped cucumber, peas, Cheddar cheese, mayonnaise, pimientos, lemon juice, and pepper. Spoon into cucumber boats.

2. For the sails, cut American cheese slice in half diagonally. Thread each triangle onto a 4-inch wooden pick. Stick each sail into cargo. Makes 2 side-dish salads.

Ants On A Log

This easy, yet nutritious snack is ideal for packing in a take-along lunch.

Peanut butter

Celery sticks

Raisins

1. Spread peanut butter into the grooves of celery sticks.

2. Place raisin "ants" on the "logs".

Smiley Sea-Creature Salad

Making this enchanting creature is almost as much fun as eating it.

½ cup low-fat (1% milkfat) cottage cheese

1 small pear

1 medium-size peach or nectarine

1 small carrot

Peanut butter

Raisins, miniature marshmallows, or nuts

Maraschino cherry

1. Line 2 salad plates with lettuce. For each salad, spoon ¼ cup cottage cheese on top of lettuce. For the body, cut pear in half. Place each pear half on cottage cheese. For the claws, cut peach into slices. Place at least 1 slice along each side of pear half next to the small end. Repeat on the other salad.

2. For the wavy tail, use a vegetable peeler to cut carrot into long, very thin strips. Place carrot strips at large end of each pear half. For the eyes, use a little peanut butter to attach raisins. For the smiley mouth, cut the maraschino cherry in half. Attach a cherry half to each pear half with a little peanut butter. Makes 2 side-dish salads.

SOUPS TO WARM THE SOUL

Does the memory of old-fashioned soups simmering on the stove make your mouth water? Soups were one of the ways grandma used up whatever vegetables and leftover meats she had on hand. She used beef bones to make stock and garden vegetables for creamy bisques or colorful vegetable soups. She enriched thick bean soups with bits of last night's roast and transformed fresh fish or shellfish into luscious chowders. Enjoy those wonderful soups of yesteryear with this tempting collection of grandma's best recipes.

Hungarian Cream of Cherry Soup (page 74)
German Pork and Kraut Soup (page 82)
Finnish Summer Vegetable Soup (page 77)

Brown Beef Stock

Brown Beef Stock

*One reason old-time soups tasted so good was that they were made
with rich, homemade stock, such as this one. If you want a lighter broth to
use in cream soups, skip the roasting step and omit the tomato sauce.*

4 pounds meaty beef, lamb, or veal bones (neck bones,
  shank crosscuts, short ribs, knuckles, or leg bones
  with marrow)

½ cup lower-sodium tomato sauce (optional)

For the stock:

14 cups cold water

4 stalks celery with leaves, cut up

4 large carrots, cut up

2 large yellow onions, thickly sliced

2 medium-size tomatoes, cut up (optional)

1 large potato, white turnip, or parsnip, peeled and
  thickly sliced

1 cup thickly sliced green onion or leek tops

4 cloves garlic, halved

4 bay leaves

1 tablespoon each dried basil leaves and thyme leaves

2 teaspoons salt

1 teaspoon whole black peppercorns

½ teaspoon whole cloves

1 Preheat the oven to 425°F. In a large shallow roasting pan, arrange meaty bones. Roast for 25 minutes. Turn the bones over. Roast for 15 minutes more. Using a pastry brush, spread tomato sauce (if using) over bones. Roast for 10 minutes more or until meat is well browned. Transfer to 10-quart stockpot.

2 To prepare the stock, pour 2 cups of the water into the roasting pan, stirring to loosen the browned bits. Transfer to stockpot. Add the remaining 12 cups of water, celery, carrots, onions, tomatoes (if using), potato, green onion tops, garlic, bay leaves, basil, thyme, salt, peppercorns, and cloves. Bring to a boil. Lower the heat and simmer, covered, for 3½ hours.

3 Using a slotted spoon, lift out bones. When bones are cool enough to handle, remove meat and reserve for another use if you like. Discard the bones.

4 To strain the stock, line a large sieve with 2 layers of 100% cotton cheesecloth. Set it in a large heat-proof bowl or container. Ladle stock through the lined sieve. Discard vegetables and seasonings. Clarify the stock if you like (tip, below).

CLARIFYING STOCK

When you plan to use stock for clear or cream soups, clarifying it first removes floating particles.

1. Strain the stock and pour it into a saucepan. Stir together ¼ cup cold water and an egg white. Pour into stock.

2. Bring to a boil. Remove from heat. Let stand for 5 minutes. Strain through a sieve lined with damp 100% cotton cheesecloth.

5 Store stock and meat in separate covered containers in the refrigerator (will keep 3 days) or in freezer (will keep 3 months). Label with type of stock, quantity, and date. Skim the solidified fat from stock before using. Makes about 12 cups stock.

Prep Time: 20 minutes Cooking Time: 4½ hours

1 Cup: Calories 21. Total Fat 1 g. Saturated Fat 0 g.
Protein 1 g. Carbohydrate 2 g. Fiber 0 g.
Sodium 371 mg. Cholesterol 3 mg.

Brown Chicken Stock Prepare as for Brown Beef Stock, substituting **4 pounds bony chicken pieces (backs, necks, and wings)** for the meaty bones and omitting the tomatoes.

1 Cup: Calories 21. Total Fat 1 g. Saturated Fat 0 g.
Protein 2 g. Carbohydrate 2 g. Fiber 0 g.
Sodium 373 mg. Cholesterol 4 mg.

Watercress Soup

*To keep watercress fresh for up to a week,
place the stems in a container of cold water
and refrigerate it in a sealed plastic bag.*

3½ **cups lower-sodium beef broth (page 67)**
 2 **cups thinly sliced fresh mushrooms**
½ **cup shredded carrot**
 2 **large green onions with tops, sliced into ½-inch lengths**
 1 **tablespoon minced fresh basil or 1 teaspoon dried basil leaves**
 1 **tablespoon lemon juice**
 1 **clove garlic, minced**
¼ **teaspoon salt**
⅛ **teaspoon black pepper**
 2 **cups bite-size pieces watercress or fresh spinach**

1 In a large saucepan, combine the beef broth, mushrooms, carrot, green onions, basil, lemon juice, garlic, salt, and pepper. Bring to a boil. Lower the heat and simmer, covered, for 3 minutes or until vegetables are just crisp-tender.

2 Stir in the watercress. Cook, uncovered, for 30 seconds more or until the watercress just starts to wilt. Makes 6 side-dish servings.

Prep Time: 20 minutes Cooking Time: 10 minutes

1 Serving: Calories 22. Total Fat 1 g. Saturated Fat 0 g.
Protein 1g. Carbohydrate 4 g. Fiber 1 g.
Sodium 109 mg. Cholesterol 0 mg.

Cream of Spinach Soup

If you like, use 1 package (10 ounces) frozen and thawed chopped spinach in place of the fresh spinach.

6 cups chopped fresh spinach
2 tablespoons butter or margarine
1 cup sliced leeks or sliced yellow onion
2 stalks celery, sliced
1¾ cups lower-sodium chicken broth (page 67)
1 teaspoon each dried mint leaves and marjoram leaves
½ teaspoon salt
¼ teaspoon black pepper
1 cup low-fat (1% milkfat) milk
3 tablespoons all-purpose flour

1 Wash the spinach. In a large saucepan, melt butter over moderately high heat. Add leeks and celery and cook for 5 minutes or until vegetables are tender, stirring often. Add the spinach, chicken broth, mint, marjoram, salt, and pepper. Bring to a boil. Lower the heat and simmer, covered, for 5 minutes. Cool slightly (do not drain).

2 In a food processor or blender, process spinach mixture, half at a time, until smooth. Return mixture to saucepan. Whisk together milk and flour; whisk into spinach mixture. Cook over moderate heat, whisking constantly, until mixture starts to thicken. Cook and whisk for 2 minutes more or until thickened. Makes 4 side-dish servings.

Prep Time: 15 minutes Cooking Time: 20 minutes

1 Serving: Calories 131. Total Fat 7 g. Saturated Fat 4 g. Protein 5 g. Carbohydrate 14 g. Fiber 3 g. Sodium 429 mg. Cholesterol 18 mg.

Cream of Asparagus Soup Prepare as for Cream of Spinach Soup, substituting **1 pound asparagus spears, cut into 1-inch pieces (3 cups)**, or **1 package (8 ounces) frozen cut asparagus, thawed,** for the spinach.

1 Serving: Calories 139. Total Fat 7 g. Saturated Fat 4 g. Protein 6 g. Carbohydrate 16 g. Fiber 4 g. Sodium 394 mg. Cholesterol 18 mg.

Dressed-Up Tomato Soup

When our great-grandmothers "dressed up" a soup, it simply meant they added cream.

4 medium-size tomatoes, chopped (2½ cups)
1¾ cups lower-sodium chicken broth (page 67)
1 cup sliced leeks or sliced yellow onion
1 can (6 ounces) lower-sodium tomato paste
2 cloves garlic, minced
1 teaspoon sugar
⅓ cup heavy cream
1 tablespoon minced fresh marjoram or thyme or 1 teaspoon dried marjoram leaves or thyme leaves
¼ teaspoon each salt and black pepper
2 teaspoons butter or margarine
1 cup thinly sliced fresh mushrooms

1 In a large saucepan, combine the tomatoes, chicken broth, leeks, tomato paste, garlic, and sugar. Bring to a boil. Lower the heat and simmer, covered, for 20 minutes or until leeks are very tender. Cool slightly (do not drain). In a food processor or blender, process mixture, half at a time, until smooth. Strain through a sieve; discard the pulp.

2 In the same saucepan, combine the heavy cream, marjoram, salt, and pepper. Gradually whisk in the tomato mixture. Cook, uncovered, over low heat for 5 minutes or until heated through, stirring occasionally.

3 Meanwhile, in a small nonstick skillet, melt the butter over moderately high heat. Add the mushrooms and cook for 3 minutes, stirring occasionally. Ladle soup into bowls. Top with mushrooms. Makes 4 side-dish servings.

Prep Time: 15 minutes Cooking Time: 35 minutes

1 Serving: Calories 167. Total Fat 10 g. Saturated Fat 6 g. Protein 4 g. Carbohydrate 19 g. Fiber 4 g. Sodium 201 mg. Cholesterol 32 mg.

Dressed-Up Tomato and Fennel Soup Prepare as for Dressed-Up Tomato Soup, substituting **1 cup chopped fennel (bulb only)** for the leeks.

1 Serving: Calories 165. Total Fat 10 g Saturated Fat 6 g. Protein 4 g. Carbohydrate 19 g. Fiber 4 g. Sodium 210 mg. Cholesterol 32 mg.

Sweet Potato Soup

Sweet Potato Soup

*Old-fashioned sweet potato soup was
delightfully thick and rich because it was made
with lots of heavy cream and butter. This more
healthful version is made with less cream, more
potatoes, and just a hint of butter for flavor.*

 1 **tablespoon butter or margarine**
 1 **large yellow onion, chopped**
 1 **large carrot, chopped**
¼ **cup minced parsley**
 2 **medium-size sweet potatoes (about 1 pound), peeled
    and cut up**
1¾ **cups lower-sodium chicken broth (page 67)**
 1 **teaspoon ground cinnamon**
¼ **teaspoon each salt and black pepper**
¼ **teaspoon ground nutmeg**
 1 **cup low-fat (1% milkfat) milk**
⅓ **cup half-and-half**

1 In a large saucepan, melt butter over moderately
high heat. Add the onion, carrot, and parsley and
cook for 5 minutes or until vegetables are tender, stirring often. Add the sweet potatoes, broth, cinnamon,
salt, pepper, and nutmeg. Bring to a boil. Lower the
heat and simmer, covered, for 20 minutes or until sweet
potatoes are tender. Cool slightly (do not drain).

2 In a food processor or blender, process sweet potato
mixture, half at a time, until smooth. Return mixture to saucepan. Stir in the milk and half-and-half.
Cook, uncovered, for 5 minutes or until heated through.
[If you'd like to serve the soup cold, cover it, then refrigerate. (It will keep for 1 week.) Before serving, stir
¼ cup low-fat (1% milkfat) milk into soup.] Makes
4 side-dish servings.

Prep Time: 15 minutes Cooking Time: 36 minutes

1 Serving: Calories 227. Total Fat 7 g. Saturated Fat 4 g.
Protein 5 g. Carbohydrate 38 g. Fiber 4 g.
Sodium 233 mg. Cholesterol 18 mg.

LOWER-SODIUM BROTH

When your recipe calls for lower-sodium beef or
chicken broth, you have three options:

◆ **Homemade Stock** Brown Beef Stock (recipe,
page 64) and Brown Chicken Stock (recipe, page
65) are both rich in flavor and low in sodium
with 371 mg. and 373 mg. of sodium per cup
respectively.

◆ **Canned Broth** You can mix ready-to-serve
canned beef or chicken broth with equal parts
water and create broths that have about 400 mg.
and about 450 mg. per cup. Or, look for canned
lower-sodium chicken broth—it has about
550 mg. sodium per cup.

◆ **Bouillon Granules** Low-sodium beef and
chicken bouillon granules make broths with
around 5 mg. and 0 mg. of sodium per cup.

Idaho Potato Chowder

This richly flavored chowder uses just enough bacon to give it old-fashioned taste.

2 strips lean bacon, chopped
1 cup finely sliced leeks or 8 large green onions with tops, finely sliced
2 cloves garlic, minced
3 medium-size potatoes, peeled and cubed
1¾ cups lower-sodium chicken broth (page 67)
½ teaspoon salt
¼ teaspoon white or black pepper
2 cups low-fat (1% milkfat) milk
3 tablespoons all-purpose flour
1 teaspoon dried basil leaves

1 In a large saucepan, cook bacon over moderate heat until crisp. Remove bacon, reserving drippings. Drain bacon on paper towels; set aside. Add leeks and garlic to reserved drippings and cook until tender. Add the potatoes, broth, salt, and pepper. Bring to a boil. Lower the heat and simmer, covered, for 20 minutes or until potatoes are tender. Using a fork, slightly mash the potatoes against the side of the saucepan.

2 In a medium-size bowl, whisk together the milk, flour, and basil; stir into potato mixture. Cook over moderate heat, stirring constantly, until mixture starts to thicken. Cook and stir for 2 minutes more or until thickened. Ladle soup into bowls. Top with bacon. Serve with corn bread. Makes 6 side-dish servings.

Prep Time: 15 minutes Cooking Time: 35 minutes

1 Serving: Calories 170. Total Fat 7 g. Saturated Fat 3 g. Protein 5 g. Carbohydrate 23 g. Fiber 2 g. Sodium 283 mg. Cholesterol 10 mg.

Potato-Vegetable Chowder Prepare as for Idaho Potato Chowder, substituting **1½ cups cubed peeled potatoes** and **1½ cups cubed peeled turnips, parsnips, or rutabagas** for the 3 cups potatoes.

1 Serving: Calories 147. Total Fat 7 g. Saturated Fat 3 g. Protein 5 g. Carbohydrate 18 g. Fiber 2 g. Sodium 297 mg. Cholesterol 10 mg.

Old-Time Vegetable Stew

Velma Patterson's recipe for vegetable stew changed with the seasons. "In the summer, she used vegetables from her garden—eggplants, sweet peppers, or tomatoes," recalls her grandson Byron. "In the fall and winter, she relied on root vegetables, such as potatoes, turnips, or parsnips."

1 small eggplant (about 1 pound), peeled and cut into ¾-inch cubes
1¾ cups lower-sodium chicken broth (page 67)
1 can (14½ ounces) lower-sodium tomatoes, undrained and cut up
2 cans (5½ ounces each) hot-style vegetable juice cocktail
1 can (8 ounces) lower-sodium tomato sauce
1 large yellow onion, chopped
1 medium-size sweet green, red, or yellow pepper, chopped
2 cloves garlic, minced
1 teaspoon dried oregano leaves
¼ teaspoon each salt and black pepper
⅓ cup minced parsley

1 In a large saucepan, combine the eggplant, broth, tomatoes, vegetable juice cocktail, tomato sauce, onion, green pepper, garlic, oregano, salt, and black pepper. Bring to a boil. Lower the heat and simmer, covered, for 25 minutes or until vegetables are crisp-tender.

2 Stir in parsley. Serve with grated Parmesan cheese. Makes 8 side-dish servings.

Prep Time: 15 minutes Cooking Time: 30 minutes

1 Serving: Calories 53. Total Fat 0 g. Saturated Fat 0 g. Protein 2 g. Carbohydrate 12 g. Fiber 3 g. Sodium 201 mg. Cholesterol 0 mg.

Turkey Vegetable Stew Prepare as for Old-Time Vegetable Stew, substituting **3 medium-size potatoes, peeled and cubed,** for the 1 small eggplant and adding **2 cups bite-size pieces cooked turkey or chicken.** Makes 4 main-dish servings.

1 Serving: Calories 282. Total Fat 4 g. Saturated Fat 1 g. Protein 25 g. Carbohydrate 37 g. Fiber 6 g. Sodium 452 mg. Cholesterol 53 mg.

Country Bean Soup

Country Bean Soup

Serve this soup the old-fashioned way—over a thick slice of bread.

1 **cup dried navy, great Northern, or lima beans, sorted and rinsed**

5 **cups lower-sodium chicken broth (page 67)**

2 **cups shredded cabbage**

2 **medium-size carrots, shredded**

1 **medium-size yellow onion, chopped**

3 **cloves garlic, minced**

3 **bay leaves**

2 **teaspoons dried oregano leaves**

1 **teaspoon dried sage leaves**

½ **teaspoon each salt and black pepper**

¼ **cup minced parsley**

1 To quick-soak beans, in a large saucepan, combine beans and 4 cups water. Bring to a boil. Lower the heat and simmer, uncovered, for 2 minutes. Remove from heat. Cover and let stand for 1 hour. (Or, for overnight method, combine beans and 4 cups water. Let stand in a cool place at least 8 hours or overnight.) Drain and thoroughly rinse beans.

2 In the same pan, combine the beans, chicken broth, cabbage, carrots, onion, garlic, bay leaves, oregano, sage, salt, and pepper. Bring to a boil. Lower the heat and simmer, covered, for 2 to 2½ hours or until beans are tender. Discard bay leaves. Using a fork, slightly mash some of the beans against side of saucepan. Stir in the parsley. Makes 4 side-dish servings.

Prep Time: 15 minutes plus soaking
Cooking Time: 2 hours 10 minutes

1 Serving: Calories 180. Total Fat 1 g. Saturated Fat 0 g.
Protein 11 g. Carbohydrate 34 g. Fiber 8 g.
Sodium 288 mg. Cholesterol 0 mg.

Country Ham and Bean Soup Prepare as for Country Bean Soup, adding **1 cup bite-size pieces cooked lower-sodium ham** with vegetables and omitting the ½ teaspoon salt. Makes 4 main-dish servings.

1 Serving: Calories 242. Total Fat 3 g. Saturated Fat 1 g.
Protein 20 g. Carbohydrate 35 g. Fiber 8 g.
Sodium 433 mg. Cholesterol 23 mg.

Emma's Hearty Vegetable Soup

Years ago, women often heated soup plates in the oven so the soup would stay hot longer at the table. Today, you can warm bowls quickly by running them under hot tap water.

3½ cups lower-sodium beef broth (page 67)
6 large carrots, sliced 1 inch thick
3 medium-size turnips or potatoes, peeled and cut into 1-inch cubes (3 cups)
12 ounces fresh green or wax beans, trimmed and cut into bite-size pieces, or 1 package (9 ounces) frozen cut green beans
1 tablespoon lower-sodium Worcestershire sauce
1 teaspoon dry mustard
¼ teaspoon each salt and black pepper
2 cans (8 ounces each) lower-sodium tomato sauce
1 cup frozen peas
2 cups sliced fresh mushrooms
2 tablespoons minced parsley

1 In a Dutch oven, combine the beef broth, carrots, turnips, green beans, Worcestershire sauce, mustard, salt, and pepper. Bring to a boil. Lower the heat and simmer, covered, for 25 minutes or until vegetables are crisp-tender.

2 Stir in tomato sauce and peas. Cook for 5 minutes, stirring occasionally. Stir in mushrooms. Sprinkle with parsley. Makes 12 side-dish servings.

Prep Time: 15 minutes Cooking Time: 35 minutes

1 Serving: Calories 62. Total Fat 1 g. Saturated Fat 0 g. Protein 3 g. Carbohydrate 14 g. Fiber 4 g. Sodium 117 mg. Cholesterol 0 mg.

Emma's Beef-Vegetable Soup Prepare as for Emma's Hearty Vegetable Soup, adding **3 cups bite-size pieces cooked beef** with the tomato sauce. Makes 8 main-dish servings.

1 Serving: Calories 231. Total Fat 7 g. Saturated Fat 2 g. Protein 25 g. Carbohydrate 21 g. Fiber 6 g. Sodium 217 mg. Cholesterol 65 mg.

Chunky Beef and Bean Soup

Grandma knew how to tell when the beans were done. She'd press one between her fingers. When the bean was soft all the way to the center, it was cooked.

1½ cups dried lima beans, sorted and rinsed
1 tablespoon vegetable oil
12 ounces boneless beef chuck roast, trimmed and cut into ¾-inch cubes
1 large yellow onion, chopped
2 cloves garlic, minced
3½ cups lower-sodium beef broth (page 67)
1¾ cups dry red wine or lower-sodium beef broth (page 67)
2 bay leaves
½ teaspoon each salt and black pepper
3 cups baby carrots
2 teaspoons each dried marjoram leaves and oregano leaves
1 medium-size sweet green pepper, chopped

1 To quick-soak beans, in a 6-quart Dutch oven, combine beans and 6 cups water. Bring to a boil. Lower the heat and simmer, uncovered, for 2 minutes. Remove from heat. Cover and let stand for 1 hour. (Or, for overnight method, combine beans and 6 cups water. Let stand in a cool place at least 8 hours or overnight.) Drain and thoroughly rinse beans.

2 In a large skillet, heat oil over moderate heat. Add half of the beef and cook until beef is browned. Remove from skillet. Add the remaining beef, the onion, and garlic. Cook until beef is browned and onion is tender.

3 In the same Dutch oven, combine beans and 2 cups fresh water. Stir in the beef mixture, broth, wine, bay leaves, salt, and black pepper. Bring to a boil. Lower the heat and simmer, covered, for 40 minutes. Add the carrots, marjoram, and oregano. Simmer, covered, for 15 minutes or until beans are almost tender. Add the green pepper and cook for 5 minutes more. Discard bay leaves. Makes 8 main-dish servings.

Prep Time: 20 minutes plus soaking Cooking Time: 1½ hours

1 Serving: Calories 249. Total Fat 5 g. Saturated Fat 1 g. Protein 17 g. Carbohydrate 27 g. Fiber 8 g. Sodium 182 mg. Cholesterol 29 mg.

Grandma Margaret's Barley Soup

Grandma Margaret's Barley Soup

*"My grandmother Margaret Gauger's barley soup was always great on
cold winter days, especially with sourdough bread," recalls Julie Rozeboom.
This thick robust soup also is good with crescent rolls or rye bread.*

3½ cups lower-sodium beef broth (page 67)

12 ounces fresh green or wax beans, trimmed and cut
into bite-size pieces, or 1 package (9 ounces) frozen
cut green beans

1 large potato, peeled and cubed

1 large yellow onion, chopped

2 large carrots, sliced

3 bay leaves

¼ teaspoon each salt and black pepper

2 cups bite-size pieces cooked beef or pork

1 can (14½ ounces) lower-sodium tomatoes, undrained
and cut up

½ cup quick-cooking barley

1 teaspoon dried rosemary leaves

1 In a large saucepan, combine the broth, green beans,
potato, onion, carrots, bay leaves, salt, and pepper.
Bring to a boil. Lower the heat and simmer, covered, for
20 minutes or until vegetables are almost tender.

2 Stir in the beef, tomatoes, barley, and rosemary.
Bring to a boil. Lower the heat and simmer, covered, for 15 minutes or until barley is tender. Discard
bay leaves. Makes 6 main-dish servings.

Prep Time: 20 minutes Cooking Time: 45 minutes

1 Serving: Calories 238. Total Fat 6 g. Saturated Fat 2 g.
Protein 23 g. Carbohydrate 27 g. Fiber 6 g.
Sodium 161 mg. Cholesterol 57 mg.

Lamb and Barley Soup Prepare as for Grandma
Margaret's Barley Soup, substituting **2 cups bite-size
pieces cooked lamb** for the beef.

1 Serving: Calories 232. Total Fat 7 g. Saturated Fat 2 g.
Protein 18 g. Carbohydrate 27 g. Fiber 6 g.
Sodium 163 mg. Cholesterol 49 mg.

Tomato-Garlic Soup

Tomato-Garlic Soup

Grandmothers often said garlic was good for what ails you. If that's true, this soup should work like magic—it has 10 cloves. Because garlic mellows as it cooks, this soup has a mild, slightly sweet flavor.

1 tablespoon olive or vegetable oil

1 tablespoon butter or margarine

2 large yellow onions, quartered and thinly sliced

10 cloves garlic, minced (1 bulb)

4 medium-size tomatoes, peeled and chopped (2½ cups)

1¾ cups lower-sodium beef broth (page 67)

1 can (8 ounces) lower-sodium tomato sauce

1 teaspoon dried thyme leaves

1 bay leaf

½ teaspoon sugar

¼ teaspoon each salt and black pepper

¼ cup minced parsley

1 In a large nonstick saucepan, heat the olive oil and butter over moderately high heat. Add onions and garlic. Lower the heat to moderately low and cook for 25 minutes or until onions are very soft and golden, stirring often.

2 Stir in tomatoes, broth, tomato sauce, thyme, bay leaf, sugar, salt, and pepper. Bring to a boil. Lower the heat and simmer, covered, for 15 minutes. Discard the bay leaf. Stir in the minced parsley. Makes 6 side-dish servings.

Prep Time: 15 minutes Cooking Time: 45 minutes

1 Serving: Calories 92. Total Fat 5 g. Saturated Fat 2 g.
Protein 2 g. Carbohydrate 12 g. Fiber 2 g.
Sodium 130 mg. Cholesterol 5 mg.

✳

Tomato-Garlic Soup with Fish Prepare as for Tomato-Garlic Soup, adding **1 pound fresh or frozen and thawed fish fillets, cut into 3/4-inch pieces.** After removing bay leaf, bring mixture to a boil. Add the fish. Lower the heat and simmer, uncovered, for 3 to 5 minutes more or until the fish flakes easily with a fork. Makes 5 main-dish servings.

1 Serving: Calories 192. Total Fat 6 g. Saturated Fat 2 g.
Protein 20 g. Carbohydrate 15 g. Fiber 3 g.
Sodium 205 mg. Cholesterol 49 mg.

Onion Soup Supreme

*There are two secrets to making this fabulous
onion soup. The first is long, slow simmering which
develops the onion and garlic flavors. The other
is to use French bread with a sturdy crust so the slices
stay intact as they float on the soup.*

1 **tablespoon butter or margarine**
1 **tablespoon olive oil**
3 **large yellow onions, thinly sliced and
   separated into rings**
2 **cloves garlic, minced**
4 **cups lower-sodium beef broth (page 67)**
1/2 **cup dry white wine, dry white vermouth, or
   lower-sodium beef broth (page 67)**
1 **tablespoon lower-sodium Worcestershire sauce**
1/4 **teaspoon each salt and black pepper**
6 **thick slices French bread**
3 **slices (1 ounce each) Gruyère or Swiss cheese, halved**

1 In a large nonstick saucepan, heat butter and oil over moderately high heat. Add onions and garlic. Lower the heat to moderately low and cook for 25 minutes or until onions are very soft and golden, stirring often.

2 Add the broth, wine, Worcestershire sauce, salt, and pepper. Bring to a boil. Lower the heat and simmer, covered, for 15 minutes.

3 Meanwhile, preheat broiler. Arrange bread on a baking sheet. Broil 4 inches from heat for 30 to 60 seconds or until toasted. Top each bread slice with a half slice of cheese. Broil for 1 minute more or until cheese melts. Ladle soup into bowls; float bread on top of soup. Serve immediately. Makes 6 side-dish servings.

Prep Time: 15 minutes Cooking Time: 45 minutes

1 Serving: Calories 238. Total Fat 10 g. Saturated Fat 4 g.
Protein 8 g. Carbohydrate 26 g. Fiber 2 g.
Sodium 388 mg. Cholesterol 21 mg.

Mama's Minestrone

*Italian grandmas had no definite rules
for what went into minestrone. It just had
to be hearty with plenty of vegetables,
white beans, and pasta or rice.*

1 **tablespoon olive oil**
1 **large yellow onion, chopped**
2 **cloves garlic, minced**
3 1/2 **cups lower-sodium beef broth (page 67)**
1 **can (15 ounces) great Northern beans, drained**
1 3/4 **cups chopped tomatoes or 1 can (14 1/2 ounces)
   Italian-style tomatoes, undrained and cut up**
2 **cups coarsely shredded cabbage**
2 **large carrots, thinly sliced**
1 **teaspoon each dried oregano leaves and basil leaves**
1/2 **teaspoon each salt and black pepper**
2 **ounces vermicelli or thin spaghetti, broken**
1 **small zucchini, halved lengthwise and sliced**

1 In a large nonstick saucepan, heat the oil over moderately high heat. Add onion and garlic and cook for 5 minutes or until onion is tender. Stir in broth, beans, tomatoes, cabbage, carrots, oregano, basil, salt, and pepper. Bring to a boil. Stir in vermicelli. Lower the heat and simmer, covered, for 15 minutes or until vegetables and pasta are tender. Stir in zucchini. Cook, uncovered, for 3 minutes more. Serve with grated Parmesan cheese. Makes 8 side-dish servings.

Prep Time: 20 minutes Cooking Time: 29 minutes

1 Serving: Calories 120. Total Fat 3 g. Saturated Fat 0 g.
Protein 5 g. Carbohydrate 21 g. Fiber 4 g.
Sodium 226 mg. Cholesterol 0 mg.

Hungarian Cream of Cherry Soup

Immigrants from Eastern Europe and the Scandinavian countries served this creamy, chilled soup as a hot-weather first course or as a light dessert.

1 cup water

¼ cup sugar

4 inches stick cinnamon

2 tablespoons cold water

1 teaspoon cornstarch

2 cups fresh or frozen and thawed pitted dark sweet cherries and/or tart red cherries

1 cup reduced-fat sour cream

½ cup dry red wine or orange juice

1 In a medium-size saucepan, bring the 1 cup water, sugar, and cinnamon to a boil. Lower the heat and simmer, uncovered, for 5 minutes. Discard cinnamon.

2 In a small bowl, whisk together the 2 tablespoons cold water and cornstarch, then whisk into the simmering sugar mixture. Cook for 2 minutes or until mixture is thickened, whisking constantly. Stir in cherries. Pour into bowl and cool to room temperature. Cover and refrigerate for 4 to 24 hours. To serve, stir in sour cream and red wine. Ladle into well-chilled bowls. Makes 6 side-dish servings.

Prep Time: 10 minutes Cooking Time: 10 minutes
Chilling Time: 4 hours

1 Serving: Calories 137. Total Fat 5 g. Saturated Fat 3 g.
Protein 2 g. Carbohydrate 19 g. Fiber 1 g.
Sodium 17 mg. Cholesterol 15 mg.

SERVING CHILLED SOUPS

An eye-catching way to serve cold soups is to nestle them in a bed of ice.

• For individual servings, use two soup bowls—a large one and small one—per person. Fill the large bowl with crushed ice and fit the small bowl into the ice. Then, ladle soup into the small bowl.

• For buffet-style serving, fill a large glass punch bowl with crushed ice and fit a smaller glass serving bowl into the ice. Then, ladle the soup into the serving bowl.

Russian Borscht

You can make a quick version of this hearty soup by substituting 1 package (10 ounces) frozen chopped spinach, thawed, for the chopped beet tops and 2 cans (15 ounces each) julienne beets, drained, for the beets.

6 medium-size beets with tops (about 2 pounds)

2 tablespoons butter or margarine

1 large yellow onion, chopped

5 cups lower-sodium beef broth (page 67)

1¾ cups chopped tomatoes or 1 can (14½ ounces) lower-sodium tomatoes, undrained and cut up

2 teaspoons dried marjoram leaves

1 teaspoon salt

1 teaspoon dried dill weed

½ teaspoon black pepper

2 cups shredded cabbage

2 cups bite-size pieces cooked beef, pork, or lower-sodium ham

2 tablespoons vinegar

1 tablespoon sugar

1 Trim leaves from beets, leaving 1 inch of stem attached. If beet tops are fresh-looking and reasonably unblemished, reserve them. (Or, substitute 2 cups finely chopped fresh spinach for the beet tops.) In a 6-quart Dutch oven, cover beets with lightly salted water. Bring to a boil. Lower the heat and simmer, covered, for 45 minutes or until tender; drain well. Cool slightly. Peel beets by slipping off skins while still warm. Cut beets into 1½x¼-inch sticks. Measure 4 cups.

2 Meanwhile, wash beet tops. Finely chop tops; measure 2 cups. In same pan, melt butter over moderately high heat. Add onion and cook for 5 minutes or until tender.

3 Add the 2 cups beet tops (or spinach), broth, tomatoes, marjoram, salt, dill weed, and pepper. Bring to a boil. Lower the heat and simmer, covered, for 5 to 10 minutes or until beet tops are tender. Stir in the cabbage, beef, vinegar, and sugar. Carefully stir in the cooked beets. Simmer, covered, for 5 to 7 minutes more or until heated through. Makes 8 main-dish servings.

Prep Time: 25 minutes Cooking Time: 1 hour 10 minutes

1 Serving: Calories 162. Total Fat 6 g. Saturated Fat 3 g.
Protein 13 g. Carbohydrate 17 g. Fiber 3 g.
Sodium 419 mg. Cholesterol 32 mg.

Russian Borscht

Chinese Noodle Soup

Chinese Noodle Soup

A traditional Chinese-American meal usually begins with a hot, light soup. Often the soup includes noodles because in Chinese culture eating them is thought to ensure a long life.

  6 **dried Chinese mushrooms**
  2 **ounces Chinese egg noodles or fine egg noodles**
3½ **cups lower-sodium chicken broth (page 67)**
1½ **cups bite-size pieces cooked chicken, pork, or lower-sodium ham**
  1 **cup thinly sliced Chinese cabbage or regular cabbage**
⅛ **teaspoon black pepper**
  1 **large green onion with top, finely sliced**
  2 **tablespoons minced parsley**

1 In a small bowl, cover mushrooms with warm water and let stand for 30 minutes. Rinse well and squeeze to drain thoroughly. Slice thinly, discarding the stems. Meanwhile, in a large saucepan, cook noodles according to package directions; drain well. Set aside.

2 In the same saucepan, bring broth to a boil. Stir in the mushrooms, chicken, cabbage, and pepper. Lower the heat and simmer, covered, for 10 minutes.

3 To serve, place noodles in soup bowls. With slotted spoon, lift mushroom mixture out of broth; place on noodles. Carefully pour broth over. Sprinkle with green onion and parsley. Makes 6 side-dish servings.

Prep Time: 15 minutes Standing Time: 30 minutes
Cooking Time: 15 minutes

1 Serving: Calories 128. Total Fat 3 g. Saturated Fat 1 g.
Protein 12 g. Carbohydrate 12 g. Fiber 1 g.
Sodium 52 mg. Cholesterol 39 mg.

Finnish Summer Vegetable Soup

Originally, this thick, creamy soup, called kesakeitto, was made with the first vegetables of summer. It usually was accompanied by open-face cold meat sandwiches.

2 **cups water**

2 **large carrots, sliced**

1 **cup fresh or frozen peas**

1 **cup fresh or frozen cut green beans**

1 **cup fresh or frozen cauliflower flowerets**

1 **medium-size potato, peeled and diced**

4 **large green onions with tops, finely sliced, or ½ cup sliced leek**

6 **small radishes, quartered**

⅛ **teaspoon salt**

1 **cup bite-size pieces fresh spinach**

2 **tablespoons butter or margarine**

2 **tablespoons all-purpose flour**

1 **tablespoon finely chopped fresh dill or 1 teaspoon dried dill weed**

¼ **teaspoon each salt and black pepper**

2 **cups low-fat (1% milkfat) milk**

1 **large egg yolk, lightly beaten**

1 In a large saucepan, combine the water, carrots, peas, green beans, cauliflower, potato, green onions, radishes, and the ⅛ teaspoon salt. Bring to a boil. Lower the heat and simmer fresh vegetables, covered, for 10 to 15 minutes or just until crisp-tender. (If the mixture contains frozen vegetables, cook according to the timings on package directions.) Stir in the spinach. Drain the vegetables, reserving 1 cup of the cooking liquid. Set aside.

2 In the same saucepan, melt the butter over moderate heat. Whisk in the flour, dill, the ¼ teaspoon salt, and pepper and cook for 1 minute. Add the 1 cup cooking liquid and the milk. Cook, whisking constantly, until mixture starts to thicken. Cook and whisk for 2 minutes.

3 Slowly stir about 1 cup of the hot mixture into the egg yolk, then return this mixture to the saucepan. Cook, stirring constantly, for 3 minutes or until mixture thickens (do not boil). Stir in the cooked vegetables; heat through. Makes 6 side-dish servings.

Prep Time: 25 minutes Cooking Time: 25 minutes

1 Serving: Calories 155. Total Fat 6 g. Saturated Fat 3 g. Protein 7 g. Carbohydrate 20 g. Fiber 4 g. Sodium 272 mg. Cholesterol 49 mg.

Greek Egg and Lemon Soup

Greek grandmas say that making a kissing sound as you stir the broth and lemon juice into the eggs prevents the mixture from curdling.

3½ **cups lower-sodium chicken broth (page 67)**

¼ **cup uncooked long-grain white rice**

3 **large eggs**

3 **tablespoons lemon juice**

2 **tablespoons minced fresh mint or parsley**

1 In a large saucepan, bring broth to a boil. Stir in rice. Lower the heat and simmer, covered, for 15 minutes or until rice is almost tender.

2 Meanwhile, in a large bowl, with an electric mixer on *High,* beat the eggs until light yellow and slightly thickened. Gradually add ¼ cup of the hot broth mixture and lemon juice, beating on *High* for 2 minutes.

3 Pour egg mixture slowly into the hot broth mixture in a thin stream, beating constantly with a fork until eggs cook and shred very finely. (Do not boil or the eggs will curdle.) Sprinkle each serving with mint. Makes 4 side-dish servings.

Prep Time: 5 minutes Cooking Time: 20 minutes

1 Serving: Calories 110. Total Fat 4 g. Saturated Fat 1 g. Protein 6 g. Carbohydrate 13 g. Fiber 0 g. Sodium 49 mg. Cholesterol 160 mg.

Turkey Frame Soup

*Wise cooks left a little meat on the turkey bones,
then used them to make turkey frame soup.*

- 8 **cups water**
- 1 **meaty turkey frame, broken up**
- 2 **medium-size yellow onions or rutabagas, quartered**
- 2 **cups loosely packed parsley sprigs or celery leaves**
- 4 **cloves garlic, quartered**
- 4 **bay leaves**
- 2 **teaspoons whole black peppercorns**
- 1 **teaspoon salt**
- 1 **large yellow onion, chopped**
- ½ **cup uncooked long-grain white rice**
- 4 **cups fresh vegetables, such as sliced carrots or celery, chopped broccoli, cauliflower flowerets, sliced mushrooms, chopped sweet green pepper, peas, or lima beans**
- 1 **teaspoon dried tarragon leaves**
- ½ **teaspoon each salt and black pepper**

1 In a 12-quart stockpot, combine the water, turkey frame, quartered onions, parsley, garlic, bay leaves, peppercorns, and the 1 teaspoon salt. Bring to a boil. Lower the heat and simmer, covered, for 2 hours.

2 Remove the turkey frame. When cool enough to handle, remove meat. Discard the bones. To strain the stock, line a large sieve with 2 layers of 100% cotton cheesecloth. Set it in a large saucepan. Ladle stock through the lined sieve. Discard the vegetables and seasonings. Skim fat from stock.

3 Bring the stock to a boil. Stir in the chopped onion and the rice. Lower heat and simmer, covered, for 15 minutes. Stir in the turkey meat, the 4 cups fresh vegetables, tarragon, the ½ teaspoon salt, and black pepper. Simmer, covered, for 15 minutes more or until the vegetables are crisp-tender, stirring occasionally. Makes 6 main-dish servings.

Prep Time: 25 minutes Cooking Time: 2¾ hours

1 Serving: Calories 217. Total Fat 4 g. Saturated Fat 1 g. Protein 21 g. Carbohydrate 26 g. Fiber 4 g. Sodium 634 mg. Cholesterol 44 mg.

Cream of Chicken Soup

*Leftover chicken was used to make a rich
creamed soup. For an extra-special touch, it
was topped with toasted almonds.*

- 1 **tablespoon butter or margarine**
- ¾ **cup finely sliced leek or 6 large green onions with tops, finely sliced**
- 1¾ **cups lower-sodium chicken broth (page 67)**
- ½ **cup half-and-half**
- ½ **teaspoon salt**
- ¼ **teaspoon white or black pepper**
- ¼ **teaspoon ground nutmeg**
- 2 **cups low-fat (1% milkfat) milk**
- ⅓ **cup all-purpose flour**
- 2 **cups finely chopped cooked chicken**

1 In a large saucepan, melt the butter over moderate heat. Add leek and cook until tender. Stir in the broth, half-and-half, salt, pepper, and nutmeg. In a small bowl, whisk together the milk and flour. Stir into the mixture in saucepan. Cook, stirring constantly, for 10 minutes or until slightly thickened and bubbly.

2 Stir in the chicken. Cook, uncovered, for 5 minutes more or until heated through. Makes 4 main-dish servings.

Prep Time: 10 minutes Cooking Time: 20 minutes

1 Serving: Calories 307. Total Fat 14 g. Saturated Fat 7 g. Protein 27 g. Carbohydrate 18 g. Fiber 1 g. Sodium 431 mg. Cholesterol 91 mg.

Cream of Chicken and Almond Soup Prepare as for Cream of Chicken Soup, adding ¼ **cup sliced almonds, toasted,** with the chicken.

1 Serving: Calories 341. Total Fat 17 g. Saturated Fat 7 g. Protein 28 g. Carbohydrate 19 g. Fiber 2 g. Sodium 432 mg. Cholesterol 91 mg.

Cream of Turkey Soup Prepare as for Cream of Chicken Soup, substituting **2 cups finely chopped cooked turkey** for the chicken.

1 Serving: Calories 293. Total Fat 12 g. Saturated Fat 7 g. Protein 27 g. Carbohydrate 18 g. Fiber 1 g. Sodium 420 mg. Cholesterol 81 mg.

Corn Chowder with Ham

Corn Chowder with Ham

"My grandma Anna Jones always used fresh corn to make this down-home chowder,"
George Granseth tells us. "First, she would cut off just the tips of the kernels with a knife.
Then, she would scrape the ear with the knife to release all the good juice."

4	medium-size fresh ears of corn or 2 cups frozen whole kernel corn
1¾	cups lower-sodium chicken broth (page 67)
1	large yellow onion, chopped
1	medium-size potato or parsnip, peeled and cubed (1 cup)
1	cup chopped sweet green, red, and/or yellow pepper
1	tablespoon minced fresh marjoram or 1 teaspoon dried marjoram leaves
¼	teaspoon each salt and white or black pepper
½	cup low-fat (1% milkfat) milk
3	tablespoons all-purpose flour
1	cup bite-size pieces cooked lower-sodium ham

1 Cut kernels off fresh corn (see above); measure 2 cups corn. In a large saucepan, combine corn, broth, onion, potato, green pepper, marjoram, salt, and white pepper. Bring to a boil. Lower the heat and simmer, covered, for 10 minutes or until potato is almost tender, stirring occasionally.

2 In a small bowl, whisk together the milk and flour. Stir into corn mixture. Cook, stirring constantly, for 2 minutes or until thickened and bubbly. Stir in ham. Cook for 2 minutes more or until heated through. Makes 4 main-dish servings.

Prep Time: 20 minutes Cooking Time: 20 minutes

1 Serving: Calories 232. Total Fat 4 g. Saturated Fat 1 g.
Protein 14 g. Carbohydrate 38 g. Fiber 4 g.
Sodium 577 mg. Cholesterol 24 mg.

Portuguese Green Soup

Portuguese Green Soup

*Caldo verde (green soup) was a specialty
of the Portuguese fishermen who settled in
New England. This recipe differs from the original
ones in that turkey kielbasa has been substituted
for Portuguese linguiça sausage and spinach
replaces Portuguese cabbage.*

1 tablespoon olive or vegetable oil
1 large yellow onion, finely chopped
2 cloves garlic, minced
3½ cups lower-sodium chicken broth (page 67)
3 medium-size potatoes, peeled and chopped
1 package (10 ounces) frozen chopped spinach, thawed
6 ounces turkey kielbasa (Polish sausage), sliced
¼ teaspoon each salt and black pepper

1 In a large saucepan, heat the oil over moderate heat. Add the onion and garlic and cook for 5 minutes or until onion is tender.

2 Add the broth and potatoes. Bring to a boil. Lower the heat and simmer, covered, for 30 minutes or until potatoes are very soft. Using a potato masher or large spoon, slightly mash the potatoes to thicken soup.

3 Stir in the spinach, kielbasa, salt, and pepper. Simmer, uncovered, for 5 minutes more or until heated through. Makes 6 side-dish servings.

Prep Time: 15 minutes Cooking Time: 45 minutes

1 Serving: Calories 163. Total Fat 6 g. Saturated Fat 2 g.
Protein 7 g. Carbohydrate 20 g. Fiber 2 g.
Sodium 339 mg. Cholesterol 19 mg.

COOKING WITH GARLIC

1. To peel garlic, place cloves on the cutting board. Lay the flat edge of your chef's knife on the cloves and whack it with your fist. Remove the skins and slice off the root ends.

2. To mince the garlic, use a smaller knife to finely chop the flattened cloves into tiny pieces.

Split Pea Soup With Kielbasa

In colonial days, a pot of pea or lentil soup often would simmer on the stove for days. Each day, leftover vegetables or bits of meat were added, making a totally new soup.

3½ **cups lower-sodium chicken broth (page 67)**
1 **cup dried green split peas, sorted and rinsed**
1 **teaspoon ground cumin**
½ **teaspoon salt**
¼ **to ½ teaspoon ground red pepper (cayenne)**
2 **large yellow onions, chopped**
1 **can (14½ ounces) lower-sodium tomatoes, undrained and cut up**
2 **large carrots, chopped**
6 **ounces turkey kielbasa (Polish sausage), sliced**
½ **cup water**

1 In a large saucepan, combine the broth, peas, cumin, salt, and red pepper. Bring to a boil. Lower the heat and simmer, covered, for 1 hour, stirring occasionally.

2 Stir in the onions, tomatoes, carrots, kielbasa, and water. Bring to a boil. Lower heat and simmer, covered, for 25 minutes more or until vegetables are tender, stirring occasionally. Makes 4 main-dish servings.

Prep Time: 15 minutes Cooking Time: 1 hour 35 minutes

1 Serving: Calories 323. Total Fat 7 g. Saturated Fat 2 g.
Protein 21 g. Carbohydrate 46 g. Fiber 8 g.
Sodium 640 mg. Cholesterol 28 mg.

Fresh Green Pea Soup

Gran usually made this flavorful soup in the spring when the first tender, young peas appeared in gardens. When selecting fresh peas, look for plump, bright green pods with medium-size peas and avoid the large ones—they're too old and tough.

1¾ **cups lower-sodium chicken broth (page 67)**
2 **pounds fresh green peas, shelled (2 cups), or 1 package (10 ounces) frozen peas**
½ **cup finely sliced leek**
1 **stalk celery, chopped**
1 **large carrot, chopped**
1 **can (12 ounces) evaporated skimmed milk**
1 **teaspoon dried mint leaves**
¼ **teaspoon salt**
⅛ **teaspoon white or black pepper**

1 In a large saucepan, combine the broth, peas, leek, celery, and carrot. Bring to a boil. Lower the heat and simmer, covered, for 15 minutes or until vegetables are very tender. Cool about 10 minutes.

2 In a food processor or blender, process pea mixture, half at a time, until smooth. Sieve, discarding pulp. Return mixture to saucepan. Stir in the milk, mint, salt, and pepper. Cook, uncovered, for 10 minutes more or until heated through. Makes 4 side-dish servings.

Prep Time: 25 minutes Cooling Time: 10 minutes
Cooking Time: 30 minutes

1 Serving: Calories 128. Total Fat 0 g. Saturated Fat 0 g.
Protein 10 g. Carbohydrate 22 g. Fiber 4 g.
Sodium 258 mg. Cholesterol 3 mg.

Scandinavian Yellow Pea Soup

When Inge Hanse came to live on a farm in North Dakota, she made many of her native Norwegian specialties. Her granddaughter, Mary Jensen, particularly loved Inge's thick yellow pea soup, which was filled with pieces of ham.

3½ **cups lower-sodium chicken broth (page 67)**
1 **cup dried yellow split peas, sorted and rinsed**
1 **meaty ham bone (1 to 1½ pounds)**
1 **teaspoon each dried marjoram leaves and thyme leaves**
2 **large yellow onions, halved crosswise and thinly sliced**
2 **stalks celery, finely chopped**
½ **teaspoon ground ginger**
¼ **teaspoon black pepper**

1 In a large saucepan, combine the broth, peas, ham bone, marjoram, and thyme. Bring to a boil. Lower the heat and simmer, covered, for 1 hour. Using a slotted spoon, lift out the ham bone. When cool enough to handle, remove ham from bone; cut ham into bite-size pieces and return to soup. Discard the bone.

2 Add the onions, celery, ginger, and pepper to soup. Bring to a boil. Lower the heat and simmer, covered, for 25 minutes or until vegetables are tender, stirring occasionally. Makes 4 main-dish servings.

Prep Time: 25 minutes Cooking Time: 1 hour 35 minutes

1 Serving: Calories 237. Total Fat 2 g. Saturated Fat 0 g.
Protein 18 g. Carbohydrate 39 g. Fiber 6 g.
Sodium 267 mg. Cholesterol 10 mg.

German Pork and Kraut Soup

Bluish-gray juniper berries are an old remedy for counteracting the wild flavor of game in dishes. In this hearty stew, the berries add a pleasant tart-sweet flavor that accents the sauerkraut perfectly.

    1 strip lean bacon, chopped
   12 ounces lean boneless pork, trimmed and cut
       into ¾-inch cubes
    1 large yellow onion, chopped
    2 cloves garlic, minced
    1 can (16 ounces) sauerkraut, undrained, or 1 package
       (16 ounces) refrigerated sauerkraut, undrained
    2 medium-size potatoes, peeled and chopped
 1¾ cups lower-sodium beef broth (page 67)
    1 can (12 ounces) reduced-calorie beer
    6 juniper berries (optional)
    3 bay leaves
    1 teaspoon paprika
    1 teaspoon fennel seeds, crushed
  ½ teaspoon caraway seeds
  ¼ teaspoon black pepper
  ¼ cup reduced-fat sour cream

1 In a large saucepan, cook bacon over moderate heat until crisp. Remove bacon, reserving drippings. Drain the bacon on paper towels; set aside.

2 Add the pork, onion, and garlic to reserved drippings. Cook over moderate heat until pork is browned and onion is tender. Add the sauerkraut, potatoes, broth, beer, juniper berries (if using), bay leaves, paprika, fennel seeds, caraway seeds, and pepper. Bring to a boil. Lower the heat and simmer, covered, for 1 hour or until pork is tender.

3 Discard the bay leaves and juniper berries. Serve soup with sour cream and bacon pieces. Makes 4 main-dish servings.

Prep Time: 20 minutes Cooking Time: 1 hour 20 minutes

1 Serving: Calories 324. Total Fat 13 g. Saturated Fat 5 g. Protein 22 g. Carbohydrate 25 g. Fiber 5 g. Sodium 867 mg. Cholesterol 73 mg.

Spicy Cheese and Beer Soup

Bring the cheese to room temperature before you add it to the soup—it will melt more quickly.

    1 tablespoon butter or margarine
    1 medium-size yellow onion, finely chopped
    1 medium-size carrot, shredded
    2 cups low-fat (1% milkfat) milk
  ¼ cup all-purpose flour
  ¼ teaspoon ground red pepper (cayenne)
 1½ cups shredded sharp American cheese (6 ounces)
    1 can (12 ounces) reduced-calorie beer
    1 cup shredded cabbage

1 In a large saucepan, melt butter over moderate heat. Add the onion and carrot and cook for 5 minutes or until tender, stirring frequently. In a small bowl, whisk together the milk, flour, and red pepper. Stir into onion mixture. Cook, stirring constantly, for 7 minutes or until thickened and bubbly.

2 Gradually add the cheese. Heat over low heat until cheese melts, stirring constantly (do not boil). Stir in the beer and cabbage; heat through. Serve with pumpernickel bread. Makes 4 main-dish servings.

Prep Time: 20 minutes Cooking Time: 18 minutes

1 Serving: Calories 309. Total Fat 18 g. Saturated Fat 11 g. Protein 15 g. Carbohydrate 18 g. Fiber 2 g. Sodium 709 mg. Cholesterol 53 mg.

GARNISHING SOUPS

Add delightful texture to soups by serving them with a garnish, such as:

- Croutons
- Popcorn
- Oyster crackers
- Chopped green onions
- Chopped sweet pepper
- Toasted thinly sliced French bread
- Snipped chives
- Carrot curls
- Sprigs of fresh herb

Hearty Clam and Tomato Soup

Hearty Clam and Tomato Soup

*New Englanders traditionally made their clam chowder with
cream, but New Yorkers loved this spicy clam and vegetable soup.*

1 **pint shucked hard-shell clams or 2 cans (6 ounces each) minced clams**

2 **strips lean bacon, chopped**

½ **cup finely sliced leek or 4 large green onions with tops, finely sliced**

1 **stalk celery, finely chopped**

2 **cloves garlic, minced**

3 **cups lower-sodium vegetable juice cocktail**

2 **medium-size potatoes, peeled and chopped**

1 **can (14½ ounces) lower-sodium tomatoes, undrained and cut up**

1 **can (11 ounces) whole kernel corn with sweet peppers**

2 **bay leaves**

2 **teaspoons dried thyme leaves**

2 **teaspoons lower-sodium Worcestershire sauce**

1 **teaspoon dried marjoram leaves**

¼ **teaspoon salt**

⅛ **teaspoon hot red pepper sauce**

1 Coarsely chop clams, reserving juice. Strain the clam juice to remove bits of shell. (Or, drain canned clams, reserving juice.) In a Dutch oven, cook bacon over moderate heat until crisp. Remove bacon, reserving drippings. Drain bacon on paper towels; set aside.

2 Add the leek, celery, and garlic to reserved drippings. Cook over moderate heat for 5 minutes or until leek is tender. Add the vegetable juice cocktail, potatoes, tomatoes, corn, bay leaves, thyme, Worcestershire sauce, marjoram, salt, and hot pepper sauce. Bring to a boil. Lower heat and simmer, covered, for 45 to 50 minutes or until the potatoes are tender.

3 Stir in clams, reserved clam juice, and bacon. Heat through, stirring occasionally. Discard bay leaves. Makes 6 main-dish servings.

Prep Time: 25 minutes Cooking Time: 1 hour

1 Serving: Calories 225. Total Fat 7 g. Saturated Fat 3 g.
Protein 12 g. Carbohydrate 28 g. Fiber 4 g.
Sodium 481 mg. Cholesterol 27 mg.

She Crab Soup

In Charleston, South Carolina, cooks used the roe and meat from female crabs in a creamy, delicately flavored soup. This lighter version substitutes milk and half-and-half for heavy cream. To simulate the roe, sprinkle sieved, hard-cooked egg yolk on top.

- **1 large yellow onion, finely chopped**
- **1 stalk celery, finely chopped**
- **¼ cup lower-sodium chicken broth (page 67)**
- **2¾ cups low-fat (1% milkfat) milk**
- **1 cup half-and-half**
- **3 tablespoons all-purpose flour**
- **½ teaspoon salt**
- **½ teaspoon ground mace**
- **¼ teaspoon white or black pepper**
- **8 ounces lump crab meat, picked over and flaked, or 1 package (8 ounces) frozen and thawed crab-flavored, salad-style fish, chopped**
- **¼ cup dry sherry, dry white wine, or half-and-half**

1 In a large saucepan, combine the onion, celery, and broth. Bring to a boil. Lower the heat and simmer, covered, for 5 minutes or until the vegetables are tender. Stir in the milk. In a small bowl, whisk together half-and-half, flour, salt, mace, and pepper. Stir into mixture in saucepan. Cook over moderate heat, stirring constantly, for 10 minutes or until thickened and bubbly.

2 Stir in the crab meat and sherry. Cook, uncovered, for 5 minutes or until heated through. Makes 4 main-dish servings.

Prep Time: 20 minutes Cooking Time: 25 minutes

1 Serving: Calories 273. Total Fat 11 g. Saturated Fat 6 g.
Protein 21 g. Carbohydrate 20 g. Fiber 1 g.
Sodium 600 mg. Cholesterol 78 mg.

✳

Lobster Bisque Prepare as for She Crab Soup, substituting **8 ounces coarsely flaked, cooked lobster or 1 package (8 ounces) frozen and thawed lobster-flavored, chunk-style fish** for the crab.

1 Serving: Calories 266. Total Fat 11 g. Saturated Fat 6 g.
Protein 20 g. Carbohydrate 20 g. Fiber 1 g.
Sodium 602 mg. Cholesterol 76 mg.

✳

Fish Bisque Prepare as for She Crab Soup, substituting **8 ounces fresh or frozen and thawed orange roughy fillets, cut into ¾-inch pieces,** for the crab. Add the fish

to thickened half-and-half mixture. Bring to a boil. Lower the heat and simmer, uncovered, for 3 to 5 minutes or until fish flakes easily with a fork. Stir in sherry.

1 Serving: Calories 261. Total Fat 11 g. Saturated Fat 6 g.
Protein 20 g. Carbohydrate 19 g. Fiber 1 g.
Sodium 416 mg. Cholesterol 62 mg.

Oyster Stew

"Grandma Velma Willard always served oyster stew on Christmas Eve," recalls granddaughter Elizabeth. "She was an expert at cooking oysters. She taught me to simmer them just until the edges start to curl."

- **1 large yellow onion, finely chopped**
- **¼ cup lower-sodium chicken broth (page 67)**
- **1 pint shucked oysters, undrained**
- **½ teaspoon salt**
- **⅛ teaspoon ground red pepper (cayenne)**
- **1¾ cups low-fat (1% milkfat) milk**
- **1 cup half-and-half**
- **½ teaspoon lower-sodium Worcestershire sauce (optional)**

1 In a large saucepan, combine the onion and broth. Bring to a boil. Lower the heat and simmer, covered, for 5 minutes or until the onion is tender. Add the oysters, salt, and red pepper. Cook for 3 to 4 minutes more or until oysters are plump and opaque.

2 Add the milk, half-and-half, and Worcestershire sauce (if using). Cook over moderate heat until the mixture is heated through, stirring often. Makes 4 main-dish servings.

Prep Time: 10 minutes Cooking Time: 20 minutes

1 Serving: Calories 230. Total Fat 12 g. Saturated Fat 6 g.
Protein 16 g. Carbohydrate 16 g. Fiber 1 g.
Sodium 455 mg. Cholesterol 82 mg.

✳

Shrimp Chowder Prepare as for Oyster Stew, substituting **12 ounces peeled, deveined, fresh or frozen and thawed medium shrimp** for the oysters. Cook until the shrimp turn opaque.

1 Serving: Calories 207. Total Fat 10 g. Saturated Fat 6 g.
Protein 19 g. Carbohydrate 11 g. Fiber 1 g.
Sodium 485 mg. Cholesterol 151 mg.

Grandma's Treats

Lickety-Split Tuna Chowder

You can put together this kid-pleasin' soup in no time.

- 1 can (10¾ ounces) condensed cream of potato or celery soup
- 1 can (10¾ ounces) condensed Manhattan-style clam chowder
- 1½ soup cans (2 cups) low-fat (1% milkfat) milk
- 1 can (6 ounces) water-packed, chunk light tuna, rinsed, drained, and flaked
- 1 jar (2 ounces) sliced pimientos, undrained (optional)
- 1½ teaspoons dried thyme leaves
- ¼ teaspoon black pepper

1. In a large saucepan, combine potato soup, clam chowder, milk, tuna, pimientos (if using), thyme, and pepper. Bring to a boil. Lower the heat and simmer, covered, for 5 minutes, stirring occasionally. Makes 4 main-dish servings.

Feel-Good Chicken Soup

Every grandmother knows nothing cures the sniffles better than homemade soup.

- 3½ cups lower-sodium chicken broth (page 67)
- 1 package (10 ounces) frozen peas and carrots
- 1 cup chopped cooked chicken
- 1½ teaspoons dried oregano leaves
- ¼ teaspoon each salt and black pepper
- ½ cup fine egg noodles

1. In a large saucepan, combine chicken broth, peas and carrots, chicken, oregano, salt, and pepper. Bring to a boil. Lower the heat; stir in the noodles. Simmer, covered, for 6 minutes or until noodles are tender, stirring occasionally. Makes 4 main-dish servings.

Chuck Wagon Soup

- 12 ounces lean ground beef
- 1 medium-size yellow onion, chopped
- 1 can (16 ounces) pork and beans in tomato sauce
- 1 can (14½ ounces) lower-sodium tomatoes, undrained and cut up
- 1½ cups lower-sodium beef broth (page 67)
- 1 tablespoon chili powder
- ¼ teaspoon each salt and black pepper
- ½ cup wagon-wheel pasta or elbow macaroni
- ¼ cup shredded Cheddar cheese

1. In a large saucepan, cook ground beef and onion until beef is browned. Drain off fat.

2. Stir in pork and beans, tomatoes, broth, chili powder, salt, and pepper. Bring to a boil. Lower the heat; stir in wagon-wheel pasta. Simmer, covered, for 15 minutes or until pasta is tender, stirring frequently. Serve with cheese. Makes 4 main-dish servings.

Letterific Tomato Soup

Let the kids spell their names with the alphabet pasta.

- 1 can (10¾ ounces) condensed Cheddar cheese soup
- 1 can (10¾ ounces) condensed tomato soup
- 1½ soup cans (2 cups) water
- ½ cup finely chopped sweet green pepper
- 1 teaspoon dried basil leaves
- ⅛ teaspoon black pepper
- ⅓ cup alphabet pasta or tiny bow-tie pasta

1. In a large saucepan, combine cheese soup, tomato soup, water, green pepper, basil, and black pepper. Bring to a boil. Lower the heat; stir in the alphabet pasta. Simmer, covered, for 10 to 12 minutes or until pasta is tender, stirring frequently. Makes 4 side-dish servings.

EGG & CHEESE DELIGHTS

*Grandma relied on farm-fresh
eggs and cheese to make economical,
flavorful dishes. She could whip
up everything from an egg-
and-potato breakfast special to a kid-
pleasing cheese sandwich to
an elegant soufflé. For picnics, gran
made deviled eggs; for a quick
supper, tender omelets; and, when the
ladies came to lunch, timbales.
Today as then, her cheese and egg dishes
are comfort food at its best.*

Asparagus-Cheese Strata (page 100)
Scotch Eggs (page 92)
French Omelet with Mushroom Sauce (page 94)

Cheese Latkes

Jewish grandmas traditionally made these crispy, golden pancakes with matzo meal. However, flour gives lighter pancakes. Serve them with strawberry preserves, maple syrup, or sour cream.

  2 large eggs
½ teaspoon vanilla
½ cup creamed (4% milkfat) cottage cheese
½ cup low-fat (1% milkfat) milk
  1 cup all-purpose flour
  1 tablespoon sugar
¼ teaspoon baking powder
¼ teaspoon ground cinnamon
⅛ teaspoon salt
  2 tablespoons vegetable oil

1 In a medium-size bowl, whisk the eggs and vanilla together. Stir in the cottage cheese and milk. In another medium-size bowl, stir together the flour, sugar, baking powder, cinnamon, and salt. Using a wooden spoon, mix the egg mixture into the flour mixture until just combined. Cover and refrigerate for 30 minutes.

2 Brush a 12-inch nonstick skillet with some of the vegetable oil. Heat over moderate heat. Using a rounded tablespoon for each latke, drop batter into skillet. Cook until latke surfaces are covered with bubbles and bottoms are golden. Flip latkes over and cook until golden. Remove from skillet and keep warm.

3 Repeat with remaining vegetable oil and remaining batter. Serve warm with strawberry preserves, maple syrup, or sour cream. Makes 4 main-dish servings.

Prep Time: 10 minutes Chilling Time: 30 minutes
Cooking Time: 12 minutes

1 Serving: Calories 265. Total Fat 11 g. Saturated Fat 2 g. Protein 11 g. Carbohydrate 30 g. Fiber 1 g. Sodium 251 mg. Cholesterol 112 mg.

Shirred Eggs Florentine

Great-grandmother often "shirred" eggs, which means to bake them in the oven. This recipe makes an easy company brunch because you can bake the eggs all at once.

  1 package (10 ounces) frozen chopped spinach, thawed
½ cup finely chopped leek or green onions
½ cup finely chopped lower-sodium ham
1½ teaspoons dried basil leaves
¼ teaspoon black pepper
  4 large eggs
¼ cup low-fat (1% milkfat) milk
½ cup shredded Gruyère or Swiss cheese (2 ounces)

1 Preheat oven to 325°F. Place the spinach in a sieve and press out as much liquid as possible. In a medium-size bowl, combine the spinach, leek, ham, basil, and pepper. Divide mixture among four 10-ounce custard cups or ramekins (tip, below).

2 Break eggs into custard cups. Add milk (tip, below). Place custard cups in a 13" x 9" x 2" baking pan and pour boiling water around custard cups to depth of 1 inch. Bake for 25 minutes or until eggs are set. Sprinkle with cheese. Makes 4 main-dish servings.

Prep Time: 15 minutes Cooking Time: 25 minutes

1 Serving: Calories 155. Total Fat 10 g. Saturated Fat 4 g. Protein 13 g. Carbohydrate 5 g. Fiber 2 g. Sodium 164 mg. Cholesterol 229 mg.

MAKING EGGS FLORENTINE

1. To make the spinach shells, press some of the spinach mixture evenly onto the bottom and partway up the sides of each custard cup.

2. Break an egg into each custard cup or ramekin. Spoon 1 tablespoon of milk over each egg.

Amish Farmer's Breakfast

Amish Farmer's Breakfast

*This potato-and-egg skillet dish was originally served at
midmorning as a second breakfast for hard-working farmers. For today's
lighter eating styles, it makes a wonderful brunch or supper dish.*

2   **strips lean bacon, chopped**

2½ **cups frozen hash brown potatoes with onions and
green peppers**

5   **large eggs**

2   **large egg whites**

¼ **cup low-fat (1% milkfat) milk**

½ **teaspoon dried chervil leaves or thyme leaves**

½ **teaspoon salt**

¼ **teaspoon black pepper**

1 In a 10-inch well-seasoned or nonstick skillet, cook
bacon over moderate heat until crisp. Remove
bacon, reserving drippings in skillet. Drain bacon on
paper towels; set aside.

2 Carefully add potatoes to reserved drippings; cook
for 8 to 10 minutes or until tender, stirring often.

3 In a large bowl, whisk together the eggs, egg whites,
milk, chervil, salt, and pepper. Pour egg mixture over
potatoes and bacon. Cook over moderate heat, without
stirring, until set on the bottom and around the edge.
(Use the corner of a pancake turner to constantly lift the
cooked edge so the uncooked eggs flow to the bottom.)
Cook for 3 minutes more or until the eggs are almost
set. Cover and cook for 1 minute or until the eggs are
set but still moist. Sprinkle with the cooked bacon.
Makes 4 main-dish servings.

Prep Time: 10 minutes Cooking Time: 20 minutes

1 Serving: Calories 247. Total Fat 15 g. Saturated Fat 6 g.
Protein 12 g. Carbohydrate 15 g. Fiber 0 g.
Sodium 494 mg. Cholesterol 277 mg.

Poached Eggs Creole

Poached Eggs Creole

*This traditional Creole sauce is made with canned stewed tomatoes
to save time. It's the perfect accent for delicate poached eggs.*

1 **can (14½ ounces) lower-sodium stewed tomatoes,
undrained and cut up**

2 **cloves garlic, minced**

⅛ **teaspoon each black pepper and white pepper**

⅛ **teaspoon ground red pepper (cayenne)**

6 **large eggs**

3 **English muffins, split and toasted**

1 In a small saucepan, combine the tomatoes, garlic,
black pepper, white pepper, and red pepper. Bring to
a boil. Lower the heat and simmer, covered, for 10 minutes, stirring occasionally.

2 Meanwhile, fill a 10-inch skillet two-thirds full with
water. Bring to a simmer over moderate heat.
Working with 1 egg at a time, break egg into a saucer,
then slide the egg into the water. Cook eggs, spooning
the water over them, for 4 to 5 minutes or until yolk is
just set; keep the water at a simmer (do not boil).

3 Using a slotted spoon, top each muffin half with
1 egg. Ladle tomato mixture over eggs. Makes
3 main-dish servings.

Prep Time: 5 minutes Cooking Time: 15 minutes

1 Serving: Calories 316. Total Fat 11 g. Saturated Fat 3 g.
Protein 18 g. Carbohydrate 36 g. Fiber 4 g.
Sodium 726 mg. Cholesterol 426 mg.

Overnight Breakfast Casseroles

Brunch dishes that could be prepared one day and popped into the oven the next morning were in great vogue in the 1950's. This company-pleasing breakfast combines sausage, eggs, and Swiss cheese.

4   ounces bulk pork sausage
6   large eggs
2   large egg whites
2   tablespoons water
1   tablespoon minced chives
1   cup low-fat (1% milkfat) milk
2   tablespoons all-purpose flour
¼   teaspoon white pepper or black pepper
⅛   teaspoon salt
½   cup shredded Swiss cheese (2 ounces)
    Paprika

1 In a 10-inch nonstick skillet, cook the sausage over moderate heat until cooked through. In a medium-size bowl, whisk together the eggs, egg whites, water, and chives. Pour over sausage in skillet. Cook, gently scrambling the eggs with a wooden spoon, for 5 minutes or just until firm yet moist. Spoon into 4 lightly greased 10-ounce custard cups.

2 In a medium-size saucepan, whisk together the milk, flour, pepper, and salt. Cook over moderate heat, whisking constantly, until mixture starts to thicken. Cook and whisk for 2 minutes more or until thickened. Stir in the Swiss cheese until melted. Spoon the cheese mixture over the eggs. Cover and refrigerate for 8 to 24 hours.

3 Preheat oven to 350°F. Bake casseroles, covered, for 40 minutes or until heated through. Sprinkle with paprika before serving. Makes 4 main-dish servings.

Prep Time: 10 minutes Cooking Time: 15 minutes
Chilling Time: 8 hours Baking Time: 40 minutes

1 Serving: Calories 267. Total Fat 17 g. Saturated Fat 7 g.
Protein 21 g. Carbohydrate 8 g. Fiber 0 g.
Sodium 444 mg. Cholesterol 347 mg.

Cheese Rice Pudding

This old-fashioned savory version of rice pudding is ideal for supper on a damp, chilly day. Serve it with buttered baby carrots and bran muffins.

1   tablespoon butter or margarine
2   tablespoons all-purpose flour
¾   teaspoon dried marjoram leaves
¼   teaspoon each salt and black pepper
1½ cups low-fat (1% milkfat) milk
1½ cups shredded Cheddar cheese (6 ounces)
3   cups cooked long-grain white rice
2   large egg whites
1   large egg

1 Preheat oven to 325°F. In a medium-size saucepan, melt butter over moderate heat. Whisk in the flour, marjoram, salt, and pepper and cook for 1 minute or until bubbly. Add the milk. Cook, whisking constantly, until the mixture starts to thicken. Stir in the Cheddar cheese until melted.

2 In a medium-size bowl, combine the rice, egg whites, and egg. Fold in the cheese mixture. Spoon into a lightly greased 8" x 8" x 2" baking dish. Bake for 30 to 35 minutes or until the center is set. Makes 6 main-dish servings.

Prep Time: 10 minutes Cooking Time: 36 minutes

1 Serving: Calories 318. Total Fat 13 g. Saturated Fat 8 g.
Protein 14 g. Carbohydrate 35 g. Fiber 1 g.
Sodium 345 mg. Cholesterol 73 mg.

CUTTING DOWN ON EGG YOLKS

As you glance through this chapter, you'll find many of the recipes call for a combination of whole eggs and egg whites rather than all whole eggs. The reason for omitting some of the egg yolks is to reduce the fat and cholesterol.

Scotch Eggs

*Scottish settlers brought the recipe for these
hearty meat-wrapped eggs to America. This
version is baked, rather than fried, to reduce
the fat. Serve the eggs warm or chill them
for picnics and tailgate lunches.*

8   ounces extra-lean ground beef
2   medium-size green onions with tops, finely chopped
½   teaspoon dried rosemary leaves
⅛   teaspoon salt
4   hard-cooked large eggs, shells removed
⅓   cup finely crushed whole-wheat crackers or lower-sodium crackers
½   cup bottled chili sauce, catsup, or spaghetti sauce

1 In a medium-size bowl, mix the ground beef, green onions, rosemary, and salt. Shape into 4 patties, each about 4 inches in diameter. Wrap a meat patty around each egg, completely encasing the egg. Place eggs on a plate. Cover and refrigerate for 2 to 4 hours.

2 Preheat oven to 400°F. Roll eggs in cracker crumbs until coated. Arrange eggs in a lightly greased shallow baking pan. Bake for 30 minutes or until meat is no longer pink. Meanwhile, in a small saucepan, heat chili sauce. Serve with eggs. Makes 4 main-dish servings.

Prep Time: 15 minutes Chilling Time: 2 hours
Cooking Time: 30 minutes

1 Serving: Calories 243. Total Fat 13 g. Saturated Fat 4 g.
Protein 19 g. Carbohydrate 13 g. Fiber 1 g.
Sodium 647 mg. Cholesterol 253 mg.

HARD COOKING EGGS

Here's how to cook and peel eggs perfectly.

♦ Place the eggs in a saucepan and cover them with cold water. Bring the water to a boil over high heat. Lower the heat and cook just below simmering for 15 minutes. Drain, then cover the warm eggs with cold water.

♦ Let the eggs stand in the water until cool enough to handle. Then, to crack the shell, gently tap each egg on the countertop and roll the egg between your hands. Finally, peel the egg from the large end down.

Rocky Top Omelet

*Years ago, puffy omelets made with whipped
egg whites were as popular as French omelets.
In this omelet, the eggs puff so much that
the surface is uneven, hence the name.*

5   large eggs
2   small apples, cored and sliced
2   tablespoons apple juice
1   tablespoon honey
⅛   teaspoon ground cinnamon
    Dash ground nutmeg
2   tablespoons water
⅛   teaspoon salt
1   tablespoon butter or margarine

1 Separate the eggs. Discard the yolk from 1 of the eggs. Place the egg whites in a clean large bowl. Place the yolks in a small bowl. Set aside.

2 Preheat the oven to 325°F. In a medium-size saucepan, combine the apple slices, apple juice, honey, cinnamon, and nutmeg. Bring to a boil. Lower the heat and simmer, uncovered, for 5 minutes or until the apples are just tender. Cover and keep apples warm.

3 With an electric mixer on *High*, beat the egg whites until frothy. Add the water and continue beating the egg whites until stiff peaks form. With a fork, beat the egg yolks and salt until combined. Fold into egg whites.

4 In a 10-inch skillet, heat the butter over moderate heat until a drop of water sizzles when dropped into skillet. Spread the egg mixture into the skillet, mounding it slightly at the edge. Cook over low heat for 8 to 10 minutes or until omelet is set and lightly browned on the bottom. Cover the skillet handle with foil and bake the omelet for 8 to 10 minutes or until a knife inserted in the center comes out clean.

5 Make a shallow cut across the top of the omelet, just to one side of center. Fold the smaller side of the omelet over the larger one. Transfer to a serving platter. Spoon the apple mixture over the omelet. Makes 2 main-dish servings.

Prep Time: 15 minutes Cooking Time: 23 minutes

1 Serving: Calories 317. Total Fat 17 g. Saturated Fat 7 g.
Protein 15 g. Carbohydrate 29 g. Fiber 2 g.
Sodium 344 mg. Cholesterol 442 mg.

Rocky Top Omelet

French Omelet
With Mushroom Sauce

The secret to making a great omelet is the right pan. In grandma's day, it was a well-seasoned iron skillet; today, it's a nonstick frying pan.

For mushroom sauce:

- 1 **tablespoon butter or margarine**
- 1 **cup thinly sliced fresh mushrooms**
- 2 **tablespoons all-purpose flour**
- ½ **teaspoon onion powder**
- ½ **teaspoon salt**
- ⅛ **teaspoon black pepper**
- 1 **cup low-fat (1% milkfat) milk**

For the omelet:

- 3 **large eggs**
- 2 **large egg whites**
- 2 **tablespoons water**
- ½ **teaspoon dried tarragon leaves**
- ⅛ **teaspoon salt**
- 1 **tablespoon butter or margarine**

HOW TO COOK OMELETS

For light, golden omelets, heat the butter until a drop of water sizzles when dropped into skillet. Pour in the egg mixture and follow these steps:

 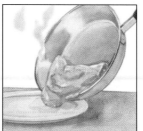

1. When the egg starts to set, use the corner of a pancake turner to lift the edge so the uncooked egg flows to the bottom of the skillet. Cook the omelet only until the egg is just set on top but still glossy.

2. Use the pancake turner to lift one side of the omelet and carefully fold the omelet in half. Tilt the skillet so the omelet is near the edge of the skillet. Then, ease the omelet onto the plate.

---

1 To prepare the mushroom sauce, in a small saucepan, melt 1 tablespoon butter over moderate heat. Add the mushrooms and cook for 3 minutes. In a small bowl, whisk together the flour, onion powder, the ½ teaspoon salt, and pepper. Stir flour mixture into mixture in saucepan. Cook for 1 minute or until bubbly. Stir in the milk. Cook, stirring constantly, for 5 minutes or until mixture is thickened and bubbly. Cover to keep warm; set aside.

2 To prepare the omelet, in a medium-size bowl, whisk together the eggs, egg whites, water, tarragon, and the ⅛ teaspoon salt. In a 10-inch nonstick skillet, heat 1 tablespoon butter over moderate heat (tip, below left). Tilt skillet to coat the surface with butter. Pour egg mixture into skillet. Cook over moderate heat for 4 minutes or just until omelet begins to set. Cook 2 minutes more or until eggs are set (tip, below left). Fold the omelet in half and transfer to a serving plate (tip, below left). Spoon the mushroom sauce over the omelet. Makes 2 main-dish servings.

Prep Time: 10 minutes Cooking Time: 15 minutes

1 Serving: Calories 320. Total Fat 21 g. Saturated Fat 10 g. Protein 19 g. Carbohydrate 15 g. Fiber 1 g. Sodium 996 mg. Cholesterol 355 mg.

Mushroom and Cheese Omelet Prepare as for French Omelet with Mushroom Sauce, omitting the mushroom sauce. In a small skillet, melt **1 tablespoon butter or margarine** over moderately high heat. Add **½ cup sliced fresh mushrooms** and cook until mushrooms are tender. Before folding omelet in half, spoon mushroom mixture down 1 side of the omelet. Sprinkle with **2 tablespoons shredded Cheddar or Swiss cheese.** Fold omelet in half.

1 Serving: Calories 263. Total Fat 21 g. Saturated Fat 11 g. Protein 15 g. Carbohydrate 2 g. Fiber 0 g. Sodium 444 mg. Cholesterol 358 mg.

French Marmalade Omelet Prepare as for French Omelet with Mushroom Sauce, omitting the mushroom sauce and the tarragon. Before folding omelet in half, spoon ¼ **cup orange marmalade, raspberry preserves, or blackberry preserves** down 1 side of the omelet. Fold omelet in half. Transfer to a serving platter. Sift **confectioners sugar** over omelet.

1 Serving: Calories 286. Total Fat 13 g. Saturated Fat 6 g. Protein 13 g. Carbohydrate 30 g. Fiber 0 g. Sodium 364 mg. Cholesterol 335 mg.

French-Toasted Cheese Sandwiches

Originally, these luscious hot sandwiches were coated in egg like French toast and then, deep fried. Today's lighter version uses egg whites and is pan-fried to give the same golden brown crust and creamy center with less fat.

For the sandwiches:

- 1 **tablespoon butter or margarine**
- ½ **cup chopped fresh mushrooms**
- ¼ **cup chopped onion**
- ⅛ **teaspoon black pepper**
- 8 **slices home-style white bread**
- 4 **slices American cheese or 2 slices Cheddar cheese (3 ounces), halved crosswise**
- 2 **slices part-skim mozzarella cheese (3 ounces), halved crosswise**

For the egg coating:

- 1 **large egg**
- 1 **large egg white**
- 3 **tablespoons low-fat (1% milkfat) milk**
  Nonstick cooking spray

1 To prepare the sandwiches, in a 10-inch nonstick skillet, melt butter over moderate heat. Cook mushrooms, onion, and pepper in butter until vegetables are tender. Remove from skillet.

2 For each sandwich, layer a slice of bread, a slice of American cheese, some of the mushroom-onion mixture, a half-slice of mozzarella cheese, and another slice of bread.

3 To prepare the egg coating, in a shallow bowl, whisk together the egg, egg white, and milk. Dip sandwiches in coating to coat on both sides. Wipe out skillet. Coat skillet with cooking spray. In the skillet, cook sandwiches, 2 at a time, over moderate heat until bread is golden and cheese begins to melt, turning once. Makes 4 main-dish servings.

Prep Time: 10 minutes Cooking Time: 13 minutes

1 Serving: Calories 428. Total Fat 18 g. Saturated Fat 9 g.
Protein 20 g. Carbohydrate 46 g. Fiber 2 g.
Sodium 729 mg. Cholesterol 89 mg.

✳

French-Toasted Cream Cheese Sandwiches

Prepare as for French-Toasted Cheese Sandwiches, omitting all of the sandwich ingredients and using

French-Toasted Cheese Sandwiches

⅓ **cup fat-free cream cheese,** ¼ **cup finely shredded carrot,** ¼ **cup finely chopped walnuts,** and **8 slices raisin-cinnamon bread.** In a small bowl, stir together cream cheese, carrot, and walnuts. Spread half of the bread slices with the cream cheese mixture. Top with remaining bread slices. Prepare the egg coating, dip sandwiches, and cook as directed in step 3 of French-Toasted Cheese Sandwiches.

1 Serving: Calories 250. Total Fat 8 g. Saturated Fat 1 g.
Protein 13 g. Carbohydrate 30 g. Fiber 3 g.
Sodium 458 mg. Cholesterol 60 mg.

EASTER EGGS

Women have been delighting their children and grandchildren with festively decorated eggs for centuries. To create these time-honored tokens of friendship and love, they used natural dyes made from fresh fruits or vegetables plus whatever decorations they had on hand. Here's how to color Easter eggs the way grandma did. It's easy and fun.

HARD COOKING EGGS FOR DYEING

1. To prepare the eggs for dyeing, dip each egg into a mild detergent solution.

2. Scrub eggs gently with a soft brush to remove the oil coating (the dye will adhere better). Rinse the eggs well.

3. Place the eggs in a stainless steel, enameled, or glass saucepan or Dutch oven (don't use aluminum or the dye won't hold on the eggs). Pour cold water over the eggs until the water is 1 inch over the top of the eggs. Bring to a boil. Lower heat and cook just below simmering for 15 minutes.

4. Drain, then cover the warm eggs with cold water. Let them stand in the water until cool enough to handle. Refrigerate until you are ready to dye the eggs.

NATURAL DYES

Fruits, vegetables, spices, herbs, and seeds provide a multitude of delightful natural colors for dyeing Easter eggs. Working with natural materials is especially enjoyable because it's not a precise science. The richness of color you obtain depends upon the concentration of the dyeing liquid, the length of time you leave the egg in the dye, and the surface of the egg itself.

To get started, here is a list of colors that can be obtained from natural materials. Remember that if you plan to eat your dyed eggs, you must use edible and chemical- and pesticide-free dyeing materials.

◆ **Pinks and Reds** For a variety of light pinkish reds, use about 2 cups cranberries, sliced beets, or red raspberries.

◆ **Orange** For a wide range of orange shades, use the skins from 4 large yellow onions.

◆ **Yellow** For delicate yellows, use 2 teaspoons ground cumin or, for a more lively yellow, try 2 teaspoons ground turmeric.

◆ **Blue** For blues that range from pale to deep teal, use about 4 cups red cabbage leaves. For shades of medium to deep blue, try 2 cups canned blueberry juice.

Dyeing Easter Eggs

1 To brew dyeing liquid from fresh fruits or vegetables, first rinse or wash them. (Omit steps 1 and 2 if you are using canned fruit juice as dyeing liquid.) Then, place the fruits or vegetables in a stainless steel, enameled, or glass saucepan. (Don't use aluminum or the dye won't hold on the eggs.) Add **2 cups cold water.** Bring to a boil. Lower the heat and simmer, covered, for 5 minutes. Remove from the heat. Cool to room temperature.

2 To strain the dyeing liquid, set a colander in a medium-size bowl and pour the cooked mixture through the colander. Discard the dyeing material. Store the strained dyeing liquid in a sealed and labeled jar in the refrigerator until you're ready to color Easter eggs. (You can brew and strain the dyeing liquid up to 2 weeks before using.)

3 Pour the brewed dyeing liquid or fruit juice into a small stainless steel, enameled, or glass saucepan. (Don't use aluminum or dye won't hold on the eggs.) Bring to a boil over medium heat. Remove from heat and stir in **1 tablespoon white vinegar.**

Carefully lower 2 to 4 eggs into the hot dyeing liquid. Let stand until the eggs reach the desired color. (Natural dyes do not "take" as quickly as commercial dyes. It may take only a few minutes or up to several hours for the eggs to dye to the color you want.)

4 Dry eggs. Once all colors of eggs are dry, lightly brush the eggs with **cooking oil.** Chill eggs (will keep for 10 days).

Eggs Goldenrod

Eggs Goldenrod

*The sieved egg yolk on top of this time-tested brunch
dish resembles the yellow flowers of the goldenrod plant.*

6 hard-cooked large eggs
1¼ cups low-fat (1% milkfat) milk
2 tablespoons all-purpose flour
1 teaspoon dried marjoram leaves
¼ teaspoon each salt and black pepper
4 frozen puff pastry shells, baked

1 Cut the hard-cooked eggs in half. Discard the yolks from 4 of the eggs. Coarsely chop yolk from 1 egg and all of the egg whites. Set aside remaining yolk.

2 In a small saucepan, whisk together the milk, flour, marjoram, salt, and pepper. Cook over moderate heat, whisking constantly, until mixture starts to thicken. Cook and whisk for 2 minutes more or until thickened. Fold in the chopped eggs.

3 Spoon into the pastry shells. Sieve some of the reserved egg yolk over each serving. Makes 4 main-dish servings.

Prep Time: 10 minutes Cooking Time: 8 minutes

1 Serving: Calories 325. Total Fat 19 g. Saturated Fat 4 g.
Protein 13 g. Carbohydrate 26 g. Fiber 1 g.
Sodium 410 mg. Cholesterol 109 mg.

Rosy Egg Salad

*Cooks of the 1930's and 1940's loved
egg salad, seasoning it with everything from
crumbled bacon to capers. This tasty version
gets its piquant flavor and rosy glow from
pimiento plus a touch of French dressing.*

   7 **hard-cooked large eggs**
   2 **tablespoons finely chopped onion**
   2 **tablespoons finely chopped celery**
   1 **tablespoon finely chopped drained canned pimientos**
 ¼ **cup reduced-fat mayonnaise**
   1 **tablespoon reduced-fat French dressing**
 ¼ **teaspoon celery seeds (optional)**
 ¼ **teaspoon salt**
 ⅛ **teaspoon black pepper**

1 Cut the hard-cooked eggs in half. Discard the yolks from 4 of the eggs. Chop the remaining egg yolks and all of the egg whites. In a large bowl, combine the chopped eggs, onion, celery, and pimientos.

2 In a small bowl, combine the mayonnaise, French dressing, celery seeds (if using), salt, and pepper. Fold mayonnaise mixture into egg mixture. To serve, spoon into lettuce cups or spread on bread. Makes 2 main-dish servings; 4 sandwiches.

Prep Time: 15 minutes

1 Serving: Calories 240. Total Fat 15 g. Saturated Fat 4 g.
Protein 17 g. Carbohydrate 10 g. Fiber 1 g.
Sodium 798 mg. Cholesterol 326 mg.

Best Deviled Eggs

*No warm-weather gathering of yesteryear
was complete without these zesty morsels—or the
inevitable squabble over who got the last one.*

 12 **hard-cooked large eggs**
 ½ **cup reduced-fat mayonnaise**
   1 **teaspoon lower-sodium Worcestershire sauce**
   1 **teaspoon tarragon vinegar or vinegar**
 ½ **teaspoon dry mustard**
 ¼ **teaspoon salt**
 ⅛ **teaspoon black pepper**
   2 **tablespoons minced parsley**

1 Cut the hard-cooked eggs in half lengthwise. Remove the yolks. Set aside the egg white halves.

2 In a large bowl, use a fork to mash the egg yolks until the consistency of fine crumbs. Stir in the mayonnaise, Worcestershire sauce, vinegar, mustard, salt, and pepper.

3 Spoon or pipe the yolk mixture into the egg white halves (tip, below). Sprinkle with the parsley. Cover and refrigerate for 1 to 6 hours. Makes 24 side-dish servings.

Prep Time: 20 minutes Chilling Time: 1 hour

1 Serving: Calories 52. Total Fat 4 g. Saturated Fat 1 g.
Protein 3 g. Carbohydrate 1 g. Fiber 0 g.
Sodium 80 mg. Cholesterol 107 mg.

Thousand Island Deviled Eggs Prepare as for Best Deviled Eggs, omitting the Worcestershire sauce and tarragon vinegar and substituting ½ **cup reduced-fat Thousand Island dressing** for the mayonnaise.

1 Serving: Calories 47. Total Fat 3 g. Saturated Fat 1 g.
Protein 3 g. Carbohydrate 1 g. Fiber 0 g.
Sodium 104 mg. Cholesterol 107 mg.

FILLING DEVILED EGGS

For home-style eggs, scoop up a rounded teaspoon of yolk mixture. Then, with a second spoon, gently mound the filling into an egg white half.

To prepare eggs for a party, spoon the yolk mixture into a pastry or decorating bag fitted with a large star tip. Then, gently squeeze the filling into the egg white halves.

Asparagus-Cheese Strata

The strata became popular during the Depression because it was an easy and economical way to use up day-old bread. We added asparagus to the traditional recipe to make a nourishing one-dish meal.

1   **package (10 ounces) frozen cut asparagus**

8   **slices day-old home-style whole-wheat bread, crusts removed**

1½ **cups shredded Muenster or part-skim mozzarella cheese (6 ounces)**

1½ **cups low-fat (1% milkfat) milk**

3   **large eggs**

2   **large egg whites**

1   **teaspoon dried dill weed**

½   **teaspoon dry mustard**

¼   **teaspoon each salt and black pepper**

1 Cook the asparagus according to package directions. Drain well. Cut bread into 2-inch squares. Line the bottom of a lightly greased 8" x 8" x 2" baking dish with half of the bread. Layer half of the Muenster cheese, the asparagus, and the remaining Muenster cheese over the bread in the dish. Top with the remaining bread.

2 In a medium-size bowl, whisk together the milk, eggs, egg whites, dill weed, mustard, salt, and pepper. Pour over the layers in the baking dish. Cover and refrigerate for 2 to 24 hours.

3 Preheat the oven to 325°F. Uncover the strata and bake for 45 to 50 minutes or until a knife inserted near the center comes out clean. Let stand 10 minutes before serving. Makes 6 main-dish servings.

Prep Time: 20 minutes   Chilling Time: 2 hours
Cooking Time: 50 minutes   Standing Time: 10 minutes

1 Serving: Calories 270. Total Fat 14 g. Saturated Fat 7 g.
Protein 17 g. Carbohydrate 21 g. Fiber 2 g.
Sodium 455 mg. Cholesterol 136 mg.

✳

Broccoli-Cheese Strata   Prepare as for Asparagus-Cheese Strata, substituting **1 cup frozen cut broccoli** for the asparagus and **1½ cups shredded Gouda cheese** for the Muenster cheese.

1 Serving: Calories 262. Total Fat 13 g. Saturated Fat 6 g.
Protein 17 g. Carbohydrate 21 g. Fiber 2 g.
Sodium 513 mg. Cholesterol 141 mg.

Italian Eggs with Peppers

Simple dishes are often the best. This recipe comes to us from the granddaughter of Sicilian-born Mary Cutaia. She often made it in the summer when green peppers were plentiful.

1   **tablespoon olive oil**

2   **large sweet green peppers, cut into thin strips**

1   **clove garlic, minced**

4   **large eggs**

4   **large egg whites**

2   **tablespoons low-fat (1% milkfat) milk**

2   **tablespoons minced fresh basil or 2 teaspoons dried basil leaves**

½   **teaspoon salt**

¼   **teaspoon black pepper**

1 In a 10-inch nonstick skillet, heat olive oil over moderately high heat. Add the green peppers and garlic and cook until the peppers are tender.

2 In a medium-size bowl, whisk together the eggs, egg whites, milk, basil, salt, and black pepper; pour over the vegetables. Cook, gently scrambling the eggs with a wooden spoon, for 4 minutes or just until firm yet moist. Serve with sliced tomatoes. Makes 4 main-dish servings.

Prep Time: 10 minutes   Cooking Time: 10 minutes

1 Serving: Calories 136. Total Fat 9 g. Saturated Fat 2 g.
Protein 10 g. Carbohydrate 4 g. Fiber 1 g.
Sodium 389 mg. Cholesterol 213 mg.

✳

Cottage Scrambled Eggs   Prepare as for Italian Eggs with Peppers, omitting the sweet green peppers and garlic and stirring ½ **cup dry-curd cottage cheese** and **4 medium-size green onions with tops, finely sliced,** into the egg mixture. In a 10-inch nonstick skillet, heat the olive oil over moderately high heat. Cook the egg mixture as directed above.

1 Serving: Calories 142. Total Fat 9 g. Saturated Fat 2 g.
Protein 13 g. Carbohydrate 2 g. Fiber 0 g.
Sodium 392 mg. Cholesterol 215 mg.

Ham and Egg Pie

Ham and Egg Pie

*It wasn't until after World War II that American cooks began calling this
savory brunch dish by its French name, quiche. Before that, it was just plain pie.*

1	**store-bought or homemade pie crust (page 337)**
1½	**cups shredded part-skim mozzarella or Swiss cheese (6 ounces)**
½	**cup finely chopped cooked lower-sodium ham**
2	**tablespoons all-purpose flour**
1½	**cups low-fat (1% milkfat) milk**
2	**large eggs**
2	**large egg whites**
½	**teaspoon dried fines herbes or basil leaves**
⅛	**teaspoon black pepper**

1 Preheat the oven to 400°F. Line a 9-inch pie plate or quiche dish with the pie crust; crimp the edge. Line the crust with foil and fill with dried beans. Bake for 15 minutes or until light brown. Cool pie crust on rack for 5 minutes; discard the foil. (Save the beans for future pastry baking.)

2 Meanwhile, in a medium-size bowl, combine the mozzarella cheese, ham, and flour. Spread in crust.

3 In the same bowl, whisk together the milk, eggs, egg whites, fines herbes, and pepper. Pour over the mixture into the crust. Cover edges of pie with foil. Bake for 20 minutes; remove foil. Bake for 15 minutes more or until the center is set. Makes 6 main-dish servings.

Prep Time: 15 minutes Cooking Time: 50 minutes

1 Serving: Calories 320. Total Fat 18 g. Saturated Fat 7 g.
Protein 18 g. Carbohydrate 21 g. Fiber 1 g.
Sodium 559 mg. Cholesterol 95 mg.

Two-Cheese Soufflé

Two-Cheese Soufflé

*In grandma's day, a puffed, golden, feather-light soufflé was
considered the hallmark of a good cook. For certain success, use American
and process Swiss cheeses. They're less likely to separate.*

  5 **large eggs**
  ³/₄ **cup low-fat (1% milkfat) milk**
  2 **tablespoons all-purpose flour**
  ¼ **teaspoon salt**
     Several dashes hot red pepper sauce
  ⅓ **cup shredded American or Colby cheese**
  ⅓ **cup shredded process Swiss or natural Swiss cheese**

1 Separate the eggs. Discard the yolks from 2 of the
eggs. Place egg whites in a clean medium-size bowl.
Place egg yolks in a small bowl. Set aside.

2 Preheat the oven to 325°F. Make a foil collar and
attach to a 1½-quart soufflé dish (tip, opposite
page). Lightly grease the foil collar and the soufflé dish.

In a small saucepan, whisk together the milk, flour, salt,
and red pepper sauce. Cook over moderate heat, stirring
constantly, until the mixture starts to thicken. Cook and
stir for 2 minutes more or until thickened and bubbly.
Add the American cheese and Swiss cheese and stir
until melted. Remove from heat.

3 Whisk egg yolks until light. Add a little of the hot
cheese mixture to yolks, then slowly whisk all of the
yolk mixture into the cheese mixture.

4 With electric mixer on *High,* beat egg whites until
soft peaks form. Stir one-fourth of the whites into
hot cheese mixture, then quickly fold in the remaining
whites. Spoon into prepared soufflé dish. Make top hat

(tip, below). Bake 45 minutes or until puffy and golden. Serve immediately. Makes 4 main-dish servings.

Prep Time: 20 minutes Cooking Time: 52 minutes

1 Serving: Calories 164. Total Fat 10 g. Saturated Fat 5 g. Protein 13 g. Carbohydrate 6 g. Fiber 0 g. Sodium 496 mg. Cholesterol 178 mg.

✳

Cheddar Chili Soufflé Prepare as for Two-Cheese Soufflé, omitting the American cheese and the Swiss cheese and adding ¾ **cup shredded sharp Cheddar cheese (3 ounces).** Stir **1 can (4 ounces) chopped green chili peppers, drained,** into the hot cheese mixture before adding the beaten egg whites.

1 Serving: Calories 190. Total Fat 11 g. Saturated Fat 6 g. Protein 14 g. Carbohydrate 8 g. Fiber 1 g. Sodium 696 mg. Cholesterol 184 mg.

SENSATIONAL SOUFFLÉS

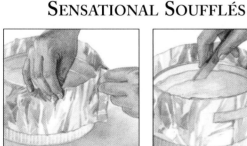 

For an extra high soufflé, add a foil collar to the dish. Cut a piece of foil large enough to wrap around the dish. Fold foil lengthwise in thirds. Wrap foil around dish, fold ends, and fasten with masking tape so collar extends 2 inches above dish.

For a more attractive soufflé, just before it goes into the oven, use a small metal spatula to score a 1-inch-deep circle in the top of the soufflé mixture 1 inch from the edge of the dish. Then, as the soufflé bakes, a top hat will form.

Egg-Artichoke Casserole

1 **jar (6½ ounces) marinated artichoke hearts**
1 **medium-size yellow onion, chopped**
3 **large eggs**
2 **large egg whites**
1½ **cups shredded sharp Cheddar cheese (6 ounces)**
½ **cup finely crushed lower-sodium crackers**
⅛ **teaspoon black pepper**

1 Preheat the oven to 350°F. Drain artichoke hearts, reserving 1 tablespoon of marinade. Chop artichoke hearts. In a medium saucepan, heat reserved marinade over moderate heat. Add onion and cook until tender.

2 In a medium-size bowl, whisk together the eggs and egg whites. Stir in the artichokes, cooked onion, Cheddar cheese, crackers, and pepper. Spoon into a lightly greased 1½-quart casserole. Bake for 35 minutes or until set and starting to brown. Serve with a tossed salad. Makes 4 main-dish servings.

Prep Time: 20 minutes Cooking Time: 40 minutes

1 Serving: Calories 363. Total Fat 24 g. Saturated Fat 11 g. Protein 20 g. Carbohydrate 19 g. Fiber 3 g. Sodium 693 mg. Cholesterol 204 mg.

Old-Fashioned Fondue

This easy soufflélike dish was called a fondue in the early 1900's and was served for lunch or supper. It wasn't until the 1950's that Americans made fondue the Swiss way by melting cheese in a chafing dish.

3 **large egg whites**
1¼ **cups low-fat (1% milkfat) milk**
1 **cup fresh bread crumbs (2 slices bread)**
⅓ **cup finely shredded Colby or Cheddar cheese**
2 **large egg yolks**
1 **tablespoon butter or margarine, melted**
½ **teaspoon dried thyme leaves**
¼ **teaspoon each salt and black pepper**

1 Preheat the oven to 325°F. In a clean medium-size bowl, with an electric mixer on *High*, beat egg whites until stiff peaks form.

2 In another medium-size bowl, whisk together the milk, bread crumbs, Colby cheese, egg yolks, butter, thyme, salt, and pepper. Fold in the stiffly beaten egg whites. Spoon mixture into a lightly greased 8-inch round baking dish.

3 Place baking dish in a shallow baking pan and pour hot water around the baking dish to a depth of 1 inch. Bake for 30 to 35 minutes or until a knife inserted near the center comes out clean. Serve with broccoli spears. Makes 3 main-dish servings.

Prep Time: 20 minutes Cooking Time: 30 minutes

1 Serving: Calories 223. Total Fat 13 g. Saturated Fat 7 g. Protein 13 g. Carbohydrate 14 g. Fiber 0 g. Sodium 478 mg. Cholesterol 169 mg.

Corn Country Croquettes

Corn Country Croquettes

*Golden brown on the outside, soft and creamy inside,
croquettes have been popular since before the Civil War. Serve
them with steamed green beans and a tossed spinach salad.*

6 **hard-cooked large eggs**
1 **can (8 ounces) lower-sodium cream-style corn**
1/3 **cup all-purpose flour**
1/2 **teaspoon onion powder**
1/4 **teaspoon each salt and black pepper**
1/4 **cup low-fat (1% milkfat) milk**
2 **tablespoons minced parsley**
1 **cup seasoned fine dry bread crumbs**
2 **large eggs, lightly beaten**
2 **tablespoons vegetable oil**

1 Cut hard-cooked eggs in half. Discard the yolks from 3 of the eggs. Finely chop the remaining egg yolks and all of the egg whites; set aside. In a small saucepan, combine the corn, flour, onion powder, salt, and pepper. Stir in milk. Cook, stirring constantly, for 5 minutes or until thickened.

2 Pour mixture into a large bowl. Stir in the finely chopped eggs and parsley. Cover and refrigerate for 1 to 24 hours.

3 Preheat oven to 300°F. Spread bread crumbs on a plate. In a shallow bowl, place the beaten eggs. Carefully drop about 1/4 cup of the chilled corn mixture onto crumbs. Shape into 1/2-inch-thick patty. Coat the patty with the bread crumbs, then with the beaten eggs, and again with the crumbs. Repeat to make 8 patties.

4 In a 10-inch nonstick skillet, heat 1 tablespoon of the oil over moderately high heat. Add 4 of the patties and cook for 8 minutes or until golden, turning frequently. Transfer to a baking sheet, cover with foil, and place in the oven to keep warm. Repeat with remaining oil and remaining patties. Makes 4 main-dish servings.

Prep Time: 20 minutes Chilling Time: 1 hour
Cooking Time: 22 minutes

1 Serving: Calories 365. Total Fat 15 g. Saturated Fat 3 g.
Protein 17 g. Carbohydrate 41 g. Fiber 4 g.
Sodium 1,097 mg. Cholesterol 267 mg.

Chilies Rellenos Bake

The traditional Tex-Mex recipe calls for these cheese-stuffed peppers to be fried in oil. This baked casserole is easier and more healthful.

4   poblano or anaheim peppers, halved lengthwise, or 2 sweet green peppers, quartered

4   ounces Colby-Monterey Jack or Cheddar cheese

3   large eggs

2   large egg whites

½   cup low-fat (1% milkfat) milk

½   cup all-purpose flour

½   teaspoon dried cilantro leaves or dried parsley

½   teaspoon baking powder

⅛   teaspoon salt

⅛   teaspoon ground red pepper (cayenne)

⅓   cup shredded Colby-Monterey Jack or Cheddar cheese

½   cup picante sauce

1 Preheat oven to 450°F. Remove stems, seeds, and veins from peppers. In a medium-size saucepan, bring a large amount of water to a boil. Add peppers and cook, uncovered, for 3 minutes. Drain peppers and invert onto paper towels. Cut the 4 ounces Colby-Monterey Jack cheese into pieces to fit inside pepper pieces. Place cheese inside pepper pieces. Arrange pepper pieces in a lightly greased 11" x 7" x 2" baking dish.

2 In a medium-size bowl, whisk together the eggs, egg whites, and milk. Whisk in the flour, cilantro, baking powder, salt, and red pepper. Pour egg mixture over pepper pieces.

3 Bake for 15 minutes or until cheese is melted and batter is puffed and golden. Sprinkle the ⅓ cup shredded Colby-Monterey Jack cheese on top. Serve with the picante sauce. Makes 4 main-dish servings.

Prep Time: 25 minutes Cooking Time: 25 minutes

1 Serving: Calories 306. Total Fat 16 g. Saturated Fat 9 g.
Protein 20 g. Carbohydrate 21 g. Fiber 2 g.
Sodium 583 mg. Cholesterol 195 mg.

Three-Cheese Grits

Native Americans showed the early settlers how to preserve corn by drying it and removing the hull. When left in kernels, the corn is called hominy. When it's ground, it's called grits. Southerners added cheese to grits, as in this old recipe.

3   cups lower-sodium chicken broth (page 67)

1   medium-size yellow onion, chopped

1   clove garlic, minced

⅛   teaspoon hot red pepper sauce

¾   cup quick-cooking hominy grits

½   cup shredded Monterey Jack or sharp American cheese (2 ounces)

½   cup shredded sharp American cheese (2 ounces)

¼   cup grated Parmesan cheese

1   large egg

2   large egg whites

1 Preheat the oven to 350°F. In a large saucepan, combine the chicken broth, onion, garlic, and hot pepper sauce. Bring to a boil. Slowly add the grits, stirring constantly. Lower the heat and simmer, uncovered, for 5 to 7 minutes or until grits are thick and smooth, stirring frequently to prevent sticking. Remove from the heat. Add the Monterey Jack cheese, American cheese, and half of the Parmesan cheese, stirring until melted. Cool slightly.

2 In a medium-size bowl, with an electric mixer on *High*, beat the egg and egg whites for 3 minutes or until light yellow and thickened. Fold half of the egg mixture into grits. Then, fold in remaining egg mixture.

3 Spoon the mixture into a lightly greased 2-quart casserole. Sprinkle with the remaining Parmesan cheese. Bake, covered, for 20 minutes. Uncover and bake 20 minutes more or until puffy and top is starting to brown. Serve with roast beef, pork, or chicken. Makes 6 side-dish servings.

Prep Time: 15 minutes Cooking Time: 50 minutes

1 Serving: Calories 194. Total Fat 8 g. Saturated Fat 5 g.
Protein 10 g. Carbohydrate 19 g. Fiber 0 g.
Sodium 293 mg. Cholesterol 56 mg.

Rinktum Tiddy

The Pennsylvania Dutch laced their Welsh rarebit with tomatoes and called it "rinktum tiddy". American cheese is used here to ensure that the sauce will be smooth and velvety, not grainy.

2 **cups low-fat (1% milkfat) milk**
¼ **cup all-purpose flour**
½ **teaspoon dry mustard**
⅛ **teaspoon white pepper or black pepper**
2 **cups shredded sharp American cheese (8 ounces)**
1 **small tomato, peeled, seeded, and finely chopped**
8 **slices whole-wheat bread, toasted and cut diagonally into triangles**

1 In a medium-size saucepan, whisk together the milk, flour, mustard, and pepper. Cook over moderate heat, whisking constantly, until mixture starts to thicken. Cook and whisk for 2 minutes more or until thickened. Stir in American cheese until melted. Stir in tomato. Serve over toast. Makes 4 main-dish servings.

Prep Time: 10 minutes Cooking Time: 10 minutes

1 Serving: Calories 460. Total Fat 22 g. Saturated Fat 13 g.
Protein 24 g. Carbohydrate 44 g. Fiber 4 g.
Sodium 1,218 mg. Cholesterol 58 mg.

Golden Curried Eggs

6 **hard-cooked large eggs**
1¼ **cups low-fat (1% milkfat) milk**
2 **tablespoons all-purpose flour**
2 **teaspoons curry powder**
¼ **teaspoon salt**
⅛ **teaspoon black pepper**
½ **cup reduced-fat sour cream**

1 Cut the hard-cooked eggs lengthwise into quarters. Discard yolks from 2 of the eggs. In a medium-size saucepan, whisk together the milk, flour, curry powder, salt, and pepper. Cook over moderate heat, whisking constantly, until mixture starts to thicken. Cook and whisk for 2 minutes more or until thickened. Whisk in the sour cream. Gently stir in the eggs. Heat through (do not boil). Serve over hot cooked rice with raisins, peanuts, and coconut. Makes 4 main-dish servings.

Prep Time: 10 minutes Cooking Time: 10 minutes

1 Serving: Calories 176. Total Fat 10 g. Saturated Fat 4 g.
Protein 12 g. Carbohydrate 9 g. Fiber 0 g.
Sodium 299 mg. Cholesterol 227 mg.

Calico Cheese Timbales

The tangy tomato sauce complements these old-time custards. Serve the timbales with broccoli or asparagus spears and a fruit salad.

1 **cup shredded Monterey Jack cheese (4 ounces)**
½ **cup shredded carrot**
2 **tablespoons grated Parmesan cheese**
2 **tablespoons all-purpose flour**
1 **cup low-fat (1% milkfat) milk**
2 **large egg whites**
1 **large egg**
½ **teaspoon dried savory leaves or basil leaves**
⅛ **teaspoon black pepper**
Quick Tomato Sauce (recipe, below)

1 Preheat the oven to 325°F. In a medium-size bowl, stir together the Monterey Jack cheese, carrot, Parmesan cheese, and flour.

2 In another medium-size bowl, whisk together the milk, egg whites, egg, savory, and pepper; stir into the cheese mixture. Pour into 4 lightly greased 6-ounce custard cups or timbale molds.

3 Place the custard cups in a shallow baking pan and pour hot water around the custard cups to a depth of 1 inch. Bake for 35 to 40 minutes or until centers are set. Unmold timbales onto plates and spoon Quick Tomato Sauce over. Makes 2 main-dish servings.

Prep Time: 20 minutes Cooking Time: 35 minutes

1 Serving: Calories 419. Total Fat 23 g. Saturated Fat 14 g.
Protein 29 g. Carbohydrate 25 g. Fiber 3 g.
Sodium 597 mg. Cholesterol 167 mg.

Quick Tomato Sauce

In a food processor or blender, process **1 cup lower-sodium stewed tomatoes, ¼ teaspoon dried savory leaves or basil leaves,** and **¼ teaspoon onion powder** until smooth. Pour mixture into a small saucepan. Cook over moderate heat until heated through. Makes 1 cup.

½ Cup: Calories 34. Total Fat 0 g. Saturated Fat 0 g.
Protein 1 g. Carbohydrate 9 g. Fiber 2 g.
Sodium 20 mg. Cholesterol 0 mg.

Grandma's Treats

Hole in One

The children can help you cut out the center of the bread.

- 2 slices home-style white bread
- 2 teaspoons butter or margarine, at room temperature
- 2 large eggs
- 1 strip lean bacon, chopped and cooked until crisp

1. With a 2-inch round cookie or biscuit cutter, cut out the center of each bread slice. (Use centers later for bread crumbs.) Spread both sides of bread slices with the butter. In a 10-inch nonstick skillet, toast bread on one side over moderate heat until golden.

2. Reduce heat to moderately low. Turn the bread over. Break an egg into the hole in each slice. Sprinkle the bacon over eggs. Cook, covered, for 5 to 6 minutes or until eggs are firm. Makes 2 main-dish servings.

Cheese Faces

In days gone by, these open-face sandwiches often were called cheese dreams.

- 4 slices home-style white bread
- 4 slices American or Cheddar cheese
- Toppers (carrot slices or shreds, zucchini slices or strips, green pepper strips, nuts, sesame seeds, and/or raisins)

1. Preheat the broiler. Top each bread slice with a slice of American cheese. Design faces using your choice of toppers. Broil sandwiches 3 to 4 inches from heat for 2 to 3 minutes or until cheese melts. Makes 4 main-dish servings.

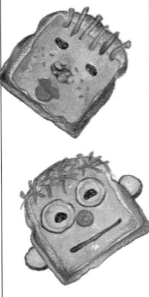

Eggs in a Nest

These scrumptious eggs will tempt even the most hard-to-please child.

- 1½ cups warm mashed potatoes
- ¼ cup reduced-fat sour cream dip with onion
- 1 tablespoon minced parsley
- 4 large eggs
- ¼ cup shredded reduced-fat Cheddar cheese (1 ounce)

1. Preheat the oven to 425°F. Combine the potatoes, sour cream dip, and parsley. Spoon potato mixture into 4 lightly greased 10-ounce custard cups. With a spoon, press the potatoes onto the bottom and halfway up the sides of each custard cup to make a "nest".

2. Break an egg into each potato nest. Place custard cups onto a baking sheet. Bake for 15 minutes or until eggs are set. Sprinkle with the Cheddar cheese. Let stand 2 minutes. Makes 4 main-dish servings.

Kid-Size Quesadillas

These tasty triangles are just the right size for a light lunch.

- ½ cup shredded part-skim mozzarella or Monterey Jack cheese (2 ounces)
- 2 flour tortillas
- Toppers (sliced olives, chopped tomato, sliced green onion, and/or chopped green pepper)

1. Sprinkle half of the mozzarella cheese on half of each tortilla. Top with your choice of the toppers. Fold tortillas in half and press gently to seal.

2. Heat a 10-inch skillet over moderate heat. Cook 1 folded tortilla for 3 minutes or until cheese melts, turning once. Repeat with remaining tortilla. Cut each tortilla into 3 triangles. Sprinkle with additional toppers if you like. Makes 2 main-dish servings.

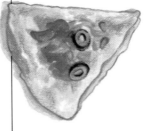

A FEAST OF MEATS

Dinner at grandma's house routinely was built around a hearty meat dish, such as pot roast, pork chops, baked ham, pot pie, or meat loaf. Grandma was an expert both at cooking meats from scratch and creatively using the leftovers. She could pound a tough steak to make it tender, bring out the best in a roast by marinating it, and turn tidbits of leftover meat into a tasty casserole. Glance through this chapter and you're sure to find several stick-to-the-ribs recipes your family will love—all made a little lighter and lower in fat than grandma's, but just as delicious.

Roast Leg of Lamb with Mint Sauce (page 150)
Italian Veal Shanks in Tomato Gravy (page 133)
Sunday-Dinner Stuffed Flank Steak (page 116)

Roast Beef With Yorkshire Pudding

Years ago, grandma made Yorkshire pudding by pouring the batter right into the drippings in the roasting pan. This lower-fat version uses only 2 tablespoons of those drippings and the batter is poured into individual custard cups.

1 **boneless beef rib eye roast, from small end (3 pounds)**
⅛ **teaspoon each salt and black pepper**

For the Yorkshire puddings:

2 **large eggs, lightly beaten**
2 **large egg whites, lightly beaten**
1½ **cups low-fat (1% milkfat) milk**
1½ **cups all-purpose flour**
¼ **teaspoon salt**
¼ **teaspoon dried thyme leaves**

For the mushroom gravy:

1½ **cups lower-sodium beef broth (page 67)**
½ **cup port or lower-sodium beef broth (page 67)**
1½ **cups sliced fresh mushrooms**
¼ **cup chopped shallots or 2 large green onions with tops, finely sliced**
½ **teaspoon dried thyme leaves**
⅛ **teaspoon each salt and black pepper**
2 **tablespoons all-purpose flour**
2 **tablespoons butter or margarine, at room temperature**

1 Preheat the oven to 350°F. Sprinkle the meat with ⅛ teaspoon salt and ⅛ teaspoon pepper, then place it on a rack in a roasting pan. Insert a roasting thermometer in the center. Roast for 45 to 60 minutes or until thermometer registers 140°F. for medium-rare or 1 to 1¼ hours or until 155°F. for medium.

2 Transfer the meat to a platter and cover with foil. Measure the pan drippings. If necessary, add vegetable oil to the drippings to measure 2 tablespoons. Increase the oven temperature to 400°F.

3 Meanwhile, to prepare the Yorkshire puddings, generously grease eight 6-ounce custard cups. Place the custard cups onto a 15½" x 10½" x 1" baking pan. In a medium-size bowl, combine the eggs, egg whites, milk, and the 2 tablespoons drippings. Add the 1½ cups flour, the ¼ teaspoon salt, and the ¼ teaspoon thyme. With a rotary beater or wire whisk, beat until smooth. Fill the custard cups ⅔ full.

4 Bake for 40 minutes or until the Yorkshire puddings are very brown and crusty. Remove from the oven and immediately pierce each with a sharp knife to release steam.

5 Meanwhile, to prepare the mushroom gravy, add the broth and port to roasting pan (tip, below), stirring to loosen the browned bits. Add the mushrooms, shallots, the ½ teaspoon thyme, ⅛ teaspoon salt, and ⅛ teaspoon pepper. Bring to a boil. Lower the heat and simmer for 3 minutes or until the mushrooms are tender.

6 In a small bowl, stir together the 2 tablespoons flour and butter. Stir into mushroom mixture. Bring to a boil over moderate heat and boil for 1 minute, stirring constantly. Slice the meat. Serve immediately with the gravy and the Yorkshire puddings. Makes 8 servings.

Prep Time: 15 minutes Cooking Time: 1 hour 25 minutes

1 Serving: Calories 362. Total Fat 16 g. Saturated Fat 7 g. Protein 28 g. Carbohydrate 24 g. Fiber 1 g. Sodium 273 mg. Cholesterol 123 mg.

USING A ROASTING PAN ON THE RANGE TOP

In the old days, cooks often made gravies or sauces right in the pan that was used to roast the meat. That method still works well, but today many pans can't take the heat of a range-top burner. Check to see if your roasting pan is made from heavy-gauge metal that is designed to be used on top of the range. If your pan is one that should not be placed on a burner:

♦ Transfer the drippings to a saucepan.

♦ Scrape the browned bits off the bottom of the pan and transfer them, too.

♦ If the browned bits are hard to scrape off, stir the liquid you'll be using to make the gravy or sauce into the pan to help loosen the bits. Then, transfer the entire mixture to the saucepan. Now, you're ready to make the gravy or sauce.

Roast Beef with Yorkshire Pudding

Mormor's Pot Roast With Garden Vegetables

"Whenever my family spent a weekend with Mormor (Alma Johnston), we would awaken to the sizzle and wonderful fragrance of pot roast browning on the stove," remembers Dorothy Anderson.

Nonstick cooking spray
1 **boneless beef chuck eye roast (2½ pounds), trimmed and tied**
2 **cups lower-sodium beef broth (page 67)**
2 **tablespoons lower-sodium tomato paste**
1 **tablespoon lower-sodium Worcestershire sauce**
2 **bay leaves**
2 **teaspoons dried marjoram leaves or thyme leaves**
½ **teaspoon salt**
¼ **teaspoon black pepper**
6 **small carrots, trimmed, or 3 medium-size carrots, halved**
6 **medium-size potatoes, peeled and halved**
1 **medium-size yellow onion, cut into 6 wedges**
1 **small rutabaga, peeled and cut into ½-inch-thick wedges**

For the gravy:
⅓ **cup cold water**
3 **tablespoons all-purpose flour**

1 Coat a Dutch oven with cooking spray. Heat the Dutch oven over moderate heat. Add the roast and cook for 10 minutes or until well browned, turning it several times. If necessary, drain off fat.

2 In a medium-size bowl, combine the beef broth, tomato paste, Worcestershire sauce, bay leaves, marjoram, salt, and pepper. Pour over the roast and bring to a boil. Lower the heat and simmer, covered, for 1¾ hours. Turn the meat over.

3 Add the carrots, potatoes, onion, and rutabaga. Cover and bring to a boil over high heat. Lower the heat and simmer, covered, for 30 to 40 minutes more or until the meat and vegetables are tender.

4 Arrange the meat and vegetables on a platter; cover with foil and keep warm. Discard the bay leaves.

5 To prepare the gravy, measure the pan juices. Skim the fat (tip, below). If necessary, add enough beef broth to the juices to measure 2 cups. Return the pan juices to the Dutch oven.

6 In a small bowl, whisk together the water and flour; add to the pan juices. Bring to a boil over moderate heat and boil for 1 minute, whisking constantly. Pour into a gravy boat and serve with the meat and vegetables. Makes 6 servings.

Prep Time: 15 minutes Cooking Time: 2 hours 40 minutes

1 Serving: Calories 377. Total Fat 8 g. Saturated Fat 3 g. Protein 33 g. Carbohydrate 44 g. Fiber 5 g. Sodium 304 mg. Cholesterol 85 mg.

Pork Pot Roast with Garden Vegetables Prepare as for Mormor's Pot Roast with Garden Vegetables, substituting **1 boneless pork double-loin roast (4½ pounds), tied,** for the beef roast and doubling all of the remaining ingredients. Use a stockpot and cook the roast for 1¼ hours, then add the vegetables and cook as in the beef roast recipe. To prepare the gravy, use 4 cups pan juices. Makes 12 servings.

1 Serving: Calories 443. Total Fat 10 g. Saturated Fat 3 g. Protein 43 g. Carbohydrate 44 g. Fiber 5 g. Sodium 306 mg. Cholesterol 100 mg.

SKIMMING FAT

For gravy that isn't greasy, it's important to remove as much fat as possible from the pan juices by skimming with a metal spoon or using a gravy skimmer. Or, try this quick method for removing fat.

1. Pour the pan juices into a metal bowl and place it in a larger bowl of ice water.

2. Let the juices stand until the fat solidifies.

3. Then, use a spoon to skim off the fat.

Pot Roast with Sour Cream Gravy

Pot Roast with Sour Cream Gravy

*Women often baked pot roast for Sunday dinner because it could cook in
the oven while the family went to church. When everyone came home, it only
took a few minutes to whip up the gravy and put dinner on the table.*

Nonstick cooking spray
1 **boneless beef chuck pot roast (2½ to 3 pounds), trimmed**
1 **can (14½ ounces) diced tomatoes, undrained**
1 **large yellow onion, chopped**
2 **large carrots, chopped**
½ **cup lower-sodium beef broth (page 67)**
2 **bay leaves**
½ **teaspoon salt**
½ **teaspoon ground cumin**
¼ **teaspoon black pepper**
½ **cup reduced-fat sour cream**
2 **tablespoons all-purpose flour**

1 Preheat oven to 350°F. Coat an ovenproof Dutch oven with cooking spray. Heat the Dutch oven over moderately high heat. Add the meat and cook for 6 to 10 minutes or until well browned, turning it several times. If necessary, drain off fat.

2 Add the tomatoes, onion, carrots, beef broth, bay leaves, salt, cumin, and pepper. Cover and bake for 2½ to 3 hours or until meat is tender, basting occasionally with liquid. Transfer the meat to a platter; cover with foil and keep warm.

3 Discard the bay leaves. Skim the fat from liquid (page 112). In a small bowl, stir together the sour cream and flour; stir into the liquid in Dutch oven. Cook over moderate heat, stirring constantly, for 3 minutes or until thickened (do not boil). Serve with the meat over hot cooked noodles. Makes 6 to 8 servings.

Prep Time: 15 minutes Cooking Time: 2 hours 40 minutes

1 Serving: Calories 349. Total Fat 13 g. Saturated Fat 5 g.
Protein 45 g. Carbohydrate 10 g. Fiber 2 g.
Sodium 448 mg. Cholesterol 137 mg.

Sauerbraten

Sauerbraten

*German grandmas braised their beef in a rich, dark,
sweet-and-sour gravy made with vinegar and gingersnaps. Cabbage
has been added to this recipe to make a one-dish meal.*

1 **boneless beef round rump roast (4 pounds), trimmed**

2 **cups water**

1½ **cups dry red wine or lower-sodium beef broth
(page 67)**

1 **cup red wine vinegar or cider vinegar**

3 **tablespoons firmly packed light brown sugar**

4 **bay leaves**

4 **parsley sprigs**

2 **teaspoons whole cloves**

1 **teaspoon whole black peppercorns**

½ **teaspoon salt**

½ **teaspoon whole allspice berries**

1 **tablespoon vegetable oil**

2 **medium-size yellow onions, sliced**

1 **small head cabbage, cored and cut into 10 wedges**

For the gravy:

1 **to 1½ cups broken gingersnaps**

1 To marinate the meat, combine the meat, water, wine, vinegar, brown sugar, bay leaves, parsley, cloves, peppercorns, salt, and allspice in a very large heavy-duty plastic bag (tip, below). Refrigerate for 1 to 2 days, turning bag occasionally.

2 Drain the meat; strain and reserve the vinegar mixture, discarding the whole spices. Pat the meat dry with paper towels. In a Dutch oven, heat the oil over moderate heat. Add the meat and cook for 10 minutes or until well browned, turning it several times.

3 Add the reserved vinegar mixture and the onions. Bring to a boil. Lower the heat and simmer, covered, for 2½ hours or until the meat is tender.

4 Transfer the meat and onions to a platter; cover with foil and keep warm. Add the cabbage to the liquid in the Dutch oven. Bring to a boil. Lower the heat and simmer, covered, for 10 minutes or until tender. Transfer the cabbage to platter; cover and keep warm.

5 To prepare gravy, stir 1 cup of the gingersnaps into the liquid in the Dutch oven. Bring to a boil over moderate heat and boil for 1 minute, stirring constantly. If necessary, add more gingersnaps to make gravy the consistency you like. Pour gravy over meat, onions, and cabbage. Serve with hot cooked noodles. Serves 10.

Prep Time: 15 minutes Marinating Time: 1 day
Cooking Time: 3 hours 5 minutes

1 Serving: Calories 349. Total Fat 11 g. Saturated Fat 3 g. Protein 40 g. Carbohydrate 17 g. Fiber 3 g. Sodium 238 mg. Cholesterol 115 mg.

MARINATING MEAT

The old-fashioned way to marinate meat was in a bowl covered by a plate, but using a plastic bag is easier and neater.

1. Place the roast, steaks, or meat cubes into a heavy-duty plastic bag. Set the bag into a deep bowl or a shallow dish. Pour the marinade over the meat in the bag.

2. Close the bag and turn it to distribute the marinade evenly over the meat. Refrigerate the meat for the time specified in the recipe. During the marinating time, turn the bag occasionally.

3. When you're ready to cook, just remove the meat from the bag.

New England Supper-in-a-Pot

If you like your meat falling-apart tender, cook the brisket longer—as much as 4 hours. Taste the cooking liquid before you add the vegetables. If it is very salty or greasy, replace half with fresh boiling water. Then, add the vegetables—they'll turn out fresher tasting.

1   **corned beef brisket (2½ to 3 pounds), rinsed and trimmed**
8   **cups water (or enough to cover meat)**
2   **bay leaves**
1   **teaspoon each whole cloves and caraway seeds**
½   **teaspoon black pepper**
6   **small potatoes**
12   **small carrots, trimmed**
6   **small turnips, peeled, sliced ½ inch thick, and cut into bite-size pieces**
1   **large yellow onion, cut into 6 wedges**
½   **small head cabbage**
12   **Brussels sprouts, trimmed**
1   **tablespoon minced parsley**

1 Place the corned beef in a large Dutch oven. Add the juices from the brisket package. Add the water, bay leaves, cloves, caraway seeds, and pepper. (If your brisket package includes a packet of spices, add it and omit the bay leaves, cloves, caraway seeds, and pepper.) Bring to a boil. Lower the heat and simmer, covered, for 2½ hours or until the meat is tender.

2 Peel a strip around each potato. Add the potatoes, carrots, turnips, and onion to Dutch oven. Bring to a boil. Lower the heat and simmer, covered, for 15 minutes. Cut the cabbage into 3 wedges; cut each wedge in half crosswise. Add the cabbage and Brussels sprouts to Dutch oven. Bring to a boil. Lower the heat and simmer, covered, for 10 minutes more or until meat is tender and vegetables are almost tender.

3 Remove the meat. Slice the meat across the grain; arrange on a platter. Arrange the vegetables around the meat. Sprinkle with the parsley. Serve with prepared horseradish or mustard. Makes 6 servings.

Prep Time: 10 minutes Cooking Time: 3¼ hours

1 Serving: Calories 543. Total Fat 25 g. Saturated Fat 8 g. Protein 30 g. Carbohydrate 52 g. Fiber 11 g. Sodium 1,534 mg. Cholesterol 125 mg.

Sunday-Dinner Stuffed Flank Steak

According to the White House Cook Book of 1887, butchers considered flank steak one of the nicest cuts, and often set it aside for their own families. Serve this colorful steak with steamed green beans and your favorite dinner rolls.

1 beef flank steak (1½ pounds), trimmed

¼ teaspoon each salt and black pepper

1 tablespoon butter or margarine

¼ cup chopped yellow onion

¼ cup chopped sweet green pepper

¼ cup shredded carrot

½ teaspoon each dried sage leaves and marjoram leaves

1½ cups dried bread cubes

2 to 3 tablespoons lower-sodium beef broth (page 67) or water

1 tablespoon vegetable oil

For the sauce:

1 cup lower-sodium beef broth (page 67)

½ cup dry red wine or lower-sodium beef broth (page 67)

¼ cup lower-sodium tomato paste

½ teaspoon each dried sage leaves and marjoram leaves

1 Sprinkle the steak with ⅛ teaspoon of the salt and ⅛ teaspoon of the black pepper. Pound both sides of the steak until steak is ½ to ¾ inch thick (tip, right). With a sharp knife, lightly score both sides of the steak.

2 In a medium-size saucepan, melt the butter over moderately high heat. Add the onion, green pepper, and carrot and cook for 5 minutes or until tender. Remove from heat. Stir in ½ teaspoon sage, ½ teaspoon marjoram, remaining ⅛ teaspoon salt, and remaining ⅛ teaspoon black pepper. Stir in the bread cubes. Drizzle with the 2 to 3 tablespoons beef broth, tossing lightly to moisten.

3 Preheat the oven to 350°F. Spread the bread mixture over the meat. Roll up and tie the meat (tip, below). In a 12-inch skillet, heat the oil over moderately high heat. Add the meat and cook for 8 minutes or until browned, turning several times to brown evenly. Transfer to a large shallow baking pan.

4 To prepare the sauce, add the 1 cup beef broth, wine, tomato paste, ½ teaspoon sage, and ½ teaspoon marjoram to the skillet. Bring to a boil, stirring to loosen the browned bits. Pour into pan around meat.

5 Cover and bake for 1¼ hours or until the meat is tender. To serve, slice the meat and arrange on a platter. Skim the fat from sauce (page 112); serve the sauce with the meat. Makes 6 servings.

Prep Time: 30 minutes Cooking Time: 1½ hours

1 Serving: Calories 283. Total Fat 14 g. Saturated Fat 5 g.
Protein 25 g. Carbohydrate 10 g. Fiber 1 g.
Sodium 267 mg. Cholesterol 64 mg.

POUNDING AND STUFFING FLANK STEAK

1. For a smooth, evenly thick steak, use the fine-toothed side of a meat mallet or the bottom of a small heavy skillet and pound the steak, starting in the center and working toward the edges.

2. To stuff the steak, spread the bread mixture over the steak and begin rolling from a short end, turning the meat slowly to keep the roll tight. Tie steak securely with cotton string.

Melt-in-Your-Mouth Filets with Mushroom Cream Sauce

Melt-in-Your-Mouth Filets
With Mushroom Cream Sauce

*Years ago, this sauce usually was made with white button mushrooms. For
an even richer flavor, you can substitute shiitake, brown, or chanterelle mushrooms.*

1   **tablespoon olive or vegetable oil**
4   **beef tenderloin steaks or 2 top loin steaks
    (1½ pounds), 1 inch thick and trimmed**

For the sauce:

1½ **cups sliced fresh mushrooms**
½   **cup sliced leek or yellow onion**
½   **cup dry white wine or lower-sodium chicken
    broth (page 67)**
⅛   **teaspoon each salt and black pepper**
½   **cup reduced-fat sour cream**
1   **tablespoon all-purpose flour**

1 In a 12-inch nonstick skillet, heat the oil over moderately high heat. Add the steaks. Lower the heat to moderate. Cook steaks for 8 to 10 minutes for medium-rare or until the steaks are the way you like them, turning them often. Transfer to a platter; cover with foil.

2 To prepare the sauce, add the mushrooms, leek, wine, salt, and pepper to the drippings in skillet. Bring to a boil. Lower the heat and simmer, uncovered, for 3 minutes or until mushrooms are tender.

3 In a small bowl, stir together the sour cream and flour. Stir into the mushroom mixture. Cook over moderate heat, stirring constantly, for 2 minutes or until thickened (do not boil). Serve the sauce over the steaks. Makes 4 servings.

Prep Time: 10 minutes Cooking Time: 15 minutes

1 Serving: Calories 360. Total Fat 20 g. Saturated Fat 7 g.
Protein 37 g. Carbohydrate 5 g. Fiber 1 g.
Sodium 160 mg. Cholesterol 117 mg.

Baked Swiss Steak

Baked Swiss Steak

*Just about everyone's grandmother made Swiss steak, and it's no
wonder. The long, slow cooking tenderizes an economical cut of meat
and the colorful vegetable sauce is delicious over noodles or rice.*

1 **pound boneless beef round steak, ³/₄ inch thick and
   trimmed**

¹/₄ **teaspoon each salt and black pepper
   Nonstick cooking spray**

2 **tablespoons all-purpose flour**

1 **can (14¹/₂ ounces) lower-sodium tomatoes,
   undrained and cut up**

2 **stalks celery, sliced ¹/₂ inch thick**

1 **large yellow onion, cut into wedges**

³/₄ **cup frozen whole kernel corn**

1¹/₂ **teaspoons dried oregano leaves**

1 Preheat the oven to 350°F. Sprinkle the steak on
both sides with the salt and pepper. Cut the steak
into 4 pieces. Pound both sides of the pieces until the
pieces are ¹/₂ inch thick (page 116).

2 Coat a 12-inch nonstick skillet with cooking spray.
Heat the skillet over moderately high heat. Add the
steak pieces and cook for 3 minutes on each side or until
browned. Transfer to a 13" x 9" x 2" baking dish.

3 Stir the flour into the drippings in skillet. Stir in the
tomatoes, celery, onion, corn, and oregano. Bring to
a boil over moderate heat and boil for 1 minute, stirring
constantly. Pour over the meat in the baking dish.

4 Cover and bake for 1¹/₄ hours or until the meat is
tender. Serve the meat and tomato mixture with
mashed potatoes or hot cooked noodles. Serves 4.

Prep Time: 20 minutes Cooking Time: 1 hour 25 minutes

1 Serving: Calories 236. Total Fat 7 g. Saturated Fat 2 g.
Protein 26 g. Carbohydrate 17 g. Fiber 4 g.
Sodium 206 mg. Cholesterol 70 mg.

Country-Fried Steak With Brown Gravy

Down-home cooks pounded steak to make it tender, floured it to seal in the juices, and served it with a spicy gravy. In some parts of the country this dish is called chicken-fried steak or smothered steak.

1 **pound boneless beef round steak, ³⁄₄ inch thick and trimmed**
3 **tablespoons all-purpose flour**
1 **teaspoon dry mustard**
¹⁄₄ **teaspoon salt**
¹⁄₈ **teaspoon ground red pepper (cayenne)**
2 **tablespoons vegetable oil**

For the gravy:
2 **cups sliced fresh mushrooms**
1 **tablespoon all-purpose flour**
³⁄₄ **cup lower-sodium beef broth (page 67)**
¹⁄₃ **cup dry red wine or tomato juice**
1 **teaspoon lower-sodium Worcestershire sauce**
¹⁄₄ **teaspoon ground sage**
   Dash ground red pepper (cayenne)

1 Cut the steak into 4 pieces. Pound both sides of the pieces until the pieces are ¹⁄₄ inch thick (page 116). In a plastic bag, combine the 3 tablespoons flour, mustard, salt, and the ¹⁄₈ teaspoon red pepper. Shake the steak pieces, 1 at a time, in flour mixture to coat.

2 In a 10-inch nonstick skillet, heat the oil over moderately high heat. Add 2 of the steak pieces and cook for 2 minutes on each side or until golden brown. Transfer to a platter; cover with foil and keep warm. Repeat with the remaining steak pieces.

3 To prepare the gravy, add the mushrooms to the drippings in skillet and cook for 3 minutes or until tender, stirring frequently. Stir in the 1 tablespoon flour. Add the beef broth, wine, Worcestershire sauce, sage, and dash red pepper. Bring to a boil over moderate heat and boil for 1 minute or until thickened, stirring constantly. Serve gravy over the steak. Makes 4 servings.

Prep Time: 15 minutes Cooking Time: 15 minutes

1 Serving: Calories 277. Total Fat 14 g. Saturated Fat 3 g.
Protein 25 g. Carbohydrate 9 g. Fiber 1 g.
Sodium 179 mg. Cholesterol 70 mg.

Liver and Onions

The secret to making this dish taste as good as grandma's is to cook the sliced onion slowly until it is sweet and almost "melted".

1 **pound calf's liver, ³⁄₈ inch thick**
1 **tablespoon butter, margarine, or olive oil**
1 **large yellow onion, thinly sliced**
¹⁄₈ **teaspoon each salt and black pepper**
2 **teaspoons lemon juice**
1 **teaspoon lower-sodium Worcestershire sauce**
2 **tablespoons minced parsley**

1 Cut the liver into thin strips; set aside. In a 10-inch nonstick skillet, melt the butter over moderate heat. Add the onion and cook for 10 minutes or until very tender, stirring frequently.

2 Add the liver. Sprinkle with the salt and pepper. Cook over moderate heat for 3 to 4 minutes or until liver is tender, stirring frequently. Transfer the liver and onions to a plate.

3 Stir the lemon juice and Worcestershire sauce into the drippings in the skillet, stirring to loosen the browned bits. Pour the mixture over the liver and onions. Sprinkle with the parsley. Makes 4 servings.

Prep Time: 10 minutes Cooking Time: 14 minutes

1 Serving: Calories 162. Total Fat 8 g. Saturated Fat 4 g.
Protein 16 g. Carbohydrate 6 g. Fiber 1 g.
Sodium 141 mg. Cholesterol 415 mg.

Beef Sirloin and Onions Prepare as for Liver and Onions, substituting **1 pound boneless beef sirloin steak, trimmed and cut into thin strips,** for the calf's liver.

1 Serving: Calories 236. Total Fat 11 g. Saturated Fat 5 g.
Protein 29 g. Carbohydrate 4 g. Fiber 1 g.
Sodium 358 mg. Cholesterol 90 mg.

Beef Pot Pie

The early English settlers made meat pies in kettles hung over the fire. To keep the pies moist, they added broth through a hole in the top crust. You can prepare this modern version easily with store-bought pie crust.

Nonstick cooking spray
1 **pound boneless beef round steak, trimmed and cut into ³/₄-inch pieces**
1 **clove garlic, minced**
1¼ **cups lower-sodium beef broth (page 67)**
½ **cup dry red wine or lower-sodium beef broth (page 67)**
1 **bay leaf**
1½ **teaspoons dried savory leaves**
½ **teaspoon dried dill weed**
¼ **teaspoon each salt and black pepper**
1½ **cups sliced fresh mushrooms**
2 **medium-size parsnips, peeled and cut into ½-inch pieces**
2 **medium-size carrots, thinly sliced**
1 **large yellow onion, cut into bite-size pieces**
1 **large sweet red or green pepper, cut into bite-size pieces**
³/₄ **cup frozen peas**
¼ **cup all-purpose flour**
1 **store-bought or homemade pie crust (page 337)**
   Low-fat (1% milkfat) milk

1 Coat a Dutch oven with cooking spray. Heat Dutch oven over moderately high heat. Add the meat and garlic and cook for 10 minutes or until meat is browned.

2 Add ³/₄ cup of the beef broth, the wine, bay leaf, savory, dill weed, salt, and black pepper. Bring to boil. Lower heat and simmer, covered, for 40 minutes.

3 Add the mushrooms, parsnips, carrots, onion, and sweet pepper. Bring to a boil. Lower the heat and simmer, covered, for 30 minutes more or until meat and vegetables are tender. Stir in peas. Discard the bay leaf.

4 Preheat the oven to 375°F. In a small bowl, stir together the remaining ½ cup beef broth and the flour; stir into the meat mixture. Bring to a boil over moderate heat and boil for 1 minute, stirring constantly. Transfer to a 1½-quart casserole.

5 Place the pie crust on top of the hot meat mixture. Trim to 1 inch beyond edge of casserole. Fold under extra crust and crimp edge. Cut slits in crust. Brush with a little milk. Bake for 20 minutes or until golden. Makes 4 servings.

Prep Time: 20 minutes Cooking Time: 1 hour 35 minutes
Baking Time: 20 minutes

1 Serving: Calories 577. Total Fat 23 g. Saturated Fat 18 g. Protein 30 g. Carbohydrate 58 g. Fiber 7 g. Sodium 448 mg. Cholesterol 70 mg.

Beef Paprikash

This dish is especially delicious served the old-world way—over hot cooked noodles dusted with poppy seeds.

Nonstick cooking spray
1½ **pounds boneless beef chuck steak, trimmed and cut into ³/₄-inch pieces**
2 **medium-size yellow onions, cut into wedges**
1 **clove garlic, minced**
1 **tablespoon all-purpose flour**
1 **tablespoon Hungarian paprika or paprika**
2 **teaspoons dried thyme leaves**
½ **teaspoon each salt and black pepper**
1 **can (14½ ounces) lower-sodium tomatoes, undrained and cut up**
1 **cup lower-sodium beef broth (page 67)**
1 **large sweet green pepper, cut into bite-size strips**
1 **cup reduced-fat sour cream**
2 **tablespoons all-purpose flour**

1 Coat a Dutch oven with cooking spray. Heat the Dutch oven over moderately high heat. Add the beef, onions, and garlic. Cook for 10 minutes or until meat is browned.

2 Stir in the 1 tablespoon flour, paprika, thyme, salt, and black pepper. Add the tomatoes, beef broth, and green pepper. Bring to a boil. Lower the heat and simmer, covered, for 1¼ to 1½ hours or until the meat is tender, stirring occasionally.

3 In a small bowl, stir together the sour cream and the 2 tablespoons flour; stir into meat mixture. Cook over moderate heat, stirring constantly, for 3 minutes or until thickened (do not boil). Serve over hot cooked noodles. Makes 6 servings.

Prep Time: 15 minutes Cooking Time: 1 hour 35 minutes

1 Serving: Calories 274. Total Fat 12 g. Saturated Fat 5 g. Protein 29 g. Carbohydrate 13 g. Fiber 2 g. Sodium 257 mg. Cholesterol 93 mg.

Spicy Texas Red

Spicy Texas Red

*In Texas, there are two rules for making chili: use
chunks of beef (not ground beef) and never add beans.*

Nonstick cooking spray

1½ **pounds boneless beef round steak, trimmed and cut
into ½-inch pieces**

3 **medium-size yellow onions, chopped**

1 **large clove garlic, minced**

2 **cans (14½ ounces each) lower-sodium tomatoes,
undrained and cut up**

2 **cans (8 ounces each) lower-sodium tomato sauce**

1 **cup lower-sodium beef broth (page 67)**

2 **tablespoons chili powder**

2 **tablespoons minced canned red jalapeño peppers**

2 **teaspoons dried oregano leaves or basil leaves**

1 **teaspoon sugar**

1 **teaspoon ground cumin**

1 **teaspoon lower-sodium Worcestershire sauce**

½ **teaspoon ground red pepper (cayenne)**

1 Coat a Dutch oven with cooking spray. Heat the
Dutch oven over moderately high heat. Add the
meat, onions, and garlic and cook for 10 minutes or
until meat is browned.

2 Stir in the tomatoes, tomato sauce, beef broth, chili
powder, jalapeño peppers, oregano, sugar, cumin,
Worcestershire sauce, and ground red pepper.

3 Bring to a boil. Lower the heat and simmer, covered, for 50 to 60 minutes or until the meat is tender. For a thicker consistency, cook, uncovered, until the
mixture is the consistency you like. Serve with hot
cooked rice. Makes 6 servings.

Prep Time: 20 minutes Cooking Time: 1 hour 5 minutes

1 Serving: Calories 241. Total Fat 8 g. Saturated Fat 3 g.
Protein 26 g. Carbohydrate 18 g. Fiber 5 g.
Sodium 146 mg. Cholesterol 70 mg.

Cornish Pasties

Cornish Pasties

*The English settlers who worked the mines in Wisconsin and Michigan carried
these meat turnovers to work in cloth lunch sacks or even in their hip pockets. Legend
says the pasties had to be sturdy enough to survive a trip down a mine shaft. This
easy recipe calls for store-bought pie crusts and makes two large pasties that serve three each.*

1 **pound boneless beef round steak, trimmed and cut
into ¼-inch pieces**

1 **medium-size potato, peeled and chopped**

1 **cup chopped peeled rutabaga or turnip**

½ **cup chopped yellow onion**

2 **tablespoons minced parsley**

1 **tablespoon lower-sodium Worcestershire sauce**

1 **clove garlic, minced**

1 **teaspoon dried basil leaves**

¼ **teaspoon salt**

⅛ **teaspoon ground red pepper (cayenne)**

2 **store-bought or homemade pie crusts (page 337)**
Low-fat (1% milkfat) milk

1 Preheat the oven to 375°F. In a medium-size bowl,
combine the meat, potato, rutabaga, onion, parsley,
Worcestershire sauce, garlic, basil, salt, and red pepper.

2 Place half of the meat mixture on half of 1 pie crust,
then fold the crust over the meat mixture, forming a
semi-circle. Crimp to seal edge. Repeat with the
remaining crust and remaining meat mixture. Cut slits
in the top of the pasties. Brush with a little milk.

3 Place on an ungreased large baking sheet. Bake for 35 to 40 minutes or until golden brown. Cut each into 3 wedges and serve with catsup or pizza sauce. Makes 6 servings.

Prep Time: 25 minutes Cooking Time: 35 minutes

1 Serving: Calories 458. Total Fat 24 g. Saturated Fat 21 g. Protein 19 g. Carbohydrate 40 g. Fiber 1 g. Sodium 411 mg. Cholesterol 47 mg.

Chicken Cornish Pasties Prepare as for Cornish Pasties, substituting **1 pound skinned and boned chicken breast halves, cut into ¼-inch pieces,** for the beef round steak.

1 Serving: Calories 438. Total Fat 22 g. Saturated Fat 21 g. Protein 19 g. Carbohydrate 40 g. Fiber 1 g. Sodium 423 mg. Cholesterol 42 mg.

Prairie Hash

If your grandmother was from the Southwest, she probably made hash with chilies and olives; from New England with beets and corned beef. If she came from the Midwest, her hash, like this old recipe, was sure to include potatoes or another root vegetable.

Nonstick cooking spray
1 tablespoon vegetable oil
3 cups chopped cooked potato, carrot, rutabaga, and/or turnip
2 cups chopped cooked beef or corned beef
1 medium-size yellow onion, chopped
½ cup chopped sweet green pepper
2 teaspoons lower-sodium Worcestershire sauce
⅛ teaspoon salt
⅛ teaspoon ground red pepper (cayenne)
½ cup catsup, chili sauce, or leftover gravy

1 Coat a 10-inch nonstick skillet with cooking spray. Add the oil to skillet. Heat oil over moderate heat. Add potato, beef, onion, green pepper, Worcestershire sauce, salt, and red pepper; stir until mixed.

2 Cook for 10 minutes or until browned, turning occasionally. Stir in the catsup. Makes 4 servings.

Prep Time: 20 minutes Cooking Time: 11 minutes

1 Serving: Calories 299. Total Fat 8 g. Saturated Fat 2 g. Protein 23 g. Carbohydrate 35 g. Fiber 2 g. Sodium 489 mg. Cholesterol 48 mg.

Mustard-Glazed Meat Loaf Special

In this home-style recipe, the beef is mixed with crackers and milk to make the loaf tender. Then, it is slathered with a special spicy brown sugar-and-mustard glaze.

1½ pounds lean ground beef
½ cup crushed lower-sodium crackers
½ cup low-fat (1% milkfat) milk
1 small yellow onion, finely chopped
⅓ cup finely chopped fresh mushrooms or sweet green pepper
2 tablespoons minced parsley
½ teaspoon salt
½ teaspoon ground sage
¼ teaspoon black pepper
2 large egg whites, lightly beaten
⅓ cup firmly packed light brown sugar
1 tablespoon lemon juice
1½ teaspoons Dijon mustard or ½ teaspoon dry mustard

1 Preheat the oven to 350°F. In a large bowl, mix the ground beef, crackers, milk, onion, mushrooms, parsley, salt, sage, black pepper, and egg whites. In a shallow baking pan, shape the meat mixture into an 8x4-inch loaf. Smooth the top.

2 Bake for 1¼ hours or until an instant-read thermometer inserted in the center registers 170°F.

3 In a small bowl, combine the brown sugar, lemon juice, and mustard. Spread over the meat loaf. Bake for 10 minutes more. Serve with mashed potatoes. Makes 6 servings.

Prep Time: 20 minutes Cooking Time: 1 hour 25 minutes

1 Serving: Calories 284. Total Fat 13 g. Saturated Fat 5 g. Protein 26 g. Carbohydrate 14 g. Fiber 0 g. Sodium 328 mg. Cholesterol 82 mg.

Mama's Meatball Sandwiches

You can make two meals at once by cooking a double-batch of meatballs and freezing half. The next time you want to make this sandwich, just thaw the meatballs in the refrigerator overnight, add them to the sausage mixture, and heat.

For the meatballs:

- 8 ounces lean ground beef
- ¼ cup fine dry bread crumbs
- 1 tablespoon low-fat (1% milkfat) milk
- ¼ teaspoon garlic powder
- ⅛ teaspoon each salt and black pepper
- 1 large egg white
  Nonstick cooking spray

For the sauce:

- 4 ounces bulk Italian sausage
- 1 small yellow onion, chopped
- ⅓ cup chopped sweet green pepper
- 1 can (8 ounces) lower-sodium tomato sauce
- 1 cup lower-sodium stewed tomatoes, undrained and cut up
- 1 teaspoon each dried basil leaves and oregano leaves
- ⅛ teaspoon each salt and black pepper
- 4 white French or Italian rolls, each 7 inches long
- ¼ cup shredded part-skim mozzarella cheese
- 1 tablespoon grated Parmesan cheese

Mama's Meatball Sandwiches

1 To prepare the meatballs, in a medium-size bowl, mix the ground beef, bread crumbs, milk, garlic powder, ⅛ teaspoon salt, ⅛ teaspoon black pepper, and egg white. Form mixture into 16 meatballs.

2 Coat a 10-inch nonstick skillet with cooking spray. Heat the skillet over moderate heat. Add the meatballs and cook for 5 minutes or until browned, turning occasionally. Remove the meatballs. Drain off fat.

3 To prepare the sauce, in the same skillet, combine the sausage, onion, and green pepper. Cook over moderately high heat until sausage is cooked through. Drain off fat. Stir in the tomato sauce, tomatoes, basil, oregano, ⅛ teaspoon salt, and ⅛ teaspoon black pepper. Return the meatballs to skillet.

4 Bring to a boil. Lower the heat and simmer, covered, for 10 minutes. Simmer, uncovered, for 5 to 10 minutes more or until the meatballs are no longer pink on the inside and the sausage mixture is thickened, stirring occasionally.

5 Preheat the broiler. With a serrated knife, cut a thin slice from the top of each roll and discard. Hollow out the rolls. Spoon the meatballs and the sausage mixture into the rolls. Sprinkle with the mozzarella cheese and Parmesan cheese. Broil the sandwiches 4 inches from the heat for 1 minute or until the cheeses melt. Makes 4 servings.

Prep Time: 15 minutes Cooking Time: 30 minutes

1 Serving: Calories 469. Total Fat 12 g. Saturated Fat 4 g.
Protein 29 g. Carbohydrate 62 g. Fiber 5 g.
Sodium 941 mg. Cholesterol 46 mg.

Heavenly Hamburgs

Hamburgers reportedly originated in Hamburg, Germany and were introduced to this country at the 1904 St. Louis Exposition. American cooks embellished the recipe by adding spices and fillings for flavor.

- 1 **pound lean ground beef**
- ¼ **cup fine dry bread crumbs**
- ½ **teaspoon dry mustard**
- ¼ **teaspoon each salt and black pepper**
- 2 **large egg whites**
- 2 **ounces Neufchâtel cream cheese, at room temperature**
- 1 **large green onion with top, finely sliced, or 2 tablespoons minced parsley**
- 1 **tablespoon chopped pitted black olives**
- 4 **hamburger buns, split and toasted**

1 Preheat the broiler or grill. In a medium-size bowl, mix the ground beef, bread crumbs, mustard, salt, pepper, and egg whites. Shape into 8 patties, each about ¼ inch thick.

2 In a small bowl, combine the Neufchâtel cheese, green onion, and olives. Fill the burgers (tip, below).

3 Broil the patties 4 inches from the heat or grill over medium-hot coals for 5 to 6 minutes on each side or until the patties are no longer pink. Serve on buns with tomato slices and lettuce leaves. Makes 4 servings.

Prep Time: 20 minutes Cooking Time: 10 minutes

1 Serving: Calories 447. Total Fat 21 g. Saturated Fat 8 g. Protein 33 g. Carbohydrate 29 g. Fiber 2 g. Sodium 593 mg. Cholesterol 89 mg.

FILLING HAMBURGERS

Spoon the filling onto the centers of half of the meat patties, spreading it to about ½ inch from the edges. Top with the remaining patties and seal well by pressing  the meat around the edges with your fingers. If necessary, reshape the burgers into even circles.

Oma's Porcupine Meatball Casserole

These old-fashioned meatballs got their name because the grains of rice swell as they cook, causing the rice to stick out like porcupine quills.

- 1 **pound lean ground beef**
- ¼ **cup uncooked long-grain white rice**
- ¼ **cup finely chopped yellow onion**
- ¼ **teaspoon each salt and black pepper**
- 2 **large egg whites**
  Nonstick cooking spray
- 2½ **cups lower-sodium beef broth (page 67)**
- 1 **can (6 ounces) lower-sodium tomato paste**
- ¼ **cup firmly packed light brown sugar**
- ¼ **cup red wine vinegar**
- 2 **medium-size potatoes, sliced ¼ inch thick**
- 2 **cups shredded red cabbage**
- 1 **tablespoon minced parsley**

1 In a medium-size bowl, mix the ground beef, rice, onion, salt, pepper, and egg whites. Form the meat mixture into 12 meatballs.

2 Coat a nonstick Dutch oven with cooking spray. Heat the Dutch oven over moderate heat. Add the meatballs and cook for 5 minutes or until browned, turning occasionally. Remove meatballs. Drain off fat. Return meatballs to Dutch oven.

3 In a medium-size bowl, stir together the beef broth, tomato paste, brown sugar, and vinegar. Pour over meatballs. Bring to a boil. Lower the heat and simmer, covered, for 5 minutes. Add the potatoes to Dutch oven. Bring to a boil. Lower the heat and simmer, covered, for 35 minutes.

4 Add the cabbage. Bring to a boil. Lower the heat and simmer, covered, for 5 to 10 minutes more or until potatoes and cabbage are tender. Transfer to a serving bowl. Sprinkle with parsley. Makes 4 servings.

Prep Time: 20 minutes Cooking Time: 1 hour 5 minutes

1 Serving: Calories 411. Total Fat 14 g. Saturated Fat 5 g. Protein 30 g. Carbohydrate 44 g. Fiber 5 g. Sodium 262 mg. Cholesterol 81 mg.

Picadillo

Picadillo

A traditional Tex-Mex dish, picadillo is a sweet, yet spicy ground beef hash.
It's delicious served over couscous or rice, but you also can use it to stuff peppers.

 1 **pound lean ground beef**
 2 **cloves garlic, minced**
 1 **can (14$\frac{1}{2}$ ounces) lower-sodium stewed tomatoes, undrained and cut up**
 1 **medium-size apple, unpeeled and chopped**
 4 **large green onions with tops, finely sliced**
$\frac{1}{3}$ **cup raisins**
$\frac{1}{4}$ **cup water**
 2 **tablespoons chopped pimiento-stuffed green olives**

 1 **tablespoon minced pickled jalapeño pepper**
 1 **tablespoon vinegar**
 1 **teaspoon sugar**
$\frac{1}{2}$ **teaspoon celery seeds**
$\frac{1}{2}$ **teaspoon each ground cinnamon and ground cumin**
$\frac{1}{4}$ **teaspoon each salt and black pepper**
$\frac{1}{8}$ **teaspoon ground cloves**
 3 **tablespoons slivered almonds, toasted (optional)**

1 In a 12-inch skillet, cook the ground beef and garlic over moderately high heat until meat is browned. Drain off fat.

2 Stir in the tomatoes, apple, green onions, raisins, water, olives, jalapeño pepper, vinegar, sugar, celery seeds, cinnamon, cumin, salt, black pepper, and cloves.

3 Bring to a boil. Lower the heat and simmer, covered, for 20 minutes. Stir in the almonds (if using). Simmer, uncovered, for 1 minute more. Serve over hot cooked rice. Makes 4 servings.

Prep Time: 20 minutes Cooking Time: 31 minutes

1 Serving: Calories 303. Total Fat 13 g. Saturated Fat 5 g. Protein 23 g. Carbohydrate 26 g. Fiber 3 g. Sodium 308 mg. Cholesterol 71 mg.

20-Minute Meatball Stew

"My grandma always made meatballs by dropping spoonfuls of the meat mixture into the bubbling stew," says Theresa Graziano. "It really takes the work out of making meatballs."

- 1 **can (11½ ounces) hot-style vegetable juice cocktail**
- 3 **tablespoons all-purpose flour**
- 1 **can (29 ounces) large-cut mixed vegetables, drained**
- 2½ **cups lower-sodium beef broth (page 67)**
- 1 **can (14½ ounces) lower-sodium stewed tomatoes, undrained and cut up**
- ½ **teaspoon dried oregano leaves**
- 8 **ounces lean ground beef**
- 2 **tablespoons plain or seasoned fine dry bread crumbs**
- 2 **tablespoons low-fat (1% milkfat) milk**
- ⅛ **teaspoon garlic salt**
- 1 **large egg white**

1 In a Dutch oven, whisk together the vegetable juice and flour. Stir in the vegetables, beef broth, tomatoes, and oregano. Bring to a boil over high heat.

2 Meanwhile, in a small bowl, mix the ground beef, bread crumbs, milk, garlic salt, and egg white.

3 Drop the meat mixture from a small spoon into the bubbling stew. Lower the heat to moderate and simmer, covered, for 6 to 7 minutes or until meatballs are no longer pink in center, stirring occasionally. Serves 4.

Prep Time: 9 minutes Cooking Time: 11 minutes

1 Serving: Calories 294. Total Fat 7 g. Saturated Fat 3 g. Protein 21 g. Carbohydrate 38 g. Fiber 10 g. Sodium 697 mg. Cholesterol 41 mg.

Sweet-and-Sour Cabbage Rolls

"When I first came to New York, a Jewish friend of mine raved about his grandmother's stuffed cabbage rolls," recalls Lee Fowler. "I couldn't understand what the fuss was about until I tasted them."

- 1 **large head cabbage**
- 1 **pound lean ground beef**
- ¾ **cup cooked long-grain white rice**
- 1 **small yellow onion, chopped**
- 2 **tablespoons minced parsley**
- ½ **teaspoon salt**
- ¼ **teaspoon ground nutmeg**
- ¼ **teaspoon black pepper**
- 2 **large egg whites**
- 1 **can (14½ ounces) lower-sodium stewed tomatoes, undrained and cut up**
- 1 **can (8 ounces) lower-sodium tomato sauce**
- ⅓ **cup raisins**
- 2 **tablespoons firmly packed light brown sugar**
- 1 **teaspoon lemon juice**

1 Preheat the oven to 350°F. Cut 8 large outer leaves from the cabbage. Chop enough of the remaining cabbage to make 6 cups and place in a 13" x 9" x 2" baking dish.

2 Cut out the heavy center veins from the reserved cabbage leaves, keeping each leaf in one piece. Plunge leaves, half at a time, into a large amount of boiling water for 3 minutes or until limp. Drain well.

3 In a medium-size bowl, mix the ground beef, rice, onion, parsley, salt, nutmeg, pepper, and egg whites. Place a scant ⅓ cup meat mixture on each cabbage leaf. Fold in the sides and roll up. Place the rolls, seam side down, on top of the chopped cabbage.

4 In a medium-size saucepan, combine the tomatoes, tomato sauce, raisins, brown sugar, and lemon juice. Bring to a boil. Pour over cabbage rolls. Bake, covered, for 1¼ hours or until meat is no longer pink in the center and cabbage is tender, basting once or twice with tomato mixture. Serve with orange slices. Serves 4.

Prep Time: 40 minutes Cooking Time: 15 minutes
Baking Time: 1¼ hours

1 Serving: Calories 340. Total Fat 6 g. Saturated Fat 2 g. Protein 26 g. Carbohydrate 50 g. Fiber 11 g. Sodium 388 mg. Cholesterol 44 mg.

Beef 'n' Noodle Casserole

*This stick-to-your-ribs dish is topped off the old-fashioned way—with buttered bread "tufts".
The butter helps the bread toast to a nice, golden brown, but you can omit it for a lower-fat dish.*

 3 **ounces wide noodles**
12 **ounces lean ground beef**
 1 **small yellow onion, chopped**
 1 **small sweet green pepper, chopped**
 1 **clove garlic, minced**
 2 **teaspoons chili powder**
 1 **teaspoon dried oregano leaves**
¼ **teaspoon each salt and black pepper**
 1 **can (14¾ ounces) lower-sodium cream-style corn**
 1 **large tomato, cut into bite-size pieces**
 1 **tablespoon butter or margarine**
 1 **cup dried bread cubes**

1 Preheat the oven to 350°F. Cook the noodles according to package directions. Drain, rinse, and drain again.

2 Meanwhile, in a 10-inch skillet, cook ground beef, onion, green pepper, and garlic over moderately high heat until meat is browned. Drain off fat. Stir in the chili powder, oregano, salt, and black pepper.

3 In a large bowl, stir together the noodles, meat mixture, corn, and tomato. Spoon into a lightly greased 1½-quart casserole. Bake, covered, for 35 minutes.

4 Meanwhile, in a small saucepan, melt the butter over moderate heat. Stir in the bread cubes until coated. Sprinkle over casserole. Bake, uncovered, for 5 to 10 minutes more or until bread cubes are toasted and casserole is heated through. Makes 3 or 4 servings.

Prep Time: 20 minutes Cooking Time: 50 minutes

1 Serving: Calories 499. Total Fat 19 g. Saturated Fat 8 g. Protein 29 g. Carbohydrate 57 g. Fiber 11 g. Sodium 380 mg. Cholesterol 104 mg.

Easy Beef Stroganoff

The classic Russian dish was made with beef tenderloin, however, American housewives adapted the recipe for ground beef.

 1 **pound lean ground beef**
 2 **cups sliced fresh mushrooms**
 1 **large yellow onion, chopped**
 1 **clove garlic, minced**
 1 **cup reduced-fat sour cream**
 3 **tablespoons all-purpose flour**
¾ **cup lower-sodium beef broth (page 67)**
 2 **tablespoons chopped pitted black olives or pimiento-stuffed green olives (optional)**
 2 **tablespoons dry sherry or catsup**
½ **teaspoon salt**
½ **teaspoon dry mustard**
¼ **teaspoon black pepper**
 2 **tablespoons minced parsley**

1 In a 10-inch skillet, cook the ground beef, mushrooms, onion, and garlic over moderately high heat until meat is browned. Drain off fat.

2 Meanwhile, in a medium-size bowl, stir together the sour cream and flour. Stir in the beef broth, olives (if using), sherry, salt, mustard, and pepper. Stir the sour cream mixture into meat mixture in skillet.

3 Cook over moderate heat, stirring constantly, for 3 minutes or until thickened (do not boil). To serve, sprinkle with parsley. Serve over hot cooked noodles or rice. Makes 4 servings.

Prep Time: 20 minutes Cooking Time: 10 minutes

1 Serving: Calories 335. Total Fat 20 g. Saturated Fat 9 g. Protein 25 g. Carbohydrate 12 g. Fiber 2 g. Sodium 390 mg. Cholesterol 94 mg.

CHOOSING GROUND BEEF

In days gone by, ground beef was labeled ground sirloin, ground round, ground chuck, or hamburger. But because modern cooks are more concerned about fat in their diets, grocery stores and butchers now often label ground beef by its fat content. The most healthful choice is ground beef that is labeled 95% or 90% lean. 95% lean ground beef contains 5 grams of fat and 90% lean contains 7 grams of fat per 3-ounce serving of cooked meat.

Hot Tamale Pie

Hot Tamale Pie

*Southwestern women applied American ingenuity to Mexican
tamales. Instead of steaming them in corn husks, they layered the spicy
ground meat mixture and cornmeal crust into a casserole dish.*

½ **cup cornmeal**

½ **cup cold water**

¼ **teaspoon salt**

⅛ **teaspoon ground red pepper (cayenne)**

1⅓ **cups water**

1 **pound lean ground beef**

1 **large yellow onion, chopped**

1 **medium-size sweet green pepper, chopped**

2 **cloves garlic, minced**

1 **can (15½ ounces) red kidney beans, drained**

1 **can (10 ounces) enchilada sauce**

1 **can (4 ounces) diced green chili peppers, undrained**

¼ **cup chopped pitted black olives**

2 **teaspoons chili powder**

½ **cup shredded reduced-fat Cheddar cheese**

1 In a small bowl, combine the cornmeal, the cold water, salt, and red pepper. In a medium-size saucepan, bring the 1⅓ cups water to a boil. Slowly add the cornmeal mixture to boiling water, stirring constantly to make sure it does not lump. Return to a boil, stirring constantly. Lower heat and cook for 10 to 15 minutes or until very thick, stirring occasionally.

2 Meanwhile, preheat the oven to 350°F. In a large skillet, cook the ground beef, onion, green pepper, and garlic until meat is browned. Drain off fat. Stir in the kidney beans, enchilada sauce, chili peppers, olives, and chili powder. Bring to a boil.

3 Spread the hot cornmeal mixture into a greased 8" x 8" x 2" baking dish. Spread the meat mixture over the cornmeal layer. Bake, covered, for 20 minutes or until heated through. Sprinkle with the Cheddar cheese. Bake, uncovered, for 2 minutes more or until the cheese is melted. Makes 6 servings.

Prep Time: 20 minutes Cooking Time: 42 minutes

1 Serving: Calories 302. Total Fat 12 g. Saturated Fat 5 g.
Protein 22 g. Carbohydrate 28 g. Fiber 7 g.
Sodium 609 mg. Cholesterol 53 mg.

Peppered Veal Stew with Dumplings

Peppered Veal Stew
With Dumplings

*Don't peek when making dumplings. If you lift the
lid before the dumplings are cooked, most of the heat escapes
and the dumplings may collapse or be doughy.*

For the stew:

- 1 **tablespoon butter, margarine, or olive oil**
- 1 **pound boneless veal, pork, or lamb, trimmed and cut into ¾-inch cubes**
- 1 **clove garlic, minced**
- ¼ **teaspoon cracked black pepper**
- 3 **tablespoons all-purpose flour**
- 3 **cups lower-sodium chicken broth (page 67)**
- 2 **cups sliced fresh mushrooms**
- 2 **medium-size carrots, sliced ½ inch thick**
- 2 **stalks celery, sliced ½ inch thick**
- 1 **cup frozen small whole onions**
- 1 **cup dry white wine or lower-sodium chicken broth (page 67)**
- 2 **bay leaves**
- 2 **teaspoons dried thyme leaves**
- 1 **teaspoon grated lemon rind (optional)**
- ¼ **teaspoon salt**
- ¼ **teaspoon ground nutmeg**

For the dumplings:

- ¾ **cup all-purpose flour**
- 1 **tablespoon chopped fresh chives or minced parsley**
- 1 **teaspoon baking powder**
- ¼ **teaspoon cracked black pepper**
  Dash salt
- ⅓ **cup low-fat (1% milkfat) milk**
- 1 **tablespoon vegetable oil**

1 To prepare the stew, in a Dutch oven, melt the butter over moderate heat. Add the meat, garlic, and ¼ teaspoon pepper and cook for 10 minutes or until meat is browned.

2 Stir in the 3 tablespoons flour. Add the chicken broth, mushrooms, carrots, celery, onions, wine, bay leaves, thyme, lemon rind (if using), the ¼ teaspoon salt, and the nutmeg. Bring to a boil. Lower the heat and simmer, covered, for 40 minutes.

3 To prepare the dumplings, in a small bowl, combine the ¾ cup flour, chives, baking powder, ¼ teaspoon pepper, and the dash salt. In another small bowl, whisk together the milk and oil. Pour milk mixture into the flour mixture. With a fork, stir until mixed.

4 Drop the batter into 4 mounds on top of bubbling stew. Simmer, covered, for 10 minutes or until toothpicks inserted in centers come out clean (do not lift lid before 10 minutes cooking). Discard bay leaves. Makes 4 servings.

Prep Time: 25 minutes Cooking Time: 1 hour 10 minutes

---

1 Serving: Calories 404. Total Fat 14 g. Saturated Fat 5 g.
Protein 26 g. Carbohydrate 34 g. Fiber 4 g.
Sodium 420 mg. Cholesterol 101 mg.

Veal Scaloppine with
Mushroom Sauce

*Italian immigrants often started restaurants in this
country, and veal scaloppine was one of the most popular
menu items. At home, grandmas served the delicacy
for company because it was both easy and elegant.*

- 1 **pound boneless veal round or sirloin steak or pork tenderloin, ¼ inch thick and trimmed**
- ⅛ **teaspoon each salt and black pepper**
- 2 **tablespoons butter or margarine**
- 1½ **cups sliced fresh mushrooms**
- 1 **small yellow onion, sliced**
- ¾ **cup lower-sodium chicken broth (page 67)**
- ⅓ **cup dry white wine or lower-sodium chicken broth (page 67)**
- 1 **tablespoon lemon juice**
- ½ **teaspoon dried rosemary leaves**
- 1 **tablespoon minced parsley**

1 Cut veal into 4 pieces. Pound both sides of veal until veal is ⅛ inch thick (page 116). Sprinkle with the salt and pepper.

2 In a 12-inch nonstick skillet, melt the butter over moderate heat. Add 2 of the veal pieces and cook for 1 to 2 minutes on each side or until tender. Transfer the veal to a platter; cover with foil and keep warm. Repeat with the remaining veal pieces.

3 Add the mushrooms and onion to the drippings in skillet. Cook over moderate heat for 4 minutes or until tender, stirring frequently. Stir in the chicken broth, wine, lemon juice, and rosemary, stirring to loosen the browned bits. Bring to a boil. Boil, uncovered, for 5 minutes or until slightly thickened. Stir in the parsley. Pour over the veal. Makes 4 servings.

Prep Time: 15 minutes Cooking Time: 15 minutes

---

1 Serving: Calories 207. Total Fat 9 g. Saturated Fat 5 g.
Protein 26 g. Carbohydrate 4 g. Fiber 1 g.
Sodium 186 mg. Cholesterol 104 mg.

Creole Veal Grillades

Creole Veal Grillades

Some Creole cooks made this dish mild, others made it spicy.
Most served it over grits, but you can use plain rice if you'd like.

1 **pound boneless veal round steak or pork tenderloin,**
   ³/4 inch thick and trimmed

1 **tablespoon vegetable oil**

1 **can (14¹/2 ounces) lower-sodium stewed tomatoes,**
   undrained and cut up

1 **medium-size yellow onion, sliced**

2 **small sweet yellow and/or green peppers, cut into**
   thin strips

1 **tablespoon minced pickled jalapeño pepper**

2 **cloves garlic, minced**

¹/2 **teaspoon salt**

¹/8 **teaspoon ground red pepper (cayenne)**

3 **cups lower-sodium chicken broth (page 67)**

³/4 **cup quick-cooking hominy grits**

4 **medium-size green onions with tops, finely chopped**

2 **tablespoons minced parsley**

1 Cut the steak into 8 pieces. Pound both sides of the veal until steak is ¹/4 inch thick (page 116).

2 In a 10-inch nonstick skillet, heat the oil over moderately high heat. Add 4 of the veal pieces and cook for 1 to 2 minutes on each side or until browned. Remove veal from skillet. Repeat with remaining veal.

3 Add the tomatoes, onion, sweet peppers, jalapeño pepper, 1 clove of the garlic, ¼ teaspoon of the salt, and ground red pepper to the skillet; stir until mixed. Return meat to skillet. Bring to a boil. Lower heat and simmer, covered, for 20 minutes or until meat is tender.

4 Meanwhile, in a medium-size saucepan, bring the chicken broth to a boil. Slowly add the grits, stirring constantly. Stir in the green onions, the remaining 1 clove garlic, and the remaining ¼ teaspoon salt. Lower heat and simmer, uncovered, for 5 to 7 minutes or until mixture is thick, stirring frequently.

5 To serve, arrange the meat on cooked grits. Spoon the tomato mixture over meat and grits. Sprinkle with parsley. Makes 4 servings.

Prep Time: 25 minutes Cooking Time: 30 minutes

1 Serving: Calories 331. Total Fat 7 g. Saturated Fat 1 g.
Protein 30 g. Carbohydrate 39 g. Fiber 7 g.
Sodium 376 mg. Cholesterol 88 mg.

Italian Veal Shanks In Tomato Gravy

Italian grandmothers slowly simmered veal shanks to make them succulent and tender. Serve this dish, called "osso buco" in Italian, with noodles, rice, or orzo (tiny pasta).

Nonstick cooking spray

3 **pounds veal or beef shanks, sawed into 2½-inch pieces (6 to 8 pieces)**

1 **tablespoon vegetable oil**

2 **medium-size carrots, chopped**

1 **large yellow onion, chopped**

1 **clove garlic, minced**

1 **can (14½ ounces) lower-sodium tomatoes, undrained and cut up**

1 **cup dry white wine or lower-sodium beef broth (page 67)**

2 **tablespoons lower-sodium tomato paste**

1 **bay leaf**

1 **teaspoon each dried thyme leaves and basil leaves**

¼ **teaspoon each salt and black pepper**

¼ **cup cold water**

2 **tablespoons all-purpose flour**

¼ **cup minced parsley**

2 **teaspoons grated lemon rind**

1 Coat a Dutch oven with cooking spray. Heat the Dutch oven over moderate heat. Add the veal shanks and cook for 10 minutes or until browned, turning them several times. Remove from pan.

2 Add the oil to Dutch oven. Heat the oil over moderate heat. Add the carrots, onion, and garlic and cook for 5 minutes or until the onion is tender. Stir in the tomatoes, wine, tomato paste, bay leaf, thyme, basil, salt, and pepper. Return the veal shanks to Dutch oven. Bring to a boil. Lower the heat and simmer, covered, for 1¼ to 1½ hours or until meat is tender.

3 Remove the veal shanks; cover with foil and keep warm. In a small bowl, stir together the cold water and flour; add to the tomato mixture. Bring to a boil over moderate heat and boil for 1 minute, stirring constantly. In another small bowl, stir together the parsley and lemon rind.

4 Spoon some of the tomato mixture over the meat, then sprinkle with the parsley mixture. Pass the remaining tomato mixture. Serve with hot cooked noodles, rice, or orzo. Makes 6 servings.

Prep Time: 15 minutes Cooking Time: 1 hour 40 minutes

1 Serving: Calories 246. Total Fat 7 g. Saturated Fat 2 g.
Protein 27 g. Carbohydrate 11 g. Fiber 3 g.
Sodium 187 mg. Cholesterol 98 mg.

SHOPPING FOR VEAL

◆ Veal differs from beef in that all veal cuts are tender because they come from young animals. However, the cuts are similar to beef cuts, but are smaller in scale.

◆ Look for veal that has a texture finer than beef and a creamy pink color.

◆ Choose cuts that have as little fat as possible. Any fat that is present should be white.

◆ Veal may be labeled either grain-fed or milk-fed. There is much controversy over the raising of animals for veal. Animal rights activists urge buying veal from organically-raised, grain-fed animals because these calves are allowed free movement and are not confined to crates. Veal from organically-raised animals also is free from antibiotic residues. If you are concerned, you can find organic veal in health food stores or some butcher shops.

Danish Fruit-Stuffed Pork Roast

Danish Fruit-Stuffed Pork Roast

This apple-and-prune-stuffed roast is traditionally served at Christmas in
Danish-American families. However, it makes a wonderful company dish any time
of year. For an extra-special touch, try making the stuffing with raisin bread.

1   **pork loin center rib roast (4 pounds), backbone loosened**

⅛   **teaspoon each salt and black pepper**

For the stuffing:

1   **cup pitted prunes**

⅔   **cup water**

3   **tablespoons butter or margarine**

1   **small yellow onion, chopped**

2   **tablespoons firmly packed light brown sugar**

1   **teaspoon grated lemon rind**

½   **teaspoon ground cinnamon**

¼   **teaspoon ground cardamom**

6   **cups dried bread cubes**

1   **large tart apple, chopped**

½   **cup apple juice**

1 Preheat the oven to 325°F. Place the roast rib side down. Cut pockets in the roast, cutting from the meaty side (tip, opposite). Sprinkle the roast with the salt and pepper.

2 To prepare the stuffing, in a small saucepan, combine the prunes and the water. Bring to a boil. Lower the heat and simmer, covered, for 10 minutes or until prunes are tender. Drain. Coarsely chop prunes; set aside.

3 In the same saucepan, melt the butter over moderate heat. Add the onion and cook for 3 minutes or until tender. Remove from heat. Stir in the brown sugar, lemon rind, cinnamon, and cardamom.

4 Place the bread cubes in a large bowl. Stir in the onion mixture, prunes, and apple. Drizzle with the apple juice, tossing lightly until moistened. Spoon about 3 tablespoons of the stuffing into each pocket of roast (tip, below). Spoon the remaining stuffing into a 1½-quart casserole; cover and refrigerate.

5 Place the roast, rib side down, in a roasting pan. Roast for 1¾ to 2¼ hours or until an instant-read thermometer inserted in the center of roast (not stuffing) registers 155°F. (Cover the roast loosely with foil after 1 hour so the stuffing doesn't overbrown.) Bake the covered casserole of stuffing alongside the roast during the last 30 to 40 minutes of roasting.

6 Let the roast stand for 15 minutes before carving. Serve the stuffing in the casserole with the roast. Makes 8 servings.

Prep Time: 35 minutes Cooking Time: 2 hours 5 minutes
Standing Time: 15 minutes

1 Serving: Calories 429. Total Fat 16 g. Saturated Fat 7 g.
Protein 35 g. Carbohydrate 35 g. Fiber 3 g.
Sodium 313 mg. Cholesterol 103 mg.

STUFFING A ROAST

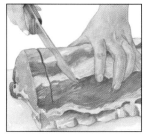 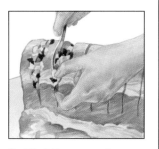

1. Using a sharp knife, cut deep slits between the rib bones of the roast. Cut through the thickest portion of the meat about halfway to the backbone and within ½ inch of the edges to make each pocket.

2. Holding a pocket open with one hand, use a small spoon to place stuffing in the slit. Lightly pack the stuffing down and keep adding stuffing until you've used about 3 tablespoons.

Plantation Pork Loin Roast with Cherry Sauce

Fresh pork was abundant on Southern plantations each year for a short time during butchering season. The women created special recipes to take advantage of the pork.

1 boneless pork single-loin roast (3 to 3½ pounds), trimmed
⅛ teaspoon each salt and black pepper

For the sauce:
4 teaspoons cornstarch
¼ teaspoon ground coriander
⅛ teaspoon ground nutmeg
1 cup cranberry juice cocktail
½ cup red currant jelly
2 cups frozen and thawed pitted tart red cherries, drained, or 1 can (16 ounces) pitted tart red cherries, drained

1 Preheat the oven to 325°F. Sprinkle the meat with the salt and pepper, then place it on a rack in a roasting pan. Insert a roasting thermometer in the center. Roast for 1¼ to 1¾ hours or until thermometer registers 155°F. Cover the meat with foil and let stand for 15 minutes before carving.

2 Meanwhile, to prepare the sauce, in a medium-size saucepan, combine the cornstarch, coriander, and nutmeg. Stir in the cranberry juice cocktail and jelly.

3 Cook over moderate heat, whisking constantly, until mixture starts to thicken. Cook for 2 minutes more or until the mixture is thickened, whisking constantly. Stir in the cherries and cook until heated through. Serve the sauce with the meat and hot cooked rice. Makes 8 to 10 servings.

Prep Time: 10 minutes Cooking Time: 1¼ hours
Standing Time: 15 minutes

1 Serving: Calories 344. Total Fat 12 g. Saturated Fat 4 g.
Protein 36 g. Carbohydrate 23 g. Fiber 1 g.
Sodium 125 mg. Cholesterol 101 mg.

Sage Pork Roast

*This hearty dish gets its robust flavor
from garlic cloves stuffed into slits in the meat
and a sprinkling of dried sage and thyme.*

- 1   boneless pork double-loin roast (3 pounds), trimmed and tied
- 2   large cloves garlic, cut into slivers
- 1   tablespoon olive or vegetable oil
- 1½   teaspoons each dried sage leaves and thyme leaves
- ½   teaspoon salt
- ¼   teaspoon freshly ground black pepper
- ½   cup dry white wine or lower-sodium chicken broth (page 67)
- 2   tablespoons minced parsley

1 Preheat the oven to 325°F. Cut about 12 small slits randomly around the meat. Insert the garlic slivers into the slits. Rub the surface of the meat with the oil. Sprinkle with the sage, thyme, salt, and pepper. Rub into the meat.

2 Place the meat on a rack in a roasting pan. Insert a roasting thermometer in the center. Roast, uncovered, for 1¾ to 2 hours or until thermometer registers 155°F. Transfer the meat to a platter. Cover the meat with foil and let stand for 15 minutes before carving.

3 Meanwhile, pour the wine into the roasting pan (page 110), stirring to loosen the browned bits. Cook over moderate heat until mixture starts to bubble. Cook until slightly thickened.

4 Slice meat; drizzle wine mixture over meat. Sprinkle with the parsley. Makes 8 servings.

Prep Time: 10 minutes   Cooking Time: 1 hour 50 minutes
Standing Time: 15 minutes

1 Serving: Calories 281. Total Fat 13 g. Saturated Fat 4 g.
Protein 35 g. Carbohydrate 1 g. Fiber 0 g.
Sodium 219 mg. Cholesterol 101 mg.

Oven Pork Barbecue

- 1   pork tenderloin (1½ pounds)
- ⅛   teaspoon each salt and black pepper
- 1   can (8 ounces) lower-sodium tomato sauce
- 1   small yellow onion, finely chopped
- 2   tablespoons vinegar
- 1   tablespoon vegetable oil
- 1   tablespoon lower-sodium Worcestershire sauce
- 1   clove garlic, minced
- 1½   teaspoons drained prepared horseradish
- 1   teaspoon dry mustard
- ½   teaspoon chili powder
- ¼   teaspoon salt
- 1   tablespoon minced parsley

1 Preheat the oven to 425°F. Sprinkle the pork with the ⅛ teaspoon salt and the pepper, then place it on a rack in a roasting pan. Roast for 40 to 50 minutes or until an instant-read thermometer inserted in the center registers 155°F.

2 Meanwhile, in a small saucepan, combine the tomato sauce, onion, vinegar, oil, Worcestershire sauce, garlic, horseradish, mustard, chili powder, and the ¼ teaspoon salt. Bring to a boil. Boil, uncovered, over moderate heat for 10 to 15 minutes or until thickened, stirring occasionally. Stir in the parsley. Set aside half of the mixture; cover and keep warm. Brush pork with the remaining half of the tomato mixture during the last 10 minutes of roasting.

3 Cover the meat with foil and let stand for 15 minutes before carving. Serve the meat with the reserved tomato mixture. Makes 6 servings.

Prep Time: 10 minutes   Cooking Time: 40 minutes
Standing Time: 15 minutes

1 Serving: Calories 182. Total Fat 7 g. Saturated Fat 2 g.
Protein 25 g. Carbohydrate 5 g. Fiber 1 g.
Sodium 203 mg. Cholesterol 67 mg.

Oven Beef Barbecue Prepare as for Oven Pork Barbecue, substituting **1 beef tenderloin (1½ pounds)** for the pork tenderloin. Roast for 55 to 65 minutes or until an instant-read thermometer inserted in the center registers 155°F., brushing with half of the tomato mixture during the last 10 minutes of roasting. Cover with foil and let stand for 15 minutes before carving.

1 Serving: Calories 219. Total Fat 11 g. Saturated Fat 3 g.
Protein 25 g. Carbohydrate 5 g. Fiber 1 g.
Sodium 208 mg. Cholesterol 71 mg.

Autumn Pot Roast

Autumn Pot Roast

*At harvest, farm cooks tucked vegetables in the root
cellar, then used them through the winter. This hearty pot roast
combines sweet potatoes, acorn squash, parsnips, and onions.*

   Nonstick cooking spray
1 **boneless pork rib end roast (3 pounds), trimmed**
1 **cup lower-sodium beef broth (page 67)**
1⅓ **cups apple juice**
2 **bay leaves**
1 **teaspoon each dried thyme leaves and marjoram
   leaves**
½ **teaspoon salt**
¼ **teaspoon ground red pepper (cayenne)**
1 **medium-size acorn or butternut squash**
4 **medium-size parsnips, peeled and quartered**
2 **cups cubed peeled sweet potato**
2 **medium-size yellow onions, cut into thin wedges**
2 **cups small whole fresh mushrooms**
3 **tablespoons all-purpose flour**

1 Coat a large Dutch oven with cooking spray. Heat the Dutch oven over moderate heat. Add the roast and cook for 10 minutes or until well browned, turning it several times. Add the broth, 1 cup of the apple juice, bay leaves, thyme, marjoram, salt, and red pepper.

2 Bring to a boil. Lower the heat and simmer, covered, for 1¾ hours. Turn the meat over. Meanwhile, cut the squash in half lengthwise; discard the seeds. Cut each half into 4 pieces. Add the squash, parsnips, sweet potato, onions, and mushrooms to Dutch oven.

3 Bring to a boil. Lower the heat and simmer, covered, for 25 to 30 minutes more or until the meat and vegetables are tender. Arrange the meat and vegetables on a platter; cover with foil and keep warm. Discard the bay leaves.

4 Measure the pan juices. Skim the fat (page 112). If necessary, add enough lower-sodium beef broth or water to the pan juices to measure 2 cups. Return the pan juices to the Dutch oven. In a small bowl, whisk together the remaining ⅓ cup apple juice and the flour; add to the pan juices. Bring to a boil over moderate heat and boil for 1 minute, whisking constantly. Serve with the meat and vegetables. Makes 8 servings.

Prep Time: 15 minutes Cooking Time: 2 hours 35 minutes

1 Serving: Calories 477. Total Fat 18 g. Saturated Fat 6 g.
Protein 36 g. Carbohydrate 44 g. Fiber 7 g.
Sodium 233 mg. Cholesterol 107 mg.

Sauerkraut and Cider Pork Chops

Sauerkraut and Cider Pork Chops

*Many women made their own sauerkraut by salting cabbage and letting
it ferment for several weeks until it had developed just the right piquant flavor.
In this dish, the sauerkraut and cider help keep the chops moist.*

Nonstick cooking spray

6 **pork loin chops with bone (2 pounds), ³/₄ inch thick and trimmed**

1 **can (16 ounces) sauerkraut, drained and rinsed, or 1 package (16 ounces) refrigerated sauerkraut, drained and rinsed**

1 **large yellow onion, sliced**

1 **cup shredded carrot**

¹/₂ **cup apple cider or apple juice**

1 **tablespoon firmly packed light brown sugar**

¹/₂ **teaspoon dried rosemary leaves**

¹/₄ **teaspoon ground ginger**

¹/₄ **teaspoon black pepper**

1 Coat a 10-inch nonstick skillet with cooking spray. Heat the skillet over moderate heat. Add 3 of the pork chops and cook for 3 minutes on each side or until browned. Remove chops. Repeat with remaining chops.

2 Add the sauerkraut, onion, carrot, apple cider, brown sugar, rosemary, ginger, and pepper to the skillet; stir until mixed.

3 Place the chops on top of sauerkraut mixture. Bring to a boil. Lower the heat and simmer, covered, for 5 to 6 minutes or until chops are no longer pink on the inside. Makes 6 servings.

Prep Time: 15 minutes Cooking Time: 20 minutes

1 Serving: Calories 201. Total Fat 7 g. Saturated Fat 2 g.
Protein 24 g. Carbohydrate 10 g. Fiber 2 g.
Sodium 355 mg. Cholesterol 67 mg.

Pork Chops With Cranberry-Sage Stuffing

To enjoy this dish any time during the year, buy an extra bag of cranberries at holiday time and tuck it in your freezer. The berries will keep for about a year.

⅓ cup chopped cranberries
1 tablespoon sugar
4 pork loin rib chops with bone (2 pounds), 1¼ inches thick and trimmed
1 tablespoon butter or margarine
⅓ cup chopped celery
¼ cup chopped yellow onion
2 tablespoons orange juice
1 teaspoon grated orange rind
½ teaspoon ground sage
1 cup dried bread cubes
⅛ teaspoon each salt and black pepper

1 Preheat the oven to 375°F. In a small bowl, stir together the cranberries and sugar; set aside. Using a sharp knife, cut a pocket in each pork chop, cutting from the meaty side toward the bone.

2 In a small saucepan, melt the butter over moderate heat. Add the celery and onion and cook for 5 minutes or until vegetables are tender. Stir in the orange juice, orange rind, sage, and cranberry mixture. Stir in the bread cubes, tossing lightly until moistened.

3 Spoon about ¼ cup of the bread mixture into each pork chop pocket and close the opening with toothpicks. Place the chops on a rack in a shallow baking pan. Sprinkle the chops with the salt and pepper. Bake for 35 to 40 minutes or until chops are no longer pink on the inside. Remove toothpicks. Makes 4 servings.

Prep Time: 25 minutes Cooking Time: 41 minutes

1 Serving: Calories 294. Total Fat 13 g. Saturated Fat 6 g. Protein 31 g. Carbohydrate 12 g. Fiber 1 g. Sodium 199 mg. Cholesterol 81 mg.

Sweet-and-Sour Pork Chops

This recipe calls for brown sugar. If yours has gotten hard, a tried-and-true way to restore the moistness is to tuck an apple wedge or a slice of bread in the sugar container, cover tightly, and let stand overnight.

Nonstick cooking spray
4 boneless pork loin chops (1 pound), ¾ inch thick and trimmed
2 medium-size carrots, thinly sliced
1 medium-size yellow onion, thinly sliced
4 lemon slices
⅔ cup apple juice
3 tablespoons firmly packed light brown sugar
3 tablespoons vinegar
1 clove garlic, minced
½ teaspoon ground ginger
¼ teaspoon each salt and black pepper
3 tablespoons cold water
4 teaspoons cornstarch

1 Coat a 10-inch skillet with cooking spray. Heat the skillet over moderate heat. Add the pork chops and cook for 3 minutes on each side or until browned.

2 Add the carrots, onion, and lemon slices. In a small bowl, combine the apple juice, brown sugar, vinegar, garlic, ginger, salt, and pepper. Pour over the pork chops and vegetables.

3 Bring to a boil. Lower the heat and simmer, covered, for 5 to 6 minutes or until chops are no longer pink on the inside. Transfer the chops and lemon slices to a platter; cover with foil and keep warm.

4 In a small bowl, stir together the cold water and cornstarch, then stir into the apple juice mixture. Cook for 2 minutes or until the mixture thickens. Spoon over the pork chops. Serve with hot cooked rice or noodles. Makes 4 servings.

Prep Time: 15 minutes Cooking Time: 15 minutes

1 Serving: Calories 263. Total Fat 8 g. Saturated Fat 3 g. Protein 27 g. Carbohydrate 22 g. Fiber 2 g. Sodium 205 mg. Cholesterol 73 mg.

Pork Chop and Rice Dinner-in-a-Dish

Community cookbooks from the 1950's featured numerous versions of this hearty pork chop, rice, and tomato casserole.

1 tablespoon vegetable oil

4 pork loin chops with bone (1½ pounds), ¾ inch thick and trimmed

1 medium-size sweet green pepper, chopped

1 medium-size yellow onion, chopped

1 can (14½ ounces) lower-sodium stewed tomatoes, undrained and cut up

2 medium-size apples, unpeeled and chopped

½ cup uncooked long-grain white rice

½ cup lower-sodium chicken broth (page 67)

1 teaspoon dried marjoram leaves

½ teaspoon ground sage

¼ teaspoon each salt and black pepper

1 Preheat the oven to 350°F. In a 10-inch skillet, heat the oil over moderate heat. Add the pork chops and cook for 3 minutes on each side or until browned. Remove the chops.

2 Add the green pepper and onion to the drippings in the skillet. Cook for 5 minutes or until the vegetables are tender. Stir in the tomatoes, apples, rice, chicken broth, marjoram, sage, salt, and black pepper. Bring to a boil.

3 Pour the tomato mixture into a 12" x 7½" x 2" baking dish. Place the chops on top. Bake, covered, for 35 minutes. Bake, uncovered, for 10 to 15 minutes more or until the pork chops are no longer pink on the inside and the rice is tender. Makes 4 servings.

Prep Time: 20 minutes Cooking Time: 1 hour

1 Serving: Calories 381. Total Fat 11 g. Saturated Fat 3 g. Protein 30 g. Carbohydrate 40 g. Fiber 4 g. Sodium 206 mg. Cholesterol 75 mg.

Nana Ann's American Chop Suey

Women from many ethnic backgrounds made Chinese food. Audrey West loved her Polish grandma's chop suey—"She used both pork and beef, but the real secret was the delicious brown gravy. It had a hint of molasses."

Nonstick cooking spray

12 ounces lean boneless pork, trimmed and cut into ½-inch cubes

4 ounces lean boneless beef or pork, trimmed and cut into ½-inch cubes

1 clove garlic, minced

1½ cups lower-sodium beef broth (page 67)

¼ cup lower-sodium soy sauce

1 tablespoon molasses

¾ teaspoon ground ginger

¼ teaspoon black pepper

2 medium-size carrots, thinly sliced

2 stalks celery, thinly sliced

2 cups sliced shiitake or other fresh mushrooms

2 cups fresh bean sprouts or 1 can (16 ounces) bean sprouts, drained

1 can (8 ounces) sliced bamboo shoots, drained

8 medium-size green onions with tops, cut into 1-inch pieces

¼ cup cold water

2 tablespoons cornstarch

1 Coat a Dutch oven with cooking spray. Heat the Dutch oven over moderate heat. Add the pork, beef, and garlic and cook for 5 to 10 minutes or until meat is browned. Add the broth, soy sauce, molasses, ginger, and pepper. Bring to a boil.

2 Lower the heat and simmer, covered, for 25 minutes or until meat is tender. Stir in the carrots and celery. Bring to a boil. Lower the heat and simmer, covered, for 10 minutes or until the vegetables are crisp-tender, stirring occasionally.

3 Stir in the mushrooms, bean sprouts, bamboo shoots, and green onions. In a small bowl, stir together the water and cornstarch, then stir into the meat mixture. Cook for 2 minutes or until mixture thickens. Serve over hot cooked rice. Makes 4 servings.

Prep Time: 20 minutes Cooking Time: 53 minutes

1 Serving: Calories 303. Total Fat 9 g. Saturated Fat 3 g. Protein 28 g. Carbohydrate 29 g. Fiber 5 g. Sodium 626 mg. Cholesterol 80 mg.

Finger-Lickin' Ribs

Finger-Lickin' Ribs

*In the early 1800's, pork ribs were considered the "leftovers" from hog butchering and
cooks looked for ways to use them up. Often, they roasted them slowly over coals and brushed
them with spicy sauces. Today, barbecued ribs are held in much more esteem.*

2½ **to 3 pounds pork loin back ribs or spareribs, cut
    into 2-rib portions**
 1 **medium-size yellow onion, chopped**
¼ **cup orange juice**
½ **cup chili sauce**
 1 **tablespoon molasses**
 1 **teaspoon grated orange rind**
½ **teaspoon dry mustard**
¼ **teaspoon ground cloves**
⅛ **teaspoon ground red pepper (cayenne)**

1 Preheat the oven to 350°F. Place the pork ribs, bone side down, in a large shallow baking pan. Bake for 1¼ to 1½ hours or until tender. Drain off fat.

2 Meanwhile, in a small saucepan, combine the onion and orange juice. Cook over moderate heat for 5 minutes or until onion is tender. Stir in the chili sauce, molasses, orange rind, mustard, cloves, and red pepper. Bring to a boil.

3 Set aside half of the chili sauce mixture. Brush the ribs with some of the remaining chili sauce mixture. Bake for 15 minutes more, brushing once or twice with the chili sauce mixture. Serve the ribs with the reserved chili sauce mixture. Makes 4 servings.

Prep Time: 10 minutes Cooking Time: 1½ hours

1 Serving: Calories 364. Total Fat 18 g. Saturated Fat 6 g.
Protein 34 g. Carbohydrate 16 g. Fiber 1 g.
Sodium 539 mg. Cholesterol 109 mg.

Heartland Pork and Apple Pie

Heartland Pork and Apple Pie

In the Midwest of years ago, where pork and apples were plentiful,
this wholesome dish provided an economical and tasty family meal. It still does.

1 **pound lean ground pork**
1 **medium-size yellow onion, chopped**
1 **stalk celery, chopped**
½ **cup fine dry bread crumbs**
½ **cup lower-sodium chicken broth (page 67)**
½ **teaspoon salt**
½ **teaspoon ground sage**
⅛ **teaspoon ground red pepper (cayenne)**
2 **store-bought or homemade pie crusts (page 337)**
2 **medium-size tart apples, peeled and thinly sliced**
2 **tablespoons sugar**
¼ **teaspoon ground allspice**
    Low-fat (1% milkfat) milk

1 Preheat the oven to 400°F. In a 10-inch skillet, cook the ground pork, onion, and celery until the meat is no longer pink. Drain off fat. Stir in the bread crumbs, chicken broth, salt, sage, and red pepper.

2 Line a 9-inch pie plate with 1 of the pie crusts; trim even with the rim. Spoon the meat mixture into the pie plate. In a medium-size bowl, combine the apples, sugar, and allspice. Spoon over the meat mixture.

3 Place the remaining pie crust over the apple mixture. Trim the crust to ½ inch beyond edge of plate.

Fold under bottom crust and crimp edge. Cut slits in top crust. Brush with a little milk. Bake for 35 to 40 minutes or until golden. Let stand for 10 minutes before serving. Makes 6 servings.

Prep Time: 20 minutes Cooking Time: 40 minutes
Standing Time: 10 minutes

1 Serving: Calories 517. Total Fat 27 g. Saturated Fat 22 g. Protein 20 g. Carbohydrate 49 g. Fiber 1 g. Sodium 586 mg. Cholesterol 55 mg.

German Meatballs In Caper Sauce

Women of German heritage usually made their meatballs with ground pork, although some added a little beef or veal. Then, they topped them with a rich, creamy sauce. This updated version is made with reduced-fat sour cream and is accented with capers and lemon juice.

1 pound lean ground pork
¼ cup fine dry bread crumbs
1 tablespoon low-fat (1% milkfat) milk
1 anchovy fillet, minced (optional)
¼ teaspoon black pepper
1 large egg white
2 tablespoons butter or margarine
2 medium-size yellow onions, sliced and separated into rings
3 tablespoons all-purpose flour
1 tablespoon firmly packed light brown sugar
1 teaspoon dried thyme leaves
1½ cups lower-sodium beef broth (page 67)
1 tablespoon lemon juice
2 tablespoons drained capers
2 tablespoons minced parsley

1 Preheat the oven to 350°F. In a medium-size bowl, mix the ground pork, bread crumbs, milk, anchovy (if using), ⅛ teaspoon of the pepper, and the egg white. Form the meat mixture into 24 meatballs.

2 Place meatballs in single layer in 15½" x 10½" x 1" baking pan. Bake for 15 to 20 minutes or until meatballs are no longer pink on the inside. Drain well.

3 Meanwhile, in a large saucepan, melt the butter over moderate heat. Add the onions and cook for

10 minutes or until tender. Stir in the flour, brown sugar, thyme, and the remaining ⅛ teaspoon pepper. Add the beef broth and lemon juice. Cook, stirring constantly, until the mixture starts to thicken. Cook and stir for 2 minutes or until thickened.

4 Stir in the capers, parsley, and meatballs. Heat through. Serve over hot cooked noodles. Makes 4 servings.

Prep Time: 20 minutes Cooking Time: 20 minutes

1 Serving: Calories 320. Total Fat 15 g. Saturated Fat 7 g. Protein 27 g. Carbohydrate 18 g. Fiber 1 g. Sodium 281 mg. Cholesterol 99 mg.

Baked Ham with Molasses Crumb Topping

This recipe is one of the oldest and best ways to prepare baked ham. If you like your dishes highly seasoned, use a spicy mustard.

1 boneless cooked lower-sodium ham (3 pounds)
2 tablespoons butter or margarine
1 tablespoon firmly packed light brown sugar
1 tablespoon molasses
1 teaspoon prepared mustard
¼ cup fine dry bread crumbs

1 Preheat the oven to 325°F. Score the top of the ham into diamonds (page 144). Place the ham on a rack in a shallow baking pan. Insert a roasting thermometer in the center. Bake for 1¼ hours.

2 Meanwhile, in a small saucepan, melt the butter over moderate heat. Stir in the brown sugar, molasses, and mustard. Stir in the bread crumbs.

3 With a large spoon, spread the crumb mixture over top of ham. Bake for 15 to 30 minutes more or until thermometer registers 135°F. Cover with foil and let stand for 15 minutes before carving. Makes 12 servings.

Prep Time: 10 minutes Cooking Time: 1½ hours
Standing Time: 15 minutes

1 Serving: Calories 156. Total Fat 7 g. Saturated Fat 3 g. Protein 18 g. Carbohydrate 5 g. Fiber 0 g. Sodium 868 mg. Cholesterol 50 mg.

Maple-Glazed Ham With Raisin Sauce

Ham was precious because it took so much of the hog to get just one piece of meat. So, women saved it for a festive occasion and then served it with a special company's–coming sauce.

1 cooked ham, shank portion (4 to 4½ pounds)
2 tablespoons whole cloves

For the maple glaze:
¼ cup maple-flavored syrup or pure maple syrup
1 tablespoon butter or margarine
1 tablespoon light corn syrup
1 tablespoon orange juice
⅛ teaspoon ground allspice
Dash ground cloves

For the raisin sauce:
¼ cup firmly packed light brown sugar
2 tablespoons cornstarch
1½ cups apple juice
1 cup raisins
3 tablespoons orange juice
1 tablespoon vinegar
1 teaspoon grated orange rind
⅛ teaspoon ground allspice

1 Preheat the oven to 325°F. Score the top of the ham into diamonds, then stud the ham with whole cloves (tip, right). Place the ham on a rack in a large shallow baking pan. Insert a roasting thermometer in the center of the thickest portion without touching bone. Bake for 1¼ hours.

2 Meanwhile, to prepare the maple glaze, in a small saucepan, combine the maple-flavored syrup, butter, corn syrup, the 1 tablespoon orange juice, ⅛ teaspoon allspice, and ground cloves. Bring to a boil; remove the pan from heat.

3 Brush the ham with some of the maple glaze. Bake for 15 minutes more or until thermometer registers 135°F., brushing once or twice with the remaining glaze. Cover ham with foil and let stand for 15 minutes before carving.

4 Meanwhile, to prepare the raisin sauce, in a medium-size saucepan, combine the brown sugar and cornstarch. Stir in the apple juice, raisins, the 3 tablespoons orange juice, vinegar, orange rind, and ⅛ teaspoon allspice.

5 Cook over moderate heat, stirring constantly, until the mixture starts to thicken. Cook and stir for 1 to 2 minutes more or until thickened. Serve the ham with the raisin sauce. Makes 10 servings.

Prep Time: 15 minutes Cooking Time: 1½ hours
Standing Time: 15 minutes

1 Serving: Calories 258. Total Fat 6 g. Saturated Fat 2 g.
Protein 21 g. Carbohydrate 30 g. Fiber 1 g.
Sodium 1,121 mg. Cholesterol 49 mg.

Maple-Glazed Ham with Apricot-Berry Sauce
Prepare as for Maple-Glazed Ham with Raisin Sauce, omitting the ingredients for the raisin sauce. To prepare the apricot-berry sauce, in a medium-size saucepan, combine ¼ **cup firmly packed light brown sugar** and **2 tablespoons cornstarch. Stir in 1½ cups orange juice.** Cook over moderate heat, stirring constantly, until mixture starts to thicken. Cook and stir for 1 to 2 minutes or until thickened. Stir in **1 can (16 ounces) unpeeled apricot halves packed in light syrup, drained and sliced;** heat through. Stir in **1½ cups sliced strawberries.**

1 Serving: Calories 241. Total Fat 6 g. Saturated Fat 2 g.
Protein 22 g. Carbohydrate 25 g. Fiber 1 g.
Sodium 1,120 mg. Cholesterol 49 mg.

SCORING HAM

Add an old-fashioned, decorative touch to baked ham by scoring the top and studding it with cloves. The scoring also allows the glaze to penetrate the meat.

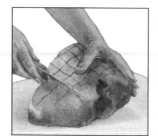 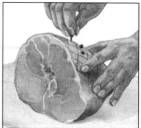

1. To score the ham, use a small sharp knife to diagonally cut ¼-inch-deep parallel lines in the top of the ham about 1 inch apart. Make another series of cuts at right angles to form diamonds.

2. Using your fingers, insert a whole clove in the middle of each of the diamonds. You may find it easier to pierce the meat first with the point of a skewer and then insert the clove.

Maple-Glazed Ham with Raisin Sauce

Company-Pleasing Ham with Plum Sauce

Company-Pleasing Ham with Plum Sauce

Many old-time recipes combined ham with fruits.
If you can't find ripe plums for this recipe (they should yield
slightly when gently squeezed), use a red apple instead.

1 **cooked center-cut ham slice (1½ pounds), 1 inch thick and trimmed**

1 **tablespoon butter or margarine**

2 **tablespoons firmly packed light brown sugar**

¾ **teaspoon dry mustard**

½ **teaspoon ground nutmeg**

⅛ **teaspoon ground cloves**

1 **can (15¼ ounces) pineapple slices packed in juice**
   Orange juice

3 **medium-size plums, sliced, or 1 large tart red apple, cored and thinly sliced**

⅓ **cup dry sherry or orange juice**

2 **tablespoons cornstarch**

1 Slash the edge of the ham slice at 1-inch intervals. In a 12-inch skillet, melt the butter over moderate heat. Stir in the brown sugar, mustard, nutmeg, and cloves. Add the ham to the skillet and cook for 5 minutes on each side or until ham is browned.

2 Drain the pineapple, reserving the juice. Set aside the pineapple slices. Add enough orange juice to the pineapple juice to measure 1 cup liquid. Pour the pineapple liquid over ham. Bring to a boil. Lower the heat and simmer, covered, for 10 minutes. Add the pineapple slices and plums. Simmer, covered, for 5 minutes more or until ham is heated through. Transfer the ham to a platter; cover with foil and keep warm.

3 In a small bowl, stir together the sherry and cornstarch, then stir into the fruit mixture. Cook for 2 minutes or until the mixture thickens. Serve the fruit mixture over ham. Makes 6 servings.

Prep Time: 15 minutes Cooking Time: 25 minutes

1 Serving: Calories 258. Total Fat 7 g. Saturated Fat 3 g. Protein 22 g. Carbohydrate 24 g. Fiber 1 g. Sodium 1,151 mg. Cholesterol 52 mg.

Baked Ham Slice With Cranberry-Honey Sauce

The center-cut ham slice is not a modern convenience—it dates back to colonial times. In New England, it often was served with cranberries.

1   cooked center-cut ham slice (1½ pounds), 1 inch thick and trimmed
1   tablespoon whole cloves
½   cup dry red wine or orange juice
¼   cup honey
½   teaspoon ground ginger
¼   teaspoon ground allspice
1½ cups cranberries
1   cup frozen small whole onions

1 Preheat the oven to 350°F. Score the top of the ham slice into diamonds, then stud the ham with the cloves (page 144). Slash the edge of ham at 1-inch intervals. Place the ham on a rack in a shallow baking pan. Bake for 30 minutes or until heated through.

2 Meanwhile, in a medium-size saucepan, combine the wine, honey, ginger, and allspice. Bring to a boil. Stir in the cranberries and onions. Return to a boil. Boil gently over moderately high heat for 5 minutes or until the cranberry skins pop. Serve the cranberry mixture over ham. Makes 6 servings.

Prep Time: 10 minutes Cooking Time: 30 minutes

1 Serving: Calories 213. Total Fat 5 g. Saturated Fat 2 g. Protein 22 g. Carbohydrate 18 g. Fiber 1 g. Sodium 1,134 mg. Cholesterol 47 mg.

Double-Duty Ham Loaf

"My grandma Anna Mae made her ham balls with ground pork and crushed graham crackers which gave them a slightly sweet flavor," recalls Kristin Heiken. This recipe does double duty because you can use it for either ham loaf or ham balls.

1½ pounds ground cooked ham
1   pound lean ground pork
¾   cup crushed graham crackers
½   cup low-fat (1% milkfat) milk
¼   cup shredded carrot
¼   cup finely chopped yellow onion
¼   teaspoon black pepper
1   large egg, lightly beaten
1   large egg white, lightly beaten
½   cup catsup
¼   cup firmly packed light brown sugar
2   tablespoons vinegar
½   teaspoon onion powder

1 Preheat the oven to 350°F. In a large bowl, mix the ground ham, ground pork, graham crackers, milk, carrot, onion, pepper, egg, and egg white. In a shallow baking pan, shape the meat mixture into a 9x5-inch loaf. Smooth the top. Bake for 1 hour. Drain off fat.

2 Meanwhile, in a small bowl, combine the catsup, brown sugar, vinegar, and onion powder. Spoon half of the mixture over the meat loaf. Bake for 15 to 30 minutes more or until an instant-read thermometer inserted in the center registers 170°F. Serve with the remaining catsup mixture. Makes 8 servings.

Prep Time: 15 minutes Cooking Time: 1¼ hours

1 Serving: Calories 293. Total Fat 10 g. Saturated Fat 3 g. Protein 31 g. Carbohydrate 19 g. Fiber 1 g. Sodium 1,158 mg. Cholesterol 104 mg.

Ham Balls Prepare as for Double-Duty Ham Loaf, shaping the meat mixture into 24 ham balls. Arrange in a 15½" x 10½" x 1" baking pan. Bake for 45 minutes; drain off fat. Spoon all of the catsup mixture over ham balls and bake for 10 minutes more.

1 Serving: Calories 293. Total Fat 10 g. Saturated Fat 3 g. Protein 31 g. Carbohydrate 19 g. Fiber 1 g. Sodium 1,158 mg. Cholesterol 104 mg.

Ham, Corn, and Macaroni au Gratin

Homemakers created many wonderful casseroles to use up leftover ham. This one is topped with a golden crust of Cheddar cheese and buttered bread crumbs.

- ½ cup elbow macaroni
- 1 tablespoon butter, margarine, or olive oil
- ½ cup chopped sweet green pepper
- ¼ cup chopped yellow onion
- 2 tablespoons all-purpose flour
- 1¼ cups low-fat (1% milkfat) milk
- ½ teaspoon dry mustard
   Dash ground red pepper (cayenne)
- 2 cups chopped cooked lower-sodium ham
- 1 cup frozen and thawed whole kernel corn
- ⅓ cup shredded Cheddar cheese
- ¾ cup fresh bread crumbs
- 1 tablespoon butter or margarine, melted
   Paprika

1 Preheat the oven to 350°F. Cook the macaroni according to package directions. Drain, rinse, and drain again.

2 Meanwhile, in a medium-size saucepan, melt 1 tablespoon butter over moderate heat. Add the green pepper and onion and cook for 5 minutes or until vegetables are tender. Stir in the flour. Add the milk, mustard, and red pepper. Cook, stirring constantly, until the mixture starts to thicken. Cook and stir for 2 minutes or until thickened.

3 Stir in the ham, corn, and cooked macaroni. Pour into an 8" x 8" x 2" baking dish. Sprinkle with the Cheddar cheese. In a small bowl, toss together the bread crumbs and the melted butter. Sprinkle over the casserole. Sprinkle with paprika. Bake for 25 to 30 minutes or until heated through. Makes 4 servings.

Prep Time: 15 minutes Cooking Time: 35 minutes

1 Serving: Calories 338. Total Fat 13 g. Saturated Fat 7 g. Protein 22 g. Carbohydrate 32 g. Fiber 2 g. Sodium 842 mg. Cholesterol 70 mg.

Beer and Brats

Beer and Brats

Hearty bratwurst dishes were popular in German-American communities all across the country. In this recipe, the sausage is simmered in beer to give it a subtle tang.

- 1 tablespoon olive or vegetable oil
- 1   medium-size yellow onion, sliced
- 1 cup reduced-calorie beer or lower-sodium beef broth (page 67)
- 1 cup lower-sodium beef broth (page 67)
- 2 tablespoons firmly packed light brown sugar
- 2 tablespoons vinegar
- 2 bay leaves
- 1 teaspoon caraway seeds
- 1 teaspoon dried thyme leaves
- 1 teaspoon lower-sodium Worcestershire sauce
- ¼ teaspoon black pepper
- 4 smoked or cooked bratwursts (12 ounces)
- 2 tablespoons all-purpose flour
- 2 tablespoons minced parsley

1 In a 10-inch skillet, heat the oil over moderate heat. Add the onion and cook for 5 minutes or until onion is tender.

2 Add the beer, ¾ cup of the broth, brown sugar, vinegar, bay leaves, caraway seed, thyme, Worcestershire sauce, and pepper. Add the bratwursts. Bring to a boil. Lower the heat and simmer, covered, for 10 minutes or until bratwursts are heated through. Transfer the bratwursts to a platter; cover with foil and keep warm. Discard the bay leaves.

3 In a small bowl, whisk together the remaining ¼ cup broth and the flour, then stir into the beer mixture. Cook over moderate heat, stirring constantly, until mixture starts to thicken. Cook and stir for 2 minutes or until thickened. Stir in the parsley. Pour the beer mixture over the bratwursts. Serve with mashed potatoes or hot cooked noodles. Makes 4 servings.

Prep Time: 10 minutes Cooking Time: 25 minutes

1 Serving: Calories 376. Total Fat 30 g. Saturated Fat 14 g. Protein 12 g. Carbohydrate 14 g. Fiber 1 g. Sodium 863 mg. Cholesterol 39 mg.

Pepper-Sausage Scramble

Before refrigeration, salt, spices, and smoke-curing were used to preserve meat as sausage. Today, folks use sausage just because they like the flavor.

Nonstick cooking spray
12 ounces cooked smoked reduced-fat sausage links, cut into ½-inch-thick slices
1 cup chopped sweet green pepper
1 medium-size yellow onion, chopped
1 clove garlic, minced
1 can (14½ ounces) lower-sodium stewed tomatoes
1 tablespoon all-purpose flour
1 cup frozen and thawed whole kernel corn
2 tablespoons minced parsley
1 tablespoon firmly packed light brown sugar
1 tablespoon vinegar
1 tablespoon prepared mustard
½ teaspoon dried marjoram leaves
¼ teaspoon black pepper

1 Coat a 10-inch nonstick skillet with cooking spray. Heat the skillet over moderately high heat. Add the sausage, green pepper, onion, and garlic and cook for 5 minutes or until vegetables are tender.

2 Drain the tomatoes, reserving the liquid. Stir the flour into the tomato liquid; add to the sausage mixture. Stir in the tomatoes, corn, parsley, brown sugar, vinegar, mustard, marjoram, and black pepper. Cook over moderate heat, stirring constantly, until mixture starts to thicken. Cook and stir for 2 minutes more or until thickened. Serve over hot cooked rice. Makes 3 or 4 servings.

Prep Time: 20 minutes Cooking Time: 12 minutes

1 Serving: Calories 380. Total Fat 23 g. Saturated Fat 8 g. Protein 20 g. Carbohydrate 30 g. Fiber 4 g. Sodium 1,165 mg. Cholesterol 80 mg.

Orange-Glazed Canadian Bacon

Made from smoked pork loin, Canadian-style bacon is closer in taste and texture to ham than bacon. You can purchase it presliced, but for best results, buy a chunk from the butcher and cut it yourself.

1 tablespoon butter or margarine
12 ounces Canadian-style bacon, sliced
⅓ cup honey
1 tablespoon orange juice
1 teaspoon grated orange rind
¼ teaspoon dry mustard
⅛ teaspoon cracked black pepper

1 In a 10-inch nonstick skillet, melt the butter over moderate heat. Add half of the Canadian-style bacon and cook for 1 minute on each side or until lightly browned. Remove bacon. Repeat with remaining bacon. Return all of the bacon to the skillet.

2 Meanwhile, in a small bowl, combine the honey, orange juice, orange rind, mustard, and pepper. Pour over bacon. Bring just to a boil. Lower the heat slightly and cook, uncovered, for 5 minutes or until the honey mixture is of glaze consistency.

3 Transfer bacon to a plate. Spoon honey mixture on top. Serve with hot cooked rice. Makes 4 servings.

Prep Time: 5 minutes Cooking Time: 10 minutes

1 Serving: Calories 213. Total Fat 7 g. Saturated Fat 3 g. Protein 13 g. Carbohydrate 24 g. Fiber 0 g. Sodium 859 mg. Cholesterol 39 mg.

Roast Leg of Lamb With Mint Sauce

New England grandmas served lamb the English way—with a refreshingly cool mint sauce. If you don't have fresh mint, you can substitute 1 tablespoon of dried mint.

1 **whole leg of lamb (5 to 6 pounds), fell removed and trimmed**

3 **tablespoons minced fresh mint**

2 **tablespoons lemon juice**

2 **tablespoons minced parsley**

1 **tablespoon grated onion or onion juice**

1 **cup mint jelly**

2 **tablespoons cornstarch**

1 **tablespoon grated lemon rind**

¾ **cup apple juice**

1 Preheat the oven to 325°F. Cut about 18 small slits randomly in the meat. Insert the mint into the slits. Rub the surface of the meat with lemon juice. Sprinkle with the parsley and onion. Pat into the meat.

2 Place the meat, fat side up, on a rack in a roasting pan. Insert a roasting thermometer in the center of the thickest portion without touching bone. Roast for 1½ to 2 hours or until thermometer registers 140°F. for medium-rare or for 2 to 2½ hours or until 155°F. for medium. Cover the meat with foil and let stand for 15 minutes before carving.

3 Meanwhile, in a small saucepan, combine the mint jelly, cornstarch, and lemon rind. Stir in apple juice. Cook over moderate heat, stirring constantly, until mixture starts to thicken. Cook and stir for 2 minutes more or until jelly melts and mixture is thickened. Serve with the meat. Makes 12 to 14 servings.

Prep Time: 15 minutes Cooking Time: 1½ hours
Standing Time: 15 minutes

1 Serving: Calories 248. Total Fat 7 g. Saturated Fat 2 g. Protein 25 g. Carbohydrate 20 g. Fiber 0 g. Sodium 70 mg. Cholesterol 79 mg.

USING A MEAT THERMOMETER

◆ For roasts, insert a roasting thermometer into the meat so the bulb rests in the center of the thickest part and does not touch bone or fat.

◆ For smaller cuts of meat or meat loaves that won't support the weight of a regular meat thermometer, check the temperature with an instant-read thermometer.

Green Chili

This favorite Southwestern dish is called "green" not because of its color, but because it uses green chili peppers rather than red.

Nonstick cooking spray

1 **pound lean boneless lamb or pork, trimmed and cut into ½-inch cubes**

1 **can (14½ ounces) diced tomatoes, undrained, or 1 can (14½ ounces) tomatoes, undrained and cut up**

1 **large sweet green pepper, chopped**

1 **large yellow onion, chopped**

1 **can (8 ounces) lower-sodium tomato sauce**

1 **can (4 ounces) diced green chili peppers, undrained**

2 **bay leaves**

1½ **teaspoons dried cilantro leaves**

1 **teaspoon dried oregano leaves**

½ **teaspoon ground sage**

¼ **teaspoon each salt and black pepper**

1 Coat a large saucepan with cooking spray. Heat the saucepan over moderately high heat. Add the lamb and cook for 5 to 10 minutes or until browned.

2 Stir in the tomatoes, green pepper, onion, tomato sauce, chili peppers, bay leaves, cilantro, oregano, sage, salt, and black pepper. Bring to a boil. Lower the heat and simmer, covered, for 50 to 60 minutes or until meat is tender. Discard the bay leaves.

3 To serve, spoon warmed canned pinto beans or hot cooked rice into serving bowls and spoon the meat mixture over beans or rice. Makes 4 servings.

Prep Time: 15 minutes Cooking Time: 1 hour

1 Serving: Calories 217. Total Fat 9 g. Saturated Fat 3 g. Protein 22 g. Carbohydrate 13 g. Fiber 3 g. Sodium 771 mg. Cholesterol 67 mg.

Company Lamb Curry

Company Lamb Curry

*Because curry powder is made from a blend of spices,
such as turmeric, cumin, and coriander, it's a good idea to
try several brands to find the blend you like best.*

1   tablespoon vegetable oil
1   pound lean boneless lamb, trimmed and cut
    into ³⁄₄-inch cubes
1   medium-size yellow onion, thinly sliced
2   tablespoons curry powder
2   cloves garlic, minced
¼   cup all-purpose flour
1½ cups chopped potato
1½ cups lower-sodium beef broth (page 67)
1   cup sliced celery
½   cup shredded carrot
1   tablespoon firmly packed light brown sugar
1   teaspoon each dry mustard and ground ginger
½   teaspoon salt
¼   teaspoon crushed red pepper

1 In a 10-inch nonstick skillet, heat the oil over moderately high heat. Add the meat, onion, curry powder, and garlic and cook for 10 minutes or until the meat is browned.

2 Stir in the flour. Stir in the potato, beef broth, celery, carrot, brown sugar, mustard, ginger, salt, and red pepper. Bring to a boil. Lower the heat and simmer, covered, for 30 to 40 minutes or until meat is tender.

3 Serve over hot cooked rice and peas. Sprinkle with your choice of raisins, coconut, chopped candied ginger, and/or peanuts. Makes 4 servings.

Prep Time: 25 minutes Cooking Time: 45 minutes

1 Serving: Calories 318. Total Fat 13 g. Saturated Fat 4 g.
Protein 23 g. Carbohydrate 28 g. Fiber 4 g.
Sodium 361 mg. Cholesterol 67 mg.

Irish Stew

*This simple lamb dish typically is
called a "white" stew because the meat
isn't browned before it's simmered.*

1 **pound lean boneless lamb, trimmed and cut
into 1-inch cubes**

4½ **cups lower-sodium beef broth (page 67)**

3 **medium-size leeks, sliced, or 1 large yellow onion,
thinly sliced**

1 **bay leaf**

½ **teaspoon salt**

¼ **teaspoon black pepper**

4 **medium-size carrots, sliced**

3 **medium-size parsnips, peeled and cut
into ½-inch pieces**

1 **teaspoon dried dill weed**

¼ **cup all-purpose flour**

1 In a Dutch oven, combine lamb, 4 cups of the broth,
leeks, bay leaf, salt, and pepper. Bring to a boil.
Lower the heat and simmer, covered, for 45 minutes.

2 Stir in the carrots and parsnips. Bring to a boil.
Lower the heat and simmer, covered, for 30 minutes
more or until the meat and vegetables are tender. Stir in
the dill weed.

3 In a small bowl, stir together the remaining ½ cup
broth and the flour, then stir into meat mixture.
Cook over moderate heat, stirring constantly, until mixture starts to thicken. Cook and stir for 2 minutes more
or until thickened. Discard bay leaf. Makes 4 servings.

Prep Time: 20 minutes Cooking Time: 1½ hours

1 Serving: Calories 372. Total Fat 10 g. Saturated Fat 3 g.
Protein 24 g. Carbohydrate 49 g. Fiber 9 g.
Sodium 385 mg. Cholesterol 67 mg.

SHOPPING FOR BONELESS LAMB

When you need boneless lamb, look for roasts
from the leg or shoulder area of the animal.
These cuts are the leanest and can be easily cut
into bite-size pieces or cubes. Lamb from very
young animals will have a pinkish red color, while
older lamb will be a darker red. The meat should
have only a thin layer of fat.

Hasenpfeffer

*German families often served hasenpfeffer,
which means "peppered hare". Originally, the
marinade helped tenderize the wild rabbit,
but with today's more tender domestic rabbit—or
chicken, it just adds a rich sweet-sour flavor.*

1 **domestic rabbit (2½ to 3 pounds), skinned, or 2½ to
3 pounds chicken breasts, thighs, and drumsticks**

1½ **cups lower-sodium beef broth (page 67)**

1 **cup dry red wine or tomato juice**

½ **cup red wine vinegar or cider vinegar**

¼ **cup firmly packed light brown sugar**

2 **bay leaves**

3 **inches stick cinnamon, broken**

1 **teaspoon each whole cloves and whole allspice
berries**

¼ **teaspoon each salt and black pepper**

1 **tablespoon vegetable oil**

1 **medium-size yellow onion, sliced**

¼ **cup cold water**

2 **tablespoons all-purpose flour**

1 Cut the rabbit into 8 pieces or remove and discard
chicken skin. Rinse; drain and pat dry. To marinate,
combine the rabbit, beef broth, wine, vinegar, brown
sugar, bay leaves, cinnamon, cloves, allspice, salt, and
pepper in a large heavy-duty plastic bag (page 115).
Refrigerate for 1 to 2 days; turn bag occasionally.

2 Drain the rabbit; strain and reserve the wine mixture, discarding the whole spices. Pat the rabbit dry
with paper towels. In a Dutch oven, heat the oil over
moderate heat. Add the rabbit and cook for 7 to 8 minutes or until browned, turning occasionally.

3 Add the reserved wine mixture and the onion. Bring
to a boil. Lower the heat and simmer, covered, for
45 to 55 minutes or until the rabbit is tender. Transfer
the rabbit and onion to a platter; cover with foil and
keep warm.

4 Skim the fat from wine mixture (page 112).
Measure 1½ cups wine mixture; return to Dutch
oven. In a small bowl, stir together the cold water and
flour; add to the wine mixture. Bring to a boil over
moderate heat and boil for 1 minute, stirring constantly. Serve with the rabbit. Makes 4 servings.

Prep Time: 20 minutes Marinating Time: 1 day
Cooking Time: 1 hour

1 Serving: Calories 429. Total Fat 15 g. Saturated Fat 3 g.
Protein 46 g. Carbohydrate 17 g. Fiber 1 g.
Sodium 269 mg. Cholesterol 135 mg.

Grandma's Treats

Little Loaves

Apricot preserves gives these mini meat loaves a hint of sweetness that kids love.

1   pound lean ground beef or pork
¼   cup fine dry bread crumbs
5   tablespoons apricot preserves
1   tablespoon prepared mustard
¼   teaspoon salt
⅛   teaspoon black pepper
1   large egg white, lightly beaten

1. Preheat the oven to 350°F. In a medium-size bowl, mix the ground beef, bread crumbs, 3 tablespoons of the apricot preserves, mustard, salt, pepper, and egg white. In an 8" x 8" x 2" baking dish, shape meat mixture into four 4x2-inch loaves. Smooth the tops.

2. Bake for 50 to 55 minutes or until an instant-read thermometer inserted in the centers registers 170°F.

3. Spread the remaining 2 tablespoons apricot preserves over loaves. Makes 4 servings.

Chili Con Carne

For a special treat, serve this chili over corn muffins.

1   pound lean ground beef
1   can (15½ ounces) red kidney beans, undrained
1   can (14½ ounces) lower-sodium stewed tomatoes, undrained and cut up
1   can (8 ounces) lower-sodium tomato sauce
1   tablespoon chili powder
1½ teaspoons onion powder
¼   cup shredded reduced-fat Cheddar cheese

1. In a large saucepan, cook the ground beef over moderately high heat until browned. Drain off fat.

2. Stir in kidney beans, tomatoes, tomato sauce, chili powder, and onion powder. Bring to a boil. Lower the heat and simmer, covered, for 10 minutes, stirring occasionally.

3. Ladle into soup bowls. Sprinkle with Cheddar cheese. Makes 4 servings.

Pigs-in-a-Blanket

Innumerable versions of this recipe have delighted children for generations.

1   package (11 ounces) refrigerated bread sticks
2   tablespoons low-fat (1% milkfat) milk
⅓   cup grated Parmesan cheese
8   reduced-fat frankfurters

1. Preheat the oven to 350°F. Unroll the bread sticks. Brush the bread sticks, 1 at a time, with milk, then roll in Parmesan cheese, shaking off excess cheese. Wrap each bread stick around a frankfurter, pressing ends to seal. Place on a lightly greased baking sheet.

2. Bake for 18 to 20 minutes or until bread sticks are golden brown. Serve with catsup and prepared mustard. Makes 8 servings.

Bacon Pizza Muffs

When you need a quick lunch, these tiny pizzas can get you out of a jam.

4   English muffins, split
1   can (8 ounces) pizza sauce
½   cup chopped Canadian-style bacon
½   cup chopped sweet green pepper or ¼ cup chopped pitted black olives
1   package (4 ounces) shredded part-skim mozzarella cheese

1. Preheat the broiler. Place the muffins onto a large shallow baking pan. Broil 5 inches from the heat for 1 to 2 minutes or until toasted.

2. Spread the pizza sauce onto the muffins. Top with the bacon and green pepper. Sprinkle with cheese.

3. Broil for 3 minutes more or until heated through and cheese is golden. Makes 4 servings.

POULTRY TO PLEASE

*Grandma had a poultry recipe
for every occasion. On special days like
Sunday or Thanksgiving, she
made roast chicken or turkey. Then, to
use up the leftovers, she served a
savory hash. On days when she had the
time, she fixed chicken and dumplings,
and, for quick meals, there always
were easy skillet dishes. This chapter is
filled with those cherished recipes,
as well as old-time ideas for goose,
pheasant, and duck.*

155

Sunday Roast Chicken with Chestnut Stuffing

Sunday Roast Chicken with Chestnut Stuffing

During the Depression, many folks could afford to serve chicken only for special meals, like Sunday dinner.

- **3 tablespoons butter or margarine**
- **1 medium-size yellow onion, chopped**
- **1 stalk celery, chopped**
- **4 cups dried bread cubes**
- **1 can (15½ ounces) chestnuts in brine, drained, rinsed, and chopped, or 2 cups chopped cooked chestnuts**
- **¼ cup pecan pieces, toasted**
- **1 teaspoon each dried thyme leaves and savory leaves**
- **½ teaspoon each salt and black pepper**
- **¾ cup lower-sodium chicken broth (page 67)**
- **1 whole broiler-fryer chicken (2½ to 3 pounds), giblets removed**
- **Chicken Gravy (recipe, opposite)**

1 In a small saucepan, melt butter over moderately high heat. Add the onion and celery and cook for 5 minutes or until vegetables are tender, stirring often. Remove the saucepan from the heat. In a large bowl, combine the bread cubes, chestnuts, pecans, thyme, savory, salt, and pepper. Stir in the onion mixture. Stir the chicken broth into bread cube mixture; toss to coat.

2 Preheat the oven to 375°F. Rinse chicken; drain and pat dry. Stuff and truss chicken (page 185). Then, place chicken, breast-side-up, on a rack in a roasting pan. Insert a roasting thermometer into thickest part of its thigh without touching bone. Spoon the remaining stuffing into a lightly greased 1½-quart casserole; cover and refrigerate. Roast chicken for 1 to 1¼ hours or until the thermometer registers 180°F. Bake the covered casserole of stuffing alongside the chicken during the last 20 to 30 minutes of roasting. Let chicken stand for 10 minutes.

3 Meanwhile, prepare Chicken Gravy. Carve chicken, discarding skin. Serve with gravy. Makes 6 servings.

Prep Time: 25 minutes Cooking Time: 1 hour 5 minutes
Standing Time: 10 minutes

1 Serving: Calories 439. Total Fat 18 g. Saturated Fat 6 g.
Protein 32 g. Carbohydrate 38 g. Fiber 4 g.
Sodium 532 mg. Cholesterol 90 mg.

Chicken Gravy

In a small saucepan, whisk together **1 can (12 ounces) evaporated skimmed milk, 2 tablespoons all-purpose flour, 1 tablespoon lower-sodium chicken or beef bouillon granules,** and **⅛ teaspoon black pepper.** Cook over moderate heat, whisking constantly, for 5 minutes or until mixture starts to thicken. Cook and whisk for 2 minutes more or until thickened. Makes 1½ cups.

¼ Cup: Calories 23. Total Fat 0 g. Saturated Fat 0 g. Protein 1 g. Carbohydrate 4 g. Fiber 0 g. Sodium 16 mg. Cholesterol 0 mg.

Herbed Bread and Cracker Stuffing

This savory stuffing is enough for a 3-pound chicken. For a 12-pound turkey, you'll need to triple the recipe.

- 2 **tablespoons butter or margarine**
- 1 **large yellow onion, chopped**
- 3 **cups toasted fresh bread crumbs**
- 1 **cup crushed lower-sodium crackers**
- ¼ **cup minced parsley**
- ½ **teaspoon each dried savory leaves and marjoram leaves**
- ¼ **teaspoon ground sage**
- ¼ **teaspoon dried rosemary leaves**
- ¼ **teaspoon black pepper**
- ½ **cup lower-sodium chicken broth (page 67)**

1 Preheat the oven to 375°F. In a medium-size saucepan, melt butter over moderately high heat. Add the onion and cook for 5 minutes or until tender. Remove the saucepan from the heat. Stir in the bread crumbs, crushed crackers, parsley, savory, marjoram, sage, rosemary, and pepper. Stir the broth into the bread crumb mixture.

2 Spoon into a lightly greased 2-quart casserole. Bake, covered, for 25 to 30 minutes or until heated through. Makes 4 side-dish servings.

Prep Time: 10 minutes Cooking Time: 31 minutes

1 Serving: Calories 233. Total Fat 10 g. Saturated Fat 4 g. Protein 5 g. Carbohydrate 32 g. Fiber 2 g. Sodium 330 mg. Cholesterol 16 mg.

Roasted Chicken with Kitchen-Garden Herbs

In the early 1900's, many cooks grew herbs in boxes on their kitchen windowsills. If you don't have fresh herbs, substitute a teaspoon of dried herb for each tablespoon of the fresh.

- 2 **tablespoons minced parsley**
- 2 **tablespoons minced fresh basil**
- 2 **tablespoons minced fresh oregano**
- 2 **teaspoons minced fresh rosemary**
- ¼ **teaspoon each salt and black pepper**
- 2 **tablespoons lemon juice**
- 1 **whole broiler-fryer chicken (2½ to 3 pounds), giblets removed**

1 In a small bowl, stir together the parsley, basil, oregano, rosemary, salt, and pepper. Stir in the lemon juice to form a paste.

2 Preheat the oven to 375°F. Rinse chicken; drain and pat dry. Truss the chicken (page 185). Then, place chicken, breast-side-up, on a rack in a roasting pan. Rub surface of chicken with the herb mixture. Insert a roasting thermometer into thickest part of its thigh without touching bone. Roast for 1 to 1¼ hours or until the thermometer registers 180°F., basting every 15 minutes. Let chicken stand for 10 minutes before carving. Makes 6 servings.

Prep Time: 10 minutes Cooking Time: 1 hour
Standing Time: 10 minutes

1 Serving: Calories 218. Total Fat 12 g. Saturated Fat 3 g. Protein 25 g. Carbohydrate 1 g. Fiber 0 g. Sodium 163 mg. Cholesterol 79 mg.

HENS VS. FRYERS

Years ago, grandma chose large, fat hens for roasting and stewing. Although you can still find roasting hens, the smaller broiler-fryer chickens have been used for the recipes in this book because they have less fat than the hens and provide fewer servings for today's smaller families.

Buttermilk Fried Chicken with Gravy (back) and Maryland Fried Chicken (front)

Buttermilk Fried Chicken with Gravy

"My Grandmother Laura's was the only fried chicken I ever really liked," remembers Trudy Foster. "She fried it first, then baked it—so it stayed crisp on the outside and juicy on the inside."

1 **broiler-fryer chicken (2½ to 3 pounds), skin and wing tips removed and cut into 8 pieces**

1 **cup self-rising flour or all-purpose flour**

1 **teaspoon paprika**

½ **teaspoon black pepper**

1 **cup low-fat (1% milkfat) buttermilk or soured milk (page 300)**

2 **tablespoons vegetable oil**

1 **cup low-fat (1% milkfat) milk**

1 Preheat the oven to 400°F. Rinse chicken; drain and pat dry. Line a 13" x 9" x 2" baking pan with foil and lightly grease it. On a sheet of wax paper, mix flour, paprika, and pepper; set aside 3 tablespoons of mixture.

2 Dip the chicken in ½ cup of the buttermilk, then roll in flour mixture on wax paper to coat. In a 12-inch nonstick skillet, heat the oil over moderately high heat. Brown the chicken in hot oil for 10 minutes or until golden, turning occasionally. Transfer chicken to prepared baking pan, reserving drippings in the skillet. Bake the chicken, uncovered, for 20 minutes or until crisp, turning once.

3 Meanwhile, measure drippings; add additional vegetable oil, if necessary, to make 2 tablespoons. Return drippings to skillet; whisk 2 tablespoons of the reserved flour mixture into the drippings. Cook over moderate heat for 1 minute or until golden. Gradually whisk in the milk. Lower heat and simmer, whisking constantly, for 5 minutes more or until slightly thickened. Stir the remaining 1 tablespoon reserved flour mixture into the remaining ½ cup buttermilk. Stir buttermilk mixture into the skillet. Cook, whisking constantly, for 1 minute more. Serve with the chicken. Makes 4 servings.

Prep Time: 20 minutes Cooking Time: 31 minutes

1 Serving: Calories 473. Total Fat 18 g. Saturated Fat 4 g. Protein 46 g. Carbohydrate 30 g. Fiber 1 g. Sodium 604 mg. Cholesterol 122 mg.

Maryland Fried Chicken

Butter gives this dish real old-fashioned flavor.

1 broiler-fryer chicken (2½ to 3 pounds), skin and wing tips removed and cut into 8 pieces
1 large egg white
2 tablespoons water
¾ cup seasoned fine dry bread crumbs
2 tablespoons butter or margarine, melted

1 Preheat the oven to 375°F. Rinse chicken; drain and pat dry. In a shallow bowl, whisk together egg white and water. Place bread crumbs on wax paper. Dip chicken into the egg white mixture, then coat with crumbs.

2 Arrange chicken in a lightly greased 13" x 9" x 2" baking pan. Drizzle with melted butter. Bake, without turning, for 50 minutes or until chicken is cooked through. Makes 4 servings.

Prep Time: 15 minutes Cooking Time: 50 minutes

1 Serving: Calories 378. Total Fat 16 g. Saturated Fat 6 g. Protein 42 g. Carbohydrate 14 g. Fiber 1 g. Sodium 346 mg. Cholesterol 133 mg.

Country Captain

"This old Southern dish was my mother's favorite for parties because she could make it way ahead and freeze it," recalls Jean Anderson. Jean's mother served it with toasted slivered almonds on top.

2½ to 3 pounds chicken breasts, thighs, and drumsticks
¾ teaspoon salt
1 tablespoon vegetable oil
3 large sweet green peppers, cut into bite-size strips
3 large yellow onions, chopped
3 cans (14½ ounces each) lower-sodium tomatoes, undrained and cut up
1 cup currants
2 teaspoons curry powder
1½ teaspoons dried thyme leaves
¼ teaspoon ground red pepper (cayenne)
¼ teaspoon black pepper
⅛ teaspoon ground cloves

1 Remove and discard chicken skin. Rinse chicken; drain and pat dry. In Dutch oven, place chicken, enough cold water to cover, and ¼ teaspoon of the salt. Bring to a boil; skim surface. Lower heat and simmer, covered, about 30 minutes or until chicken is cooked through. Remove chicken from liquid and discard liquid. Cool the chicken; remove and discard the bones. Cut the meat into bite-size pieces.

2 In a 12-inch skillet, heat oil over moderately high heat. Add the green peppers and onions and cook for 5 minutes or until tender. Stir in tomatoes, currants, curry powder, thyme, red pepper, black pepper, cloves, and the remaining ½ teaspoon salt. Bring to a boil. Lower heat and simmer, covered, for 15 minutes. Stir chicken into tomato mixture; heat through. Serve over hot cooked rice. Makes 4 to 6 servings.

Prep Time: 25 minutes Cooking Time: 1 hour 5 minutes

1 Serving: Calories 465. Total Fat 12 g. Saturated Fat 2 g. Protein 40 g. Carbohydrate 54 g. Fiber 12 g. Sodium 531 mg. Cholesterol 100 mg.

Brunswick Chicken Stew

Originally, this dish was made with squirrel or rabbit, but today, most folks stick with chicken.

2½ to 3 pounds chicken breasts, thighs, and drumsticks
4 cups water
1 large yellow onion, chopped
2 bay leaves
½ teaspoon salt
1 can (14½ ounces) lower-sodium tomatoes, undrained and cut up
1 package (10 ounces) frozen lima beans, thawed
1 cup frozen corn
½ cup chopped cooked lower-sodium ham
¼ cup minced parsley
1 tablespoon lower-sodium Worcestershire sauce
¼ teaspoon ground red pepper (cayenne)

1 Remove and discard chicken skin. Rinse chicken; drain and pat dry. In Dutch oven, combine chicken, water, onion, bay leaves, and salt. Bring to boil; skim surface. Lower heat and simmer, covered, about 30 minutes or until chicken is cooked through. Remove chicken. Cool the chicken; remove and discard the bones. Cut meat into bite-size pieces.

2 Add the tomatoes, lima beans, corn, ham, parsley, Worcestershire sauce, and red pepper to Dutch oven. Return to a boil. Lower the heat and simmer, covered, for 10 minutes. Discard bay leaves. Stir in chicken pieces and heat through. Makes 5 or 6 servings.

Prep Time: 20 minutes Cooking Time: 50 minutes

1 Serving: Calories 307. Total Fat 8 g. Saturated Fat 2 g. Protein 36 g. Carbohydrate 24 g. Fiber 7 g. Sodium 501 mg. Cholesterol 90 mg.

When Is Chicken Cooked?

Grandma always knew when chicken was done, but you may not have her experience. Start checking the chicken a little before the suggested cooking time in the recipe. The chicken is cooked through when you cut into it and it is no longer pink on the inside and the juices run clear. White meat cooks faster than dark, so remove these pieces when they're done and keep them warm.

Skillet Chicken Paprika

Hungarian grandmas traditionally made this creamy chicken dish with rose-colored Hungarian paprika, which is quite spicy. But the milder, bright red paprika found in most supermarkets also works well.

2½ to 3 pounds chicken breasts, thighs, and drumsticks
1 tablespoon vegetable oil
1 cup sliced celery
1 medium-size yellow onion, sliced
2 tablespoons paprika
¼ teaspoon each salt and black pepper
1¼ cups lower-sodium chicken broth (page 67)
½ cup reduced-fat sour cream
2 tablespoons all-purpose flour

1 Remove and discard chicken skin. Rinse chicken; drain and pat dry. In a 12-inch nonstick skillet, heat the oil over moderately high heat. Brown chicken in hot oil for 10 minutes or until golden, turning occasionally. Remove chicken from skillet.

2 Add the celery and onion to drippings in skillet. Cook for 5 minutes or until tender. Stir in the paprika, salt, and pepper. Cook and stir for 1 minute. Stir in the broth. Return the chicken to the skillet. Bring to a boil. Lower the heat and simmer, covered, about 30 minutes or until chicken is cooked through.

3 Remove chicken from skillet. Cover; keep warm. In a small bowl, whisk together the sour cream and flour; stir into mixture in skillet. Cook over moderate

heat, stirring constantly, until mixture starts to thicken. Cook and stir for 1 minute more (do not boil). Serve over chicken and hot cooked noodles. Serves 4 to 6.

Prep Time: 15 minutes Cooking Time: 55 minutes

1 Serving: Calories 320. Total Fat 15 g. Saturated Fat 5 g. Protein 36 g. Carbohydrate 10 g. Fiber 2 g. Sodium 256 mg. Cholesterol 112 mg.

Chicken Molé

Southwestern women often cooked classic Mexican dishes for their families. This version of chicken molé is made with cocoa, which gives the sauce a pleasant bite.

2½ to 3 pounds chicken breasts, thighs, and drumsticks
2 tablespoons butter, margarine, or olive oil
1 medium-size yellow onion, chopped
1 small sweet green pepper, cut in thin strips
2 cloves garlic, minced
2 large tomatoes, chopped
¾ cup lower-sodium chicken broth (page 67)
1 tablespoon unsweetened cocoa
¼ teaspoon salt
¼ teaspoon ground cinnamon
¼ teaspoon crushed red pepper
¼ cup cold water
2 tablespoons cornstarch

1 Remove and discard chicken skin. Rinse chicken; drain and pat dry. In a 12-inch nonstick skillet, melt butter over moderate heat. Brown chicken in hot butter for 10 minutes or until golden, turning occasionally. Remove chicken from skillet.

2 Add onion, green pepper, and garlic to drippings in skillet. Cook for 5 minutes or until vegetables are tender. Stir in tomatoes, broth, cocoa, salt, cinnamon, and red pepper. Return chicken to skillet. Bring to a boil. Lower the heat and simmer, covered, about 30 minutes or until chicken is cooked through.

3 Remove chicken from skillet. Cover and keep warm. In a small bowl, whisk together the cold water and cornstarch; stir into mixture in skillet. Cook for 2 minutes more or until thickened. Serve over chicken and hot cooked rice. Makes 4 to 6 servings.

Prep Time: 20 minutes Cooking Time: 53 minutes

1 Serving: Calories 311. Total Fat 14 g. Saturated Fat 6 g. Protein 35 g. Carbohydrate 12 g. Fiber 2 g. Sodium 285 mg. Cholesterol 116 mg.

Chicken-Oyster Gumbo

Chicken-Oyster Gumbo

Originally gumbo was a native African dish made with okra and called quingombo
(okra in the African language of Bantu). In Louisiana, cooks adapted this stew to local
ingredients and shortened its name. Gumbo has been a Creole favorite ever since.

⅓ cup all-purpose flour

3 tablespoons vegetable oil

2½ to 3 pounds chicken breasts, thighs, and drumsticks
　　Nonstick cooking spray

1 tablespoon vegetable oil

2 stalks celery, sliced

1 medium-size sweet red or green pepper, chopped

1 medium-size yellow onion, thinly sliced

1 clove garlic, minced

2½ cups lower-sodium chicken broth (page 67)

1 can (14½ ounces) lower-sodium tomatoes,
　　undrained and cut up

¼ to ½ teaspoon ground red pepper (cayenne)

¼ teaspoon each salt and black pepper

1 cup okra pods cut into 1-inch pieces,
　　or 1 cup frozen sliced okra

1 can (8 ounces) oysters, drained

1 For roux, in a large heavy saucepan, stir together the flour and the 3 tablespoons oil until smooth. Cook over moderate heat, stirring constantly, for 5 to 7 minutes or until the roux is dark brown. Remove from heat.

2 Remove and discard chicken skin. Rinse chicken; drain and pat dry. Coat a Dutch oven with cooking spray. Add the 1 tablespoon oil and heat over moderately high heat. Brown chicken in hot oil for 10 minutes or until golden, turning occasionally. Remove from Dutch oven. Add celery, sweet red pepper, onion, and garlic to Dutch oven. Cook for 5 minutes or until vegetables are tender. Stir in the roux and heat until bubbly. Gradually stir in chicken broth. Stir in tomatoes, ground red pepper, salt, and black pepper.

3 Return chicken to Dutch oven. Bring to a boil. Lower heat and simmer, covered, about 30 minutes or until the chicken is cooked through. Stir in okra and oysters. Cook for 10 minutes more or until okra is tender. Serve over hot cooked rice. Makes 5 or 6 servings.

Prep Time: 20 minutes Cooking Time: 1 hour 5 minutes

1 Serving: Calories 362. Total Fat 18 g. Saturated Fat 3 g.
Protein 32 g. Carbohydrate 18 g. Fiber 4 g.
Sodium 269 mg. Cholesterol 93 mg.

Arroz con Pollo

Arroz con Pollo

Grandmas of Spanish ancestry season this classic dish with saffron.
Mexican-Americans prefer the flavor of green chilies, while Cuban and
Puerto Rican cooks add sweet peppers and olives, as in this recipe.

2½ to 3 pounds chicken breasts, thighs, and drumsticks
   Nonstick cooking spray
 1 tablespoon vegetable oil
 1 cup uncooked long-grain white rice
 2 cloves garlic, minced
 2 cups lower-sodium chicken broth (page 67)
 1 can (14½ ounces) lower-sodium tomatoes, undrained and cut up
 1 large sweet green pepper, chopped
 ½ cup chopped cooked lower-sodium ham
 ¾ teaspoon hot red pepper sauce
 ¼ teaspoon salt
 ¼ cup sliced black olives

1 Remove and discard chicken skin. Rinse chicken; drain and pat dry. Coat a Dutch oven with cooking spray. Add the oil and heat over moderately high heat. Brown the chicken in hot oil for 10 minutes or until golden, turning occasionally. Remove chicken from Dutch oven. Add the rice and garlic to Dutch oven. Cook and stir over moderate heat for 5 minutes or until the rice just starts to brown.

2 Stir chicken broth, tomatoes, green pepper, ham, pepper sauce, and salt into Dutch oven. Return chicken to Dutch oven. Bring to a boil. Lower the heat and simmer, covered, about 30 minutes or until chicken is cooked through and rice is tender. Stir in olives; heat through. Makes 6 servings.

Prep Time: 15 minutes   Cooking Time: 50 minutes

1 Serving: Calories 333. Total Fat 9 g. Saturated Fat 2 g.
Protein 28 g. Carbohydrate 32 g. Fiber 2 g.
Sodium 317 mg. Cholesterol 74 mg.

Chicken Marengo

Reportedly first created for Napoleon in honor of the 1800 Battle of Marengo, this chicken, tomato, and mushroom dish has been popular in America since the turn of the century. Serve it over noodles or rice.

2½ to 3 pounds chicken breasts, thighs, and drumsticks
⅓ cup all-purpose flour
¼ teaspoon salt
⅛ teaspoon black pepper
2 tablespoons vegetable oil
1½ cups lower-sodium chicken broth (page 67)
2 medium-size tomatoes, chopped
2 cups sliced fresh mushrooms
1 medium-size yellow onion, chopped
2 cloves garlic, minced
1½ teaspoons dried thyme leaves
¼ teaspoon each salt and black pepper
¼ cup dry sherry or lower-sodium chicken broth (page 67)
2 tablespoons all-purpose flour
¼ cup minced parsley

1 Remove and discard chicken skin. Rinse chicken; drain and pat dry. On a sheet of wax paper, combine the ⅓ cup flour, ¼ teaspoon salt, and ⅛ teaspoon pepper. Coat chicken pieces with flour mixture. In a 12-inch nonstick skillet, heat the oil over moderately high heat. Brown the chicken in the hot oil for 10 minutes or until golden, turning occasionally. Drain well.

2 In a large bowl, combine the broth, tomatoes, mushrooms, onion, garlic, thyme, ¼ teaspoon salt, and ¼ teaspoon pepper. Add to skillet. Bring to a boil. Lower the heat and simmer, covered, about 30 minutes or until chicken is cooked through. Remove chicken from skillet. Cover and keep warm.

3 In a small bowl, whisk together the sherry and the 2 tablespoons flour; stir into mixture in skillet. Cook over moderate heat, stirring constantly, until mixture starts to thicken. Cook and stir for 2 minutes more or until thickened. Stir in parsley. Serve with chicken. Makes 4 to 6 servings.

Prep Time: 25 minutes Cooking Time: 50 minutes

1 Serving: Calories 365. Total Fat 15 g. Saturated Fat 3 g. Protein 37 g. Carbohydrate 18 g. Fiber 2 g. Sodium 360 mg. Cholesterol 100 mg.

Down-Home Chicken with Parsley Dumplings

The old-fashioned way to serve this dish was with the meat on the bone. However, if you prefer, you can remove the chicken and cut it into bite-size pieces before adding the dumplings.

2½ to 3 pounds chicken breasts, thighs, and drumsticks
3 cups lower-sodium chicken broth (page 67)
2 medium-size yellow onions, sliced
2 stalks celery, cut into ½-inch slices
1½ teaspoons poultry seasoning
½ teaspoon garlic powder
½ teaspoon each salt and black pepper
¼ cup cold water
2 tablespoons all-purpose flour

For the dumplings:
1 cup all-purpose flour
2 tablespoons minced parsley
1 teaspoon baking powder
¼ teaspoon salt
⅓ cup low-fat (1% milkfat) milk
2 tablespoons vegetable oil

1 Remove and discard chicken skin. Rinse chicken; drain and pat dry. In a Dutch oven, combine chicken, broth, onions, celery, poultry seasoning, garlic powder, the ½ teaspoon salt, and the pepper. Bring to a boil. Lower the heat and simmer, covered, about 30 minutes or until chicken is cooked through. In a small bowl, whisk together the cold water and the 2 tablespoons flour. Stir into chicken mixture. Cook, stirring constantly, until mixture starts to thicken. Cook and stir for 2 minutes more or until thickened.

2 To prepare dumplings, in a medium-size bowl combine the 1 cup flour, parsley, baking powder, and the ¼ teaspoon salt. In a small bowl, whisk together the milk and oil. Pour milk mixture into flour mixture. With a fork, stir until mixed. Drop into 4 mounds on top of the bubbling chicken mixture. Simmer, covered, for 10 minutes or until toothpicks inserted in centers of dumplings come out clean (do not lift lid before 10 minutes cooking). Makes 4 servings.

Prep Time: 20 minutes Cooking Time: 50 minutes

1 Serving: Calories 436. Total Fat 15 g. Saturated Fat 3 g. Protein 39 g. Carbohydrate 35 g. Fiber 2 g. Sodium 636 mg. Cholesterol 101 mg.

Chicken and Noodles

*"I remember going to Grandma
Martin's for chicken and noodles," recalls
octogenarian Mildred Steffens. "She always served
it with biscuits on the side, but other families
I knew served it over mashed potatoes."*

2½ **to 3 pounds chicken breasts, thighs, and drumsticks**
  4 **cups lower-sodium chicken broth (page 67)**
  2 **large carrots, cut into ½-inch slices**
  1 **large yellow onion, chopped**
  1 **teaspoon celery seed (optional)**
 ¼ **teaspoon each salt and pepper**
  1 **package (8 ounces) frozen noodles or 6 ounces
    medium-size regular noodles**
 ¼ **cup cold water**
  2 **tablespoons all-purpose flour**

1 Remove and discard chicken skin. Rinse chicken; drain and pat dry. In a Dutch oven, combine chicken, broth, carrots, onion, celery seed (if using), salt, and pepper. Bring to a boil. Lower the heat and simmer, covered, about 30 minutes or until chicken is cooked through. Remove chicken from broth mixture. Set broth mixture aside. Cool chicken; remove and discard bones. Cut meat into bite-size pieces.

2 Bring broth mixture to a boil over high heat. Add noodles. Return to a boil. Lower the heat and simmer, covered, for 20 minutes for frozen noodles (6 minutes for regular noodles).

3 Add chicken pieces. In a small bowl, whisk together the cold water and flour. Stir into the chicken mixture. Cook, stirring constantly, until mixture starts to thicken. Cook and stir for 2 minutes more or until the mixture is thickened. Serve over mashed potatoes. Makes 4 servings.

Prep Time: 20 minutes Cooking Time: 1 hour 10 minutes

1 Serving: Calories 420. Total Fat 10 g. Saturated Fat 2 g.
Protein 40 g. Carbohydrate 42 g. Fiber 3 g.
Sodium 241 mg. Cholesterol 130 mg.

Turkey and Noodles Prepare as for Chicken and Noodles, substituting **1 pound turkey breast tenderloin** for the chicken. Simmer the turkey with the carrots, onion, celery seed (if using), salt, and pepper about 25 minutes or until the turkey is cooked through. Remove the turkey from broth mixture. Set broth mixture aside. Cool turkey; cut into bite-size pieces. Cook noodles and thicken as directed in steps 2 and 3 of Chicken and Noodles.

1 Serving: Calories 329. Total Fat 3 g. Saturated Fat 0 g.
Protein 32 g. Carbohydrate 42 g. Fiber 3 g.
Sodium 203 mg. Cholesterol 103 mg.

Chicken with Homemade Noodles Prepare as for Chicken and Noodles, but omit the noodles and make the homemade noodles as follows. In a medium-size bowl, combine **1 large egg, lightly beaten; 3 tablespoons low-fat (1% milkfat) milk; and ¼ teaspoon salt.** Stir in **1¼ cups all-purpose flour** to form a stiff dough. Roll out and cut noodles (tip, below). Let stand at room temperature for 2 hours to dry. To store noodles, place in an airtight container and refrigerate up to 3 days. (Or, place in a freezer container and freeze.)

Add the homemade noodles to the boiling broth mixture. Return to a boil. Lower the heat and simmer, covered, for 10 minutes. Add chicken pieces and thicken as directed in step 3 of Chicken and Noodles.

1 Serving: Calories 425. Total Fat 9 g. Saturated Fat 3 g.
Protein 41 g. Carbohydrate 42 g. Fiber 3 g.
Sodium 386 mg. Cholesterol 154 mg.

HOW TO CUT NOODLES

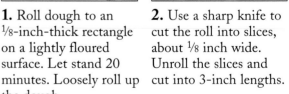

1. Roll dough to an ⅛-inch-thick rectangle on a lightly floured surface. Let stand 20 minutes. Loosely roll up the dough.

2. Use a sharp knife to cut the roll into slices, about ⅛ inch wide. Unroll the slices and cut into 3-inch lengths.

Chicken with Homemade Noodles

Chicken and Sausage Casserole

Serve this Cajun-style dish over rice or noodles. For a thicker stew, mix 2 tablespoons all-purpose flour with ¼ cup water and add it in step 2, after the chicken has cooked. Cook and stir until thickened.

2 large sweet green peppers, halved and thinly sliced
1 large yellow onion, halved and thinly sliced
4 ounces sweet bulk Italian sausage
4 cloves garlic, minced
2½ to 3 pounds chicken breasts, thighs, and drumsticks
1 tablespoon vegetable oil
1 can (28 ounces) plum tomatoes, undrained and coarsely chopped
2 tablespoons red wine vinegar or cider vinegar
¼ teaspoon salt

1 In a Dutch oven, combine green peppers, onion, sausage, and garlic. Cook and stir until sausage is cooked through. Remove sausage mixture and drain.

2 Remove and discard chicken skin. Rinse chicken; drain. Dry. Wipe out pan; add oil. Heat over moderately high heat. Brown chicken in oil for 10 minutes; turn often. Stir in sausage mixture, tomatoes, vinegar, and salt. Bring to boil. Lower heat; simmer, covered, about 30 minutes or until chicken is cooked through. Stir often. Serve over cooked rice or noodles. Serves 4.

Prep Time: 20 minutes Cooking Time: 50 minutes

1 Serving: Calories 374. Total Fat 15 g. Saturated Fat 4 g. Protein 43 g. Carbohydrate 16 g. Fiber 3 g. Sodium 690 mg. Cholesterol 123 mg.

CUTTING UP A CHICKEN

Cutting a whole chicken into parts, like grandma did, usually saves money.

1. Remove leg by cutting between thigh and body; bend back thigh. Cut hip joint. Cut joint to separate thigh and drumstick.

2. Remove wing by cutting skin between wing and body; bend back wing until shoulder joint breaks. Cut through joint.

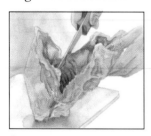

3. Separate breast from back by cutting through ribs on each side. Bend halves apart; cut apart.

4. Halve breast by cutting lengthwise along one side of breastbone. Cut back in half.

Nana's Chicken Stew

Farm-fresh cream gave old-fashioned chicken stews a wonderful richness. This version uses half-and-half to cut the fat, while keeping the luscious flavor.

2½ to 3 pounds chicken breasts, thighs, and drumsticks
3½ cups water
2 teaspoons dried dill weed
½ teaspoon salt
¼ teaspoon black pepper
4 carrots, sliced ½ inch thick
2 medium-size potatoes, cut into 1-inch cubes
2 parsnips, peeled and sliced ½ inch thick
½ cup cold water
3 tablespoons all-purpose flour
⅓ cup half-and-half

1 Remove and discard chicken skin. Rinse chicken; drain and pat dry. In Dutch oven, combine chicken, the 3½ cups water, dill weed, salt, and pepper. Bring to a boil. Lower the heat and simmer, covered, for 5 minutes. Stir in carrots, potatoes, and parsnips. Return to a boil. Lower heat and simmer, covered, for 20 minutes or until chicken is cooked through. Remove chicken and vegetables to a serving bowl.

2 Whisk together the ½ cup cold water and the flour; whisk into mixture in Dutch oven. Cook, whisking constantly, for 2 minutes. Stir in the half-and-half. Bring to a boil; cook for 1 minute. Serve with the chicken and vegetables. Makes 4 servings.

Prep Time: 25 minutes Cooking Time: 40 minutes

1 Serving: Calories 417. Total Fat 10 g. Saturated Fat 4 g. Protein 41 g. Carbohydrate 40 g. Fiber 6 g. Sodium 424 mg. Cholesterol 119 mg.

Savory Chicken and Biscuits

Savory Chicken and Biscuits

"Grandmother's chicken stew warmed both body and soul,"
recalls Jim Dwyer. "She always topped it with heart-shaped biscuits."

1 **pound skinned and boned chicken thighs or breasts, cut into 1-inch pieces**

1 **large yellow onion, cut into 1-inch chunks**

8 **ounces fresh mushrooms, quartered**

1 **cup lower-sodium chicken broth (page 67)**

3 **cloves garlic, minced**

1 **teaspoon dried rosemary leaves**

¼ **teaspoon each salt and black pepper**

2 **tablespoons cornstarch mixed with ¼ cup cold water**

1 **cup fresh or frozen peas**

1 **jar (4 ounces) sliced pimientos, drained**

For the biscuits:

½ **cup low-fat (1% milkfat) buttermilk or soured milk (page 67)**

½ **teaspoon dried minced onion or minced onion**

1 **cup all-purpose flour**

1 **teaspoon baking powder**

¼ **teaspoon baking soda**

⅛ **teaspoon salt**

3 **tablespoons butter or margarine**

1 Preheat oven to 375°F. In large saucepan, combine the chicken, onion chunks, mushrooms, broth, garlic, rosemary, the ¼ teaspoon salt, and the pepper. Bring to a boil. Lower the heat and simmer, uncovered, for 3 minutes. Stir in cornstarch mixture. Cook for 2 minutes. Stir in the peas and pimientos; set aside.

2 To prepare biscuits, combine buttermilk and dried onion; set aside. In large bowl, stir together the flour, baking powder, baking soda, and the ⅛ teaspoon salt. Using a pastry blender, cut in butter until mixture resembles coarse crumbs. Stir in buttermilk mixture just until combined.

3 On a lightly floured surface, pat dough into a 9-inch circle. Using a 2-inch heart-shaped or round cutter, cut 9 biscuits. Bring chicken mixture to a boil; transfer to 2-quart casserole. Arrange biscuits on top. Bake for 20 to 25 minutes or until chicken is cooked through and biscuits are golden. Makes 4 servings.

Prep Time: 25 minutes Cooking Time: 35 minutes

1 Serving: Calories 459. Total Fat 18 g. Saturated Fat 8 g.
Protein 30 g. Carbohydrate 43 g. Fiber 6 g.
Sodium 641 mg. Cholesterol 101 mg.

Chicken-on-Sunday Bake

*When this tasty chicken casserole first
appeared in community cookbooks, the baking
time was at least 2 hours so it could cook
while everyone went to church.*

10 **chicken thighs**

1½ **cups low-fat (1% milkfat) milk**

1 **can (10¾ ounces) reduced-fat cream of
mushroom soup**

1 **can (10¾ ounces) reduced-fat cream of
chicken soup**

1 **cup uncooked long-grain white rice**

1 **small yellow onion, chopped**

⅛ **teaspoon black pepper**

1 Preheat the oven to 350°F. Remove and discard
chicken skin. Rinse chicken; drain and pat dry.
Arrange chicken thighs in a lightly greased 13" x 9" x 2"
baking dish. In a medium-size bowl, combine the milk,
cream of mushroom soup, cream of chicken soup, rice,
onion, and pepper. Spoon the mixture over chicken.

2 Bake, covered, for 45 minutes. Uncover and bake
15 minutes more or until chicken is cooked through.
Makes 5 servings.

Prep Time: 10 minutes Cooking Time: 1 hour

1 Serving: Calories 477. Total Fat 15 g. Saturated Fat 5 g.
Protein 35 g. Carbohydrate 46 g. Fiber 1 g.
Sodium 610 mg. Cholesterol 112 mg.

Gran's Oven-Barbecued Chicken

*In the 1800's, meat roasted over an outdoor
pit was called "barbecued". By the 1940's, the
word barbecued was applied to any meat
or chicken with a zesty red sauce. Usually the
dish was baked in the oven.*

1 **tablespoon vegetable oil**

1 **medium-size yellow onion, finely chopped**

1 **cup lower-calorie, lower-sodium catsup**

¼ **cup firmly packed light brown sugar**

¼ **cup cider vinegar**

2 **teaspoons lower-sodium Worcestershire sauce**

2 **teaspoons prepared mustard**

¼ **teaspoon ground red pepper (cayenne)**

2½ **to 3 pounds chicken breasts, thighs, and drumsticks**

Gran's Oven-Barbecued Chicken

1 Preheat oven to 375°F. In a small saucepan, heat oil
over moderately high heat. Add onion and cook for
5 minutes or until onion is tender. Stir in the catsup,
brown sugar, vinegar, Worcestershire sauce, mustard,
and red pepper. Bring to a boil. Lower the heat and
simmer, covered, for 10 minutes.

2 Remove and discard chicken skin. Rinse chicken;
drain and pat dry. Arrange chicken in a lightly
greased 13" x 9" x 2" baking dish. Spoon catsup mixture
over chicken. Bake, covered, for 20 minutes. Uncover
and bake 15 to 20 minutes more or until chicken is
cooked through. Makes 4 servings.

Prep Time: 15 minutes Cooking Time: 55 minutes

1 Serving: Calories 348. Total Fat 11 g. Saturated Fat 2 g.
Protein 35 g. Carbohydrate 28 g. Fiber 1 g.
Sodium 142 mg. Cholesterol 100 mg.

Thyme-and-Chicken Fricassee

In grandma's day, fricassees started with an old hen, that had to be simmered for hours to make it tender, and ended with a rich cream sauce. This modern version uses chicken breasts, so it's quicker cooking, and evaporated skimmed milk to cut the fat.

4   **skinned and boned chicken breast halves (about 5 ounces each)**
⅓ **cup all-purpose flour**
1   **teaspoon dried thyme leaves**
½ **teaspoon paprika**
¼ **teaspoon salt**
⅛ **teaspoon black pepper**
¼ **cup low-fat (1% milkfat) milk**
1   **tablespoon vegetable oil**
1   **medium-size yellow onion, chopped**
½ **cup lower-sodium chicken broth (page 67)**
2   **bay leaves**
½ **teaspoon celery seed**
¼ **teaspoon each salt and black pepper**
1   **can (12 ounces) evaporated skimmed milk**
2   **tablespoons all-purpose flour**

1 Rinse chicken; drain and pat dry. On a sheet of wax paper, mix the ⅓ cup flour, thyme, paprika, ¼ teaspoon salt, and ⅛ teaspoon pepper. Dip chicken pieces in milk, then coat with flour mixture.

2 In a 10-inch nonstick skillet, heat oil over moderately high heat. Brown chicken in hot oil for 2 minutes on each side; transfer to a plate. Add onion to skillet. Cook for 3 minutes or until onion is tender.

3 Stir broth, bay leaves, celery seed, ¼ teaspoon salt, and ¼ teaspoon pepper into skillet. Return chicken along with any juices to the skillet. Bring to a boil. Lower the heat and simmer, covered, for 10 minutes or until chicken is cooked through. Discard the bay leaves. Remove the chicken from skillet. Cover; keep warm.

4 In a medium bowl, whisk together the evaporated skimmed milk and the 2 tablespoons flour. Stir into mixture in skillet. Cook over moderate heat, stirring constantly, until mixture starts to thicken. Cook and stir for 2 minutes more or until thickened. Serve with chicken over hot cooked noodles. Makes 4 servings.

Prep Time: 15 minutes Cooking Time: 25 minutes

1 Serving: Calories 329. Total Fat 7 g. Saturated Fat 1 g.
Protein 40 g. Carbohydrate 24 g. Fiber 1 g.
Sodium 442 mg. Cholesterol 88 mg.

Chicken Kiev

This classic Russian dish was a favorite at fancy restaurants. However, many women served it at home for dinner parties. In this adaptation, the chicken is baked instead of fried (to cut the fat), but it is filled with butter and herbs for authentic flavor.

¼ **cup butter or margarine, at room temperature**
2   **tablespoons minced parsley**
2   **tablespoons minced fresh chives or green onion tops**
1   **clove garlic, minced**
⅛ **teaspoon black pepper**
4   **skinned and boned chicken breast halves (about 5 ounces each)**
¼ **cup all-purpose flour**
¼ **teaspoon salt**
2   **large egg whites**
2   **tablespoons water**
½ **cup fine dry bread crumbs**
1   **tablespoon butter or margarine**

1 In a small bowl, combine the ¼ cup butter, parsley, chives, garlic, and pepper. Cover and chill in the freezer for 20 to 30 minutes or until butter is firm.

2 Meanwhile, rinse chicken; drain and pat dry. Pound both sides of chicken breasts with side of meat mallet or bottom of small heavy skillet until breasts are ⅛ inch thick. Spoon some of the butter mixture onto each chicken breast. Roll chicken breasts up to encase butter mixture; secure with wooden picks.

3 On a sheet of wax paper, combine flour and salt. In a small bowl, whisk together the egg whites and water. Place bread crumbs on a sheet of wax paper. Coat chicken rolls with the flour mixture, then dip in the egg white mixture and coat with the bread crumbs. Wrap rolls in plastic wrap and refrigerate for 1 to 24 hours.

4 Preheat the oven to 400°F. In 10-inch nonstick skillet, melt the 1 tablespoon butter over moderately high heat. Brown chicken rolls in hot butter for 5 minutes or until golden, turning occasionally. Transfer chicken rolls to a lightly greased 8" x 8" x 2" baking dish. Bake for 15 minutes or until chicken is cooked through. Serve with rice pilaf. Makes 4 servings.

Prep Time: 20 minutes Chilling Time: 1 hour 20 minutes
Cooking Time: 21 minutes

1 Serving: Calories 342. Total Fat 16 g. Saturated Fat 8 g.
Protein 33 g. Carbohydrate 16 g. Fiber 1 g.
Sodium 455 mg. Cholesterol 109 mg.

Chicken Chow Mein

Chicken Chow Mein

Chinese–American grandmas will tell you that the difference between chop suey and chow mein is that chow mein is served over crisp chow mein noodles while chop suey is served over rice. To cut 10 grams of fat per serving, opt for chop suey with the rice.

4 **skinned and boned chicken breast halves (about 5 ounces each), cut into bite-size strips**

Nonstick cooking spray

2 **tablespoons vegetable oil**

2 **stalks celery, cut into 1-inch pieces**

2 **medium-size yellow onions, halved and sliced**

2 **cloves garlic, minced**

1¼ **cups lower-sodium chicken broth (page 67)**

¼ **cup lower-sodium soy sauce**

2 **tablespoons cornstarch**

1 **tablespoon firmly packed light brown sugar**

1 **can (14 ounces) mixed Chinese vegetables, drained**

1 **can (8 ounces) sliced water chestnuts, drained**

3 **cups chow mein noodles**

1 Rinse chicken; drain and pat dry. Coat a wok or heavy 12-inch skillet with cooking spray. In the wok or skillet, heat 1 tablespoon of the oil over moderately high heat. Add the chicken and stir-fry for 3 minutes or until cooked through. Using a slotted spoon, remove the chicken from wok. Cover and keep warm.

2 Heat the remaining 1 tablespoon of oil in the wok. Add the celery, onions, and garlic. Stir-fry for 2 minutes or until almost tender.

3 In a small bowl, whisk together the chicken broth, soy sauce, cornstarch, and brown sugar. Add to the wok along with the Chinese vegetables and water chestnuts. Bring to a boil and cook for 1 minute or until the sauce thickens and the vegetables are heated through.

4 Return the cooked chicken along with any juices to the wok. Bring to a boil and cook 1 minute or until heated through. Spoon chicken mixture over chow mein noodles. Makes 4 servings.

Prep Time: 20 minutes Cooking Time: 12 minutes

1 Serving: Calories 486. Total Fat 21 g. Saturated Fat 3 g. Protein 35 g. Carbohydrate 40 g. Fiber 5 g. Sodium 840 mg. Cholesterol 78 mg.

Golden Chicken Scallops

In this old recipe, chicken breasts are pounded into thin scallops to help them cook quickly and evenly.

- **4** skinned and boned chicken breast halves (about 5 ounces each)
- ¼ cup all-purpose flour
- **1** large egg
- **2** tablespoons low-fat (1% milkfat) milk
- ¾ cup seasoned fine dry bread crumbs
- ¼ teaspoon each salt and black pepper
- **2** tablespoons vegetable oil
- ½ medium-size lemon

1 Rinse chicken; drain and pat dry. Pound the chicken breasts with side of meat mallet or bottom of small heavy skillet until they are ½ inch thick. Place the flour on a sheet of wax paper. In a small bowl, whisk together the egg and milk. On another sheet of wax paper, combine bread crumbs, salt, and pepper. Coat the chicken breasts with the flour, then dip in egg mixture and coat with the bread crumb mixture.

2 In a 12-inch nonstick skillet, heat oil over moderate heat. Cook chicken breasts in hot oil for 4 minutes on each side or until chicken is cooked through. Arrange the chicken on a platter. Squeeze lemon over chicken. Serve with asparagus spears. Makes 4 servings.

Prep Time: 10 minutes Cooking Time: 9 minutes

1 Serving: Calories 348. Total Fat 12 g. Saturated Fat 2 g.
Protein 35 g. Carbohydrate 23 g. Fiber 0 g.
Sodium 818 mg. Cholesterol 132 mg.

Stacked Chicken Enchiladas With Salsa Verde

The tomatillos used in this traditional Tex–Mex sauce sometimes are called green tomatoes, but they're actually a completely different fruit. Look for them at a Mexican food specialty store.

- **Salsa Verde (recipe, right) or 1½ cups green salsa**
- **1** cup reduced-fat sour cream
- **1** large yellow onion, chopped
- **1** medium-size sweet green pepper, chopped
- ¼ cup water
- **2** cups chopped cooked chicken breast
- **1** cup shredded part-skim mozzarella cheese (4 ounces)
- **6** 7-inch flour tortillas

1 Preheat the oven to 350°F. Prepare the Salsa Verde. In food processor or blender, process 1 cup of the Salsa Verde or green salsa and the sour cream until smooth. Set aside.

2 In a small saucepan, combine the onion, green pepper, and water. Cook, covered, for 5 minutes or until vegetables are tender. Drain vegetables. In a medium-size bowl, stir together the onion mixture, chicken, and ¾ cup of the mozzarella cheese.

3 Place 1 flour tortilla in the bottom of a lightly greased 9" x 9" x 2" baking dish. Top with a generous ½ cup of the chicken mixture and a generous 3 tablespoons of the salsa-sour cream mixture. Repeat layers with the remaining tortillas, remaining chicken mixture, and remaining salsa-sour cream mixture to make a stack. Spread the remaining ½ cup Salsa Verde or green salsa over tortillas. Sprinkle with the remaining ¼ cup mozzarella cheese. Cover loosely with foil. Bake for 25 minutes. Remove foil; bake for 5 minutes more. Cut stack into quarters to serve. Serve with a tossed salad. Makes 4 servings.

Prep Time: 25 minutes Cooking Time: 45 minutes

1 Serving: Calories 531. Total Fat 21 g. Saturated Fat 9 g.
Protein 38 g. Carbohydrate 49 g. Fiber 7 g.
Sodium 1,118 mg. Cholesterol 98 mg.

Salsa Verde

In a food processor or blender, process **2 cans (13 ounces each)** drained tomatillos, **2 cans (4 ounces each)** undrained chopped green chili peppers, **4 sprigs fresh cilantro or parsley, 4 cloves garlic,** and ⅛ **teaspoon ground red pepper (cayenne)** until smooth. Transfer mixture to a small saucepan. Bring to a boil. Lower the heat and simmer, covered, for 5 minutes. Cool to room temperature. (This salsa also is good chilled and served as a dip with vegetable dippers or baked tortilla wedges.) Makes 1½ cups.

1 Tablespoon: Calories 13. Total Fat 0 g. Saturated Fat 0 g.
Protein 0 g. Carbohydrate 3 g. Fiber 1 g.
Sodium 111 mg. Cholesterol 0 mg.

Chicken Croquettes with Creamy Gravy

Our great-grandmothers often served croquettes for ladies luncheons. In this up-to-date recipe, the croquettes are baked instead of fried and served with a luscious, basil-seasoned gravy.

 3 tablespoons butter or margarine
 1 medium-size yellow onion, finely chopped
 2 tablespoons minced parsley
½ cup all-purpose flour
¼ teaspoon salt
⅛ teaspoon ground red pepper (cayenne)
¼ cup lower-sodium chicken broth (page 67)
 2 tablespoons low-fat (1% milkfat) milk
1½ cups ground cooked chicken breast
⅓ cup plain or seasoned fine dry bread crumbs
 1 large egg, lightly beaten
½ cup plain or seasoned fine dry bread crumbs
   Creamy Gravy (recipe, above right)

1 In a small saucepan, melt the butter over moderate heat. Add the onion and cook for 5 minutes or until onion is tender. Stir in the parsley. In a small bowl, combine the flour, salt, and red pepper. Stir into mixture in saucepan. Cook for 1 minute or until bubbly. Add the chicken broth and milk. Cook, stirring constantly, until mixture starts to thicken. Cook and stir for 2 minutes more or until thickened.

2 Pour mixture into a large bowl. Stir in ground chicken and the ⅓ cup bread crumbs. Cover and refrigerate for at least 1 hour. Using your hands, shape ¼ cup of the mixture into a ¾-inch-thick wedge or patty. Repeat with the remaining mixture to form a total of 8 wedges or patties.

3 Preheat the oven to 375°F. Place egg in a shallow dish. Place the ½ cup bread crumbs on a sheet of wax paper. Coat wedges with bread crumbs, then dip in the egg and coat again with the crumbs. Arrange wedges in lightly greased shallow baking pan. Bake for 25 to 30 minutes or until wedges are golden and heated through. Serve with Creamy Gravy. Serves 4.

Prep Time: 30 minutes Chilling Time: 1 hour
Cooking Time: 40 minutes

1 Serving: Calories 373. Total Fat 16 g. Saturated Fat 9 g.
Protein 20 g. Carbohydrate 35 g. Fiber 2 g.
Sodium 702 mg. Cholesterol 118 mg.

Creamy Gravy

In a small saucepan, melt **1 tablespoon butter or margarine** over moderate heat. Whisk in **2 tablespoons all-purpose flour**, **½ teaspoon dried basil leaves**, **¼ teaspoon salt**, and **dash white or black pepper**. Cook for 1 minute or until bubbly. Add **1 cup low-fat (1% milkfat) milk**. Cook, whisking constantly, until the mixture starts to thicken. Cook and whisk for 2 minutes more or until thickened. Makes 1 cup.

¼ Cup: Calories 66. Total Fat 4 g. Saturated Fat 2 g.
Protein 2 g. Carbohydrate 6 g. Fiber 0 g.
Sodium 193 mg. Cholesterol 10 mg.

Quick Curried Chicken with Apples

Curried dishes were brought to America by the early English settlers, but it wasn't until after World War II that they became really popular.

 2 tablespoons butter or margarine
 1 large yellow onion, halved and thinly sliced
 1 small sweet green pepper, chopped
 1 small tart apple, cored and chopped
 2 cloves garlic, minced
 1 tablespoon curry powder
 5 tablespoons all-purpose flour
 1 tablespoon sugar
¼ teaspoon each salt and black pepper
 1 cup apple juice
 1 cup lower-sodium chicken broth (page 67)
 2 tablespoons cider vinegar
2½ cups bite-size pieces cooked chicken breast

1 In a medium-size saucepan, melt butter over moderate heat. Add the onion, green pepper, apple, garlic, and curry powder. Cook for 5 minutes or until onion and green pepper are tender. Stir in the flour, sugar, salt, and black pepper. Add the apple juice, broth, and vinegar. Cook, stirring constantly, until the mixture starts to thicken. Cook and stir for 2 minutes or until thickened.

2 Stir chicken into mixture in saucepan; heat through. Serve over hot cooked rice with chutney. Serves 4.

Prep Time: 15 minutes Cooking Time: 15 minutes

1 Serving: Calories 322. Total Fat 10 g. Saturated Fat 5 g.
Protein 33 g. Carbohydrate 25 g. Fiber 2 g.
Sodium 269 mg. Cholesterol 100 mg.

Chicken Croquettes with Creamy Gravy

Lazy Day Chicken Puff

Serve this golden soufflélike dish with a tossed spinach salad and a colorful combination of steamed or stir-fried vegetables.

> 5 **large eggs**
> ³⁄₄ **cup low-fat (1% milkfat) milk**
> 2 **tablespoons all-purpose flour**
> ½ **teaspoon dry mustard**
> ¼ **teaspoon white or black pepper**
> ⅛ **teaspoon salt**
> 3 **tablespoons grated Parmesan cheese**
> 2 **tablespoons minced parsley**
> 2 **cups chopped cooked chicken breast**

1 Preheat the oven to 325°F. Separate the eggs. Discard the yolks from 2 of the eggs. Place the egg whites in a clean large bowl. Place the yolks in a small bowl. Set aside. Lightly grease just the bottom of a 2-quart casserole. Set aside.

2 In a medium-size saucepan, whisk together the milk, flour, mustard, pepper, and salt. Cook over moderate heat, whisking constantly, for 2 minutes or until mixture is thickened and bubbly. Stir in the Parmesan cheese and parsley.

3 Whisk egg yolks until light. Slowly stir about half of the hot mixture into egg yolks, then return this mixture to the saucepan. Cook, whisking constantly, for 1 minute or until mixture is thickened (do not boil). Stir in the chicken.

4 With an electric mixer on *High*, beat the egg whites until soft peaks form. Stir one-quarter of the whites into the chicken mixture, then quickly fold in the remaining whites. Spoon into the prepared casserole. Bake for 40 minutes or until a knife inserted in center comes out clean. Serve immediately. Makes 4 servings.

Prep Time: 15 minutes Cooking Time: 43 minutes

1 Serving: Calories 255. Total Fat 11 g. Saturated Fat 4 g. Protein 31 g. Carbohydrate 6 g. Fiber 0 g. Sodium 313 mg. Cholesterol 228 mg.

COOKED POULTRY MADE EASY

When you need cooked poultry, but don't have any leftovers on hand:

♦ Stop by the deli counter of your supermarket and purchase a whole cooked chicken.

♦ Look for packaged frozen cooked chicken in your grocer's freezer case.

♦ Poach some chicken or turkey breast. For 2 cups of cut-up cooked chicken, place 12 ounces of skinned and boned chicken breast or turkey breast in a large skillet. Add just enough water to cover the poultry. Bring to a boil. Lower the heat and simmer, covered, for 12 to 14 minutes or until poultry is cooked through.

Chicken Livers with Mushrooms and Onions

As far back as 1896, the Boston Cooking School Cook Book instructed women to pair chicken livers with mushrooms and onions.

> 1 **pound chicken livers, quartered**
> ¼ **cup all-purpose flour**
> 2 **tablespoons vegetable oil**
> 2 **cups sliced fresh mushrooms**
> 1 **large onion, thinly sliced**
> ¼ **cup lower-sodium chicken broth (page 67)**
> ½ **teaspoon dried basil leaves, crushed**
> ¼ **teaspoon each salt and black pepper**
> 2 **tablespoons minced parsley**

1 Rinse chicken livers; drain and pat dry. Place the flour on a sheet of wax paper. Coat livers with flour.

2 In a 12-inch nonstick skillet, heat oil over moderately high heat. Add chicken livers, mushrooms, and onion. Cook, stirring constantly, for 5 minutes or until the chicken livers are just slightly pink inside. Stir in the broth, basil, salt, and pepper. Bring to a boil. Lower the heat and simmer, covered, for 5 minutes. Sprinkle with parsley. Serve with hot cooked rice. Makes 4 servings.

Prep Time: 10 minutes Cooking Time: 12 minutes

1 Serving: Calories 181. Total Fat 10 g. Saturated Fat 1 g. Protein 13 g. Carbohydrate 10 g. Fiber 1 g. Sodium 160 mg. Cholesterol 293 mg.

Cornish Hens with Ham and Wild Rice Stuffing

Cornish Hens with Ham and Wild Rice Stuffing

*Rock Cornish hens were developed in the 1950's when American breeders
crossed the Cornish hen from England with the American Plymouth rock hen.*

   ¾ **cup uncooked wild rice**
1½ **cups lower-sodium chicken broth (page 67)**
   1 **tablespoon butter or margarine**
   1 **cup sliced fresh mushrooms**
   1 **medium-size yellow onion, chopped**
  ¼ **cup diced cooked lower-sodium ham**
  ¼ **cup chopped pecans, toasted (optional)**
   1 **teaspoon each dried thyme leaves and marjoram
      leaves**
   1 **teaspoon grated orange rind**
  ¼ **teaspoon each salt and black pepper**
   2 **Cornish game hens (1 pound each)**

1 Place wild rice in a wire strainer. Run cold water through the rice, lifting rice with fingers to clean thoroughly. In a small saucepan, bring broth to a boil over high heat. Stir in wild rice. Return to a boil. Lower the heat and simmer, covered, for 40 minutes or until most of the broth is absorbed. Drain off liquid. Meanwhile, in a medium-size saucepan, melt butter over moderate heat. Add the mushrooms and onion and cook for 5 minutes or until tender. In a large bowl, combine wild rice, mushroom mixture, ham, pecans (if using), thyme, marjoram, orange rind, salt, and pepper.

2 Preheat the oven to 375°F. Rinse hens; drain and pat dry. Remove and discard giblets and neck if present. Stuff and truss hens (page 185). Place hens, breast side up, on a rack in a roasting pan. Cover hens loosely with foil. Spoon remaining stuffing into a lightly greased 1½-quart casserole; cover and refrigerate.

3 Roast hens for 30 minutes. Uncover hens. Roast for 30 to 45 minutes more or until hens are cooked through, basting occasionally with pan drippings. Bake the covered casserole of stuffing alongside the hens during the last 20 minutes of roasting. To serve, halve hens lengthwise, discarding skin. Makes 4 servings.

Prep Time: 15 minutes Cooking Time: 45 minutes
Roasting Time: 1 hour

1 Serving: Calories 421. Total Fat 14 g. Saturated Fat 5 g.
Protein 45 g. Carbohydrate 29 g. Fiber 2 g.
Sodium 662 mg. Cholesterol 127 mg.

Holiday Roast Turkey with Old-Fashioned Corn Bread Stuffing

Holiday Roast Turkey with Old-Fashioned Corn Bread Stuffing

Old-fashioned cooks sometimes added eggs and baking powder to their corn bread stuffing to give it a fluffier texture. The stuffing in this recipe is a delicious example.

3 tablespoons butter or margarine
1 large yellow onion, chopped
5 cups crumbled corn bread
5 cups toasted fresh bread crumbs
1 teaspoon baking powder
1 teaspoon poultry seasoning
¼ teaspoon black pepper
¾ cup lower-sodium chicken broth (page 67)
1 large egg, lightly beaten
1 fresh or frozen and thawed turkey (12 pounds)
1 tablespoon vegetable oil
   Giblet Gravy (recipe, opposite)

1 In a medium-size saucepan, melt the butter over moderate heat. Add the onion and cook for 5 minutes or until tender. Remove from the heat. In a very large bowl, combine the corn bread, bread crumbs, baking powder, poultry seasoning, and pepper. Stir in the onion mixture. In small bowl, whisk together broth and egg. Stir into the corn bread mixture. Toss to coat well.

2 Preheat oven to 325°F. Rinse turkey; drain and pat dry. Remove neck and giblets; set aside to make the Giblet Gravy. Stuff and truss turkey (page 185). Place, breast-side-up, on a rack in a large roasting pan. Brush with oil. Insert roasting thermometer in turkey thigh without touching bone. Spoon remaining stuffing into a lightly greased 2-quart casserole; cover and refrigerate.

3 Roast turkey for 3 to 3½ hours or until the thermometer registers 180°F., basting often and covering with foil to prevent overbrowning if necessary. Bake the covered casserole of stuffing alongside turkey during the last 30 minutes of roasting, adding an additional 2 to 3 tablespoons chicken broth if stuffing is dry. Let turkey stand for 15 to 20 minutes before carving.

4 Meanwhile, cook neck and giblets for Giblet Gravy. Reserve 2 tablespoons of the pan drippings from roast turkey for Giblet Gravy. Prepare gravy. Carve turkey, discarding skin (tip, right). Serve turkey and dressing with gravy. Makes 12 servings.

Prep Time: 20 minutes Cooking Time: 6 minutes
Roasting Time: 3 hours Standing Time: 15 minutes

1 Serving with Gravy: Calories 649. Total Fat 22 g.
Saturated Fat 7 g. Protein 78 g. Carbohydrate 31 g. Fiber 2 g.
Sodium 705 mg. Cholesterol 316 mg.

Giblet Gravy

Rinse the turkey **neck** and **giblets**. Refrigerate the liver. In a large saucepan, combine the remaining giblets, neck, and **4 cups water**. Add **1 medium-size yellow onion, cut into wedges; 1 large carrot, cut into chunks; 2 sprigs parsley; ½ teaspoon salt; and ¼ teaspoon white or black pepper.** Bring to a boil. Lower the heat and simmer, covered, for 40 minutes. Add liver. Continue cooking for 20 minutes more or until tender. Strain broth, reserving 1⅓ cups. Reserve giblets and neck; discard vegetables. When cool enough to handle, remove meat from neck; discard neck bones. Finely chop the neck meat and giblets; set aside.

In a Dutch oven, whisk together reserved pan drippings, **1 can (12 ounces) evaporated skimmed milk, ⅓ cup all-purpose flour, ¼ teaspoon salt, and ¼ teaspoon white or black pepper.** Cook over moderate heat until bubbly. Add the reserved broth. Cook, whisking constantly, until the mixture starts to thicken. Cook and whisk for 2 minutes more or until thickened. Stir in neck meat and giblets; heat through. Makes 3 cups.

¼ Cup: Calories 77. Total Fat 2 g. Saturated Fat 1 g.
Protein 7 g. Carbohydrate 6 g. Fiber 0 g.
Sodium 147 mg. Cholesterol 102 mg.

HOW TO CARVE A TURKEY

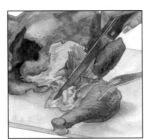

1. To remove one leg, pull drumstick away from the body and cut between the thigh and the body. Cut through the joint that connects the thighbone to back. Repeat with the other leg. To separate each thigh from each drumstick, cut through joint that connects the thigh to drumstick.

2. Remove the wings by cutting through the joints where the wing bones are attached to the back. Carve the breast meat into thin slices. (The slices still will be attached at the bottom.)

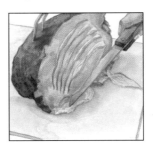

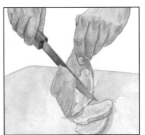

3. Loosen the breast meat slices by making a cut horizontally into the breast. To serve the remainder of the breast, cut smaller slices following the arc of the breastbone on each side of the bird.

4. If you want to slice the meat from the drumsticks, hold the drumstick upright, large end down. Slice the meat parallel to the bone, working the knife under the tendons. Rotate the leg, as necessary to get even slices.

THANKSGIVING DINNER

*A*lthough Thanksgiving was celebrated by the Pilgrims, it wasn't until 1789 that President Washington declared the first nationwide celebration, and not until 1863 that President Lincoln made it a national holiday. Since then, Americans have passed on the spirit of Thanksgiving Day to their children and grandchildren by "giving thanks" with an elaborate meal. This year, add a historical touch to your traditional dinner by serving a colonial fruit drink called a shrub or an old-time hot mulled cider. They're the perfect prelude to a truly old-fashioned Thanksgiving feast.

Thanksgiving Dinner
(For 12)

Sparkling Cranberry Shrub and/or Mulled Cranberry Cider
(Opposite)

Farm-Fresh Marinated Vegetables
(Page 27)

Holiday Roast Turkey with
Old-Fashioned Corn Bread Stuffing
(Page 176)

Cranberry Relish in Orange Cups
(Page 270)

Candied Yams and Apples
(Page 262)

Green Beans with Onion
(Page 242)

Nutty Crescents
(Page 312)

Spicy Pumpkin Chiffon Pie
(Page 336)

Apple Cider Pie
(Page 331)

SPARKLING CRANBERRY SHRUB

Shrubs served in colonial days were fruit-based drinks liberally spiked with brandy or rum. Today, cooks usually leave the spirits out so they can enjoy the refreshing taste of the fruit.

  4 **cups (2 pints) raspberry sherbet, softened**
  3 **cups cranberry juice cocktail**
 ¼ **cup lemon juice**
  3 **cups chilled ginger ale (24 ounces)**

1. Spoon half of the sherbet into a blender. Pour in half of the cranberry juice and half of the lemon juice. Process until smooth. Pour into 6 glasses. Repeat with remaining sherbet, remaining cranberry juice, and remaining lemon juice.

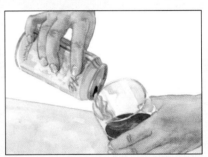

2. Carefully pour some of the ginger ale down the side of each glass. Stir to muddle slightly. Makes twelve 6-ounce servings.

MULLED CRANBERRY CIDER

Cider was a favorite of early American settlers. It often was served mulled, which means heated with sugar and spices. The children enjoyed theirs fresh or "sweet," while the adults drank "hard" or fermented cider.

  8 **cups (2 quarts) cranberry juice cocktail**
  3 **cups frozen unsweetened red raspberries, thawed and slightly mashed**
  6 **cinnamon sticks, each 3 inches long**
1½ **teaspoons whole cloves**
  1 **vanilla bean, split**
  4 **cups (1 quart) apple cider, at room temperature**

1. In a large saucepan, bring the cranberry juice, raspberries, cinnamon sticks, cloves, and vanilla bean to a boil over high heat. Lower the heat and simmer, uncovered, for 15 minutes.

2. Strain through a tea strainer or a sieve lined with 100% cotton cheesecloth into a large heat-proof pitcher. Carefully pour in cider. Stir gently. Makes twelve 8-ounce servings.

Turkey Pot Pie

Turkey Pot Pie

*When it came to making turkey or chicken pot pies, grandma's
rule was—anything goes. Some grandmas topped their pies with
dumplings. Others used pastry as in this recipe.*

1½ **pounds turkey tenderloin steaks, cut into 1-inch
pieces**
1 **large potato, peeled and cubed**
2 **medium-size carrots, sliced**
1 **medium-size yellow onion, halved and thinly sliced**
½ **cup water**
¼ **teaspoon salt**

1 **can (12 ounces) evaporated skimmed milk**
⅓ **cup all-purpose flour**
1 **teaspoon dried thyme leaves**
¼ **teaspoon each salt and white or black pepper**
1 **store-bought or homemade pie crust (page 337)**
   Low-fat (1% milkfat) milk

1 Rinse turkey; drain and pat dry. In a large saucepan, place the turkey, potato, carrots, onion, water, and ¼ teaspoon salt. Bring to a boil. Lower the heat and simmer, covered, for 15 minutes or until the turkey is cooked through. Drain, reserving the cooking liquid.

2 Preheat the oven to 350°F. In the same saucepan, whisk together the evaporated skimmed milk, flour, thyme, ¼ teaspoon salt, and pepper. Stir in the reserved cooking liquid. Cook over moderate heat, whisking constantly, until the mixture starts to thicken. Cook and whisk for 2 minutes more or until thickened and bubbly. Stir in the turkey mixture.

3 Spoon the turkey mixture into a lightly greased 2-quart casserole. Place the pie crust on top of mixture in casserole (tip, below). Trim to 1 inch beyond edge of casserole. Fold under extra crust and crimp edge. Cut slits in crust. Brush with a little milk. Bake for 20 to 25 minutes or until pie crust is golden. Let stand for 5 minutes before serving. Makes 6 servings.

Prep Time: 20 minutes Cooking Time: 25 minutes
Baking Time: 20 minutes Standing Time: 5 minutes

1 Serving: Calories 384. Total Fat 11 g. Saturated Fat 10 g.
Protein 33 g. Carbohydrate 37 g. Fiber 1 g.
Sodium 439 mg. Cholesterol 75 mg.

MOVING PIE CRUST WITH EASE

Positioning rolled-out homemade pie crust on top of a pie can sometimes be tricky. Here's how to move the pie crust without tearing it.

 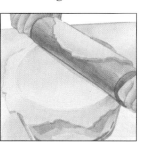

1. Transfer the pie crust to a rolling pin by lifting the edge of the crust over the top of the rolling pin. Then, gently roll up the crust.

2. After positioning the rolling pin at 1 edge of the filled casserole, slowly unroll the crust over the casserole.

Turkey Hash

Chicken hash was one of Thomas Jefferson's favorite breakfast dishes. This version has been adapted so you can use leftover turkey. If you have 2 cups of leftover potatoes, too, chop them and use them in place of the 2 medium potatoes.

2 medium-size potatoes, peeled and chopped
2 tablespoons butter or margarine
1 medium-size yellow onion, chopped
1 small sweet green or red pepper, chopped
2 cups chopped cooked turkey
½ teaspoon dried rosemary leaves
¼ teaspoon black pepper
⅛ teaspoon salt
¼ cup lower-sodium chicken broth (page 67)

1 In a small saucepan, cover potatoes with water. Bring to a boil over high heat. Lower the heat and simmer, covered, for 15 minutes or until potatoes are tender. Drain.

2 In a 10-inch skillet, melt butter over moderate heat. Add the onion and green pepper and cook for 5 minutes or until tender. Stir in potatoes, turkey, rosemary, black pepper, and salt. Cook, stirring constantly, for 5 minutes. Stir in chicken broth. Cook and stir for 2 minutes more or until hash is desired consistency. Makes 3 servings.

Prep Time: 20 minutes Cooking Time: 33 minutes

1 Serving: Calories 365. Total Fat 14 g. Saturated Fat 7 g.
Protein 36 g. Carbohydrate 24 g. Fiber 2 g.
Sodium 253 mg. Cholesterol 107 mg.

Chicken Hash Prepare as for Turkey Hash substituting **2 cups chopped cooked chicken** for the turkey and **¼ cup leftover or canned chicken gravy** for the chicken broth.

1 Serving: Calories 402. Total Fat 17 g. Saturated Fat 7 g.
Protein 36 g. Carbohydrate 25 g. Fiber 2 g.
Sodium 385 mg. Cholesterol 122 mg.

Scalloped Turkey

The earliest scalloped dishes featured poultry, meat, or vegetables baked with bread or cracker crumbs. Later, bread cubes and stuffing mix became popular.

- 2 tablespoons butter or margarine, melted
- 1 teaspoon onion powder
- ½ teaspoon garlic powder
- ½ teaspoon poultry seasoning
- ¼ teaspoon black pepper
- 3 cups home-style white or whole-wheat bread cubes
- 1½ cups lower-sodium chicken broth (page 67)
- 2 tablespoons all-purpose flour
- 1 teaspoon dried marjoram leaves
- ¼ teaspoon salt
- ⅛ teaspoon black pepper
- 3 large eggs, lightly beaten
- 2 cups chopped cooked turkey breast or chicken breast
- 1 jar (2½ ounces) sliced mushrooms, drained

1 Preheat the oven to 375°F. In a small bowl, combine melted butter, onion powder, garlic powder, poultry seasoning, and ¼ teaspoon pepper. In a large bowl, toss the bread cubes with the butter mixture. Spread the mixture in a large shallow baking pan. Bake for 10 minutes or until the bread cubes are toasted, stirring often. Reduce the oven temperature to 325°F.

2 Meanwhile, in a medium-size saucepan, whisk together the broth, flour, marjoram, salt, and ⅛ teaspoon pepper. Cook over moderate heat, whisking constantly, until mixture starts to thicken. Cook and whisk for 2 minutes more or until thickened. In a small bowl, slowly stir about ½ cup of the chicken broth mixture into the eggs, then return this mixture to the saucepan. Cook, whisking constantly, for 2 minutes or until mixture is thickened (do not boil).

3 Spread half of the bread cubes in a lightly greased 8" x 8" x 2" baking dish. Top with the turkey and mushrooms, then with the remaining bread cubes. Pour chicken broth mixture over all. Bake, covered, for 25 minutes. Uncover and bake for 5 minutes more or until a knife inserted near center comes out clean. Makes 4 servings.

Prep Time: 15 minutes Cooking Time: 40 minutes

1 Serving: Calories 292. Total Fat 11 g. Saturated Fat 5 g.
Protein 29 g. Carbohydrate 17 g. Fiber 1 g.
Sodium 447 mg. Cholesterol 236 mg.

Turkey Loaf with Mushroom Sauce

In the days when serving turkey was considered a splurge, women made this comforting dish to use up the precious leftovers.

For the turkey loaf:
- 2 cups finely chopped cooked turkey or chicken
- 1 cup fresh bread crumbs
- 2 tablespoons chopped drained canned pimientos
- ½ teaspoon celery seed
- ½ teaspoon salt
- ⅛ teaspoon white or black pepper
- ¾ cup low-fat (1% milkfat) milk
- 2 large egg whites
- 1 large egg

For the mushroom sauce:
- 1½ cups sliced fresh mushrooms
- ½ cup lower-sodium chicken broth (page 67)
- 1 can (12 ounces) evaporated skimmed milk
- 3 tablespoons all-purpose flour
- ⅛ teaspoon white or black pepper
- 2 tablespoons minced parsley
- 1 teaspoon lemon juice

1 To prepare the turkey loaf, preheat the oven to 325°F. In a large mixing bowl, combine the turkey, bread crumbs, pimientos, celery seed, salt, and ⅛ teaspoon pepper. Whisk together the milk, egg whites, and egg. Pour over turkey mixture. Mix thoroughly until combined. Press turkey mixture into a lightly greased 8" x 4" x 2" loaf pan. Bake for 45 to 50 minutes or until loaf is set in center.

2 Meanwhile, to prepare the mushroom sauce, in a medium-size saucepan, combine mushrooms and chicken broth. Bring to a boil. Lower heat and simmer, covered, for 1 minute or until mushrooms are tender.

3 In a small bowl, whisk together the evaporated skimmed milk, flour, and ⅛ teaspoon pepper. Add to mushroom mixture. Cook over moderate heat, whisking constantly, until mixture starts to thicken. Cook and whisk for 2 minutes more or until thickened. Stir in parsley and lemon juice. Serve mushroom sauce over turkey loaf. Makes 4 servings.

Prep Time: 20 minutes Cooking Time: 45 minutes

1 Serving: Calories 311. Total Fat 8 g. Saturated Fat 2 g.
Protein 34 g. Carbohydrate 25 g. Fiber 1 g.
Sodium 551 mg. Cholesterol 121 mg.

Turkey Tetrazzini

Turkey Tetrazzini

*This dish was first made in a restaurant using chicken and was named for an
opera star of the 1890's, Luisa Tetrazzini. Over the years, countless cooks made the
dish at home resulting in numerous delicious recipes, like this turkey version.*

- 6 ounces spaghetti
- 1 can (12 ounces) evaporated skimmed milk
- ½ cup low-fat (1% milkfat) milk
- 2 tablespoons all-purpose flour
- 1 teaspoon lower-sodium Worcestershire sauce
- ¼ teaspoon each salt and white or black pepper
- ½ cup shredded Cheddar cheese (2 ounces)
- 2 cups chopped cooked turkey breast or chicken breast
- 1 jar (2½ ounces) sliced mushrooms, drained
- 2 tablespoons chopped drained canned pimientos (optional)
- ⅓ cup fresh bread crumbs
- ¼ cup grated Parmesan cheese

1 Preheat the oven to 350°F. Cook spaghetti according to package directions; drain and keep warm.

2 Meanwhile, in a medium-size saucepan, whisk together evaporated skimmed milk, low-fat milk, flour, Worcestershire sauce, salt, and pepper. Cook over moderate heat, whisking constantly, until the mixture starts to thicken. Cook and whisk for 2 minutes more or until thickened. Stir in the Cheddar cheese until melted. Stir in turkey, mushrooms, and pimientos (if using).

3 Place half of the spaghetti into a lightly greased 2-quart casserole. Top with half of the turkey mixture. Repeat layers. In a small bowl, combine the bread crumbs and Parmesan cheese. Sprinkle bread crumb mixture over casserole. Bake, uncovered, for 30 minutes or until heated through. Makes 4 servings.

Prep Time: 15 minutes Cooking Time: 40 minutes

1 Serving: Calories 458. Total Fat 9 g. Saturated Fat 5 g.
Protein 41 g. Carbohydrate 51 g. Fiber 2 g.
Sodium 569 mg. Cholesterol 84 mg.

Turkey Club Sandwich

Turkey Club Sandwich

There are two theories on how this perennial sandwich favorite got its name.
Some say it was dubbed a club sandwich because it was served in club cars of trains.
Others insist it was because the double-decker was a must on country club menus.

4 **strips lean bacon, halved**

12 **slices home-style white or whole-wheat sandwich bread, toasted**

½ **cup reduced-fat mayonnaise**

8 **lettuce leaves**

1 **large tomato, thinly sliced**

8 **ounces thinly sliced cooked turkey breast or chicken breast**

8 **tiny sweet pickles (optional)**

8 **pimiento-stuffed green olives (optional)**

1 In a 10-inch skillet, cook bacon over moderate heat until crisp. Drain on paper towels; set aside.

2 Spread 1 side of each bread slice with some of the mayonnaise. Place a lettuce leaf on the mayonnaise side of 4 bread slices. Top each with some of the sliced tomato and 2 half-strips bacon. Add another slice of bread, mayonnaise side up. Top with remaining lettuce leaves. Divide turkey among sandwiches. Top with remaining bread slices, mayonnaise side down.

3 Cut sandwiches in half diagonally. Thread a pickle and an olive (if using) onto each of 8 wooden picks. Poke a pick into each sandwich half. Makes 4 servings.

Prep Time: 15 minutes Cooking Time: 5 minutes

1 Serving: Calories 400. Total Fat 13 g. Saturated Fat 3 g.
Protein 26 g. Carbohydrate 45 g. Fiber 2 g.
Sodium 700 mg. Cholesterol 62 mg.

Turkey Salad Sandwiches

This turkey salad is made the old-fashioned way—by grinding the meat, instead of cutting it into bite-size pieces. This makes the filling easier to spread and less messy to eat.

2 cups ground cooked turkey or chicken
1 can (8 ounces) crushed pineapple packed in juice, drained
¼ cup finely chopped almonds, toasted
¼ cup finely chopped celery
¼ cup reduced-fat mayonnaise
2 tablespoons reduced-fat sour cream
1 teaspoon lemon juice
¼ teaspoon salt
12 slices home-style white or whole-wheat bread
6 lettuce leaves

1 In a medium-size bowl, combine turkey, pineapple, almonds, celery, mayonnaise, sour cream, lemon juice, and salt. Spread the turkey mixture on half of the bread slices. Top with the lettuce leaves and the remaining bread slices. Makes 6 servings.

Prep Time: 20 minutes

1 Serving: Calories 297. Total Fat 10 g. Saturated Fat 2 g.
Protein 19 g. Carbohydrate 33 g. Fiber 2 g.
Sodium 451 mg. Cholesterol 40 mg.

Roast Goose with Currant Stuffing

A goose gives off more fat during roasting than most other poultry. So have a bulb baster ready to draw off the drippings.

1 large yellow onion, chopped
1 large tart apple, chopped
¼ cup lower-sodium chicken broth (page 67)
6 cups toasted fresh bread crumbs
½ cup currants or chopped raisins
¼ cup slivered almonds, toasted
¼ cup minced parsley
1 teaspoon dried sage leaves
¼ teaspoon each salt and black pepper
⅓ cup lower-sodium chicken broth (page 67)
1 goose (7 to 8 pounds), giblets removed

1 In a small saucepan, combine the onion, apple, and ¼ cup broth. Bring to a boil. Lower heat and simmer for 5 minutes or until onion and apple are tender.

2 In large mixing bowl, combine onion mixture, bread crumbs, currants, almonds, parsley, sage, salt, and pepper. Toss ⅓ cup broth with bread crumb mixture.

3 Preheat the oven to 350°F. Rinse goose; drain and pat dry. Prick the skin on the lower breast, legs, and around the wings with a skewer. Stuff and truss goose (tip, below). Then, place goose, breast-side-up, on a rack in large roasting pan. Insert a roasting thermometer in its thigh without touching bone. Spoon remaining stuffing into a lightly greased 1½-quart casserole; cover and refrigerate.

4 Roast goose for 2 to 2½ hours or until the thermometer registers 175°F., draining fat often. Bake the covered casserole of stuffing alongside the goose during the last 30 minutes of roasting. Let the goose stand for 15 to 20 minutes. Carve goose, discarding the skin. Makes 6 servings.

Prep Time: 20 minutes Cooking Time: 8 minutes
Roasting Time: 2 hours Standing Time: 15 minutes

1 Serving: Calories 673. Total Fat 28 g. Saturated Fat 9 g.
Protein 64 g. Carbohydrate 41 g. Fiber 3 g.
Sodium 467 mg. Cholesterol 319 mg.

TRUSSING POULTRY

 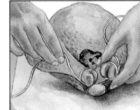

1. Start by spooning some of the stuffing loosely into the neck cavity. Pull the neck skin over the opening and secure it with a small skewer.

2. Next, spoon more stuffing into the body cavity. If there's a band of skin that crosses tail, slip ends of the drumsticks under it. If not, tie drumsticks together with cotton string. Finally, tuck the wing tips under the back.

Smothered Pheasant

Years ago, birds of all kinds were "smothered" under a thick sauce. Jeanette Davidson remembers her Grandmother Fanny Gunlack's chicken recipe. "Steaming hot and covered in a rich cream sauce—my gosh," she exclaims. "It was good!"

6 tablespoons all-purpose flour
¾ teaspoon salt
⅛ teaspoon black pepper
1 ready-to-cook pheasant or broiler-fryer chicken (2½ to 3 pounds), skin and wing tips removed and quartered
1 tablespoon vegetable oil
1 large yellow onion, halved lengthwise and sliced
1 cup lower-sodium chicken broth (page 67)
1 tablespoon butter or margarine
1½ cups sliced fresh mushrooms
¼ teaspoon black pepper
1 can (12 ounces) evaporated skimmed milk
Paprika

1 On a sheet of wax paper, combine 3 tablespoons of the flour, ¼ teaspoon of the salt, and the ⅛ teaspoon pepper. Rinse pheasant; drain and pat dry. Coat the pheasant pieces with flour mixture (tip, above right). In a 12-inch nonstick skillet, heat the oil over moderately high heat. Brown the pheasant pieces in hot oil for 10 minutes or until golden, turning occasionally. Arrange the onion slices over pheasant. Pour the chicken broth into the skillet. Bring to a boil. Lower the heat and simmer, covered, about 30 minutes or until the pheasant is cooked through.

2 Meanwhile, in a medium-size saucepan, melt the butter over moderate heat. Add the mushrooms and cook for 3 minutes or until tender. Stir in the remaining 3 tablespoons flour, the remaining ½ teaspoon salt, and the ¼ teaspoon pepper. Cook for 1 minute or until bubbly. Add the evaporated skimmed milk. Cook, stirring constantly, until mixture starts to thicken. Cook and stir for 2 minutes more or until thickened. Serve the mushroom mixture over pheasant and onion. Sprinkle with paprika. Makes 4 servings.

Prep Time: 20 minutes Cooking Time: 41 minutes

1 Serving: Calories 371. Total Fat 12 g. Saturated Fat 4 g.
Protein 42 g. Carbohydrate 22 g. Fiber 1 g.
Sodium 581 mg. Cholesterol 104 mg.

FLOURING POULTRY

Coating pheasant or other poultry with a thin layer of seasoned flour adds flavor, preserves moistness, and aids in browning. Simply roll the pieces, one at a time, in the flour mixture. Make sure each piece is completely covered, patting on more of the flour mixture as necessary.

Salmi of Duck

Salmi is an old-fashioned word for a hearty stew made with game, wine, and butter.

1 ready-to-cook duck (4 to 4½ pounds), skin and wing tips removed and quartered
2 tablespoons butter or margarine
2 tablespoons all-purpose flour
1½ teaspoons dried thyme leaves
¼ teaspoon salt
⅛ teaspoon ground cloves
⅛ teaspoon black pepper
¾ cup lower-sodium beef broth (page 67)
½ cup dry red wine or lower-sodium beef broth (page 67)

1 Preheat the oven to 375°F. Rinse duck; drain and pat dry. In a 12-inch nonstick skillet, melt butter over moderate heat. Brown the duck in hot butter for 10 minutes or until golden, turning occasionally. Transfer duck to lightly greased 9" x 9" x 2" baking dish.

2 Whisk flour, thyme, salt, cloves, and pepper into drippings in skillet. Cook for 1 minute or until bubbly. Whisk in beef broth and wine. Cook, whisking constantly, until mixture starts to thicken. Cook and whisk for 2 minutes more or until thickened. Pour mixture over duck pieces. Bake, covered, for 50 to 60 minutes or until duck is cooked through. Skim fat. Serve duck and wine mixture over hot cooked rice. Makes 4 servings.

Prep Time: 15 minutes Cooking Time: 1 hour 5 minutes

1 Serving: Calories 304. Total Fat 18 g. Saturated Fat 8 g.
Protein 26 g. Carbohydrate 4 g. Fiber 0 g.
Sodium 265 mg. Cholesterol 111 mg.

Grandma's Treats

Cock-a-Doodle-Do Bake

8 chicken legs
  (1¾ pounds)

⅓ cup all-purpose flour

1 teaspoon dried
  Italian seasoning

1 tablespoon vegetable
  oil

1 cup spaghetti sauce

1. Preheat the oven to 375°F. Remove and discard chicken skin. Rinse legs; drain. Pat dry. On a sheet of wax paper, combine flour and Italian seasoning. Coat legs with flour mixture.

2. In a 10-inch nonstick skillet, heat the oil over moderately high heat. Brown legs in hot oil for 10 minutes or until golden, turning occasionally.

3. Arrange legs in a lightly greased 8" x 8" x 2" baking dish. Pour spaghetti sauce over legs. Bake, covered, for 30 to 35 minutes or until legs are cooked through. Serve with grated Parmesan cheese. Makes 4 to 8 servings.

Chicken and Cheese Subs

With this easy recipe, youngsters can have subs just like from a sandwich shop.

2 tablespoons reduced-fat mayonnaise

1 teaspoon prepared mustard

4 white French rolls, each 6 inches long

4 lettuce leaves

6 ounces thinly sliced cooked chicken

4 slices (¾ ounce each) reduced-fat American cheese

4 slices (¾ ounce each) reduced-fat process Swiss cheese

12 slices sweet or dill pickle

1. In a small bowl, combine the mayonnaise and mustard. Split French rolls and spread with mustard mixture.

2. Top each roll bottom with a lettuce leaf, some of the chicken, a slice of American cheese, and a slice of Swiss cheese. Arrange 3 pickle slices on each sandwich. Top with roll top. Serves 4.

Henny Penny Pockets

1 cup chopped cooked chicken

¼ cup reduced-fat sour cream

¼ cup shredded reduced-fat Cheddar cheese (1 ounce)

⅛ teaspoon garlic powder

  Dash black pepper

1 package (10 ounces) refrigerated biscuits

1 large egg white, lightly beaten

1. Preheat the oven to 400°F. In a medium-size bowl, combine the chicken, sour cream, Cheddar cheese, garlic powder, and pepper.

2. Press or roll each biscuit to a 4-inch circle on a lightly floured surface. Spoon 1 rounded tablespoon of the chicken mixture on 1 side of each circle. Brush water on the edges of circles. Fold each biscuit over chicken mixture, forming a semi-circle. Use a fork to crimp the edges. Brush with egg white.

3. Place on a lightly greased baking sheet. Bake for 8 to 10 minutes or until golden. Makes 10.

Chicken Littles

Kids of all ages will love these crispy chip-coated miniature drumsticks.

16 chicken drummettes

⅔ cup crushed potato chips

½ teaspoon chili powder

¼ teaspoon onion powder

⅛ teaspoon black pepper

2 tablespoons butter or margarine, melted

1. Preheat the broiler. Remove and discard chicken skin. Rinse chicken; drain and pat dry. On a sheet of wax paper, combine the potato chips, chili powder, onion powder, and pepper. Dip chicken in melted butter, then coat with potato chip mixture. Place in a lightly greased baking pan.

2. Broil 3 inches from heat for 3 minutes. Turn and broil 3 to 5 minutes more or until chicken is cooked through. Makes 4 to 8 servings.

FROM OCEAN & LAKE

When it came to cooking the catch of the day, grandma knew dozens of ways. She would fry cornmeal-coated catfish, roll pike fillets around bread stuffing, wrap salmon in pastry, or dress-up broiled scrod with lemon and butter. When shellfish were plentiful, she simmered sole, scallops, and lobster for bouillabaisse; whisked together shrimp pie; sautéed scampi in wine; and stirred up a roux to season crab or shrimp gumbo. Try these old-fashioned recipes and rediscover how good home-cooked seafood can be.

Minnesota Stuffed Fish (page 190)
Scampi in White Wine (page 204)
Fish Fillets with Fresh Tomato Sauce (page 196)

189

Minnesota Stuffed Fish

*Polish women who settled in Minnesota,
traditionally served this hearty bread, mushroom,
and apple stuffing with Northern Pike.
However, it's also superb with whitefish, cod,
orange roughy, or red snapper.*

1 **drawn fresh or frozen and thawed pike, whitefish, cod, orange roughy, or red snapper (about 4 pounds)**

2 **tablespoons butter or margarine**

1 **large yellow onion, chopped**

1 **stalk celery, sliced**

1 **teaspoon dried thyme leaves**

½ **teaspoon salt**

¼ **teaspoon black pepper**

6 **slices home-style white bread, toasted and cut into cubes (4 cups)**

1 **medium-size tart cooking apple, peeled and chopped**

1 **jar (2½ ounces) sliced mushrooms, drained**

⅓ **to ⅔ cup lower-sodium chicken broth (page 67)**

1 **tablespoon butter or margarine, melted**

1 Preheat the oven to 350°F. Rinse fish and pat dry. In a large skillet, melt the 2 tablespoons butter over moderate heat. Add the onion and celery and cook for 5 minutes or until onion is tender. Stir in the thyme, salt, and pepper. In a large bowl, combine bread cubes, apple, and mushrooms. Stir in onion mixture. Drizzle with enough of the broth to moisten, tossing lightly.

2 To stuff the fish, fill the cavity with bread mixture, lightly patting to flatten evenly. (If all of the mixture does not fit into fish, place remaining in a covered casserole and refrigerate.) Tie or skewer the fish closed. Place stuffed fish onto a lightly greased, large shallow baking pan. Brush outside of fish with the 1 tablespoon melted butter.

3 Cover the fish loosely with foil. Bake for 50 to 60 minutes or until fish flakes when tested with a fork. Bake the covered casserole of bread mixture alongside the fish during the last 20 to 25 minutes of baking time. Makes 6 servings.

Prep Time: 20 minutes Cooking Time: 56 minutes

1 Serving: Calories 272. Total Fat 8 g. Saturated Fat 4 g.
Protein 31 g. Carbohydrate 18 g. Fiber 2 g.
Sodium 474 mg. Cholesterol 73 mg.

Country Fried Fish

*Many African-American grandmas insisted
that the only way to serve catfish was to coat it
with cornmeal and panfry it, so it turned
out crispy. This modern version is oven-fried to
reduce the fat but still give a crunchy coating.*

½ **cup Tartar Sauce (recipe, right)**

4 **pan-dressed fresh or frozen and thawed catfish or other small fish (8 to 10 ounces each)**

⅓ **cup low-fat (1% milkfat) buttermilk**

1 **large egg white, lightly beaten**

⅓ **cup fine dry bread crumbs**

⅓ **cup yellow or white cornmeal**

½ **teaspoon each paprika and garlic salt**

2 **tablespoons butter or margarine, melted**

1 **tablespoon lemon juice**

1 Prepare Tartar Sauce. Cover and refrigerate while preparing the fish.

2 Preheat the oven to 500°F. Remove and discard fish skin. Rinse fish and pat dry. In a pie plate or shallow dish, combine buttermilk and egg white. In another pie plate or shallow dish, combine bread crumbs, cornmeal, paprika, and garlic salt. Using tongs, dip each fish into egg mixture. Roll in cornmeal mixture to coat well.

3 Place fish on lightly greased wire rack in a large shallow baking pan. In a small bowl, combine butter and lemon juice. Drizzle butter mixture over the fish. Bake for 12 to 14 minutes or until coating is golden and the fish flakes when tested with a fork. Serve with the Tartar Sauce. Makes 4 servings.

Prep Time: 20 minutes Cooking Time: 12 minutes

1 Serving: Calories 408. Total Fat 24 g. Saturated Fat 7 g.
Protein 26 g. Carbohydrate 22 g. Fiber 1 g.
Sodium 697 mg. Cholesterol 90 mg.

Oven-Fried Fish Fillets Prepare as for Country Fried Fish, substituting **1½ pounds fresh or frozen and thawed catfish or other fish fillets (½ to 1 inch thick)** for the pan-dressed catfish and **⅔ cup crushed lower-sodium crackers** for the bread crumbs and cornmeal. Separate fillets or cut into 4 serving-size portions. Measure thickness of fish. Coat fillets and bake as above, allowing 8 to 10 minutes per ½-inch thickness of fish.

1 Serving: Calories 466. Total Fat 27 g. Saturated Fat 8 g.
Protein 29 g. Carbohydrate 25 g. Fiber 1 g.
Sodium 793 mg. Cholesterol 99 mg.

Tartar Sauce

In a medium-size bowl, combine **1 cup reduced-fat mayonnaise**, ¼ **cup finely chopped dill pickle or dill pickle relish**, **1 finely chopped large green onion with top**, **1 tablespoon drained capers**, **1 teaspoon Dijon mustard**, ½ **teaspoon dried thyme leaves**, and **dash ground red pepper (cayenne)**. Cover and refrigerate (will keep for 1 week). Makes about 1¼ cups (ten 2-tablespoon servings).

1 Serving: Calories 60. Total Fat 5 g. Saturated Fat 1 g.
Protein 0 g. Carbohydrate 4 g. Fiber 0 g.
Sodium 202 mg. Cholesterol 6 mg.

Halibut with Egg Sauce

In the early days, halibut were so plentiful that fishermen along the Eastern shore considered them a nuisance. Cooks dressed up the bland fish with a delicious parslied egg sauce.

4 **fresh or frozen and thawed halibut, salmon, shark, or swordfish steaks, 1 inch thick (about 8 ounces each)**
1 **tablespoon butter or margarine, melted**
1 **tablespoon lemon juice**
½ **teaspoon garlic powder**
¼ **teaspoon salt**
⅛ **teaspoon black pepper**
   Egg Sauce (recipe, right)

1 Preheat the broiler. Rinse fish and pat dry. In a small bowl, combine the butter, lemon juice, garlic powder, salt, and pepper.

2 Arrange fish on lightly greased rack of broiler pan. Brush fish with half of the butter mixture. Broil 5 inches from the heat for 5 minutes. Using a wide spatula, carefully turn fish over. Brush with remaining butter mixture. Broil 5 to 7 minutes more or until fish flakes when tested with a fork. Serve with Egg Sauce. Makes 4 servings.

Prep Time: 10 minutes Cooking Time: 10 minutes

1 Serving: Calories 348. Total Fat 14 g. Saturated Fat 5 g.
Protein 48 g. Carbohydrate 6 g. Fiber 0 g.
Sodium 384 mg. Cholesterol 191 mg.

Halibut with Egg Sauce

Egg Sauce

In a medium-size saucepan, whisk together ½ **cup half-and-half**, **2 tablespoons all-purpose flour**, ½ **teaspoon dry mustard**, and ⅛ **teaspoon each salt and black pepper**. Whisk in ½ **cup lower-sodium chicken broth (page 67)**. Cook over moderate heat, whisking constantly, for 7 minutes or until mixture is thickened and bubbly. Stir in **2 chopped hard-cooked large eggs** and **1 tablespoon minced parsley**; heat through. Makes about 1½ cups (about four ⅓-cup servings).

1 Serving: Calories 96. Total Fat 6 g. Saturated Fat 3 g.
Protein 5 g. Carbohydrate 5 g. Fiber 0 g.
Sodium 111 mg. Cholesterol 117 mg.

Poached Salmon with Dill Sauce

Poached Salmon with Dill Sauce

Years ago, salmon was frequently simmered in a lightly flavored broth mixture, called a court bouillon, which kept the fish sweet and moist. This classic cooking technique fits right in with today's lighter eating.

4 **fresh or frozen and thawed salmon or halibut steaks,**
  ³/₄ inch thick (about 6 ounces each)

1 **cup dry white wine or lower-sodium chicken**
  broth (page 67)

1 **small yellow onion, thickly sliced**

2 **lemon slices**

4 **sprigs parsley**

4 **whole black peppercorns**

For the dill sauce:

1 **tablespoon butter or margarine**

1 **tablespoon all-purpose flour**

2 **teaspoons finely chopped fresh dill or ³/₄ teaspoon**
  dried dill weed

½ **teaspoon sugar**

⅛ **teaspoon salt**

1 **large egg yolk, lightly beaten**

1 **teaspoon lemon juice**

1 Rinse fish and pat dry. To poach the fish, in a large skillet, combine the wine, onion, lemon slices, parsley, and peppercorns. Bring to a boil. Arrange the salmon in a single layer in the wine mixture. Bring to a boil. Lower the heat and simmer, covered, for 5 to 8 minutes or until the fish flakes when tested with a fork. Use a slotted spatula to carefully remove the salmon from the skillet; keep warm. Strain and reserve 1 cup of the cooking liquid.

2 To prepare the dill sauce, in a small saucepan, melt the butter over moderate heat. Whisk in the flour, dill, sugar, and salt and cook for 1 minute or until bubbly. Add the reserved cooking liquid. Cook, whisking constantly, until the mixture starts to thicken. Slowly stir about ½ cup of the hot mixture into the egg yolk, then return this mixture to the saucepan. Cook, stirring constantly, for 1 to 2 minutes or until the mixture thickens (do not boil). Stir in the lemon juice.

3 Spoon some of the dill sauce over the salmon. Pass the remaining sauce. Makes 4 servings.

Prep Time: 10 minutes Cooking Time: 15 minutes

1 Serving: Calories 350. Total Fat 17 g. Saturated Fat 4 g.
Protein 33 g. Carbohydrate 4 g. Fiber 0 g.
Sodium 178 mg. Cholesterol 163 mg.

Salmon Coulibiac

*This pastry-wrapped salmon was considered
the height of chic in the 1950's. Serve it warm as
the centerpiece for a buffet. Or, chill the coulibiac
and serve it for a picnic with sour cream.*

For the filling:

2 **cups sliced fresh mushrooms**

1 **cup sliced leek or 8 large green onions with
  tops, sliced**

¼ **cup water**

3 **hard-cooked large eggs, yolks discarded**

1 **cup cooked long-grain white rice**

¼ **cup minced parsley**

1 **teaspoon dried dill weed**

¼ **teaspoon each salt and black pepper**

1 **can (14¾ ounces) salmon, picked through, rinsed,
  drained, and flaked**

For the pastry:

1 **package (17¼ ounces) frozen puff pastry
  sheets, thawed 20 minutes**

2 **large egg whites, lightly beaten**

1 **tablespoon water**

1 Preheat the oven to 400°F. To prepare the filling, in a large saucepan, combine mushrooms, leek, and the ¼ cup water; cook, covered, for 5 minutes or until leek is tender. Drain well. Chop the hard-cooked egg whites. Stir the chopped egg whites, the rice, parsley, dill weed, salt, and pepper into the mushroom mixture. Carefully add the salmon. Toss to mix.

2 To prepare the pastry, on a lightly floured surface, roll 1 sheet of the puff pastry into a 14x10-inch rectangle. Place onto a foil-lined 15" x 10" x 1" baking pan. Roll remaining sheet of puff pastry into a 12x8-inch rectangle. Cut slits in top of pastry or prick with a fork for escape of steam; set aside. Combine beaten egg whites and the 1 tablespoon water; brush a little of the egg white mixture over pastry on baking pan. Spread filling over pastry (tip, right).

3 Moisten edges of pastry on baking pan with egg white mixture; place second rectangle of pastry over filling. Overlap edges of pastry (tip, right). Using a fork,

press the edges together to seal. Brush pastry lightly with egg white mixture. Bake for 20 to 25 minutes or until the pastry is golden. Makes 6 servings.

Prep Time: 25 minutes Cooking Time: 25 minutes

1 Serving: Calories 472. Total Fat 26 g. Saturated Fat 1 g.
Protein 17 g. Carbohydrate 42 g. Fiber 1 g.
Sodium 744 mg. Cholesterol 17 mg.

Old-World Coulibiac Prepare as for Salmon Coulibiac, but omit the canned salmon and poach **1 pound fresh or frozen and thawed salmon fillets or steaks, ¾ inch thick,** as follows. Rinse fish and pat dry. In a large skillet, combine **1 cup lower-sodium chicken broth (page 67); 1 small carrot, sliced; 1 small yellow onion, thickly sliced; 1 stalk celery, sliced; 4 whole black peppercorns;** and **2 bay leaves.** Bring to a boil. Arrange the fish in a single layer in the broth mixture. Return to a boil. Lower the heat and simmer, covered, for 5 to 8 minutes or until the fish flakes when tested with a fork. Use a slotted spatula to carefully remove fish from skillet; cool. Remove and discard skin and bones. Use a fork to flake fish. Prepare filling and pastry and bake as directed in Salmon Coulibiac.

1 Serving: Calories 598. Total Fat 28 g. Saturated Fat 1 g.
Protein 26 g. Carbohydrate 59 g. Fiber 2 g.
Sodium 573 mg. Cholesterol 32 mg.

ASSEMBLING COULIBIAC

 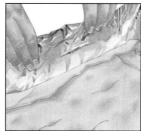

1. Spoon the salmon filling down the center of the pastry. Evenly spread the filling to within 1 inch of the edges of the pastry.

2. Holding onto the foil on 1 side of the pastry, lift the foil until the edge of the bottom pastry overlaps the edge of the top pastry. Repeat on the 3 remaining sides.

Fish Steaks Teriyaki

Fish Steaks Teriyaki

*Japanese immigrants to the West Coast introduced Americans to teriyaki
sauce. If you want to grill—rather than broil—the steaks, use a grill basket to
make turning the fish easy. If you don't have one, place a piece of lightly
greased heavy foil over the grill rack and make slits, so the fat will drain away.
When it's time to turn the fish, use tongs or a metal spatula.*

**4 fresh or frozen and thawed halibut, shark, or
swordfish steaks, 1 inch thick (about 8 ounces each)**

For the marinade:

¼ cup water

¼ cup lower-sodium soy sauce

**¼ cup dry sherry or lower-sodium chicken broth
(page 67)**

1 tablespoon sugar

2 teaspoons dry mustard

1 teaspoon ground ginger

3 cloves garlic, minced

1 Rinse fish and pat dry. To prepare the marinade, in
a jar with a tight-fitting lid, combine the water, soy
sauce, dry sherry, sugar, mustard, ginger, and garlic.
Cover; shake well. Pour marinade into a large heavy-
duty plastic bag. Add fish. Close bag. Refrigerate for
2 to 3 hours, turning bag occasionally.

2 Preheat the broiler. Drain fish, reserving marinade.
Arrange fish on lightly greased rack of a broiler pan.
Brush fish with reserved marinade. Broil 5 inches from
the heat for 5 minutes. Using a wide spatula, carefully
turn fish over. Brush with reserved marinade. Broil 5 to
7 minutes more or until fish flakes when tested with a
fork. Makes 4 servings.

Prep Time: 10 minutes Chilling Time: 2 hours
Cooking Time: 10 minutes

1 Serving: Calories 251. Total Fat 6 g. Saturated Fat 1 g.
Protein 44 g. Carbohydrate 7 g. Fiber 0 g.
Sodium 622 mg. Cholesterol 66 mg.

Citrusy Sole

Traditional fish dishes were often quite simple, using just fresh herbs and citrus to enhance, not overpower, the delicate fish.

1½ **pounds fresh or frozen and thawed sole, flounder, orange roughy, or haddock fillets, ¼ to ½ inch thick**

½ **cup orange juice**

2 **large green onions with tops, thinly sliced**

2 **tablespoons minced parsley**

2 **tablespoons lemon or lime juice**

1 **teaspoon dried tarragon leaves**

1 **teaspoon grated orange rind**

1 **teaspoon grated lemon or lime rind**

¼ **teaspoon salt**

  Paprika

1 Rinse fish and pat dry. In a jar with a tight-fitting lid, combine orange juice, green onions, parsley, lemon juice, tarragon, orange rind, lemon rind, and salt. Cover; shake well. Pour juice mixture into large heavy-duty plastic bag. Add the fish. Close the bag; refrigerate for 6 hours or overnight, turning the bag occasionally.

2 Preheat broiler. Drain fish, reserving juice mixture. Place fish on lightly greased rack of a broiler pan. Tuck under thin edges of fillets. Broil 5 inches from heat for 3 to 6 minutes or until fish flakes when tested with a fork, brushing once with juice mixture. Sprinkle generously with paprika. Serves 4.

Prep Time: 15 minutes Chilling Time: 6 hours
Cooking Time: 3 minutes

1 Serving: Calories 156. Total Fat 2 g. Saturated Fat 0 g.
Protein 29 g. Carbohydrate 5 g. Fiber 0 g.
Sodium 258 mg. Cholesterol 80 mg.

Yankee Scrod

From Maine to Connecticut, Yankees prized the sweet, succulent scrod, which are young cod weighing about 1½ to 2 pounds each. If they're not available in your area, substitute flounder or perch.

1½ **pounds fresh or frozen and thawed scrod, flounder, or perch fillets, 1 inch thick**

2 **tablespoons lemon juice**

1 **tablespoon butter or margarine, melted**

1 **teaspoon grated lemon rind**

½ **teaspoon dried thyme leaves**

¼ **teaspoon salt**

⅛ **teaspoon black pepper**

½ **cup fine dry bread crumbs**

1 Preheat the broiler. Rinse the fish and pat dry. In a small bowl, stir together the lemon juice, butter, lemon rind, thyme, salt, and pepper. Set aside.

2 Place the fish on lightly greased rack of a broiler pan. Tuck under thin edges of the fillets. Broil 5 inches from the heat for 5 minutes, brushing twice with the lemon-butter mixture. Turn the fish; brush with the lemon-butter mixture. Broil for 4 minutes. Sprinkle the bread crumbs over the fish. Broil for 1 minute more or until the fish flakes when tested with a fork and the bread crumbs are golden. Serve with hot boiled potatoes. Makes 4 servings.

Prep Time: 10 minutes Cooking Time: 10 minutes

1 Serving: Calories 215. Total Fat 5 g. Saturated Fat 2 g.
Protein 30 g. Carbohydrate 10 g. Fiber 1 g.
Sodium 393 mg. Cholesterol 88 mg.

SHOPPING FOR FISH

For great-tasting fish, begin with the right form so you don't overcook or undercook it. Here's how to be sure to buy fish at the peak of its freshness.

◆ When a recipe calls for a whole fish, it will usually list one of two common forms. The first is the **drawn fish,** which is a fish with only the internal organs removed. The second is the **dressed or pan-dressed fish,** which is a fish with the scales, head, tail, and fins—as well as the internal organs—removed. The term pan-dressed usually is used with smaller fish.

◆ If your recipe uses **fish steaks,** look for crosswise slices from a dressed fish. Steaks usually are cut from large fish.

◆ When you need a **fillet,** buy a boneless, lengthwise slice from the side of a fish.

◆ As you select fish of all forms, follow your nose—fish should smell fresh.

◆ Before you purchase a whole fish, make sure the skin is shiny and taut and the flesh is firm and elastic. The eyes, if present, should be clear, bright, and bulging. The gills should be dry (not slippery) and bright in color.

Fish Fillets with Fresh Tomato Sauce

When grandma made sauces with tomatoes, she often added a pinch of sugar to mellow the bitterness from the seeds.

- 4 **fresh or frozen and thawed sole or flounder fillets, ¼ to ½ inch thick (about 6 ounces each)**
- 1 **teaspoon dried basil leaves**
- ⅛ **teaspoon each salt and black pepper**
- 1 **tablespoon butter or margarine**
- 1 **medium-size yellow onion, chopped**
- 2 **tablespoons finely chopped shallots**
- 3 **cloves garlic, minced**
- 4 **medium-size tomatoes, peeled and chopped (2½ cups)**
- ½ **cup dry white wine or lower-sodium chicken broth (page 67)**
- 1 **teaspoon sugar**
- 1 **tablespoon minced parsley**

1 Rinse fish and pat dry. Sprinkle each fish fillet with the basil, salt, and pepper. Roll up fillets. Secure each roll with toothpicks.

2 In a large skillet, melt butter over moderate heat. Add the onion, shallots, and garlic and cook for 5 minutes or until onion is tender. Gradually stir in the tomatoes and wine. Add the sugar. Bring to a boil. Lower the heat and simmer, uncovered, for 15 minutes.

3 Place fish rolls, seam side down, into tomato mixture. Simmer, covered, for 8 to 10 minutes or until fish flakes when tested with a fork. To serve, carefully remove toothpicks and spoon tomato mixture over fish. Sprinkle with parsley. Serve with hot cooked rice or noodles. Makes 4 servings.

Prep Time: 20 minutes Cooking Time: 34 minutes

1 Serving: Calories 257. Total Fat 6 g. Saturated Fat 2 g. Protein 37 g. Carbohydrate 10 g. Fiber 2 g. Sodium 246 mg. Cholesterol 98 mg.

Broiled Shad With Mushrooms

Dutch settlers roasted shad on a plank of wood, a technique they learned from the Indians. This old recipe has been adapted to the broiler.

- 1½ **pounds fresh or frozen and thawed shad (tip, below left), sole, or flounder fillets, ¼ to ½ inch thick**
- 1 **tablespoon butter or margarine, melted**
- 1 **tablespoon lemon juice**
- 1 **tablespoon finely chopped yellow onion**
- 1 **tablespoon drained prepared horseradish**
- 1 **tablespoon Dijon mustard**
- ¼ **teaspoon salt**
- ⅛ **teaspoon black pepper**
- 1 **tablespoon butter or margarine**
- 2 **cups sliced fresh mushrooms**

1 Preheat the broiler. Rinse fish and pat dry. In a small bowl, stir together 1 tablespoon melted butter, lemon juice, onion, horseradish, Dijon mustard, salt, and pepper.

2 Place the fish on lightly greased rack of a broiler pan. Tuck under thin edges of fillets. Brush with lemon mixture. Broil 5 inches from heat for 3 to 6 minutes or until fish flakes when tested with a fork, brushing once with lemon mixture.

3 Meanwhile, in a medium-size skillet, melt 1 tablespoon butter over moderate heat. Add the mushrooms and cook for 3 minutes or until tender. Serve mushrooms on top of fish. Makes 4 servings.

Prep Time: 10 minutes Cooking Time: 3 minutes

1 Serving: Calories 353. Total Fat 26 g. Saturated Fat 9 g. Protein 26 g. Carbohydrate 3 g. Fiber 1 g. Sodium 365 mg. Cholesterol 122 mg.

LOW-FAT FISH

Different varieties of fish vary significantly in fat content. For example, in the recipe at right, you can save 19 grams of fat per serving by using low-fat sole or flounder instead of the high-fat shad. For easy reference, here's a listing of some low-, moderate-, and high-fat fish.

- **Low-Fat Fish** Catfish, cod, cusk, flounder, grouper, haddock, halibut, monkfish, orange roughy, perch, pike, redfish, red snapper, shark, sole, turbot, and whiting.
- **Moderate-Fat Fish** Carp, mahimahi, pollock, pompano, sea bass, and swordfish.
- **High-Fat Fish** Bluefish, butterfish, mackerel, salmon, shad, trout, tuna, and whitefish.

Broiled Shad with Mushrooms

Fish Packets with Garden Vegetables

Our great grandmothers often cooked fish "en papillote"—meaning in paper—to keep it moist and tender. Although they probably used parchment paper, this recipe calls for more commonly available aluminum foil.

1½ **pounds fresh or frozen and thawed whitefish, haddock, lake trout, or red snapper fillets, ¾ to 1 inch thick**

2 **medium-size carrots, cut into 1½x½-inch sticks**

2 **stalks celery, thinly sliced**

1 **small red onion, thinly sliced and separated into rings**

2 **tablespoons butter or margarine, at room temperature**

1 **tablespoon minced parsley**

1 **tablespoon lemon juice**

¼ **teaspoon salt**

¼ **teaspoon garlic powder**

⅛ **teaspoon ground red pepper (cayenne)**

1 Preheat the oven to 425°F. Rinse fish and pat dry. Cut into 4 serving-size portions. In a medium-size saucepan, bring ½ inch of water to a boil over high heat. Add the carrots, celery, and onion and cook for 3 to 4 minutes or just until tender. Drain well.

2 Lightly grease four 14x12-inch pieces of heavy foil. To assemble fish bundles, place 1 fish portion on each piece of foil, tucking under thin edges of the fillets. In a small bowl, stir together the butter, parsley, lemon juice, salt, garlic powder, and red pepper. Spread butter mixture over fish portions. Top with vegetable mixture, dividing equally among fish portions.

3 Bring the foil up over the fish and close all edges with tight double folds. Place foil packets on a shallow baking pan. Bake for 18 to 20 minutes or until fish flakes when tested with a fork (carefully open foil to check doneness). To serve, place packets on plates. With kitchen shears, open packets by cutting a large X on the top of each, then pull back foil. Eat directly from foil. Serve with sourdough bread. Makes 4 servings.

Prep Time: 20 minutes Cooking Time: 26 minutes

1 Serving: Calories 319. Total Fat 16 g. Saturated Fat 5 g. Protein 34 g. Carbohydrate 8 g. Fiber 2 g. Sodium 312 mg. Cholesterol 121 mg.

German Panned Fish

This old German recipe makes an easy one-dish meal—just add bread and a salad.

1½ **pounds fresh or frozen and thawed flounder, turbot, or orange roughy fillets, ½ to ¾ inch thick**

6 **medium-size potatoes (about 2 pounds total), thinly sliced**

1 **large yellow onion, thinly sliced**

¾ **teaspoon salt**

½ **teaspoon black pepper**

2 **tablespoons olive oil**

For the mustard sauce:

1 **tablespoon butter or margarine**

2 **medium-size green onions with tops, thinly sliced**

2 **tablespoons all-purpose flour**

1⅓ **cups low-fat (1% milkfat) milk**

¼ **cup half-and-half**

2 **tablespoons Dijon mustard**

2 **tablespoons dry Riesling, other dry white wine, or water**

2 **teaspoons lemon juice**

1 Preheat oven to 400°F. Rinse fish; pat dry. Cut into ¾-inch cubes; refrigerate. In large saucepan, cover potatoes with water. Bring to a boil over high heat. Lower heat and simmer, covered, for 5 minutes. Drain.

2 Arrange potatoes and onion slices in lightly greased 13" x 9" x 2" baking pan. Sprinkle with ½ teaspoon of the salt and ¼ teaspoon of the pepper. Drizzle with oil. Toss gently to coat vegetables. Bake, uncovered, for 45 minutes or until potatoes are crisp, turning mixture twice. Gently stir fish into mixture. Bake for 5 to 7 minutes more or until fish flakes when tested with a fork.

3 Meanwhile, in a small saucepan, melt butter over moderately high heat. Cook green onions in butter for 3 minutes or until tender. Stir in the flour, the remaining ¼ teaspoon salt, and the remaining ¼ teaspoon pepper. Cook for 1 minute or until bubbly. Stir in the milk and half-and-half. Cook over moderate heat, stirring constantly, until mixture starts to thicken. Cook and stir for 2 minutes more or until thickened. In small bowl, combine mustard, wine, and lemon juice. Stir into the milk mixture. Serve with fish mixture. Serves 4.

Prep Time: 25 minutes Cooking Time: 1 hour 5 minutes

1 Serving: Calories 471. Total Fat 15 g. Saturated Fat 5 g. Protein 36 g. Carbohydrate 47 g. Fiber 3 g. Sodium 798 mg. Cholesterol 96 mg.

New England Kedgeree

New England Kedgeree

*New England seamen brought this curried fish recipe back
from India. It makes a wonderful supper on a cold, damp night,
served with a green vegetable and chunks of hot, crusty bread.*

½ cup long-grain white rice
1 pound smoked haddock or cod fillets
2 bay leaves
4 whole black peppercorns
1 tablespoon butter or margarine
1 large yellow onion, chopped
1 teaspoon curry powder
¼ teaspoon ground red pepper (cayenne)
2 hard-cooked large eggs, sieved
2 tablespoons minced parsley

1 In a medium-size saucepan, cook the rice according to the package directions, omitting the salt.

2 Meanwhile, in a large nonstick skillet, place fish in a single layer. Cover with cold water. Add bay leaves and peppercorns. Bring to a boil. Lower the heat and simmer, covered, for 8 to 10 minutes or until fish flakes when tested with a fork. Drain fish; discard cooking liquid and seasonings. Cool fish slightly. Remove and discard skin and bones. Use a fork to flake fish. Set aside.

3 In the same skillet, melt butter over moderate heat. Add onion and cook for 5 minutes or until tender. Stir in the curry powder and red pepper. Cook and stir for 1 minute. Stir in the cooked rice and half of the sieved egg. Add fish; gently stir to combine. Heat through, stirring constantly. To serve, sprinkle with the remaining sieved egg and parsley. Makes 4 servings.

Prep Time: 10 minutes Cooking Time: 35 minutes

1 Serving: Calories 304. Total Fat 7 g. Saturated Fat 3 g.
Protein 34 g. Carbohydrate 24 g. Fiber 1 g.
Sodium 929 mg. Cholesterol 201 mg.

Seafood-Stuffed Flounder

Seafood-Stuffed Flounder

*This elegant party dish can be made with either scallops or shrimp. To make sure
your fish rolls look party perfect, choose fish fillets that are uniform in size and thickness.*

2 **pounds fresh or frozen and thawed skinless flounder,
orange roughy, sole, or other fish fillets, ¼ to ½ inch
thick**

1 **pound fresh or frozen and thawed sea scallops
or 1 pound peeled, deveined, fresh or frozen and
thawed large shrimp**

1 **package (10 ounces) frozen chopped spinach**

1 **medium-size yellow onion, chopped**

1 **cup lower-sodium herb stuffing mix**

½ **cup reduced-fat sour cream**

¼ **cup grated Parmesan cheese**

1 **large egg, lightly beaten
Paprika**

1 Rinse fish and pat dry. In a large saucepan, bring
4 cups water to a boil; add scallops and cook for 1 to
3 minutes or just until the scallops turn opaque. Drain
scallops; cut into quarters. Cook the spinach and onion
according to the directions on the spinach package;
drain well, pressing out excess liquid with paper towels.
In a medium-size bowl, using a heavy spoon, slightly
crush the stuffing mix. Stir in the spinach-onion mixture, stuffing mix, sour cream, Parmesan cheese, and
egg. Mix well. Carefully stir in scallops.

2 Preheat the oven to 375°F. Measure length of fillets.
Cut long fillets or overlap thinner ends of 2 short
fillets to make pieces 7 to 8 inches in length. Spread

about ½ cup of the scallop mixture evenly on top of each fish piece. Roll fish pieces up, starting from narrow ends. Secure each roll with toothpicks. Place rolls, seam side down, in a lightly greased 13" x 9" x 2" baking dish.

3 Bake for 20 to 25 minutes or until the fish flakes when tested with a fork. To serve, carefully remove toothpicks and sprinkle fish rolls with paprika. Serves 8.

Prep Time: 20 minutes Cooking Time: 10 minutes
Baking Time: 20 minutes

1 Serving: Calories 204. Total Fat 6 g. Saturated Fat 2 g. Protein 28 g. Carbohydrate 9 g. Fiber 1 g. Sodium 358 mg. Cholesterol 97 mg.

Norwegian Fish Pudding with Shrimp Sauce

Norwegian women served mild-flavored fish with a delicate dilled shrimp sauce. Be sure to use fresh, not frozen, fish because it contains a natural gelatin that helps give this pudding body and a smooth texture.

1 **tablespoon fine dry bread crumbs**
1 **pound fresh skinless halibut or cod fillets, ¼ to ½ inch thick**
1⅓ **cups half-and-half**
2 **tablespoons cornstarch**
¼ **teaspoon each salt and white pepper**
¼ **teaspoon ground nutmeg**
  Shrimp Sauce (recipe, above right)

1 Preheat the oven to 350°F. Sprinkle the bottom and sides of a lightly greased 8" x 4" x 2" loaf pan with bread crumbs, tilting to spread evenly. Set aside.

2 Rinse fish and pat dry. Cut fish into 2-inch pieces. In a small bowl, whisk together the half-and-half, cornstarch, salt, white pepper, and nutmeg. In a food processor or blender, process fish and cornstarch mixture, half at a time, until smooth. Spread fish mixture into prepared loaf pan. Sharply rap pan on the counter to eliminate air pockets. Cover pan with foil.

3 Place loaf pan into a 13" x 9" x 2" baking pan. Pour boiling water into baking pan around the loaf pan to a depth of 1½ inches. Bake for 30 to 40 minutes or until a knife inserted in the center comes out clean. Place loaf

pan on a wire rack; let stand, covered, for 10 minutes. Carefully pour off any liquid around pudding. Unmold onto a warm serving platter. Spoon Shrimp Sauce over pudding. Serve with green beans. Makes 4 servings.

Prep Time: 15 minutes Cooking Time: 30 minutes
Standing Time: 10 minutes

1 Serving: Calories 316. Total Fat 13 g. Saturated Fat 7 g. Protein 33 g. Carbohydrate 15 g. Fiber 0 g. Sodium 471 mg. Cholesterol 121 mg.

Shrimp Sauce

In a small saucepan, whisk together **1¼ cups low-fat (1% milkfat) milk, 2 tablespoons all-purpose flour, ½ teaspoon dried dill weed, ¼ teaspoon salt, and ⅛ teaspoon white pepper.** Cook over moderate heat, stirring constantly, for 8 minutes or until thickened and bubbly. Stir in **4 ounces cooked, peeled medium-size shrimp.** Cook until shrimp are heated through, stirring once. Makes about 1½ cups (about four ⅓-cup servings).

1 Serving: Calories 75. Total Fat 1 g. Saturated Fat 1 g. Protein 9 g. Carbohydrate 7 g. Fiber 0 g. Sodium 236 mg. Cholesterol 58 mg.

JUDGING FISH DONENESS

Here's how to tell when fish is cooked just right.

◆ Perfectly cooked fish is opaque all the way through to the center and the juices are milky. Test the fish with a fork at its thickest point. It should separate into flakes.

◆ Undercooked fish will be translucent in the center and the juices still will be clear. When you test it with a fork, the fish will be too firm to flake easily.

◆ Overcooked fish will be opaque, but there will be few, if any, juices. When you test it with a fork, the fish will be dry and crumbly.

Bouillabaisse, American-Style

In France, this classic fish stew was made with as many as a dozen different kinds of Mediterranean seafood, including eel, sea bass, mussels, and scallops. Americans adapted the recipe to use local seafood, such as rock lobster, sole, and clams.

8 ounces fresh or frozen and thawed sole, flounder, or halibut fillets

8 ounces fresh or frozen and thawed sea scallops

1 frozen and partially thawed small rock lobster tail (8 ounces) or 8 ounces lobster meat

1 tablespoon olive oil

1 large yellow onion, chopped

2 cloves garlic, minced

3½ cups lower-sodium chicken broth (page 67)

1¾ cups chopped tomatoes or 1 can (14½ ounces) lower-sodium tomatoes, undrained and cut up

1 cup dry white wine or lower-sodium chicken broth (page 67)

2 tablespoons minced parsley

2 bay leaves

1 teaspoon dried thyme leaves

1 teaspoon fennel seeds or celery seeds

½ teaspoon salt

¼ teaspoon thread saffron, crushed (optional)

⅛ teaspoon ground red pepper (cayenne)

1 can (6½ ounces) minced clams

Bouillabaisse, American-Style

1 Rinse fish, scallops, and lobster and pat dry. Cut fish into 2-inch pieces. Halve large scallops. Halve lobster tail lengthwise, then cut crosswise into 6 portions.

2 In a large saucepan, heat oil over moderate heat. Add the onion and garlic and cook for 5 minutes or until onion is tender. Stir in the chicken broth, tomatoes, wine, parsley, bay leaves, thyme, fennel seeds, salt, saffron (if using), and red pepper. Bring to a boil. Lower the heat and simmer, covered, for 30 minutes.

3 Line a large sieve with 2 layers of 100% cotton cheesecloth. Set it in a large saucepan. Strain the vegetable mixture through the lined sieve. Discard the vegetables and seasonings.

4 Bring strained liquid to a boil. Add the fish, scallops, lobster, and clams. Return to a boil. Lower the heat and simmer, uncovered, for 4 to 5 minutes or until fish flakes when tested with a fork and scallops and lobster turn opaque, stirring occasionally. Serve with French bread. Makes 6 servings.

Prep Time: 25 minutes Cooking Time: 55 minutes

1 Serving: Calories 175. Total Fat 4 g. Saturated Fat 1 g. Protein 19 g. Carbohydrate 8 g. Fiber 1 g. Sodium 443 mg. Cholesterol 49 mg.

Cajun Crayfish Étouffée

Crayfish are freshwater shellfish that taste like slightly sweet shrimp. If crayfish aren't available, substitute shrimp.

12 ounces peeled, fresh or frozen and thawed crayfish tails or large shrimp
3 tablespoons all-purpose flour
3 tablespoons olive or vegetable oil
1 large yellow onion, chopped
1 medium-size sweet green pepper, chopped
2 stalks celery, sliced
4 large green onions with tops, sliced
3 cloves garlic, minced
½ teaspoon salt
½ teaspoon hot red pepper sauce
4 medium-size tomatoes, peeled and chopped

1 Rinse shrimp and pat dry. For roux, in a large heavy saucepan, stir together flour and oil until smooth. Cook over moderate heat, stirring constantly, for 5 to 7 minutes or until roux is dark brown.

2 Add the onion, green pepper, celery, green onions, garlic, salt, and hot pepper sauce. Cook for 8 to 10 minutes or until vegetables are just tender, stirring frequently. Gradually stir in tomatoes. Bring to a boil. Add the shrimp. Lower the heat and simmer, covered, for 5 minutes or just until the shrimp turn opaque, stirring occasionally. Serve with hot cooked rice. Serves 4.

Prep Time: 20 minutes Cooking Time: 23 minutes

1 Serving: Calories 226. Total Fat 12 g. Saturated Fat 1 g.
Protein 16 g. Carbohydrate 17 g. Fiber 3 g.
Sodium 447 mg. Cholesterol 121 mg.

Shrimp and Corn Pie

This old-fashioned savory custard is a Louisiana seafood specialty. Serve it with sliced tomatoes and crusty bread.

½ cup evaporated skimmed milk
2 large egg whites
1 large egg
1 teaspoon lower-sodium Worcestershire sauce
¼ teaspoon salt
⅛ teaspoon black pepper
12 ounces cooked, peeled shrimp, halved crosswise
2 cups frozen corn, thawed

1 Preheat the oven to 350°F. In a large bowl, whisk together the evaporated skimmed milk, egg whites, egg, Worcestershire sauce, salt, and pepper. Stir in the shrimp and corn.

2 Spoon the mixture into a 9-inch pie plate. Bake for 30 minutes or until the center is almost set. Let stand 5 minutes before serving. Makes 4 servings.

Prep Time: 10 minutes Cooking Time: 30 minutes
Standing Time: 5 minutes

1 Serving: Calories 203. Total Fat 2 g. Saturated Fat 1 g.
Protein 27 g. Carbohydrate 21 g. Fiber 2 g.
Sodium 412 mg. Cholesterol 220 mg.

SHRIMP PRIMER

◆ **Forms of Shrimp** Raw shrimp in the shell are available either whole or headless in both fresh or frozen forms. Peeled and deveined raw shrimp also come fresh or frozen. Cooked shrimp are sold in the shell and peeled. Look for them fresh in the fish case or frozen in the freezer case.

◆ **How Much to Buy** If you're buying shrimp in the shell rather than already peeled, use these guidelines. A pound of shrimp in the shell will yield about 12 ounces of peeled shrimp. Or, 1½ pounds shrimp in the shell will be about 1 pound after peeling.

◆ **Sizes of Shrimp** The bigger the shrimp, the fewer per pound and, generally, the more they cost. Shrimp come in a range of sizes from miniature (over 100 per pound) to colossal (10 or fewer per pound). For large shrimp, you'll get 21 to 30 per pound.

◆ **Selecting Shrimp** When purchasing shrimp, make sure they smell fresh and are translucent, moist, and firm. If shrimp smell of ammonia or have blackened edges or spots on their shells, they are of poor quality.

◆ **Storing Fresh Shrimp** Once you get shrimp home, rinse them under cold running water and drain them. Then, place the shrimp in a covered container and refrigerate for no more than 2 days.

Shrimp Creole

Creole cooks insist that the only way to make this New Orleans classic is with jumbo Gulf Coast shrimp. However, smaller shrimp work just fine.

- **12** ounces peeled, deveined, fresh or frozen and thawed large shrimp
- **2** tablespoons olive or vegetable oil
- **1** large yellow onion, chopped
- **1** medium-size sweet green pepper, chopped
- **2** stalks celery, sliced
- **3** cloves garlic, minced
- **1¾** cups chopped tomatoes or 1 can (14½ ounces) lower-sodium tomatoes, undrained and cut up
- **1** teaspoon dried thyme leaves
- **2** bay leaves
- **¼** teaspoon each salt and black pepper
- **¼** teaspoon ground red pepper (cayenne)

1 Rinse shrimp and pat dry. In a large skillet, heat the oil over moderate heat. Add the onion, green pepper, celery, and garlic and cook for 8 to 10 minutes or until vegetables are just tender.

2 Stir in the tomatoes, thyme, bay leaves, salt, black pepper, and red pepper. Bring to a boil. Lower the heat and simmer, uncovered, for 10 minutes.

3 Stir the shrimp into tomato mixture. Bring to a boil. Lower the heat and simmer, covered, for 5 minutes more or just until the shrimp turn opaque, stirring occasionally. Discard the bay leaves. Serve with hot cooked rice. Makes 4 servings.

Prep Time: 20 minutes Cooking Time: 30 minutes

1 Serving: Calories 165. Total Fat 8 g. Saturated Fat 1 g.
Protein 15 g. Carbohydrate 10 g. Fiber 2 g.
Sodium 298 mg. Cholesterol 121 mg.

✳

Fish Creole Prepare as for Shrimp Creole, substituting **12 ounces fresh or frozen and thawed fish fillets, cut into ¾-inch pieces,** for the shrimp.

1 Serving: Calories 202. Total Fat 9 g. Saturated Fat 1 g.
Protein 18 g. Carbohydrate 10 g. Fiber 2 g.
Sodium 211 mg. Cholesterol 31 mg.

Scampi in White Wine

In Italy, this dish was made with scampi—tiny relatives of the lobster. Italian immigrants to America adapted the recipe for shrimp. To keep either scampi or shrimp tender, cook them just until they turn opaque.

- **1½** pounds fresh or frozen and thawed large scampi or shrimp, peeled and deveined with tails left on
- **2** tablespoons butter or margarine
- **¼** cup minced parsley
- **1** teaspoon dried basil leaves
- **3** cloves garlic, minced
- **¼** cup dry white wine or nonalcoholic dry white wine
- **1** tablespoon lemon juice
- **1** teaspoon grated lemon rind
- **¼** teaspoon salt
- **⅛** teaspoon black pepper

1 Rinse scampi and pat dry. In a large nonstick skillet, melt the butter over moderate heat. Add the parsley, basil, and garlic and cook for 1 minute.

2 Stir in the scampi, wine, lemon juice, lemon rind, salt, and pepper. Cook, covered, for 4 to 5 minutes or just until the scampi turn opaque, stirring occasionally. Serve with lemon wedges. Makes 4 servings.

Prep Time: 15 minutes Cooking Time: 6 minutes

1 Serving: Calories 149. Total Fat 7 g. Saturated Fat 4 g.
Protein 18 g. Carbohydrate 2 g. Fiber 0 g.
Sodium 380 mg. Cholesterol 177 mg.

DEVEINING SHRIMP

1. To remove the vein from a shrimp, use a small sharp knife to make a slit along its back, exposing the vein.

2. Lift the vein from the slit with the tip of the knife, then rinse the shrimp under running water.

Louisiana Seafood Gumbo

Louisiana Seafood Gumbo

*Creole cooks used a roux, a mixture of flour and fat, to thicken
many of their dishes and to add a rich "browned" flavor. To make sure your
roux is brown enough, cook it until it's the color of a tarnished penny.*

8 ounces peeled, deveined, fresh or frozen and thawed
  large shrimp

3 tablespoons all-purpose flour

3 tablespoons olive or vegetable oil

1 large yellow onion, chopped

1 medium-size sweet red or green pepper, chopped

4 cloves garlic, minced

3½ cups lower-sodium chicken broth (page 67)

2 cups fresh or frozen and thawed okra pods, sliced

2 bay leaves

1 teaspoon dried thyme leaves

½ teaspoon salt

½ teaspoon ground red pepper (cayenne)

8 ounces smoked turkey sausage or andouille sausage,
  cut into ½-inch slices

8 ounces lump crab meat, picked over and flaked,
  or 1 package (6 ounces) frozen crab meat

½ pint shucked oysters, undrained

1 Rinse shrimp and pat dry; refrigerate. For roux, in a
heavy Dutch oven, stir together flour and oil until
smooth. Cook over moderate heat, stirring constantly,
for 5 to 7 minutes or until roux is dark brown.

2 Add onion, sweet red pepper, and garlic. Cook for
8 to 10 minutes or just until vegetables are tender,
stirring frequently. Gradually stir in broth. Stir in okra,
bay leaves, thyme, salt, and ground red pepper. Bring to
a boil. Lower heat and simmer, covered, for 20 minutes.

3 Add the sausage. Simmer, covered, for 10 minutes.
Add the shrimp, crab, and oysters. Bring to a boil.
Lower the heat and simmer, uncovered, for 5 minutes
or just until the shrimp and crab turn opaque. Discard
bay leaves. Spoon off fat. Serve with hot cooked rice
and hot red pepper sauce. Makes 6 servings.

Prep Time: 25 minutes Cooking Time: 1 hour

1 Serving: Calories 320. Total Fat 15 g. Saturated Fat 3 g.
Protein 28 g. Carbohydrate 17 g. Fiber 3 g.
Sodium 770 mg. Cholesterol 153 mg.

Lobster Thermidor

Lobster Thermidor

*In colonial times, lobster was so plentiful that it was
considered poor man's food. By the 1800's, it was reserved for
special occasions and frequently served in a rich cream sauce.*

4 **frozen and thawed small rock lobster tails
(8 ounces each)**

1 **tablespoon butter or margarine**

1 **cup sliced fresh mushrooms**

4 **shallots, chopped, or ¼ cup finely chopped onion**

¾ **cup half-and-half**

2 **tablespoons all-purpose flour**

1 **teaspoon dry mustard**

½ **teaspoon salt**

⅛ **teaspoon ground red pepper (cayenne)**

¾ **cup low-fat (1% milkfat) milk**

2 **large egg yolks, lightly beaten**

2 **tablespoons dry sherry or lower-sodium chicken
broth (page 67)**

2 **tablespoons grated Parmesan cheese**

1 Rinse lobster tails. In a Dutch oven, bring 8 cups water to a boil. Add lobster tails; return to a boil. Lower the heat and simmer, uncovered, for 6 to 10 minutes or until shells turn bright red and meat is opaque. Drain well. Cool slightly. Place each lobster tail with meat side up. Remove the meat from the shells (tip, below). Place shells in a shallow baking pan. Cut meat into 1-inch chunks.

2 Preheat the broiler. In a medium-size skillet, melt the butter over moderate heat. Add the mushrooms and shallots and cook for 3 minutes, stirring occasionally. Remove from heat. Stir in lobster.

3 In a medium-size saucepan, whisk together the half-and-half, flour, dry mustard, salt, and red pepper. Add the milk. Cook over moderate heat, whisking constantly, for 8 minutes or until mixture is thickened and bubbly. Slowly stir about ½ cup of the hot mixture into the egg yolks, then return this mixture to the saucepan. Cook, whisking constantly, for 3 minutes or until mixture thickens (do not boil). Stir in the mushroom mixture and dry sherry; heat through.

4 Spoon the hot lobster mixture into the lobster shells. Sprinkle the Parmesan cheese over lobster mixture in shells. Broil 5 inches from the heat for 2 to 3 minutes or until the Parmesan cheese is melted and lightly browned. Makes 4 servings.

Prep Time: 20 minutes Cooking Time: 37 minutes

1 Serving: Calories 329. Total Fat 16 g. Saturated Fat 9 g.
Protein 32 g. Carbohydrate 12 g. Fiber 1 g.
Sodium 1,179 mg. Cholesterol 230 mg.

OPENING LOBSTER TAILS

Place lobster tail underside up. With kitchen shears, cut away the thin undershell of the tail to expose the meat. Carefully pull the meat from the shell with a sturdy fork.

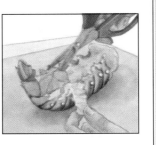

Deviled Crab

Maryland natives grew up on deviled crab. The "deviled" flavor of this recipe comes from ground red pepper, hot red pepper sauce, and mustard.

1 tablespoon butter or margarine

1 small sweet green pepper, chopped

4 large green onions with tops, finely sliced, or ½ cup finely sliced leek

1 stalk celery, sliced

2 cloves garlic, minced

2 cups low-fat (1% milkfat) milk

¼ cup all-purpose flour

1 teaspoon dry mustard

¼ teaspoon salt

¼ teaspoon ground red pepper (cayenne)

⅛ teaspoon hot red pepper sauce

1 pound lump crab meat, picked over and flaked, or 1 package (8 ounces) frozen and thawed, crab-flavored, salad-style fish, chopped

1 tablespoon butter or margarine, melted

½ cup fine dry bread crumbs

1 Preheat the oven to 350°F. In a medium-size saucepan, melt 1 tablespoon butter over moderate heat. Add the green pepper, green onions, celery, and garlic and cook for 5 minutes or until vegetables are tender, stirring often. In a small bowl, whisk together the milk, flour, dry mustard, salt, ground red pepper, and red pepper sauce. Stir into mixture in saucepan. Cook, stirring constantly, for 8 minutes or until thickened and bubbly. Stir in crab meat.

2 Spoon mixture into 4 lightly greased 10-ounce ramekins or individual casseroles. Toss the 1 tablespoon melted butter with the bread crumbs. Sprinkle buttered crumbs on top of the crab mixture. Bake for 15 to 20 minutes or until heated through and browned on top. Makes 4 servings.

Prep Time: 20 minutes Cooking Time: 29 minutes

1 Serving: Calories 256. Total Fat 9 g. Saturated Fat 5 g.
Protein 19 g. Carbohydrate 25 g. Fiber 2 g.
Sodium 577 mg. Cholesterol 61 mg.

Sea Scallop Kabobs

Sea Scallop Kabobs

*For evenly cooked kabobs, make sure the pieces are loosely threaded onto the skewers.
If you push the pieces too close together, they won't get done where they touch.*

8 ounces fresh or frozen and thawed cod, halibut,
   or monkfish steaks, 1 inch thick

8 ounces fresh or frozen and thawed sea scallops

For the marinade:

¼ cup orange juice

2 tablespoons olive or vegetable oil

1 tablespoon lime or lemon juice

2 cloves garlic, minced

For the coating:

½ cup fine dry bread crumbs

1 teaspoon dried thyme leaves

¼ teaspoon salt

⅛ teaspoon black pepper

For the kabobs:

8 small fresh mushrooms

½ large sweet green pepper, cut into 1-inch squares

½ large sweet red pepper, cut into 1-inch squares

1 medium-size orange

1 Remove and discard skin from fish. Rinse fish and scallops and pat dry. Halve large scallops. Cut fish into 2-inch pieces. To prepare the marinade, in a jar with a tight-fitting lid, combine the orange juice, oil, lime juice, and garlic. Cover; shake well. Pour marinade into a large heavy-duty plastic bag. Add scallops and fish. Close bag. Refrigerate for 6 to 8 hours, turning bag occasionally.

2 To prepare the coating, in a small shallow bowl, stir together the bread crumbs, thyme, salt, and black pepper. Set aside.

3 To prepare the kabobs, in a medium-size bowl, pour boiling water over the mushrooms and sweet pepper squares. Let stand for 2 minutes; drain well on paper towels. Meanwhile, cut orange into 8 wedges, then halve each wedge crosswise.

4 Preheat the broiler. Drain scallops and fish; discard marinade. Roll scallops and fish pieces in the coating to coat well. On 8 long metal skewers, alternately thread scallops, fish pieces, sweet pepper squares, mushrooms, and orange pieces. Arrange kabobs on lightly greased rack of a broiler pan.

5 Broil 5 inches from the heat for 10 to 12 minutes or just until scallops are opaque and fish flakes when tested with a fork, turning once. Makes 4 servings.

Prep Time: 25 minutes Chilling Time: 6 hours
Cooking Time: 10 minutes

1 Serving: Calories 206. Total Fat 7 g. Saturated Fat 1 g. Protein 18 g. Carbohydrate 20 g. Fiber 2 g. Sodium 482 mg. Cholesterol 32 mg.

Crispy Fried Scallops

Then, as now, the trick to cooking light, crisp scallops is to keep the vegetable oil nice and hot so the coating doesn't soak up too much fat.

Spicy Cocktail Sauce (recipe, right) or purchased tartar sauce
1 pound fresh or frozen and thawed sea scallops
⅓ cup all-purpose flour
⅛ teaspoon black pepper
2 large egg whites
⅓ cup fine dry bread crumbs, finely crushed lower-sodium crackers, or cornmeal
Vegetable oil

1 Prepare Spicy Cocktail Sauce. Cover and refrigerate for at least 2 hours.

2 Rinse scallops and thoroughly pat dry with paper towels. Halve large scallops. On a sheet of wax paper, combine the flour and pepper. In a small bowl, lightly beat the egg whites. Roll scallops in flour mixture to coat well; shake off excess flour mixture. Dip flour-coated scallops into egg whites. Roll scallops in bread crumbs.

3 Preheat the oven to 300°F. In a deep-fat fryer or a medium-size heavy saucepan, heat 2 inches of vegetable oil to 375°F or until a 1-inch cube of bread browns in 30 seconds. Fry scallops, a few at a time, in the hot oil for 1½ to 2 minutes or until golden, turning once. Using a slotted spoon, remove scallops and drain well on paper towels. Transfer to a shallow baking pan and keep warm in oven while frying remaining scallops. Serve with Spicy Cocktail Sauce and lemon wedges. Makes 4 servings.

Prep Time: 15 minutes Chilling Time: 2 hours
Cooking Time: 20 minutes

1 Serving: Calories 350. Total Fat 18 g. Saturated Fat 2 g. Protein 22 g. Carbohydrate 26 g. Fiber 1 g. Sodium 771 mg. Cholesterol 34 mg.

Spicy Cocktail Sauce

In a small saucepan, combine **¼ cup water, 2 tablespoons finely chopped yellow onion,** and **1 clove garlic, minced.** Cook, covered, for 5 minutes or until onion is tender; drain. Stir in **½ cup bottled chili sauce; ½ cup lower-calorie, lower-sodium catsup; 1 tablespoon drained prepared horseradish; 2 teaspoons lemon juice; 2 teaspoons lower-sodium Worcestershire sauce; ½ teaspoon dry mustard;** and **⅛ teaspoon ground red pepper (cayenne).** Bring to a boil. Lower heat and simmer, uncovered, for 2 minutes. Transfer to a small bowl. Cool. Cover and refrigerate for at least 2 hours (will keep for 1 week). Makes about 1 cup (eight 2-tablespoon servings).

1 Serving: Calories 39. Total Fat 0 g. Saturated Fat 0 g. Protein 1 g. Carbohydrate 9 g. Fiber 1 g. Sodium 247 mg. Cholesterol 0 mg.

New England Clam Cakes

New England Clam Cakes

Since colonial times, folks all along the Eastern seaboard have made this old-fashioned delicacy. Early cooks went to the trouble of shucking, cooking, and mincing fresh clams, but today, using canned clams makes short work of this recipe.

- 2 **large egg whites, lightly beaten**
- 2/3 **cup seasoned fine dry bread crumbs**
- 2 **tablespoons finely chopped chives or green onion tops**
- 2 **teaspoons Dijon mustard**
- 1 **teaspoon lower-sodium Worcestershire sauce**
- 2 **cans (6½ ounces each) minced clams, drained**
- 1 **tablespoon butter or margarine, melted**

1 Preheat the oven to 450°F. In a medium-size bowl, combine the egg whites, ⅓ cup of the bread crumbs, chives, mustard, and Worcestershire sauce. Stir in the clams. Cover and refrigerate for 20 minutes. In a shallow dish, toss the melted butter with the remaining ⅓ cup bread crumbs.

2 Using about ⅓ cup of the clam mixture for each, shape into four 3-inch round patties. Coat each patty with the bread crumb mixture. Place on a lightly greased baking sheet. Bake for 10 to 12 minutes or until golden. Serve with lemon wedges. Makes 4 servings.

Prep Time: 15 minutes Chilling Time: 20 minutes
Cooking Time: 10 minutes

1 Serving: Calories 205. Total Fat 5 g. Saturated Fat 2 g.
Protein 21 g. Carbohydrate 18 g. Fiber 0 g.
Sodium 721 mg. Cholesterol 51 mg.

Lobster Cakes Prepare as for New England Clam Cakes, substituting **2 cans (6½ ounces each) lobster meat, drained,** for the minced clams.

1 Serving: Calories 195. Total Fat 4 g. Saturated Fat 2 g.
Protein 22 g. Carbohydrate 16 g. Fiber 0 g.
Sodium 973 mg. Cholesterol 69 mg.

Seattle Clam Hash

Legend says that New Englanders who came to the Northwest couldn't live without their hash. So when they didn't have corned beef, they used clams instead.

1¼ pounds potatoes
 2 cans (6½ ounces each) minced clams, drained
 2 strips lean bacon, chopped
 1 large yellow onion, chopped
 2 tablespoons butter or margarine
 ¼ cup low-fat (1% milkfat) milk
 1 teaspoon dry mustard
 ½ teaspoon salt
 ¼ teaspoon black pepper

1 In a medium-size saucepan, cover the potatoes with water. Bring to a boil over high heat. Lower the heat and simmer, covered, for 20 to 25 minutes or until tender. Drain. Cool potatoes slightly; peel and cube. In a large bowl, combine potatoes and clams. Set aside.

2 Meanwhile, in a large nonstick skillet, cook bacon over moderate heat until crisp. Remove bacon, reserving 1 tablespoon drippings. Drain the bacon on paper towels. Add onion to reserved drippings in the skillet. Cook over moderate heat for 5 minutes or until the onion is tender. Add bacon pieces and onion to potato mixture; toss to combine. Wipe skillet clean with paper towels.

3 In the same skillet, melt butter over moderate heat. Remove from heat. With a spatula, pat the potato-clam mixture evenly into the skillet, leaving a ½-inch space around edge. Cook over moderate heat for 10 minutes or until brown on the bottom. Turn hash in large portions. In a small bowl, combine milk, dry mustard, salt, and pepper. Pour milk mixture over hash and let it soak in. Cook over low heat for 10 to 15 minutes or until brown on the bottom. Serve with sliced tomatoes. Makes 4 servings.

Prep Time: 15 minutes Cooking Time: 50 minutes

1 Serving: Calories 330. Total Fat 12 g. Saturated Fat 6 g.
Protein 16 g. Carbohydrate 39 g. Fiber 4 g.
Sodium 536 mg. Cholesterol 50 mg.

Yankee Red Fish Hash Prepare as for Seattle Clam Hash, substituting **1 cup flaked, cooked fish** and **1 can (8¼ ounces) beets, drained and finely chopped,** for the 2 cans minced clams.

1 Serving: Calories 320. Total Fat 12 g. Saturated Fat 6 g.
Protein 13 g. Carbohydrate 42 g. Fiber 6 g.
Sodium 591 mg. Cholesterol 40 mg.

Nana's Scalloped Oysters

Years ago, oysters often were served as part of holiday menus because winter was when oysters were most plentiful. When buying shucked oysters, look for fresh smelling ones that are in clear, not cloudy, liquid.

 1 cup crushed lower-sodium crackers
 1 cup fresh bread crumbs (2 slices)
 2 tablespoons butter or margarine, melted
 1 pint shucked oysters, undrained
 ¼ cup low-fat (1% milkfat) milk
 1 teaspoon lower-sodium Worcestershire sauce
 ¼ teaspoon each salt and black pepper
 2 tablespoons butter or margarine
 1 large yellow onion, chopped
 1 medium-size sweet green pepper, chopped
 ¼ cup all-purpose flour

1 Preheat the oven to 425°F. In a medium-size bowl, combine crackers and bread crumbs; toss 2 tablespoons melted butter with crumb mixture. Sprinkle ¼ cup of the crumb mixture into bottom of a lightly greased 1½-quart casserole. Set aside remaining crumbs. Drain the oysters, reserving ¼ cup of oyster liquor (add milk, if necessary, to measure ¼ cup liquid). In a small bowl, combine the oysters, the reserved oyster liquor, milk, Worcestershire sauce, salt, and black pepper. Set aside.

2 In a medium-size saucepan, melt 2 tablespoons butter over moderate heat. Add the onion and green pepper and cook for 5 minutes or until tender. Stir in the flour. Stir in the oyster mixture; cook until bubbly.

3 Spoon half of the oyster mixture into prepared dish. Sprinkle with half of remaining crumb mixture. Top with remaining oyster mixture. Sprinkle with remaining crumb mixture. Bake for 25 minutes or until heated through. Makes 8 side-dish or 3 main-dish servings.

Prep Time: 15 minutes Cooking Time: 35 minutes

1 Side-Dish Serving: Calories 156. Total Fat 8 g.
Saturated Fat 4 g. Protein 5 g. Carbohydrate 16 g. Fiber 1 g.
Sodium 295 mg. Cholesterol 32 mg.

Tuna Pie with Biscuits

Community cookbooks feature numerous recipes for biscuit-topped pot pies, which were particularly popular in the 1940's and 1950's.

 1 **package (6) refrigerated biscuits**
 2 **tablespoons butter or margarine**
 1 **large yellow onion, chopped**
 1 **medium-size sweet green or red pepper, chopped**
 2 **stalks celery, sliced**
 1 **cups lower-sodium chicken broth (page 67)**
1½ **teaspoons dried thyme leaves**
 ¼ **teaspoon each salt and black pepper**
1½ **cups low-fat (1% milkfat) milk**
 ½ **cup all-purpose flour**
 2 **cans (6 ounces each) water-packed, chunk light tuna, rinsed, drained, and flaked, or 1 can (14¾ ounces) salmon, picked through, rinsed, drained, and flaked**

1 Preheat the oven to 400°F. Cut the biscuits in half crosswise. Set aside.

2 In a large saucepan, melt the butter over moderate heat. Add the onion, green pepper, and celery and cook for 5 minutes or until tender. Stir in the broth, thyme, salt, and black pepper. In a small bowl, whisk together the milk and flour. Stir into mixture in saucepan. Cook, stirring constantly, for 8 minutes or until thickened and bubbly. Stir in the tuna.

3 Immediately spoon the tuna mixture into a 2-quart casserole. Quickly place the biscuit halves on top of the hot tuna mixture. Bake for 12 minutes or until biscuits are done. Let stand for 5 minutes before serving. Makes 6 servings.

Prep Time: 15 minutes Cooking Time: 26 minutes
Standing Time: 5 minutes

1 Serving: Calories 225. Total Fat 6 g. Saturated Fat 3 g. Protein 18 g. Carbohydrate 25 g. Fiber 1 g. Sodium 527 mg. Cholesterol 28 mg.

Salmon Loaf

Use easy-to-flake pink and chum salmon in salmon loaves or patties and save the more costly red sockeye and chinook salmon for salads or special main dishes.

 1 **can (14¾ ounces) salmon, rinsed and drained**
 1 **tablespoon lemon juice**
 ¼ **cup water**
 4 **large green onions with tops, finely sliced**
 1 **teaspoon dried dill weed**
 1 **teaspoon dry mustard**
 ¼ **teaspoon salt**
 ⅛ **teaspoon black pepper**
 1 **large egg, lightly beaten**
 ½ **cup low-fat (1% milkfat) milk**
 1 **cup fresh bread crumbs (2 slices)**

1 Preheat the oven to 350°F. Using a fork, flake the salmon, discarding the skin and bones (tip, below). Sprinkle salmon with the lemon juice.

2 In a small saucepan, combine the water and green onions; cook, covered, for 5 minutes or until tender. Drain well. Stir in dill weed, mustard, salt, and pepper.

3 In a medium-size bowl, combine the egg and milk. Stir in the onion mixture and bread crumbs. Add salmon and mix thoroughly. Pat salmon mixture into a lightly greased 7½" x 3½" x 2" loaf pan. Bake for 35 to 40 minutes or until set in center. Let stand 5 minutes, then unmold onto serving platter. Serve with plain low-fat yogurt or reduced-fat sour cream. Makes 4 servings.

Prep Time: 15 minutes Cooking Time: 40 minutes
Standing Time: 5 minutes

1 Serving: Calories 147. Total Fat 6 g. Saturated Fat 2 g. Protein 14 g. Carbohydrate 8 g. Fiber 1 g. Sodium 491 mg. Cholesterol 77 mg.

REMOVING SALMON BONES

Canned salmon typically contains edible bones. Whether you remove the bones or not is a matter of preference. For dishes such as the Salmon Loaf above, removing the bones will give a smoother texture. However, the bones are rich in calcium, so you may opt to leave them in casseroles and most other dishes.

Grandma's Treats

Shrimp-Filled Croissants

Another day make these satisfying sandwiches with a 6-ounce can of tuna instead of the shrimp.

- **1 can (4 ¼ ounces) shrimp, rinsed and drained**
- **¼ cup finely chopped sweet green pepper**
- **¼ cup shredded carrot**
- **¼ cup reduced-fat mayonnaise**
- **2 teaspoons Dijon mustard**
- **2 croissants, split**
- **4 thin cucumber slices**

1. In a medium-size bowl, combine the shrimp, green pepper, and carrot. Stir in the mayonnaise and mustard. Cover and refrigerate for 20 minutes.

2. Line croissant bottoms with lettuce. Spoon the filling over lettuce. Top each sandwich with 2 thin cucumber slices and a croissant top. Makes 2 servings.

Salmon Patties

These crispy fish "burgers" are a delightful change-of-pace from beef.

- **1 can (7 ½ ounces) salmon, rinsed and drained**
- **1 large egg white, lightly beaten**
- **¼ cup low-fat (1% milkfat) milk**
- **½ cup finely crushed lower-sodium crackers**
- **½ teaspoon dry mustard**
- **½ teaspoon paprika**
- **4 hamburger buns, split and toasted**

1. Using a fork, flake the salmon, discarding the skin and bones (tip, opposite). In a medium-size bowl, combine the egg white and milk. Stir in the crackers, mustard, and paprika. Add the salmon; mix well to combine. Refrigerate for 20 minutes. Pat salmon mixture into 4 fish shapes or shape mixture into four 3-inch round patties.

2. Preheat the broiler. Place patties on lightly greased rack of a broiler pan. Broil

5 inches from the heat for 6 minutes; turn and broil for 3 minutes more. Serve patties on lettuce-lined buns with tomato slices. Makes 4 servings.

Sailor's Telescopes

These savory spyglasses are just the right size for junior mariners to handle.

- **1 can (6 ounces) water-packed, chunk light tuna, chilled, rinsed, drained, and flaked**
- **4 ounces reduced-fat soft-style cream cheese, at room temperature**
- **⅓ cup finely chopped celery**
- **8 slices home-style white or whole-wheat bread**

1. In a medium-size bowl, stir together the tuna, cream cheese, and celery.

2. Trim crusts from bread. Roll each slice lightly with a rolling pin until flattened.

3. To make telescopes, spread about 2 tablespoons of the tuna mixture on each bread slice. Roll up. Makes 4 servings.

Mexican-Style Fish Sticks

Your little ones are sure to shout "Ole!" when they taste these south-of-the-border fish sticks.

- **2 packages (8 ounces each) frozen fish sticks**
- **1 can (9 ounces) plain bean dip (optional)**
- **½ cup chunky salsa**
- **¼ cup shredded Monterey Jack cheese (2 ounces)**

1. Bake fish sticks according to package directions.

2. Meanwhile, in a small saucepan, combine the bean dip (if using) and salsa; heat through. Spoon over the fish sticks. Sprinkle with Monterey Jack cheese. Makes 4 servings.

ROBUST GRAINS, BEANS, & PASTA

No matter what her roots, grandma was sure to have a grain, bean, or pasta recipe that recalled her heritage. New England grandmas fried jonnycakes. Native Americans simmered wild rice. Nanas from Italy made lasagna and Southern grannies served up grits. In this chapter, you'll find an assortment of these traditional ethnic and regional favorites as well as all-American standards, such as macaroni and cheese and baked beans.

215

Wild Rice with Apples

*Native Americans of the Great Lakes
region showed European settlers how to cook
a local marsh-grass seed. The settlers
called it wild "rice" because the grass grows
in water like regular rice.*

 1 **cup uncooked wild rice**
 2 **cups lower-sodium chicken broth (page 67)**
 1 **tablespoon olive or vegetable oil**
 1 **large yellow onion, chopped**
 1 **stalk celery, thinly sliced**
 1 **medium-size tart apple, chopped**
 ¼ **cup minced parsley**
 ¼ **cup chopped pecans or walnuts, toasted**
 1 **teaspoon dried marjoram leaves**
 ¼ **teaspoon each salt and pepper**

1 Place the wild rice in a wire strainer. Run cold water through rice, lifting the rice with fingers to clean thoroughly.

2 In a medium-size saucepan, bring the chicken broth to a boil over high heat. Stir in the wild rice. Return to a boil. Lower the heat and simmer, covered, for 40 minutes or until most of the broth is absorbed. Drain off liquid.

3 Meanwhile, in a large saucepan, heat the oil over moderate heat. Add the onion and celery and cook for 5 minutes or until the vegetables are tender. Stir in the apple, parsley, pecans, marjoram, salt, and pepper. Cook for 2 minutes more, sitting frequently.

4 Stir the cooked wild rice into the apple mixture. Cook for 2 to 3 minutes or until heated through. Makes 6 side-dish servings.

Prep Time: 15 minutes Cooking Time: 42 minutes

1 Serving: Calories 186. Total Fat 6 g. Saturated Fat 1 g.
Protein 5 g. Carbohydrate 30 g. Fiber 3 g.
Sodium 100 mg. Cholesterol 0 mg.

Charleston Red Rice

*Folklore says rice first came to the South
when a ship from Madagascar was blown off
course and landed in Charleston. The folks
there took good care of the captain and his crew.
As a gift, he left a small amount of rice.*

 ½ **cup uncooked long-grain white rice**
 3 **strips lean bacon, chopped**
 1 **large yellow onion, chopped**
 1 **large sweet red pepper, chopped**
 1¾ **cups chopped tomatoes or 1 can (14½ ounces) lower-sodium tomatoes, undrained and cut up**
 1 **teaspoon sugar**

1 In a medium-size saucepan, cook the rice according to the package directions, omitting the butter.

2 Meanwhile, in a large saucepan, cook the bacon over moderate heat until crisp. Remove bacon, reserving 2 tablespoons of the drippings. Drain the bacon on paper towels; set aside. Cook the onion and red pepper in the reserved drippings for 5 minutes or until the vegetables are tender.

3 Add the cooked rice, tomatoes, and sugar to the onion mixture. Bring to a boil. Lower the heat and simmer, uncovered, for 10 minutes or until heated through. Stir in the bacon. Serve with roast meats or poultry. Makes 6 side-dish servings.

Prep Time: 15 minutes Cooking Time: 35 minutes

1 Serving: Calories 145. Total Fat 7 g. Saturated Fat 3 g.
Protein 3 g. Carbohydrate 19 g. Fiber 1 g.
Sodium 260 mg. Cholesterol 7 mg.

COOKING RICE TO PERFECTION

♦ To tell when long-grain white or brown rice is cooked, squeeze a grain between your fingers. There should be no hard core. Also, the grains should be whole with no splitting.

♦ For wild rice, cook the rice until most of the liquid is absorbed. Then, bite into a grain of rice. It should be tender with just a hint of chewiness.

Chinese Fried Rice

Chinese Fried Rice

"My Chinese grandmother told me that the secret to making fried rice is to chill the cooked rice first," says Maymay Quey Lin. "Chilling dries out the rice slightly so it doesn't stick together when you fry it."

 8 **dried mushrooms**
¼ **cup lower-sodium chicken broth (page 67)**
 3 **tablespoons lower-sodium soy sauce**
 1 **large egg, lightly beaten**
½ **teaspoon ground ginger**
¼ **teaspoon black pepper**
 2 **tablespoons vegetable oil**
 1 **medium-size yellow onion, halved lengthwise and thinly sliced**
 2 **stalks celery, sliced diagonally**
 2 **cloves garlic, minced**
 4 **cups cooked short- or long-grain white rice, well chilled**
½ **cup peanuts**

1 In a small bowl, cover mushrooms with warm water and let stand for 30 minutes. Rinse well and squeeze to drain thoroughly. Chop mushrooms, discarding the stems. In a small bowl, whisk together chicken broth, soy sauce, egg, ginger, and pepper.

2 In a heavy 12-inch skillet or wok, heat oil over moderately high heat. Add onion, celery, and garlic. Stir-fry for 3 to 4 minutes or until almost tender. Add mushrooms; stir-fry for 1 minute. Stir in rice. While stirring rice mixture constantly, drizzle egg mixture over rice. Cook for 5 to 7 minutes or until egg is cooked and rice is heated through, stirring frequently. Sprinkle with the peanuts. Makes 4 main-dish servings.

Prep Time: 15 minutes Standing Time: 30 minutes
Cooking Time: 10 minutes

1 Serving: Calories 419. Total Fat 18 g. Saturated Fat 2 g.
Protein 13 g. Carbohydrate 53 g. Fiber 4 g.
Sodium 891 mg. Cholesterol 53 mg.

✳

Pork Fried Rice Prepare as for Chinese Fried Rice, adding **2 cups chopped cooked pork or chicken** with the cooked rice. Makes 6 main-dish servings.

1 Serving: Calories 377. Total Fat 16 g. Saturated Fat 3 g.
Protein 25 g. Carbohydrate 35 g. Fiber 2 g.
Sodium 630 mg. Cholesterol 76 mg.

Curried Rice Pilaf

Middle Eastern and Southern grandmas browned rice in butter to give it a rich, nutty flavor.

- **1 tablespoon butter or margarine**
- **¾ cup uncooked long-grain white rice**
- **1 tablespoon olive or vegetable oil**
- **1 medium-size yellow onion, finely chopped**
- **1 stalk celery, thinly sliced**
- **1½ teaspoons curry powder**
- **1¾ cups lower-sodium chicken broth (page 67)**
- **½ teaspoon salt**
- **⅛ teaspoon black pepper**
- **½ cup raisins**
- **⅓ cup coarsely chopped pecans, toasted**

1 In a large saucepan, melt the butter over moderate heat. Add the rice and cook for 5 minutes or until lightly browned. Remove the rice from the saucepan.

2 In the same saucepan, heat the oil over moderate heat. Add the onion, celery, and curry powder and cook for 5 minutes or until vegetables are tender.

3 Stir in the rice. Add the chicken broth, salt, and pepper. Bring to a boil. Lower the heat and simmer, covered, for 20 minutes or until rice is tender and liquid is absorbed. Stir in the raisins and pecans. Cook, uncovered, for 3 to 4 minutes more or until heated through. Makes 6 side-dish servings.

Prep Time: 10 minutes Cooking Time: 40 minutes

1 Serving: Calories 225. Total Fat 9 g. Saturated Fat 2 g. Protein 3 g. Carbohydrate 34 g. Fiber 2 g. Sodium 206 mg. Cholesterol 5 mg.

Mushroom Rice Pilaf Prepare as for Curried Rice Pilaf, substituting **1 teaspoon dried thyme leaves** for the 1½ teaspoons curry powder, omitting the raisins, and adding **1 cup sliced fresh mushrooms** with the onion and celery.

1 Serving: Calories 184. Total Fat 9 g. Saturated Fat 2 g. Protein 3 g. Carbohydrate 24 g. Fiber 1 g. Sodium 204 mg. Cholesterol 5 mg.

Pilaf with Pistachio And Pine Nuts

This rice-and-nut combination was a favorite of Thomas Jefferson. Make it with all pine nuts or all pistachio nuts, if you prefer.

- **1½ cups lower-sodium chicken broth (page 67)**
- **3 teaspoons butter or margarine**
- **½ teaspoon salt**
- **¼ teaspoon ground mace or ground allspice**
- **⅔ cup uncooked long-grain white rice**
- **¼ cup pistachio nuts or chopped pecans**
- **¼ cup pine nuts or slivered almonds**

1 In a medium-size saucepan, bring the chicken broth, 1 teaspoon of the butter, the salt, and mace to a boil over high heat. Stir in the rice. Lower the heat and simmer, covered, for 20 minutes or until the rice is tender and liquid is absorbed. Transfer rice to a warm serving bowl.

2 Meanwhile, in a small skillet, melt the remaining 2 teaspoons butter over moderate heat. Add the pistachio nuts and pine nuts and cook for 1 to 2 minutes or until light golden, stirring frequently. Sprinkle the nuts over the rice. Serve with roast pork or chicken. Makes 4 side-dish servings.

Prep Time: 5 minutes Cooking Time: 25 minutes

1 Serving: Calories 219. Total Fat 9 g. Saturated Fat 3 g. Protein 5 g. Carbohydrate 30 g. Fiber 2 g. Sodium 299 mg. Cholesterol 8 mg.

FREEZING COOKED RICE

Shortcut meal preparation by keeping some cooked rice in the freezer to serve with meals.

◆ Cook the rice as you normally would and freeze it in an airtight freezer container or plastic bag. You can keep the rice up to 6 months.

◆ To reheat the frozen rice, place it in a saucepan and add 2 tablespoons of water for each cup of rice. Cover and cook rice over moderately high heat for 5 minutes or until rice is heated through.

Turkish Pilaf

Turkish Pilaf

In the 1896 Boston Cooking School Cook Book, Turkish pilaf
was a simple mixture of rice and stewed tomatoes. As the years
passed, it was enriched with currants, nuts, and spices.

1   **tablespoon butter or margarine**

¾   **cup uncooked long-grain white rice**

1   **tablespoon olive or vegetable oil**

1   **large yellow onion, finely chopped**

1¾   **cups lower-sodium beef broth (page 67)**

½   **teaspoon salt**

¼   **teaspoon each ground cinnamon and ground allspice or mace**

1¾   **cups chopped tomatoes or 1 can (14½ ounces) lower-sodium tomatoes, undrained and cut up**

⅓   **cup currants or raisins**

⅓   **cup slivered almonds or pine nuts, toasted**

1 In large saucepan, melt the butter over moderate heat. Add rice and cook for 5 minutes or until lightly browned. Remove rice from saucepan. In the same saucepan, heat the oil over moderate heat. Add the onion and cook for 5 minutes or until onion is tender.

2 Stir in the rice. Add the beef broth, salt, cinnamon, and allspice. Bring to a boil. Lower the heat and simmer, covered, for 20 minutes or until rice is tender and liquid is absorbed. Stir in the tomatoes, currants, and almonds. Return to a boil. Lower the heat and simmer, covered, for 2 to 3 minutes more or until heated through. Makes 6 side-dish servings.

Prep Time: 15 minutes   Cooking Time: 42 minutes

1 Serving: Calories 217. Total Fat 9 g. Saturated Fat 2 g.
Protein 5 g. Carbohydrate 32 g. Fiber 3 g.
Sodium 208 mg. Cholesterol 5 mg.

Shrimp Pilaf Prepare as for Turkish Pilaf, adding **12 ounces cooked, peeled shrimp** with the currants and almonds. Makes 6 main-dish servings.

1 Serving: Calories 273. Total Fat 9 g. Saturated Fat 2 g.
Protein 16 g. Carbohydrate 32 g. Fiber 3 g.
Sodium 334 mg. Cholesterol 116 mg.

Rice Cakes with Mushroom-Walnut Sauce

Rice Cakes with Mushroom-Walnut Sauce

*Grandmas usually made rice patties as a way to use up leftover
rice. You can serve these delicious patties as a side dish with chicken, roast
beef, or fish, or as a main dish with a salad, vegetable, and rolls.*

For the rice cakes:

- ½ cup uncooked long-grain white rice
- ¼ cup finely chopped yellow onion
- ¼ cup finely chopped sweet green, red, or yellow pepper
- ¼ cup seasoned fine dry bread crumbs
- 1 large egg, lightly beaten
- ⅛ teaspoon ground red pepper (cayenne)
- 2 tablespoons vegetable oil

For the sauce:

- 1 tablespoon butter or margarine
- 1 cup sliced fresh mushrooms
- ¼ cup finely sliced green onions with tops
- 2 tablespoons all-purpose flour
- ¼ teaspoon salt
- ⅛ teaspoon black pepper
- 1 cup lower-sodium beef broth (page 67)
- ¼ cup chopped walnuts, toasted

1 To prepare the rice cakes, in a medium-size saucepan, cook the rice according to the package directions, omitting the butter. While the rice is still warm, stir in the onion, green pepper, bread crumbs, egg, and ground red pepper. Using about ½ cup for each patty, shape mixture into 4 patties, each about ¾ inch thick. Cover; refrigerate 1 hour.

2 In a 12-inch nonstick skillet, heat oil over moderate heat. Cook patties in hot oil for 3 minutes. Using a wide spatula, carefully turn patties. Cook for 3 minutes more or until patties are golden. Transfer patties to a serving platter and keep warm.

3 Meanwhile, to prepare the sauce, in a medium-size saucepan, melt the butter over moderate heat. Add mushrooms and green onions; cook for 3 minutes. Stir in flour, salt, and black pepper. Cook for 1 minute. Stir in the beef broth. Cook, stirring constantly, for 5 minutes or until thickened. Stir in walnuts. Serve sauce over patties. Makes 4 side-dish or 2 main-dish servings.

Prep Time: 25 minutes Chilling Time: 1 hour
Cooking Time: 30 minutes

1 Side-Dish Serving: Calories 301. Total Fat 16 g.
Saturated Fat 3 g. Protein 7 g. Carbohydrate 32 g. Fiber 2 g.
Sodium 649 mg. Cholesterol 61 mg.

New Orleans Dirty Rice

Creole cooks gave this zesty dish its name because the chopped chicken livers make the rice look "dirty".

1¼ cups lower-sodium beef broth (page 67)
¼ teaspoon salt
2 bay leaves
½ cup uncooked long-grain white rice
3 tablespoons all-purpose flour
3 tablespoons vegetable oil
1 large yellow onion, finely chopped
1 medium-size sweet green pepper, finely chopped
1 stalk celery, finely sliced
2 cloves garlic, minced
8 ounces chicken livers, coarsely chopped
1 teaspoon dried thyme leaves or oregano leaves
⅛ teaspoon ground red pepper (cayenne)
¼ cup minced parsley

1 In medium-size saucepan, bring broth, salt, and bay leaves to boil. Stir in rice. Lower heat and simmer, covered, for 20 minutes or until rice is tender and liquid is absorbed. Discard bay leaves. Using a fork, fluff rice.

2 Meanwhile, for roux, in heavy Dutch oven, stir flour and oil until smooth. Cook over moderate heat, stirring constantly, 5 to 7 minutes or until dark brown. Add onion, green pepper, celery, and garlic and cook 8 to 10 minutes or until vegetables are tender; stir frequently. Add chicken livers, thyme, and red pepper. Cook, covered, over moderately low heat for 6 to 8 minutes or until livers are slightly pink, stirring often.

3 Stir rice and parsley into liver mixture. Cook, uncovered, for 1 to 2 minutes more or until heated through. Makes 6 side-dish or 3 main-dish servings.

Prep Time: 20 minutes Cooking Time: 25 minutes

1 Side-Dish Serving: Calories 177. Total Fat 8 g.
Saturated Fat 1 g. Protein 6 g. Carbohydrate 20 g. Fiber 1 g.
Sodium 108 mg. Cholesterol 98 mg.

Bulgur Wheat Pilaf

Bulgur gives this savory pilaf a subtle chewy texture. Look for it in the rice or grains section of the supermarket.

1 tablespoon butter or margarine
1 medium-size sweet red or green pepper, chopped
6 green onions with tops, sliced
2 cloves garlic, minced
¾ cup bulgur
1¾ cups lower-sodium chicken broth (page 67)
1 teaspoon dried thyme leaves
¼ teaspoon each salt and black pepper

1 In a large saucepan, melt butter over moderate heat. Add green pepper, green onions, and garlic; cook for 5 minutes or until vegetables are tender, stirring often. Stir in bulgur. Add broth, thyme, salt, and black pepper. Bring to boil. Lower heat; simmer, covered, 15 minutes or until bulgur is tender and liquid is absorbed. Makes 4 side-dish servings.

Prep Time: 10 minutes Cooking Time: 25 minutes

1 Serving: Calories 131. Total Fat 3 g. Saturated Fat 2 g.
Protein 3 g. Carbohydrate 23 g. Fiber 5 g.
Sodium 169 mg. Cholesterol 8 mg.

Chicken Bulgur Pilaf Prepare as for Bulgur Wheat Pilaf, adding **2 cups chopped cooked chicken or turkey** and ¼ **cup sliced almonds, toasted,** to cooked bulgur mixture. Heat through. Makes 4 main-dish servings.

1 Serving: Calories 298. Total Fat 12 g. Saturated Fat 4 g.
Protein 25 g. Carbohydrate 25 g. Fiber 6 g.
Sodium 230 mg. Cholesterol 70 mg.

New England Barley Casserole

Barley first came to America with the Pilgrims. Pearl barley gets its name because, after the hull is removed, the barley is polished or pearled. It comes in both regular and quick-cooking forms.

- 1 **tablespoon butter or margarine**
- 1 **tablespoon olive or vegetable oil**
- ¾ **cup quick-cooking barley**
- 1 **medium-size yellow onion, chopped**
- 2 **cups sliced fresh mushrooms**
- 2 **cups lower-sodium beef broth (page 67)**
- ½ **cup cashews, chopped, or peanuts, halved**
- ½ **teaspoon salt**
- ¼ **teaspoon black pepper**
- ¼ **cup minced parsley**

1 Preheat the oven to 350°F. In a large saucepan, heat the butter and oil over moderate heat until butter is melted. Add barley and onion and cook for 5 minutes or until onion is tender, stirring frequently. Add mushrooms. Cook for 2 minutes more.

2 Add beef broth, cashews, salt, and pepper. Bring to a boil. Pour into 1½-quart casserole. Bake, covered, for 45 minutes or until barley is tender, stirring once or twice. Stir in parsley. Makes 4 side-dish servings.

Prep Time: 10 minutes Cooking Time: 1 hour

1 Serving: Calories 255. Total Fat 15 g. Saturated Fat 4 g.
Protein 7 g. Carbohydrate 30 g. Fiber 4 g.
Sodium 406 mg. Cholesterol 8 mg.

Old-Fashioned Oatmeal with Raisins

The secret to this old-time breakfast favorite is toasting the oats, which adds a rich color and flavor.

- 1½ **cups old-fashioned rolled oats**
- 1 **cup raisins, currants, or mixed dried fruit bits**
- ¼ **cup firmly packed light brown sugar**
- 1 **teaspoon ground cinnamon**
- ½ **teaspoon salt**
- 3 **cups water**

1 Preheat the oven to 350°F. Spread the oats in a shallow baking pan. Bake for 15 to 20 minutes or until oats are lightly browned, stirring occasionally.

2 In a small bowl, combine oats, raisins, brown sugar, cinnamon, and salt. In medium-size saucepan, bring water to a boil. Gradually stir in oat mixture. Simmer, uncovered, for 5 to 7 minutes or until thickened, stirring often. Remove from heat. Cover; let stand for 3 minutes. Serve with milk. Makes 4 side-dish servings.

Prep Time: 5 minutes Cooking Time: 25 minutes
Standing Time: 3 minutes

1 Serving: Calories 276. Total Fat 2 g. Saturated Fat 0 g.
Protein 6 g. Carbohydrate 62 g. Fiber 5 g.
Sodium 276 mg. Cholesterol 0 mg.

Southern Fried Grits

This Southern classic is great for today because you can prepare the grits ahead and fry them up hot and toasty in the morning.

- 2 **cups water**
- ¼ **teaspoon salt**
- ½ **cup quick-cooking hominy grits**
- 1 **tablespoon butter or margarine**
- 2 **tablespoons low-fat (1% milkfat) milk**
- 1 **large egg, lightly beaten**
- ⅓ **cup all-purpose flour**
- 2 **tablespoons vegetable oil**

1 In a medium-size saucepan, bring the water and the salt to a boil. Slowly add grits to boiling water, stirring constantly. Lower the heat and simmer, uncovered, for 5 to 7 minutes or until grits are thick and smooth, stirring frequently to prevent sticking. Stir in the butter.

2 Spread hot mixture into lightly greased 8" x 4" x 2" loaf pan. Cool to room temperature. Cover and refrigerate at least 6 hours (will keep for 1 day). Turn out of pan onto a cutting board. Cut into 8 slices. Cut slices in half diagonally.

3 In a shallow dish, stir together the milk and egg. On a sheet of wax paper, place the flour. Dip the slices of the grits mixture into the milk-egg mixture, then coat with the flour.

4 In a large nonstick skillet, heat oil over moderate heat. Cook slices in hot oil for 3 to 5 minutes. Using a wide spatula, carefully turn slices and cook 3 to 5 minutes more or until golden. Drain on paper towels. Serve with maple syrup. Makes 8 side-dish servings.

Prep Time: 15 minutes Cooking Time: 17 minutes
Cooling Time: 1 hour Chilling Time: 6 hours

1 Serving: Calories 112. Total Fat 6 g. Saturated Fat 1 g.
Protein 2 g. Carbohydrate 13 g. Fiber 1 g.
Sodium 91 mg. Cholesterol 31 mg.

Southern Fried Grits

Rhode Island Jonnycakes

*Some cooks make these cornmeal pancakes
with a little sugar; others think plain is best, but all
Rhode Islanders spell jonnycake without a "h".*

- **1 cup stone-ground white cornmeal**
- **1 teaspoon sugar (optional)**
- **½ teaspoon salt**
- **1¼ cups boiling water**
- **½ cup low-fat (1% milkfat) milk**
- **2 tablespoons vegetable oil**

1 In a medium-size bowl, combine cornmeal, sugar (if using), and salt. In a thin steady stream, pour boiling water into cornmeal mixture, stirring constantly. (Batter will be very thick.). When the water is absorbed, stir in the milk. (Batter will be thin.)

2 Heat a 12-inch nonstick griddle or skillet over moderate heat and brush with a little of the oil. Using about ¼ cup batter for each jonnycake, pour batter onto the griddle. (Batter will spread to about 5 inches.) Cook about 2 minutes on each side or until golden and crisp around edges. (If jonnycakes aren't browning quickly enough, increase heat to moderately high.) Serve with butter and maple syrup. Makes 8 side-dish servings.

Prep Time: 10 minutes Cooking Time: 17 minutes

1 Serving: Calories 100. Total Fat 4 g. Saturated Fat 0 g.
Protein 2 g. Carbohydrate 14 g. Fiber 1 g.
Sodium 141 mg. Cholesterol 1 mg.

Hasty Pudding

*Colonial cooks turned mush into hasty pudding by
adding cream or milk. For a special breakfast, they served
it with brown sugar, maple syrup, or molasses.*

- **1 cup cornmeal**
- **1 cup cold water**
- **½ teaspoon salt**
- **2½ cups water**
- **6 teaspoons butter or margarine**

1 In a small bowl, combine cornmeal, the cold water, and salt. In a medium-size saucepan, bring the 2½ cups water to a boil. Slowly add cornmeal mixture to boiling water, stirring constantly so it does not lump. Return to a boil, stirring constantly. Lower the heat and simmer, covered, for 10 to 15 minutes or until very thick, stirring occasionally. Ladle into bowls. Top each serving with 1 teaspoon of the butter. Sprinkle with a little ground nutmeg if you like. Serve with half-and-half or milk. Makes 6 side-dish servings.

Prep Time: 5 minutes Cooking Time: 20 minutes

1 Serving: Calories 118. Total Fat 4 g. Saturated Fat 2 g.
Protein 2 g. Carbohydrate 18 g. Fiber 2 g.
Sodium 222 mg. Cholesterol 10 mg.

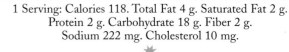

Fried Cornmeal Mush Prepare as for Hasty Pudding. Pour the hot mixture into an 8" x 4" x 2" loaf pan. Cover and refrigerate for at least 6 hours (will keep for 1 day). Turn out of loaf pan onto a cutting board. Cut into ½-inch-thick slices. In a 12-inch nonstick skillet, melt half of the butter or margarine over moderate heat. Add half of the slices; cook for 12 to 15 minutes. Using a wide spatula, carefully turn slices and cook 12 to 15 minutes more or until crisp and brown. Repeat with the remaining butter or margarine and the remaining slices. Serve with honey or maple syrup.

1 Serving: Calories 101. Total Fat 2 g. Saturated Fat 1 g.
Protein 2 g. Carbohydrate 18 g. Fiber 2 g.
Sodium 202 mg. Cholesterol 5 mg.

Italian Polenta

*Italian grandmas made their cornmeal mush with
cheese and topped it with tomato sauce.*

- **1 cup cornmeal**
- **1 cup cold water**
- **½ teaspoon salt**
- **2½ cups water**
- **¼ cup grated Parmesan cheese**

1 In a small bowl, combine cornmeal, the cold water, and salt. In a medium-size saucepan, bring the 2½ cups water to a boil. Slowly add cornmeal mixture to boiling water, stirring constantly so it does not lump. Return to a boil, stirring constantly. Lower the heat and simmer, covered, for 10 to 15 minutes or until very thick, stirring occasionally. Stir in the Parmesan cheese. Pour the hot mixture into a 9-inch pie plate. Cover and refrigerate for at least 2 hours (will keep for 1 day).

2 Preheat oven to 350°F. Bake, uncovered, for 20 minutes or until heated through. Serve in wedges with warmed spaghetti sauce. Makes 6 side-dish servings.

Prep Time: 5 minutes Cooking Time: 20 minutes
Chilling Time: 2 hours Baking Time: 20 minutes

1 Serving: Calories 103. Total Fat 2 g. Saturated Fat 1 g.
Protein 4 g. Carbohydrate 18 g. Fiber 2 g.
Sodium 256 mg. Cholesterol 3 mg.

Baked Spinach Gnocchi

Baked Spinach Gnocchi

Over the years, Italian-style dumplings were made with everything
from potato to semolina and spinach, like this tasty recipe. Serve gnocchi as
you would pasta with your favorite spaghetti sauce.

1 package (10 ounces) frozen chopped spinach
1/4 cup finely chopped yellow onion
2 cups low-fat (1% milkfat) milk
1/2 cup semolina or quick-cooking farina
1 teaspoon dried basil leaves
2 cloves garlic, minced
2 tablespoons butter or margarine
2 large eggs, lightly beaten
2/3 cup grated Parmesan cheese

1 Cook the spinach and onion according to directions on spinach package; drain well, pressing out excess liquid with paper towels.

2 Meanwhile, in a medium-size mixing bowl, stir together 3/4 cup of the milk, the semolina, basil, and garlic. In a medium-size saucepan, bring the remaining 1 1/4 cups milk and the butter to a boil over moderately high heat. Slowly add the semolina mixture to the boiling milk, stirring constantly. Cook, uncovered, for 3 to 5 minutes or until very thick.

3 Remove from heat. Stir about 1 cup of the mixture into eggs; return mixture to the saucepan. Stir in the spinach mixture and 1/3 cup of the Parmesan cheese. Pour into a lightly greased 8" x 8" x 2" baking dish. Cover; refrigerate at least 4 hours (will keep for 1 day).

4 Preheat the oven to 425°F. Turn chilled mixture out of baking dish onto a cutting board. Cut into diamond-shaped pieces. Sprinkle pieces with remaining 1/3 cup Parmesan cheese. Place on a lightly greased baking sheet. Bake for 20 to 25 minutes or until golden. Makes 8 side-dish or 4 main-dish servings.

Prep Time: 15 minutes Cooking Time: 10 minutes
Chilling Time: 4 hours Baking Time: 20 minutes

1 Side-Dish Serving: Calories 156. Total Fat 8 g.
Saturated Fat 4 g. Protein 9 g. Carbohydrate 13 g. Fiber 2 g.
Sodium 252 mg. Cholesterol 70 mg.

Kasha and Noodles

Kasha and Noodles

This age-old Jewish specialty has a nutty flavor that
goes well with main dishes, such as meatballs or chicken. The
egg coats the grains of kasha so they don't stick together.

6 **ounces curly or plain egg noodles**
2 **tablespoons olive or vegetable oil**
1 **large yellow onion, chopped**
2 **cups thinly sliced fresh mushrooms**
¾ **cup kasha (toasted buckwheat groats)**
1 **large egg, lightly beaten**
1¾ **cups lower-sodium chicken broth (page 67)**
½ **teaspoon salt**
¼ **teaspoon black pepper**

1 Cook the noodles according to package directions. Drain, rinse, and drain again; transfer noodles to a warm bowl and keep warm.

2 Meanwhile, in a large saucepan, heat the oil over moderate heat. Add the onion and mushrooms and cook for 5 minutes or until the onion is tender. In a small bowl, combine the kasha and egg, stirring well to coat each grain.

3 Push the onion mixture to one side of the saucepan; add kasha mixture to the other side. Cook over moderately high heat, stirring constantly, for 3 to 4 minutes or until the kasha grains have separated. Stir in the chicken broth, salt, and pepper.

4 Bring to a boil. Lower the heat and simmer, covered, for 12 to 15 minutes or until the kasha is tender. Stir in the cooked noodles; heat through. Makes 8 side-dish servings.

Prep Time: 10 minutes Cooking Time: 30 minutes

1 Serving: Calories 174. Total Fat 5 g. Saturated Fat 1 g.
Protein 6 g. Carbohydrate 27 g. Fiber 3 g.
Sodium 146 mg. Cholesterol 44 mg.

Vermont-Style Baked Beans

The trick to making great baked beans is long, slow cooking. This recipe is the way folks in Vermont like beans—sweetened with pure maple syrup.

- 6 **cups water**
- 1½ **cups dried navy or great Northern beans, soaked (tip, below right)**
- 1 **large yellow onion, chopped**
- 2 **strips lean bacon, chopped and cooked until crisp**
- ¼ **cup firmly packed light brown sugar**
- ¼ **cup pure maple syrup**
- 1 **tablespoon dry mustard**
- ¼ **teaspoon each salt and black pepper**

1 In a large saucepan, combine the water and the soaked beans. Bring to a boil. Lower the heat and simmer, covered, for 1½ to 2 hours or until beans are tender. Drain beans, reserving 1 cup liquid.

2 Preheat the oven to 300°F. In a 2-quart casserole or bean pot, combine cooked beans, onion, and bacon. Stir in ½ cup of the reserved liquid, brown sugar, maple syrup, dry mustard, salt, and pepper. Bake, covered, for 2 to 2½ hours or until desired consistency, stirring occasionally and adding more reserved liquid, if needed. Makes 6 side-dish servings.

Prep Time: 10 minutes plus soaking
Cooking Time: 1 hour 40 minutes Baking Time: 2 hours

1 Serving: Calories 239. Total Fat 2 g. Saturated Fat 1 g. Protein 11 g. Carbohydrate 46 g. Fiber 10 g. Sodium 128 mg. Cholesterol 2 mg.

Boston Baked Beans Prepare as for Vermont-Style Baked Beans, substituting ¼ **cup molasses** for the maple syrup.

1 Serving: Calories 240. Total Fat 2 g. Saturated Fat 1 g. Protein 11 g. Carbohydrate 46 g. Fiber 10 g. Sodium 132 mg. Cholesterol 2 mg.

Last-Minute Baked Beans Prepare as for Vermont-Style Baked Beans, substituting **3 cans (15 ounces each) navy or great Northern beans, undrained,** for the cooked beans and omitting the bean liquid. Bake, covered, for 1 to 1½ hours or until desired consistency. Makes 8 side-dish servings.

1 Serving: Calories 209. Total Fat 2 g. Saturated Fat 0 g. Protein 10 g. Carbohydrate 40 g. Fiber 9 g. Sodium 296 mg. Cholesterol 1 mg.

Midwestern Lima Bean Pot

- 6 **cups water**
- 1½ **cups dried lima beans, soaked (tip, below)**
- 1 **large yellow onion, chopped**
- ½ **cup bite-size pieces cooked ham (optional)**
- ⅓ **cup molasses**
- ⅓ **cup bottled chili sauce**
- 1 **tablespoon vinegar**
- 1 **teaspoon dry mustard**
- ⅛ **teaspoon ground red pepper (cayenne)**

1 In a large saucepan, combine the water and the soaked beans. Bring to a boil. Lower the heat and simmer, covered, for 1 to 1¼ hours or until beans are tender. Drain beans, reserving 1 cup liquid.

2 Preheat the oven to 300°F. In a 2-quart casserole or bean pot, combine the cooked beans, onion, and ham. Stir in reserved liquid, molasses, chili sauce, vinegar, mustard, and red pepper. Bake, covered, for 1 hour, stirring occasionally. Uncover; bake for 1 hour more or until desired consistency. Makes 6 side-dish servings.

Prep Time: 10 minutes plus soaking
Cooking Time: 1 hour 10 minutes Baking Time: 2 hours

1 Serving: Calories 233. Total Fat 1 g. Saturated Fat 0 g. Protein 11 g. Carbohydrate 48 g. Fiber 10 g. Sodium 214 mg. Cholesterol 0 mg.

SOAKING DRIED BEANS

The old-fashioned way of fixing dried beans was to soak them overnight. However, you can save time by using the quick-soak method. Either way, first sort the beans, discarding any shriveled or moldy ones. Then, rinse beans and drain them.

◆ To soak dried beans overnight, place them in a large saucepan or Dutch oven. Add enough cold water to cover the beans. Cover the saucepan. Let stand at room temperature at least 8 hours or overnight. Drain and thoroughly rinse the beans.

◆ To quick-soak dried beans, place them in a large saucepan or Dutch oven. Add enough cold water to cover. Bring to a boil. Lower the heat and simmer, uncovered, for 2 minutes. Remove from heat. Cover and let stand for 1 hour. Drain and thoroughly rinse the beans.

Swedish Brown Beans

Swedish Brown Beans

Serve these robust sweet-and-sour-flavored beans as a side dish with pork or lamb chops or with cheese, crackers, and fruit for a light supper. Look for the traditional Swedish brown beans at a large supermarket or a food specialty store.

4	cups water
1½	cups dried Swedish brown beans or pinto beans, soaked (page 227)
¼	cup white vinegar
¼	cup dark corn syrup
1	tablespoon firmly packed light brown sugar
½	teaspoon salt
¼	teaspoon ground cinnamon (optional)

1 In a large saucepan, combine the water and the soaked beans. Bring to a boil. Lower the heat and simmer, covered, for 1½ to 2 hours or until beans are tender. Drain beans, reserving 1 cup liquid.

2 Preheat the oven to 300°F. In a 2-quart casserole or bean pot, combine cooked beans, ½ cup of the reserved liquid, the vinegar, corn syrup, brown sugar, salt, and cinnamon (if using). Bake, covered, for 1½ to 2 hours or until desired consistency, stirring occasionally and adding more of the reserved liquid, if needed. Makes 6 side-dish servings.

Prep Time: 5 minutes plus soaking
Cooking Time: 1 hour 40 minutes Baking Time: 1½ hours

1 Serving: Calories 206. Total Fat 1 g. Saturated Fat 0 g. Protein 10 g. Carbohydrate 42 g. Fiber 10 g. Sodium 202 mg. Cholesterol 0 mg.

Santa Fe Refried Beans

Refried beans is a misnomer. These Southwestern beans were never fried twice, but were simmered on the stove, then mashed and fried just once.

1½	cups dried pinto, pink, or red kidney beans, sorted and rinsed
4	cups water
1	large yellow onion, chopped
3	cloves garlic, minced
1	cup salsa
¾	teaspoon salt

1 In a large saucepan, combine the beans, the water, onion, and garlic. Bring to a boil. Lower the heat and simmer, covered, for 2 to 2½ hours or until beans are very tender. Cool slightly (do not drain).

2 In a food processor or blender, process bean mixture, half at a time, until smooth. Return bean mixture to the saucepan. Stir in salsa and salt. Cook, uncovered, over moderate heat for 5 minutes or until desired consistency, stirring constantly. Serve with reduced-fat sour cream and reduced-fat shredded Cheddar cheese. Makes 6 side-dish or 3 main-dish servings.

Prep Time: 15 minutes Cooking Time: 2¼ hours

1 Side-Dish Serving: Calories 183. Total Fat 1 g. Saturated Fat 0 g. Protein 10 g. Carbohydrate 35 g. Fiber 10 g. Sodium 526 mg. Cholesterol 0 mg.

White Beans and Ham

Thrifty women created this delicious recipe to take advantage of leftover ham. Serve it with burgers or as a main dish with corn bread and a fruit salad.

4	cups water
1½	cups dried navy or great Northern beans, soaked (page 227)
1	cup bite-size pieces cooked lower-sodium ham
1	large yellow onion, chopped
2	stalks celery, sliced
3	bay leaves
¼	teaspoon each salt and black pepper
⅛	teaspoon ground cloves (optional)

1 In a Dutch oven, combine the water and the soaked beans. Bring to a boil. Lower the heat and simmer, covered, for 1 to 1½ hours or until the beans are tender. Drain beans, reserving 1½ cups liquid. Remove 2 cups of beans from Dutch oven; using a fork, slightly mash these beans. Return mashed beans to Dutch oven.

2 Stir in the reserved liquid, ham, onion, celery, bay leaves, salt, pepper, and cloves (if using). Bring to a boil. Lower the heat and simmer, covered, for 30 minutes or until vegetables are tender, stirring occasionally. Discard the bay leaves. Makes 8 side-dish or 4 main-dish servings.

Prep Time: 15 minutes plus soaking Cooking Time: 1¾ hours

1 Side-Dish Serving: Calories 152. Total Fat 2 g. Saturated Fat 1 g. Protein 11 g. Carbohydrate 23 g. Fiber 8 g. Sodium 248 mg. Cholesterol 10 mg.

Hoppin' John

Southerners serve this dish on New Year's Day to ensure good luck throughout the year. This custom is thought to have its beginnings in the African tradition of preparing dried bean dishes on feast days as "offerings to the gods".

2½ **cups water**
1 **cup dried black-eyed peas or cowpeas, sorted and rinsed**
½ **cup uncooked long-grain white rice**
¼ **teaspoon salt**
3 **strips lean bacon, chopped**
1 **large yellow onion, chopped**
2 **cloves garlic, minced**
⅛ **teaspoon hot red pepper sauce**

1 In a large saucepan, bring the water and black-eyed peas to a boil over moderately high heat. Lower the heat and simmer, covered, for 40 to 45 minutes or until peas are tender. Drain.

2 Meanwhile, in a medium-size saucepan, cook the rice according to the package directions, using the ¼ teaspoon salt and omitting the butter. In a large skillet, cook the bacon over moderate heat until crisp. Remove bacon, reserving drippings. Drain the bacon on paper towels; set aside.

3 Add the onion and garlic to reserved drippings and cook until onion is tender. Stir in the cooked peas, cooked rice, and red pepper sauce. Cook for 2 to 3 minutes more or until heated through. To serve, sprinkle with the cooked bacon. Serve with roast pork or ham. Makes 6 side-dish servings.

Prep Time: 10 minutes Cooking Time: 55 minutes

1 Serving: Calories 216. Total Fat 6 g. Saturated Fat 2 g. Protein 9 g. Carbohydrate 33 g. Fiber 4 g. Sodium 165 mg. Cholesterol 6 mg.

✳

Easy Hoppin' John Prepare as for Hoppin' John, substituting **1 can (15 ounces) black-eyed peas, pinto beans, or red kidney beans, rinsed and drained,** for the cooked black-eyed peas.

1 Serving: Calories 200. Total Fat 6 g. Saturated Fat 2 g. Protein 8 g. Carbohydrate 29 g. Fiber 7 g. Sodium 311 mg. Cholesterol 6 mg.

Black Beans and Rice

Some South American grandmas made this traditional dish with ham; others served it meatless. Whichever way you choose, top it with sour cream, sliced green onions, and orange or lime wedges.

2 **cups lower-sodium beef broth (page 67)**
1⅓ **cups dried black beans, soaked (page 227)**
½ **cup water**
2 **bay leaves**
1 **large yellow onion, chopped**
1 **large sweet green pepper, chopped**
½ **cup bite-size pieces cooked lower-sodium ham**
2 **cloves garlic, minced**
1 **tablespoon vinegar or lemon juice**
¼ **teaspoon black pepper**
¼ **teaspoon hot red pepper sauce**
1 **cup uncooked long-grain white rice**

1 In a Dutch oven, combine the beef broth, the soaked beans, water, and bay leaves. Bring to a boil. Lower the heat and simmer, covered, for 1¾ to 2 hours or until the beans are tender. Discard bay leaves.

2 Stir the onion, green pepper, ham, garlic, vinegar, black pepper, and red pepper sauce into the bean mixture. Bring to a boil. Lower the heat and simmer, covered, for 15 minutes.

3 Meanwhile, cook the rice according to package directions, omitting the butter and salt. Spoon bean mixture over hot cooked rice. Serve with additional hot red pepper sauce. Makes 4 main-dish servings.

Prep Time: 10 minutes plus soaking Cooking Time: 2¼ hours

1 Serving: Calories 471. Total Fat 3 g. Saturated Fat 1 g. Protein 24 g. Carbohydrate 87 g. Fiber 16 g. Sodium 218 mg. Cholesterol 12 mg.

HOW MANY BEANS?

When a recipe calls for dried beans, keep in mind that 8 ounces of uncooked beans measures about 1¼ cups. This amount will yield 3 to 3½ cups of cooked beans. If you want to substitute canned beans for cooked dried beans in a recipe, a 15-ounce can has about 1¾ cups.

Louisiana Red Beans and Rice

Bayou cooks served this hearty dish on Monday because they made it with the bone from Sunday's baked ham.

4 cups water

1¼ cups dried red beans or red kidney beans, soaked (page 227)

1 meaty ham hock (1 to 1½ pounds)

1 large yellow onion, chopped

2 stalks celery, sliced

2 bay leaves

2 cloves garlic, minced

1½ teaspoons dried thyme leaves

¼ teaspoon each salt and black pepper

1 cup uncooked long-grain white rice

¼ cup minced parsley

1 In a Dutch oven, combine the water, the soaked beans, and ham hock. Bring to a boil. Lower the heat and simmer, covered, for 1 to 1½ hours or until beans are tender. Drain beans, reserving 2 cups liquid. Remove 2 cups of the beans from Dutch oven. Using a fork or potato masher, slightly mash these beans. Return mashed beans to Dutch oven. Remove ham bone. When bone is cool, remove meat. Discard bone. Cut meat into bite-size pieces; return to Dutch oven.

2 Stir in the reserved liquid, onion, celery, bay leaves, garlic, thyme, salt, and pepper. Bring to a boil. Lower the heat and simmer, covered, for 30 minutes or until vegetables are tender, stirring occasionally. Discard bay leaves. Meanwhile, cook the rice according to package directions, omitting butter and salt. Spoon bean mixture over rice. Sprinkle with parsley. Serve with corn bread. Makes 6 main-dish servings.

Prep Time: 20 minutes plus soaking
Cooking Time: 1 hour 40 minutes

1 Serving: Calories 433. Total Fat 12 g. Saturated Fat 4 g.
Protein 25 g. Carbohydrate 55 g. Fiber 9 g.
Sodium 262 mg. Cholesterol 53 mg.

Quick Red Beans and Rice Prepare as for Louisiana Red Beans and Rice, substituting **2 cans (15½ ounces each) red beans or red kidney beans, rinsed and drained,** for the cooked red beans; **½ cup bite-size pieces cooked lower-sodium ham** for the ham hock; and **1½ cups water** for the 2 cups reserved liquid.

1 Serving: Calories 315. Total Fat 2 g. Saturated Fat 1 g.
Protein 15 g. Carbohydrate 58 g. Fiber 12 g.
Sodium 241 mg. Cholesterol 8 mg.

Louisiana Red Beans and Rice

MINCING PARSLEY

To mince parsley easily, place a few sprigs in a glass measuring cup and snip them, right in the cup, with kitchen shears. The lines on the side of the cup will tell you how much you've minced.

Lentils and Sausage

Lentils and Sausage

*If you can't find smoked turkey sausage, use another
reduced-fat smoked sausage or substitute lower-sodium ham.*

2½ cups lower-sodium beef broth (page 67)
1 cup dried lentils, sorted and rinsed
6 ounces smoked turkey sausage, sliced
1 large potato, peeled and cubed
1 large yellow onion, chopped
2 cloves garlic, minced
1 teaspoon dried basil leaves
½ teaspoon salt
¼ teaspoon black pepper

1 In a large saucepan, bring the beef broth to a boil over high heat. Stir in the lentils. Lower the heat and simmer, covered, for 20 minutes.

2 Add the sausage, potato, onion, garlic, basil, salt, and pepper. Bring to a boil. Lower the heat and simmer, covered, for 20 minutes or until lentils and potato are tender. Makes 4 main-dish servings.

Prep Time: 15 minutes Cooking Time: 50 minutes

1 Serving: Calories 284. Total Fat 7 g. Saturated Fat 2 g.
Protein 20 g. Carbohydrate 38 g. Fiber 7 g.
Sodium 606 mg. Cholesterol 28 mg.

West-Coast Lentil Casserole

1¾ cups lower-sodium chicken broth (page 67)
2 bay leaves
1 cup dried lentils or split peas, sorted and rinsed
1 tablespoon vegetable oil
1 large yellow onion, chopped
1 large carrot, finely chopped
2 cloves garlic, minced
¼ cup lower-calorie, lower-sodium catsup
2 tablespoons firmly packed light brown sugar
1 teaspoon dry mustard
1 teaspoon dried oregano leaves

1 In a medium-size saucepan, bring the chicken broth and bay leaves to a boil over high heat. Stir in the lentils. Lower the heat and simmer, covered, for 20 minutes. Discard bay leaves.

2 Preheat the oven to 350°F. Meanwhile, in a medium-size skillet, heat the oil over moderate heat. Add the onion, carrot, and garlic and cook for 5 minutes or until the vegetables are tender. Stir in the catsup, brown sugar, dry mustard, and oregano.

3 In a 1½-quart casserole, combine lentils and onion mixture. Bake, covered, for 25 minutes. Makes 6 side-dish servings.

Prep Time: 15 minutes Cooking Time: 25 minutes
Baking Time: 25 minutes

1 Serving: Calories 159. Total Fat 3 g. Saturated Fat 0 g.
Protein 8 g. Carbohydrate 27 g. Fiber 5 g.
Sodium 11 mg. Cholesterol 0 mg.

USING LENTILS

◆ Years ago, lentils typically were greenish-brown. Today, however, yellow and red ones also are available. They taste just the same as the green variety, but they add a more colorful touch to soups, stews, and casseroles. Look for them in large supermarkets or Middle Eastern food specialty stores.

◆ Before using lentils, sort through them, selecting only the plump ones and discarding any shriveled or spotted ones. Then, rinse the lentils before cooking them.

Cheesiest Ever Macaroni and Cheese

Grandmas made sinfully rich macaroni and cheese from scratch, long before boxed was invented. This recipe uses the old-fashioned technique of baking the macaroni in a custard.

1 tablespoon fine dry bread crumbs
8 ounces elbow macaroni
1 large yellow onion, coarsely chopped
2½ cups shredded extra-sharp Cheddar cheese (10 ounces)
1 cup low-fat (1% milkfat) milk
2 large eggs
1 large egg white
¼ teaspoon black pepper
1 can (3 ounces) french-fried onions (optional)

1 Preheat oven to 350°F. Sprinkle the bottom and sides of a lightly greased 2-quart casserole with the bread crumbs, tilting casserole to coat evenly. Set aside.

2 In a large saucepan, bring 3 quarts of water to a boil; add the macaroni and onion and cook for 5 to 6 minutes or just until macaroni is tender but still firm to the bite. Drain, rinse, and drain again.

3 Arrange a third of the macaroni mixture in the prepared casserole. Spoon 1 cup of the Cheddar cheese over macaroni mixture. Repeat with another third of the macaroni mixture and another 1 cup of the Cheddar cheese. Top with remaining macaroni mixture. In a medium-size bowl, whisk together the milk, eggs, egg white, and pepper. Pour over macaroni mixture.

4 Bake, covered, for 30 minutes or until a knife inserted near the center comes out clean. Remove from oven. Sprinkle with the remaining ½ cup Cheddar cheese. Spoon french-fried onions (if using) around the outside edge. Bake, uncovered, for 5 minutes more or until cheese is melted. Makes 6 main-dish servings.

Prep Time: 20 minutes Cooking Time: 20 minutes
Baking Time: 35 minutes

1 Serving: Calories 387. Total Fat 19 g. Saturated Fat 11 g.
Protein 21 g. Carbohydrate 33 g. Fiber 1 g.
Sodium 355 mg. Cholesterol 122 mg.

Greek Pastitsio

Greek Pastitsio

Greek immigrants brought the recipe for this layered lamb-and-macaroni casserole with them from the old country. Serve it, as you would lasagna, accompanied by a green salad and French bread or bread sticks.

 6 ounces elbow macaroni

 2 large eggs

 ½ cup feta cheese, cubed (2 ounces), or ⅓ cup grated Parmesan cheese

 ¼ cup low-fat (1% milkfat) milk

For the meat filling:

 12 ounces lean ground lamb or ground beef

 1 large yellow onion, chopped

 1¾ cups chopped tomatoes or 1 can (14½ ounces) lower-sodium tomatoes, undrained and cut up

 1 teaspoon dried oregano leaves

 ¼ teaspoon ground cinnamon

 ⅛ teaspoon each salt and black pepper

 ⅔ cup grated Parmesan cheese

For the sauce:

 1½ cups low-fat (1% milkfat) milk

 2 tablespoons all-purpose flour

 ¼ teaspoon each salt and black pepper

 ¼ cup grated Parmesan cheese

1 Preheat the oven to 350°F. Cook the macaroni according to package directions. Drain, rinse, and drain again; transfer to a warm bowl. Separate the eggs. In a small bowl, lightly beat the yolks; set aside for the sauce. Stir the egg whites, feta cheese, and the ¼ cup milk into the macaroni. Set aside.

2 Meanwhile, to prepare the meat filling, in a large skillet, cook the lamb and onion over moderately high heat until meat is browned. Drain off fat. Stir in the tomatoes, oregano, cinnamon, the ⅛ teaspoon salt, and the ⅛ teaspoon pepper. Bring to a boil. Lower the heat and simmer, covered, for 5 minutes. Remove from heat. Stir in the ⅔ cup Parmesan cheese. Layer half of the macaroni mixture in a lightly greased 8" x 8" x 2" baking dish. Top with the meat filling, then with the remaining macaroni mixture.

3 To prepare the sauce, in a medium-size saucepan, whisk together the 1½ cups milk, the flour, the ¼ teaspoon salt, and the ¼ teaspoon pepper. Cook over moderate heat, whisking constantly, for 8 minutes or

until mixture is thickened and bubbly. Slowly stir about 1 cup of the hot mixture into the lightly beaten egg yolks, then return this mixture to the saucepan. Cook, stirring constantly, for 3 minutes or until mixture thickens. (Do not boil.) Stir in the ¼ cup Parmesan cheese.

4 Pour the sauce over the macaroni layer. Bake for 30 to 35 minutes or until heated through. Let stand 10 minutes before serving. Makes 6 main-dish servings.

Prep Time: 20 minutes Cooking Time: 30 minutes
Baking Time: 30 minutes Standing Time: 10 minutes

1 Serving: Calories 422. Total Fat 20 g. Saturated Fat 10 g.
Protein 28 g. Carbohydrate 32 g. Fiber 2 g.
Sodium 742 mg. Cholesterol 142 mg.

Salmon Noodle Casserole

Creamy one-dish meals made with salmon first became popular in the 1930's. You can substitute tuna or chicken for the salmon, if you prefer.

4 ounces medium-size noodles
1 tablespoon olive or vegetable oil
1 medium-size yellow onion, chopped
1 medium-size sweet green pepper, chopped
1 stalk celery, sliced
⅓ cup all-purpose flour
⅛ teaspoon black pepper
3½ cups low-fat (1% milkfat) milk
½ cup shredded Swiss cheese (2 ounces)
1 can (14¾ ounces) pink salmon, picked through, rinsed, drained, and flaked; or 2 cans (6 ounces each) water-packed, chunk light tuna, rinsed, drained, and flaked; or 2 cups cooked chicken
⅓ cup grated Parmesan cheese

1 Preheat oven to 350°F. Cook the noodles according to the package directions. Drain, rinse, and drain again; return to the saucepan and cover.

2 Meanwhile, in a large saucepan, heat the oil over moderate heat. Add the onion, green pepper, and celery and cook for 5 minutes or until the vegetables are tender. Stir in the flour and black pepper. Add the milk. Cook, stirring constantly, for 10 minutes or until the mixture is thickened and bubbly. Stir in the Swiss cheese until melted. Stir in the cooked noodles. Carefully stir in the salmon.

3 Spoon the mixture into a lightly greased 8" x 8" x 2" baking dish. Top with the Parmesan cheese. Bake for 25 minutes or until heated through. Makes 4 main-dish servings.

Prep Time: 20 minutes Cooking Time: 42 minutes

1 Serving: Calories 432. Total Fat 16 g. Saturated Fat 6 g.
Protein 32 g. Carbohydrate 40 g. Fiber 2 g.
Sodium 665 mg. Cholesterol 50 mg.

Noodles Romanoff

Many old cookbooks featured this Eastern European noodle dish made with sour cream and poppy seeds. Serve it in place of potatoes with roast pork, grilled chicken, or poached fish.

4 ounces curly or plain egg noodles
1 tablespoon olive or vegetable oil
1 large yellow onion, chopped
2 cloves garlic, minced
1 carton (12 ounces) low-fat (1% milkfat) cottage cheese
1 cup reduced-fat sour cream
2 teaspoons poppy seeds
¼ teaspoon salt
⅛ teaspoon hot red pepper sauce
¼ cup fine dry bread crumbs
1 tablespoon butter or margarine, melted

1 Preheat oven to 350°F. Cook the noodles according to package directions. Drain, rinse, and drain again; transfer to a warm large bowl.

2 Meanwhile, in a medium-size skillet, heat the oil over moderate heat. Add the onion and garlic and cook for 5 minutes or until onion is tender. Add onion mixture to noodles. Stir in the cottage cheese, sour cream, poppy seeds, salt, and red pepper sauce.

3 Spoon into a lightly greased 8" x 8" x 2" baking dish. In a small bowl, combine the bread crumbs and melted butter. Sprinkle over the noodle mixture. Bake for 25 minutes or until heated through. Makes 6 side-dish servings.

Prep Time: 15 minutes Cooking Time: 40 minutes

1 Serving: Calories 224. Total Fat 11 g. Saturated Fat 5 g.
Protein 11 g. Carbohydrate 20 g. Fiber 1 g.
Sodium 396 mg. Cholesterol 38 mg.

Rose's Lasagna

"My Grandma Rose always made her sauce for lasagna from scratch," recalls Rosemary Corsiglia. "But I save time by using one of the new gourmet spaghetti sauces, then adding sausage, onion, and some garlic for flavor."

For the meat sauce:
- 8 ounces bulk Italian sausage or lean ground beef
- 1 large yellow onion, chopped
- 2 cloves garlic, minced
- 4 cups spaghetti sauce

For the ricotta filling:
- 1½ cups part-skim ricotta cheese or low-fat (1% milkfat) cottage cheese, drained
- ⅓ cup grated Parmesan cheese or Romano cheese
- ¼ cup minced parsley
- 1 large egg white, lightly beaten

For the casserole:
- 9 no-boil lasagna noodles
- 2 cups shredded part-skim mozzarella or provolone cheese (8 ounces)

1 Preheat the oven to 350°F. To prepare the meat sauce, in a large saucepan, cook the sausage, onion, and garlic over moderately high heat until sausage is browned. Remove from saucepan and drain well. Wipe out the saucepan. Return the meat mixture to saucepan. Stir in spaghetti sauce. Bring to a boil. Lower heat and simmer, covered, for 5 minutes, stirring occasionally.

2 Meanwhile, to prepare the ricotta filling, in a medium-size mixing bowl, stir together the ricotta cheese, Parmesan cheese, parsley, and egg white.

3 To prepare the casserole, spread 2 cups of the meat sauce over bottom of a lightly greased 13" x 9" x 2" baking dish. Place 3 dry noodles, side by side, on top of sauce (do not overlap). Spread with half of the ricotta filling. Spoon 1½ cups of the meat sauce over (tip, above right). Sprinkle with one-third of the mozzarella cheese. Repeat layers of noodles, ricotta filling, meat sauce, and mozzarella. Then, top with the remaining noodles, meat sauce, and mozzarella.

4 Bake, covered, for 35 to 40 minutes or until noodles are tender. Uncover; bake for 5 minutes more. Let stand 10 minutes. Makes 8 main-dish servings.

Prep Time: 20 minutes Cooking Time: 15 minutes
Baking Time: 40 minutes Standing Time: 10 minutes

1 Serving: Calories 386. Total Fat 18 g. Saturated Fat 9 g.
Protein 26 g. Carbohydrate 28 g. Fiber 3 g.
Sodium 964 mg. Cholesterol 55 mg.

LAYERING LASAGNA

To assemble the lasagna, spoon some meat sauce over the layer of ricotta filling. Then, use a spatula or the back of a spoon to spread the meat sauce into an even layer.

Spinach-Stuffed Shells With Mushroom Sauce

- 8 jumbo shells or 4 manicotti shells

For the spinach filling:
- 1 package (10 ounces) frozen chopped spinach
- 2 large green onions with tops, finely sliced
- ⅔ cup part-skim ricotta cheese
- ⅓ cup grated Parmesan cheese
- 1 large egg, lightly beaten

For the mushroom sauce:
- 1 tablespoon olive or vegetable oil
- 2 cups sliced fresh mushrooms
- 3 tablespoons all-purpose flour
- ¼ teaspoon each salt and black pepper
- ⅛ teaspoon ground nutmeg
- 1¼ cups low-fat (1% milkfat) milk
- ½ cup reduced-fat sour cream

1 Cook pasta shells according to package directions. Drain, rinse, and drain again; invert shells on foil.

2 Preheat the oven to 350°F. Meanwhile, to prepare the spinach filling, cook the spinach and green onions according to the directions on the spinach package; drain well, pressing out excess liquid with paper towels. In a medium-size bowl, combine the spinach-onion mixture, ricotta cheese, Parmesan cheese, and egg. Mix well. To stuff the jumbo shells, spoon about 2 tablespoons of the filling into each shell. (Use about ¼ cup of the filling in each manicotti shell.) Place the shells in a lightly greased 8" x 8" x 2" baking dish. Bake, covered, for 15 minutes.

3 While shells are baking, to prepare the mushroom sauce, in a medium-size saucepan, heat the oil over moderate heat. Add the mushrooms and cook for 2 minutes or just until tender. In a small bowl, whisk together 2 tablespoons of the flour, the salt, pepper, and nutmeg. Stir the flour mixture into mushrooms. Cook for 1 minute or until bubbly. Add the milk. Cook, stirring constantly, for 8 minutes or until the mixture is thickened and bubbly.

4 In a small bowl, stir together the sour cream and the remaining 1 tablespoon flour. Gradually stir about half of the hot mixture into the sour cream mixture, then return this mixture to the saucepan. Heat through. (Do not boil.)

5 Pour the sauce over the shells. Bake, uncovered, for 15 minutes more or until heated through. Makes 4 main-dish servings.

Prep Time: 25 minutes Cooking Time: 1 hour

1 Serving: Calories 375. Total Fat 16 g. Saturated Fat 7 g. Protein 20 g. Carbohydrate 39 g. Fiber 3 g. Sodium 447 mg. Cholesterol 87 mg.

Three Cheese Fettuccine

How Italian-Americans made pasta depended on what part of Italy their ancestors called home. This cheese-sauced fettuccine is typical of northern Italy, while tomato-sauced pastas are more common in southern Italy.

- 2 **cups broccoli flowerets**
- 2 **cups thinly sliced carrots**
- 1 **tablespoon olive or vegetable oil**
- 1 **cup thinly sliced leek or 8 large green onions with tops, finely sliced**
- 2 **cloves garlic, minced**
- ¼ **cup all-purpose flour**
- 1 **teaspoon dried marjoram leaves or oregano leaves**
- ¼ **teaspoon black pepper**
- 2½ **cups low-fat (1% milkfat) milk**
- ¾ **cup shredded Gouda or fontina cheese**
- ¾ **cup shredded Swiss cheese (3 ounces)**
- ½ **cup grated Parmesan cheese**
- 12 **ounces dried fettuccine or linguine**

1 In a large saucepan, bring ½ inch of water to a boil over high heat. Add the broccoli and carrots. Lower the heat and simmer, covered, for 8 to 10 minutes or until crisp-tender. Drain.

Three Cheese Fettuccine

2 In a large saucepan, heat the oil over moderate heat. Add the leek and garlic and cook until leek is tender. Stir in flour, marjoram, and pepper and cook for 1 minute or until bubbly. Add the milk. Cook, stirring constantly, until mixture starts to thicken. Stir in the Gouda cheese, Swiss cheese, and ¼ cup of the Parmesan cheese. Stir broccoli and carrots into cheese mixture. Cover and keep warm.

3 Meanwhile, in a Dutch oven, cook fettuccine according to package directions. Drain; return fettuccine to the Dutch oven. Add cheese mixture to fettuccine and toss gently until well mixed. Sprinkle with the remaining ¼ cup Parmesan cheese. Serve immediately. Makes 6 main-dish servings.

Prep Time: 20 minutes Cooking Time: 20 minutes

1 Serving: Calories 480. Total Fat 16 g. Saturated Fat 8 g. Protein 24 g. Carbohydrate 61 g. Fiber 4 g. Sodium 425 mg. Cholesterol 54 mg.

Sunday Night Spaghetti

"Every Sunday night, one of us grandkids would take a turn going to Grandma Anna's for supper," remembers Maureen Roach. "She served spaghetti with a rich, thick sauce that had carrot in it to take out the bitterness."

12 ounces bulk Italian sausage or bulk pork sausage
12 ounces lean ground beef
2 cups sliced fresh mushrooms
1 large yellow onion, chopped
1 medium-size carrot, shredded
1 stalk celery, thinly sliced
3 cloves garlic, minced
2 cans (14½ ounces each) lower-sodium tomatoes, undrained and cut up
1 can (6 ounces) lower-sodium tomato paste
½ cup dry red wine or lower-sodium beef broth (page 67)
¼ cup minced parsley
1 teaspoon each dried basil leaves and oregano leaves
½ teaspoon salt
¼ teaspoon black pepper
12 ounces regular or thin spaghetti

1 In a Dutch oven, cook sausage and ground beef over moderately high heat until meat is browned. Using a slotted spoon, remove meat from Dutch oven; drain well. Add the mushrooms, onion, carrot, celery, and garlic to pan drippings and cook for 5 minutes or until the vegetables are tender; remove from the Dutch oven and drain well.

2 Wipe out Dutch oven. Return meat and vegetable mixture to Dutch oven. Stir in tomatoes, tomato paste, wine, parsley, basil, oregano, salt, and pepper. Bring to a boil. Lower the heat and simmer for 30 to 45 minutes or until desired consistency, stirring often.

3 Meanwhile, cook spaghetti according to package directions. Drain, rinse, and drain again; transfer to a warm bowl. Spoon the sauce over pasta. Makes 6 main-dish servings.

Prep Time: 20 minutes Cooking Time: 50 minutes

1 Serving: Calories 502. Total Fat 15 g. Saturated Fat 5 g.
Protein 27 g. Carbohydrate 61 g. Fiber 7 g.
Sodium 527 mg. Cholesterol 58 mg.

Pasta and Beans

Italian grandmas served this hearty soup for lunch with cheese and bread. If cannellini beans aren't available, substitute great Northerns.

4 ounces elbow macaroni
1 tablespoon olive or vegetable oil
1 large yellow onion, halved lengthwise and thinly sliced
1 medium-size sweet green pepper, chopped
1 large carrot, shredded
2 cloves garlic, minced
1¾ cups chopped tomatoes or 1 can (14½ ounces) lower-sodium tomatoes, undrained and cut up
1 teaspoon each dried oregano leaves and basil leaves
½ teaspoon salt
¼ teaspoon black pepper
1 can (15 ounces) cannellini beans or great Northern beans, rinsed and drained

1 Cook the macaroni according to package directions. Drain, rinse, and drain again; return the cooked macaroni to the saucepan.

2 Meanwhile, in a Dutch oven, heat the oil over moderate heat. Add the onion, green pepper, carrot, and garlic and cook for 5 minutes or until vegetables are tender. Stir in the tomatoes, oregano, basil, salt, and black pepper. Bring to a boil. Lower the heat and simmer, covered, for 10 minutes.

3 Stir in the cooked macaroni and the beans. Cook, covered, for 5 minutes more or until heated through. Serve with grated Parmesan cheese and minced parsley. Makes 4 main-dish servings.

Prep Time: 20 minutes Cooking Time: 25 minutes

1 Serving: Calories 358. Total Fat 6 g. Saturated Fat 0 g.
Protein 12 g. Carbohydrate 64 g. Fiber 4 g.
Sodium 560 mg. Cholesterol 0 mg.

Grandma's Treats

Sugar 'n' Spice Porridge

Youngsters are sure to start the day off right with this comforting hot cereal.

1½ cups low-fat (1% milkfat) milk

2 tablespoons butter or margarine

⅓ cup chopped pitted dates or raisins

3 tablespoons sugar

¼ teaspoon salt

¼ teaspoon ground cardamom or ground cinnamon

⅛ teaspoon ground nutmeg

⅓ cup quick-cooking farina

1. In a medium-size saucepan, bring the milk and butter to a boil over moderately high heat. Stir in the dates, sugar, salt, cardamom, and nutmeg.

2. Slowly add farina to the boiling milk, stirring constantly. Cook for 30 seconds. Remove from heat. Let stand for 1 minute. Serve with milk. Makes 2 servings.

Mexican Tacos

Half the fun of these south-of-the-border sandwiches is sprinkling on lots of toppings.

8 corn taco shells

1 can (16 ounces) refried beans

½ cup salsa

1 cup shredded lettuce

1 cup shredded reduced-fat Cheddar or Monterey Jack cheese (4 ounces)

1 large tomato, finely chopped

1. Preheat the oven to 300°F. Place the taco shells in a shallow baking pan. Bake for 8 to 10 minutes or until hot and crispy.

2. Meanwhile, in a small saucepan, stir together the refried beans and salsa. Cook over moderate heat for 2 to 3 minutes or until heated through, stirring frequently.

3. Fill the taco shells with the bean mixture. Top with the lettuce, cheese, and tomato. Makes 4 servings.

Frank and Bean Sandwiches

Kids will be delighted with this novel way of eating franks and beans.

4 slices home-style whole-wheat or white bread

1 can (16 ounces) baked beans

2 frankfurters, sliced

4 slices (1½ ounces each) reduced-fat Swiss or American cheese

1. Preheat the oven to 425°F. Place bread slices in an ungreased shallow baking pan.

2. In a small bowl, stir together the beans and frankfurters. Spread the bean mixture over bread to cover each slice completely, mounding slightly in the center.

3. Bake for 10 minutes or until heated through. Place a cheese slice on top of each bean sandwich. Bake for 2 to 3 minutes more or until the cheese melts. Makes 4 servings.

Spanish Rice

This festive side dish adds pizzazz to plain burgers or chicken.

1 can (14½ ounces) stewed tomatoes, undrained and cut up

½ cup water

½ teaspoon chili powder

¼ teaspoon garlic powder

½ cup uncooked long-grain white rice

½ cup shredded reduced-fat Cheddar cheese

1. In a medium-size saucepan, combine the tomatoes, water, chili powder, and garlic powder.

2. Bring to a boil over moderately high heat. Stir in the rice. Lower the heat and simmer, covered, for 20 minutes or until the rice is tender.

3. Top with the Cheddar cheese. Makes 3 or 4 servings.

BOUNTY FROM THE GARDEN

If grandma needed vegetables for dinner, she didn't head for the supermarket. A country grandma just stepped out her door and gathered something from the garden, while a city gran stopped by the corner market. The dishes she prepared depended on what was in season. In springtime, she cooked asparagus; in summer, corn; in fall, assorted squashes and pumpkin. Whatever the vegetable, grandma dressed it up with simple seasonings and sauces. This chapter brings you the most memorable of her time-honored recipes.

Asparagus Goldenrod (page 242)
Okra with Corn and Tomatoes (page 253)
Orange-Raisin Carrots (page 246)

Bernice's Asparagus

"My grandmother stir-fried asparagus with a little water so the pieces stayed a nice, bright green," recalls Kenneth Lee. "Sometimes, she'd serve it with butter and lemon juice, or as in this recipe, with tomato."

Nonstick cooking spray
1 **pound fresh asparagus spears, cut into 2-inch pieces**
⅓ **cup water**
1 **large tomato, seeded and chopped**
2 **teaspoons lemon juice**
½ **teaspoon dried rosemary leaves or basil leaves**
⅛ **teaspoon salt**
Dash black pepper

1 Coat a 10-inch nonstick skillet with cooking spray. Heat skillet over moderately high heat. Add asparagus; cook for 3 minutes, stirring constantly. Add the water. Cook and stir for 3 to 4 minutes more or until asparagus is crisp-tender and water is evaporated. Lower heat to moderate.

2 Stir in the tomato, lemon juice, rosemary, salt, and pepper. Cook for 1 minute more or until tomato is heated through, stirring occasionally. Makes 4 servings.

Prep Time: 15 minutes Cooking Time: 8 minutes

1 Serving: Calories 43. Total Fat 1 g. Saturated Fat 0 g. Protein 3 g. Carbohydrate 8 g. Fiber 3 g. Sodium 83 mg. Cholesterol 0 mg.

Asparagus Goldenrod

An early version of this elegant egg-topped side dish, appeared in the 1909 White House Cook Book. Serve it with broiled steak for an extra-special meal.

1 **pound fresh or frozen asparagus spears**
1 **tablespoon butter or margarine**
1 **tablespoon all-purpose flour**
1 **teaspoon grated lemon rind**
⅛ **teaspoon each salt and black pepper**
¾ **cup low-fat (1% milkfat) milk**
3 **large egg whites**
2 **large egg yolks**
⅛ **teaspoon salt**
⅛ **teaspoon ground allspice**

1 In a large saucepan, bring ½ inch of water to a boil over high heat. Add fresh asparagus. Lower the heat and simmer, covered, for 4 to 8 minutes or until crisp-tender. (Or, cook frozen asparagus according to package

directions.) Drain; arrange asparagus on an ovenproof platter or in a 9-inch round baking dish.

2 Preheat the oven to 350°F. In the same saucepan, melt the butter over moderate heat. Whisk in flour, lemon rind, ⅛ teaspoon salt, and pepper and cook for 1 minute or until bubbly. Add milk. Cook, whisking constantly, until mixture starts to thicken. Cook and whisk for 2 minutes or until thickened. Pour over asparagus.

3 In a clean large bowl, with electric mixer on *High,* beat the egg whites until stiff peaks form; set aside. In a small bowl, with electric mixer on *High,* beat egg yolks, ⅛ teaspoon salt, and allspice for 3 minutes or until light yellow and thickened. Fold into beaten egg whites. Gently spoon over sauce and asparagus. Bake for 15 minutes or until egg mixture is golden. Serves 4.

Prep Time: 20 minutes Cooking Time: 30 minutes

1 Serving: Calories 120. Total Fat 6 g. Saturated Fat 3 g. Protein 9 g. Carbohydrate 9 g. Fiber 2 g. Sodium 242 mg. Cholesterol 116 mg.

Green Beans with Onion

"When I visited my Grandma Sallie in Florida, we always had lots of good Southern cooking." says Flora Szatkowski. "I particularly remember all-vegetable dinners of home-grown tomatoes, corn on the cob, string beans, and turnip greens."

1 **pound fresh green beans or 1 package (16 ounces) frozen whole green beans**
1 **tablespoon olive or vegetable oil**
1 **medium-size yellow onion, sliced**
½ **teaspoon each dried marjoram leaves and oregano leaves**
¼ **teaspoon salt**
⅛ **teaspoon ground red pepper (cayenne)**

1 In a large saucepan, bring ½ inch of water to a boil over high heat. Add fresh whole beans. Lower the heat and simmer, covered, for 15 to 20 minutes or until crisp-tender. (Or, cook the frozen beans according to package directions.) Drain, removing the beans.

2 In the same saucepan, heat the oil over moderate heat. Add the onion and cook for 8 to 10 minutes or until tender and browned. Stir in the beans, marjoram, oregano, salt, and red pepper. Heat through. Serves 6.

Prep Time: 5 minutes Cooking Time: 30 minutes

1 Serving: Calories 50. Total Fat 2 g. Saturated Fat 0 g. Protein 2 g. Carbohydrate 7 g. Fiber 3 g. Sodium 91 mg. Cholesterol 0 mg.

Spanish Green Beans

Spanish Green Beans

This old-fashioned combination of beans and tomatoes is especially good made with fresh beans. Snapping them into bite-size pieces with your fingers is easy, in fact it has a kind of natural rhythm that's calming. If the beans are too limp to snap, use a knife.

12 ounces fresh green beans, snapped into 1-inch pieces, or 3 cups frozen cut green beans

1 tablespoon olive or vegetable oil

1 medium-size yellow onion, chopped

½ cup chopped sweet green pepper

1 clove garlic, minced

1 can (14½ ounces) diced tomatoes, undrained, or 1 can (14½ ounces) tomatoes, undrained and cut up

½ teaspoon dried oregano leaves

¼ teaspoon dried rosemary leaves

⅛ teaspoon each salt and black pepper

2 teaspoons cornstarch

1 In a medium-size saucepan, bring ½ inch of water to a boil over high heat. Add the fresh beans. Lower the heat and simmer, covered, for 15 to 20 minutes or until crisp-tender. (Or, cook the frozen beans according to package directions.) Drain, removing the beans.

2 In the same saucepan, heat the oil over moderate heat. Add the onion, green pepper, and garlic and cook for 5 minutes or until vegetables are tender.

3 Drain the tomatoes, reserving the liquid. Add the tomatoes to cooked onion. Stir in the beans, oregano, rosemary, salt, and black pepper.

4 In a small bowl, stir together the reserved tomato liquid and the cornstarch, then stir into the bean mixture. Bring to a boil over moderate heat, stirring constantly. Cook for 2 minutes or until mixture is thickened, stirring constantly. Serve with grilled chicken. Makes 4 servings.

Prep Time: 15 minutes Cooking Time: 33 minutes

1 Serving: Calories 92. Total Fat 4 g. Saturated Fat 1 g. Protein 3 g. Carbohydrate 14 g. Fiber 4 g. Sodium 308 mg. Cholesterol 0 mg.

Orange-Glazed Beets and Broccoli Polonaise

Orange-Glazed Beets

*Old-time cookbooks advise cooking
whole beets with the stem end left on so they
don't "bleed" while they're cooking.*

1¼   **pounds fresh beets or 2 cans (16 ounces each) diced beets, drained**

⅓   **cup lower-calorie orange marmalade**

1   **tablespoon cornstarch**

1   **tablespoon honey**

1   **tablespoon cider vinegar**

⅛   **teaspoon ground cinnamon**
Dash ground allspice

1 Trim fresh beets ½ inch above the stems. In a large saucepan, cover the beets with lightly salted water. Bring to a boil over high heat. Lower the heat and simmer, covered, for 40 to 45 minutes or until almost tender. Drain, removing the beets. Cool slightly. Peel by slipping off skins while still warm; cut into ½-inch cubes. (Or, use canned diced beets.)

2 In the same saucepan, stir together the marmalade, cornstarch, honey, vinegar, cinnamon, and allspice. Bring to a boil over moderate heat, stirring constantly.

3 Stir in the beets. Cook for 3 to 4 minutes or until beets are heated through, stirring occasionally. Makes 4 servings.

Prep Time: 20 minutes Cooking Time: 55 minutes

1 Serving: Calories 114. Total Fat 0 g. Saturated Fat 0 g.
Protein 2 g. Carbohydrate 27 g. Fiber 2 g.
Sodium 101 mg. Cholesterol 0 mg.

Broccoli Polonaise

*Many grandmothers served vegetables
polonaise-style which means topped with a mixture
of butter, bread crumbs, parsley, and
hard-cooked egg. You also can serve this topping
over steamed asparagus or cauliflower.*

1   **pound fresh broccoli spears or 1 package (16 ounces) frozen broccoli spears**

1   **tablespoon butter or margarine**

⅓   **cup seasoned fine dry bread crumbs**

2   **tablespoons minced parsley**

½   **teaspoon grated lemon rind**

⅛   **teaspoon ground red pepper (cayenne)**

1   **hard-cooked large egg, finely chopped**

1 In a large saucepan, bring ½ inch of water to a boil over high heat. Add the fresh broccoli. Lower the heat and simmer, covered, for 8 to 10 minutes or until crisp-tender. (Or, cook the frozen broccoli according to package directions.) Drain and arrange the broccoli on a platter.

2 Meanwhile, in a small saucepan, heat the butter over moderate heat until lightly browned. Stir in the bread crumbs, parsley, lemon rind, ground red pepper, and hard-cooked egg. Spoon over the cooked broccoli. Makes 4 servings.

Prep Time: 10 minutes Cooking Time: 13 minutes

1 Serving: Calories 110. Total Fat 5 g. Saturated Fat 2 g.
Protein 6 g. Carbohydrate 12 g. Fiber 4 g.
Sodium 147 mg. Cholesterol 61 mg.

Broccoli with Olives and Anchovies

*Although broccoli was grown in colonial
Williamsburg and at Thomas Jefferson's Monticello
estate, it wasn't until the 1920's that the dark
green vegetable became popular. Because this broccoli
dish uses olives and anchovies, there's
no need for added salt.*

1   **pound fresh broccoli spears or 1 package (16 ounces) frozen cut broccoli**

6   **medium-size green onions with tops, finely sliced**

2   **cloves garlic, minced**

2   **tablespoons chopped canned anchovy fillets**

¼   **teaspoon black pepper**

2   **tablespoons sliced pitted black olives**

1   **tablespoon olive or vegetable oil**

1 Cut broccoli flowerets from stalks; cut the remaining broccoli stalks into 1-inch pieces. In a large saucepan, bring ½ inch of water to a boil over high heat. Add the broccoli, green onions, garlic, anchovies, and pepper. Lower the heat and simmer, covered, for 8 to 10 minutes or until broccoli is crisp-tender. (Or, cook frozen broccoli, onions, garlic, anchovies, and pepper according to directions on broccoli package.) Drain.

2 Add the olives and oil to broccoli mixture; toss until mixed. Makes 6 servings.

Prep Time: 15 minutes Cooking Time: 13 minutes

1 Serving: Calories 50. Total Fat 3 g. Saturated Fat 1 g.
Protein 3 g. Carbohydrate 5 g. Fiber 3 g.
Sodium 78 mg. Cholesterol 0 mg.

German Red Cabbage

*To keep red cabbage an attractive rosy color,
always cook it with something acidic, like
vinegar or lemon juice. This sweet-and-sour dish
is especially good with broiled pork chops.*

1 **tablespoon olive or vegetable oil**
5 **cups coarsely shredded red cabbage**
¼ **cup apple or currant jelly**
¼ **cup dry red wine or lower-sodium chicken broth (page 67)**
4 **teaspoons cider vinegar**
⅛ **teaspoon each salt and black pepper**
⅛ **teaspoon ground cloves**
2 **medium-size apples, cored and cut into 1-inch chunks**
1 **tablespoon all-purpose flour**

1 In a 12-inch skillet, heat the oil over moderate heat. Add the cabbage and cook for 5 minutes. Stir in the apple jelly, 2 tablespoons of the red wine, the vinegar, salt, pepper, and cloves. Stir in apples. Bring to a boil. Lower the heat and simmer, covered, for 10 minutes or until the cabbage is crisp-tender, stirring frequently.

2 In a small bowl, stir together the remaining 2 tablespoons red wine and the flour, then stir into cabbage mixture. Cook over moderate heat, stirring constantly, until mixture starts to thicken. Cook and stir for 2 minutes more or until thickened. Makes 4 servings.

Prep Time: 15 minutes Cooking Time: 25 minutes

1 Serving: Calories 156. Total Fat 4 g. Saturated Fat 1 g.
Protein 1 g. Carbohydrate 29 g. Fiber 4 g.
Sodium 81 mg. Cholesterol 0 mg.

Orange-Raisin Carrots

8 **medium-size carrots, sliced**
⅓ **cup raisins**
⅓ **cup orange juice**
1 **tablespoon firmly packed light brown sugar**
1 **teaspoon cornstarch**
½ **teaspoon grated orange rind**
¼ **teaspoon ground ginger**

1 In a large saucepan, bring ½ inch of water to a boil over high heat. Add the carrots. Lower the heat and simmer, covered, for 7 to 9 minutes or until carrots are crisp-tender. Drain.

2 Meanwhile, in a small saucepan, stir together the raisins, orange juice, brown sugar, cornstarch, orange rind, and ginger. Bring to a boil over moderate heat, stirring constantly. Cook for 2 minutes or until mixture is thickened, stirring constantly.

3 Pour over the carrots; toss until mixed. Serve with grilled or broiled burgers. Makes 4 servings.

Prep Time: 15 minutes Cooking Time: 12 minutes

1 Serving: Calories 120. Total Fat 0 g. Saturated Fat 0 g.
Protein 2 g. Carbohydrate 30 g. Fiber 4 g.
Sodium 89 mg. Cholesterol 0 mg.

Nan's Circles and Squares

*This old-timey medley of carrots, sweet
pepper, and green olives goes well with any simple
main dish, such as grilled chicken, steak, or fish.*

1 **tablespoon butter or margarine**
1 **large yellow onion, sliced**
1 **medium-size sweet red or green pepper, chopped**
6 **medium-size carrots, sliced**
½ **cup apple juice**
1 **teaspoon dried basil leaves**
¼ **teaspoon salt**
⅛ **teaspoon black pepper**
1 **teaspoon cornstarch**
2 **tablespoons cut-up pimiento-stuffed green olives**
1 **tablespoon minced parsley**

1 In a large saucepan, melt the butter over moderate heat. Add the onion and red pepper and cook for 5 minutes or until vegetables are tender. Stir in carrots, ¼ cup of the apple juice, basil, salt, and black pepper.

2 Bring to a boil. Lower the heat and simmer, covered, for 7 to 9 minutes or until carrots are crisp-tender.

3 In a small bowl, stir together the remaining ¼ cup apple juice and the cornstarch, then stir into the simmering carrot mixture. Cook for 2 minutes or until mixture is thickened. Remove from heat. Stir in the olives. Sprinkle with parsley. Makes 4 servings.

Prep Time: 15 minutes Cooking Time: 20 minutes

1 Serving: Calories 109. Total Fat 3 g. Saturated Fat 2 g.
Protein 2 g. Carbohydrate 19 g. Fiber 3 g.
Sodium 271 mg. Cholesterol 8 mg.

Fancy-Fixin's Cauliflower

Fancy-Fixin's Cauliflower

In Pudd'nhead Wilson's Calendar, Mark Twain proclaims,
"Cauliflower is nothing but cabbage with a college education." This zesty
recipe dresses up the "educated" vegetable with a tangy sauce.

1 **small head cauliflower or 3 cups frozen cauliflower**
1 **tablespoon olive or vegetable oil**
1 **stalk celery, thinly sliced**
2 **tablespoons cider vinegar**
2 **tablespoons lower-sodium chicken broth (page 67) or water**
1 **tablespoon chopped drained canned pimientos**
1 **teaspoon sugar**
¼ **teaspoon dried thyme leaves**
⅛ **teaspoon black pepper**

1 Cut fresh cauliflower into flowerets. In a large saucepan, bring ½ inch of lightly salted water to a boil over high heat. Add the cauliflower. Lower the heat and simmer, covered, for 8 to 10 minutes or until crisp-tender. (Or, cook the frozen cauliflower according to package directions.) Drain; transfer cauliflower to a serving bowl.

2 Meanwhile, in a small saucepan, heat the oil over moderate heat. Add the celery and cook for 5 minutes or until tender. Stir in the vinegar, chicken broth, pimientos, sugar, thyme, and pepper. Drizzle over the cauliflower and toss until mixed. Makes 4 servings.

Prep Time: 10 minutes Cooking Time: 13 minutes

1 Serving: Calories 58. Total Fat 4 g. Saturated Fat 1 g.
Protein 2 g. Carbohydrate 6 g. Fiber 2 g.
Sodium 22 mg. Cholesterol 0 mg.

Saucy Peas and New Potatoes, a variation of Saucy Celery

Saucy Celery

*Grandma never worried when her celery turned limp. She just soaked
it in ice water for 10 minutes or so and it was good as new.*

8 **stalks celery, sliced ¾ inch thick**
1 **large yellow onion, cut into thin wedges**
1 **cup evaporated skimmed milk or low-fat
    (1% milkfat) milk**
1 **tablespoon all-purpose flour**
¼ **teaspoon salt**
⅛ **teaspoon ground nutmeg**
    Dash black pepper

1 In a large saucepan, bring ½ inch of water to a boil over high heat. Add the celery and onion. Lower the heat and simmer, covered, for 10 to 12 minutes or until celery is crisp-tender. Drain; transfer to serving bowl.

2 Meanwhile, in a small saucepan, whisk together the evaporated skimmed milk, flour, salt, nutmeg, and pepper. Cook over moderate heat, whisking constantly, until mixture starts to thicken. Cook and whisk for 2 minutes more or until thickened.

3 Pour over the celery and onion; stir until mixed. Makes 4 servings.

Prep Time: 10 minutes Cooking Time: 15 minutes

1 Serving: Calories 87. Total Fat 0 g. Saturated Fat 0 g.
Protein 6 g. Carbohydrate 15 g. Fiber 2 g.
Sodium 307 mg. Cholesterol 2 mg.

Saucy Peas and New Potatoes Prepare as for Saucy Celery, substituting **1 pound tiny new potatoes** and **1 package (10 ounces) frozen peas** for the celery and the onion. Cut any large potatoes in half. Cook the potatoes for 10 minutes, then add the peas and cook for 5 minutes more or until tender. Prepare sauce and combine as directed in steps 2 and 3 of Saucy Celery.

1 Serving: Calories 222. Total Fat 0 g. Saturated Fat 0 g.
Protein 11 g. Carbohydrate 44 g. Fiber 6 g.
Sodium 273 mg. Cholesterol 2 mg.

Country-Style Escalloped Corn

A favorite old-fashioned way to prepare vegetables was to scallop them, which means baked with cream or milk and topped with bread or cracker crumbs.

1 tablespoon butter or margarine
1 large yellow onion, chopped
1 stalk celery, finely chopped
1 large egg, lightly beaten
1 large egg white
¾ cup crushed lower-sodium crackers
¾ cup low-fat (1% milkfat) milk
2 tablespoons chopped drained canned pimientos (optional)
1 teaspoon dry mustard
¼ teaspoon salt
⅛ teaspoon ground red pepper (cayenne)
1 can (14¾ ounces) lower-sodium cream-style corn, undrained
1 can (8¾ ounces) lower-sodium whole kernel corn, drained
2 teaspoons butter or margarine, melted

1 Preheat the oven to 350°F. In a small saucepan, melt the 1 tablespoon butter over moderate heat. Add the onion and celery and cook for 5 minutes or until vegetables are tender.

2 In a medium-size bowl, combine the egg, egg white, ½ cup of the crackers, milk, pimientos (if using), mustard, salt, and red pepper. Stir in onion mixture, cream-style corn, and whole kernel corn. Pour into a lightly greased 1½-quart casserole.

3 In a small bowl, stir together the remaining ¼ cup crackers and the 2 teaspoons melted butter. Sprinkle over corn mixture. Bake for 60 to 65 minutes or until a knife inserted near center comes out clean. Serves 5.

Prep Time: 15 minutes Cooking Time: 66 minutes

1 Serving: Calories 208. Total Fat 7 g. Saturated Fat 3 g.
Protein 7 g. Carbohydrate 33 g. Fiber 6 g.
Sodium 263 mg. Cholesterol 54 mg.

Escalloped Corn with Mushrooms Prepare as for Country-Style Escalloped Corn, cooking **1 cup sliced fresh mushrooms** with the onion and celery.

1 Serving: Calories 211. Total Fat 7 g. Saturated Fat 3 g.
Protein 7 g. Carbohydrate 33 g. Fiber 6 g.
Sodium 263 mg. Cholesterol 54 mg.

Creamy Corn Puddin'

The secret to the fresh-from-the-garden flavor of this custardy side dish is to scrape the ear after you have cut off the corn. This releases the milky juices.

3 medium-size fresh ears of corn or 1½ cups frozen whole kernel corn
1 tablespoon butter or margarine
1 small yellow onion, chopped
4 large egg whites
2 large egg yolks
1 tablespoon sugar
1 tablespoon all-purpose flour
¼ teaspoon salt
⅛ teaspoon ground nutmeg
⅛ teaspoon ground red pepper (cayenne)
1½ cups low-fat (1% milkfat) milk

1 Preheat the oven to 350°F. Cut kernels off fresh corn (page 251). Measure 1½ cups corn.

2 In a small saucepan, bring ½ inch of water to a boil over high heat. Add the fresh or frozen corn. Lower the heat and simmer, covered, for 5 minutes or until tender. Drain, removing the corn.

3 In the same saucepan, melt the butter over moderate heat. Add the onion and cook for 5 minutes or until tender; set aside.

4 In a clean small bowl, with an electric mixer on *High,* beat the egg whites until stiff peaks form; set aside. In a large bowl, with electric mixer on *High,* beat the egg yolks for 3 minutes or until light yellow and thickened. Stir in the corn, onion mixture, sugar, flour, salt, nutmeg, and red pepper. Stir in the milk. Fold in the beaten egg whites.

5 Pour into an 8" x 8" x 2" baking dish. Bake for 35 to 40 minutes or until a knife inserted near the center comes out clean. Makes 6 servings.

Prep Time: 20 minutes Cooking Time: 16 minutes
Baking Time: 35 minutes

1 Serving: Calories 131. Total Fat 5 g. Saturated Fat 2 g.
Protein 7 g. Carbohydrate 17 g. Fiber 1 g.
Sodium 185 mg. Cholesterol 79 mg.

Southern Fried Corn

Southern Fried Corn

*Southern grandmas made this home-style favorite with
cream, but this more healthful version uses canned evaporated
skimmed milk to create the same wonderful flavor.*

6 **medium-size fresh ears of corn or 3 cups frozen
whole kernel corn**

2 **strips lean bacon, chopped**

1 **medium-size yellow onion, chopped**

½ **cup chopped sweet red or green pepper**

1 **teaspoon all-purpose flour**

¼ **teaspoon salt**

⅛ **teaspoon black pepper**

½ **cup evaporated skimmed milk or low-fat
(1% milkfat) milk**

1 Cut kernels off fresh corn (tip, opposite). Measure 3 cups corn.

2 In a 10-inch nonstick skillet, cook bacon over moderate heat until crisp. Remove bacon, reserving drippings. Drain the bacon on paper towels; set aside.

3 Add the corn, onion, and red pepper to reserved drippings. Cook over moderate heat, stirring constantly, for 8 minutes or until the corn is tender and lightly browned.

4 Stir in the flour, salt, and black pepper. Add the milk. Cook, stirring constantly, until mixture starts to thicken. Cook and stir for 2 minutes more or until thickened. Sprinkle with the bacon pieces. Serve with broiled chicken. Makes 4 servings.

Prep Time: 15 minutes Cooking Time: 18 minutes

1 Serving: Calories 211. Total Fat 7 g. Saturated Fat 2 g.
Protein 8 g. Carbohydrate 35 g. Fiber 4 g.
Sodium 260 mg. Cholesterol 7 mg.

CUTTING CORN OFF THE COB

1. To cut the kernels off the cob, place 1 ear of corn at a time in a shallow pan. Holding the ear of corn at an angle, use a sharp knife to cut across the tips of the kernels, working from the top down.

2. Next, scrape the ear with the dull side of the knife to release the milky juices into pan.

End-of-Summer Stuffed Eggplant

For a light supper, serve this flavorful mushroom-stuffed eggplant as a main dish. It's enough for two people.

1 large eggplant (1½ pounds)
1 tablespoon olive or vegetable oil
2 cups sliced fresh mushrooms
1 medium-size yellow onion, chopped
1 clove garlic, minced
1 small tomato, chopped
⅓ cup chopped cooked lower-sodium ham
1½ teaspoons dried basil leaves
¼ teaspoon salt
⅛ teaspoon black pepper
¾ cup crushed lower-sodium crackers
1 tablespoon grated Romano cheese

1 Preheat the oven to 375°F. Cut a thin slice off 1 side of eggplant; discard. Hollow out the eggplant, leaving a ½-inch-thick shell. Chop the eggplant pulp; measure 1½ cups. In a large saucepan, bring ½ inch of water to a boil over high heat. Add the eggplant pulp. Lower the heat and simmer, covered, for 5 to 8 minutes or until tender. Drain, removing the eggplant.

2 In the same saucepan, heat the oil over moderate heat. Add the mushrooms, onion, and garlic and cook for 5 minutes or until onion is tender. Stir in the tomato, ham, basil, salt, pepper, and eggplant pulp. Set aside 1 tablespoon of the crackers; stir the remaining crackers into the mushroom mixture.

3 Spoon the mushroom mixture into the eggplant shell. Sprinkle with the reserved crackers and the Romano cheese. Place the eggplant in a shallow baking dish and pour hot water around eggplant to a depth of ½ inch. Bake for 45 minutes or until heated through. Makes 4 servings.

Prep Time: 25 minutes Cooking Time: 16 minutes
Baking Time: 45 minutes

1 Serving: Calories 146. Total Fat 7 g. Saturated Fat 1 g. Protein 6 g. Carbohydrate 16 g. Fiber 2 g. Sodium 374 mg. Cholesterol 10 mg.

Wilted Greens

Come spring, tender young spinach and lettuce leaves were wilted in hot oil and spices. Grandma called them a "mess-'o'-greens".

1 tablespoon olive or vegetable oil
8 medium-size green onions with tops, finely sliced
3 tablespoons firmly packed light brown sugar
1 teaspoon all-purpose flour
⅛ teaspoon salt
   Dash ground red pepper (cayenne)
3 tablespoons red wine vinegar or cider vinegar
2 tablespoons water
6 cups bite-size pieces romaine
6 cups bite-size pieces fresh spinach

1 In a 12-inch skillet, heat the oil over moderate heat. Add the green onions and cook for 3 minutes or until tender.

2 Stir in the brown sugar, flour, salt, and red pepper. Add the vinegar and water. Cook, stirring constantly, until mixture starts to thicken. Cook and stir for 2 minutes more or until thickened. Remove from heat.

3 Add the romaine and spinach. Toss for 30 to 60 seconds or until the greens just start to wilt. Serve with roast veal or pork. Makes 4 servings.

Prep Time: 20 minutes Cooking Time: 8 minutes

1 Serving: Calories 95. Total Fat 4 g. Saturated Fat 1 g. Protein 4 g. Carbohydrate 13 g. Fiber 4 g. Sodium 148 mg. Cholesterol 0 mg.

Shaker Hominy Cakes

2 Add the hominy mixture to the flour mixture all at once and stir just until combined.

3 Heat a 12-inch nonstick griddle or skillet over moderate heat and brush with a little of the vegetable oil. Using about ¼ cup batter for each cake, pour the batter onto the griddle. Cook for 3 minutes or just until covered with bubbles. Flip over and cook for 2 minutes more or until golden. Makes 12 cakes.

Prep Time: 10 minutes Cooking Time: 16 minutes

1 Cake: Calories 111. Total Fat 3 g. Saturated Fat 1 g.
Protein 3 g. Carbohydrate 17 g. Fiber 1 g.
Sodium 260 mg. Cholesterol 19 mg.

Mushrooms Paprika

*Old-timers boast of the days when
wild mushrooms were so plentiful they could
gather a bucketful before breakfast.*

  1 **tablespoon olive or vegetable oil**
  8 **cups sliced fresh mushrooms**
  1 **large yellow onion, chopped**
 ⅔ **cup reduced-fat sour cream**
 ⅔ **cup low-fat (1% milkfat) milk**
  4 **teaspoons all-purpose flour**
 ½ **teaspoon paprika**
 ¼ **teaspoon salt**
 ⅛ **teaspoon ground red pepper (cayenne)**

1 In a 12-inch skillet, heat the oil over moderately high heat. Add mushrooms and onion and cook for 3 minutes or until vegetables are tender, stirring often.

2 Meanwhile, in a small bowl, stir together the sour cream, milk, flour, paprika, salt, and red pepper. Stir into the mushroom mixture. Cook over moderate heat, stirring constantly, until mixture starts to thicken. Cook and stir for 2 minutes more or until thickened. Serves 6.

Prep Time: 15 minutes Cooking Time: 10 minutes

1 Serving: Calories 99. Total Fat 6 g. Saturated Fat 3 g.
Protein 4 g. Carbohydrate 9 g. Fiber 2 g.
Sodium 115 mg. Cholesterol 11 mg.

Dilled Mushrooms Prepare as for Mushrooms Paprika, substituting ½ **teaspoon dried dill weed** for the paprika.

1 Serving: Calories 99. Total Fat 6 g. Saturated Fat 3 g.
Protein 4 g. Carbohydrate 9 g. Fiber 2 g.
Sodium 115 mg. Cholesterol 11 mg.

Shaker Hominy Cakes

*Shakers made hominy to preserve fresh corn.
The women soaked corn in lye, boiled it, rubbed
off the hulls, and then, boiled the corn again.
They served hominy cakes for breakfast or
at dinner as a vegetable.*

  1 **can (14½ ounces) hominy, drained**
1¼ **cups all-purpose flour**
  2 **teaspoons baking powder**
  1 **teaspoon sugar**
 ½ **teaspoon salt**
  1 **large egg, lightly beaten**
1¼ **cups low-fat (1% milkfat) milk**
  2 **tablespoons vegetable oil**

1 In a large bowl, with a pastry blender or a potato masher, mash the hominy until the size of small peas. In another large bowl, stir together the flour, baking powder, sugar, and salt. In a medium-size bowl, combine the egg, milk, and oil; stir in the hominy.

Okra with Corn And Tomatoes

*A Southern and Creole favorite,
okra adds a delicious asparaguslike flavor
to this hearty vegetable dish.*

1 **package (10 ounces) frozen whole kernel corn**
2 **cups fresh or frozen okra pods**
2 **medium-size tomatoes, cut up**
1 **medium-size yellow onion, chopped**
1 **stalk celery, thinly sliced**
¼ **cup chopped cooked lower-sodium ham (optional)**
¼ **cup water**
1 **teaspoon dried oregano leaves**
¼ **teaspoon salt**
¼ **teaspoon ground red pepper (cayenne)**

1 In a 10-inch skillet, combine the corn, fresh or frozen okra, tomatoes, onion, celery, ham (if using), water, oregano, salt, and red pepper. Bring mixture to a boil over high heat.

2 Lower the heat and simmer, covered, for 10 minutes or until vegetables are tender, stirring occasionally. Simmer, uncovered, for 5 minutes more or until most of the liquid has evaporated. Makes 6 servings.

Prep Time: 10 minutes Cooking Time: 20 minutes

1 Serving: Calories 75. Total Fat 0 g. Saturated Fat 0 g.
Protein 3 g. Carbohydrate 18 g. Fiber 4 g.
Sodium 105 mg. Cholesterol 0 mg.

STORING VEGETABLES

♦ To get the most from your fresh produce, store vegetables in plastic or paper bags that are open or vented, not airtight, so the vegetables can "breathe". Always wash and cut up vegetables as you need them, not before.

♦ Store perishable vegetables, such as tomatoes, cucumbers, sweet peppers, broccoli, cauliflower, carrots, beets, summer squash, and green onions, in the vegetable drawer of your refrigerator.

♦ Keep sturdier vegetables—like potatoes, sweet potatoes, onions, and winter squashes, such as acorn or butternut—in a cool, dry place with plenty of air circulation.

Glazed Onions

Onions were one of the first crops the colonists planted when they came to America. This old recipe features onions cooked in a buttery, sweet, golden glaze.

3 **large yellow onions, sliced and separated into rings**
2 **tablespoons butter or margarine**
2 **tablespoons sugar**
¼ **teaspoon ground ginger**
Dash salt

1 In a large saucepan, bring ½ inch of water to a boil over high heat. Add the onions. Lower the heat and simmer, covered, for 10 minutes or until tender. Drain.

2 Meanwhile, in a 10-inch skillet, melt the butter over moderate heat. Stir in the sugar, ginger, and salt until sugar is dissolved. Add the onions. Cook, uncovered, for 2 to 3 minutes or until onions are glazed and most of the liquid has evaporated, stirring frequently. Makes 4 servings.

Prep Time: 10 minutes Cooking Time: 17 minutes

1 Serving: Calories 104. Total Fat 6 g. Saturated Fat 4 g.
Protein 1 g. Carbohydrate 13 g. Fiber 1 g.
Sodium 93 mg. Cholesterol 16 mg.

Glazed Carrots Prepare as for Glazed Onions, substituting **8 medium-size carrots, sliced,** for the onions and ¼ **teaspoon dried mint leaves** for the ginger. Cook the carrots in water for 7 to 9 minutes or until tender, then continue as directed in step 2 of Glazed Onions.

1 Serving: Calories 134. Total Fat 6 g. Saturated Fat 4 g.
Protein 2 g. Carbohydrate 20 g. Fiber 3 g.
Sodium 177 mg. Cholesterol 16 mg.

Glazed Parsnips Prepare as for Glazed Onions, substituting **6 medium-size parsnips, sliced,** for the onions and **2 tablespoons firmly packed light brown sugar** for the sugar. Cook parsnips in water for 7 to 9 minutes or until tender, then continue as directed in step 2 of Glazed Onions.

1 Serving: Calories 181. Total Fat 6 g. Saturated Fat 4 g.
Protein 2 g. Carbohydrate 32 g. Fiber 6 g.
Sodium 106 mg. Cholesterol 16 mg.

Over-Stuffed Onions and Over-Stuffed Peppers

Over-Stuffed Onions

*The mild, sweet onion varieties, like Vidalia
and Walla Walla, are ideal in this dish, where they are
stuffed with Parmesan cheese and bread crumbs.
Serve the onions with roast beef or lamb.*

- 4 **medium-size yellow onions**
- 1 **tablespoon olive or vegetable oil**
- 1 **cup shredded carrot**
- ¾ **cup toasted fresh bread crumbs (1½ slices)**
- 2 **tablespoons grated Parmesan cheese**
- 1 **tablespoon minced parsley**
- ½ **teaspoon dried thyme leaves**
- ⅛ **teaspoon salt**
  Dash black pepper
- 1 **to 2 tablespoons water**

1 Preheat the oven to 350°F. Hollow out each onion (tip, right); reserve the onion pulp. In a large saucepan, bring ½ inch of water to a boil over high heat. Add the onion shells and cook for 5 minutes. Drain, inverting the onions on paper towels. Chop the reserved onion pulp; measure ½ cup.

2 In the same saucepan, heat the oil over moderate heat. Add the ½ cup onion pulp and the carrot and cook for 5 minutes or until vegetables are tender. Remove from heat. Stir in the bread crumbs, Parmesan cheese, parsley, thyme, salt, and pepper. Drizzle with enough of the water to moisten, tossing lightly.

3 Spoon the bread crumb mixture into the onion shells. Place in an 8" x 8" x 2" baking dish. Bake, covered loosely with foil, for 20 to 25 minutes or until the onions are tender and the bread crumb mixture is heated through. Makes 4 servings.

Prep Time: 20 minutes Cooking Time: 35 minutes

1 Serving: Calories 126. Total Fat 5 g. Saturated Fat 1 g.
Protein 4 g. Carbohydrate 18 g. Fiber 2 g.
Sodium 191 mg. Cholesterol 3 mg.

✳

Over-Stuffed Peppers Prepare as for Over-Stuffed Onions, substituting **2 small sweet red, yellow, and/or green peppers, halved lengthwise,** for the onions, and chopped sweet pepper for the onion pulp.

1 Serving: Calories 89. Total Fat 5 g. Saturated Fat 1 g.
Protein 3 g. Carbohydrate 10 g. Fiber 2 g.
Sodium 178 mg. Cholesterol 3 mg.

HOLLOWING OUT ONIONS

Cut a thin slice from the top of each onion. Hold the onion at an angle. Use a small spoon to remove the pulp from the center of the onion, leaving a ⅜-inch shell.

Braised Peas With Lettuce

*Farm wives gathered fresh greens from
the garden, rinsed them off, and used the water
clinging to the leaves to help steam the peas.
If you use fresh peas for this recipe, add a few pods to
the pot. They will keep the peas bright green.*

- 3 **leaf lettuce leaves**
- 2 **packages (10 ounces each) frozen peas or 4 cups fresh shelled peas**
- 8 **medium-size green onions with tops, finely sliced**
- 1 **bay leaf**
- 1 **tablespoon water**
- 1 **teaspoon sugar**
- ⅛ **teaspoon each salt and black pepper**
- 2 **tablespoons minced parsley**
- 1 **tablespoon butter or margarine**

1 Place the lettuce leaves in the bottom of a 10-inch skillet. Add the peas, green onions, and bay leaf. Sprinkle with the water, sugar, salt, and pepper.

2 Bring to a boil over high heat. Lower the heat and simmer, covered, for 10 to 15 minutes or until peas are crisp-tender.

3 Drain peas well. Discard the lettuce and bay leaf. Toss peas with parsley and butter. Makes 4 servings.

Prep Time: 10 minutes Cooking Time: 12 minutes

1 Serving: Calories 138. Total Fat 3 g. Saturated Fat 2 g.
Protein 7 g. Carbohydrate 21 g. Fiber 8 g.
Sodium 214 mg. Cholesterol 8 mg.

NATURALLY GOOD TREATS

Years ago, drying was a simple and efficient way to put away food for the winter. Women cut up fruits and vegetables, strung the pieces on thread, hung the strands by the fireplace to dry, and stored them in a cool place.

Introduce the youngsters at your house to the fun of this old-fashioned technique. Start by drying apple slices and toasting pumpkin seeds in your oven. Then, let the kids stir together these two naturally good snacks.

SHAKE-A-SACK APPLE SNACK

- **2 cups Homemade Dried Apples (recipe, below), quartered, or store-bought dried apple chunks**
- **1 package (6 or 7 ounces) dried peaches or apricots, halved and cut into 1/2-inch pieces**
- **2 cups bite-size wheat-, rice-, corn-, or bran-square cereal**
- **1 cup puffed corn cereal or tiny marshmallows**
- **1 cup coconut**
- **1 cup slivered almonds (optional), toasted**

1. In a large heavy-duty plastic bag, combine Homemade Dried Apples, dried peaches, wheat-square cereal, puffed corn cereal, coconut, and almonds (if using). Close bag and seal. Shake until well mixed. Makes 8 to 9 cups.

HOMEMADE DRIED APPLES

1 Core **4 medium-size tart cooking apples**. Peel apples if you like. Slice the apples into rings, about 1/4-inch thick.

2 To keep the apple rings from browning, in a large bowl, combine **2 cups cold water** and **2 tablespoons lemon juice**. Add the apple rings, making sure each apple ring gets coated with the water-lemon mixture. Let stand for 5 minutes. Drain well; pat apple rings dry with paper towels.

3 Preheat oven to 300°F. Lightly coat 2 wire racks with **nonstick cooking spray**. Arrange the apple rings in a single layer on the wire racks, making sure

rings do not touch or overlap. Set each rack on a baking sheet. Bake for 15 minutes. Reverse positions of the baking sheets in the oven, moving the baking sheet from the top oven rack to the bottom oven rack and vice versa. Bake for 15 minutes more. Turn off the oven. Let the apple rings dry in the oven, with the door closed, for 3 hours. Remove from oven.

4 To store, place apple rings in large heavy-duty plastic bag. Close bag. Makes about 4 cups.

Pumpkin-Patch Party Mix

    4 **cups air-popped popcorn**
       Toasted Fresh Pumpkin Seeds (recipe, below) or 3 cups shelled sunflower nuts
    2 **cups honey graham cereal, round sweetened bran cereal, or round toasted oat cereal**
  1½ **cups lightly salted dry-roasted mixed nuts or peanuts**
  1½ **cups candy corn or gumdrops**
  1½ **cups raisins**

1. In a large bowl, stir together the popped popcorn, Toasted Fresh Pumpkin Seeds, honey graham cereal, mixed nuts, candy corn, and raisins.

2. To store, place in a tightly covered container. Makes about 12 cups.

Toasted Fresh Pumpkin Seeds

1 Remove the seeds from a pumpkin, leaving behind as much of the fiber as you can. Immediately place the seeds in a large bowl of water to avoid any fiber drying on the seeds.

2 Transfer the pumpkin seeds to a colander. Thoroughly rinse the pumpkin seeds under cold running water, rubbing the seeds

between your fingers until the pulp and strings are washed off. Drain well.

3 Preheat the oven to 300°F. In a medium-size mixing

bowl, combine **3 cups of the pumpkin seeds, 2 tablespoons vegetable oil,** and **1 teaspoon salt;** stir to coat well. Spread the seeds onto a baking sheet. Bake for 65 to 70 minutes or until lightly browned and crisp, stirring often to brown the seeds evenly. Cool to room temperature. (The seeds also are good salted and eaten as a snack.) To store, place in a tightly covered container (will keep for 1 week). Makes 3 cups.

4 Spoon half of the potato mixture into 4 mounds in the skillet; flatten tops slightly. Cook for 4 to 5 minutes on each side or until browned, turning carefully. Cover and keep warm. Repeat with remaining potato mixture, adding more oil if necessary. Makes 4 servings.

Prep Time: 15 minutes Chilling Time: 1 hour
Cooking Time: 47 minutes

1 Serving: Calories 247. Total Fat 7 g. Saturated Fat 2 g. Protein 6 g. Carbohydrate 42 g. Fiber 3 g. Sodium 342 mg. Cholesterol 8 mg.

CHOOSING POTATOES

Grandma used one kind of potato for all types of cooking. But today, you have more choices.

• **Mashing** Use russets, round-whites, or the yellow varieties. They will give moist, fluffy mashed potatoes.

• **Baking** Choose russets, the yellow varieties, or the blue or purple varieties.

• **Making Salads** Select waxy potatoes, such as round-reds, round-whites, or long-whites.

• **Boiling** Buy round-reds or long-whites for varieties that hold their shape well.

• **Frying** Rely on russets or round-reds.

Potatoes Lyonnaise

This old-fashioned recipe called for lots of butter. To reduce the fat, this version uses a small amount of olive oil instead.

3 medium-size potatoes (about 1 pound total), thinly sliced
1 medium-size yellow onion, thinly sliced and separated into rings
1 tablespoon olive or vegetable oil
½ teaspoon salt
¼ teaspoon black pepper
2 tablespoons minced parsley

1 Preheat the oven to 425°F. In a medium-size saucepan, cover the potatoes with water. Bring to a boil over high heat. Lower the heat and simmer, covered, for 12 to 15 minutes or until potatoes are almost tender. Drain well; pat dry with paper towels.

2 Spread the potatoes and onion in a lightly greased 15½" x 10½" x 1" baking pan. Drizzle with the oil. Sprinkle with the salt and pepper. Bake, covered, for 15 minutes or until onion is tender. Bake, uncovered, for 15 to 20 minutes more or until potatoes and onion are browned. Sprinkle with parsley. Makes 3 servings.

Prep Time: 15 minutes Cooking Time: 52 minutes

1 Serving: Calories 183. Total Fat 5 g. Saturated Fat 1 g. Protein 3 g. Carbohydrate 33 g. Fiber 4 g. Sodium 367 mg. Cholesterol 0 mg.

Gran's Potato Pancakes

"My family liked these pancakes so much that grandma made extra mashed potatoes to fry up the next day," says Shirley Tokheim. "She always was careful when turning the pancakes so that the tasty brown crust wouldn't stick to the skillet."

6 medium-size potatoes (about 2 pounds total)
¼ cup low-fat (1% milkfat) milk
1 tablespoon butter or margarine
½ teaspoon salt
¼ teaspoon paprika
¼ teaspoon black pepper
4 medium-size green onions with tops, finely chopped
2 large egg whites, lightly beaten
Nonstick cooking spray
1 tablespoon vegetable oil

1 Peel and quarter potatoes. In a large saucepan, cover the potatoes with water. Bring to a boil over high heat. Lower the heat and simmer, covered, for 20 to 25 minutes or until tender. Drain.

2 In a medium-size bowl, with the electric mixer on *Low*, beat potatoes until almost smooth. Add milk, butter, salt, paprika, and pepper. Beat until light and fluffy. Cover and refrigerate for at least 1 hour.

3 Stir the green onions and egg whites into potato mixture until well mixed. Coat a 10-inch nonstick skillet with cooking spray. Add the oil to skillet. Heat the oil over moderate heat.

Herbed Oven-Style Potatoes Prepare as for Potatoes Lyonnaise, sprinkling ½ **teaspoon dried oregano leaves,** ¼ **teaspoon dried rosemary leaves,** and **1 clove garlic, minced,** over the potatoes and onion with the salt and pepper.

1 Serving: Calories 185. Total Fat 5 g. Saturated Fat 1 g. Protein 3 g. Carbohydrate 34 g. Fiber 4 g. Sodium 367 mg. Cholesterol 0 mg.

Old-Time Scalloped Potatoes

Old-Time Scalloped Potatoes

Hearty meals at grandma's house often featured these stick-to-the-ribs
potatoes, which are baked in a creamy sauce and topped with cheese.

4 **medium-size potatoes (about 1⅓ pounds total), peeled and thinly sliced**
1 **medium-size yellow onion, chopped**
¼ **cup water**
¼ **teaspoon each salt and black pepper**
¼ **teaspoon celery seeds (optional)**
1½ **cups low-fat (1% milkfat) milk**
3 **tablespoons all-purpose flour**
2 **tablespoons minced parsley**
½ **cup shredded reduced-fat Cheddar cheese (2 ounces)**

1 In a large saucepan, cover the potatoes with water. Bring to a boil over high heat. Lower the heat and simmer, covered, for 12 to 15 minutes or until potatoes are almost tender. Drain.

2 Preheat the oven to 350°F. Meanwhile, in a small saucepan, combine the onion and the ¼ cup water. Bring to a boil. Lower the heat and simmer, covered, for 5 minutes or until tender. Drain. Stir in the salt, pepper, and celery seeds (if using). In a small bowl, whisk together the milk and flour. Stir into the onion mixture. Cook over moderate heat, stirring constantly, until mixture starts to thicken. Cook and stir for 2 minutes or until thickened. Stir in the parsley.

3 Place half of the potatoes in a lightly greased 1½-quart casserole. Cover with half of the milk mixture. Add the remaining potatoes and remaining milk mixture. Bake for 20 minutes or until heated through. Sprinkle with the Cheddar cheese. Serves 4.

Prep Time: 20 minutes Cooking Time: 42 minutes

1 Serving: Calories 228. Total Fat 4 g. Saturated Fat 2 g.
Protein 10 g. Carbohydrate 38 g. Fiber 2 g.
Sodium 288 mg. Cholesterol 14 mg.

Colcannon

Colcannon

*Colcannon is an old Irish favorite. Your family will love this dish because
the mashed potatoes mellow the strong flavor of the cabbage.*

4 **medium-size potatoes (about 1⅓ pounds total)**
3 **cups chopped cabbage**
8 **medium-size green onions with tops, finely sliced**
2 **to 3 tablespoons low-fat (1% milkfat) milk**
1 **tablespoon butter or margarine**
½ **teaspoon salt**
¼ **teaspoon black pepper**
2 **tablespoons minced parsley**

1 Peel and quarter potatoes. In a large saucepan, cover the potatoes with water. Bring to a boil over high heat. Lower the heat and simmer, covered, for 20 to 25 minutes or until tender. Drain.

2 Meanwhile, in a medium-size saucepan, bring ½ inch of water to a boil over high heat. Add the cabbage and green onions. Lower the heat and simmer, covered, for 8 to 10 minutes or until the cabbage is tender. Drain.

3 In a medium-size bowl, with an electric mixer on *Low,* beat the potatoes until almost smooth. Add the milk, butter, salt, and pepper. Beat until light and fluffy. Stir in the cooked cabbage mixture and parsley. Makes 4 servings.

Prep Time: 20 minutes Cooking Time: 30 minutes

1 Serving: Calories 163. Total Fat 3 g. Saturated Fat 2 g.
Protein 4 g. Carbohydrate 31 g. Fiber 3 g.
Sodium 319 mg. Cholesterol 8 mg.

German Potato Dumplings

Many a grandma made dumplings without a written recipe. To test the dough, she dropped a spoonful into boiling water. If the dumpling fell apart, she would beat in a little more flour.

3 medium-size potatoes (about 1 pound total)
1 medium-size yellow onion, chopped
2 teaspoons butter or margarine
½ cup fresh bread crumbs (1 slice)
4 strips lean bacon, chopped
2 slices white sandwich bread, cut into ½-inch cubes
1 large egg
¼ teaspoon salt
¼ teaspoon ground nutmeg
⅛ teaspoon white or black pepper
2 cups all-purpose flour

1 Peel and quarter potatoes. In a large saucepan, cover the potatoes and onion with water. Bring to a boil over high heat. Lower the heat and simmer, covered, for 20 to 25 minutes or until potatoes are tender. Drain.

2 Meanwhile, in a 10-inch skillet, melt the butter over moderate heat. Add the bread crumbs and cook for 3 to 5 minutes or until toasted and browned, stirring frequently. Remove and set aside. In the same skillet, cook bacon over moderate heat until crisp. Remove bacon, reserving 1 tablespoon drippings. Drain bacon on paper towels; set aside. Add bread cubes to reserved drippings and cook for 2 to 3 minutes or until crisp and browned, stirring frequently. Remove bread cubes.

3 In large bowl, with electric mixer on *Low*, beat potatoes and onion until almost smooth. Add egg, salt, nutmeg, and pepper. Beat until fluffy. Using a wooden spoon, beat in the flour until a soft dough forms.

4 With floured fingers, shape the dough into 1-inch balls. Make a hole in the center of each ball, insert a few pieces of bacon and a bread cube in each hole, then reshape into a ball. Meanwhile, half fill a Dutch oven with water; bring to a boil. Drop half of the dumplings into the boiling water and cook for 15 minutes. Remove dumplings and drain on paper towels; cover and keep warm. Repeat with remaining dumplings. Sprinkle bread crumbs over dumplings. Serve with pot roast. Makes 8 servings.

Prep Time: 25 minutes Cooking Time: 1 hour

1 Serving: Calories 239. Total Fat 6 g. Saturated Fat 2 g.
Protein 7 g. Carbohydrate 40 g. Fiber 2 g.
Sodium 198 mg. Cholesterol 34 mg.

Sweet Potato Pecan Casserole

For this recipe, select sweet potatoes with deep orange skin and meat. They are moist and great for mashing. The tan-skinned sweet potatoes have yellow flesh, a drier texture, and are better for baking.

4 medium-size sweet potatoes (about 2 pounds total)
2 large egg whites
2 tablespoons honey or firmly packed light brown sugar
1 tablespoon butter or margarine
¼ teaspoon salt
⅛ teaspoon ground nutmeg
2 tablespoons finely chopped pecans

1 Peel and quarter sweet potatoes. In a large saucepan, cover the sweet potatoes with water. Bring to a boil over high heat. Lower the heat and simmer, covered, for 20 to 25 minutes or until tender. Drain.

2 Preheat the oven to 350°F. In a large bowl, with an electric mixer on *Low*, beat the potatoes until almost smooth. Add the egg whites, honey, butter, salt, and nutmeg. Beat until light and fluffy.

3 Spoon the sweet potato mixture into an 8-inch round baking pan. Sprinkle with pecans. Bake for 25 minutes or until heated through. Makes 4 servings.

Prep Time: 15 minutes Cooking Time: 55 minutes

1 Serving: Calories 332. Total Fat 6 g. Saturated Fat 2 g.
Protein 6 g. Carbohydrate 65 g. Fiber 5 g.
Sodium 220 mg. Cholesterol 8 mg.

Marshmallow-Topped Sweet Potato Casserole
Prepare as for Down-Home Sweet Potato Casserole, substituting ½ cup tiny marshmallows for the pecans. Sprinkle the marshmallows over potato mixture the last 15 minutes of baking.

1 Serving: Calories 325. Total Fat 4 g. Saturated Fat 2 g.
Protein 6 g. Carbohydrate 69 g. Fiber 5 g.
Sodium 223 mg. Cholesterol 8 mg.

Candied Yams and Apples

*In this country, true yams were seldom
available; what grandmother used was probably
the deep orange variety of sweet potato.*

3 **medium-size sweet potatoes (about 1½ pounds total)
or 2 cans (18 ounces each) sweet potatoes, drained
and cut up**
2 **medium-size tart cooking apples, cored and sliced**
⅓ **cup firmly packed light brown sugar**
2 **tablespoons apple juice**
1 **tablespoon butter or margarine**
¼ **teaspoon ground allspice**
⅛ **teaspoon ground nutmeg**

1 Peel and slice fresh sweet potatoes. In a large
saucepan, cover the potatoes with water. Bring to a
boil over high heat. Lower the heat and simmer, covered, for 8 to 10 minutes or until potatoes are almost
tender. Drain. (Or, use canned sweet potatoes.)

2 Meanwhile, in a 12-inch skillet, combine the apple
slices, brown sugar, apple juice, butter, allspice, and
nutmeg. Bring just to a boil over moderate heat. Lower
the heat slightly and cook, uncovered, for 3 to 5 minutes
or until apples are almost tender and juice mixture is
slightly thickened, stirring occasionally. Gently stir in
the sweet potatoes.

3 Cook, uncovered, for 5 to 10 minutes more or until
apples are tender and sweet potatoes are heated
through, spooning the juice mixture over potatoes occasionally. Makes 6 servings.

Prep Time: 10 minutes Cooking Time: 23 minutes

1 Serving: Calories 197. Total Fat 2 g. Saturated Fat 1 g.
Protein 2 g. Carbohydrate 43 g. Fiber 4 g.
Sodium 38 mg. Cholesterol 5 mg.

Candied Yams and Oranges Prepare as for Candied Yams and Apples, omitting the apples and substituting **2 tablespoons orange juice** for the apple juice.
After heating sweet potatoes in the juice mixture, gently stir in **2 medium-size oranges, peeled and sectioned.**

1 Serving: Calories 191. Total Fat 2 g. Saturated Fat 1 g.
Protein 2 g. Carbohydrate 41 g. Fiber 4 g.
Sodium 38 mg. Cholesterol 5 mg.

Summer Squash With Sour Cream

*When choosing yellow summer
squash, press your fingernail into the skin.
It should pierce the skin easily.*

1 **pound yellow summer squash or zucchini,
thinly sliced**
1 **medium-size yellow onion, halved and thinly sliced**
¾ **cup reduced-fat sour cream**
1 **tablespoon all-purpose flour**
2 **tablespoons low-fat (1% milkfat) milk**
½ **teaspoon dried dill weed**
¼ **teaspoon salt**
Dash ground red pepper (cayenne)

1 In a large saucepan, bring ½ inch of water to a boil
over high heat. Add the squash and onion. Lower
the heat and simmer, covered, for 3 to 5 minutes or until
squash is crisp-tender. Drain.

2 Meanwhile, in a small saucepan, stir together the
sour cream and flour. Stir in the milk, dill weed, salt,
and red pepper. Cook and stir over low heat until heated through (do not boil). Pour over the vegetables; stir
until mixed. Makes 4 servings.

Prep Time: 10 minutes Cooking Time: 8 minutes

1 Serving: Calories 96. Total Fat 6 g. Saturated Fat 3 g.
Protein 3 g. Carbohydrate 9 g. Fiber 2 g.
Sodium 157 mg. Cholesterol 18 mg.

DRESSING UP VEGETABLES

Grandma frequently served cooked vegetables
seasoned only with butter, salt, and pepper, but
for special occasions you might want to add a
little something extra.

◆ Sprinkle toasted nuts or sesame seeds over
cooked sliced carrots, cut green beans, or halved
brussels sprouts.

◆ Top steamed broccoli or asparagus spears with
chopped black olives.

◆ Snip a little fresh basil over cooked corn, sliced
beets, or cauliflower flowerets.

◆ Sauté garlic in a little olive oil and spoon it over
steamed sliced zucchini or pea pods.

Scalloped Tomatoes with Cheese

Scalloped Tomatoes with Cheese

*Years ago, many Americans thought tomatoes were poisonous, and it
wasn't until the mid-to-late-1800's that cooks began using them. Scalloped
tomatoes first appeared in cookbooks around the turn of the century.*

1 tablespoon olive or vegetable oil
1 large yellow onion, chopped
1 large sweet green pepper, chopped
1 clove garlic, minced
2 cans (14½ ounces each) lower-sodium tomatoes, undrained
2 tablespoons all-purpose flour
2 teaspoons sugar
1 teaspoon dried thyme leaves
½ teaspoon dried oregano leaves
¼ teaspoon salt
⅛ teaspoon black pepper
2 cups toasted fresh bread crumbs (4 slices)
⅓ cup shredded reduced-fat Cheddar cheese (1½ ounces)

1 Preheat the oven to 350°F. In a large saucepan, heat the oil over moderate heat. Add the onion, green pepper, and garlic and cook for 5 minutes or until the vegetables are tender. Drain the tomatoes, reserving the liquid. Cut up the tomatoes and add to the onion mixture. Bring to a boil.

2 In a small bowl, stir together the tomato liquid and the flour, then stir into the tomato mixture. Stir in the sugar, thyme, oregano, salt, and black pepper. Cook over moderate heat, stirring constantly, until mixture starts to thicken. Cook and stir for 2 minutes more or until thickened.

3 Place half of the tomato mixture in a 1½-quart casserole. Cover with half of bread crumbs. Repeat layers with remaining tomato mixture and remaining crumbs. Bake for 15 minutes or until bubbly. Sprinkle with cheese. Bake for 1 to 2 minutes more or until cheese melts. Serve with meat or poultry. Serves 6.

Prep Time: 15 minutes Cooking Time: 35 minutes

1 Serving: Calories 144. Total Fat 5 g. Saturated Fat 1 g.
Protein 5 g. Carbohydrate 22 g. Fiber 4 g.
Sodium 247 mg. Cholesterol 5 mg.

Creamed White Turnips

Sugar is used like a spice in this recipe—there's just enough to mellow the turnips, but not enough to sweeten them. For best results, use small, young turnips. They will have a mild, sweet flavor and a crisp, rather than woody, texture.

1¼ **pounds turnips**
2 **tablespoons finely chopped fresh chives or green onion tops (optional)**
2 **tablespoons low-fat (1% milkfat) milk**
1 **teaspoon sugar**
¼ **teaspoon salt**
   Dash white or black pepper

1 Peel and quarter turnips. In a medium-size saucepan, cover the turnips with water. Bring to a boil over high heat. Lower the heat and simmer, covered, for 30 to 35 minutes or until very tender. Drain.

2 In a medium-size bowl, with an electric mixer on *Low*, beat the turnips until almost smooth. Add the chives (if using), the milk, sugar, salt, and pepper. Beat until light and fluffy. Makes 3 servings.

Prep Time: 10 minutes Cooking Time: 40 minutes

1 Serving: Calories 43. Total Fat 0 g. Saturated Fat 0 g. Protein 2 g. Carbohydrate 11 g. Fiber 4 g. Sodium 273 mg. Cholesterol 0 mg.

Vegetable Mix-Up

Thrifty housewives made this hash with leftover vegetables from a pot roast or boiled dinner.

   Nonstick cooking spray
1 **tablespoon butter or margarine**
3 **cups chopped cooked carrots, parsnips, turnips, and/or cabbage**
2 **cups chopped cooked potatoes**
1 **medium-size yellow onion, chopped**
1 **teaspoon dried marjoram leaves**
¼ **teaspoon salt**
¼ **teaspoon ground sage**
⅛ **teaspoon black pepper**
⅓ **cup lower-sodium chicken broth (page 67)**

1 Coat a 10-inch nonstick skillet with cooking spray. Add the butter to skillet. Melt the butter over moderate heat. Add the carrots, potatoes, onion, marjoram, salt, sage, and pepper; stir until mixed.

2 Cook the mixture for 10 minutes or until browned, turning occasionally. Stir in the chicken broth. Makes 6 servings.

Prep Time: 15 minutes Cooking Time: 11 minutes

1 Serving: Calories 125. Total Fat 2 g. Saturated Fat 1 g. Protein 2 g. Carbohydrate 25 g. Fiber 4 g. Sodium 118 mg. Cholesterol 5 mg.

Fried Apples

Fried apples were an old-time favorite served with breakfast or with a roast for dinner.

1 **tablespoon butter or margarine**
3 **medium-size tart cooking apples, cored and cut into thin wedges**
2 **tablespoons firmly packed light brown sugar**
¼ **teaspoon ground nutmeg or ground cinnamon**

1 In a 10-inch nonstick skillet, melt the butter over moderately high heat. Add the apples and cook for 3 minutes or until lightly browned, stirring frequently.

2 Stir in the brown sugar and nutmeg. Lower the heat to moderately low and cook, covered, for 2 to 3 minutes more or until apples are tender. Makes 4 servings.

Prep Time: 10 minutes Cooking Time: 6 minutes

1 Serving: Calories 104. Total Fat 3 g. Saturated Fat 2 g. Protein 0 g. Carbohydrate 20 g. Fiber 2 g. Sodium 31 mg. Cholesterol 8 mg.

Fried Apples with Onion Prepare as for Fried Apples, adding **1 medium-size yellow onion, thinly sliced**, with the apples.

1 Serving: Calories 111. Total Fat 3 g. Saturated Fat 2 g. Protein 0 g. Carbohydrate 22 g. Fiber 2 g. Sodium 32 mg. Cholesterol 8 mg.

Grandma's Treats

Calico Peas

Team this colorful pea-and-pimiento combo with roast chicken or beef.

- 1 package (10 ounces) frozen peas
- 1 small yellow onion, cut into thin wedges
- 1 tablespoon butter or margarine
- 1 tablespoon chopped drained canned pimientos
- 1/4 teaspoon dried dill weed
- 1/8 teaspoon each salt and black pepper

1. In a medium-size saucepan, bring 1/2 inch of water to a boil over high heat. Add the peas and

onion. Lower the heat and simmer, covered, for 5 minutes or until peas and onion are crisp-tender. Drain.

2. Stir the butter, pimientos, dill weed, salt, and pepper into vegetables, tossing until butter is melted. Makes 3 or 4 servings.

Cinnamon Sweet Potato Rounds

Serve these sweet and cinnamony potato circles with burgers.

- 3 medium-size sweet potatoes (about 1½ pounds total), peeled and thinly sliced
- 2 tablespoons butter or margarine, melted
- 2 tablespoons sugar
- 1/4 teaspoon ground cinnamon

1. Preheat the oven to 425°F. In a large saucepan, cover the sweet potatoes with water. Bring to a boil over high heat. Lower the heat and simmer, covered, for 5 to 8 minutes or until sweet potatoes are almost tender. Drain well; pat dry with paper towels.

2. Spread the sweet potato slices in a lightly greased 15½" x 10½" x 1" baking pan. Drizzle with the melted butter. Bake for 10 minutes or until butter is hot and bubbly.

3. In a small bowl, stir together the sugar and cinnamon; sprinkle over sweet potatoes. Bake for 5 to 10 minutes more or until sweet potatoes are glazed. Makes 3 or 4 servings.

Tex-Mex Baked Potatoes

These dressed-up baked potatoes are both nourishing and tasty.

- 4 medium-size baking potatoes (about 2 pounds total)
- 1/2 cup taco sauce
- 1/2 cup shredded reduced-fat Cheddar cheese (2 ounces)
- 1 cup shredded lettuce
- 1 small tomato, chopped

1. Preheat the oven to 425°F. Prick the potatoes with a fork. Bake for 40 to 60 minutes or until tender.

2. Gently roll each potato under your hand; cut a crisscross in the top of each potato. Press the ends and push up.

3. Meanwhile, in a small saucepan, heat the taco sauce until warm. Spoon over the potatoes. Sprinkle with the cheese; top with the lettuce and tomato. Makes 4 servings.

Bundled-Up Corn

The youngsters can help you wrap up the ears of corn.

- 2 tablespoons butter or margarine, at room temperature
- 1 teaspoon grated lemon rind
- 1/4 teaspoon each salt and black pepper
- 4 medium-size fresh ears of corn, broken in half

1. Preheat the oven to 450°F. In a small bowl, stir together the butter, lemon rind, salt, and pepper.

2. Place 2 half ears of corn on a piece of heavy foil. Repeat with the remaining corn. Spread the corn with the butter mixture; wrap corn in the foil.

3. Bake for 30 minutes or until corn is tender. Remove foil. To serve, insert corn holders in the ends of each ear. Makes 4 servings.

Bread-and-Butter Pickles '29

GRANDMA'S SAUCES & TRIMMINGS

*Often, what made grandma's
meals so delightful were all the little
extras she served alongside.
Rich sauces, smooth gravies, tangy
dressings, creamy butters,
flavorful relishes, crisp pickles, and
fruit-packed preserves were all
part of grandma's bag of tricks for
making everyday meals truly special.
In this chapter, you'll discover
such old-time favorites as Buttery
Basting Sauce, Cranberry Relish
in Orange Cups, Hot Bacon Dressing,
Perfect Peach Preserves, Iowa Corn
Relish, and much, much more.*

267

Onion Herb Sauce over meat loaf

Onion Herb Sauce

The secret to making this recipe is to let the flour brown but not burn. This wonderfully flavorful sauce makes an ideal accompaniment to meat and poultry.

1 **tablespoon butter or margarine**
¼ **cup finely chopped yellow onion**
1 **clove garlic, minced**
1 **tablespoon all-purpose flour**
½ **teaspoon dried thyme leaves**
⅛ **teaspoon salt**
   Dash black pepper
⅔ **cup lower-sodium beef broth (page 67)**

1 In a small saucepan, melt the butter over moderate heat. Add the onion and garlic and cook for 5 minutes or until onion is tender.

2 Stir in the flour, thyme, salt, and pepper. Cook the mixture, stirring constantly, for 10 minutes or until flour is browned.

3 Add the beef broth. Cook, stirring constantly, until mixture starts to thicken. Cook and stir for 2 minutes more or until thickened. If you prefer a smoother sauce, strain through a sieve and discard the onion pulp. Serve sauce with meat or poultry. Makes about ⅔ cup.

Prep Time: 5 minutes Cooking Time: 20 minutes

2 Tablespoons: Calories 31. Total Fat 2 g. Saturated Fat 1 g.
Protein 0 g. Carbohydrate 2 g. Fiber 0 g.
Sodium 79 mg. Cholesterol 6 mg.

✳

Sherried Onion Herb Sauce Prepare as for Onion Herb Sauce, reducing the beef broth to ½ cup and adding **1 tablespoon dry sherry or dry red wine**. Makes about ½ cup.

2 Tablespoons: Calories 41. Total Fat 3 g. Saturated Fat 2 g.
Protein 0 g. Carbohydrate 3 g. Fiber 0 g.
Sodium 98 mg. Cholesterol 8 mg.

Double Mustard Sauce

Danish immigrants served mustard sauce with boiled cod; cooks from the British Isles with finnan haddie (smoked haddock). You'll enjoy it with ham, poultry, fish, Brussels sprouts, or potatoes.

2   teaspoons butter or margarine
2   tablespoons finely chopped yellow onion
1   teaspoon firmly packed light brown sugar
3/4 teaspoon dry mustard
1/8 teaspoon white or black pepper
1   cup evaporated skimmed milk
1   tablespoon all-purpose flour
1   tablespoon Dijon mustard
1   teaspoon vinegar

1 In a small saucepan, melt butter over moderate heat. Add onion and cook for 5 minutes or until tender.

2 Stir in the brown sugar, dry mustard, and pepper. In a small bowl, stir together the evaporated skimmed milk and flour. Stir into the mixture in saucepan. Cook, stirring constantly, until mixture starts to thicken. Cook and stir for 2 minutes more or until thickened. Remove saucepan from heat.

3 Stir in the Dijon mustard and vinegar. Serve sauce with meat, poultry, fish, or vegetables. Makes 1 cup.

Prep Time: 5 minutes Cooking Time: 13 minutes

2 Tablespoons: Calories 43. Total Fat 1 g. Saturated Fat 1 g.
Protein 3 g. Carbohydrate 5 g. Fiber 0 g.
Sodium 94 mg. Cholesterol 4 mg.

✳

Mustard Sauce with Capers   Prepare as for Double Mustard Sauce, adding **1 tablespoon drained capers.**

2 Tablespoons: Calories 44. Total Fat 1 g. Saturated Fat 1 g.
Protein 3 g. Carbohydrate 5 g. Fiber 0 g.
Sodium 112 mg. Cholesterol 4 mg.

✳

Mustard Sauce with Dill   Prepare as for Double Mustard Sauce, adding 1/4 **teaspoon dried dill weed.**

2 Tablespoons: Calories 43. Total Fat 1 g. Saturated Fat 1 g.
Protein 3 g. Carbohydrate 5 g. Fiber 0 g.
Sodium 94 mg. Cholesterol 4 mg.

Horseradish Sauce

New Englanders often served roast beef with horseradish sauce instead of gravy. This recipe also goes well with steak, burgers, or lamb chops.

1   cup reduced-fat sour cream
1/2 cup reduced-fat mayonnaise
1/4 cup drained prepared horseradish
1   tablespoon cider vinegar
1   teaspoon sugar
1/4 teaspoon dried thyme leaves (optional)
1/8 teaspoon each salt and white or black pepper

1 In a small bowl, stir together the sour cream, mayonnaise, horseradish, vinegar, sugar, thyme (if using), salt, and pepper.

2 Cover and refrigerate for at least 1 hour (will keep for 1 week). Serve the sauce with meat or fish. Makes 1 3/4 cups.

Prep Time: 5 minutes Chilling Time: 1 hour

2 Tablespoons: Calories 47. Total Fat 4 g. Saturated Fat 2 g.
Protein 1 g. Carbohydrate 3 g. Fiber 0 g.
Sodium 74 mg. Cholesterol 9 mg.

Mock Hollandaise Sauce

Community cookbooks featured numerous adaptations of classic hollandaise. You can use this easy eggless sauce without heating, or serve it warm.

1/2 cup reduced-fat sour cream
1/2 cup reduced-fat mayonnaise
2   tablespoons low-fat (1% milkfat) milk
2   tablespoons lemon juice
1   teaspoon grated lemon rind
1   teaspoon Dijon mustard
    Dash ground red pepper (cayenne)

1 In a small bowl, combine the sour cream, mayonnaise, milk, lemon juice, lemon rind, mustard, and red pepper. Serve immediately. Or, transfer mixture to a saucepan and cook over low heat just until warm, stirring occasionally; do not boil. Serve with poultry, fish, eggs, asparagus, or artichokes. Makes 1 1/4 cups.

Prep Time: 5 minutes

2 Tablespoons: Calories 48. Total Fat 4 g. Saturated Fat 1 g.
Protein 1 g. Carbohydrate 3 g. Fiber 0 g.
Sodium 81 mg. Cholesterol 8 mg.

Cumberland Sauce

*This old-fashioned sweet-and-sour sauce
is great with ham, lamb, game birds, and venison.
To avoid any bitterness, be sure to remove
both the orange's outer white membrane and the
membrane between the segments.*

- 3 **oranges**
- 4 **teaspoons cornstarch**
- ½ **teaspoon dry mustard**
- ¼ **teaspoon ground ginger**
- ½ **cup currant or apple jelly**
- 1 **tablespoon port, dry sherry, or orange juice**
- 1 **tablespoon lemon juice**
- ½ **teaspoon grated lemon rind**

1 Grate ½ teaspoon orange rind. Peel and section 2 oranges over a bowl to catch the juice. Squeeze juice from remaining 1 orange. Measure juice. If necessary, add enough water to the juice to measure ¾ cup.

2 In a small saucepan, whisk together the cornstarch, mustard, and ginger. Whisk in the ¾ cup orange juice, the orange rind, currant jelly, port, lemon juice, and lemon rind.

3 Bring to a boil over moderate heat, whisking occasionally. Cook for 2 minutes or until mixture is thickened, whisking constantly. Stir in orange sections. Serve with meat or poultry. Makes 1¾ cups.

Prep Time: 15 minutes Cooking Time: 7 minutes

---

2 Tablespoons: Calories 46. Total Fat 0 g. Saturated Fat 0 g.
Protein 0 g. Carbohydrate 12 g. Fiber 1 g.
Sodium 4 mg. Cholesterol 0 mg.

Cranberry Relish In Orange Cups

*Native Americans showed the European
settlers how to sweeten cranberries with maple
syrup. Later, women made cranberry relish
with sugar and served it in orange cups.*

- 3 **oranges**
- ½ **cup firmly packed light brown sugar**
- ½ **cup orange juice**
- ¼ **cup water**
- 1 **tablespoon finely chopped crystallized ginger**
- ¼ **teaspoon ground ginger**
- **Dash ground cloves**
- 2 **cups cranberries**

1 Cut the oranges in half, making a zigzag edge (tip, below). Remove pulp (tip, below). Cover and store orange shells in the refrigerator (will keep for 1 day).

2 In a large saucepan, stir together the brown sugar, orange juice, water, crystallized ginger, ground ginger, and cloves. Bring the mixture to a boil over high heat, stirring until the sugar is dissolved. Lower the heat to moderately high and cook, uncovered, for 3 minutes, stirring occasionally.

3 Add the cranberries. Return to a boil over high heat. Lower heat to moderately high and cook for 2 to 3 minutes or until skins pop, stirring occasionally.

4 Transfer to a covered container and refrigerate for at least 1 hour before serving. Store in the refrigerator (will keep for 1 week). To serve, spoon into orange shells. Serve with meat or poultry. Makes 6 servings.

Prep Time: 15 minutes Cooking Time: 12 minutes
Chilling Time: 1 hour

---

1 Serving: Calories 76. Total Fat 0 g. Saturated Fat 0 g.
Protein 0 g. Carbohydrate 19 g. Fiber 1 g.
Sodium 5 mg. Cholesterol 0 mg.

MAKING ORANGE CUPS

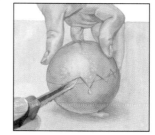 

1. With a small serrated knife, score a line around the middle of each orange. Then, using the line as a guide, cut each orange in half in a zigzag pattern to make a decorative edge.

2. To loosen the pulp from the shell, cut around the inside of each orange half with the knife. Using a small spoon, carefully remove and discard the pulp, leaving the orange shell intact.

Buttery Basting Sauce on fish

Buttery Basting Sauce

Grandma often basted meats to keep them moist. She used a spoon, but today a small brush makes the job much easier. This easy basting sauce adds a tangy citrus flavor to grilled or roasted meat, fish, seafood, or poultry.

4 teaspoons butter or margarine

2 tablespoons lime juice

1 teaspoon grated lime rind

½ teaspoon dried marjoram leaves, basil leaves, or oregano leaves

½ teaspoon dry mustard

½ teaspoon lower-sodium Worcestershire sauce

⅛ teaspoon crushed red pepper

1 In a small saucepan, melt the butter over moderate heat. Remove from heat.

2 Stir in the lime juice, lime rind, marjoram, mustard, Worcestershire sauce, and red pepper. Use to baste 1 pound meat, fish, seafood, or poultry during cooking. Makes ¼ cup (enough for 4 servings).

Prep Time: 5 minutes Cooking Time: 1 minute

1 Serving: Calories 39. Total Fat 4 g. Saturated Fat 2 g.
Protein 0 g. Carbohydrate 1 g. Fiber 0 g.
Sodium 42 mg. Cholesterol 10 mg.

From top to bottom: Curried Mayonnaise, Homemade-and-Healthier Mayonnaise, and Piquant Mayonnaise

Homemade-and-Healthier Mayonnaise

This sandwich spread has the tanginess and smooth texture of the original, but only half of the fat.

1 **package (1¾ ounces) powdered fruit pectin**
1 **teaspoon dry mustard**
⅛ **teaspoon salt**
⅛ **teaspoon ground red pepper (cayenne)**
¾ **cup evaporated skimmed milk**
1 **large egg**
⅔ **cup vegetable oil**
1 **tablespoon vinegar or lemon juice**

1 In a small saucepan, whisk together the pectin, mustard, salt, and red pepper. Slowly add the evaporated skimmed milk, whisking constantly. Whisk in the egg until combined. Cook over moderate heat, whisking constantly, until mixture just starts to bubble. Pour into a blender container. Refrigerate for 15 minutes.

2 With blender running slowly, pour oil in a very thin but steady stream through the hole in lid. Stop and scrape down the sides occasionally. Add vinegar; cover and blend until combined. Transfer to covered container and refrigerate for at least 1½ hours before serving. (The mixture may not be as stiff as commercial mayonnaise.) Store in refrigerator (will keep for 1 week). Serve as a sandwich spread. Makes about 1¾ cups.

Prep Time: 8 minutes Cooking Time: 5 minutes
Chilling Time: 1¾ hours

1 Tablespoon: Calories 61. Total Fat 5 g. Saturated Fat 0 g.
Protein 1 g. Carbohydrate 2 g. Fiber 0 g.
Sodium 23 mg. Cholesterol 8 mg.

Curried Mayonnaise Prepare as for Homemade-and-Healthier Mayonnaise, adding **2 finely sliced large green onions with tops, 1½ teaspoons curry powder, and ¼ teaspoon garlic powder.**

1 Tablespoon: Calories 61. Total Fat 5 g. Saturated Fat 0 g.
Protein 1 g. Carbohydrate 3 g. Fiber 0 g.
Sodium 23 mg. Cholesterol 8 mg.

Piquant Mayonnaise Prepare as for Homemade-and-Healthier Mayonnaise, adding ⅓ **cup bottled chili sauce, 2 tablespoons dill or sweet pickle relish, and 2 tablespoons minced parsley.** Serve as a sandwich spread or salad dressing. Makes 2¼ cups.

1 Tablespoon: Calories 51. Total Fat 4 g. Saturated Fat 0 g.
Protein 1 g. Carbohydrate 3 g. Fiber 0 g.
Sodium 58 mg. Cholesterol 6 mg.

Refreshing Cucumber Buttermilk Dressing

Bring out the best in salads with this old-fashioned dressing. It also makes a delicious topper for baked potatoes or a tangy dip for vegetables.

½ **cup low-fat (1% milkfat) buttermilk or soured milk (page 300)**
½ **cup shredded cucumber**
¼ **cup reduced-fat mayonnaise**
2 **medium-size green onions with tops, finely sliced**
1 **tablespoon sugar**
1 **tablespoon white wine vinegar**
⅛ **teaspoon salt**
Dash black pepper

1 In a small bowl, stir together buttermilk, cucumber, mayonnaise, green onions, sugar, vinegar, salt, and pepper. Cover and refrigerate for at least 1 hour (will keep for 1 week). Serve on salad greens or vegetable salads. Makes 1¼ cups (ten 2-tablespoon servings).

Prep Time: 10 minutes Chilling Time: 1 hour

2 Tablespoons: Calories 26. Total Fat 1 g. Saturated Fat 0 g.
Protein 0 g. Carbohydrate 3 g. Fiber 0 g.
Sodium 71 mg. Cholesterol 2 mg.

Hot Bacon Dressing

Warm and tangy, this dressing is perfect drizzled over spinach, leaf lettuce, or other salad greens.

1 **strip lean bacon, chopped**
⅓ **cup thinly sliced leek or yellow onion**
¼ **cup red wine vinegar**
2 **tablespoons honey**
½ **teaspoon dry mustard**
⅛ **teaspoon cracked black pepper**

1 In a small saucepan, cook the bacon over moderate heat until crisp. Remove bacon, reserving drippings. Drain the bacon on paper towels; set aside.

2 Add the leek to reserved drippings and cook for 3 minutes or until tender. Stir in the vinegar, honey, mustard, and pepper. Bring to a boil.

3 Serve immediately on salad greens. Sprinkle with bacon. Makes ½ cup (four 2-tablespoon servings).

Prep Time: 10 minutes Cooking Time: 10 minutes

2 Tablespoons: Calories 64. Total Fat 3 g. Saturated Fat 1 g.
Protein 1 g. Carbohydrate 10 g. Fiber 0 g.
Sodium 41 mg. Cholesterol 3 mg.

French Vinaigrette Dressing

Over the years, women created many wonderful variations of this classic dressing.

¼ **cup olive or vegetable oil**

3 **tablespoons cider or white vinegar**

3 **tablespoons lemon juice**

4 **teaspoons sugar**

½ **teaspoon dry mustard or 1 teaspoon Dijon mustard**

½ **teaspoon dried basil leaves or thyme leaves**

½ **teaspoon paprika**

1 In a jar with a tight-fitting lid, combine the oil, vinegar, lemon juice, sugar, mustard, basil, and paprika. Cover and shake well, then refrigerate for at least 1 hour (will keep for 1 week).

2 To serve, shake the dressing well. Serve on salad greens or vegetable or fruit salads. Makes ⅔ cup (five 2-tablespoon servings).

Prep Time: 5 minutes Chilling Time: 1 hour

2 Tablespoons: Calories 115. Total Fat 11 g. Saturated Fat 1 g. Protein 0 g. Carbohydrate 5 g. Fiber 0 g. Sodium 0 mg. Cholesterol 0 mg.

✳

Honey French Dressing Prepare as for French Vinaigrette Dressing, substituting **4 teaspoons honey** for the sugar. Serve on fruit salads.

2 Tablespoons: Calories 119. Total Fat 11 g. Saturated Fat 1 g. Protein 0 g. Carbohydrate 6 g. Fiber 0 g. Sodium 1 mg. Cholesterol 0 mg.

✳

Chiffonade Dressing Prepare as for French Vinaigrette Dressing, adding ⅓ **cup drained, canned diced beets or chopped sweet red pepper** and **1 chopped hard-cooked large egg white.** Makes 1¼ cups (ten 2-tablespoon servings). Serve on greens or vegetable salads.

2 Tablespoons: Calories 60. Total Fat 5 g. Saturated Fat 1 g. Protein 0 g. Carbohydrate 3 g. Fiber 0 g. Sodium 22 mg. Cholesterol 0 mg.

✳

India Dressing Prepare as for French Vinaigrette Dressing, adding **1 chopped hard-cooked large egg white, 2 tablespoons chopped chutney,** and ½ **teaspoon curry powder.** Makes 1 cup (eight 2-tablespoon servings). Serve on greens or vegetable salads.

2 Tablespoons: Calories 81. Total Fat 7 g. Saturated Fat 1 g. Protein 1 g. Carbohydrate 5 g. Fiber 0 g. Sodium 23 mg. Cholesterol 0 mg.

Tart Lemon Dressing

The sweet, yet sour, combination of honey and lemon in this salad dressing tastes especially good with greens such as escarole, spinach, Swiss chard, or kale.

½ **cup lemon juice**

¼ **cup honey**

¼ **cup olive or vegetable oil**

1 **teaspoon grated gingerroot**

½ **teaspoon grated lemon rind**

¼ **teaspoon paprika**

1 In a jar with a tight-fitting lid, combine the lemon juice, honey, oil, gingerroot, lemon rind, and paprika. Cover and shake well, then refrigerate for at least 1 hour (will keep for 1 week).

2 To serve, shake the dressing well. Serve on salad greens or fruit salads. Makes 1 cup (eight 2-tablespoon servings).

Prep Time: 10 minutes Chilling Time: 1 hour

2 Tablespoons: Calories 96. Total Fat 7 g. Saturated Fat 1 g. Protein 0 g. Carbohydrate 10 g. Fiber 0 g. Sodium 1 mg. Cholesterol 0 mg.

Pineapple Cream Dressing

This slightly sweet dressing was a favorite for fruit salads in the 1940's and 1950's.

1½ **cups plain low-fat yogurt**

1 **can (8 ounces) crushed pineapple packed in juice, undrained**

¼ **cup low-fat (1% milkfat) milk**

2 **tablespoons firmly packed light brown sugar**

¼ **teaspoon ground allspice**

1 In a small bowl, stir together the yogurt, pineapple, milk, brown sugar, and allspice. Cover and refrigerate for at least 1 hour (will keep for 1 week).

2 Serve on fruit salads. Makes 2¼ cups (eighteen 2-tablespoon servings).

Prep Time: 5 minutes Chilling Time: 1 hour

2 Tablespoons: Calories 26. Total Fat 0 g. Saturated Fat 0 g. Protein 1 g. Carbohydrate 5 g. Fiber 0 g. Sodium 17 mg. Cholesterol 1 mg.

Cool Mint Dressing over fruit

Cool Mint Dressing

*Grandma prepared this dressing in summer when she had fresh
mint. Make it early in the day so it has time to develop a full mint
flavor. Do not substitute dried mint; it will alter the flavor.*

⅓ **cup red wine vinegar**

¼ **cup firmly packed light brown sugar**

¼ **cup olive or vegetable oil**

8 **sprigs fresh mint**

1 **teaspoon grated lime rind**

½ **teaspoon poppy seeds**

   Dash ground red pepper (cayenne)

1 In a jar with a tight-fitting lid, combine the vinegar,
brown sugar, oil, mint, lime rind, poppy seeds, and
red pepper. Cover and shake well, then refrigerate for at
least 8 hours (will keep for 1 week).

2 To serve, discard the mint and shake the dressing
well. Serve on fruit salads. Makes ¾ cup (six
2-tablespoon servings).

Prep Time: 5 minutes Chilling Time: 8 hours

2 Tablespoons: Calories 106. Total Fat 9 g. Saturated Fat 1 g.
Protein 0 g. Carbohydrate 7 g. Fiber 0 g.
Sodium 8 mg. Cholesterol 0 mg.

Perfect Peach Preserves over waffles

Perfect Peach Preserves

*For best flavor, Georgia cooks always made these preserves with lusciously
ripe peaches. If your store-bought peaches are not quite ripe enough, place them
in a paper bag and store them at room temperature for a day or two.*

5　cups sugar

3　pounds peaches

2　tablespoons lime or lemon juice

1　teaspoon grated lime or lemon rind

½　teaspoon ground ginger

⅛　teaspoon ground allspice

1　package (1¾ ounces) powdered fruit pectin

½　teaspoon butter or margarine

1 Prepare 7 half-pint jars and lids (page 278). Measure sugar into a bowl; set aside. Peel, pit, and finely chop enough of the peaches to measure 4 cups; transfer to a 6- to 8-quart kettle or Dutch oven. Stir in the lime juice, lime rind, ginger, and allspice. Stir in the fruit pectin and butter.

2 Bring to a full rolling boil over high heat, stirring constantly. Quickly stir in the sugar. Return to a full rolling boil and boil for 1 minute, stirring constantly. Remove from heat. Skim off foam.

3 Immediately ladle into the prepared jars, filling to within ⅛ inch of tops. Wipe jar rims and threads. Quickly cover with lids; screw firmly. To seal, invert the jars for 5 minutes, then turn upright. To set preserves, let stand at room temperature for 24 hours. Check the seal on each jar (page 278). Store in a cool, dark place (will keep for 1 year). Makes 7 half-pints.

Prep Time: 30 minutes　Cooking Time: 7 minutes
Standing Time: 24 hours

1 Tablespoon: Calories 39. Total Fat 0 g. Saturated Fat 0 g.
Protein 0 g. Carbohydrate 10 g. Fiber 0 g.
Sodium 0 mg. Cholesterol 0 mg.

EASY FREEZER JAMS

Years ago, grandma boiled the fruit for jam and sealed the jars with paraffin. Today, there's an easier way—you can make freezer jam. Recipes for these jams are specially formulated so that you don't have to go to the trouble of cooking the fruit. Freezer jams are perfect for today's tastes and busy schedules because they have a great fresh fruit flavor and take less time to make. If you choose to make a freezer recipe, expect the jam to be softer set than a store-bought version.

Raspberry-Blueberry Freezer Jam

*Although grandma crushed berries
by hand, you can use a food processor if you like.
To get bits of fruit in the jam, be careful not
to puree the berries. Just quickly turn the processor
on and off several times to chop them.*

1½   **pints red raspberries or blackberries**
1½   **pints blueberries**
  3   **tablespoons lime juice**
  ½   **teaspoon grated lime rind**
5¼   **cups sugar**
  1   **package (1¾ ounces) powdered fruit pectin**
  ¾   **cup water**

1 Prepare freezer containers and lids (page 278). Using a pastry blender or a potato masher, crush the raspberries and blueberries, 1 cup at a time. Measure 3 cups crushed fruit; transfer to a large bowl.

2 Stir in the lime juice and lime rind. Stir in the sugar. Let stand for 10 minutes, stirring occasionally.

3 In a small saucepan, stir together the pectin and water (may be lumpy). Bring to a boil over high heat, stirring constantly. Boil for 1 minute, stirring constantly. Remove from heat. Stir into the fruit mixture. Continue stirring for 3 minutes or until sugar is dissolved (a few sugar crystals may remain).

4 Immediately ladle into containers, filling to within ½ inch of tops. Wipe edges; quickly cover with lids. To set jam, let stand at room temperature for 24 hours.

5 Store in the freezer (will keep for 1 year) or in the refrigerator (will keep for 3 weeks). Makes 6¾ cups.

Prep Time: 20 minutes Cooking Time: 3 minutes
Standing Time: 10 minutes; 24 hours

1 Tablespoon: Calories 41. Total Fat 0 g. Saturated Fat 0 g.
Protein 0 g. Carbohydrate 11 g. Fiber 0 g.
Sodium 0 mg. Cholesterol 0 mg.

Rosy Rhubarb Jam

*"Each spring, after Grandma Anna
made her rhubarb jam, she'd invite us over for thin
Scandinavian pancakes, topped with lots of
jam and whipped cream," says Gummi Vidarsson.
"This was the best dessert we'd have all year."*

  5   **cups granulated sugar**
1½   **cups firmly packed light brown sugar**
2½   **pounds rhubarb stalks (trimmed), finely chopped**
  1   **cup water**
  1   **package (1¾ ounces) powdered fruit pectin**
  1   **teaspoon grated lemon rind**
  ½   **teaspoon butter or margarine**
      Few drops red food coloring (optional)

1 Prepare 7 half-pint jars and lids (page 278). Measure the sugars into a bowl; set aside.

2 In a large saucepan, combine the rhubarb and water. Bring to a boil over high heat. Lower the heat and simmer, covered, for 2 minutes. Measure 4½ cups rhubarb mixture; transfer to a 6- to 8-quart kettle or Dutch oven.

3 Stir in the pectin, lemon rind, butter, and food coloring (if using). Bring to a full rolling boil over high heat, stirring constantly. Quickly stir in the sugars. Return to a full rolling boil and boil for 1 minute, stirring constantly. Remove from heat. Skim off any foam.

4 Immediately ladle into jars, filling to within ⅛ inch of tops. Wipe jar rims and threads. Quickly cover with lids; screw firmly. To seal, invert the jars for 5 minutes, then turn upright. To set jam, let stand at room temperature for 24 hours. Check the seal on each jam jar (page 278).

5 Store in a cool, dark place (will keep for 1 year). Makes 7 half-pints.

Prep Time: 25 minutes Cooking Time: 14 minutes
Standing Time: 24 hours

1 Tablespoon: Calories 47. Total Fat 0 g. Saturated Fat 0 g.
Protein 0 g. Carbohydrate 12 g. Fiber 0 g.
Sodium 3 mg. Cholesterol 0 mg.

high heat, stirring constantly. Quickly stir in the sugar. Return to a full rolling boil and boil for 1 minute, stirring constantly. Stir in the pecans. Remove from heat. Skim off foam.

2 Immediately ladle into jars, filling to within ⅛ inch of tops. Wipe jar rims and threads. Quickly cover with lids; screw firmly. To seal, invert jars for 5 minutes, then turn upright. To set conserves, let stand at room temperature for 24 hours. Check the seal on each jar (tip, left). Store in cool, dark place (will keep for 1 year). Makes 6 half-pints.

Prep Time: 25 minutes Cooking Time: 7 minutes
Standing Time: 24 hours

1 Tablespoon: Calories 42. Total Fat 1 g. Saturated Fat 0 g. Protein 0 g. Carbohydrate 10 g. Fiber 0 g. Sodium 1 mg. Cholesterol 0 mg.

Blue-Ribbon Grape Jelly

Farm wives relied on the natural pectin in grapes to set jelly. Today, commercial pectin gives the set.

4½ cups sugar
3 cups unsweetened grape juice
1 cup cranberry juice cocktail
3 tablespoons lemon juice
2 teaspoons grated lemon rind
1 package (1¾ ounces) powdered fruit pectin
½ teaspoon butter or margarine

1 Prepare 6 half-pint jars and lids (tip, above left). Measure the sugar into a bowl; set aside. In a 6- to 8-quart kettle or Dutch oven, combine grape juice, cranberry juice, lemon juice, and lemon rind.

2 Stir in pectin and butter. Bring to a full rolling boil over high heat, stirring constantly. Quickly stir in sugar. Return to full rolling boil and boil for 1 minute, stirring constantly. Remove from heat. Skim off foam.

3 Immediately ladle into the prepared jars, filling to within ⅛ inch of tops. Wipe jar rims and threads. Quickly cover with the lids; screw firmly. To seal, invert the jars for 5 minutes, then turn upright. To set the jelly, let stand at room temperature for 24 hours. Check the seal on each jar (tip, above left). Store in a cool, dark place (will keep for 1 year). Makes 6 half-pints.

Prep Time: 15 minutes Cooking Time: 7 minutes
Standing Time: 24 hours

1 Tablespoon: Calories 45. Total Fat 0 g. Saturated Fat 0 g. Protein 0 g. Carbohydrate 11 g. Fiber 0 g. Sodium 1 mg. Cholesterol 0 mg.

PRESERVING HINTS

• **Choosing Jars** Use only glass jars and lids specifically made for canning. Follow the manufacturers' directions for assembling lids and seals. Decorative jelly glasses (see Grape Jelly, photo opposite) cannot be used for room-temperature storage because they have loose tops that can't be sealed. If you use them, omit the inverting step. When jelly is set, refrigerate for up to 3 weeks.

• **Preparing Jars and Lids** Wash jars and lids in hot sudsy water and rinse well. Heat the lids by pouring boiling water over and letting them stand in the hot water until you use them. (For pickles, let both the lids and jars stand in boiling water.)

• **Checking the Seal** After your cooked jams or jellies or processed pickles have completely cooled, check the seal of each jar by pressing the middle of the lid with your finger. If the dip in the lid holds when you lift your finger, the jar is sealed. If the lid springs back up, the jar is not sealed. Store any unsealed jars in the refrigerator (will keep for 3 weeks).

• **Preparing Freezer Containers and Lids** Wash plastic containers or glass jars and their lids in hot sudsy water; rinse thoroughly. Then, rinse them a second time by pouring boiling water over them.

Plum Conserves

What's a conserve? It's a jam made with two or three different fruits plus raisins and nuts.

3 cups sugar
2 pounds plums
1 orange
1 cup golden raisins
1 package (1¾ ounces) powdered fruit pectin
3 tablespoons finely chopped crystallized ginger
½ teaspoon ground coriander
½ teaspoon butter or margarine
½ cup coarsely chopped pecans

1 Prepare 6 half-pint jars and lids (tip, above). Measure sugar into a bowl; set aside. Finely chop plums, orange (with peel), and raisins; transfer to a 6- to 8-quart kettle or Dutch oven. Stir in the pectin, ginger, coriander, and butter. Bring to a full rolling boil over

Blue-Ribbon Grape Jelly and Plum Conserves on biscuits

Spicy Apple Butter on hot cereal

Spicy Apple Butter

When America was largely rural, making apple butter was often
a social event. Families would get together to peel apples, simmer the
aromatic butter in large kettles, and share the latest news.

4 **pounds tart cooking apples, quartered**

4 **cups unsweetened pineapple or apple juice**

1½ **cups sugar**

½ **cup honey**

1½ **teaspoons ground cinnamon**

1 **teaspoon ground cardamom**

½ **teaspoon ground mace**

1 In a 6- to 8-quart kettle or Dutch oven, combine the apples and pineapple juice. Bring to a boil. Lower the heat and simmer, covered, for 30 minutes, stirring occasionally. Press through a food mill or a sieve, discarding the peels and cores. Measure 8 to 9 cups pulp.

2 Return the pulp to kettle. Stir in the sugar, honey, cinnamon, cardamom, and mace. Bring to a boil. Lower heat and simmer, uncovered, for 2 to 2½ hours or until very thick, stirring frequently. Place the kettle in a sink of ice water; let stand to cool, stirring frequently.

3 Prepare freezer containers and lids (page 278). Ladle the apple mixture into containers, filling to within ½ inch of tops. Wipe edges; cover with lids.

4 Store in the freezer (will keep for 1 year) or in the refrigerator (will keep for 3 weeks). Makes 5 cups.

Prep Time: 25 minutes   Cooking Time: 2¾ hours

1 Tablespoon: Calories 39. Total Fat 0 g. Saturated Fat 0 g.
Protein 0 g. Carbohydrate 10 g. Fiber 0 g.
Sodium 0 mg. Cholesterol 0 mg.

Maple Butter

One way grandma added an extra-special touch to her homemade breads was with flavored butters.

- ½ **cup butter or margarine, at room temperature**
- 2 **tablespoons maple-flavored syrup or pure maple syrup**
- 1 **teaspoon grated lemon rind**

1 In a small bowl, with an electric mixer on *Low*, beat the butter, syrup, and lemon rind until creamy.

2 Store in a covered container in the refrigerator (will keep for 2 weeks). Let stand at room temperature for 30 minutes before serving. Serve on breads, pancakes, or toast. Makes ½ cup.

Prep Time: 5 minutes

1 Teaspoon: Calories 38. Total Fat 4 g. Saturated Fat 2 g. Protein 0 g. Carbohydrate 1 g. Fiber 0 g. Sodium 40 mg. Cholesterol 10 mg.

Herb Mustard Butter Prepare as for Maple Butter, omitting the syrup and lemon rind and adding **1 tablespoon Dijon mustard** and **½ teaspoon dried thyme leaves.** Serve on French bread, meats, poultry, fish, or cooked vegetables.

1 Teaspoon: Calories 35. Total Fat 4 g. Saturated Fat 2 g. Protein 0 g. Carbohydrate 0 g. Fiber 0 g. Sodium 55 mg. Cholesterol 10 mg.

USING A WATER-BATH CANNER

As soon as the lid is screwed on each jar, use canning tongs to place it on the rack in the canner of boiling water. Make sure the jars do not touch. Replace the canner cover after you add each jar.

After the jars have finished processing, use hot pads to lift the rack and jars out of the canner. Remove the jars from the rack and let them cool on a board or towel.

Bread-and-Butter Pickles

In the old days, women made pickles to preserve their garden bounty all year long; today, cooks make them for that old-time, homemade flavor.

- 10 **cups sliced medium-size cucumbers**
- 5 **medium-size yellow onions, sliced**
- 2 **medium-size sweet red and/or yellow peppers, sliced crosswise into rings**
- ⅓ **cup pickling salt**
- 3 **cloves garlic, halved**
  - **Cracked ice**
- 3 **cups sugar**
- 2 **cups cider vinegar**
- 4 **teaspoons mustard seeds**
- 1½ **teaspoons coriander seeds**
- 1½ **teaspoons whole black peppercorns**
- ¾ **teaspoon celery seeds**
- ¾ **teaspoon ground turmeric**

1 In a large bowl, stir together the cucumbers, onions, sweet peppers, pickling salt, and garlic. Stir in a large amount of cracked ice. Let stand for 3 hours; drain well. Discard the garlic.

2 Prepare 5 pint jars and lids (page 278). Fill a water-bath canner half full of water. Cover and bring to a boil over high heat. In another large kettle, bring additional water to a boil.

3 Meanwhile, in a 6- to 8-quart kettle or Dutch oven, stir together the sugar, vinegar, mustard seeds, coriander seeds, peppercorns, celery seeds, and turmeric. Add the cucumber mixture. Bring to a boil.

4 Immediately ladle the cucumber mixture and liquid into jars, filling to within ½ inch of tops. Wipe jar rims and threads. Quickly cover with lids; screw firmly. Place the jars on the rack in canner (tip, left). Fill canner with additional boiling water so that the water reaches 1 inch over jar tops. Cover and bring to a rolling boil. Process for 10 minutes (page 282). Remove jars; cool (tip, left). Check seal on each jar (page 278).

5 Store in a cool, dark place (will keep for 1 year). Makes 5 pints.

Prep Time: 45 minutes Standing Time: 3 hours
Cooking Time: 35 minutes

¼ Cup: Calories 15. Total Fat 0 g. Saturated Fat 0 g. Protein 0 g. Carbohydrate 4 g. Fiber 0 g. Sodium 113 mg. Cholesterol 0 mg.

PICKLING POINTERS

• **Filling the Jars** Pack the pickle solids and liquid into each jar, making sure the liquid covers the solids and leaving the recommended amount of headspace.

• **Removing Air Bubbles** Gently work a thin plastic knife down the sides of the jars. Add more of the liquid, if needed, and cover jars.

• **Processing** Keep the water in the canner boiling gently, adding more boiling water if the level drops. If the water stops boiling, stop counting processing time, turn up the heat, and wait for the water to return to a rolling boil before resuming counting.

Easy Beet Pickles

"My Grandmother Martin's beet pickles were my favorite," remembers Bonnie Premo. "They always were firm and had a delicious spicy flavor."
Here's how to make your own spicy beet pickles the easy way—with canned beets.

½ cup cider vinegar
⅓ cup sugar
⅓ cup water
½ teaspoon ground cinnamon
¼ teaspoon ground allspice
¼ teaspoon caraway seeds
⅛ teaspoon salt
⅛ teaspoon ground cloves
2 cans (14½ ounces each) sliced beets, drained

1 In large saucepan, stir together vinegar, sugar, water, cinnamon, allspice, caraway seeds, salt, and cloves. Bring to a boil over high heat, stirring occasionally.

2 Stir in the beets. Return to a boil. Lower the heat and simmer, covered, for 5 minutes.

3 Transfer to a covered container and refrigerate for at least 24 hours before serving. Store in the refrigerator (will keep for 1 month). Use a slotted spoon to serve. Makes 2 cups.

Prep Time: 5 minutes Cooking Time: 13 minutes
Chilling Time: 24 hours

¼ Cup: Calories 17. Total Fat 0 g. Saturated Fat 0 g.
Protein 0 g. Carbohydrate 4 g. Fiber 1 g.
Sodium 119 mg. Cholesterol 0 mg.

Deep-South Watermelon Rind Pickles

These old-fashioned Southern favorites are unlike any store-bought pickles—they're a wonderful blend of four spices and a hint of lemon.

5 pounds watermelon rind
6 cups water
⅓ cup pickling salt
3 cups sugar
1½ cups white vinegar
1½ cups water
1 cinnamon stick, 3 inches long, broken
3 1 x ⅛-inch slices gingerroot
2 teaspoons whole allspice berries
1 teaspoon whole cloves
1 small lemon, halved and thinly sliced

1 Cut the green and pink parts from watermelon rind; discard green and pink parts. Cut the white part of the rind into 1-inch pieces; measure 9 cups. Transfer the rind to a large bowl. Combine the 6 cups water and pickling salt; pour over watermelon rind (add more water, if necessary, to cover rind). Let stand at room temperature for 8 hours or overnight. Drain; rinse rind.

2 In a Dutch oven, cover watermelon rind with cold water. Bring to a boil. Lower the heat and simmer, covered, for 20 to 25 minutes or until tender. Drain.

3 Meanwhile, in a 6- to 8-quart kettle or Dutch oven, stir together the sugar, vinegar, the 1½ cups water, cinnamon, gingerroot, allspice, and cloves. Bring to a boil. Lower the heat and simmer, uncovered, for 10 minutes. Strain through a sieve, discarding the spices. Return the hot sugar mixture to the kettle.

4 Add the watermelon rind and lemon to the kettle. Bring to a boil. Lower the heat and simmer, covered, for 25 minutes or until rind is clear.

5 Meanwhile, prepare 3 pint jars and lids (page 278). Fill a water-bath canner half full of water. Cover and bring to a boil over high heat. In another large kettle, bring additional water to a boil.

Deep-South Watermelon Rind Pickles

Layered Pepper and Cabbage Slaw

Dill seeds sometimes were called "meetin' seeds" because children chewed the seeds during church to help stay awake. They also were used to flavor pickles, relishes, and slaws.

1 cup sugar
1 cup white vinegar
½ cup water
2 cloves garlic, minced
1 tablespoon dill seeds
2 teaspoons dry mustard
1 teaspoon dried thyme leaves
¼ teaspoon each salt and black pepper
6 cups shredded cabbage
1 small yellow onion, chopped
2 large sweet red and/or yellow peppers, chopped
1 tablespoon chopped canned red jalapeño pepper

1 In a medium-size bowl, combine the sugar, vinegar, water, garlic, dill seeds, mustard, thyme, salt, and black pepper.

2 In a large bowl, combine cabbage and onion. Pour two-thirds of vinegar mixture over cabbage mixture; toss to coat. Cover and refrigerate for at least 8 hours.

3 Meanwhile, in a medium-size bowl, combine the sweet peppers and jalapeño pepper. Pour the remaining vinegar mixture over pepper mixture; toss to coat. Cover and refrigerate for at least 8 hours.

4 In a storage jar or bowl, layer one-third of the cabbage mixture, half of the pepper mixture, another one-third of the cabbage mixture, the remaining pepper mixture, and the remaining cabbage mixture. Pour in any remaining vinegar mixture.

5 Cover and store in the refrigerator (will keep for 1 week). Use a slotted spoon to serve. Serve with grilled chicken. Makes 6½ cups.

Prep Time: 30 minutes Chilling Time: 8 hours

¼ Cup: Calories 24. Total Fat 0 g. Saturated Fat 0 g. Protein 0 g. Carbohydrate 6 g. Fiber 1 g. Sodium 18 mg. Cholesterol 0 mg.

6 Immediately ladle the rind and hot sugar mixture into the prepared jars, filling to within ½ inch of tops. Wipe jar rims and threads. Quickly cover with lids; screw firmly. Place the jars on the rack in canner (page 281). Fill canner with additional boiling water so that the water reaches 1 inch over jar tops. Cover and bring to a rolling boil. Process for 10 minutes (tip, opposite page). Remove the jars and cool (page 281). Check the seal on each jar (page 278).

7 Store in a cool, dark place (will keep for 1 year). Makes 3 pints.

Prep Time: 30 minutes Standing Time: 8 hours
Cooking Time: 1 hour 25 minutes

¼ Cup: Calories 45. Total Fat 0 g. Saturated Fat 0 g. Protein 1 g. Carbohydrate 10 g. Fiber 0 g. Sodium 99 mg. Cholesterol 0 mg.

Fiesta Onion Relish

Spoon this colorful, old-time relish on burgers or serve it alongside grilled pork chops. To speed up the job of chopping the vegetables, use a food processor fitted with the steel blade. Use short, on-and-off pulses to cut the vegetables into tiny pieces.

1 **cinnamon stick, 3 inches long, broken**

1 **teaspoon each whole cloves and whole allspice berries**

¼ **teaspoon crushed red pepper**

½ **cup sugar**

½ **cup white vinegar**

¼ **cup water**

2 **large yellow onions, chopped**

2 **medium-size carrots, chopped**

⅓ **cup raisins**

1 **large sweet green pepper, chopped**

3 **tablespoons drained canned sliced pimientos**

1 Enclose the cinnamon, cloves, allspice, and red pepper in a spice bag (tip, right). In a large saucepan, stir together the sugar, vinegar, and water. Stir in the spice bag, onions, carrots, and raisins.

2 Bring to a boil over high heat. Lower the heat to moderately high and boil gently, uncovered, for 5 minutes. Remove from heat.

3 Stir in the green pepper and pimientos. Transfer to a covered container and refrigerate for at least 8 hours before serving. Store in the refrigerator (will keep for 1 week). Discard the spice bag before serving. Use a slotted spoon to serve. Makes 4½ cups.

Prep Time: 25 minutes Cooking Time: 10 minutes
Chilling Time: 8 hours

¼ Cup: Calories 32. Total Fat 0 g. Saturated Fat 0 g.
Protein 0 g. Carbohydrate 8 g. Fiber 1 g.
Sodium 7 mg. Cholesterol 0 mg.

Making a Spice Bag

Assemble a spice bag by placing the cinnamon, cloves, allspice, and crushed red pepper in the center of a 3-inch square of 100% cotton cheesecloth. Bring up the corners; tie securely with cotton string.

Chow-Chow

This spicy vegetable combination is a descendant of the mustard-flavored relish made by Chinese immigrants who helped build the transcontinental railroad. Serve it on burgers or grilled chicken sandwiches.

1 **cup firmly packed light brown sugar**

1 **cup vinegar**

½ **cup water**

2 **teaspoons dry mustard**

1 **teaspoon celery seeds**

1 **teaspoon whole allspice berries**

½ **teaspoon ground turmeric**

1½ **cups cauliflower cut into small pieces**

1 **large yellow onion, chopped**

2 **cups chopped cabbage**

2 **large sweet red, yellow, or green peppers, chopped**

2 **medium-size green or red tomatoes, seeded and chopped**

1 In a large saucepan, stir together the brown sugar, vinegar, water, mustard, celery seeds, allspice, and turmeric. Stir in the cauliflower and onion.

2 Bring to a boil over high heat. Lower the heat to moderately high and boil gently, uncovered, for 3 minutes. Remove from heat.

3 Stir in the cabbage, sweet peppers, and tomatoes. Transfer to covered container; refrigerate for at least 8 hours before serving. Store in refrigerator (will keep for 1 week). Use slotted spoon to serve. Makes 6½ cups.

Prep Time: 25 minutes Cooking Time: 8 minutes
Chilling Time: 8 hours

¼ Cup: Calories 28. Total Fat 0 g. Saturated Fat 0 g.
Protein 1 g. Carbohydrate 7 g. Fiber 1 g.
Sodium 6 mg. Cholesterol 0 mg.

Sauerkraut Hamburger Relish

Sauerkraut Hamburger Relish

For a milder-flavored relish, place the sauerkraut in a sieve, rinse it under
cold running water to wash off some of the saltiness, and drain it well.

¼ **cup sugar**

¼ **cup vinegar**

2 **tablespoons water**

1 **teaspoon dried savory leaves or basil leaves**

1 **teaspoon lower-sodium Worcestershire sauce**

¼ **teaspoon crushed red pepper**

1 **can (8 ounces) lower-sodium sauerkraut, drained**

1 **medium-size tomato, seeded and chopped**

¾ **cup seeded and chopped cucumber**

2 **medium-size green onions with tops, finely sliced**

1 In a medium-size bowl, stir together the sugar, vinegar, water, savory, Worcestershire sauce, and red pepper. Stir in the sauerkraut, tomato, cucumber, and green onions.

2 Transfer to a covered container and refrigerate for at least 2 hours before serving. Store in the refrigerator (will keep for 1 week). Use a slotted spoon to serve. Makes 3 cups.

Prep Time: 15 minutes Chilling Time: 2 hours

¼ Cup: Calories 17. Total Fat 0 g. Saturated Fat 0 g.
Protein 0 g. Carbohydrate 4 g. Fiber 0 g.
Sodium 30 mg. Cholesterol 0 mg.

Gingery Pear and Pepper Relish over a pork chop

Gingery Pear and Pepper Relish

A Southern specialty, this chutney-like relish is a
delicious combination of currants, onion, pears, peppers, and
crystallized ginger. Serve it with pork, ham, or poultry.

²⁄₃ **cup cider vinegar**

½ **cup firmly packed light brown sugar**

⅓ **cup currants or raisins**

2 **tablespoons chopped crystallized ginger**

1 **teaspoon dry mustard**

¼ **teaspoon ground allspice**

⅛ **teaspoon ground red pepper (cayenne)**

1 **large yellow onion, chopped**

5 **medium-size pears, cored and chopped**

2 **medium-size sweet red, yellow, or green peppers,**
chopped

1 In a large saucepan, stir together the vinegar, brown sugar, currants, ginger, mustard, allspice, and ground red pepper. Stir in the onion.

2 Bring to a boil over high heat. Lower the heat to moderately high and boil gently, uncovered, for 3 minutes. Remove from heat.

3 Stir in the pears and sweet peppers. Transfer to a covered container and refrigerate for at least 8 hours before serving. Store in the refrigerator (will keep for 1 week). Use a slotted spoon to serve. Makes 6 cups.

Prep Time: 25 minutes Cooking Time: 8 minutes
Chilling Time: 8 hours

¼ Cup: Calories 35. Total Fat 0 g. Saturated Fat 0 g.
Protein 0 g. Carbohydrate 9 g. Fiber 1 g.
Sodium 1 mg. Cholesterol 0 mg.

SCORING A CUCUMBER

To give cucumber slices a decorative scored edge, draw the tines of a fork length-wise down the side of a whole cucumber, making grooves about 1/16 inch deep. Turn the cucumber slightly and repeat. Continue scoring all around the cucumber. Then, slice the cucumber crosswise; discard ends.

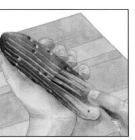

Corn and Cukes

This super-simple refrigerator relish goes together in minutes. It's delicious with meats, poultry, grilled fish, and sandwiches.

2   **packages (10 ounces each) frozen whole kernel corn**
3/4 **cup sugar**
2/3 **cup white vinegar**
2   **tablespoons water**
1   **teaspoon dried marjoram leaves**
1/4 **teaspoon salt**
    Few dashes hot red pepper sauce
2   **small cucumbers**
1   **medium-size sweet red or green pepper, chopped**
1   **cup small whole fresh mushrooms**

1 In a large saucepan, cook the corn according to package directions. Drain. Stir in the sugar, vinegar, water, marjoram, salt, and red pepper sauce.

2 Bring to a boil over high heat. Lower the heat to moderately high and boil gently, uncovered, for 3 minutes. Remove from heat.

3 Score and slice the cucumbers (tip, above). Stir the cucumbers, sweet pepper, and mushrooms into corn mixture. Transfer to a covered container and refrigerate for at least 8 hours before serving. Store in the refrigerator (will keep for 1 week). Use a slotted spoon to serve. Makes 6¾ cups.

Prep Time: 10 minutes Cooking Time: 15 minutes
Chilling Time: 8 hours

¼ Cup: Calories 35. Total Fat 0 g. Saturated Fat 0 g.
Protein 1 g. Carbohydrate 9 g. Fiber 1 g.
Sodium 15 mg. Cholesterol 0 mg.

Iowa Corn Relish

Grandma waited for fresh corn to make her relish. This never-fail recipe uses frozen corn, so you can make it any time.

1   **package (10 ounces) frozen whole kernel corn**
1   **medium-size yellow onion, finely chopped**
1/3 **cup sugar**
1   **tablespoon cornstarch**
1   **teaspoon celery seeds**
1   **teaspoon ground turmeric**
1/4 **teaspoon salt**
1/8 **teaspoon ground red pepper (cayenne)**
1/2 **cup vinegar**
1/4 **cup water**
1   **large tomato, seeded and chopped**
1   **large sweet green pepper, chopped**

1 In a large saucepan, cook the corn and onion according to the directions on the corn package. Drain, removing the corn mixture.

2 In the same saucepan, stir together the sugar, cornstarch, celery seeds, turmeric, salt, and red pepper. Stir in the vinegar and water. Stir in the corn mixture, tomato, and green pepper.

3 Bring to a boil over high heat, stirring constantly. Lower the heat to moderate and cook for 2 minutes or until mixture is thickened, stirring constantly.

4 Transfer to a covered container and refrigerate for at least 2 hours before serving. Store in the refrigerator (will keep for 1 month). Serve with burgers or grilled chicken. Makes 4¼ cups.

Prep Time: 15 minutes Cooking Time: 15 minutes
Chilling Time: 2 hours

¼ Cup: Calories 39. Total Fat 0 g. Saturated Fat 0 g.
Protein 1 g. Carbohydrate 10 g. Fiber 1 g.
Sodium 34 mg. Cholesterol 0 mg.

Rosy Tomato Relish

Be sure to seed the tomatoes. This will keep them from watering out as the relish chills.

½ **cup red wine vinegar**
⅓ **cup firmly packed light brown sugar**
1 **cinnamon stick, 3 inches long, broken**
2 **teaspoons mustard seeds**
1 **teaspoon grated orange rind**
½ **teaspoon ground ginger**
⅛ **teaspoon ground cloves**
2 **medium-size tart cooking apples, chopped**
1 **large yellow onion, chopped**
4 **medium-size tomatoes, seeded and chopped**

1 In a large saucepan, stir together the vinegar, brown sugar, cinnamon, mustard seeds, orange rind, ginger, and cloves. Stir in the apples and onion.

2 Bring to a boil over high heat. Lower the heat to moderately high and boil gently, uncovered, for 3 minutes. Remove from heat.

3 Stir in the tomatoes. Transfer to a covered container and refrigerate for at least 8 hours before serving. Store in the refrigerator (will keep for 1 week). Discard the cinnamon before serving. Use a slotted spoon to serve. Serve with roast pork or broiled pork chops. Makes 5½ cups.

Prep Time: 25 minutes Cooking Time: 8 minutes
Chilling Time: 8 hours

¼ Cup: Calories 20. Total Fat 0 g. Saturated Fat 0 g. Protein 0 g. Carbohydrate 5 g. Fiber 1 g. Sodium 4 mg. Cholesterol 0 mg.

County Fair Cherries

Shaker women were famous for their homemade spiced cherries. Over time, their recipes were dressed up a bit, as in this version which uses both orange juice and brandy.

½ **cup sugar**
½ **cup orange juice**
2 **tablespoons vinegar**
1 **teaspoon grated orange rind**
¼ **teaspoon ground cinnamon**
⅛ **teaspoon ground mace**
2 **pounds dark sweet cherries, pitted, or 2 packages (16 ounces each) frozen pitted dark sweet cherries**
2 **tablespoons brandy, dry sherry, or orange juice**

1 In a large saucepan, stir together the sugar, orange juice, vinegar, orange rind, cinnamon, and mace. Stir in the fresh or frozen cherries.

2 Bring to a boil over high heat. Lower the heat to moderately high and boil gently, uncovered, for 5 minutes. Remove from heat. Stir in the brandy.

3 Transfer to a covered container and refrigerate for at least 8 hours before serving. Store in the refrigerator (will keep for 1 week). Use a slotted spoon to serve. Serve with roast chicken or turkey. Makes 3 cups.

Prep Time: 20 minutes Cooking Time: 10 minutes
Chilling Time: 8 hours

¼ Cup: Calories 64. Total Fat 1 g. Saturated Fat 0 g. Protein 1 g. Carbohydrate 14 g. Fiber 1 g. Sodium 0 mg. Cholesterol 0 mg.

Spiced Honey Apple Rings

Old-time cooks brightened up plates of roast pork or chicken with these colorful, sweetly glazed apple slices.

2 **cups cranberry juice cocktail**
½ **cup honey**
½ **teaspoon ground cinnamon**
¼ **teaspoon ground allspice**
⅛ **teaspoon ground cloves**
4 **medium-size tart red cooking apples, cored and cut crosswise into ½-inch-thick slices**

1 In a 10-inch skillet, stir together the cranberry juice, honey, cinnamon, allspice, and cloves. Bring to a boil over high heat. Lower the heat to moderately high and boil gently, uncovered, for 5 minutes.

2 Add the apples. Return to a boil. Lower the heat and simmer, covered, for 8 to 10 minutes or just until tender, spooning the honey mixture over apples occasionally. Serve warm or chilled.

3 Store in a covered container in the refrigerator (will keep for 1 month). Use a slotted spoon to serve. Makes 6 servings.

Prep Time: 10 minutes Cooking Time: 20 minutes

1 Serving: Calories 77. Total Fat 0 g. Saturated Fat 0 g. Protein 0 g. Carbohydrate 20 g. Fiber 2 g. Sodium 1 mg. Cholesterol 0 mg.

Grandma's Treats

Chunky Homemade Peanut Butter

Show the youngsters that peanut butter doesn't have to come from a jar. For a special fresh fruit flavor, add the grated orange rind.

- **2 cups unsalted dry roasted peanuts**
- **¼ teaspoon salt**
- **½ cup chopped unsalted dry roasted peanuts**
- **½ teaspoon grated orange rind (optional)**

1. In a food processor, process the 2 cups peanuts and the salt for 5 minutes or until smooth and spreadable. Stop occasionally to scrape side of bowl so mixture is evenly blended.

2. Stir in the ½ cup chopped peanuts and orange rind (if using).

3. Transfer to covered container; refrigerate for at least 1 hour before serving. Store in the refrigerator (will keep for 1 month). Makes 1¼ cups.

Fluffy Apricot Butter

A spoonful of this fruity butter will make toast or pancakes extra special.

- **¾ cup butter or margarine, at room temperature**
- **¼ cup finely chopped fresh or canned apricots**
- **2 tablespoons confectioners sugar**
- **1 teaspoon lemon juice**
- **½ teaspoon grated lemon rind**

1. In a medium-size bowl, with an electric mixer on *Low,* beat the butter until creamy.

2. Add the apricots, confectioners sugar, lemon juice, and lemon rind. Beat until well mixed.

3. Store in a covered container in the refrigerator (will keep for 2 weeks). Let stand at room temperature for 30 minutes before serving. Serve on breads, pancakes, or toast. Makes 1 cup.

Fruit Leather

The kids will love biting into this chewy snack.

- **4 ounces dried peaches**
- **4 ounces dried apricots**
- **2 cups water**
- **1 teaspoon vanilla**
- **¼ teaspoon ground allspice**
- **1 teaspoon sugar (optional)**

1. In a medium-size saucepan, combine the peaches and apricots; add the water. Bring to a boil. Lower the heat and simmer, covered, for 30 minutes or until fruit is very tender. Drain and cool.

2. Preheat the oven to 300°F. In a food processor or blender, process fruit mixture, vanilla, and allspice until smooth.

3. Line a 15½" x 10½" x 1" baking pan with foil; lightly grease the foil. Spread the fruit mixture evenly over foil. Bake for 25 minutes. Without opening door, turn off oven and let dry for 8 hours or overnight.

4. Remove the foil and fruit leather from pan; peel the fruit leather off foil. Sprinkle with the sugar (if using). Starting from a short end, roll up fruit leather. Wrap in foil and store in the refrigerator (will keep for 2 months). To serve, unroll and tear off pieces. Makes 4 to 6 servings.

Raisin-Orange Applesauce

Applesauce tastes even better when it's served warm.

- **1 jar (23 ounces) unsweetened applesauce**
- **⅓ cup raisins**
- **¼ cup orange marmalade**
- **¼ teaspoon ground cinnamon (optional)**

1. In a large saucepan, stir together the applesauce, raisins, orange marmalade, and cinnamon (if using).

2. Cook over moderately high heat for 5 minutes or until heated through, stirring frequently. Makes 2¾ cups.

NOT BY BREAD ALONE

The aroma of bread baking

is what many of us remember most

about a visit to grandma's house.

For dinner, she made tender muffins,

crusty loaves, or flaky biscuits.

As snacks, she offered delicate coffee

cakes, crispy fritters, and buttery scones.

And then, there were her

unforgettable feather-light, homemade

pancakes, waffles, and French toast.

Those old-fashioned breads

are still right for today, especially when

made with less fat and filled with

nourishing whole grains, dried fruits,

and a sprinkling of nuts.

From front to back: Apricot-Nut Loaf and Irish Soda Bread

Irish Soda Bread

*A favorite with Irish settlers who
came to America, this bread is a cross between
a biscuit and a coffee cake. Serve it slightly
warm and spread with jam.*

1⅓ **cups all-purpose flour**
 ⅔ **cup whole-wheat flour**
 2 **tablespoons firmly packed light brown sugar**
 1 **teaspoon baking powder**
 1 **teaspoon caraway seeds (optional)**
 ½ **teaspoon baking soda**
 ¼ **teaspoon salt**
 3 **tablespoons butter or margarine**
 2 **large egg whites**
 ¾ **cup low-fat (1% milkfat) buttermilk or soured milk
    (page 300)**
 ⅓ **cup currants**
1½ **teaspoons grated orange rind**

1 Preheat the oven to 375°F. In a large bowl, stir
together the all-purpose flour, whole-wheat flour,
brown sugar, baking powder, caraway seeds (if using),
baking soda, and salt.

2 Using a pastry blender or 2 knives, cut in the butter
until the mixture resembles coarse crumbs.

3 In a medium-size bowl, combine the egg whites,
buttermilk, currants, and orange rind. Add to the
flour mixture all at once and stir just until a soft dough
forms. Knead on a lightly floured surface for 30 seconds. Shape into a 6-inch round loaf on a lightly
greased baking sheet.

4 Using a very sharp knife or razor blade, make a
crisscross slash in the top of loaf. Brush loaf top
with a little additional buttermilk.

5 Bake for 30 minutes or until the bread is golden.
Transfer the loaf to a wire rack to cool. Makes
1 loaf (12 servings).

Prep Time: 20 minutes Cooking Time: 30 minutes

1 Serving: Calories 126. Total Fat 3 g. Saturated Fat 2 g.
Protein 4 g. Carbohydrate 21 g. Fiber 2 g.
Sodium 193 mg. Cholesterol 9 mg.

Apricot-Nut Loaf

*Years ago, this fruit bread often was
served at afternoon teas. For even slices that
don't crumble, make sure the bread is
completely cool before you cut it.*

   Boiling water
 1 **package (6 ounces) dried apricots, chopped**
 2 **cups all-purpose flour**
 ¾ **cup granulated sugar**
 1 **tablespoon baking powder**
 ¼ **teaspoon salt**
 2 **large egg whites**
 ⅔ **cup apricot nectar or orange juice**
 3 **tablespoons vegetable oil**
 2 **teaspoons grated orange rind**
 ½ **cup finely chopped pecans or walnuts**
 3 **to 4 teaspoons orange juice**
 ½ **cup sifted confectioners sugar**

1 Preheat the oven to 350°F. In a small bowl, pour
enough boiling water over apricots to cover; let
stand for 5 minutes. Drain and set aside.

2 Meanwhile, in a large bowl, stir together the flour,
granulated sugar, baking powder, and salt. In a
medium-size bowl, combine the egg whites, apricot
nectar, oil, and orange rind. Add to the flour mixture all
at once and stir just until combined. Fold in the apricots
and chopped pecans.

3 Spoon into a lightly greased 8" x 4" x 2" loaf pan.
Bake for 50 to 55 minutes or until a toothpick
inserted in the center comes out clean. Cool the bread
in pan on a wire rack for 5 minutes; remove from pan.

4 In a small bowl, gradually stir the orange juice into
the confectioners sugar until mixture is thin enough
to drizzle. Drizzle over loaf. Cool completely. Makes
1 loaf (16 servings).

Prep Time: 20 minutes Standing Time: 5 minutes
Cooking Time: 50 minutes

1 Serving: Calories 187. Total Fat 5 g. Saturated Fat 0 g.
Protein 3 g. Carbohydrate 34 g. Fiber 2 g.
Sodium 134 mg. Cholesterol 0 mg.

Granny's Moist Apple-Prune Bread

This spicy bread is delicious spread with cream cheese.

- 2 cups all-purpose flour
- ½ cup granulated sugar
- ½ cup firmly packed light brown sugar
- 1½ teaspoons baking powder
- 1 teaspoon ground cinnamon
- ½ teaspoon ground ginger
- ¼ teaspoon baking soda
- ¼ teaspoon salt
- 2 large egg whites
- 1 cup shredded peeled apple
- ⅓ cup apple juice
- 3 tablespoons vegetable oil
- 1 teaspoon grated lemon rind
- ½ cup chopped pitted prunes

1 Preheat the oven to 350°F. In a large bowl, stir together the flour, granulated sugar, brown sugar, baking powder, cinnamon, ginger, baking soda, and salt.

2 In a medium-size bowl, combine the egg whites, shredded apple, apple juice, oil, and lemon rind. Add to the flour mixture all at once and stir just until combined. Fold in the prunes.

3 Spoon into a lightly greased 8" x 4" x 2" loaf pan. Bake for 55 to 60 minutes or until a toothpick inserted in the center comes out clean. Cool the bread in the pan on a wire rack for 5 minutes; remove from pan. Cool completely. Makes 1 loaf (16 servings).

Prep Time: 20 minutes Cooking Time: 55 minutes

1 Serving: Calories 143. Total Fat 3 g. Saturated Fat 0 g. Protein 2 g. Carbohydrate 28 g. Fiber 1 g. Sodium 108 mg. Cholesterol 0 mg.

HOW TO MAKE PERFECT QUICK BREADS

♦ For quick breads and muffins with smooth edges and no crusty rims, grease the pans on the bottom and only halfway up the sides. This way the batter will cling to the sides of the pan rather than sliding back down during baking.

♦ To make sure quick breads and muffins have rounded—not peaked—tops and don't crumble, mix the liquid and dry ingredients just until combined. Don't overmix. The batter should have a few lumps when you spoon it into the pan.

♦ For even quick bread slices, completely cool the bread before slicing and use a serrated knife.

♦ To store quick breads and muffins, wrap them in foil or seal them in plastic bags and store them at room temperature. They will keep for 3 days. To store them longer, wrap them in heavy foil or seal them in freezer bags and place them in the freezer. They will keep for 3 months.

Gingerbread Muffins

In times past, gingerbread was served as a bread with meals, not as a dessert. These slightly spicy muffins are great for breakfast or as an accompaniment to roast meats, poultry, or fish.

- 1½ cups all-purpose flour
- 1 cup whole-bran cereal
- ⅓ cup firmly packed light brown sugar
- 2 teaspoons baking powder
- ¾ teaspoon each ground cinnamon and ground ginger
- ½ teaspoon baking soda
- ⅛ teaspoon ground cloves
- 2 large egg whites
- 1 cup low-fat (1% milkfat) milk
- ¼ cup molasses
- 3 tablespoons vegetable oil
- ¾ cup chopped pitted dates

1 Preheat the oven to 400°F. Lightly grease 12 regular-size muffin cups or line with paper liners.

2 In a large bowl, stir together the flour, bran cereal, brown sugar, baking powder, cinnamon, ginger, baking soda, and cloves. In a medium-size bowl, combine the egg whites, milk, molasses, and oil. Add to the flour mixture all at once and stir just until combined. Fold in the chopped dates.

3 Fill each muffin cup about ¾ full. Bake for 16 to 18 minutes or until brown. Serve warm. Makes 12.

Prep Time: 15 minutes Cooking Time: 16 minutes

1 Muffin: Calories 178. Total Fat 4 g. Saturated Fat 0 g. Protein 4 g. Carbohydrate 34 g. Fiber 3 g. Sodium 196 mg. Cholesterol 1 mg.

Blueberry Streusel Muffins

Blueberry Streusel Muffins

*Originally, muffins were a rather plain bread. Over the years,
however, Americans started making them sweeter and more like a cake.
This blueberry-filled version has a delicious sugar-and-spice topping.*

For the streusel topping:
- ¼ **cup firmly packed light brown sugar**
- 2 **tablespoons all-purpose flour**
- ½ **teaspoon ground cinnamon**
- ¼ **teaspoon ground allspice**
- 1 **tablespoon butter or margarine**

For the muffins:
- 2 **cups all-purpose flour**
- ½ **cup granulated sugar**
- 1 **tablespoon baking powder**
- ⅛ **teaspoon salt**
- 2 **large egg whites**
- ¾ **cup low-fat (1% milkfat) milk**
- 3 **tablespoons butter or margarine, melted**
- ½ **teaspoon grated lime rind**
- ¾ **cup fresh or frozen blueberries**

1 Preheat the oven to 400°F. Lightly grease 12 regular-size muffin cups or line with paper liners. To prepare the streusel topping, in a medium-size bowl, stir together the brown sugar, the 2 tablespoons flour, the cinnamon, and allspice. Using a pastry blender or 2 knives, cut in the 1 tablespoon butter until the mixture resembles coarse crumbs. Set aside.

2 To prepare the muffins, in a large bowl, stir together the 2 cups flour, the granulated sugar, baking powder, and salt. In another medium-size bowl, combine the egg whites, milk, the 3 tablespoons melted butter, and the lime rind. Add to the flour mixture all at once and stir just until combined. Fold in blueberries.

3 Fill each muffin cup about ¾ full. Sprinkle with the streusel topping. Bake for 20 to 22 minutes or until golden. Serve warm. Makes 12 muffins.

Prep Time: 20 minutes Cooking Time: 20 minutes

1 Muffin: Calories 173. Total Fat 4 g. Saturated Fat 3 g.
Protein 3 g. Carbohydrate 31 g. Fiber 1 g.
Sodium 202 mg. Cholesterol 11 mg.

Cinnamon-Pecan Coffee Cake and German Apple Kuchen

Cinnamon-Pecan Coffee Cake

This coffee cake recipe is ideal for a brunch buffet because it makes so many servings. If you'd like to make it one day and serve it the next, place it in a tightly covered container and store it at room temperature.

2½ cups all-purpose flour
1½ cups firmly packed light brown sugar
⅓ cup butter or margarine
¼ cup chopped pecans
2 teaspoons baking powder
1 teaspoon ground cinnamon
½ teaspoon baking soda
½ teaspoon ground ginger
⅛ teaspoon salt
2 large egg whites
1 large egg, lightly beaten
1½ cups reduced-fat sour cream
1 teaspoon grated lemon rind
1 cup chopped dried figs or raisins

For the glaze:
1 cup sifted confectioners sugar
2 teaspoons lemon juice
1 to 2 tablespoons low-fat (1% milkfat) milk

1 Preheat the oven to 350°F. In a large bowl, stir together the flour and brown sugar. Using a pastry blender or 2 knives, cut in the butter until the mixture resembles coarse crumbs. Remove ½ cup of the flour mixture and stir the pecans into it; set aside. Stir the baking powder, cinnamon, baking soda, ginger, and salt into the remaining flour mixture. In a medium-size bowl, combine the egg whites, egg, sour cream, and lemon rind. Add to the cinnamon mixture all at once and stir just until combined. Fold in the figs.

2 Spread the batter into a lightly greased 13" x 9" x 2" baking pan. Sprinkle with the pecan mixture. Bake for 30 to 35 minutes or until a toothpick inserted in the center comes out clean. To prepare glaze, in small bowl, stir together the confectioners sugar and lemon juice. Stir in the milk until mixture is thin enough to drizzle. Drizzle over coffee cake. Serve warm or cool. Serves 18.

Prep Time: 20 minutes Cooking Time: 30 minutes

1 Serving: Calories 230. Total Fat 7 g. Saturated Fat 4 g.
Protein 4 g. Carbohydrate 38 g. Fiber 2 g.
Sodium 163 mg. Cholesterol 29 mg.

Cape Cod Cranberry Coffee Cake

Cranberries were called "crane berries" because they were eaten by cranes living near the bogs. The berries also were nicknamed "bounce berries" because they bounce when ripe.

For the cranberry filling:

1½ cups chopped cranberries

¼ cup water

⅔ cup sugar

2 tablespoons cornstarch

For the streusel topping:

¼ cup sugar

¼ cup all-purpose flour

1 tablespoon butter or margarine

1 tablespoon sliced almonds (optional)

For the coffee cake:

1½ cups all-purpose flour

½ cup sugar

½ teaspoon baking powder

¼ teaspoon baking soda

¼ teaspoon ground nutmeg

3 tablespoons butter or margarine

2 large egg whites

½ cup low-fat (1% milkfat) buttermilk or soured milk (page 300)

1 teaspoon vanilla

1 To prepare the cranberry filling, in a small saucepan, combine the cranberries and water. Bring to a boil. Lower the heat and simmer, covered, for 5 minutes or until tender. In a small bowl, stir together the ⅔ cup sugar and cornstarch, then stir into cranberry mixture. Cook over moderate heat, stirring constantly, for 4 minutes or until mixture is thickened. Remove from heat.

2 Preheat oven to 350°F. To prepare streusel topping, in medium-size bowl, stir together the ¼ cup sugar and the ¼ cup flour. Using a pastry blender or 2 knives, cut in the 1 tablespoon butter until mixture resembles coarse crumbs. Stir in almonds (if using). Set aside.

3 To prepare the coffee cake, in a large bowl, stir together the 1½ cups flour, the ½ cup sugar, baking powder, baking soda, and nutmeg. Using a pastry blender or 2 knives, cut in the 3 tablespoons butter until the mixture resembles coarse crumbs. In a small bowl, combine the egg whites, buttermilk, and vanilla. Add to flour mixture all at once and stir just until combined.

4 Spread two-thirds of the batter into a lightly greased 9-inch round baking pan. Spread the cranberry filling over batter. Drop the remaining batter in small mounds on top of cranberry filling. Sprinkle with the streusel topping. Bake for 35 to 40 minutes or until golden. Serve warm. Makes 9 servings.

Prep Time: 20 minutes Cooking Time: 45 minutes

1 Serving: Calories 282. Total Fat 6 g. Saturated Fat 3 g. Protein 4 g. Carbohydrate 55 g. Fiber 1 g. Sodium 141 mg. Cholesterol 15 mg.

German Apple Kuchen

German and Austrian grandmas often served kuchen at coffee klatches, where friends shared the latest news.

1 large tart cooking apple, peeled and thinly sliced

1½ cups all-purpose flour

⅔ cup granulated sugar

2 teaspoons baking powder

⅛ teaspoon salt

2 large egg whites

½ cup apple juice

3 tablespoons vegetable oil

1 teaspoon grated lemon rind

⅓ cup firmly packed light brown sugar

1 tablespoon light corn syrup

2 teaspoons butter or margarine

1 teaspoon lemon juice

½ teaspoon ground cinnamon

1 In a small saucepan, bring ½ inch of water to a boil over high heat. Add apple. Lower heat and simmer, covered, for 2 minutes or just until tender. Drain well.

2 Preheat the oven to 375°F. In a large bowl, stir together the flour, granulated sugar, baking powder, and salt. In a medium-size bowl, combine the egg whites, apple juice, oil, and lemon rind. Add to the flour mixture all at once and stir just until combined.

3 Spread the batter into a lightly greased 9" x 9" x 2" baking pan. Top with the apple slices. In a small saucepan, combine the brown sugar, corn syrup, butter, lemon juice, and cinnamon. Bring to a boil. Quickly drizzle over apple slices. Bake for 25 to 30 minutes or until a toothpick inserted in the center comes out clean. Serve warm. Makes 9 servings.

Prep Time: 20 minutes Cooking Time: 32 minutes

1 Serving: Calories 226. Total Fat 6 g. Saturated Fat 1 g. Protein 3 g. Carbohydrate 42 g. Fiber 1 g. Sodium 165 mg. Cholesterol 2 mg.

Bacon Buttermilk Corn Bread

Buttermilk was the liquid leftover after butter was churned. Grandma used it in corn bread and other baked goods to add a delightful tang. What's more, it's very low in fat.

2   strips lean bacon, chopped
Vegetable oil (optional)
1⅓   cups cornmeal
⅔   cup all-purpose flour
2   tablespoons sugar (optional)
1   tablespoon baking powder
¼   teaspoon baking soda
Dash salt
2   large egg whites
1   large egg, lightly beaten
1   cup low-fat (1% milkfat) buttermilk or soured milk (page 300)

1 Preheat the oven to 425°F. In a small saucepan, cook the bacon over moderate heat until crisp. Remove bacon, reserving drippings. Drain the bacon on paper towels; set aside.

2 Measure the drippings. If necessary, add vegetable oil to the drippings to measure 3 tablespoons; set aside. In a large bowl, stir together the cornmeal, flour, sugar (if using), baking powder, baking soda, and salt.

3 In a medium-size bowl, combine the egg whites, egg, buttermilk, the 3 tablespoons drippings, and the bacon pieces. Add to the flour mixture all at once and stir just until combined.

COLORFUL CORNMEAL

Cornmeal is available in several colors. Typically, Southerners prefer white cornmeal, while Northerners use yellow. Blue cornmeal is popular in the Southwest. All the colors can be used interchangeably, since the flavor and texture of the different types are virtually the same. But when you're choosing, keep in mind that blue cornmeal may make some dishes look unusual.

4 Pour the batter into a lightly greased 8" x 8" x 2" baking pan. Bake for 22 to 24 minutes or until golden. Serve warm. Makes 9 servings.

Prep Time: 15 minutes   Cooking Time: 27 minutes

1 Serving: Calories 182. Total Fat 7 g. Saturated Fat 2 g. Protein 6 g. Carbohydrate 25 g. Fiber 2 g. Sodium 290 mg. Cholesterol 28 mg.

Spoon Bread

The consistency of this fluffy, creamy, cornmeal dish is more like a pudding than a bread. Serve it in place of potatoes with any meal.

2¼   cups low-fat (1% milkfat) milk
¾   cup cornmeal
1   tablespoon butter or margarine, melted
¾   teaspoon baking powder
¼   teaspoon salt
⅛   teaspoon ground red pepper (cayenne) (optional)
1   large egg yolk, lightly beaten
3   large egg whites

1 Preheat the oven to 325°F. In a large saucepan, whisk together 1½ cups of the milk and the cornmeal. Bring to a boil over high heat. Lower the heat and cook, uncovered, for 1 to 2 minutes or until mixture is very thick and pulls away from side of pan, whisking constantly. Remove from heat.

2 Whisk in the remaining ¾ cup milk, the butter, baking powder, salt, and red pepper (if using). Whisk 1 cup of the cornmeal mixture into the egg yolk, then return all to the saucepan.

3 In a small bowl, with an electric mixer on *High*, beat the egg whites until stiff peaks form. Gently fold into cornmeal mixture.

4 Pour into a lightly greased 1½-quart casserole. Bake for 50 to 60 minutes or until a knife inserted near center comes out clean. Serve immediately. Serves 6.

Prep Time: 10 minutes   Cooking Time: 56 minutes

1 Serving: Calories 137. Total Fat 4 g. Saturated Fat 2 g. Protein 7 g. Carbohydrate 18 g. Fiber 1 g. Sodium 245 mg. Cholesterol 44 mg.

Parmesan Spoon Bread Prepare as for Spoon Bread, omitting the salt and stirring ¼ **cup grated Parmesan cheese** into the cooked cornmeal mixture.

1 Serving: Calories 156. Total Fat 5 g. Saturated Fat 3 g. Protein 8 g. Carbohydrate 18 g. Fiber 1 g. Sodium 233 mg. Cholesterol 48 mg.

Cheese and Carrot Biscuits, a variation of Sour Cream Biscuits

Sour Cream Biscuits

Southern grandmas will tell you good biscuits should be crusty on the outside and soft and crumbly
on the inside. Northern grandmas insist biscuits should be high, light, and flaky, like these.

1²/₃ **cups all-purpose flour**
 ¹/₃ **cup cornmeal**
  1 **tablespoon sugar**
  1 **tablespoon baking powder**
  1 **teaspoon dried minced onion or minced onion**
 ¹/₂ **teaspoon cream of tartar**
 ¹/₈ **teaspoon salt**
     Dash ground red pepper (cayenne)
 ¹/₃ **cup shortening, butter, or margarine**
 ¹/₂ **cup reduced-fat sour cream**
 ¹/₂ **cup low-fat (1% milkfat) milk**

1 Preheat the oven to 450°F. In a large bowl, stir together the flour, cornmeal, sugar, baking powder, onion, cream of tartar, salt, and red pepper. Using a pastry blender or 2 knives, cut in the shortening until the mixture resembles coarse crumbs. Add sour cream and milk all at once and stir just until a soft dough forms.

2 Knead on a lightly floured surface for 30 seconds, then pat or roll until ³/₄ inch thick. Using a 2¹/₂-inch biscuit cutter, cut into 12 to 14 biscuits, rerolling and cutting the scraps. Place on an ungreased baking sheet.

3 Brush the tops with a little additional milk if you like. Bake for 10 to 12 minutes or until golden. Serve warm. Makes 12 to 14 biscuits.

Prep Time: 15 minutes Cooking Time: 10 minutes

1 Biscuit: Calories 150. Total Fat 7 g. Saturated Fat 2 g.
Protein 3 g. Carbohydrate 19 g. Fiber 1 g.
Sodium 154 mg. Cholesterol 4 mg.

Cheese and Carrot Biscuits Prepare as for Sour Cream Biscuits, omitting onion and adding ¹/₃ **cup shredded reduced-fat Cheddar cheese, 2 tablespoons shredded carrot,** and ¹/₂ **teaspoon dried thyme leaves.**

1 Biscuit: Calories 162. Total Fat 8 g. Saturated Fat 3 g.
Protein 4 g. Carbohydrate 19 g. Fiber 1 g.
Sodium 179 mg. Cholesterol 7 mg.

Oatmeal Biscuits

"If you don't own a biscuit cutter, use a water tumbler with straight sides," recommends octogenarian Lillian Lindahl.

1¼ **cups all-purpose flour**

¾   **cup old-fashioned (5 minutes) or quick-cooking (1 minute) rolled oats**

1   **tablespoon sugar**

1   **tablespoon baking powder**

½   **teaspoon cream of tartar**

¼   **teaspoon baking soda**

¼   **teaspoon ground cinnamon**

⅛   **teaspoon salt**

⅓   **cup butter or margarine**

¾   **cup low-fat (1% milkfat) buttermilk or soured milk (tip, below)**

1 Preheat the oven to 450°F. In a large bowl, stir together the flour, oats, sugar, baking powder, cream of tartar, baking soda, cinnamon, and salt. Using a pastry blender or 2 knives, cut in the butter until the mixture resembles coarse crumbs. Add the buttermilk all at once and stir just until a soft dough forms.

2 Knead on a lightly floured surface for 30 seconds, then pat or roll until ¾ inch thick. Using a 2½-inch biscuit cutter, cut into 12 to 14 biscuits, rerolling and cutting the scraps of dough.

3 Place on an ungreased baking sheet. Brush the tops with a little additional buttermilk if you like. Bake for 10 to 12 minutes or until golden. Makes 12 to 14.

Prep Time: 15 minutes Cooking Time: 10 minutes

1 Biscuit: Calories 124. Total Fat 6 g. Saturated Fat 3 g. Protein 3 g. Carbohydrate 16 g. Fiber 1 g. Sodium 238 mg. Cholesterol 15 mg.

MAKING SOURED MILK

If you don't have buttermilk, mix up some soured milk to use as a substitute.

1. To make 1 cup of soured milk, place 1 tablespoon of lemon juice or vinegar in a 1-cup glass measuring cup.

2. Add enough low-fat (1% milkfat) milk to measure 1 cup; stir until mixed. Let the mixture stand for 5 minutes before using.

Currant Scones

Currant Scones

Recipes for scones came to America with immigrants from Scotland, England, and Wales. Traditionally scones are made with heavy cream, but this adaptation uses low-fat yogurt.

2   **cups all-purpose flour**

¼   **cup sugar**

2   **teaspoons baking powder**

½   **teaspoon baking soda**
     Dash salt

3   **tablespoons butter or margarine**

1   **large egg white**

½   **cup vanilla low-fat yogurt**

½   **cup currants or raisins**

1½ **teaspoons grated orange rind**
     Low-fat (1% milkfat) milk

1 Preheat the oven to 425°F. In a large bowl, stir together the flour, sugar, baking powder, baking soda, and salt. Using a pastry blender or 2 knives, cut in the butter until the mixture resembles coarse crumbs. In a small bowl, combine the egg white, yogurt, currants, and orange rind. Add to the flour mixture all at once and stir just until a soft dough forms.

2 Knead on a lightly floured surface for 30 seconds, then pat or roll into an 8-inch circle. Place on a lightly greased baking sheet. Using a sharp knife, score the circle into 8 wedges.

3 Brush with a little milk and sprinkle with a little additional sugar. Bake for 18 to 20 minutes or until golden. Serve warm. Makes 8 scones.

Prep Time: 15 minutes Cooking Time: 18 minutes

1 Scone: Calories 218. Total Fat 5 g. Saturated Fat 3 g. Protein 5 g. Carbohydrate 39 g. Fiber 2 g. Sodium 280 mg. Cholesterol 12 mg.

Herbed Cheese Scones

To avoid yellow specks on top of scones and other quick breads, make sure to stir the dry ingredients thoroughly so the baking powder and soda are well distributed.

2   cups all-purpose flour
3   tablespoons firmly packed light brown sugar
2   teaspoons baking powder
1/2 teaspoon baking soda
1/2 teaspoon dry mustard
1/2 teaspoon dried rosemary leaves
1/4 teaspoon ground sage
1/8 teaspoon ground red pepper (cayenne)
    Dash salt
3   tablespoons butter or margarine
1   large egg white
1   cup dry-curd cottage cheese
1/3 cup low-fat (1% milkfat) milk

1 Preheat the oven to 425°F. In a large bowl, stir together the flour, brown sugar, baking powder, baking soda, mustard, rosemary, sage, red pepper, and salt. Using a pastry blender or 2 knives, cut in the butter until the mixture resembles coarse crumbs.

2 In a medium-size bowl, combine the egg white, cottage cheese, and milk. Add to the flour mixture all at once and stir just until a soft dough forms.

3 Knead on a lightly floured surface for 30 seconds, then pat or roll into an 8-inch circle. Place on a lightly greased baking sheet. Using a sharp knife, score the circle into 8 wedges. Brush the dough with a little additional milk. Bake for 22 to 25 minutes or until golden. Serve warm. Makes 8 scones.

Prep Time: 15 minutes Cooking Time: 22 minutes

1 Scone: Calories 188. Total Fat 5 g. Saturated Fat 3 g. Protein 7 g. Carbohydrate 29 g. Fiber 1 g. Sodium 277 mg. Cholesterol 13 mg.

Perfect Popovers

For no-fail popovers, start with a piping hot pan. Steady the muffin pan with a pot holder and pour the batter from a pitcher.

2   large egg whites
1   large egg, lightly beaten
1   cup low-fat (1% milkfat) milk
1   tablespoon olive or vegetable oil
1   cup all-purpose flour
1/2 teaspoon dried parsley or oregano leaves
1/8 teaspoon salt

1 Preheat the oven to 400°F. Generously grease the bottoms and sides of 12 regular-size muffin cups. Heat the pan in the oven.

2 Meanwhile, in a medium-size bowl, combine the egg whites, egg, milk, and oil. Add the flour, parsley, and salt. With a rotary beater or wire whisk, beat the mixture until smooth.

3 Fill each hot muffin cup about half full. Bake on the lowest oven rack for 25 minutes or until very brown and crusty. Remove pan from the oven and immediately pierce each popover with a sharp knife to release steam. Serve immediately. Makes 12 popovers.

Prep Time: 15 minutes Cooking Time: 25 minutes

1 Popover: Calories 65. Total Fat 2 g. Saturated Fat 0 g. Protein 3 g. Carbohydrate 9 g. Fiber 0 g. Sodium 47 mg. Cholesterol 19 mg.

Cinnamon French Toast with Apricot Sauce

Cinnamon French Toast with Apricot Sauce

In the old days, grandma made French toast to use up day-old bread. Today, folks
serve it because it tastes so good, especially with a homemade apricot sauce.

For the French toast:

- 4 **large egg whites**
- 2 **large eggs, lightly beaten**
- 1 **cup low-fat (1% milkfat) milk**
- 1 **tablespoon firmly packed light brown sugar**
- 1 **teaspoon vanilla**
- ½ **teaspoon ground cinnamon**
- ¼ **teaspoon ground nutmeg**
- 8 **slices French bread, 1 inch thick, or day-old home-style white bread**
- 1 **tablespoon butter or margarine**

For the apricot sauce:

- 1 **can (5½ ounces) apricot nectar**
- 2 **teaspoons cornstarch**
- 1 **tablespoon firmly packed light brown sugar**
- 1 **teaspoon lemon juice**
- ¼ **teaspoon grated lemon rind**

1 To prepare the French toast, in a shallow bowl, combine the egg whites, eggs, milk, 1 tablespoon brown sugar, vanilla, cinnamon, and nutmeg. Dip half of the bread slices into egg mixture, letting them soak about 30 seconds on each side. In a 12-inch nonstick skillet, melt half of the butter over moderate heat. Add soaked bread. Cook for 3 minutes on each side or until golden. Repeat with the remaining bread and remaining butter.

2 Meanwhile, to prepare the apricot sauce, in a small saucepan, whisk together the apricot nectar and cornstarch. Whisk in 1 tablespoon brown sugar, lemon juice, and lemon rind. Bring to a boil over moderate heat, whisking constantly. Cook and whisk for 2 minutes or until mixture is thickened. Serve over the French toast. Makes 8 servings.

Prep Time: 15 minutes Cooking Time: 13 minutes

1 Serving: Calories 172. Total Fat 4 g. Saturated Fat 2 g.
Protein 8 g. Carbohydrate 26 g. Fiber 1 g.
Sodium 288 mg. Cholesterol 58 mg.

Apple Fritters

These light morsels are delicious as a snack or with a meal.

1³⁄₄ cups all-purpose flour

¹⁄₃ cup cornmeal

2 tablespoons sugar

2 teaspoons baking powder

¹⁄₈ teaspoon salt

2 large egg whites

1 large tart cooking apple, finely chopped

1 cup low-fat (1% milkfat) milk

¹⁄₂ cup shredded reduced-fat Cheddar cheese (2 ounces)
Vegetable oil

¹⁄₃ cup sugar

¹⁄₂ teaspoon ground nutmeg

1 In a large bowl, stir together the flour, cornmeal, the 2 tablespoons sugar, the baking powder, and salt. In a medium-size bowl, combine egg whites, apple, milk, and cheese. Add to flour mixture all at once and stir just until combined.

2 In deep 12-inch skillet, heat 1 inch of oil over moderately high heat to 375°F. or until a 1-inch cube of bread browns in 30 seconds. Carefully drop the batter by heaping tablespoons, several at a time, into hot oil. Cook for 3 to 4 minutes or until golden, turning once. Using slotted spoon, remove and drain on paper towels.

3 In a paper or plastic bag, combine the ¹⁄₃ cup sugar and nutmeg. Add the hot fritters, several at a time, and shake to coat. Serve warm. Makes about 30 fritters.

Prep Time: 20 minutes Cooking Time: 25 minutes

1 Fritter: Calories 80. Total Fat 3 g. Saturated Fat 0 g.
Protein 2 g. Carbohydrate 11 g. Fiber 0 g.
Sodium 63 mg. Cholesterol 2 mg.

Buckwheat Pancakes

Buckwheat gives these cakes a hearty, old-time flavor.

¹⁄₂ cup buckwheat flour

¹⁄₃ cup all-purpose flour

1 teaspoon baking powder

¹⁄₂ teaspoon baking soda
Dash salt

2 large egg whites

1 cup low-fat (1% milkfat) buttermilk or soured milk (page 300)

2 tablespoons olive or vegetable oil

1 tablespoon molasses

1 In a medium-size bowl, stir together the buckwheat flour, all-purpose flour, baking powder, baking soda, and salt. In another medium-size bowl, combine the egg whites, buttermilk, oil, and molasses. Add to the flour mixture all at once and stir just until combined.

2 Heat a 12-inch nonstick griddle or skillet over moderate heat and brush with a little additional oil. Using about ¹⁄₄ cup batter for each pancake, pour the batter onto the griddle. Cook for 3 minutes or just until covered with bubbles. Flip over and cook for 2 minutes more or until brown. (If the batter becomes too thick, stir in a little additional buttermilk.) Makes 6 pancakes.

Prep Time: 10 minutes Cooking Time: 12 minutes

1 Pancake: Calories 126. Total Fat 5 g. Saturated Fat 1 g.
Protein 4 g. Carbohydrate 16 g. Fiber 1 g.
Sodium 270 mg. Cholesterol 3 mg.

Cornmeal Griddle Cakes

Whether you call them griddle cakes, pancakes, flapjacks, or batter cakes, the secret to turning out a perfect batch is to make sure the griddle is nice and hot. To test it, sprinkle a few drops of water on the surface—they should bounce.

1 cup all-purpose flour

¹⁄₂ cup cornmeal

1 tablespoon sugar

2¹⁄₂ teaspoons baking powder

¹⁄₄ teaspoon salt

2 large egg whites

1¹⁄₄ cups low-fat (1% milkfat) milk

¹⁄₂ cup frozen and thawed whole kernel corn

2 tablespoons olive or vegetable oil

1 In a large bowl, stir together the flour, cornmeal, sugar, baking powder, and salt. In a medium-size bowl, combine the egg whites, milk, corn, and oil. Add to flour mixture all at once and stir just until combined.

2 Heat a 12-inch nonstick griddle or skillet over moderate heat and brush with a little additional oil. Using about ¹⁄₄ cup batter for each pancake, pour the batter onto the griddle. Cook for 3 minutes or just until covered with bubbles. Flip over and cook for 2 minutes more or until golden. Makes 8 or 9 pancakes.

Prep Time: 10 minutes Cooking Time: 17 minutes

1 Pancake: Calories 153. Total Fat 4 g. Saturated Fat 1 g.
Protein 5 g. Carbohydrate 25 g. Fiber 1 g.
Sodium 253 mg. Cholesterol 2 mg.

Banana Waffles

*The Dutch introduced waffles to colonial
New York. It soon became the custom to give each
new bride a waffle iron with her initials and
wedding date worked into the design.*

1¼ cups all-purpose flour
⅔ cup whole-wheat flour
1 tablespoon baking powder
½ teaspoon ground allspice or ground cinnamon
    Dash salt
2 large egg whites
1 large egg, lightly beaten
2 cups low-fat (1% milkfat) milk
½ cup mashed ripe banana
¼ cup olive or vegetable oil
¼ cup chopped pecans or walnuts (optional)

1 Preheat a lightly greased waffle iron. In a large bowl, stir together the all-purpose flour, whole-wheat flour, baking powder, allspice, and salt. In a medium-size bowl, combine the egg whites, egg, milk, banana, oil, and pecans (if using). Add to the flour mixture all at once and stir just until combined.

2 Using 1 to 1¼ cups batter for each waffle, pour the batter onto the grids. Close lid quickly; do not open during baking. Bake according to the manufacturer's directions. Use a fork to lift the waffle off grid. (If the batter becomes too thick, add a little additional milk.) Makes fourteen 4-inch squares (7 servings).

Prep Time: 15 minutes Cooking Time: 16 minutes

1 Serving: Calories 249. Total Fat 10 g. Saturated Fat 2 g.
Protein 8 g. Carbohydrate 33 g. Fiber 2 g.
Sodium 289 mg. Cholesterol 33 mg.

KEEPING THE FIRST BATCH WARM

Here's how to keep the first batch of waffles, fritters, pancakes, or French toast warm, while you are cooking the rest.

• Arrange waffles and fritters in a single layer on a wire rack that is set on top of a baking sheet. Place the baking sheet in the oven at 300°F.

• Place pancakes or French toast on an ovenproof plate. Place the plate in the oven at 300°F.

Country-Style Whole Grain Bread

*This savory wheat-and-rye bread is
ideal for all types of sandwiches, from a turkey
club to sliced roast beef to tuna salad.*

2 tablespoons butter or margarine
1 large yellow onion, finely chopped
½ cup lukewarm water (105° to 115°F.)
2 packages active dry yeast
¼ cup firmly packed light brown sugar
1¼ cups low-fat (1% milkfat) milk
1½ teaspoons dried marjoram leaves
½ teaspoon salt
1 cup whole-wheat flour
1 cup rye flour
3 to 3½ cups all-purpose flour

1 In a small saucepan, melt the butter over moderate heat. Add the onion and cook for 5 minutes or until tender. Set aside. Meanwhile, in a large bowl, combine the water, yeast, and 1 tablespoon of the brown sugar. Let stand for 10 minutes or until foamy. Stir in the remaining brown sugar, the milk, marjoram, and salt. Using a wooden spoon, beat in onion mixture, whole-wheat flour, and rye flour, then beat in enough of the all-purpose flour, 1 cup at a time, to make a soft dough.

2 Knead the dough on a lightly floured surface for 6 to 8 minutes or until smooth and elastic, adding only as much of the remaining flour as needed. Transfer the dough to a large buttered bowl, turning to coat with the butter. Cover loosely and let rise in a warm place for 45 minutes to 1¼ hours or until doubled in size.

3 Punch down the dough; divide in half. Cover and let rest for 10 minutes. Shape each half into a loaf. Place the loaves, smooth sides up, in 2 lightly greased 8" x 4" x 2" or 9" x 5" x 3" loaf pans. Cover and let rise for 30 to 45 minutes more or until doubled in size.

4 Preheat the oven to 375°F. Bake for 35 to 40 minutes or until golden and the bread sounds hollow when tapped on the bottom. (If the loaves seem to be browning too quickly, lay foil loosely over tops.) Turn out onto wire racks to cool. Dust with additional all-purpose flour if you like. Makes 2 loaves (32 servings).

Prep Time: 45 minutes Rising Time: 1¼ hours
Cooking Time: 41 minutes

1 Serving: Calories 84. Total Fat 1 g. Saturated Fat 1 g.
Protein 3 g. Carbohydrate 16 g. Fiber 1 g.
Sodium 47 mg. Cholesterol 2 mg.

Old-World Braided Bread with Honey Glaze

Old-World Braided Bread with Honey Glaze

When braiding bread, be sure to weave the ropes of dough loosely so they have room to expand during rising.

²⁄₃ **cup lukewarm water (105° to 115°F.)**

2 **packages active dry yeast**

¾ **cup sugar**

2 **large egg whites**

1 **large egg**

²⁄₃ **cup low-fat (1% milkfat) milk**

3 **tablespoons butter or margarine, melted**

1 **teaspoon ground cardamom**

½ **teaspoon salt**

¼ **teaspoon ground mace**

1½ **cups raisins**

5¼ **to 5¾ cups all-purpose flour**

2 **tablespoons honey**

1 **teaspoon toasted wheat germ (optional)**

1 In a large bowl, combine the water, yeast, and 1 tablespoon of the sugar. Let stand for 10 minutes or until foamy. Stir in the remaining sugar, egg whites, egg, milk, butter, cardamom, salt, and mace. Using a wooden spoon, beat in the raisins, then beat in enough of the flour, 1 cup at a time, to make a soft dough.

2 Knead the dough on a lightly floured surface for 6 to 8 minutes or until smooth and elastic, adding only as much of the remaining flour as needed. Transfer the dough to a large buttered bowl, turning to coat with the butter. Cover loosely and let rise in a warm place for 1 to 1½ hours or until doubled in size.

3 Punch down the dough; divide into 6 pieces. Cover and let rest for 10 minutes. Roll each piece into a 14x1-inch rope. Place 3 ropes side-by-side on a lightly greased baking sheet. Pinch the top ends together, braid, then tuck the ends under. Repeat with remaining 3 ropes. Cover and let rise for 45 minutes to 1 hour more or until doubled in size.

4 Preheat the oven to 350°F. Bake for 25 to 30 minutes or until golden and bread sounds hollow when tapped on the bottom. (If the loaves seem to be browning too quickly, lay foil loosely over tops.) Brush with honey; sprinkle with wheat germ (if using). Transfer to wire racks to cool. Makes 2 loaves (24 servings).

Prep Time: 50 minutes Rising Time: 1¾ hours
Cooking Time: 25 minutes

1 Serving: Calories 182. Total Fat 2 g. Saturated Fat 1 g.
Protein 4 g. Carbohydrate 37 g. Fiber 1 g.
Sodium 72 mg. Cholesterol 13 mg.

Poppy Seed Pinwheels

Poppy Seed Pinwheels

*Women of European ancestry used poppy seed filling to give
their breads an attractive swirl and pleasing crunch. Look for the
prepared filling in the baking section of your supermarket.*

²⁄₃ **cup lukewarm water (105° to 115°F.)**

  2 **packages active dry yeast**

  2 **tablespoons firmly packed light brown sugar**

  2 **large egg whites**

  1 **large egg**

²⁄₃ **cup low-fat (1% milkfat) milk**

  3 **tablespoons butter or margarine, melted**

½ **teaspoon salt**

  2 **cups whole-wheat flour**

2½ **to 3 cups all-purpose flour**

  1 **can (12½ ounces) poppy seed cake and pastry filling**

1 In a large bowl, combine the water, yeast, and brown sugar. Let stand for 10 minutes or until foamy. Stir in the egg whites, egg, milk, butter, and salt. Using a wooden spoon, beat in the whole-wheat flour, then beat in enough of the all-purpose flour, 1 cup at a time, to make a soft dough.

2 Knead the dough on a lightly floured surface for 6 to 8 minutes or until smooth and elastic, adding only as much of the remaining flour as needed. Transfer the dough to a large buttered bowl, turning to coat with the butter. Cover loosely; let rise in a warm place for 45 minutes to 1¼ hours or until doubled in size.

3 Punch down the dough; divide in half. Cover and let rest for 10 minutes. Roll each half into a 14x7-inch rectangle. Spread half of the poppy seed filling over each rectangle to within ½ inch of edges. Starting at a short side, roll up the dough jelly-roll style. Place, smooth sides up, in 2 lightly greased 8" x 4" x 2" loaf pans. Cover and let rise for 30 to 45 minutes more or until doubled in size.

4 Preheat the oven to 375°F. Bake for 25 to 30 minutes or until golden and bread sounds hollow when tapped on the bottom. (If the loaves seem to be browning too quickly, lay foil loosely over the tops.) Turn out onto wire racks to cool. Makes 2 loaves (32 servings).

Prep Time: 45 minutes Rising Time: 1¼ hours
Cooking Time: 25 minutes

1 Serving: Calories 112. Total Fat 2 g. Saturated Fat 1 g.
Protein 3 g. Carbohydrate 19 g. Fiber 1 g.
Sodium 59 mg. Cholesterol 10 mg.

Crusty French Loaves

This loaf has a chewy crust and soft inside, just like the ones grandma used to make.

½ **cup lukewarm water (105° to 115°F.)**
2 **packages active dry yeast**
1 **tablespoon sugar**
1⅓ **cups water**
¾ **teaspoon salt**
4¾ **to 5¼ cups all-purpose flour**
   Cornmeal
1 **large egg white**
1 **tablespoon water**

1 In a large bowl, combine the ½ cup water, the yeast, and sugar. Let stand for 10 minutes or until foamy. Stir in the 1⅓ cups water and the salt. Using a wooden spoon, beat in enough of the flour, 1 cup at a time, to make a soft dough.

2 Knead the dough on a lightly floured surface for 8 to 10 minutes or until smooth and elastic, adding only as much of the remaining flour as needed. Transfer the dough to a large buttered bowl, turning to coat with the butter. Cover loosely and let rise in a warm place for 45 minutes to 1¼ hours or until doubled in size.

3 Punch down the dough; divide into thirds. Cover and let rest for 10 minutes. Roll each third into a 13x8-inch rectangle. Starting at a long side, roll up the dough jelly-roll style. Taper the ends. Place loaves, smooth sides up, on lightly greased baking sheets sprinkled with a little cornmeal. Cover and let rise for 30 to 45 minutes more or until doubled in size.

4 Preheat the oven to 450°F; place a pan of boiling water on the bottom rack. In a small bowl, combine the egg white and the 1 tablespoon water; brush over loaves. Make a slash in each loaf (tip, below).

5 Place 1 or 2 loaves on the middle oven rack. (Refrigerate remaining loaves until ready to bake.) Bake loaves for 16 to 18 minutes or until golden and the bread sounds hollow when tapped on bottom. (If the loaves seem to be browning too quickly, lay pieces of foil loosely over tops.) Transfer to wire racks to cool. Makes 3 loaves (24 servings).

Prep Time: 50 minutes Rising Time: 1¼ hours
Cooking Time: 32 minutes

1 Serving: Calories 95. Total Fat 0 g. Saturated Fat 0 g.
Protein 3 g. Carbohydrate 20 g. Fiber 1 g.
Sodium 70 mg. Cholesterol 0 mg.

Mini French Loaves Prepare as for Crusty French Loaves, dividing the dough into 12 pieces. Shape each piece into a 4-inch-long loaf, tapering the ends. Bake for 12 minutes. Makes 12 mini loaves (24 servings).

1 Serving: Calories 95. Total Fat 0 g. Saturated Fat 0 g.
Protein 3 g. Carbohydrate 20 g. Fiber 1 g.
Sodium 70 mg. Cholesterol 0 mg.

FINISHING FRENCH LOAVES

To make the traditional slashes in French bread, use a very sharp knife or a razor blade and cut a slash about ¼ inch deep down the center of each unbaked loaf. Bake as directed.

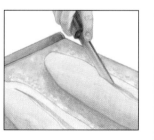

Honey Oatmeal Bread

Honey Oatmeal Bread

*"My husband grew up with homemade bread, but he didn't really
appreciate it until he left home," says Joanne Boeckman. "After eating store-bought
for a while, he realized that fresh baked bread was a real treat."*

½ cup lukewarm water (105° to 115°F.)

2 packages active dry yeast

1 cup low-fat (1% milkfat) milk

¼ cup honey

3 tablespoons butter or margarine, melted

½ teaspoon salt

2 cups old-fashioned (5 minutes) or quick-cooking
   (1 minute) rolled oats

3¾ to 4¼ cups all-purpose flour

1 large egg white

1 tablespoon water

1 tablespoon old-fashioned (5 minutes)
   or quick-cooking (1 minute) rolled oats

1 In a large bowl, combine the ½ cup water and the yeast. Let stand for 10 minutes or until foamy. Stir in the milk, honey, butter, and salt. Using a wooden spoon, beat in the 2 cups oats, then beat in enough of the flour, 1 cup at a time, to make a soft dough.

2 Knead the dough on a lightly floured surface for 6 to 8 minutes or until smooth and elastic, adding only as much of the remaining flour as needed. Transfer the dough to a large buttered bowl, turning to coat with the butter. Cover loosely and let rise in a warm place for 1 to 1½ hours or until doubled in size.

3 Punch down the dough; divide in half. Cover and let rest for 10 minutes. Shape each half into a 6-inch round loaf. Place the loaves, smooth sides up, on a lightly greased large baking sheet. Cover and let rise for 1 to 1¼ hours more or until doubled in size.

4 Preheat the oven to 375°F. In a small bowl, combine the egg white and the 1 tablespoon water; brush over loaves. Sprinkle tops with the 1 tablespoon oats. Bake for 35 minutes or until golden and bread sounds hollow when tapped on the bottom. (If loaves brown too quickly, lay pieces of foil loosely over tops.) Transfer to wire racks to cool. Makes 2 loaves (32 servings).

Prep Time: 40 minutes Rising Time: 2 hours
Cooking Time: 35 minutes

1 Serving: Calories 96. Total Fat 2 g. Saturated Fat 1 g.
Protein 3 g. Carbohydrate 17 g. Fiber 1 g.
Sodium 51 mg. Cholesterol 3 mg.

Molasses Oatmeal Bread Prepare as for Honey Oatmeal Bread, substituting ¼ **cup molasses** for honey.

1 Serving: Calories 95. Total Fat 2 g. Saturated Fat 1 g.
Protein 3 g. Carbohydrate 17 g. Fiber 1 g.
Sodium 52 mg. Cholesterol 3 mg.

Open Sesame Loaves

*With its decorative crisscross top and creamy filling,
this coffee cake is special enough for company.*

½ **cup lukewarm water (105° to 115°F.)**
1 **package active dry yeast**
½ **cup sugar**
4 **large egg whites**
¾ **cup low-fat (1% milkfat) milk**
3 **tablespoons butter or margarine, melted**
½ **teaspoon salt**
3¾ **to 4¼ cups all-purpose flour**
2 **packages (8 ounces each) Neufchâtel cream cheese**
2 **teaspoons grated lemon rind**
1 **teaspoon vanilla**
4 **teaspoons sesame seeds**

1 In a large bowl, combine the water, yeast, and 1 tablespoon of the sugar. Let stand for 10 minutes or until foamy. Stir in 3 tablespoons of the sugar, 2 of the egg whites, the milk, butter, and salt. Using a wooden spoon, beat in enough of the flour, 1 cup at a time, to make a soft dough.

2 Knead the dough on a lightly floured surface for 6 to 8 minutes or until smooth and elastic, adding only as much of the remaining flour as needed. Transfer the dough to a large buttered bowl, turning to coat with the butter. Cover loosely and let rise in a warm place for 1½ to 2 hours or until doubled in size.

3 Punch down the dough; divide in half. Cover and let rest for 10 minutes. Meanwhile, in a medium-size bowl, with an electric mixer on *Medium,* beat the remaining ¼ cup sugar, the remaining 2 egg whites, the Neufchâtel cheese, lemon rind, and vanilla until combined. Roll each half of the dough into a 12x9-inch rectangle. Carefully transfer each rectangle to a lightly greased baking sheet.

4 Spread half of the Neufchâtel cheese mixture in a 3-inch-wide strip down the center of each rectangle to within ½ inch of ends. Make cuts from the edges of cheese mixture to edges of dough (tip, below). Fold dough strips across cheese mixture and press to seal (tip, below). Cover and let rise for 45 minutes to 1 hour more or until doubled in size.

5 Preheat the oven to 350°F. Brush the loaves with a little additional milk and sprinkle with the sesame seeds. Bake for 23 to 25 minutes or until golden. (If the loaves seem to be browning too quickly, lay pieces of foil loosely over the tops.) Transfer to wire racks to cool. Makes 2 loaves (24 servings).

Prep Time: 50 minutes Rising Time: 2¼ hours
Cooking Time: 23 minutes

1 Serving: Calories 159. Total Fat 6 g. Saturated Fat 4 g.
Protein 5 g. Carbohydrate 20 g. Fiber 1 g.
Sodium 148 mg. Cholesterol 19 mg.

HOW TO MAKE SESAME LOAVES

1. On the long sides of each rectangle of dough, use a sharp knife to cut dough into strips, cutting from the edge of cheese mixture to edge of dough. Space cuts 1 inch apart.

2. To shape loaf, grasp a dough strip with your fingers, fold it across cheese mixture, and lay it at an angle. Repeat with strip from opposite side. Continue until all strips are folded. Press strips together in center to seal.

Cheese Bread

⅔ cup lukewarm water (105° to 115°F.)
2 packages active dry yeast
2 tablespoons sugar
2 large egg whites
¾ cup water
½ teaspoon salt
¼ teaspoon ground red pepper (cayenne)
1½ cups shredded reduced-fat Cheddar cheese (6 ounces)
4 to 4½ cups all-purpose flour

1 In a large bowl, combine the ⅔ cup water, the yeast, and sugar. Let stand for 10 minutes or until foamy. Stir in egg whites, the ¾ cup water, salt, and red pepper. Using wooden spoon, beat in cheese, then beat in enough of the flour, 1 cup at a time, to make soft dough.

2 Knead the dough on a lightly floured surface for 6 to 8 minutes or until smooth and elastic, adding only as much of the remaining flour as needed. Transfer the dough to a large buttered bowl, turning to coat with the butter. Cover loosely and let rise in a warm place for 45 minutes to 1¼ hours or until doubled in size.

3 Punch down the dough; divide in half. Cover and let rest for 10 minutes. Shape each half into a loaf (tip, below). Place the loaves, smooth sides up, in 2 lightly greased 8" x 4" x 2" loaf pans. Cover and let rise for 30 to 45 minutes more or until doubled in size.

4 Preheat the oven to 350°F. Bake for 35 to 40 minutes or until golden and bread sounds hollow when tapped on the bottom. (If loaves seem to be browning too quickly, lay pieces of foil loosely over tops.) Turn out onto wire racks to cool. Makes 2 loaves (32 servings).

Prep Time: 45 minutes Rising Time: 1¼ hours
Cooking Time: 35 minutes

1 Serving: Calories 79. Total Fat 1 g. Saturated Fat 1 g. Protein 4 g. Carbohydrate 13 g. Fiber 1 g. Sodium 75 mg. Cholesterol 4 mg.

SHAPING CHEESE BREAD

♦ **To pat the dough into a loaf,** gently pull it into an 8x4-inch rectangle and tuck the ends under.

♦ **To roll the dough into a loaf,** roll the dough to a 12x8-inch rectangle. Starting from a short end, roll up the rectangle; pinch the ends to seal.

Hot Cross Buns

English grandmas served these frosted rolls on Good Friday.

½ cup lukewarm water (105° to 115°F.)
2 packages active dry yeast
½ cup granulated sugar
2 large egg whites
1 large egg
½ cup low-fat (1% milkfat) milk
¼ cup butter or margarine, melted
¾ teaspoon ground cinnamon
½ teaspoon salt
¼ teaspoon ground mace or ground nutmeg
¾ cup currants or raisins
4¼ to 4¾ cups all-purpose flour
1 cup sifted confectioners sugar
½ teaspoon vanilla
2 to 3 teaspoons low-fat (1% milkfat) milk

1 In a large bowl, combine water, yeast, and 1 tablespoon of the granulated sugar. Let stand for 10 minutes or until foamy. Stir in remaining granulated sugar, egg whites, egg, ½ cup milk, butter, cinnamon, salt, and mace. Using a spoon, beat in currants, then beat in enough of the flour, 1 cup at a time, to make soft dough.

2 Knead the dough on a lightly floured surface for 4 to 6 minutes or until smooth and elastic, adding only as much of the remaining flour as needed. Transfer the dough to a large buttered bowl, turning to coat with the butter. Cover loosely and let rise in a warm place for 1 to 1½ hours or until doubled in size. Punch down; divide into 18 pieces. Cover and let rest for 10 minutes. Shape each piece into a ball. Place balls, smooth sides up, on lightly greased baking sheets. Cover and let rise for 30 to 45 minutes more or until doubled in size.

3 Preheat the oven to 350°F. Brush the buns with a little additional milk. Using a very sharp knife or razor blade, make a cross-shaped slash in the top of each bun. Bake for 14 to 16 minutes or until golden. Transfer to wire racks; cool for 10 minutes. Meanwhile, in a small bowl, stir together the confectioners sugar and vanilla. Stir in the 2 to 3 teaspoons milk until mixture is of thick drizzling consistency. Drizzle over the slashes in buns. Serve warm or cool. Makes 18 buns.

Prep Time: 50 minutes Rising Time: 1½ hours
Cooking Time: 14 minutes Cooling Time: 10 minutes

1 Bun: Calories 202. Total Fat 3 g. Saturated Fat 2 g. Protein 5 g. Carbohydrate 39 g. Fiber 2 g. Sodium 100 mg. Cholesterol 19 mg.

Pumpernickel-Raisin Rolls

Pumpernickel-Raisin Rolls

"Grandma would bake rolls early Sunday morning before church,"
recalls Elaine Hammer Walser, "always making extra so Grandpa could invite
company home for dinner. And, he always did. Sometimes there would be
two extra people, sometimes six. Grandma always had enough rolls."

½ cup lukewarm water (105° to 115°F.)
2 packages active dry yeast
1¼ cups low-fat (1% milkfat) milk
3 tablespoons molasses
2 tablespoons butter or margarine, melted
2 teaspoons grated orange rind
1 teaspoon fennel seeds, crushed
½ teaspoon salt
2 cups rye flour
¾ cup raisins
2½ to 3 cups all-purpose flour

1 In a large bowl, combine water and yeast. Let stand for 10 minutes or until foamy. Stir in milk, molasses, butter, orange rind, fennel seeds, and salt. Using spoon, beat in rye flour and raisins, then beat in enough of the all-purpose flour, 1 cup at a time, to make a soft dough.

2 Knead dough on a lightly floured surface for 6 to 8 minutes or until smooth and elastic, adding only as much remaining flour as needed. Transfer to a large buttered bowl, turning to coat with butter. Cover loosely; let rise in warm place 1 to 1½ hours or until doubled.

3 Punch down the dough; divide into 24 pieces. Cover and let rest for 10 minutes. Shape each piece into a ball. Place balls, smooth sides up, in 3 lightly greased 8-inch round baking pans. Cover and let rise for 30 to 45 minutes more or until doubled in size. Preheat the oven to 350°F. Bake for 16 to 18 minutes or until brown. Serve warm or cool. Makes 24 rolls.

Prep Time: 45 minutes Rising Time: 1½ hours
Cooking Time: 16 minutes

1 Roll: Calories 116. Total Fat 1 g. Saturated Fat 1 g.
Protein 3 g. Carbohydrate 23 g. Fiber 2 g.
Sodium 63 mg. Cholesterol 3 mg.

Nutty Crescents

*Women made many different rolls from their
basic white bread dough. They folded rounds in half
for Parker House rolls, twisted ropes into knots
or rosettes, and for special occasions, rolled triangles
of dough sprinkled with nuts into crescents.*

½ **cup lukewarm water (105° to 115°F.)**
1 **package active dry yeast**
¼ **cup sugar**
3 **large egg whites**
1 **large egg**
½ **cup low-fat (1% milkfat) milk**
3 **tablespoons butter or margarine, melted**
½ **teaspoon salt**
4¼ **to 4¾ cups all-purpose flour**
1 **tablespoon water**
⅓ **cup finely chopped pecans, toasted**
1 **tablespoon sugar (optional)**

1 In a large bowl, combine the ½ cup water, the yeast,
and 1 tablespoon of the sugar. Let stand for 10 minutes or until foamy. Stir in another 3 tablespoons of the
sugar, 2 of the egg whites, the egg, milk, butter, and salt.
Using a wooden spoon, beat in enough of the flour,
1 cup at a time, to make a soft dough.

2 Knead the dough on a lightly floured surface for
6 to 8 minutes or until smooth and elastic, adding
only as much of the remaining flour as needed. Transfer
the dough to a large buttered bowl, turning to coat with
the butter. Cover loosely and let rise in a warm place for
1 to 1½ hours or until doubled in size.

3 Punch down the dough; divide in half. Cover and let
rest for 10 minutes. Roll each half into a 12-inch
circle. In a small bowl, combine the remaining 1 egg
white and the 1 tablespoon water; brush half over each
circle. Sprinkle each circle with half of the pecans and
half of the 1 tablespoon sugar (if using). Cut each circle
into 12 wedges. Starting at the wide end of each wedge,
roll toward point.

4 Place, points down, on lightly greased baking sheets.
Cover; let rise for 20 to 35 minutes or until doubled.
Preheat oven to 375°F. Bake for 12 to 15 minutes or
until golden. Serve warm or cool. Makes 24.

Prep Time: 50 minutes Rising Time: 1 hour 20 minutes
Cooking Time: 12 minutes

1 Roll: Calories 120. Total Fat 3 g. Saturated Fat 1 g.
Protein 3 g. Carbohydrate 20 g. Fiber 1 g.
Sodium 72 mg. Cholesterol 13 mg.

Kolaches with Prune-Nut Filling

*Czechoslovakian families served these fruit-
filled rolls for snacks and with meals. "Instead of the
traditional rounds, Grandma Gensic spread the
filling over the dough, rolled it up, and shaped it into
a huge horseshoe," recalls granddaughter Patti.*

½ **cup lukewarm water (105° to 115°F.)**
2 **packages active dry yeast**
½ **cup granulated sugar**
1 **large egg**
½ **cup low-fat (1% milkfat) milk**
3 **tablespoons butter or margarine, melted**
1½ **teaspoons grated lemon rind**
½ **teaspoon salt**
¾ **teaspoon ground nutmeg**
3¾ **to 4¼ cups all-purpose flour**
1½ **cups water**
1 **cup finely chopped pitted prunes**
¼ **cup chopped walnuts**
2 **tablespoons firmly packed light brown sugar**
Confectioners sugar

1 In a large bowl, combine the ½ cup water, the yeast,
and 1 tablespoon of the granulated sugar. Let stand
for 10 minutes or until foamy. Stir in the remaining
granulated sugar, the egg, milk, butter, 1 teaspoon of the
lemon rind, salt, and ½ teaspoon of the nutmeg. Using
a wooden spoon, beat in enough of the flour, 1 cup at a
time, to make a soft dough.

2 Knead the dough on a lightly floured surface for
4 to 6 minutes or until smooth and elastic, adding
only as much of the remaining flour as needed. Transfer
the dough to a large buttered bowl, turning to coat with
the butter. Cover loosely and let rise in a warm place for
1 to 1½ hours or until doubled in size.

3 Meanwhile, in a medium-size saucepan, combine
the 1½ cups water and the prunes. Bring to a boil.
Lower the heat and simmer, covered, for 10 minutes or
until tender. Drain. In a small bowl, stir together the
prunes, walnuts, brown sugar, the remaining ½ teaspoon lemon rind, and the remaining ¼ teaspoon nutmeg. Set the mixture aside.

Kolaches with Prune-Nut Filling

4 Punch down the dough; divide into 24 pieces. Cover and let rest for 10 minutes. Shape each piece into a ball. Flatten each to a circle 2½ inches in diameter. Place on lightly greased baking sheets. Cover and let rise for 30 to 45 minutes more or until doubled in size.

5 Preheat the oven to 375°F. With your thumb, make an indentation in the center of each circle. Spoon about 2 teaspoons of the prune mixture into each indentation. Brush the edges with a little additional milk. Bake for 10 to 12 minutes or until golden. Transfer to wire racks to cool. Lightly sift confectioners sugar over tops. Makes 24.

Prep Time: 50 minutes Rising Time: 1½ hours
Cooking Time: 25 minutes

1 Kolache: Calories 135. Total Fat 3 g. Saturated Fat 1 g.
Protein 3 g. Carbohydrate 25 g. Fiber 2 g.
Sodium 66 mg. Cholesterol 13 mg.

Old-Fashioned Dinner Rolls

"Grandma Lizzie would bring her fresh dinner rolls to all the family get-togethers," remembers Vicki Euken. "They were light, evenly shaped, tender, and a real hit. She had a knack for turning simple bread into something extra special."

½ cup lukewarm water (105° to 115°F.)
1 package active dry yeast
⅓ cup sugar
1 large egg
¾ cup low-fat (1% milkfat) buttermilk or soured milk (page 300)
3 tablespoons butter or margarine, melted
½ teaspoon salt
⅓ cup cornmeal
4 to 4½ cups all-purpose flour
1 tablespoon toasted wheat germ, poppy seeds, or sesame seeds (optional)

1 In a large bowl, combine the water, yeast, and 1 tablespoon of the sugar. Let stand for 10 minutes or until foamy. Stir in the remaining sugar, the egg, buttermilk, butter, and salt. Using a wooden spoon, beat in the cornmeal, then beat in enough of the flour, 1 cup at a time, to make a soft dough.

2 Knead the dough on a lightly floured surface for 6 to 8 minutes or until smooth and elastic, adding only as much of the remaining flour as needed. Transfer the dough to a large buttered bowl, turning to coat with the butter. Cover loosely and let rise in a warm place for 1¼ to 1¾ hours or until doubled in size.

3 Punch down the dough; divide into 24 pieces. Cover and let rest for 10 minutes. Shape each piece into a ball. Place balls, smooth sides up, in 3 lightly greased 9-inch round baking pans. Cover and let rise for 30 to 45 minutes more or until doubled in size.

4 Preheat the oven to 375°F. Brush the rolls with a little additional buttermilk; sprinkle with the wheat germ (if using). Bake for 10 to 12 minutes or until golden. Serve warm or cool. Makes 24 rolls.

Prep Time: 45 minutes Rising Time: 1¾ hours
Cooking Time: 10 minutes

1 Roll: Calories 114. Total Fat 2 g. Saturated Fat 1 g.
Protein 3 g. Carbohydrate 21 g. Fiber 1 g.
Sodium 70 mg. Cholesterol 13 mg.

Lola's Perfect Cinnamon Rolls

At the Mapes house, everyone liked both iced cinnamon rolls and caramel rolls so Grandma Lola combined both into one delightful recipe.

½ **cup lukewarm water (105° to 115°F.)**
2 **packages active dry yeast**
1 **cup granulated sugar**
2 **large egg whites**
1 **large egg**
1 **cup low-fat (1% milkfat) milk**
¼ **cup butter or margarine, melted**
¾ **teaspoon salt**
5½ **to 6 cups all-purpose flour**
⅔ **cup firmly packed light brown sugar**
½ **cup light corn syrup**
3 **tablespoons butter or margarine, melted**
2 **teaspoons ground cinnamon**
2 **teaspoons grated orange rind**
⅔ **cup raisins, currants, or chopped nuts**

For the glaze:
1½ **cups sifted confectioners sugar**
1½ **teaspoons vanilla**
3 **to 4 teaspoons orange juice**

1 In a large bowl, combine the water, yeast, and 1 tablespoon of the granulated sugar. Let stand for 10 minutes or until foamy. Stir in another 7 tablespoons of the granulated sugar, the egg whites, egg, milk, the ¼ cup butter, and salt. Using a wooden spoon, beat in enough of the flour, 1 cup at a time, to make soft dough.

2 Knead the dough on a lightly floured surface for 6 to 8 minutes or until smooth and elastic, adding only as much of the remaining flour as needed. Transfer to a large buttered bowl, turning to coat with butter. Cover loosely and let rise in a warm place for 1 to 1½ hours or until doubled in size. In a small bowl, stir together the brown sugar, corn syrup, and 3 tablespoons butter; spread evenly in two 13" x 9" x 2" baking pans.

3 Punch down the dough; divide in half. Cover and let rest for 10 minutes. Roll each half into a 12x9-inch rectangle. Brush each with a little additional milk. Stir together the remaining ½ cup granulated sugar, cinnamon, and orange rind; sprinkle half over each rectangle. Sprinkle each with half of the raisins. Starting at a long side of each, roll up jelly-roll style. Slice each into 12 pieces; place in prepared pans. Cover and let rise for

30 to 45 minutes or until doubled in size. Preheat oven to 350°F. Bake for 16 to 18 minutes or until golden.

4 Let the rolls stand in the pans on wire racks for 1 minute before inverting onto baking sheets. To prepare the glaze, in a small bowl, stir together the confectioners sugar and vanilla. Stir in the orange juice until mixture is thin enough to drizzle. Invert rolls again, then drizzle with glaze. Serve warm. Makes 24.

Prep Time: 55 minutes Rising Time: 1½ hours
Cooking Time: 16 minutes

1 Roll: Calories 251. Total Fat 4 g. Saturated Fat 2 g.
Protein 4 g. Carbohydrate 50 g. Fiber 1 g.
Sodium 125 mg. Cholesterol 18 mg.

Angel Biscuits

These biscuits are called "angel" because the yeast, baking powder, and baking soda make them extra light.

⅓ **cup lukewarm water (105° to 115°F.)**
1 **package active dry yeast**
1 **tablespoon firmly packed light brown sugar**
2½ **cups all-purpose flour**
1½ **teaspoons baking powder**
½ **teaspoon baking soda**
¼ **teaspoon salt**
¼ **teaspoon dried dill weed or savory leaves**
⅓ **cup shortening**
¾ **cup low-fat (1% milkfat) buttermilk or soured milk (page 300)**

1 Preheat the oven to 450°F. In a small bowl, combine the water, yeast, and brown sugar. Let stand for 10 minutes or until foamy. In a large bowl, stir together the flour, baking powder, baking soda, salt, and dill weed. Using a pastry blender or 2 knives, cut in the shortening until the mixture resembles coarse crumbs. Add the yeast mixture and buttermilk all at once and stir just until a soft dough forms.

2 Knead on a lightly floured surface for 30 seconds, then pat or roll until ½ inch thick. Using a 2½-inch biscuit cutter, cut into 20 to 22 biscuits, rerolling and cutting the scraps of dough. Place on ungreased baking sheets. Bake for 7 to 9 minutes or until golden. Serve warm. Makes 20 to 22 biscuits.

Prep Time: 25 minutes Cooking Time: 7 minutes

1 Biscuit: Calories 94. Total Fat 4 g. Saturated Fat 1 g.
Protein 2 g. Carbohydrate 13 g. Fiber 1 g.
Sodium 105 mg. Cholesterol 1 mg.

Grandma's Treats

Pancakes with Raisin Faces

Flapjacks, with silly faces on top, are fun to eat.

1¼ cups packaged regular pancake mix

¼ cup cornmeal

1 large egg, lightly beaten

1 cup orange juice

Vegetable oil

Shredded coconut

Raisins

Maraschino cherry halves

1. In a large bowl, stir together the pancake mix and cornmeal. In a medium-size bowl, combine the egg and orange juice. Add to the cornmeal mixture all at once and stir just until combined.

2. Heat a 12-inch nonstick griddle or skillet over moderate heat and brush with a little oil. Using about ¼ cup batter for each pancake, pour batter onto griddle. For hair, sprinkle some coconut on top edges of pancakes. Cook just until covered with

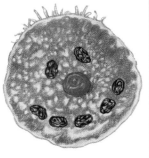

bubbles. Flip over and cook until golden. Transfer to plates.

3. For each pancake, add raisins for the eyes and mouth and a cherry half for the nose. Serve with syrup. Makes 8.

Hoecake Corn Bread

Let the children dip this panfried Southern corn bread in maple syrup, honey, or molasses.

1½ cups cornmeal

¼ teaspoon salt

1½ cups boiling water

Vegetable oil

1. In a medium-size bowl, stir together the cornmeal and salt. Slowly add the boiling water to the cornmeal mixture, stirring until mixed.

2. In a 12-inch skillet, heat ⅛ inch of oil over moderately high heat. Spoon the cornmeal mixture in 6 mounds into the skillet; flatten the tops slightly but keep the edges irregular.

3. Cook for 2 to 3 minutes on each side or until golden. Using a slotted spatula, remove the corn bread and drain on paper towels. Serve with maple syrup, honey, or molasses. Makes 6 servings.

Puffy Breakfast Surprise

When the grandchildren come to visit, delight them with this oven pancake.

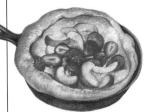

1 tablespoon butter or margarine

2 large eggs

2 large egg whites

⅔ cup low-fat (1% milkfat) milk

½ cup all-purpose flour

1 teaspoon grated orange rind

¼ teaspoon ground cinnamon

⅛ teaspoon salt

Confectioners sugar

1½ cups fresh or frozen and thawed peach slices

1 cup halved fresh or frozen and thawed strawberries

1. Preheat the oven to 400°F. In a 10-inch ovenproof skillet, melt the butter in the oven.

2. Meanwhile, in a medium-size bowl, with rotary beater, beat eggs and egg whites until combined. Add the milk, flour, orange rind, cinnamon, and salt. Beat until smooth.

3. Remove skillet from oven; tilt to coat the sides with butter. Pour in the batter. Bake for

25 minutes or until puffed and golden.

4. Lightly sift confectioners sugar over. Top with the peaches and strawberries. Serves 4.

Chocolate Sticky Rolls

⅓ cup fudge ice-cream topping

1 tablespoon butter or margarine, melted

2 tablespoons chopped peanuts

1 package (11 ounces) refrigerated bread sticks

1. Preheat the oven to 350°F. In a 9-inch round baking pan, stir together the fudge topping and melted butter. Sprinkle with the peanuts.

2. Separate the coiled bread sticks (do not unroll). Arrange on top of the mixture in pan. Bake for 22 minutes or until golden.

3. Let the rolls stand in the pan on a wire rack for 2 to 3 minutes; invert onto a serving plate. Serve warm. Makes 8 rolls.

THE SWEET TOUCH

Whatever the meal, grandma's desserts provided the perfect ending. For birthday dinners, she made luscious cakes. At picnics, she cut wedges of flaky pie. Come Sunday dinner, shortcake graced the table. On weekdays, she served cookies for lunch and cobblers or fruit compotes for supper. For snacks, she made her scrumptious candies, such as taffy, divinity, peanut brittle, or fudge. So go ahead, indulge your sweet tooth, and give some of gran's delectable recipes a try.

Angel Food Cake with
Stirred Custard Sauce (page 325)

Fresh Strawberry-Orange Sherbet (page 346)

Peach Cider Pie (page 331)

Snickerdoodles (page 354)

Blackberry Jam Cake with Cream Cheese Frosting

Blackberry Jam Cake with Cream Cheese Frosting

Jam cake was a favorite in the South, especially in Tennessee and Kentucky. President Andrew Jackson reportedly loved blackberries so much, he always served blackberry jam cake for Christmas.

2½ **cups all-purpose flour**

1½ **teaspoons baking powder**

1½ **teaspoons ground cinnamon**

1 **teaspoon ground nutmeg**

½ **teaspoon baking soda**

¼ **teaspoon salt**

½ **cup low-fat (1% milkfat) buttermilk or soured milk (page 300)**

1 **teaspoon vanilla**

1½ **cups sugar**

½ **cup butter or margarine, at room temperature**

2 **large egg whites**

1 **large egg**

1½ **cups seedless blackberry, red raspberry, or strawberry jam**

Cream Cheese Frosting (recipe, opposite)

1 Preheat the oven to 350°F. Lightly grease two 9-inch round cake pans, then dust with flour; line the bottoms with wax paper. In a small bowl, stir together the 2½ cups flour, the baking powder, cinnamon, nutmeg, baking soda, and salt. In a cup, combine the buttermilk and vanilla.

2 In a large bowl, with an electric mixer on *Medium,* cream the sugar and butter until light yellow and fluffy, scraping side of bowl often. Add the egg whites and beat well. Add egg and beat well. Beat in ¾ cup of the blackberry jam. Using a wooden spoon, stir in one-third of the flour mixture, then half of the buttermilk mixture. Repeat, then stir in remaining flour mixture.

3 Spread the batter evenly into the prepared pans. Bake for 25 to 30 minutes or until toothpicks inserted in the centers come out clean. Place the pans upright on wire racks for 10 minutes. Using a narrow metal spatula, loosen sides of cake layers from the pans, then invert the cakes onto the racks. Peel off the wax paper and let cakes cool completely.

4 While the cakes cool, make the Cream Cheese Frosting. Place 1 cake layer, upside down, onto a serving plate. Using an icing spatula or a wide knife, spread the remaining ¾ cup blackberry jam over the top of the first layer. Top with the second layer, right side up. Frost the top, then the side of cake with the frosting. Serve or cover and store in refrigerator. Serves 16.

Prep Time: 25 minutes Cooking Time: 25 minutes
Cooling Time: 2½ hours

1 Serving with Frosting: Calories 408. Total Fat 8 g.
Saturated Fat 5 g. Protein 4 g. Carbohydrate 82 g.
Fiber 1 g. Sodium 238 mg. Cholesterol 34 mg.

Ask-For-Seconds Cake With Fudge Frosting

Layer cake recipes made their way into grandma's kitchen in the 1880's. Before then, baking powder wasn't common, and the heat from the cookstove was too uneven for these fragile cakes.

2½   cups all-purpose flour
2½   teaspoons baking powder
⅛   teaspoon salt
1½   cups low-fat (1% milkfat) milk
1   tablespoon vanilla
⅛   teaspoon yellow food coloring (optional)
1⅔   cups sugar
½   cup butter or margarine, at room temperature
2   large egg whites
1   large egg
   Fudge Frosting (recipe, right)

1 Preheat the oven to 350°F. Lightly grease two 8-inch round cake pans, then dust with flour; line bottoms with wax paper. In a small bowl, stir together the 2½ cups flour, the baking powder, and salt. In cup, combine the milk, vanilla, and food coloring (if using).

2 In a large bowl, with an electric mixer on *Medium*, cream the sugar and butter until light yellow and fluffy. Add the egg whites and beat well. Add the egg and beat well. Using a wooden spoon, stir in one-third of the flour mixture, then half of the milk mixture. Repeat, then stir in the remaining flour mixture.

3 Spread batter evenly into prepared pans. Bake for 25 to 30 minutes or until toothpicks inserted in centers come out clean. Place pans upright on wire racks for 10 minutes. Loosen sides from pans, then invert cakes onto racks. Peel off paper; cool cakes completely.

4 When the cakes are cool, make the Fudge Frosting. Place 1 cake layer, upside down, onto a serving plate. Using an icing spatula or a wide knife, work quickly to frost the top of this layer. Top with the second layer, right side up. Frost top, then the side of the cake with the remaining frosting. Makes 16 servings.

Prep Time: 40 minutes Cooking Time: 25 minutes
Cooling Time: 2½ hours

1 Serving with Frosting: Calories 391. Total Fat 10 g.
Saturated Fat 4 g. Protein 5 g. Carbohydrate 72 g.
Fiber 2 g. Sodium 182 mg. Cholesterol 30 mg.

Cream Cheese Frosting

In a large bowl, with an electric mixer on *Medium*, beat ½ package (4 ounces) Neufchâtel cream cheese, 4 teaspoons low-fat (1% milkfat) milk, and 2 teaspoons vanilla until fluffy. Gradually add 1 box (16 ounces) confectioners sugar, sifted (4½ cups), beating until frosting is smooth and of spreading consistency. Makes about 2 cups frosting or enough to frost tops and sides of two 8- or 9-inch round cake layers or a 13" x 9" x 2" cake.

2 Tablespoons: Calories 129. Total Fat 2 g. Saturated Fat 1 g.
Protein 1 g. Carbohydrate 29 g. Fiber 0 g.
Sodium 30 mg. Cholesterol 5 mg.

Fudge Frosting

In a medium-size saucepan, place 2 cups miniature marshmallows, ½ cup unsweetened cocoa, ½ cup low-fat (1% milkfat) milk, and ¼ cup vegetable oil. Cook over low heat until the marshmallows melt and the mixture is smooth, stirring constantly. Remove from heat. Transfer the chocolate mixture to a large bowl; let stand for 5 minutes. With an electric mixer on *Medium*, gradually add 1 box (16 ounces) confectioners sugar, sifted (4½ cups), and 1 tablespoon vanilla, beating for 3 minutes or until frosting starts to lose its gloss and is of spreading consistency. Use immediately. Makes about 2 cups frosting or enough to frost tops and sides of two 8- or 9-inch round cake layers or a 13" x 9" x 2" cake.

2 Tablespoons: Calories 170. Total Fat 4 g. Saturated Fat 1 g.
Protein 1 g. Carbohydrate 35 g. Fiber 1 g.
Sodium 7 mg. Cholesterol 0 mg.

Whisky Cake

Whisky Cake

*Southern grandmas used the finest bourbons to make this old-fashioned
cake, which was often served during the holidays. The perfect whisky cake is
moist and dense with lots of nuts and sometimes raisins, too.*

2 cups raisins
2 cups chopped walnuts
2½ cups all-purpose flour
2 teaspoons ground cardamom or ground cinnamon
1 teaspoon baking powder
¼ teaspoon baking soda
¼ teaspoon salt
1⅔ cups firmly packed light brown sugar
¾ cup butter or margarine, at room temperature
4 large egg whites
1 large egg
½ cup bourbon, Scotch whisky, or apple cider

1 Lightly grease a 9" x 9" x 2" baking pan. To keep cake from overbrowning, line pan with parchment paper; lightly grease paper. In a medium-size bowl, pour enough boiling water over the raisins to cover. Let stand for 30 minutes or until water cools to room temperature; drain well. In a medium-size bowl, toss drained raisins and walnuts with ½ cup of the flour.

2 Preheat the oven to 325°F. In another medium-size bowl, stir together the remaining 2 cups flour, the cardamom, baking powder, baking soda, and salt. In a large bowl, with an electric mixer on *Medium*, cream the brown sugar and butter until light and fluffy, scraping

side of bowl often. Add the egg whites and beat well. Add the egg and beat well. Using a wooden spoon, stir in one-third of the flour mixture, then half of the bourbon. Repeat, then stir in the remaining flour mixture. Fold in the raisin mixture.

3 Spread batter evenly into prepared pan; smooth the surface. Bake about 55 minutes or until a toothpick inserted in the center comes out clean. Place the pan upright on a wire rack for 20 minutes. Using a narrow metal spatula, loosen sides of cake from the pan, then invert the cake onto the rack. Cool completely. Remove the paper. Makes 20 servings.

Prep Time: 25 minutes Standing Time: 30 minutes
Cooking Time: 55 minutes Cooling Time: 3 hours

1 Serving: Calories 311. Total Fat 15 g. Saturated Fat 5 g. Protein 5 g. Carbohydrate 39 g. Fiber 2 g. Sodium 160 mg. Cholesterol 29 mg.

Applesauce Cake with Caramel Frosting

"If you asked Grandma Stella how she made apple cake, she'd say 'use about 2 cups of flour and a pinch of salt,'" remembers Connie Behrens. "What's more, she baked on a wood stove that didn't have a temperature gauge. She'd check the temperature with her hand and she never burned or undercooked anything."

2½ **cups all-purpose flour**
2 **teaspoons ground cinnamon**
1½ **teaspoons baking powder**
½ **teaspoon baking soda**
¼ **teaspoon salt**
1½ **cups sugar**
½ **cup butter or margarine, at room temperature**
1 **large egg**
1 **large egg white**
1½ **cups unsweetened applesauce**
½ **cup currants or raisins**
½ **cup chopped pecans or walnuts, toasted**
  Caramel Frosting (recipe, right)

1 Preheat the oven to 350°F. Lightly grease a 13" x 9" x 2" baking pan, then dust with flour. In a medium-size bowl, stir together the 2½ cups flour, the cinnamon, baking powder, baking soda, and salt.

2 In a large bowl, with an electric mixer on *Medium,* cream the sugar and butter until light yellow and fluffy, scraping side of bowl often. Add the egg and beat well. Add the egg white and beat well. Using a wooden spoon, stir in one-third of the flour mixture, then half of the applesauce. Repeat, then stir in the remaining flour mixture. Stir in currants and pecans.

3 Spread the batter evenly into the prepared pan. Bake for 30 to 35 minutes or until a toothpick inserted in the center comes out clean. Place the pan upright on a wire rack. Cool completely.

4 When cake has cooled for 1½ hours, make the Caramel Frosting. Using an icing spatula or wide knife, work quickly to frost top of cake. (Or, omit Caramel Frosting and serve cake with frozen and thawed whipped dessert topping.) Makes 20 servings.

Prep Time: 25 minutes Cooking Time: 30 minutes
Cooling Time: 2½ hours

1 Serving with Frosting: Calories 290. Total Fat 8 g. Saturated Fat 4 g. Protein 3 g. Carbohydrate 53 g. Fiber 1 g. Sodium 166 mg. Cholesterol 26 mg.

Caramel Frosting

In medium-size saucepan, combine ¾ **cup firmly packed light brown sugar,** ½ **cup low-fat (1% milkfat) milk,** and **2 tablespoons butter or margarine.** Cook over moderate heat, whisking constantly, until mixture comes to a boil. Cook for 2 minutes, whisking constantly. Remove from the heat. Transfer to a large bowl; let stand for 1 hour or until mixture cools to room temperature. With an electric mixer on *Medium,* gradually add **3 cups sifted confectioners sugar,** beating until frosting is smooth and of spreading consistency. Use frosting immediately. Makes about 1½ cups frosting or enough to frost the top of a 13" x 9" x 2" cake.

1 Tablespoon: Calories 92. Total Fat 1 g. Saturated Fat 1 g. Protein 0 g. Carbohydrate 21 g. Fiber 0 g. Sodium 17 mg. Cholesterol 3 mg.

Devilish Chocolate Cake With Chocolate Buttercream Frosting

This cake was named "devil's food" because it had so much baking soda the batter turned red. Today, most recipes use less soda so the batter is a rich, brown color.

2½ **cups all-purpose flour**
⅔ **cup unsweetened cocoa**
1½ **teaspoons baking soda**
⅛ **teaspoon salt**
1⅔ **cups low-fat (1% milkfat) buttermilk or soured milk (page 300)**
2 **teaspoons vanilla**
1¾ **cups sugar**
½ **cup butter or margarine, at room temperature**
2 **large egg whites**
Chocolate Buttercream Frosting (recipe, right)

1 Preheat oven to 350°F. Lightly grease two 9-inch round cake pans, then dust with flour; line bottoms with wax paper. In small bowl, stir together the 2½ cups flour, the cocoa, baking soda, and salt. In cup, combine buttermilk and vanilla. In large bowl, with an electric mixer on *Medium*, cream sugar and butter until light yellow and fluffy, scraping side of bowl often. Add egg whites; beat well. Using wooden spoon, stir in one-third of the flour mixture, then half of the buttermilk mixture. Repeat, then stir in the remaining flour mixture.

2 Spread the batter evenly into prepared pans. Bake for 25 to 30 minutes or until toothpicks inserted in the centers come out clean. Place the pans upright on wire racks for 10 minutes. Using a narrow metal spatula, loosen sides of layers from pans, then invert cakes onto the racks. Peel off paper; cool cakes completely.

3 While the cakes cool, make the Chocolate Buttercream Frosting. Place 1 cake layer, upside down, onto a serving plate. Using an icing spatula or a wide knife, frost the top of the layer. Top with the second layer, right side up. Frost the top, then the side of the cake with remaining frosting. (To freeze, place the unwrapped frosted cake in the freezer until firm. Then, wrap and return it to the freezer. Unwrap the cake before thawing.) Makes 16 servings.

Prep Time: 25 minutes Cooking Time: 25 minutes
Cooling Time: 2½ hours

1 Serving with Frosting: Calories 383. Total Fat 11 g. Saturated Fat 7 g. Protein 5 g. Carbohydrate 70 g. Fiber 3 g. Sodium 270 mg. Cholesterol 28 mg.

Chocolate Buttercream Frosting

In a large bowl, with an electric mixer on *Low* to *Medium*, beat ⅓ **cup butter or margarine, at room temperature**, and ¼ **cup unsweetened cocoa** until light and fluffy. Gradually add **1 box (16 ounces) confectioners sugar, sifted (4½ cups)**; ⅓ **cup low-fat (1% milkfat) milk**; ¼ **cup unsweetened cocoa**; and **2 teaspoons vanilla**, beating until frosting is smooth and of spreading consistency. Makes about 2 cups frosting or enough to frost tops and sides of two 8- or 9-inch round cake layers.

2 Tablespoons: Calories 153. Total Fat 4 g. Saturated Fat 3 g. Protein 1 g. Carbohydrate 30 g. Fiber 1 g. Sodium 42 mg. Cholesterol 11 mg.

Brownie Pudding Cake

The batter in this old, community-cookbook favorite separates as it's baked, making a layer of pudding with a cake on top. This luscious version is low in fat because it uses cocoa instead of baking chocolate.

1½ **cups all-purpose flour**
¾ **cup granulated sugar**
½ **cup unsweetened cocoa**
2 **teaspoons baking powder**
⅛ **teaspoon salt**
¾ **cup low-fat (1% milkfat) milk**
2 **tablespoons vegetable oil**
2 **teaspoons vanilla**
1 **cup firmly packed light brown sugar**
1¾ **cups boiling water**

1 Preheat oven to 350°F. In an ungreased 9" x 9" x 2" baking pan, combine the flour, granulated sugar, ¼ cup of the cocoa, the baking powder, and salt. Add the milk, oil, and vanilla. Stir just until smooth. Spread the batter evenly in the pan.

2 Sprinkle with the brown sugar and the remaining ¼ cup cocoa. Pour the boiling water over batter. Bake for 30 to 35 minutes or until toothpick inserted in center of the cake layer comes out clean. Serve warm with vanilla ice cream or frozen yogurt. Serves 10.

Prep Time: 10 minutes Cooking Time: 30 minutes

1 Serving: Calories 225. Total Fat 4 g. Saturated Fat 1 g. Protein 3 g. Carbohydrate 47 g. Fiber 2 g. Sodium 141 mg. Cholesterol 1 mg.

Praline Pound Cake

Praline Pound Cake

Grandma made pound cakes with a pound each of butter, flour, and sugar. Modern
recipes, like this delicate nut-flavored one, use much less butter and sugar.

 2 **large eggs**
1¾ **cups all-purpose flour**
 1 **teaspoon baking powder**
½ **teaspoon baking soda**
⅔ **cup low-fat (1% milkfat) milk**
 2 **teaspoons vanilla**
¾ **cup butter or margarine, at room temperature**
½ **cup granulated sugar**
½ **cup firmly packed light brown sugar**
 1 **cup coarsely chopped pecans, toasted**

1 Separate the eggs. Discard the yolk from 1 of the eggs. Set aside. Preheat the oven to 325°F. Lightly grease a 9" x 5" x 3" loaf pan, then dust with flour. In a small bowl, stir together the 1¾ cups flour, baking powder, and baking soda. In cup, combine milk and vanilla.

2 In a large bowl, with an electric mixer on *Medium*, cream the butter, granulated sugar, and brown sugar

until light and fluffy, scraping side of bowl often. Add the egg whites and beat well. Add the egg yolk and beat well. Using a wooden spoon, stir in one-third of the flour mixture, then half of the milk mixture. Repeat, then stir in the remaining flour mixture. Stir in pecans.

3 Spread the batter evenly into the prepared pan. Bake for 55 to 60 minutes or until a toothpick inserted in the center comes out clean. Place the pan upright on a wire rack for 10 minutes. Using a narrow metal spatula, loosen sides of cake from the pan, then invert cake onto the rack. Cool completely. Serve with sliced strawberries, vanilla ice cream, or frozen yogurt. Serves 16.

Prep Time: 20 minutes Cooking Time: 55 minutes
Cooling Time: 3 hours

1 Serving: Calories 232. Total Fat 15 g. Saturated Fat 6 g.
Protein 3 g. Carbohydrate 23 g. Fiber 1 g.
Sodium 173 mg. Cholesterol 50 mg.

Orange Chiffon Cake with Spice 'n' Orange Frosting

Orange Chiffon Cake with Spice 'n' Orange Frosting

Women in the late 1940's were eager to try chiffon cakes because they
were a recent innovation. The delicate cakes, often citrus-flavored, were made
by folding stiffly beaten egg whites into a vegetable-oil batter.

1	**cup egg whites (6 or 7 large)**
2	**cups all-purpose flour**
1½	**cups sugar**
1	**tablespoon baking powder**
¼	**teaspoon salt**
¾	**cup orange juice**
½	**cup vegetable oil**
1	**tablespoon grated orange rind**
1	**teaspoon vanilla**
½	**cup egg yolks (6 or 7 large)**
½	**teaspoon cream of tartar**
	Spice 'n' Orange Frosting (recipe, opposite)

1 In a clean large bowl, place the egg whites. Let stand at room temperature for 30 minutes. Preheat the oven to 325°F. In a small bowl, stir together the flour, ¾ cup of the sugar, the baking powder, and salt. In a cup, combine orange juice, oil, orange rind, and vanilla.

2 In a very large bowl, with an electric mixer on *High*, beat egg yolks for 2 to 4 minutes or until thick. Add the oil mixture; beat until well combined. Set aside.

3 Add the cream of tartar to the egg whites. With very clean beaters and the mixer on *Medium to High*, beat the egg whites until soft peaks form. Gradually add the remaining ¾ cup sugar, 2 tablespoons at a time, beating until stiff peaks form.

4 Use a rubber spatula to gently fold one-third of egg whites into yolk mixture, then fold in all of flour mixture, and finally the remaining egg whites. Gently spoon evenly into *ungreased* 10-inch angel food cake pan. Bake on lowest oven rack for 50 to 55 minutes or until top springs back when lightly touched. Immediately invert cake in pan, standing pan on its legs or resting center tube over tall-necked bottle. Cool completely. While cake cools, make Spice 'n' Orange Frosting. Using narrow metal spatula, loosen side of cake from pan. Remove from pan. Frost cake with frosting. Serve or cover and store in refrigerator. Serves 16.

Prep Time: 30 minutes Standing Time: 30 minutes
Cooking Time: 50 minutes Cooling Time: 3 hours

1 Serving with Frosting: Calories 280. Total Fat 11 g. Saturated Fat 3 g. Protein 4 g. Carbohydrate 41 g. Fiber 1 g. Sodium 149 mg. Cholesterol 80 mg.

Angel Food Cake with Stirred Custard Sauce

Before the invention of electric mixers, women beat the egg whites for angel food cake by hand. Some were so expert they could beat the whites on a large platter instead of in a bowl.

1½ cups egg whites (9 or 10 large)
1½ cups sifted confectioners sugar
1 cup all-purpose flour
⅛ teaspoon salt
2 teaspoons vanilla
1½ teaspoons cream of tartar
1 cup granulated sugar
  Stirred Custard Sauce (recipe, right)

1 In clean very large bowl, place egg whites. Let stand at room temperature for 30 minutes. Preheat oven to 350°F. Onto a piece of wax paper, sift together confectioners sugar, flour, and salt. Sift 2 more times.

2 Add vanilla and cream of tartar to egg whites. With very clean beaters and electric mixer on *Medium to High,* beat egg whites until soft peaks form. Gradually add the granulated sugar, 2 tablespoons at a time, beating until stiff peaks form. Sift about one-fourth of the flour mixture over egg whites, then use rubber spatula to gently fold in. Repeat sifting and folding in of remaining flour mixture, using one-fourth of flour mixture each time. Gently spoon evenly into an *ungreased* 10-inch angel food cake pan. Using narrow metal spatula, cut through batter to break any large air bubbles.

3 Bake on lowest oven rack for 35 to 40 minutes or until top springs back when lightly touched. Immediately invert cake in pan, standing pan on its legs or resting center tube over a tall-necked bottle. Cool completely. While cake cools, make Stirred Custard Sauce. Using a narrow metal spatula, loosen side of cake from pan. Remove cake from pan. Spoon sauce over cake. Serve with sliced fruit and berries. Serves 16.

Prep Time: 25 minutes Standing Time: 30 minutes
Cooking Time: 35 minutes Cooling Time: 3 hours

1 Serving with Sauce: Calories 163. Total Fat 2 g. Saturated Fat 1 g. Protein 4 g. Carbohydrate 33 g. Fiber 0 g. Sodium 63 mg. Cholesterol 54 mg.

Spice 'n' Orange Frosting

In a small saucepan, whisk together ¾ **cup orange juice,** ¼ **cup sugar, 1 tablespoon cornstarch,** ¼ **teaspoon ground cinnamon,** and ¼ **teaspoon ground nutmeg.** Bring to a boil over moderate heat, whisking constantly. Cook for 2 minutes or until mixture is thickened, whisking constantly. Stir in **1 teaspoon grated orange rind.** Cover surface with plastic wrap and refrigerate until completely chilled. Transfer the orange mixture to a large bowl. Carefully fold in **1 container (8 ounces) frozen and thawed reduced-fat whipped dessert topping.** Makes about 4 cups.

¼ Cup: Calories 55. Total Fat 2 g. Saturated Fat 2 g. Protein 0 g. Carbohydrate 8 g. Fiber 0 g. Sodium 0 mg. Cholesterol 0 mg.

Stirred Custard Sauce

Whisk together **4 large egg yolks** and ¼ **cup sugar** until creamy. In medium-size heavy saucepan, heat 1⅔ **cups low-fat (1% milkfat) milk** over moderate heat. Slowly stir about ½ cup of the hot milk into sugar mixture, then return this mixture to the saucepan. Cook, stirring often, for 10 minutes or until mixture coats metal spoon. Quickly stir in **1 teaspoon vanilla.** Place saucepan in a bath of ice water for 1 to 2 minutes, stirring constantly. Transfer mixture to a small bowl. Cover surface with plastic wrap; refrigerate. Makes about 2 cups.

2 Tablespoons: Calories 38. Total Fat 2 g. Saturated Fat 1 g. Protein 2 g. Carbohydrate 4 g. Fiber 0 g. Sodium 15 mg. Cholesterol 54 mg.

Best-Ever Shortcake

Best-Ever Shortcake

*"Grandma Lola used eggs, butter, cream, and milk from her farm. Her shortcake
biscuits were very rich and tender and she always topped them with fresh
picked strawberries," recalls Jeanette Davidson. For birthdays and other special occasions,
you can bake this shortcake in heart-shaped pans—there's enough to serve 16.*

3   **cups all-purpose flour**

²⁄₃   **cup sugar**

1   **tablespoon baking powder**

²⁄₃   **cup butter or margarine**

1   **cup low-fat (1% milkfat) milk**

2   **large egg whites**

1   **large egg**

6   **cups fresh or frozen and thawed, sliced,
    strawberries or sliced, peeled, peaches**

¹⁄₄   **cup sugar**

For the whipped cream topping:

2   **cups heavy cream**

¹⁄₄   **cup sugar**

1   **teaspoon vanilla**

¹⁄₂   **teaspoon almond extract**

1 Preheat the oven to 450°F. Lightly grease 2 heart-shaped cake pans or two 8-inch round cake pans.

2 In a large bowl, stir together the flour, the ²/₃ cup sugar, and the baking powder. Using a pastry blender or 2 knives, cut in the butter until the mixture resembles coarse crumbs. In a small bowl, combine the milk, egg whites, and egg. Add to the flour mixture all at once and stir just until mixture is moistened.

3 Spread dough evenly into the prepared pans. Bake for 14 to 17 minutes or just until toothpicks inserted in centers come out clean (do not overbake). Place pans upright on wire racks for 10 minutes. Using narrow metal spatula, loosen sides of cake layers from pans.

4 Meanwhile, toss the fruit with ¼ cup sugar, then let stand to form juice. To prepare the whipped cream topping, in a large chilled bowl, combine the heavy cream, ¼ cup sugar, the vanilla, and almond extract. With a rotary beater or chilled beaters and an electric mixer on *Medium,* beat until soft peaks form.

5 To assemble the shortcake, place 1 warm cake layer on a serving plate. Top with half of the fruit mixture. Top with the second warm cake layer, right side up. Top with remaining fruit mixture. Serve with the whipped cream topping. Makes 16 servings.

Prep Time: 25 minutes Cooking Time: 14 minutes
1 Serving with Topping: Calories 343. Total Fat 20 g. Saturated Fat 12 g. Protein 5 g. Carbohydrate 38 g. Fiber 2 g. Sodium 201 mg. Cholesterol 76 mg.

Frosted Shortcake Prepare as for Best-Ever Shortcake, decreasing from 6 cups to 2 cups sliced strawberries or peaches and omitting the ¼ cup sugar tossed with the fruit. Also, omit the whipped cream topping and prepare an icing as follows. In a large bowl, stir together **1 box (16 ounces) confectioners sugar, sifted (4½ cups); ¼ cup low-fat (1% milkfat) milk; and 1 teaspoon vanilla.** Stir in **1 to 2 tablespoons additional milk,** 1 teaspoon at a time, until icing is thin enough to drizzle. To assemble the shortcake, cool the cakes completely. Place 1 cake layer on a serving plate. Drizzle the layer with half of the icing; top with the fruit. Top with the second cake layer, right side up. Drizzle with the remaining icing.

1 Serving with Icing: Calories 318. Total Fat 9 g. Saturated Fat 5 g. Protein 4 g. Carbohydrate 57 g. Fiber 1 g. Sodium 192 mg. Cholesterol 35 mg.

Peach Upside-Down Cake

"Grandma's upside-down cake was moist and full of fruit with a wonderful aroma and a great golden color. It never lasted long on my grandparents' busy farm," recalls Natalie Pagel.

1 can (8¼ ounces) peach slices packed in juice or 1 can (8½ ounces) unpeeled apricot halves
2 tablespoons light corn syrup
1 tablespoon butter or margarine
1⅓ cups all-purpose flour
2 teaspoons baking powder
¼ teaspoon ground nutmeg
1 cup low-fat (1% milkfat) milk
1 teaspoon vanilla
¼ cup firmly packed light brown sugar
²/₃ cup granulated sugar
¼ cup butter or margarine, at room temperature
1 large egg

1 Preheat the oven to 350°F. Drain the peaches, reserving 1 tablespoon of the juice. In a 9-inch round cake pan, place the reserved peach juice, corn syrup, and the 1 tablespoon butter. Place the pan in the oven and heat until the butter melts. Meanwhile, in a small bowl, stir together the flour, baking powder, and nutmeg. In a cup, combine the milk and vanilla.

2 Remove the pan from oven. Stir the brown sugar into the melted butter mixture. Arrange the peach slices in the pan; set aside.

3 In a large bowl, with an electric mixer on *Medium,* cream the granulated sugar and the ¼ cup butter until light yellow and fluffy, scraping side of bowl often. Add the egg and beat well. Using a wooden spoon, stir in one-third of the flour mixture, then half of the milk mixture. Repeat, then stir in remaining flour mixture.

4 Carefully pour the batter evenly over the peach slices. Bake for 35 to 40 minutes or until a toothpick inserted in the center comes out clean. Place the pan upright on a wire rack for 5 minutes. Using a narrow metal spatula, loosen side of cake layer from the pan, then invert the cake onto a serving plate. Serve warm. Makes 10 servings.

Prep Time: 15 minutes Cooking Time: 35 minutes
Cooling Time: 5 minutes
1 Serving: Calories 217. Total Fat 7 g. Saturated Fat 4 g. Protein 3 g. Carbohydrate 37 g. Fiber 1 g. Sodium 182 mg. Cholesterol 38 mg.

GINGERBREAD COTTAGE

Since Victorian days, making a gingerbread house at Christmas time has been a popular project for the whole family to enjoy. This one takes several hours to complete. Youngsters will enjoy the process more if you build it in stages— baking one day, decorating the next, and doing other activities while waiting for the icing to set.

MATERIALS

17x14-inch baking sheet

Decorating bag with tip with ¼-inch round opening

Sharp knife

Rolling pin

Poster board (cut into pattern pieces shown at right)

Two 14x10-inch doilies

11x11-inch medium-weight cardboard

Transparent tape

Rubber spatula

Suggested candies:
Gumdrops
Peppermint rounds
Candy-coated chocolate pieces
Red cinnamon candies
Spearmint leaves
Nonpareils
Candy buttons

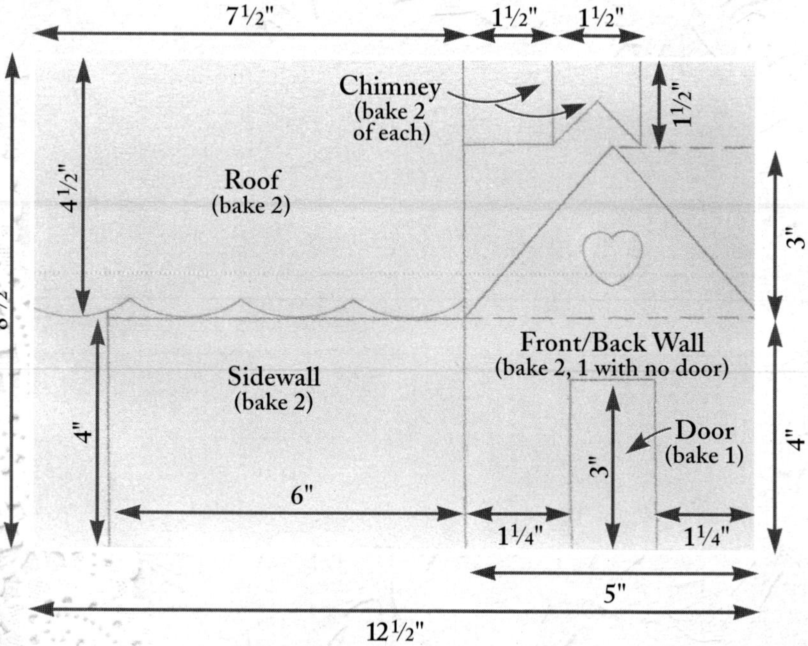

7½" 1½" 1½"

Chimney (bake 2 of each)

1½"

4½"

Roof (bake 2)

3"

8½"

3"

Sidewall (bake 2)

Front/Back Wall (bake 2, 1 with no door)

4"

Door (bake 1)

4"

3"

6"

1¼" 1¼"

5"

12½"

GINGERBREAD

1 cup shortening
1 cup granulated sugar
1 cup dark molasses
¼ cup water
6 cups all-purpose flour
2 teaspoons each ground ginger and ground cinnamon
1 teaspoon salt

For the icing:
3 large egg whites
¾ teaspoon cream of tartar
1 box (16 ounces) confectioners sugar, sifted (4½ cups)
Shredded coconut (optional)

1. In a large bowl, with an electric mixer on high, beat the shortening, granulated sugar, molasses, and water until smooth and creamy. In another large bowl, combine the flour, ginger, cinnamon, and salt. Add the dry ingredients to the creamed mixture. Mix to form a stiff dough. Wrap the dough in plastic wrap; refrigerate for 1 hour.

2. Preheat the oven to 350°F. Lightly grease the 17x14-inch baking sheet. Place half of the dough on the baking sheet. Using a floured rolling pin, roll out dough to cover baking sheet. (Steady pan by setting it on a dish towel.) Lay pattern pieces on the dough, as shown below, and cut around them with a sharp knife. Carefully remove dough around patterns. Remove poster board. Bake dough pieces for 15 to 20 minutes or until dark brown. Cool on baking sheet for 10 minutes; remove to a rack to finish cooling. Repeat with remaining dough, except omit the door piece and cut back wall without a door.

ASSEMBLY

1 To prepare the icing, let the egg whites stand at room temperature for 30 minutes. In a medium-size bowl, with an electric mixer on *High,* beat the egg whites and cream of tartar until frothy. Gradually beat in the confectioners sugar; continue beating for 7 to 10 minutes or until very stiff. Cover and refrigerate until ready to use.

2 Overlap the 2 doilies on the cardboard; tape in place. Using a rubber spatula, swirl half of the icing almost to the edge of

the doilies, building up edges. Sprinkle with coconut (if using); allow to set for 10 minutes. Cover remaining icing with a damp paper towel and refrigerate until needed. Using the decorating bag and tip, pipe icing on the bottom and inside edges of front wall and set in place on base. Pipe icing around the bottom and outside edges of one sidewall and place against the front wall to form an L shape, as shown below left. Repeat this procedure with the other side and the back to form a rectangle. (For added strength, pipe extra icing along the inside joints of cottage.) Allow to set for 1 hour or until icing is very hard.

3 Pipe icing along all top edges, reinforcing corners with extra icing. Position 1 roof piece at a time on the house. With someone holding the roof, reinforce the peak with a line of icing. Allow icing to set for 5 to 10 minutes.

4 To make the chimney, pipe icing on 2 square pieces, as shown above; position the pointed pieces between them to form a square, pressing lightly. When chimney is firm (about 30 minutes), set in place on the roof; reinforce seams and fill in cracks with icing. Set the door in place.

5 Pipe icing decoratively on roof, under eaves, and around window. Decorate with candies as you like, using icing to glue candies in place. To make icicles, pipe icing strings along the edges of the roof and chimney.

Deep-Dish Cherry Pie

Deep-Dish Cherry Pie

*Old-fashioned, deep-dish pies were baked in a casserole with just one crust on top. To catch
any juice that bubbles over, put the casserole in the oven on a baking sheet.*

1 cup sugar
¼ cup all-purpose flour
1 teaspoon lime juice
¼ teaspoon grated lime rind
4 cups fresh or frozen pitted tart red cherries
1 store-bought or homemade pie crust (page 337)
Low-fat (1% milkfat) milk

1 Preheat the oven to 375°F. In a large bowl, stir
together the sugar, flour, lime juice, and lime rind.
Add the cherries; toss until cherries are coated. (If using
frozen cherries, let the mixture stand for 15 to 30 minutes or until cherries are partially thawed but still icy,
stirring occasionally.) Pour the cherry mixture into a
1½-quart casserole.

2 Place the pie crust on top of the cherry mixture.
Trim crust to 1 inch beyond edge of casserole. Fold
under the extra crust and crimp edge (page 332). Cut
slits in the crust. Brush with a little milk; sprinkle with
a little additional sugar.

3 Bake for 50 to 55 minutes or until crust is golden.
Cool on a wire rack for 1 hour before serving. Serve
warm with vanilla frozen yogurt. Makes 8 servings.

Prep Time: 20 minutes Cooking Time: 50 minutes
Cooling Time: 1 hour

1 Serving: Calories 271. Total Fat 8 g. Saturated Fat 8 g.
Protein 2 g. Carbohydrate 50 g. Fiber 1 g.
Sodium 108 mg. Cholesterol 0 mg.

Apple Cider Pie

*The directions for making apple pie in most
early cookbooks were simple: toss the
apples with sugar and bake them in pastry. The
authors assumed cooks knew what to do.*

- ¾ cup apple cider or apple juice
- ½ cup chopped pitted dates or raisins
- 1 tablespoon cornstarch
- ½ teaspoon ground ginger
- ½ teaspoon grated lemon rind
- 2 store-bought or homemade pie crusts (page 337)
- ½ cup sugar
- 1 tablespoon all-purpose flour
- 5 cups thinly sliced, peeled, tart cooking apples

1 Preheat the oven to 375°F. In a small saucepan, stir together the apple cider, dates, cornstarch, ginger, and lemon rind. Bring to a boil over moderate heat, stirring constantly. Cook for 2 minutes or until mixture is thickened, stirring constantly. Remove from heat.

2 Line a 9-inch pie plate with 1 of the pie crusts. Trim crust even with edge of pie plate. In a large bowl, stir together the sugar and flour. Add the apples; toss until apples are coated. Spoon the apple mixture into crust. Spoon the cider mixture over apple mixture.

3 Cut slits in the remaining pie crust; place on top of cider mixture. Trim top crust to ½ inch beyond edge of pie plate. Fold top crust under bottom crust and crimp edge (page 332). Sprinkle with a little additional sugar. Bake for 40 to 45 minutes or until apples are tender and crust is golden. (If the edge of the crust seems to be browning too quickly, cover with foil.) Cool on a wire rack for 2 hours before serving. Makes 8 servings.

Prep Time: 30 minutes Cooking Time: 45 minutes
Cooling Time: 2 hours

1 Serving: Calories 377. Total Fat 15 g. Saturated Fat 15 g.
Protein 2 g. Carbohydrate 59 g. Fiber 2 g.
Sodium 211 mg. Cholesterol 0 mg.

Peach Cider Pie Prepare as for Apple Cider Pie, **substituting 5 cups fresh or frozen and thawed, thinly sliced, peeled, peaches** for the apples and increasing the flour to 2 tablespoons.

1 Serving: Calories 387. Total Fat 15 g. Saturated Fat 15 g.
Protein 3 g. Carbohydrate 62 g. Fiber 3 g.
Sodium 211 mg. Cholesterol 0 mg.

Cinnamon Apple Crumb Pie

- ½ cup firmly packed light brown sugar
- 1 tablespoon all-purpose flour
- 1¼ teaspoons ground cinnamon
- ½ teaspoon ground cardamom
- 6 cups thinly sliced, peeled, tart cooking apples
- 1 store-bought or homemade pie crust (page 337)
- ⅔ cup firmly packed light brown sugar
- ½ cup all-purpose flour
- 2 tablespoons butter or margarine

1 Preheat the oven to 375°F. In a large bowl, stir together the ½ cup brown sugar, the 1 tablespoon flour, ¾ teaspoon of the cinnamon, and the cardamom. Add the apples; toss until apples are coated.

2 Line a 9-inch pie plate with the pie crust. Trim crust to ½ inch beyond edge of pie plate. Fold under extra crust and crimp edge (page 332). Spoon the apple mixture into crust. In a medium-size bowl, stir together the ⅔ cup brown sugar, ½ cup flour, and the remaining ½ teaspoon cinnamon. Cut in the butter (tip, below). Sprinkle over the apple mixture.

3 Bake for 40 to 45 minutes or until apples are tender and crumb topping is golden. Cool on a wire rack for 2 hours before serving. Makes 8 servings.

Prep Time: 25 minutes Cooking Time: 40 minutes
Cooling Time: 2 hours

1 Serving: Calories 306. Total Fat 11 g. Saturated Fat 9 g.
Protein 2 g. Carbohydrate 52 g. Fiber 2 g.
Sodium 143 mg. Cholesterol 8 mg.

CUTTING IN BUTTER

Using a pastry blender, cut the butter into the brown sugar mixture until the pieces look like coarse crumbs.

Or, use two table knives to cut crisscross through the mixture until the butter is in coarse crumbs.

Strawberry Rhubarb Pie

Good cooks adjusted the flour in their pies using more if the fruit was very juicy, a little less if it wasn't ripe. If your berries are still firm, use the 3 tablespoons flour.

   1 **cup sugar**
   3 **to 4 tablespoons all-purpose flour**
 ½ **teaspoon grated lemon rind**
 ⅛ **teaspoon ground nutmeg**
   3 **cups fresh or frozen unsweetened strawberries, sliced**
2½ **cups fresh or frozen, unsweetened, sliced, rhubarb**
   2 **store-bought or homemade pie crusts (page 337)**

1 Preheat oven to 375°F. In large bowl, combine sugar, flour, lemon rind, and nutmeg. Add fruit; toss until coated. (If using any frozen fruit, let mixture stand 15 to 30 minutes or until fruit is partially thawed but still icy; stir often.) Line 9-inch pie plate with 1 of the pie crusts. Trim even with edge of plate. Pour fruit mixture into crust. Cut slits in remaining crust; place on fruit. Trim top crust to ½ inch beyond edge of plate. Fold top crust under bottom crust; crimp edge (tip, below).

2 Bake for 45 to 50 minutes (70 to 80 minutes for frozen fruit) or until crust is golden. (If edge of crust seems to be browning too quickly, cover with foil.) Cool on a wire rack for 2½ hours before serving. Serves 8.

Prep Time: 20 minutes Cooking Time: 45 minutes
Cooling Time: 2½ hours

1 Serving: Calories 374. Total Fat 15 g. Saturated Fat 15 g.
Protein 3 g. Carbohydrate 57 g. Fiber 2 g.
Sodium 213 mg. Cholesterol 0 mg.

CRIMPING PIE CRUSTS

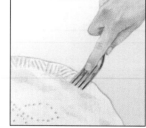 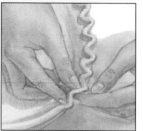

For a flat edge, use the tines of a fork to lightly press the edge, as shown. If the fork starts to stick, dip it into flour.

For a high edge, place an index finger and thumb inside the pastry. Press with the index finger of the other hand, as shown.

Green Tomato Pie

When the first frost came early, housewives often had lots of green tomatoes on their hands. To use them up, they made this homespun dessert that tastes similar to mincemeat pie.

   5 **cups thinly sliced, peeled, green tomatoes (about 2 pounds)**
   1 **cup raisins**
 ¼ **cup orange juice**
   1 **tablespoon lemon juice**
   1 **cup sugar**
   3 **tablespoons all-purpose flour**
   2 **teaspoons grated orange rind**
   1 **teaspoon ground cinnamon**
 ½ **teaspoon ground allspice**
   2 **store-bought or homemade pie crusts (page 337)**

1 Preheat the oven to 375°F. In a large saucepan, combine the green tomatoes, raisins, orange juice, and lemon juice. Bring to a boil. Lower the heat and simmer, covered, for 5 minutes. Using a slotted spoon, remove the tomato slices and place in a bowl.

2 In a small bowl, whisk together the sugar, flour, orange rind, cinnamon, and allspice. Stir into the juice mixture. Bring to a boil over moderate heat, whisking constantly. Cook for 2 minutes or until mixture is thickened, stirring constantly; remove from heat. Gently stir in the tomatoes. Cool for 10 minutes.

3 Meanwhile, line a 9-inch pie plate with 1 of the pie crusts. Trim crust even with edge of pie plate. Pour tomato mixture into crust. Cut slits in remaining pie crust; place on top of tomato mixture. Trim top crust to ½ inch beyond edge of pie plate. Fold top crust under bottom crust; crimp edge (tip, left). Sprinkle with a little additional sugar.

4 Bake for 40 to 45 minutes or until crust is golden. (If the edge of the crust seems to be browning too quickly, cover with foil.) Cool on a wire rack for 1 hour before serving. Makes 8 servings.

Prep Time: 25 minutes Cooking Time: 55 minutes
Cooling Time: 1 hour 10 minutes

1 Serving: Calories 443. Total Fat 15 g. Saturated Fat 15 g.
Protein 4 g. Carbohydrate 75 g. Fiber 3 g.
Sodium 228 mg. Cholesterol 0 mg.

Sour Cream Raisin Pie

To make sure your egg whites beat up nice and stiff, separate the eggs, one at a time; place each white into a small bowl and then transfer it to a large bowl. This way if any yolk gets into the white, you only ruin one white instead of the whole batch.

1 store-bought or homemade pie crust (page 337)

For the filling:

 3/4 **cup raisins**
 1 **cup firmly packed light brown sugar**
 1/2 **cup all-purpose flour**
 3/4 **teaspoon ground cinnamon**
 1/4 **teaspoon ground nutmeg**
 1 **can (12 ounces) evaporated skimmed milk**
 1/3 **cup low-fat (1% milkfat) milk**
 2 **large egg yolks**
 1 **cup reduced-fat sour cream**
 1 **teaspoon vanilla**

For the meringue:

 4 **large egg whites**
 1/2 **teaspoon vanilla**
 1/2 **teaspoon cream of tartar**
 1/2 **cup granulated sugar**

Sour Cream Raisin Pie

1 Preheat the oven to 450°F. Line a 9-inch pie plate with pie crust. Trim crust to 1/2 inch beyond edge of pie plate. Fold under extra crust and crimp edge (tip, opposite). Using tines of a fork, prick bottom and sides of crust. Bake for 10 to 12 minutes or until golden; set aside. Lower the oven temperature to 350°F.

2 Meanwhile, to prepare the filling, pour boiling water over raisins and let stand for 5 minutes. Drain and set aside. In a large saucepan, whisk together the brown sugar, flour, cinnamon, and nutmeg. Whisk in the evaporated skimmed milk and the low-fat milk. Bring to a boil over moderately high heat, whisking constantly. Lower the heat to moderate and cook for 2 minutes or until the mixture is thickened, whisking constantly. Remove from the heat.

3 In a small bowl, whisk the egg yolks until light. Add a little of the hot milk mixture to yolks, then slowly whisk all of the yolk mixture into the milk mixture in the saucepan. Return just to boiling. Cook for 2 minutes more, whisking constantly. Remove from heat. Stir in the sour cream, the 1 teaspoon vanilla, and the raisins. Cover; set aside.

4 To prepare the meringue, in a clean large bowl, with an electric mixer on *High,* beat the egg whites, the 1/2 teaspoon vanilla, and the cream of tartar until soft peaks form. Gradually add the granulated sugar, beating until stiff peaks form.

5 Pour the hot filling into the baked crust. Top with the meringue, spreading evenly and sealing to edge of crust. Bake for 15 minutes. Cool on a wire rack for 2 1/2 hours. Serve or cover and store in the refrigerator. Makes 8 servings.

Prep Time: 20 minutes Cooking Time: 35 minutes
Cooling Time: 2 1/2 hours

1 Serving: Calories 416. Total Fat 13 g. Saturated Fat 10 g.
Protein 9 g. Carbohydrate 68 g. Fiber 1 g.
Sodium 210 mg. Cholesterol 67 mg.

Lemon Chess Pie

A favorite in New England and the South, chess pie often was served for afternoon tea rather than with a meal.

1 **store-bought or homemade pie crust (page 337)**
3 **large egg whites**
2 **large eggs**
1 **cup firmly packed light brown sugar**
⅓ **cup low-fat (1% milkfat) milk**
¼ **cup granulated sugar**
2 **tablespoons lemon juice**
1 **tablespoon cornmeal**
1 **tablespoon all-purpose flour**
1 **tablespoon butter or margarine, melted**
2 **teaspoons grated lemon rind**
2 **teaspoons vanilla**

1 Preheat oven to 400°F. Line a 9-inch pie plate with pie crust. Trim crust to ½ inch beyond edge of pie plate. Fold under extra crust and crimp edge (page 332). Line crust with foil and fill with dried beans. Bake for 15 minutes or until light brown. Cool crust on wire rack for 5 minutes; discard foil. (Save beans for future pastry baking.) Lower oven temperature to 350°F.

2 Meanwhile, in a large bowl, using a rotary beater or fork, beat the egg whites and eggs just until mixed. Whisk in brown sugar, milk, granulated sugar, lemon juice, cornmeal, flour, butter, lemon rind, and vanilla. Pour into crust. Bake for 40 to 45 minutes or until knife inserted in center comes out clean. (If edge is browning too quickly, cover with foil.) Cool on wire rack 1 hour. Serve or cover and store in refrigerator. Serves 8.

Prep Time: 15 minutes Cooking Time: 55 minutes
Cooling Time: 1 hour

1 Serving: Calories 265. Total Fat 10 g. Saturated Fat 9 g.
Protein 4 g. Carbohydrate 39 g. Fiber 0 g.
Sodium 168 mg. Cholesterol 58 mg.

Banana Cream Pie

For best results, use firm, yet ripe, bananas in this rich pie.

1 **store-bought or homemade pie crust (page 337)**
½ **cup sugar**
¼ **cup cornstarch**
2½ **cups low-fat (1% milkfat) milk**
2 **large egg yolks**
1 **tablespoon vanilla**
2 **medium-size bananas, sliced**

For the meringue:
4 **large egg whites**
½ **teaspoon vanilla**
½ **teaspoon cream of tartar**
½ **cup sugar**

1 Preheat the oven to 450°F. Line a 9-inch pie plate with pie crust. Trim crust to ½ inch beyond edge of pie plate. Fold under extra crust and crimp edge (page 332). Using tines of a fork, prick bottom and sides of crust. Bake for 10 to 12 minutes or until golden; set aside. Lower the oven temperature to 350°F.

2 Meanwhile, to prepare the filling, in a large saucepan, whisk together ½ cup sugar and the cornstarch. Whisk in the milk. Bring to a boil over moderately high heat, whisking constantly. Lower the heat to moderate and cook for 2 minutes or until mixture is thickened, whisking constantly. Remove from heat.

3 In a small bowl, whisk the egg yolks until light. Add a little of the hot milk mixture to yolks, then slowly whisk all of the yolk mixture into the milk mixture in the saucepan. Return just to boiling. Cook for 2 minutes more, whisking constantly. Remove from heat. Stir in the 1 tablespoon vanilla. Cover and set aside. Arrange bananas on bottom of baked crust; set aside.

4 To prepare the meringue, in a clean large bowl, with an electric mixer on *High*, beat the egg whites, the ½ teaspoon vanilla, and the cream of tartar until soft peaks form. Gradually add ½ cup sugar, beating until stiff peaks form.

5 Pour the hot filling over bananas. Top with the meringue, spreading evenly and sealing to edge of crust. Bake for 15 minutes. Cool on a wire rack for 2½ hours. Serve or cover and store in the refrigerator. Makes 8 servings.

Prep Time: 25 minutes Cooking Time: 25 minutes
Cooling Time: 2½ hours

1 Serving: Calories 318. Total Fat 10 g. Saturated Fat 8 g.
Protein 6 g. Carbohydrate 51 g. Fiber 1 g.
Sodium 174 mg. Cholesterol 56 mg.

Chocolate Banana Cream Pie Prepare as for Banana Cream Pie, using ¾ **cup sugar** instead of ½ cup in the filling and whisking ⅓ **cup unsweetened cocoa** into the sugar-cornstarch mixture.

1 Serving: Calories 350. Total Fat 10 g. Saturated Fat 9 g.
Protein 7 g. Carbohydrate 60 g. Fiber 2 g.
Sodium 175 mg. Cholesterol 56 mg.

Walnut Maple Pie

Walnut Maple Pie

Grandma used whatever nuts she had on hand, which is how this delicious variation of pecan pie came to be. Hazelnuts, macadamia nuts, cashews, or peanuts also work well.

  1 **store-bought or homemade pie crust (page 337)**
  2 **large egg whites**
  1 **large egg**
  1 **cup maple-flavored syrup or pure maple syrup**
  ½ **cup firmly packed light brown sugar**
  2 **tablespoons all-purpose flour**
  1 **tablespoon butter or margarine, melted**
  1½ **teaspoons vanilla**
  ½ **cup chopped walnuts**

1 Preheat oven to 400°F. Line a 9-inch pie plate with pie crust. Trim crust to ½ inch beyond edge of pie plate. Fold under extra crust and crimp edge (page 332). Line crust with foil and fill with dried beans. Bake for 15 minutes or until light brown. Cool crust on a wire rack for 5 minutes; discard foil. (Save beans for future pastry baking.) Lower oven temperature to 350°F.

2 Meanwhile, in a large bowl, using a rotary beater or fork, beat the egg whites and egg just until mixed. Whisk in the maple-flavored syrup, brown sugar, flour, butter, and vanilla just until smooth. Stir in the walnuts.

3 Pour the syrup mixture into baked crust. Bake for 40 to 45 minutes or until a knife inserted in the center comes out clean. (If the edge of the crust seems to be browning too quickly, cover with foil.) Cool on a wire rack for 1 hour. Serve with frozen vanilla yogurt or cover and store in the refrigerator. Makes 8 servings.

Prep Time: 15 minutes Cooking Time: 55 minutes
Cooling Time: 1 hour

1 Serving: Calories 342. Total Fat 14 g. Saturated Fat 9 g.
Protein 4 g. Carbohydrate 51 g. Fiber 0 g.
Sodium 170 mg. Cholesterol 31 mg.

Spicy Pumpkin Chiffon Pie

Spicy Pumpkin Chiffon Pie

In the 1950's, an inventive cook created a fluffy mixture by folding
beaten egg whites into a creamy pie filling. The result was so light and airy it
looked like a pile of chiffon and so the name for this recipe was coined.

1¼ **cups finely crushed gingersnaps and/or finely crushed graham crackers**
  2 **tablespoons granulated sugar**
  4 **large egg whites**
  2 **tablespoons butter or margarine, melted**
  2 **envelopes unflavored gelatin (2 teaspoons each)**
1¼ **cups evaporated skimmed milk**
  1 **can (16 ounces) pumpkin**
½ **cup firmly packed light brown sugar**
  1 **teaspoon ground cinnamon**
  1 **teaspoon grated lemon rind**
¼ **teaspoon ground ginger**
⅛ **teaspoon ground cloves**
⅔ **cup granulated sugar**

1 Preheat the oven to 375°F. In a small bowl, stir together the gingersnaps and the 2 tablespoons granulated sugar. In another small bowl, combine 1 of the egg whites and the melted butter. Add to the crumb mixture and stir until combined. Press into the bottom and up the sides of a lightly greased 9-inch pie plate. Bake for 4 to 5 minutes or until edge of crust is starting to brown. Cool on a wire rack.

2 Meanwhile, in a medium-size saucepan, sprinkle the gelatin over milk; let stand for 1 minute. Cook over low heat for 5 minutes or until gelatin dissolves completely, whisking constantly. Remove from heat.

3 In a large bowl, combine the pumpkin, brown sugar, cinnamon, lemon rind, ginger, and cloves. Stir in the gelatin mixture. Refrigerate the mixture for 30 minutes, stirring occasionally.

4 In a clean large heavy saucepan, with an electric mixer on *High,* beat the remaining 3 egg whites and the ⅔ cup granulated sugar over low heat for 6 minutes or until stiff peaks form. Fold into the pumpkin mixture. If necessary, refrigerate until the mixture mounds slightly when dropped from a spoon. Spoon the pumpkin mixture into the baked crumb crust. Cover and refrigerate for at least 4 hours or until set. Serves 8.

Prep Time: 30 minutes Cooking Time: 10 minutes
Chilling Time: 4½ hours

1 Serving: Calories 278. Total Fat 5 g. Saturated Fat 2 g. Protein 8 g. Carbohydrate 52 g. Fiber 2 g. Sodium 227 mg. Cholesterol 9 mg.

Homemade Pie Crust

Some grandmas made pie crust with vegetable oil instead of lard or shortening. An oil-based crust is perfect for today because it's lower in saturated fat. It's also easier, because you just stir the ingredients together.

For 1-crust pastry:

1¼ cups all-purpose flour
⅛ teaspoon salt
¼ cup vegetable oil
3 tablespoons cold water

For 2-crust pastry:

2⅓ cups all-purpose flour
¼ teaspoon salt
½ cup vegetable oil
6 tablespoons cold water

1 To prepare the pastry, in a large bowl, stir together the flour and salt. In a small bowl, combine the oil and water (do not stir). Add to flour mixture all at once and stir lightly with a fork just until moistened. If necessary, stir in up to 1 tablespoon additional water, ½ teaspoon at a time, as needed to moisten. For 1-crust pie, shape as directed in Step 2. For 2-crust pie, shape as directed in step 3.

2 For a 1-crust pie, form the pastry into a ball, then flatten slightly. Place the ball of pastry between sheets of wax paper. Roll from the center outward into a 12-inch circle. Peel off top paper. Fit crust, pastry side down, into a 9-inch pie plate. Remove wax paper. Trim the crust to ½ inch beyond edge of pie plate. Fold under extra crust and crimp edge (page 332). Fill and bake as directed in recipe.

3 For a 2-crust pie, form the pastry into 2 balls, then flatten slightly. Place each ball of pastry between sheets of wax paper. Roll each from the center outward into a 12-inch circle. Peel off top papers. Fit 1 crust, pastry side down, into a 9-inch pie plate. Remove wax paper. Trim crust even with edge of pie plate. Fill pastry-lined pie plate with desired filling. Peel paper off the remaining crust; cut slits in crust and place on top of filling. Remove the remaining wax paper. Trim top crust to ½ inch beyond edge of pie plate. Fold top crust under bottom crust and crimp edge (page 332). Bake as directed in pie recipe. Makes 8 servings.

Prep Time: 18 minutes

⅛ of 1-Crust Pastry: Calories 131. Total Fat 7 g. Saturated Fat 1 g. Protein 2 g. Carbohydrate 15 g. Fiber 1 g. Sodium 34 mg. Cholesterol 0 mg.

⅛ of 2-Crust Pastry: Calories 253. Total Fat 14 g. Saturated Fat 1 g. Protein 4 g. Carbohydrate 28 g. Fiber 1 g. Sodium 67 mg. Cholesterol 0 mg.

STORE-BOUGHT CRUST

Supermarkets now carry a variety of easy-to-use pie crust products.

• **Refrigerated pastry** Found in supermarket dairy cases, each package of refrigerated pastry contains two 12-inch pastry crusts (enough for two 9-inch, 1-crust pies or one 9-inch, 2-crust pie). Because the crusts are already rolled out, they are easy to use.

• **Pie crust mix** This product comes in 1-crust and 2-crust sizes. You'll find it in the baking aisle of the supermarket. To prepare the crusts, all you do is add water, mix the dough, and roll it out.

• **Frozen pie crusts** A deep-dish frozen unbaked pie crust is the equivalent of 1 homemade pie crust. The shallow frozen unbaked pie crusts do not hold as much filling, so they are not recommended for the recipes in this book.

Summer Pudding

*England settlers brought the recipe for
this old-fashioned dessert to America. Be sure
to let it stand overnight so the bread soaks
up all the flavorful fruit juices.*

- 4 **cups sliced fresh strawberries**
- 2 **cups fresh or frozen and thawed blueberries**
- 1 **cup sugar**
- 1 **cup orange juice**
- 1 **teaspoon grated orange rind**
- 3 **cups fresh or frozen and thawed rhubarb cut into ½-inch pieces**
- 12 **slices dried home-style bread, crusts removed**
- 1½ **cups reduced-fat frozen and thawed whipped dessert topping**

1 In a large bowl, toss strawberries and blueberries with ¼ cup of the sugar; set aside and allow berries to form juice. Meanwhile, in a large saucepan, combine the remaining ¾ cup sugar, the orange juice, and orange rind. Bring to a boil over moderately high heat, stirring constantly. Add the rhubarb. Lower the heat and simmer, covered, for 5 to 7 minutes or until rhubarb is very tender. Remove from heat. Stir in the strawberry-blueberry mixture. Set aside.

2 Halve the bread slices diagonally to make triangles. Line the bottom of a 2-quart bowl (preferably a glass one) with some of the bread triangles, fitting the pieces close together by carefully arranging and trimming as needed (reserve the trimmings). Completely line the side of the bowl with some of the remaining bread triangles and fit reserved trimmings into any open spaces.

3 Using slotted spoon, lift the fruit mixture from the juice and carefully spoon the fruit into bread-lined bowl. Completely cover fruit with the remaining bread triangles and fit reserved trimmings into any open spaces. Slowly pour the juice around the edge and over the bread. Cover surface with wax paper or plastic wrap.

4 Set the bowl onto a dinner plate, then invert a plate that is slightly smaller than the diameter of the bowl

on top of the wax paper; press down firmly. Place a light weight on top of the inverted plate. Refrigerate for 12 to 24 hours.

5 To serve, remove the weight, inverted plate, and the wax paper. Loosen the side of the pudding from the bowl with a narrow metal spatula; unmold pudding onto a serving platter. Spoon some of the dessert topping onto each serving. Makes 12 servings.

Prep Time: 30 minutes Chilling Time: 12 hours

1 Serving: Calories 195. Total Fat 2 g. Saturated Fat 1 g.
Protein 3 g. Carbohydrate 41 g. Fiber 3 g.
Sodium 139 mg. Cholesterol 0 mg.

Ambrosia

*Southerners believe this fruit dessert lives
up to its name, which means food for the gods. It's
a must on many a Christmas dinner table.*

- 4 **medium-size oranges**
- **Orange juice**
- 2 **small bananas, sliced**
- 1½ **cups fresh pineapple chunks or 1 can (15¼ ounces) pineapple tidbits or chunks packed in juice, drained**
- 2 **tablespoons sifted confectioners sugar**
- 1 **tablespoon brandy or dry sherry (optional)**
- 2 **tablespoons coconut**

1 Grate ½ teaspoon orange rind. Peel and section oranges over a bowl to catch the juice. Measure the juice. If necessary, add enough additional orange juice to measure ¼ cup. Set aside. Dip the banana slices into a little orange juice, turning to coat.

2 To serve, evenly divide the oranges, bananas, and pineapple among 6 sherbet dishes.

3 In a small bowl, stir together the orange rind, the ¼ cup orange juice, the confectioners sugar, and brandy (if using). Spoon some of the juice mixture over each serving. Cover and refrigerate for 1 to 2 hours. Sprinkle with coconut before serving. Makes 6 servings.

Prep Time: 20 minutes Chilling Time: 1 hour

1 Serving: Calories 113. Total Fat 1 g. Saturated Fat 1 g.
Protein 1 g. Carbohydrate 27 g. Fiber 3 g.
Sodium 6 mg. Cholesterol 0 mg.

Mixed Melon Compote

Mixed Melon Compote

A light fruit dessert was the perfect way to end a hearty meal.

2 cups fresh strawberries, quartered

¼ small cantaloupe, seeded and scooped into balls

¼ small honeydew melon, seeded and scooped into balls

2 small plums, pitted and sliced

⅔ cup apple juice

3 tablespoons firmly packed light brown sugar

2 teaspoons lemon juice

½ teaspoon grated lemon rind

¼ teaspoon ground cinnamon

1 In a large bowl, combine the strawberries, cantaloupe, honeydew melon, and plums. In a small bowl, stir together the apple juice, brown sugar, lemon juice, lemon rind, and cinnamon. Pour the juice mixture over the fruit mixture; toss gently to coat. Cover and refrigerate for at least 1 hour, stirring once.

2 To serve, evenly divide the fruit mixture with juices among 6 sherbet dishes. Serve with cookies. Makes 6 servings.

Prep Time: 20 minutes Chilling Time: 1 hour

1 Serving: Calories 74. Total Fat 0 g. Saturated Fat 0 g.
Protein 1 g. Carbohydrate 19 g. Fiber 2 g.
Sodium 9 mg. Cholesterol 0 mg.

✸

Mixed Citrus Compote Prepare as for Mixed Melon Compote, substituting **4 medium-size oranges, peeled and sectioned; 3 medium-size apples, cubed; and 2 medium-size grapefruit, peeled and sectioned;** for the fresh strawberries, cantaloupe, honeydew melon, and plums.

1 Serving: Calories 138. Total Fat 0 g. Saturated Fat 0 g.
Protein 2 g. Carbohydrate 35 g. Fiber 4 g.
Sodium 3 mg. Cholesterol 0 mg.

Peach Cobbler

Peach Cobbler

"Grandma's peach cobbler tasted better than anything you could imagine,
sweet with a surprising tartness and creamy yet crunchy at the same time," declares
Linda Wicker. "It was like baked sunshine right out of the oven."

1 cup peach nectar, apricot nectar, or apple juice

⅓ cup sugar

4 teaspoons all-purpose flour

½ teaspoon ground nutmeg

3 cups fresh or frozen and thawed, sliced, peeled, peaches

½ teaspoon grated lemon rind

⅔ cup all-purpose flour

2 tablespoons old-fashioned (5 minutes) or quick-cooking (1 minute) rolled oats

2 tablespoons sugar

1 teaspoon baking powder

2 tablespoons butter or margarine

2 tablespoons low-fat (1% milkfat) milk

1 large egg white

1 Preheat the oven to 400°F. In a medium-size saucepan, whisk together the peach nectar, the ⅓ cup sugar, the 4 teaspoons flour, and ¼ teaspoon of the nutmeg. Cook over moderate heat, whisking constantly, until mixture starts to thicken. Cook and whisk for 2 minutes more or until thickened. Stir in peaches and lemon rind. Cook until bubbly. Keep warm.

2 In a medium-size bowl, stir together the ⅔ cup flour, the oats, the 2 tablespoons sugar, the baking powder, and the remaining ¼ teaspoon nutmeg. Using a pastry blender or 2 knives, cut in the butter until the mixture resembles coarse crumbs. In a small bowl, combine the milk and egg white. Add to the oat mixture and stir until a dough forms.

3 Spoon hot peach mixture into a 9-inch round baking pan. Spoon dough into 4 even mounds on top of hot peach mixture. Bake for 18 to 22 minutes or until a toothpick inserted near the center of 1 of the mounds comes out clean. Serve warm with whipped cream or reduced-fat whipped topping. Makes 4 servings.

Prep Time: 25 minutes Cooking Time: 30 minutes

1 Serving: Calories 332. Total Fat 6 g. Saturated Fat 4 g. Protein 5 g. Carbohydrate 66 g. Fiber 4 g. Sodium 203 mg. Cholesterol 16 mg.

Blueberry Cobbler Prepare as for Perfect Peach Cobbler, substituting **3 cups fresh or frozen and thawed blueberries** for the peaches.

1 Serving: Calories 338. Total Fat 7 g. Saturated Fat 4 g. Protein 5 g. Carbohydrate 67 g. Fiber 4 g. Sodium 210 mg. Cholesterol 16 mg.

Apple Brown Betty

Some grandmas made their betty with torn soft bread; others made it with dried bread cubes or crumbs. But they all used lots of juicy apples and a hint of citrus and spice.

- 4 **cups thinly sliced, peeled, tart cooking apples**
- ½ **cup granulated sugar or firmly packed light brown sugar**
- 1 **tablespoon all-purpose flour**
- ½ **teaspoon grated orange rind**
- 8 **slices dried home-style bread, crusts removed, cut into ½-inch cubes**
- 1 **tablespoon granulated sugar or firmly packed light brown sugar**
- ⅛ **teaspoon ground cinnamon**

1 Preheat the oven to 375°F. In a large bowl, stir together the apples, the ½ cup sugar, the flour, and orange rind. Add half of the bread cubes; toss until well mixed. Spoon into a 9-inch round baking pan. Bake for 15 minutes.

2 Meanwhile, in a medium-size bowl, combine the remaining bread cubes, the 1 tablespoon sugar, and the cinnamon. Sprinkle over apple mixture. Bake for 10 to 15 minutes more or until the fruit is tender and the topping is golden. Serve warm. Makes 4 servings.

Prep Time: 20 minutes Cooking Time: 25 minutes

1 Serving: Calories 313. Total Fat 2 g. Saturated Fat 0 g. Protein 4 g. Carbohydrate 71 g. Fiber 3 g. Sodium 270 mg. Cholesterol 1 mg.

Three-Berry Slump

A slump or grunt is an old-time New England dessert of sweetened berries with dumplings on top. If you like, use 2½ cups of one berry instead of a combination.

- 1 **cup water**
- 1 **cup fresh or frozen and thawed blueberries**
- ¾ **cup fresh or frozen and thawed raspberries or strawberries**
- ¾ **cup fresh or frozen and thawed blackberries**
- ⅓ **cup firmly packed light brown sugar**
- 2 **tablespoons cold water**
- 1 **tablespoon cornstarch**
- 1 **teaspoon vanilla**
- ½ **cup all-purpose flour**
- 2 **tablespoons firmly packed light brown sugar**
- ½ **teaspoon baking soda**
- ¼ **teaspoon ground cardamom or ground nutmeg**
- 2 **tablespoons butter or margarine**
- ¼ **cup low-fat (1% milkfat) buttermilk or soured milk (page 300)**

1 In a large saucepan, combine the 1 cup water, blueberries, raspberries, blackberries, and the ⅓ cup brown sugar. Bring to a boil. Lower the heat and simmer, covered, for 5 minutes, stirring occasionally.

2 Meanwhile, in a small bowl, whisk together the 2 tablespoons cold water and the cornstarch. Stir into the berry mixture. Bring to a boil over moderate heat, stirring constantly. Stir in the vanilla. Remove from heat. Cover; keep warm.

3 In a medium-size bowl, stir together the flour, the 2 tablespoons brown sugar, the baking soda, and cardamom. Using a pastry blender or 2 knives, cut in butter until mixture resembles coarse crumbs. Add buttermilk to flour mixture and stir until a dough forms.

4 Spoon the dough into 4 even mounds on top of the hot berry mixture. Simmer, covered, for 10 minutes or until a toothpick inserted near the center of 1 of the mounds comes out clean. (Do not lift lid before 10 minutes cooking.) Makes 4 servings.

Prep Time: 15 minutes Cooking Time: 20 minutes

1 Serving: Calories 233. Total Fat 6 g. Saturated Fat 4 g. Protein 3 g. Carbohydrate 42 g. Fiber 4 g. Sodium 241 mg. Cholesterol 17 mg.

Blackberry Dumplings

Blackberry Dumplings

*Shaker women wrapped fresh fruit in pastry, baked the dumplings in
the oven, and served them with a sauce or warmed maple syrup.*

 1 **package (11 ounces) pie crust mix**
2½ **cups fresh or frozen and thawed blackberries**
 ¼ **cup sugar**
 ¼ **cup all-purpose flour**
 ¼ **teaspoon ground nutmeg**
 1 **tablespoon low-fat (1% milkfat) milk**
    Orange Sauce (recipe, opposite) (optional)

1 Preheat the oven to 400°F. Line a baking sheet with foil. Lightly grease the foil. Set aside. Prepare the pie crust as directed on the package. On a lightly floured surface, roll pie crust to a 24x12-inch rectangle. Cut into eight 6-inch squares.

2 In a large bowl, toss the blackberries with the sugar, flour, and nutmeg. Spoon some of the blackberry mixture onto the center of each pie crust square.

3 Lightly moisten the edges of each square with water. Bring the corners of each square to the center over berries; pinch seams. Place onto prepared baking sheet. Brush the dumplings with the milk. Bake for 20 to 25 minutes or until dumplings are golden. Serve warm with Orange Sauce (if using). Makes 8 servings.

Prep Time: 25 minutes Cooking Time: 20 minutes

1 Serving: Calories 265. Total Fat 13 g. Saturated Fat 3 g.
Protein 3 g. Carbohydrate 35 g. Fiber 3 g.
Sodium 295 mg. Cholesterol 0 mg.

Apple Dumplings Prepare as for Blackberry Dumplings, substituting **2½ cups chopped, peeled, tart cooking apples** for the blackberries.

1 Serving: Calories 261. Total Fat 12 g. Saturated Fat 3 g.
Protein 3 g. Carbohydrate 35 g. Fiber 2 g.
Sodium 295 mg. Cholesterol 0 mg.

Orange Sauce

In a small saucepan, whisk together **1¼ cups orange juice, ¼ cup sugar, 4 teaspoons cornstarch, ½ teaspoon grated orange rind,** and **¼ teaspoon ground nutmeg.** Bring to a boil over moderate heat, whisking constantly. Cook for 2 minutes or until mixture is thickened, whisking constantly. Makes about 1 cup.

2 Tablespoons: Calories 47. Total Fat 0 g. Saturated Fat 0 g.
Protein 0 g. Carbohydrate 12 g. Fiber 0 g.
Sodium 1 mg. Cholesterol 0 mg.

Sautéed Bananas with Buttered Rum Glaze

Brennan's restaurant in New Orleans made bananas Foster famous and, before long, housewives were creating their own versions of the elegant, but easy, dessert. It's especially good spooned over vanilla frozen yogurt.

6 **medium-size bananas**
2 **tablespoons butter or margarine**
½ **cup firmly packed light brown sugar**
¼ **cup raisins**
2 **tablespoons light corn syrup**
¼ **cup orange juice**
2 **tablespoons rum or orange juice**

1 Peel the bananas; cut in half crosswise, then lengthwise. Set aside.

2 In a 12-inch nonstick skillet, melt the butter over moderate heat. Add the brown sugar, raisins, and corn syrup. Slowly stir in the orange juice. Bring to a boil, stirring constantly.

3 Carefully add the bananas. Cook for 3 to 4 minutes or just until bananas are heated through, stirring occasionally. Stir in the rum. Makes 6 servings.

Prep Time: 10 minutes Cooking Time: 8 minutes

1 Serving: Calories 240. Total Fat 4 g. Saturated Fat 3 g.
Protein 2 g. Carbohydrate 50 g. Fiber 3 g.
Sodium 54 mg. Cholesterol 10 mg.

Shaker Baked Apples

Many old-time recipes instruct the cook to cut a strip of peel from around the top of each apple. This keeps the apple skins from splitting during baking.

4 **medium-size tart cooking apples, cored**
½ **cup currants or raisins**
2 **tablespoons honey**
½ **teaspoon apple pie spice or ground cinnamon**
½ **teaspoon grated lemon rind**
½ **cup apple juice**

1 Preheat the oven to 350°F. Peel a strip from the top of each apple. Place the apples into a 9-inch round baking pan.

2 In a small bowl, combine the currants, honey, apple pie spice, and lemon rind. Spoon the currant mixture into the centers of the apples. Pour the apple juice into the baking pan.

3 Bake for 40 to 45 minutes or until the apples are just tender, basting occasionally with the apple juice in bottom of dish. Serve warm with low-fat (1% milkfat) milk or reduced-fat vanilla ice cream. Makes 4 servings.

Prep Time: 15 minutes Cooking Time: 40 minutes

1 Serving: Calories 180. Total Fat 1 g. Saturated Fat 0 g.
Protein 1 g. Carbohydrate 47 g. Fiber 4 g.
Sodium 3 mg. Cholesterol 0 mg.

HOMEMADE ICE CREAM

*B**ack before families had refrigerators with
freezers, ice was a precious commodity. Ice
wagons made regular deliveries to people in
town, but rural folks had to go into town and pick
ice up at the icehouse. That's why, back then, families
made and ate more ice cream in the winter—when there
was plenty of "free" ice—than they did in the summer.*

*Today, store-bought ice cream is a year-round treat. But
for birthdays, anniversarys, graduations, housewarmings,
and other special occasions, it's fun to make old-fashioned
ice cream just like grandma did. The extra-special good
taste will remind your family and friends
of the simple pleasures of yesteryear.*

PEACH ICE CREAM

- 4 **large egg yolks**
- 1 **cup sugar**
- 2 **cups low-fat (1% milkfat) milk**
- 3 **cups pureed, fresh or frozen and thawed, peeled, peaches**
- 1 **tablespoon vanilla**
- ½ **teaspoon salt**
- 2 **cups half-and-half**

1. In a large heavy saucepan, whisk together the egg yolks and sugar
until pale, smooth, and creamy. Whisk in the milk. Cook over moderate
heat, whisking constantly, for 8 to 10 minutes or until mixture coats
a metal spoon. Remove from heat. Place saucepan in a bath of ice water
for 2 to 3 minutes, stirring constantly.

2. Transfer the milk mixture to a large bowl. Stir in the peaches, vanilla,
and salt. Cover surface with plastic wrap; refrigerate for 30 minutes,
stirring occasionally. Stir in the half-and-half.

MATERIALS

**4- or 5-quart ice cream
freezer**
Crushed ice
Rock salt

TO FREEZE ICE CREAM

1 Pour the ice cream mixture into the freezer can of a 4- or 5-quart ice cream freezer. Fit the can into the outer freezer bucket. Insert the dasher, then cover with the freezer can lid. Fit the electric motor or hand crank into place.

2 Add alternate layers of crushed ice and rock salt. (Follow the manufacturer's directions for the proportions.) Be sure to place the ice cream freezer where it can drain during freezing. Freeze until done according to manufacturer's directions, adding ice and salt occasionally as ice melts.

3 If using an electric freezer, unplug. Carefully drain off water through the drain hole in outer freezer bucket. Remove the motor or crank. Before opening the can, make sure the ice and salt are below the level of the can lid so that no melted ice seeps into the can. Wipe the can and lid with a damp paper towel. Leaving freezer can in the bucket, remove the lid and dasher. Use a rubber spatula or spoon to scrape the dasher.

4 To ripen ice cream, cover the top of the freezer can with a sheet of waxed paper. Before replacing lid on can, plug the hole in the lid with some waxed paper. Pack the outer freezer bucket with ice and salt, covering the top of the ice cream can. (Follow manufacturer's directions for the proportions.) Then cover the ice- and salt-packed ice cream freezer with several layers of newspapers. Let stand for 4 hours. Drain off water and add extra salt and ice as necessary during ripening. Makes 8 cups (sixteen ½-cup servings).

Strawberry Ice Cream
Prepare as for Peach Ice Cream, substituting **strawberries or raspberries** for the peaches. (Sieve the berries after pureeing to remove the seeds; discard the seeds, then measure 3 cups puree.) Add **1 teaspoon grated orange rind** with the fruit. Makes 8 cups (sixteen ½-cup servings).

Double Chocolate Ice Cream
Prepare as for Peach Ice Cream, omitting the peaches, substituting **2 cups chocolate low-fat (2% milkfat) milk** for the low-fat (1% milkfat) milk, and adding **1 cup light chocolate-flavored syrup** with the vanilla. Makes 7 cups (fourteen ½-cup servings).

Fresh Strawberry-Orange Sherbet

Nothing was better on a hot summer day than sherbet made in a hand-crank ice cream freezer.

2 **cups sugar**

2 **cups orange juice**

4 **cups pureed fresh strawberries or raspberries**

1 In a medium-size saucepan, combine the sugar and orange juice. Bring to a boil over moderate heat, stirring constantly with a wooden spoon to dissolve sugar. Remove from heat. Transfer the orange mixture to a large bowl. Refrigerate for 30 minutes.

2 Meanwhile, using a wire strainer, sieve the pureed berries to remove the seeds; discard seeds. Stir the strawberries into the orange mixture.

3 Pour the berry-orange mixture into the freezer can of a 4- or 5-quart ice cream freezer. Fit the can into the outer freezer bucket. Insert the dasher, then cover with the freezer can lid. Fit electric motor or hand crank into place. Add ice and salt (page 345). Freeze according to manufacturer's directions. Makes 8 cups (sixteen ½-cup servings).

Prep Time: 10 minutes Chilling Time: 30 minutes
Freezing Time: 35 minutes

1 Serving: Calories 123. Total Fat 0 g. Saturated Fat 0 g. Protein 0 g. Carbohydrate 31 g. Fiber 1 g. Sodium 1 mg. Cholesterol 0 mg.

Indian Pudding

In colonial days, Indian pudding was a simple cornmeal mush sweetened with molasses.
In later years, it was dressed up with everything from sugar and eggs to raisins and spices.

2 **cups low-fat (1% milkfat) milk**

¼ **cup dark molasses**

¼ **cup cornmeal**

2 **large egg whites**

3 **tablespoons firmly packed light brown sugar**

1 **tablespoon butter or margarine, melted**

½ **teaspoon ground cinnamon or pumpkin pie spice**

⅛ **teaspoon salt**

¼ **cup raisins**

1 **tablespoon chopped crystallized ginger (optional)**

1 Preheat the oven to 300°F. In a medium-size saucepan, combine the milk and molasses. Stir in the cornmeal. Cook, stirring constantly, over moderate heat for 5 to 6 minutes or until thick. Set aside.

2 In a medium-size bowl, combine the egg whites, brown sugar, butter, cinnamon, and salt. Stir into the cornmeal mixture. Stir in the raisins and ginger (if using). Spoon mixture into an 8-inch round baking dish. Bake for 45 minutes. Makes 4 servings.

Prep Time: 10 minutes Cooking Time: 50 minutes

1 Serving: Calories 228. Total Fat 4 g. Saturated Fat 3 g. Protein 7 g. Carbohydrate 42 g. Fiber 1 g. Sodium 197 mg. Cholesterol 13 mg.

Scandinavian Rice Pudding

Scandinavian women made rice pudding without eggs and cooked it in a saucepan, like porridge. To keep the rice snowy white, they added the raisins at the end.

2½ **cups low-fat (1% milkfat) milk**

⅓ **cup uncooked long-grain white rice**

¼ **cup sugar**

¼ **teaspoon salt**

¼ **teaspoon ground cinnamon**

⅓ **cup raisins**

1 **teaspoon vanilla**

1 In a medium-size saucepan, bring the milk just to a boil. Stir in the rice, sugar, salt, and cinnamon. Return to boiling. Lower the heat and simmer, covered, for 45 minutes or until most of the milk is absorbed and the rice is creamy, stirring occasionally.

2 Meanwhile, in a small bowl, pour enough boiling water over raisins to cover. Let stand for 10 minutes or until raisins are plump; drain well.

3 Stir the raisins and vanilla into the rice mixture. Cover and let stand on a wire rack for 5 minutes. Serve warm. Makes 3 servings.

Prep Time: 5 minutes Cooking Time: 55 minutes
Standing Time: 5 minutes

1 Serving: Calories 282. Total Fat 2 g. Saturated Fat 1 g. Protein 9 g. Carbohydrate 57 g. Fiber 1 g. Sodium 284 mg. Cholesterol 8 mg.

Jewish Noodle Pudding

Jewish Noodle Pudding

*Jewish grandmas made one version of this traditional dessert without
dairy products so it could be enjoyed with a meat meal. Other recipes, like this one,
included sour cream, milk, or cheese and were eaten with a dairy meal.*

4 **large egg whites**

1 **large egg**

1 **container (8 ounces) reduced-fat sour cream**

½ **cup low-fat (1% milkfat) milk**

¼ **cup sugar**

2 **tablespoons all -purpose flour**

1 **teaspoon vanilla**

¼ **teaspoon ground cinnamon**

⅛ **teaspoon ground allspice**

3 **ounces wide noodles, cooked and drained**

½ **cup chopped, peeled, tart cooking apple**

⅓ **cup mixed dried fruit bits or raisins**

2 **tablespoons sugar**

⅛ **teaspoon ground cinnamon**

1 Preheat the oven to 350°F. In a large bowl, stir together the egg whites, egg, sour cream, milk, the ¼ cup sugar, flour, vanilla, the ¼ teaspoon cinnamon, and allspice. Stir in the noodles, apple, and fruit bits.

2 Spoon the noodle mixture into a lightly greased 1½-quart casserole. In a small bowl, combine the 2 tablespoons sugar and the ⅛ teaspoon cinnamon.

3 Bake for 15 minutes. Stir mixture. Sprinkle the sugar-cinnamon mixture over the noodles. Bake for 12 to 15 minutes more or until the noodle mixture is almost set in the center. Remove from oven. Let stand on a wire rack for 5 minutes. Makes 4 servings.

Prep Time: 25 minutes Cooking Time: 27 minutes
Standing Time: 5 minutes

1 Serving: Calories 325. Total Fat 9 g. Saturated Fat 5 g.
Protein 11 g. Carbohydrate 50 g. Fiber 1 g.
Sodium 121 mg. Cholesterol 93 mg.

Christmas Plum Pudding with Brandied Cider Sauce

Christmas Plum Pudding with Brandied Cider Sauce

*Although often confused with fruitcake, this classic Christmas dessert tastes
more like a rich, dense spice cake. This version uses butter instead of the traditional
suet and can be made with your choice of candied fruit, currants, or raisins.*

1¼ cups all-purpose flour	4 large egg whites
1 teaspoon grated orange rind	½ cup apple cider or apple juice
1 teaspoon ground cinnamon	¾ cup raisins
¾ teaspoon baking powder	½ cup shredded carrot
½ teaspoon ground ginger	⅓ cup candied cherries, halved, or currants or raisins
⅛ teaspoon ground cloves	⅓ cup chopped candied pineapple, currants, or raisins
½ cup firmly packed light brown sugar	⅓ cup pecan halves
¼ cup butter or margarine, at room temperature	Brandied Cider Sauce (recipe, opposite)

1 Lightly grease a 1½-quart steamed pudding mold or casserole. In a medium-size bowl, stir together the flour, orange rind, cinnamon, baking powder, ginger, and cloves.

2 In a large bowl, with an electric mixer on *Medium,* cream the brown sugar and butter until light and fluffy, scraping side of bowl often. Add the egg whites and beat well. Using a wooden spoon, stir in one-third of the flour mixture, then half of the apple cider. Repeat, then stir in the remaining flour mixture. Stir in the raisins, carrot, cherries, pineapple, and pecans.

3 Spoon the batter evenly into the prepared mold. Cover mold with foil. Tie foil in place with string.

4 Place mold on a rack in a Dutch oven. Pour boiling water into the Dutch oven until the water is halfway up the side of the mold. Cook, covered, over low heat for 2 to 2½ hours or until a toothpick inserted in the center comes out clean.

5 Place mold upright on a wire rack and let stand for 10 minutes. Using a narrow metal spatula, loosen side of plum pudding from the mold, then invert the pudding onto a serving plate. Serve warm with Brandied Cider Sauce; top with vanilla ice cream if you like. (Or, cover and refrigerate the pudding—will keep for 1 week. To reheat the pudding, steam as directed in step 4 for 1 hour or until heated through.) Serves 8.

Prep Time: 25 minutes Cooking Time: 2 hours
Standing Time: 10 minutes

1 Serving: Calories 347. Total Fat 10 g. Saturated Fat 4 g.
Protein 5 g. Carbohydrate 61 g. Fiber 2 g.
Sodium 148 mg. Cholesterol 17 mg.

Brandied Cider Sauce

In a small saucepan, whisk together ¾ **cup apple cider or apple juice,** ¼ **cup firmly packed light brown sugar,** and **1 tablespoon cornstarch.** Bring to a boil over moderate heat, whisking constantly. Cook for 2 minutes or until the mixture is thickened, whisking constantly. Stir in **2 tablespoons brandy or apple juice** and **1 teaspoon butter or margarine.** Makes about ¾ cup.

1½ Tablespoons: Calories 44. Total Fat 1 g. Saturated Fat 0 g.
Protein 0 g. Carbohydrate 8 g. Fiber 0 g.
Sodium 7 mg. Cholesterol 1 mg.

Chocolate Bread Pudding

Grandma made bread pudding to use up stale bread. If you don't have any, cut fresh bread into cubes, cover them with paper towels, and air-dry at room temperature for 8 to 12 hours.

4 **cups dried home-style bread or French bread cubes**
2 **cups chocolate low-fat (2% milkfat) milk or low-fat (1% milkfat) milk**
1 **cup sugar**
⅓ **cup unsweetened cocoa**
1 **teaspoon ground cinnamon**
2 **large egg whites**
1 **large egg**
2 **tablespoons butter or margarine, melted**
1 **tablespoon vanilla**
⅓ **cup chopped pecans (optional)**

1 Preheat oven to 350°F. Lightly grease an 8" x 8" x 2" baking dish. In a large bowl, place the bread cubes. Pour the chocolate milk over bread cubes; stir and mash until the bread is well soaked. (Mixture should be very moist but not soupy. If needed, add more chocolate milk, 1 tablespoon at a time, until bread is well soaked.)

2 In a small bowl, combine the sugar, cocoa, and cinnamon. In a medium-size bowl, use a rotary beater to beat together the egg whites, egg, butter, and vanilla. Add the sugar mixture, then beat until combined. Stir in the pecans (if using). Add the egg mixture to the bread mixture. Gently stir until combined.

3 Turn the mixture into the prepared dish. Bake, covered, for 30 minutes. Uncover and bake for 10 to 15 minutes more or until almost set in the center. Let stand on a wire rack for 5 minutes. Serve with frozen and thawed reduced-fat whipped dessert topping or reduced-fat vanilla ice cream. Makes 9 servings.

Prep Time: 15 minutes Cooking Time: 40 minutes
Standing Time: 5 minutes

1 Serving: Calories 223. Total Fat 5 g. Saturated Fat 3 g.
Protein 6 g. Carbohydrate 40 g. Fiber 2 g.
Sodium 173 mg. Cholesterol 35 mg.

Double Fudge Brownies

A surefire method for getting brownies out of the pan is to line the pan with foil before adding the batter. Then, once the brownies are cooled, lift the entire block out of the pan and cut it into squares or rectangles.

¾ **cup all-purpose flour**
⅓ **cup unsweetened cocoa**
¼ **teaspoon baking powder**
 1 **cup granulated sugar**
½ **cup butter or margarine, at room temperature**
 2 **large egg whites**
 1 **large egg**
 1 **teaspoon vanilla**
½ **cup miniature semisweet chocolate chips**
½ **cup coarsely chopped walnuts (optional)**
   Confectioners sugar

1 Preheat the oven to 350°F. In a medium-size bowl, combine the flour, cocoa, and baking powder. In a large bowl, with an electric mixer on *Medium*, cream the granulated sugar and butter until light yellow and fluffy, scraping side of bowl often. Add the egg whites, egg, and vanilla, beating well.

2 Using a wooden spoon, stir in the flour mixture just until flour disappears. Stir in the chocolate chips and walnuts (if using).

3 Spoon evenly into a lightly greased 8" x 8" x 2" baking pan; smooth the surface. Bake for 25 to 30 minutes or until a toothpick inserted in the center comes out clean and brownies begin to pull away from edges of pan. Cool on a wire rack. Lightly sift confectioners sugar over top. Makes 16 brownies.

Prep Time: 15 minutes Cooking Time: 25 minutes

1 Brownie: Calories 157. Total Fat 8 g. Saturated Fat 5 g. Protein 2 g. Carbohydrate 21 g. Fiber 1 g. Sodium 78 mg. Cholesterol 29 mg.

BAKING WITH MARGARINE

• For best results when baking, use a stick product that says "margarine" on the label. Check carefully to be sure you aren't buying soft-style, diet, or spread margarine products. Also, don't use products sold in tubs. All these products have extra water which will cause your cookies to fail.

♦ Corn-oil margarine is fine for baking but it makes a softer cookie dough than butter. For shaped, sliced, or cutout cookies, chill doughs made with this margarine in the freezer a few hours or until easy to handle.

Hermits

This recipe dates back to colonial New England.

 2 **cups all-purpose flour**
 1 **teaspoon baking soda**
 1 **teaspoon ground cinnamon**
¼ **teaspoon ground allspice or ground nutmeg**
½ **cup sugar**
½ **cup butter or margarine, at room temperature**
½ **cup molasses**
 2 **large egg whites**
 1 **large egg**
½ **cup currants or raisins**
⅓ **cup finely chopped walnuts or pecans**

1 Preheat the oven to 375°F. In a medium-size bowl, combine the flour, baking soda, cinnamon, and allspice. In a large bowl, with an electric mixer on *Medium*, cream the sugar and butter until light yellow and fluffy, scraping side of bowl often. Add the molasses, egg whites, and egg; beat well. Using a wooden spoon, stir in the flour mixture just until flour disappears. Fold in the currants and walnuts.

2 Drop dough by rounded tablespoonfuls, 2 inches apart, onto lightly greased baking sheets. Bake for 8 to 9 minutes or until edges are brown. Remove cookies and cool on wire racks. Lightly sift confectioners sugar over if you like. Makes about 36 cookies.

Prep Time: 15 minutes Cooking Time: 24 minutes

1 Cookie: Calories 87. Total Fat 3 g. Saturated Fat 2 g. Protein 1 g. Carbohydrate 13 g. Fiber 0 g. Sodium 68 mg. Cholesterol 13 mg.

Favorite Oatmeal Cookies

Favorite Oatmeal Cookies

*Grandma dropped her cookie dough from a spoon, but a small
ice cream scoop can make the job go quicker and easier.*

- 2 **cups all-purpose flour**
- 2 **teaspoons ground cinnamon**
- 1 **teaspoon baking powder**
- 1 **teaspoon baking soda**
- 2 **cups sugar**
- 1 **cup butter or margarine, at room temperature**
- 1/4 **cup low-fat (1% milkfat) milk**
- 2 **large egg whites**
- 2 **large eggs**
- 2 **teaspoons vanilla**
- 3 **cups old-fashioned (5 minutes) or quick-cooking (1 minute) rolled oats**

1 Preheat the oven to 375°F. In a medium-size bowl, combine the flour, cinnamon, baking powder, and baking soda. In a large bowl, with an electric mixer on *Medium*, cream the sugar and butter until light yellow and fluffy, scraping side of bowl often. Add the milk, egg whites, eggs, and vanilla, beating well. Using a wooden spoon, stir in the flour mixture just until flour disappears. Stir in the oats.

2 Drop dough by rounded tablespoonfuls, 2 inches apart, onto ungreased baking sheets. Bake for 8 to 10 minutes or until edges are light brown. Remove cookies and cool on wire racks. Makes about 42.

Prep Time: 15 minutes Cooking Time: 32 minutes

1 Cookie: Calories 125. Total Fat 5 g. Saturated Fat 3 g.
Protein 2 g. Carbohydrate 18 g. Fiber 1 g.
Sodium 93 mg. Cholesterol 22 mg.

Raisin 'n' Walnut Oatmeal Cookies Prepare as for Favorite Oatmeal Cookies, adding **1½ cups raisins or 1 package (8 ounces) chopped pitted dates** and **1 cup coarsely chopped walnuts** with the oats. Makes about 48 cookies.

1 Cookie: Calories 141. Total Fat 6 g. Saturated Fat 3 g.
Protein 2 g. Carbohydrate 21 g. Fiber 1 g.
Sodium 82 mg. Cholesterol 19 mg.

Sour Cream Sugar Cookies

Sour Cream Sugar Cookies

"Grandmother Helen made cookies for all the holidays," reminisces Paula Secker. "Her Valentine's Day cookies were my favorite. She always made them heart shaped with pink frosting and packed them in a coffee tin. Whenever I saw that coffee tin, I knew exactly what was in it and who it was from."

  3 **cups all-purpose flour**
1¼ **teaspoons baking powder**
  ½ **teaspoon baking soda**
  ½ **teaspoon ground nutmeg or ground cinnamon (optional)**
  ⅛ **teaspoon salt**
1½ **cups granulated sugar**
  ½ **cup butter or margarine, at room temperature**
  1 **cup reduced-fat sour cream**
  1 **large egg**
  2 **teaspoons vanilla**
For the glaze:
  2 **cups sifted confectioners sugar**
  3 **tablespoons low-fat (1% milkfat) milk**
  ½ **teaspoon vanilla**
   Paste or liquid food coloring (optional)

1 In a medium-size bowl, combine the flour, baking powder, baking soda, nutmeg (if using), and salt. In a large bowl, with an electric mixer on *Medium*, cream the granulated sugar and butter, beating until fluffy, scraping side of bowl often.

2 Add the sour cream, egg, and the 2 teaspoons vanilla, beating well. Using a wooden spoon, stir in the flour mixture just until flour disappears. Divide the dough into 3 equal pieces. Wrap each piece of dough in plastic wrap. Refrigerate for 1 hour or until thoroughly chilled and easy to handle.

3 Preheat the oven to 375°F. On a lightly floured surface, roll out 1 piece of dough to ¼ inch thickness and cut into shapes with cookie cutters. With a spatula, transfer the cookies to ungreased cookie sheets, placing them 2 inches apart. Bake for 8 to 10 minutes or until the edges are firm and bottoms are lightly browned. Remove cookies and cool on wire racks. Repeat with remaining dough.

4 To prepare the glaze, in a medium-size bowl, stir together confectioners sugar, half of the milk, the ½ teaspoon vanilla, and a little food coloring (if using).

Gradually stir in enough of the remaining milk to make mixture of glazing consistency. Spread the top of each cooled cookie with some of the glaze. Allow glaze to dry completely. Store cookies in an airtight container (do not freeze glazed cookies). Makes about 36 cookies.

Prep Time: 40 minutes Chilling Time: 1 hour
Cooking Time: 24 minutes

1 Serving: Calories 127. Total Fat 4 g. Saturated Fat 2 g. Protein 2 g. Carbohydrate 22 g. Fiber 0 g. Sodium 73 mg. Cholesterol 15 mg.

Peanut Butter Icebox Cookies

"My Grandma Emma's peanut butter cookies always smelled and tasted wonderful," says Marge Steenson. "She taught me her special way of slicing them. She'd keep the roll of dough evenly rounded by giving it a quarter turn after slicing off each cookie."

  2 **cups all-purpose flour**
  ¾ **teaspoon baking soda**
  ½ **cup butter or margarine, at room temperature**
  ½ **cup chunky peanut butter**
  ⅓ **cup granulated sugar**
  ⅓ **cup firmly packed light brown sugar**
  ¼ **cup low-fat (1% milkfat) milk**
  1 **teaspoon vanilla**

1 In a medium-size bowl, combine the flour and baking soda. In a large bowl, with an electric mixer on *Medium*, cream the butter and peanut butter until well mixed. Add the granulated sugar and brown sugar and beat until light and fluffy, scraping side of bowl often. Add the milk and vanilla, beating well. Using a wooden spoon, stir in flour mixture just until flour disappears.

2 Shape the cookie dough into two 6-inch-long rolls. Wrap each roll of dough in plastic wrap. Refrigerate for 4 to 48 hours.

3 Preheat the oven to 375°F. Using a sharp knife, cut the rolls of dough into ¼-inch-thick slices. Place the slices 1 inch apart onto ungreased baking sheets. Bake for 7 to 8 minutes or until edges are firm and light brown. Remove cookies and cool on wire racks. Makes about 36 cookies.

Prep Time: 20 minutes Chilling Time: 4 hours
Cooking Time: 21 minutes

1 Serving: Calories 82. Total Fat 4 g. Saturated Fat 2 g. Protein 2 g. Carbohydrate 9 g. Fiber 0 g. Sodium 71 mg. Cholesterol 7 mg.

Snickerdoodles

This old-fashioned cookie with its unusual name first appeared in cookbooks in the mid to late 1800's. Depending on the recipe, it can be either a soft or crisp cookie, but it always is sprinkled with or rolled in cinnamon-sugar and has a crackly top.

- 3 **cups all-purpose flour**
- 1 **teaspoon baking soda**
- ½ **teaspoon ground nutmeg or ground cinnamon (optional)**
- ¼ **teaspoon cream of tartar**
- 1 **cup firmly packed light brown sugar**
- ½ **cup butter or margarine, at room temperature**
- 2 **large egg whites**
- 1 **large egg**
- 1 **teaspoon vanilla**
- ⅓ **cup currants**
- ⅓ **cup chopped walnuts**
- 3 **tablespoons granulated sugar**
- 1½ **teaspoons ground cinnamon**

1 In a medium-size bowl, combine the flour, baking soda, nutmeg (if using), and cream of tartar. In a large bowl, with an electric mixer on *Medium,* cream the brown sugar and butter until light and fluffy, scraping side of bowl often.

2 Add the egg whites, egg, and vanilla; beat well. Using a wooden spoon, stir in the flour mixture just until flour disappears. Stir in the currants and walnuts. Cover and refrigerate for 3 to 4 hours.

3 Preheat the oven to 350°F. In a small bowl, stir together the granulated sugar and cinnamon. Shape the dough into 1-inch balls. Roll in the sugar-cinnamon mixture. Place the balls 2 inches apart onto lightly greased baking sheets. Using the bottom of a drinking glass, slightly flatten each ball of dough.

4 Bake for 8 to 10 minutes or until edges are firm and light brown. Cool on baking sheets for 1 minute. Remove cookies and cool on wire racks. Makes about 48 cookies.

Prep Time: 20 minutes Chilling Time: 3 hours
Cooking Time: 32 minutes

1 Cookie: Calories 71. Total Fat 3 g. Saturated Fat 1 g.
Protein 1 g. Carbohydrate 11 g. Fiber 0 g.
Sodium 51 mg. Cholesterol 10 mg.

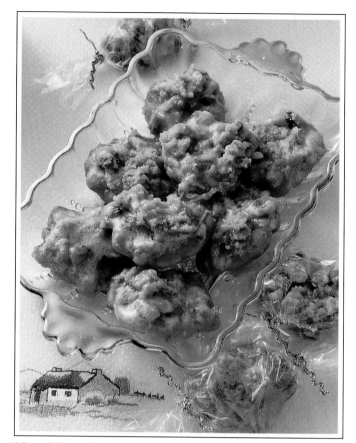

New Orleans Pralines

New Orleans Pralines

This candy is an old New Orleans favorite. Be sure the nuts are at room temperature (or slightly warm if just toasted) when you stir them into the sugar syrup. If they're cold, they'll cool down the syrup and the candy will harden too quickly.

- 1½ **cups granulated sugar**
- 1 **cup low-fat (1% milkfat) milk**
- ¾ **cup firmly packed light brown sugar**
- 3 **tablespoons butter or margarine**
- 2 **teaspoons vanilla**
- 1 **cup coarsely chopped pecans, toasted (optional)**

1 Line a baking sheet with foil. Lightly butter the foil. In a large heavy saucepan, combine the granulated sugar, milk, brown sugar, butter, and vanilla. Bring to a boil over moderately high heat, stirring constantly with a wooden spoon to dissolve sugar. (Avoid splashing mixture onto side of the pan.) Boil for 3 minutes. If using a candy thermometer, clip to side of pan, making sure bulb is immersed but not touching bottom of pan.

2 Cook over moderate heat, stirring occasionally, to 240°F. on candy thermometer, soft-ball stage (15 to 18 minutes). (Or, use this cold water test. Using spoon, drop a small amount of hot mixture into very cold, but not icy, water. Dip your fingers into the water and form mixture into a ball. Remove ball from water; it should immediately flatten and run between your fingers.)

3 Remove pan from heat; remove the thermometer from saucepan. Stir in the pecans (if using). Stir vigorously with the wooden spoon until mixture is slightly thick, beginning to look cloudy, and the pecans stay suspended in candy mixture (4 to 5 minutes).

4 Working quickly, drop by teaspoonfuls onto the prepared foil, spreading each to 1½ inches. If mixture becomes too stiff, stir in very hot water, a few drops at a time, until it is a softer consistency. Cool 30 minutes or until candies are firm and no longer glossy. To store, wrap each piece in plastic wrap. Makes about 32 pieces.

Prep Time: 15 minutes Cooking Time: 28 minutes
Cooling Time: 30 minutes

1 Piece: Calories 62. Total Fat 1 g. Saturated Fat 1 g.
Protein 0 g. Carbohydrate 13 g. Fiber 0 g.
Sodium 16 mg. Cholesterol 3 mg.

Old-Fashioned Taffy

Taffy pulls are fondly remembered by folks who grew up during the first half of this century. The suspense of waiting for the syrup to cook and then cool to just the right stage was almost unbearable. When the pulling finally began, it was almost magical to see how the candy turned from translucent to creamy.

2 **cups sugar**
1 **cup dark corn syrup**
1 **cup water**
1 **teaspoon salt**
2 **tablespoons butter or margarine**
2 **teaspoons vanilla**

1 Butter a 15½" x 10½" x 1" baking pan; set aside. In a large heavy saucepan, combine the sugar, corn syrup, water, and salt. Bring to a boil over moderately high heat, stirring constantly with a wooden spoon to dissolve sugar. (Avoid splashing mixture onto side of the pan.) Boil for 2 minutes. If using a candy thermometer, clip to side of pan, making sure bulb is immersed but not touching bottom of pan.

2 Cook over moderate heat, without stirring, to 265°F. on candy thermometer, hard-ball stage (15 to 20 minutes). (Or, use this cold water test. Using a spoon, drop a small amount of hot mixture into very cold, but not icy, water. Dip your fingers into the water and form the mixture into a ball. Remove the ball from the water; it should not flatten but can be deformed by pressure.)

3 Remove the pan from heat; remove the thermometer from the saucepan. Immediately stir in the butter and vanilla. Quickly pour mixture into prepared pan. Set the pan on a wire rack and cool just until taffy mixture can be handled easily (15 to 20 minutes). Carefully check hot taffy mixture to avoid getting burned. It may be cool on surface, but extremely hot underneath, so gather up mixture carefully. You will need 3 helpers.

4 With well-buttered hands, divide taffy into fourths and carefully shape warm taffy mixture into 4 balls. With each person working 1 ball, pull, fold, and twist mixture until it turns a creamy color and is stiff and quite difficult to pull (12 to 16 minutes). To keep taffy from sticking, lightly butter your hands as necessary.

5 Taffy is ready to snip when the end cracks off as it is tapped against a work surface (tip, below). Twist and pull each piece of pulled taffy into a long strand about ½ inch thick. Using buttered kitchen scissors, snip each strand of taffy into bite-size pieces. Let stand at room temperature for 2 hours to harden.

6 To store, wrap each piece of taffy in plastic wrap. (This prevents the taffy from becoming soft and sticky.) Makes about 1½ pounds (48 pieces).

Prep Time: 35 minutes Cooking Time: 25 minutes
Cooling Time: 15 minutes Standing Time: 2 hours

1 Piece: Calories 56. Total Fat 0 g. Saturated Fat 0 g.
Protein 0 g. Carbohydrate 14 g. Fiber 0 g.
Sodium 60 mg. Cholesterol 1 mg.

MAKING TAFFY

To tell if the taffy is ready to snip, tap it on your work surface. If the candy cracks, cut it into pieces. If it doesn't crack, pull it a few more minutes.

Divine Divinity

Divine Divinity

*"Grandma Dorothy's divinity melts in your mouth! I ask for it
every year," says Michelle Thiering. "I place my order at Thanksgiving
and on Christmas Eve, it's ready and waiting for me to dig in."*

2½ **cups sugar**

⅔ **cup light corn syrup**

½ **cup water**

2 **large egg whites**

1½ **teaspoons vanilla**

⅔ **cup coarsely chopped pecans or walnuts or chopped
red or green candied cherries (optional)**

1 Line a baking sheet with waxed paper. In a large heavy saucepan, combine the sugar, corn syrup, and water. Bring to a boil over moderately high heat, stirring constantly with a wooden spoon to dissolve sugar. (Avoid splashing mixture onto side of the pan.) Boil for 3 minutes. If using a candy thermometer, carefully clip to side of the pan, making sure the bulb is immersed but not touching the bottom of the pan.

2 Cook over moderate heat, without stirring, to 260°F. on candy thermometer, hard-ball stage (15 to 18 minutes). (Or, use this cold water test. Using a spoon, drop a small amount of hot mixture into very cold, but not icy, water. Dip your fingers into the water and form the mixture into a ball. Remove the ball from the water; it should not flatten but can be deformed by pressure.)

3 Remove pan from heat; remove the thermometer from saucepan. In a large bowl, with very clean beaters and an electric mixer on *Medium to High*, beat the egg whites until stiff peaks form. Slowly pour hot syrup mixture in a fine stream over egg whites, beating with electric mixer on *High* for 3 minutes and scraping the side of the bowl occasionally.

4 Add the vanilla. Continue beating with the electric mixer on *High* just until candy starts to lose its gloss and holds soft peaks (5 to 6 minutes), scraping the side of the bowl occasionally. Stir in nuts (if using).

5 Working quickly, drop by teaspoonfuls onto waxed paper. If the divinity becomes too stiff, beat in very hot water, a few drops at a time, until it is a softer consistency. Cool completely. To store, cover tightly. Makes about 36 pieces.

Prep Time: 20 minutes Cooking Time: 25 minutes

1 Piece: Calories 72. Total Fat 0 g. Saturated Fat 0 g.
Protein 0 g. Carbohydrate 19 g. Fiber 0 g.
Sodium 11 mg. Cholesterol 0 mg.

MAKING DIVINITY

◆ Choose a dry day. Because sugar absorbs moisture from the air, divinity may never set up if you try to make it on a humid day.

◆ Start with room temperature egg whites. They beat up to a greater volume than cold egg whites.

◆ Use a heavy-duty, freestanding electric mixer. Beating divinity puts a strain on a mixer's motor. Portable mixers and lightweight freestanding mixers may not have heavy enough motors.

◆ Follow the recipe directions carefully. Timing is important. Adding the hot syrup too quickly or not beating the candy mixture long enough can cause divinity to fail. Overbeating the divinity will cause it to set up before you can drop it into individual pieces.

Old-Time Peanut Brittle

The key to perfect brittle is adding baking soda. It reacts with the caramelized sugar to make the candy porous and not too hard—so it's easy to eat.

¾ **cup sugar**
¾ **cup light corn syrup**
¼ **cup water**
3 **tablespoons butter or margarine, at room temperature**
1½ **cups shelled raw peanuts or coarsely chopped raw cashews**
2 **teaspoons vanilla**
1 **teaspoon baking soda**

1 Butter a large baking sheet; set aside. In a large heavy saucepan, combine the sugar, corn syrup, water, and butter. Bring to a boil over moderately high heat, stirring constantly with a wooden spoon to dissolve sugar. (Avoid splashing mixture onto side of the pan.) Boil for 3 minutes. If using a candy thermometer, carefully clip to the side of the pan, making sure the bulb is immersed but not touching the bottom of pan.

2 Cook over moderate heat, stirring occasionally, to 240°F. on candy thermometer, soft-ball stage (10 to 12 minutes). (Or, use this cold water test. Using a spoon, drop small amount of hot mixture into very cold, but not icy, water. Dip your fingers into water and form mixture into a ball. Remove ball from water; it should immediately flatten and run between your fingers.)

3 Stir in peanuts. Cook over moderate heat, stirring constantly, to 300°F. on candy thermometer, hard-crack stage (10 to 15 minutes). (Using a spoon, drop a small amount of hot mixture into very cold, but not icy, water. It should separate into hard, brittle threads that snap easily.) Watch carefully so mixture does not burn.

4 Remove the pan from heat; remove the thermometer from the saucepan. Immediately stir vanilla and baking soda into hot mixture, stirring constantly until light and foamy. Quickly pour and spread mixture onto prepared baking sheet.

5 With 2 forks, lift and pull candy into 14x12-inch rectangle. Pull gently to avoid tearing. Cool completely on wire rack. Break candy into pieces. To store, cover tightly. Makes about 1 pound (50 pieces).

Prep Time: 20 minutes Cooking Time: 30 minutes

1 Piece: Calories 57. Total Fat 3 g. Saturated Fat 1 g.
Protein 1 g. Carbohydrate 7 g. Fiber 0 g.
Sodium 39 mg. Cholesterol 2 mg.

Mamie Eisenhower Fudge

When Mamie Eisenhower came to the White House, she brought along a recipe for fudge that called for marshmallow creme. Her candy was so creamy the President reportedly called it the "million dollar" fudge.

1 package (12 ounces) semisweet chocolate chips
1 package (11½ ounces) milk chocolate chips
1 jar (7 ounces) marshmallow creme
1½ cups chopped walnuts
2 teaspoons vanilla
4 cups sugar
1 can (12 ounces) evaporated skimmed milk
2 tablespoons butter or margarine

1 Line a 13" x 9" x 2" baking pan with foil, extending the foil over edges of pan. Lightly butter foil; set aside. In a large bowl, combine the semisweet chocolate chips, milk chocolate chips, marshmallow creme, walnuts, and vanilla.

2 In a heavy large saucepan, stir together the sugar, evaporated skimmed milk, and butter. Bring to boil over moderate heat, stirring constantly with a wooden spoon to dissolve sugar. (Avoid splashing mixture onto side of the pan.) Lower the heat to moderately low. Stir and boil for 12 minutes. Remove from heat.

3 Carefully pour the boiling mixture over the chocolate mixture. Stir until the chocolate is melted and the mixture is creamy and well combined. Quickly turn the fudge into prepared pan. While fudge is warm, use the tip of a small knife to score into 1-inch squares.

4 When fudge is firm, lift it out of pan; cut into squares (tip, above right). To store, cover tightly and refrigerate. Makes about 3½ pounds (117 pieces).

Prep Time: 20 minutes Cooking Time: 20 minutes

1 Piece: Calories 75. Total Fat 3 g. Saturated Fat 1 g. Protein 1 g. Carbohydrate 12 g. Fiber 0 g. Sodium 9 mg. Cholesterol 1 mg.

CUTTING FUDGE

By lining the pan with foil, you can remove the fudge quickly and easily.

◆ When the candy is firm, grasp the foil and lift the block of fudge out of the pan.

◆ Remove the foil and place the candy on a cutting board.

◆ Using a long-bladed serrated knife, such as a bread knife, cut along the lines scored in the fudge. To get a smooth even cut, place one hand on the knife handle and the other on the top of the blade, then press down evenly until the knife cuts through the candy.

Peanutty Fudge

For smooth, creamy fudge, be sure to knead it thoroughly to blend the ingredients.

1 box (16 ounces) confectioners sugar, sifted (4½ cups)
⅔ cup unsweetened cocoa
⅔ cup chunky peanut butter
2 tablespoons butter or margarine, at room temperature
½ cup low-fat (1% milkfat) milk
1 teaspoon vanilla
½ cup finely chopped peanuts (optional)

1 Line an 8" x 8" x 2" baking pan with foil, extending foil over edges of pan. Lightly butter the foil; set aside. Sift together the confectioners sugar and cocoa into a medium-size bowl.

2 In large bowl, with electric mixer on *Medium*, cream peanut butter and butter until creamy. Add cocoa mixture; beat until fluffy, scraping bowl often. Add milk and vanilla; beat well. Stir in peanuts (if using).

3 Turn the mixture out onto a work surface and knead for 3 to 4 minutes or until well combined.

4 Press the fudge into the prepared pan. Using the tip of a small knife, score into 1-inch squares. When fudge is firm, lift it out of pan; cut into squares (tip, above). To store, cover tightly and refrigerate. Makes about 2 pounds (64 pieces).

Prep Time: 25 minutes

1 Piece: Calories 49. Total Fat 2 g. Saturated Fat 1 g. Protein 1 g. Carbohydrate 8 g. Fiber 0 g. Sodium 18 mg. Cholesterol 1 mg.

Grandma's Treats

Rocky Road Candy

When grandma wanted to make an easy sweet treat, she relied on this no-fuss candy.

- 1 package (11½ ounces) milk chocolate chips
- ⅓ cup vegetable oil
- 1 bag (10½ ounces) miniature marshmallows
- ¾ cup coarsely chopped walnuts or pecans

1. Line an 8" x 8" x 2" baking pan with foil, extending foil over edges of pan. Lightly butter foil; set aside.

2. In a large saucepan, combine the chocolate chips and oil. Heat over low heat until chips are melted and mixture is smooth, stirring constantly. Remove from heat.

3. Stir in the marshmallows and walnuts. Spread the mixture evenly in the prepared pan. Cover and refrigerate for 4 hours or until firm.

4. Grasp the foil and lift candy out of pan. Cut candy into squares. To store, cover tightly and refrigerate. Makes about 36 pieces.

Surprise Packages

- 1 can (20 ounces) reduced-calorie cherry pie filling
- ¼ cup chopped almonds
- 2 teaspoons lemon juice
- ½ teaspoon ground cinnamon
- 2 store-bought refrigerated pie crusts

1. Preheat oven to 425°F. In small bowl, stir together the pie filling, almonds, lemon juice, and cinnamon.

2. Place 1 of the crusts on an ungreased large baking sheet. Spoon half of the cherry mixture on half of this crust, then fold crust over the mixture, forming a semicircle. Using back of a fork, crimp the edge. Repeat with the remaining crust and remaining cherry mixture.

3. Cut slits in the tops of the crusts. Brush with a little milk and sprinkle with a little sugar if you like.

4. Bake for 20 minutes or until crusts are golden. (If the edges seem to be browning too quickly, cover with foil.) Serve warm. Makes 8 servings.

Ice-Cream Cone Cakes

These fun-to-eat cones are a new twist on old-fashioned cake and ice cream.

- 14 flat-bottom ice-cream cones
- 1 package (1-layer-size) devil's food or yellow cake mix
- Reduced-fat ice cream, any flavor

1. Preheat the oven to 350°F. Place the ice-cream cones in a large shallow baking pan. Prepare the cake mix according to package directions. Pour the cake batter into cones, filling to within 1 inch of tops.

2. Bake for 20 to 25 minutes or until toothpicks inserted in the centers come out clean. Remove the cakes from pan. Cool on wire racks.

3. Place a large scoop of ice cream on top of each cake. Makes 14.

Chocolate Haystacks

This recipe is sure to please today's kids.

- 3 cups old-fashioned (5 minutes) or quick-cooking (1 minute) rolled oats
- 1 cup shredded coconut
- ½ cup coarsely chopped pecans or walnuts
- 1½ cups sugar
- ½ cup low-fat (1% milkfat) milk
- ⅓ cup unsweetened cocoa
- ¼ cup butter or margarine
- 1 teaspoon vanilla

1. Line a baking sheet with wax paper; set aside. In a large bowl, stir together the oats, coconut, and pecans.

2. In a medium-size heavy saucepan, combine the sugar, milk, cocoa, butter, and vanilla. Bring to a boil over moderate heat, stirring constantly with a wooden spoon to dissolve sugar.

3. Pour the hot milk mixture over the oat mixture and stir until combined. Drop by rounded tablespoonfuls onto the prepared baking sheet. Refrigerate until firm. Transfer to a covered container; refrigerate. Makes about 36 pieces.

ACKNOWLEDGMENTS

Our thanks to: Photographers: Michael Molkenthin (Cover); Alan Richardson (Pages 167, 328).
Illustrator: Linda Gist (Pages 37, 328). Public Library of Des Moines.
Grateful acknowledgment is made to the following source for permission to adapt the following recipe. "German Panned Fish" adapted from THE NEW GERMAN COOKBOOK by Jean Anderson and Hedy Wurz. Copyright© 1993 by Jean Anderson and Hedy Wurz. Reprinted by permission of HarperCollins Publishers, Inc.

INDEX

Page numbers in *italic* type refer to photographs.

Page numbers in *italic* type refer to photographs.

melt-in-your-mouth filets with, cream sauce, 117, *117*
paprika, 252
rice cakes with, -walnut sauce, 220, *220*
rice pilaf, 218
spinach-stuffed shells with, sauce, 236
turkey loaf with, sauce, 182
veal scaloppine with, sauce, 131

Mustard
-glazed meat loaf special, 123
herb, butter, 281
sauce, double, 269
sauce with capers, 269
sauce with dill, 269

N

Nana Ann's American chop suey, 140
Nana's chicken stew, 166
Nana's scalloped oysters, 211
Nan's circles and squares, 246
New England barley casserole, 222
New England clam cakes, 210, *210*
New England kedgeree, 199, *199*
New England supper-in-a-pot, 115
New Orleans dirty rice, 221
New Orleans pralines, 354, *354*
Noodle(s)
beef 'n', casserole, 128
chicken and, 164
chicken with homemade, 164, *165*
how to cut, 164
kasha and, 226, *226*
pudding, Jewish, 347, *347*
Romanoff, 235
salmon, casserole, 235
soup, Chinese, 76, *76*
turkey and, 164
Norwegian fish pudding with shrimp sauce, 201
Nuts, toasting, 14
Nutty cheese balls, 10, 14
Nutty crescents, *290*, 312

O

Oatmeal biscuits, 300
Oatmeal with raisins, old-fashioned, 222
Okra with corn and tomatoes, *240*, 253
Old-country bacon and potato salad, 44
Old-fashioned dinner rolls, 313
Old-fashioned fondue, 103
Old-fashioned oatmeal with raisins, 222
Old-fashioned pirozhkis, 20, *21*
Old-fashioned taffy, 355
Old-time peanut brittle, 357
Old-time scalloped potatoes, 259, *259*
Old-time vegetable stew, 68
Old-world braided bread with honey glaze, 305, *305*
Old-world coulibiac, 193
Oma's porcupine meatball casserole, 125

Omelets
French marmalade, 94
French, with mushroom sauce, *86*, 94
how to cook, 94
mushroom and cheese, 94
rocky top, 92, *93*
Onion(s)
beef sirloin and, 119
chicken livers with mushrooms and, 174
dip, curried, *12*, 13
fried apples with, 264
glazed, 253
green beans with, 242
herb sauce, 268, *268*
hollowing out, 255
liver and, 119
over-stuffed, *254*, 255
relish, fiesta, *267*, 284
sherried, herb sauce, 268
soup supreme, 73
Open-face chicken tea sandwiches, 36
Open sesame loaves, 309
Orange(s)
applesauce, raisin-, 289
candied yams and, 262
chiffon cake with spice 'n', frosting, 324, *324*
in Cumberland sauce, *266*, 270
cups, cranberry relish in, 270
eggnog punch, 31, *31*
-glazed beets, *244*, 245
-glazed Canadian bacon, 149
making, cups, 270
-raisin carrots, *241*, 246
sauce, 343
sherbet, fresh strawberry-, *317*, 346
Oven beef barbecue, 136
Oven-fried fish fillets, 190
Oven pork barbecue, 136
Overnight breakfast casseroles, 91
Overnight fruit salad, 55
Over-stuffed onions, *254*, 255
Over-stuffed peppers, *254*, 255
Oyster(s)
gumbo, chicken-, 161, *161*
nana's scalloped, 211
stew, 84

P, Q

Pancakes
buckwheat, 303
cornmeal griddle cakes, 303
gran's potato, 258
puffy breakfast surprise, 315
with raisin faces, 315
Parmesan spoon bread, 298
Parsley, mincing, 231
Parsnips, glazed, 253
Party perfect oven-fried vegetables, 28
Pasta and beans, 238
Pasties, chicken Cornish, 123
Pasties, Cornish, 122, *122*
Pastitsio, Greek, 234, *234*
Pâte, country, 17
Pâte sandwiches, easy, *34*, 35

Pea(s)
braised, with lettuce, 255
calico, 265
saucy, and new potatoes, 248, *248*
Peach(es)
cider pie, *316*, 331
cobbler, 340, *340*
in fruit leather, 289
ice cream, 344, *344*
preserves, perfect, 276, *276*
upside-down cake, 327
Peanut brittle, old-time, 357
Peanut butter, chunky homemade, 289
Peanut butter icebox cookies, 353
Peanutty fudge, 358
Pear and pepper relish, gingery, 286, *286*
Pepper(s)
and cabbage slaw, layered, 283
and olive antipasto, sweet, 26, *26*
over-stuffed, *254*, 255
relish, gingery pear and, 286, *286*
-sausage scramble, 149
Peppered veal stew with dumplings, *130*, 131
Perfect peach preserves, 276, *276*
Perfect popovers, 301
Pheasant, smothered, 186
Picadillo, 126, *126*
Pickles
bread-and-butter, *267*, 281
deep-south watermelon rind, 282, *283*
easy beet, 282
pickling pointers, 282
Pie crust
crimping, 332
homemade, 337
moving, with ease, 181
store-bought, 337
Pies (dessert), 330-337
apple cider, 331
banana cream, 334
chocolate banana cream, 334
cinnamon apple crumb, 331
deep-dish cherry, 330, *330*
green tomato, 332
lemon chess, 334
peach cider, *316*, 331
sour cream raisin, 333, *333*
spicy pumpkin chiffon, 336, *336*
strawberry rhubarb, 332
walnut maple, 335, *335*
Pies (savory)
beef pot, 120
ham and egg, 101, *101*
heartland pork and apple, 142, *142*
tuna, with biscuits, 212
turkey pot, 180, *180*
Pigs-in-a-blanket, 153
Pilafs
bulgur wheat, 221
chicken bulgur, 221
curried rice, 218
mushroom rice, 218
shrimp, 219
Turkish, 219, *219*
with pistachio and pine nuts, 218

Page numbers in *italic* type refer to photographs.

Page numbers in *italic* type refer to photographs.

Page numbers in *italic* type refer to photographs.